lonely pla

D1085746

HIKING & TRAMPING IN
New
Zealand

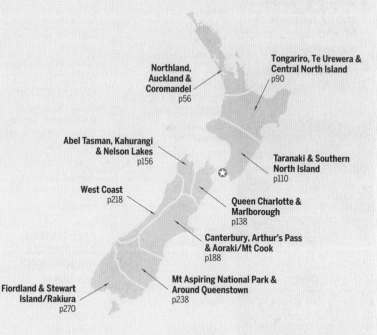

Northland,
Auckland &
Coromandel
p56

Tongariro, Te Urewera &
Central North Island
p90

Abel Tasman, Kahurangi
& Nelson Lakes
p156

Taranaki & Southern
North Island
p110

West Coast
p218

Queen Charlotte &
Marlborough
p138

Canterbury, Arthur's Pass
& Aoraki/Mt Cook
p188

Fiordland & Stewart
Island/Rakiura
p270

Mt Aspiring National Park &
Around Queenstown
p238

Andrew Bain, Jim DuFresne

PLAN YOUR TRIP

OTURERE HUT P100

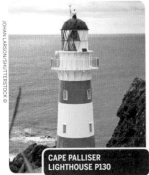

CAPE PALLISER
LIGHTHOUSE P130

ON THE TRACK

Contents

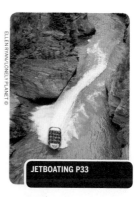

JETBOATING P33

ELLEN RYAN/LONELY PLANET ©

Welcome to New Zealand

There may be no country on earth as naturally diverse as New Zealand. Here glaciers leak through rainforest, volcanoes form a beating heart, sun-blazed beaches frame coastal national parks, and ice-tipped mountains hack at the sky.

Jewels of Nature

It's the extraordinary natural architecture that lures trampers, but NZ also comes jewelled with one of the planet's finest and most extensive track networks. The natural drama all around the country is worthy of the theatre, but the boards you'll tread are tracks that climb through mountain passes, or trace the lines of rivers or lakes, or disappear momentarily into the soft sand of long beaches.

Hut Havens

Almost 1000 huts dot the trails, which are headlined by a Great Walks system that has long been envied and mimicked by the rest of the world. Even in the most remote reaches, huts await – often with historical tales as engrossing as the views. DOC maintains more than 950 huts in its national parks, conservation areas and reserves. While many were purpose-built for trampers and climbers, others stand as a legacy to industries such as forestry, farming, mining and deer culling. Today they form a network that offers cheap, character-filled accommodation in the most unlikely places, a unique and highly treasured feature of the NZ backcountry.

Easy Does It

Reward here doesn't always require effort. Certainly, you can slog it to the top of hard-earned alpine passes such as Cascade Saddle for mountain views beyond excellence, but there are equally worthy prizes that can be found in committing just a few hours to walk to points beneath the hanging terminus of Rob Roy Glacier, or along empty and wild bays around the northern tip of Coromandel Peninsula.

Space Invaders

Evidence of what awaits comes in the numbers. There are just 4.8 million New Zealanders, scattered across more than 260,000 sq km: bigger than the UK with one-fourteenth of the population. Filling in the large gaps in between are the sublime mountains, forests, lakes, beaches and fiords that have made NZ one of the world's most desirable hiking destinations. Stand on a Fiordland pass with mountains rearing above, beside a dazzling volcanic lake in Tongariro, or on an Abel Tasman beach lined with forest, and you'll see why NZ tramping tracks have labels such as 'finest walk in the world' and 'best day walk in the world'. And yet those very tracks may not even be the best in the country.

By Andrew Bain, Writer

They call them Great Walks for a reason, but any time I'm on one of these showpiece tramps, I find my eye wandering elsewhere on the map. The New Zealand landscape reads like an open invitation to explore on foot – into that valley, onto that pass, along that beach. Like few other places on earth, you can wake with a hankering to hike a particular landscape – be it mountains or beach, forest or alpine – and find that there are possibilities in quick reach of wherever you stand in the country.

For more about our writers, see p352

Hiking & Tramping in New Zealand

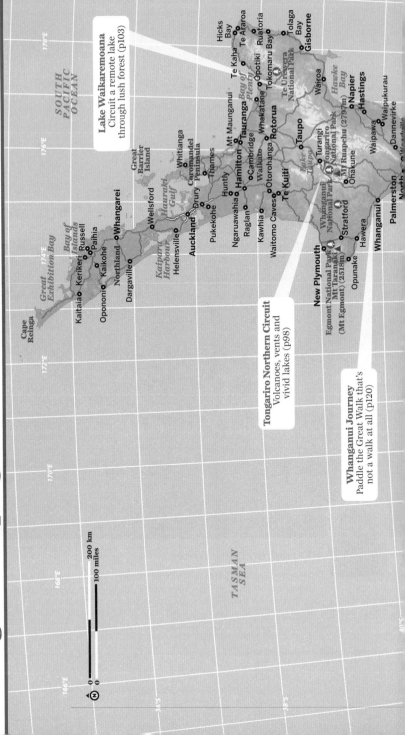

Lake Waikaremoana
Circuit a remote lake through lush forest (p103)

Tongariro Northern Circuit
Volcanoes, vents and vivid lakes (p98)

Whanganui Journey
Paddle the Great Walk that's not a walk at all (p120)

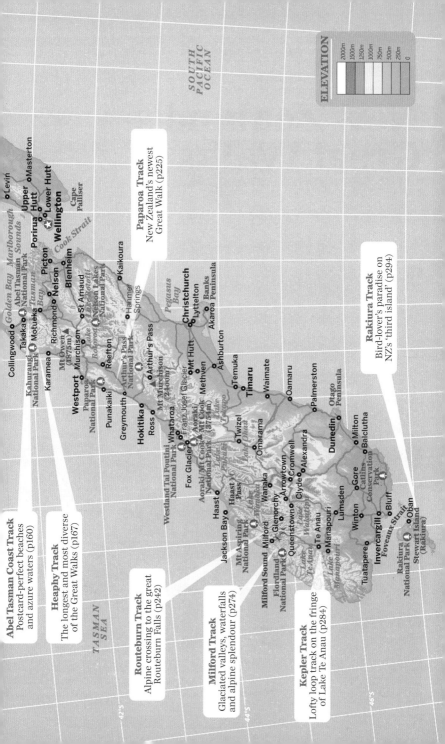

Abel Tasman Coast Track
Postcard-perfect beaches and azure waters (p160)

Heaphy Track
The longest and most diverse of the Great Walks (p167)

Paparoa Track
New Zealand's newest Great Walk (p225)

Rakiura Track
Bird-lover's paradise on NZ's 'third island' (p294)

Routeburn Track
Alpine crossing to the great Routeburn Falls (p242)

Milford Track
Glaciated valleys, waterfalls and alpine splendour (p274)

Kepler Track
Lofty loop track on the fringe of Lake Te Anau (p284)

ELEVATION

2000m
1500m
1250m
1000m
750m
500m
250m
0

New Zealand's Great Walks

Abel Tasman Coast Track

1 Routinely touted as New Zealand's most beautiful Great Walk, the Abel Tasman Coast Track (p160) is also the most popular. Located in the country's smallest national park, this track brings together great weather, granite cliffs, golden sands and a bushy backdrop. Spot seals and birds, explore fascinating estuaries, hidden inlets and freshwater pools, study bizarre rock formations and significant trees...or simply laze around on that beach towel you packed. Water taxis and kayak trips offer endless options for maximising enjoyment.

Tongariro Northern Circuit

2 New Zealand's oldest national park is also home to one of its most dynamic and imposing Great Walks. The Tongariro Northern Circuit (p98) loops among a trio of volcanoes that provided one of the most dramatic backdrops in *Lord of the Rings*, and wears dazzling lakes, steaming vents, lava bombs and craters like bling. Add in a couple of waterfalls and the country's only desert and you get a sense of what makes this a truly great walk.

Right: Taranaki Falls (p98), Tongariro National Park

Lake Waikaremoana

3 Remote, immense and shrouded in mist, Te Urewera encompasses the North Island's largest tract of virgin forest. The park's highlight is Lake Waikaremoana ('Sea of Rippling Waters'), a deep crucible of water encircled by the Lake Waikaremoana track (p103). This tramp passes through ancient rainforest and reedy inlets, and traverses gnarly ridges, including the famous Panekiri Bluff, from where there are stupendous views of the lake and endless forested peaks and valleys.

Whanganui Journey

4 The Great Walk you can have when you're not having a walk, the Whanganui Journey (p120) is actually a canoe or kayak trip along the Whanganui River, NZ's longest navigable waterway. It's a journey through sheer gorges, where the reflections can almost induce vertigo, and over short bouncy rapids. The forest is dense and the views are immense. Along the way it passes the folly-like Bridge to Nowhere, numerous bush campsites and the only DOC hut in the country that's also used as a *marae* (Māori meeting house).

Heaphy Track

5 This wild and wonderful historic crossing (p167) from Golden Bay to the West Coast dishes up the most diverse scenery of any of the Great Walks, taking in dense forest, tussock-covered downs, caves, secluded valleys and beaches dusted in salt spray and fringed by nikau palms. It's a mighty wilderness, and if time's at a premium you can always mountain bike it (in winter and spring, at least)...

Kepler Track

6 One of three Great Walks within Fiordland National Park, the Kepler Track (p284) was built to take pressure off the Milford and Routeburn. Many trampers now say it rivals both of them. This high crossing takes you from the peaceful, beech-forested shores of Lake Te Anau and Lake Manapouri before bumping across the alpine tops of Mt Luxmore. Expect towering limestone bluffs, razor-edged ridges, vast views and crazy caves. The Kepler is a truly spectacular way to appreciate the grandeur of NZ's largest national park.

TIMMIESTERPHOTOGRAPHY/GETTY IMAGES ©

Milford Track

7 The finest walk in the world? Somebody once thought so, and wrote as much in a London newspaper...and so the mythology of the Milford Track (p274) was born. If it's hyperbole, it's only by degrees, for this track is a compendium of all good mountain things: gin-clear streams (pictured above), dense rainforest, an unforgettable alpine pass and Sutherland Falls; one of the highest waterfalls in the world.

Routeburn Track

8 NZ's second-most popular Great Walk is truly a mountain spectacular. The Routeburn Track (p242) climbs high onto alpine slopes linking Fiordland and Mt Aspiring National Parks, providing seemingly endless views, though nearer-to-hand sights such as thundering waterfalls, bizarre rock formations, alpine tarns and peculiar plant life will likely capture your attention just as much. The track is regularly compared, and rated against, the Milford Track, but it is its own little piece of walking wonder.

Rakiura Track

9 Following the Foveaux Strait coast and shore of Paterson Inlet on tranquil Stewart Island, this leisurely loop (p294) offers a rewarding combination of waterside scenery, notable native trees and ferns, and historic relics of bygone days. Bird-watchers will be all atwitter, with a diverse range of species to be seen and heard. These include big-winged coastal birds such as sooty shearwaters and mollymawks, as well as little blue penguins; beaky waders such as dotterels, herons and godwits in the inlet; and forest birds such as kiwis, bellbirds, parakeets, kereru and kaka.

Paparoa Track

10 Slated to open in 2019, the Paparoa Track (p225) will become NZ's 10th Great Walk. The 55km shared-use trail (tramping and mountain biking) will cross the West Coast's Paparoa Range, connecting two existing tramps – the Croesus Track and the Inland Pack Track. It takes in the alpine tops of the range, thick swaths of rainforest and the limestone cliffs of the Pororari River, as well as diverting along a side trail to the site of the former Pike River Mine, where 29 miners were killed in an accident in 2010.

JUDITH LIENERT/SHUTTERSTOCK ©

Need to Know

For more information, see Survival Guide (p319)

Currency
New Zealand dollar ($)

Language
English, Māori

Visas
Citizens of Australia,
the UK and 58 other
countries don't need
visas for NZ (length-of-
stay allowances vary);
see www.immigration.
govt.nz.

Money
Credit cards are used for
most purchases in NZ,
and are accepted in most
hotels and restaurants.
ATMs widely available in
cities and larger towns.

Mobile Phones
European phones will
work on NZ's network,
but not most American
or Japanese phones. Use
global roaming or a local
SIM card and prepaid
account.

Time
New Zealand time
(GMT/UTC plus 12
hours)

When to Go

Northland/Auckland
TRAMP Year-Round

Central North Island
TRAMP Nov–Apr

Nelson/Marlborough
TRAMP Year-Round

Arthur's Pass National Park
TRAMP Nov–Mar

Mt Aspiring/Fiordland
National Parks
TRAMP Nov–Apr

High Season
(Dec–Feb)
➡ Normally the
best, most-settled
weather.
➡ Tramping high
season starts just
before Christmas.
➡ Huts and tracks
can get busy.

Shoulder
(Oct–Nov &
Feb–Mar)
➡ Tracks are less
busy.
➡ Fine weather
lingers into April.
➡ Most low-level
tracks can be walked
October through
April.

Low Season
(Jun–Aug)
➡ Weather at its
coldest and wettest;
river levels high.
➡ Many high-
altitude tracks closed
because of avalanche
danger.
➡ Some low-level
walks possible, with
solitude guaranteed.

Tramping Costs

Lodges, huts & campsites: Free–$80

➡ Great Walk hut: $24-80

➡ Backcountry hut: free–$15

➡ Campsite: free–$18

Track transport $25–250

➡ Shuttle bus, one way up to an hour: $5–50

➡ Shuttle bus, longer return-trip: $45–135

➡ Boat transfer: $25–105

➡ Flight: $149–250

Guided trips & private tracks: More than $150

➡ Day tramp: $185–433

➡ Private track (2–3 nights): $175–260

➡ Great Walk (3–4 nights): $1375–2130

Note: these costs do not reflect the pricing trial, which will increase Great Walk hut fees for international visitors.

Useful Websites

Department of Conservation (DOC; www.doc.govt.nz) Parks, reserves, tramps, huts, camping and conservation.

Mountain Safety Council (www.mountainsafety.org.nz) Staying safe in NZ's outdoors.

Federated Mountain Clubs of NZ (www.fmc.org.nz) Umbrella organisation for tramping and mountaineering clubs.

100% Pure New Zealand (www.newzealand.com) Official tourism site.

Lonely Planet (lonelyplanet.com) Destination information, hotel bookings and traveller forum.

MetService (www.metservice.com) Weather forecasts and warnings.

Te Ara (www.teara.govt.nz) The 'Encyclopedia of NZ'.

Exchange Rates

Australia	A$1	NZ$1.10
Canada	C$1	NZ$1.14
China	Y10	NZ$2.21
Euro zone	€1	NZ$1.72
Japan	¥100	NZ$1.29
Singapore	S$1	NZ$1.08
UK	UK£1	NZ$1.97
US	US$1	NZ$1.46

For current exchange rates, see www.xe.com.

Track Standards

NZ's tracks literally range from easy strolls in the park to full-on, multiday adventures across untamed, unmarked mountainous terrain. Our authors adhere to the following guidelines:

Easy A walk on flat terrain or with minor elevation changes, usually over short distances on well-travelled tracks with no navigational difficulties.

Moderate A walk with challenging terrain, often involving longer distances and steep climbs.

Demanding A walk with long daily distances and difficult terrain with significant elevation change. May involve challenging route-finding and high-altitude travel.

Each track is also graded in accordance with the official DOC (www.doc.govt.nz) categories:

Walking Track Gentle walking from a few minutes to a day on mostly well-formed tracks.

Great Walk/Easy Tramping Track Comfortable multiday tramping on generally well-formed tracks.

Tramping Track Challenging day or multiday tramping on mostly unformed tracks. Moderate to high backcountry skills and experience required.

Route Challenging multiday tramping on unformed and natural tracks. Navigation and high-level backcountry skills and experience required.

The Hut System

➡ DOC maintains more than 950 huts in its national parks, conservation areas and reserves. While many were purpose-built for trampers and climbers, others stand as a legacy to industries such as forestry, farming, mining and deer culling. Today they form a network that offers cheap accommodation in the most unlikely places, a unique and highly treasured feature of the NZ backcountry.

➡ Huts come in all shapes and sizes. The flashest are generally Great Walk Huts, large multiroomed buildings equipped with such comforts as solar lighting, kitchen sinks, gas cookers, flush toilets and a hut warden. But even at the bottom end of the scale – in bivvies and basic huts – you'll still get a mattress, some kind of water supply, a toilet (possibly a long drop) and a fireplace, all going well.

➡ With some exceptions, such as Great Walk huts and campsites, huts and campsites are paid for with Backcountry Hut tickets and passes. These should be purchased in advance online, or at DOC offices, i-SITEs or outdoor gear shops.

➡ Each hut ticket costs $5. You simply deposit the appropriate number of ticket butts in the box at the hut when you arrive. If you plan to do a lot of tramping, a Backcountry Hut Pass (six months/one year $92/122), valid for Serviced and Standard Huts, might prove a wise investment.

➡ In late 2018, DOC introduced a differential pricing trial. International visitors can expect to pay higher rates than locals on some of the Great Walks.

If You Like...

Volcanoes

The New Zealand landscape has serious indigestion. Straddling the collision boundary of two major tectonic plates, it regularly burps, steams, bubbles and hisses to life.

Tongariro Northern Circuit
This spectacular four-day loop circumnavigates Mt Ngauruhoe, passing through desert-like lands and always in sight of Ngauruhoe's conical shape. (p98)

Tongariro Alpine Crossing
The abbreviated version of the Northern Circuit is a compendium of volcanic features – luminous lakes, steaming vents, angry red craters. (p95)

Rangitoto Island Loop A day trip from Auckland takes you onto the volcanic island of Rangitoto, which is blanketed in 600-year-old black lava. (p67)

Mt Taranaki Summit Stand atop this slumbering volcano with its near-perfect volcanic figure at the end of a challenging but achievable 1570m climb. (p123)

Wildlife

Isolated from the rest of the world, New Zealand is a veritable menagerie of unique animals that evolved without the interference of predatory mammals. Brace yourself for freaky critters!

Kaikoura Coast Track Look to the sea for dolphins, seals and soaring seabirds, and inland for riflemen, bellbirds, grey warblers and long-tailed cuckoos. (p151)

Rakiura Track Stewart Island contains the largest and most diverse bird populations in NZ; the tokoeka (kiwi) population alone is around 15,000. (p294)

Heaphy Track Get thee to Kahurangi for a field trip of curiosities – giant snails, bats, weta (insects), spiders, beetles and 60 native bird species. (p167)

St Arnaud Range Track The feathery fruits of the Rotoiti Nature Recovery Project's labour include kaka (parrots), bellbirds, tomtits, robins, riflemen and kiwi. (p180)

Glaciers

They're the rivers that flow in slow motion, and they lace New Zealand's Southern Alps, feeding the brilliantly coloured lakes and rivers and providing ice-perfect views.

Hooker Valley Track Pooled at the foot of NZ's highest mountain is Hooker Lake, typically with icebergs cruising about its silty waters. (p213)

Rob Roy Track Sit for a while at the upper lookout and you're almost guaranteed to see an avalanche or two from the hanging glacier across the valley. (p256)

Rees-Dart Track Detour out from Dart Hut towards Cascade Saddle and you'll get to wander along the edge of Dart Glacier. (p250)

Mountain Climbs

New Zealand errs on the mountainous side, with a spine of alpine peaks on the South Island, creating a wealth of lofty but achievable summits.

Mueller Hut Route This 1040m climb is a quintessential alpine experience, with geological wonders, fascinating plant life and a hut with million-dollar views. (p210)

Roys Peak From Lake Wanaka's shores it's a 1200m ascent to superb views over the lake and a multitude of mighty mountains. (p262)

Avalanche Peak The Arthur's Pass views will have you debating whether the Tongariro Alpine Crossing really is the country's best day walk. (p200)

Ben Lomond How often can you walk from the centre of a busy town to find a 1400m climb with views this good? (p260)

Mountain Passes

They're the beacons through the mountains – the passes that lure you out of the valleys to high vantage points and onwards into other valleys.

Cascade Saddle Ascend from the Matukituki Valley and return the same way, or exit via the Rees-Dart Track. (p253)

Milford Track A memorial cairn, tarns, a shelter and breathtaking views all sit high on Mackinnon Pass. (p274)

Routeburn Track The view from 1255m-high Harris Saddle is spectacular enough; detour to 1515m Conical Hill and things look better still. (p242)

Gillespie Pass Circuit This remote track crosses a 1500m pass overlooked by towering peaks. (p257)

Sunrise Track Rise gently through beech forest on this family-friendly trail that rewards with far-reaching views from Armstrong Saddle. (p124)

Rivers

Whether they're roaring, braided glacial rivers or waterways with pools so clear they look pasted into the landscape, rivers are a defining feature – and typically the guiding lines – of NZ tramping.

Whanganui Journey This Great Walk is actually a 145km paddle down NZ's longest navigable river, through the lush wilds of Whanganui National Park. (p120)

Pelorus Track So scenic it starred in *The Hobbit,* the Pelorus River is followed for two days during this three-day tramp. (p146)

Karangahake Gorge A narrow gorge filled with gold relics, a cycle trail and a day walk along the Ohinemuri River's banks. (p82)

Top: Mueller Glacier, Hooker Valley Track (p212)

Bottom: Fur seal, Kaikoura Coast Track (p151)

Milford Track Primarily a journey along two wilderness rivers – Clinton and Arthur – past deep pools and through riverbank rainforest. (p274)

Beaches

With around 15,000km of coastline, NZ boasts more bays and beaches than you can shake a bucket and spade at. They're less bikini-clad with golden sands, and more...um...windswept and interesting.

Te Paki Coastal Track The vast expanse of Ninety Mile Beach gets the glory, but just around the corner are beautiful white-sand beaches. (p59)

Heaphy Track Smooth seas and soft sand are so bland! If you're looking for some coastal drama, you can't beat a wild-west beach. (p167)

Abel Tasman Coast Track No need to Photoshop this postcard paradise. These golden sands and blue bays are for real. (p160)

Coromandel Walkway Bookended by beaches and with intermission at a rocky and wild beach, this day walk is a coastal spectacular. (p76)

Waterfalls

Water*falls*? It certainly does, especially in the mountains where the rain gauge can top 11,000mm annually. That's a lot of falling water...

Tongariro Northern Circuit Tumbling 20m over an old lava flow, Wairere Stream plunges headlong over Taranaki Falls into a boulder-ringed pool. (p98)

Rob Roy Track Tear your eyes from the hanging glaciers and you'll notice a pair of high waterfalls pouring off the cliffs by the upper lookout. (p256)

Routeburn Track This truly great track boasts the truly great Routeburn Falls. (p242)

Milford Track One of the world's loftiest waterfalls, Sutherland Falls hops, skips and jumps 580m into a pool a short trip from the track. (p274)

History

New Zealand's backcountry history generally involved gold-mining, logging and plenty of 'number 8 wire' (Kiwi ingenuity).

Aotea Track This track follows routes laid down by loggers who came to Great Barrier Island seeking kauri trees, leaving relics in their wake. (p70)

Karangahake Gorge History here ranges from 'windows' cut into mountains to discard rock debris, to the world's first use of cyanide to extract gold from crushed ore. (p82)

Hollyford Track A typically hare-brained scheme of the era, Jamestown was always a long shot. Cue colourful characters and a dash of drama. (p279)

Old Ghost Road Terrain so brutal the track wasn't completed by the gold miners who tried to build it; 130 years later it was finished by professional builders. (p221)

Loop Hikes

There's such a sense of completion in a loop walk: making it all the way back to where you started, without the complication of transport connections or the déjà vu of backtracking.

Pouakai Circuit This two-day circuit features spectacular views of Mt Taranaki from the top of the Pouakai Range. (p118)

Putangirua Pinnacles Wander up a creek bed to a crumbling badlands, then up a ridge for views over the North Island's southernmost stretch of coastline. (p130)

Gillespie Pass Circuit Disappear deep into Mt Aspiring National Park's quiet northern end, crossing an alpine pass to link two remote valleys. (p257)

Kepler Track This memorable Fiordland alpine crossing takes in eye-popping sights such as towering bluffs, razor-edged ridges and crazy caves. (p284)

Mountain Biking

Major investment has seen the Nga Haerenga/New Zealand Cycle Trail grow to 22 different trails covering more than 2500km. Some are shared with trampers, others pass very near to trails.

Coromandel Walkway Branching off the coastal tramping route is a dedicated mountain-bike track, climbing 500m to roll along hilltops above the peninsula's northern tip. (p76)

Karangahake Gorge This day walk shares much of its course with the Hauraki Rail Trail, the gentlest of the New Zealand Cycle Trail routes. (p82)

Queen Charlotte Track Good on foot, excellent on bike, this Marlborough Sounds track is open to mountain bikers almost year-round. (p141)

Heaphy Track Coast down to the coast on this Great Walk that opens to bike riders from May to November. (p167)

Old Ghost Road The longest bit of singletrack (85km) in the country has precipitous alpine riding and skills-testing switchbacks. (p221)

Itineraries

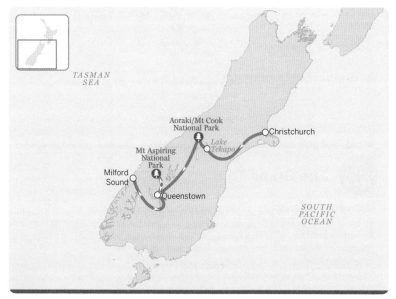

 ## Southern Highlights

Wing into **Christchurch** and stock up on supplies before heading for some of the South Island's best tracks.

Head south past gorgeous **Lake Tekapo**, taking in the obligatory view at the Church of the Good Shepherd, before continuing on to **Aoraki/Mt Cook National Park**. Warm up your tramping legs on the easy hike through the Hooker Valley before giving them a sterner test on the Mueller Hut Route, staying up high in one of NZ's loftiest huts.

Drive on over Lindis Pass into the adrenaline bowl that is **Queenstown**. Get perspective from atop Ben Lomond, and detour out past Wanaka into **Mt Aspiring National Park** to climb to a glacial extravaganza on the Rob Roy Track. Only in Queenstown can you then give your legs a rest by taking a bungy jump, or by skimming across Lake Wakatipu in a shark-shaped vessel.

Cross the Southern Alps on the Routeburn Track before taking a day off to ogle, cruise or kayak **Milford Sound**, before returning to Queenstown along the Greenstone Caples Track, which horseshoes through two distinctly different valleys – take your pick – that meet near the shores of Lake Wakatipu.

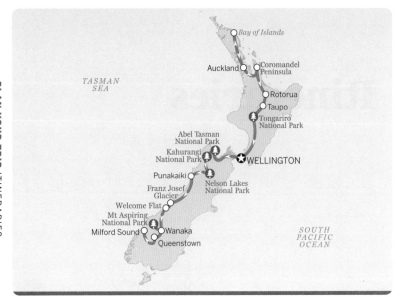

 The Grand Tour

Kick off your tramping bonanza in metropolitan **Auckland**. Warm up with a day hike on the volcanic island of Rangitoto, before driving north to the beautiful **Bay of Islands**. Set out on foot from its shores to rugged, lighthouse-tipped Cape Brett, getting a different perspective on the famed Hole in the Rock along the way.

Head south to the sun-soaked **Coromandel Peninsula** to explore its myriad attractions as well as venturing in to Kauaeranga Valley to scale the Pinnacles. Travel south, getting steamed and sulphured at **Rotorua** and **Taupo** before donning the backpack again among the volcanic landscapes of **Tongariro National Park**. Savour them on the Tongariro Northern Circuit, or, if time is tight, traverse the much heralded Tongariro Alpine Crossing.

Head to **Wellington** to wander through the national museum, Te Papa, before crossing Cook Strait to the South Island. Stretch your arms now as well as your legs in **Abel Tasman National Park**, home to the most popular of NZ's Great Walks as well as golden beaches and turquoise waters begging to be kayaked.

Two more national parks – **Kahurangi** and **Nelson Lakes** – lie nearby. Tramp the Heaphy or Lake Angelus Tracks on your way to the wild West Coast. Follow the stunning coast road, pausing at the Pancake Rocks at **Punakaiki**.

Keep on trucking south towards glacier country. Take a guided glacier walk onto **Franz Josef Glacier** before tramping into **Welcome Flat** for a well-earned soak in the hot springs. Having cleared Haast Pass, head for lakeside **Wanaka**, from where you can head into **Mt Aspiring National Park** along the Matukituki Valley, veering away onto the Rob Roy Track to find a dramatic grandstand position beneath a hanging glacier.

Head over the Crown Range to the self-branded 'adventure capital of the world', **Queenstown**. Take your pick from some of NZ's most fabulous tramps – the Routeburn, Greenstone Caples and Rees-Dart. Head round to the almost-mythical **Milford Sound**, arriving by vehicle through the Homer Tunnel or on foot along the Milford Track, the tramp once described as the finest walk in the world. Finish by heading back to Queenstown, where you can wind down in one of its many inviting bars.

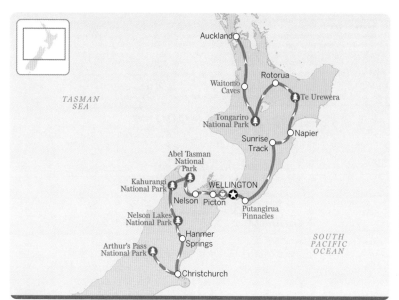

The Gentle Option

Ease into things with a couple of days in **Christchurch**, before heading inland and upland to **Arthur's Pass National Park**, where Bealey Spur rewards trampers with a simple climb that's blessed with views. Head north to the hot pools of **Hanmer Springs** before continuing to **Nelson Lakes National Park**, spending your days on the Mt Robert or St Arnaud Range climbs, and your nights in local accommodation. Meander through the Motueka Valley, popping in to the Tableland in **Kahurangi National Park** before hitting **Abel Tasman National Park** and the most idyllic of NZ's Great Walks. You might want to hang around for a few days to get a different perspective on the park from a kayak or boat.

Indulge in the fine local food and wine in **Nelson**, then wind your way eastwards to **Picton** along the scenic Queen Charlotte Drive. Cruise through the Marlborough Sounds, then hit the Queen Charlotte Track while your bags are ferried ahead of you by water taxi. Take a restorative tour of Marlborough's world-class wineries before hopping the ferry to **Wellington**.

Stroll into cinematic excellence at **Putangirua Pinnacles**, with plenty of time left in the day to visit the lighthouse and seals at Cape Palliser. Head north to discover one of the easiest ways to an alpine pass in NZ on the **Sunrise Track** before stopping for a couple of days in art-deco **Napier** in sunny Hawke's Bay. Gorge yourself on the region's ample produce, then burn off the calories on its flat cycling trails.

Venture into mystical **Te Urewera** to complete the Lake Waikaremoana Great Walk then soak up some Māori culture and a good dose of sulphur at the many geothermal delights of **Rotorua**. Be sure to soak away any tramping aches in a hot spring here.

Swing across to Taupo, the lakeside resort just a stone's throw from **Tongariro National Park** and the legendary Tongariro Alpine Crossing. Check out the twinkling glowworms of **Waitomo Caves** before heading to **Auckland**, finishing your journey with an easy day tramp on volcanic Rangitoto Island or heading further north for a couple of days on the rewarding and dramatic Cape Brett Track.

Alpine Explorer
3 WEEKS

Start in vibrant **Nelson** before heading off on this tour along the spine of NZ's Southern Alps. Drive to **Nelson Lakes National Park**, where the Lake Angelus Track climbs up Robert Ridge for sweeping views of the Southern Alps.

Wend your way through the wild **Buller Gorge**, which doubles as the starting point for one of NZ's newest tramping tracks, the Old Ghost Road – if time is tight, you can always mountain bike it.

Take in the Pancake Rocks at **Punakaiki** as you briefly touch the west coast, before heading east to **Arthur's Pass National Park** to scale Avalanche Peak.

East of the pass, stick close to the mountains on the Inland Scenic Route through to Tekapo and **Aoraki/Mt Cook National Park**, where you can climb to Mueller Hut for views of NZ's highest mountain, or stroll through the Hooker Valley for

Swing through Wanaka and into **Mt Aspiring National Park**, climbing high to Cascade Saddle or low (but with high views) on the Rob Roy Track. Finally, make an alpine crossing on the Routeburn Track before finishing in **Queenstown**.

North Island Wonders
3 WEEKS

Begin in **Auckland** and head south to the geothermal hot spot of **Rotorua**, where geysers, bubbling mud, steaming vents and Māori cultural performances await.

Venture into densely forested **Te Urewera** and tramp the Great Walk around Lake Waikaremoana, before driving to **Taupo** to do a skydive, raft a river or catch a trout.

Nearby is volcanic **Tongariro National Park**, home to the famed Tongariro Alpine Crossing, almost universally claimed as NZ's best day tramp. Then retire the boots for a few days as you splash into the Great Walk that's actually a river paddle: the 145km Whanganui Journey through the North Island's largest lowland wilderness, **Whanganui National Park**.

Truck west to **Egmont National Park** and the near-symmetrical cone of Mt Taranaki. Tracks abound on the mountain, but it's worth tramping the Pouakai Crossing to decide for yourself whether it's actually better than the Tongariro Alpine Crossing. Loop back to Auckland via **Waitomo Caves**, where you can ogle at glowworms or don a wet suit and abseil and river-tube deep into subterranean passages and caverns.

Plan Your Trip
Choosing Your Tramp

There are many considerations when choosing a tramp in New Zealand, be it the terrain (do the mountains call, or is it sand and sea that beckons?), the views, or your own level of experience.

Select a track that suits your level of fitness and experience. If you're tramping with others, consider the ability of all group members. We've graded each tramp, from easy to demanding, to help you choose the most suitable ones for you. The DOC website (www.doc.govt.nz) also grades tracks according to a national track standard. Talking to people who have recently completed a tramp is also a great way to source information.

Many of NZ's most famous tracks are located in mountainous regions, and in winter these will be too dangerous or challenging to all but the most-experienced and well-equipped trampers using specialised winter equipment. There are, however, tracks that can be completed in shoulder seasons or year-round. Choose the right tramp for the right time of year, but be prepared to alter your plans if the weather isn't right.

If it's your first tramp, or you've just arrived in the country, the DOC Day Hikes (p66) and Great Walks (p8) are an ideal introduction. Every one of them is incredibly scenic, and they're also well signposted and maintained, and (during the Great Walks season) monitored by hut wardens who will pass on weather reports, track-condition updates and helpful advice.

Go With Those in the Know

If possible tramp with someone else, or in a group, for safety in numbers (and, potentially, more fun).

Hiking companions can be found by lingering around DOC visitors centres, or online through sites such as Meetup (www.meetup.com) or numerous tramping clubs affiliated with the Federated Mountain Clubs (www.fmc.org.nz).

The Mountain Safety Council (www.mountain-safety.org.nz) produces a range of excellent resources, almost all of which are free. Its 29-part Get Outdoors video series on YouTube is highly recommended if you're considering any tramping in NZ.

If you're preparing for a specific trip, the Mountain Safety Council has a range of activity-specific guides, as well as e-Learning tools.

CHOOSING YOUR TRAMP

TRACK	DURATION	DIFFICULTY	BEST TIME TO GO	GETTING THERE
NORTHLAND, AUCKLAND & COROMANDEL				
Te Paki Coastal Track (p59)	3 days	easy	year-round	shuttle bus
Cape Brett Track (p63)	2 days	moderate	year-round	water taxi
Rangitoto Island Loop (p66)	4-5 hours	easy	year-round	ferry
Aotea Track (p70)	3 days	moderate	Oct-May	shuttle bus
Coromandel Walkway (p76)	6-7 hours	moderate	year-round	shuttle bus
Kauaeranga Kauri Trail (p78)	2 days	moderate	Oct-May	private
Karangahake Gorge (p82)	5-6 hours	easy	year-round	tourist train
TONGARIRO, TE UREWERA & CENTRAL NORTH ISLAND				
Tongariro Alpine Crossing (p95)	7-8 hours	moderate	Dec-Mar	shuttle bus
Tongariro Northern Circuit (p98)	4 days	moderate	Dec-Mar	shuttle bus
Lake Waikaremoana (p103)	4 days	easy-moderate	Nov-Apr	shuttle bus, boat
TARANAKI & SOUTHERN NORTH ISLAND				
Around the Mountain Circuit (p115)	5 days	moderate-demanding	Oct-May	shuttle bus
Pouakai Circuit (p118)	2 days	moderate	Oct-May	shuttle bus
Pouakai Crossing (p121)	7½-9½ hours	moderate	Oct-May	shuttle bus
Mt Taranaki Summit (p123)	8-10 hours	moderate-demanding	Jan-Mar	shuttle bus
Sunrise Track (p124)	4½-5½ hours	easy-moderate	Nov-Mar	private
Mt Holdsworth–Jumbo Circuit (p127)	3 days	moderate-demanding	Oct-May	private
Putangirua Pinnacles (p130)	3 hours	easy-moderate		bus, private
QUEEN CHARLOTTE & MARLBOROUGH				
Queen Charlotte Track (p141)	4 days	moderate	Nov-Dec & Feb-Apr	boat, shuttle bus
Pelorus Track (p146)	3 days	moderate	Oct-Apr	shuttle bus
Kaikoura Coast Track (p151)	2 days	easy-moderate	Dec-Mar	bus
ABEL TASMAN, KAHURANGI & NELSON LAKES				
Abel Tasman Coast Track (p160)	5 days	easy	Mar-May	bus, boat
Heaphy Track (p167)	5 days	moderate	Nov-Apr	shuttle bus, plane
Tableland Circuit (p172)	3 days	moderate	Nov-Apr	shuttle bus
Lake Angelus Track (p179)	2 days	moderate	Nov-Apr	shuttle bus, boat
St Arnaud Range Track (p180)	5 day	moderate	Nov-Apr	bus
Travers-Sabine Circuit (p181)	5 days	moderate-demanding	Nov-Apr	shuttle bus, boat

WHY GO?

Tramp spectacular beaches and the rugged coast around New Zealand's northern tip

Roll along a narrow cape with classic Bay of Island views and a night in a lighthouse keepers' cottage

Climb a volcano and tramp through lava fields, enjoying one of the best views of central Auckland

Wander a rugged island with historic kauri dams and hot springs

A remote tramp along the northern tip of the Coromandel Peninsula, combining lush bush and wild coast

Step back in time with logging and gold-mining relics on the forested hills of the Coromandel Peninsula

Explore a deep gorge lined and punctured with gold-mining relics

The best day walk in NZ? You decide as you hike past vibrant lakes and furious craters in a bleakly volcanic landscape

Tramp past volcanoes and through a spectacular thermal area on this Great Walk

Enjoy beaches, swimming and fishing on this Great Walk

Hike a lap around Mt Taranaki, taking in waterfalls, views and Fathams Peak.

Short walk that delivers brilliant views of Mt Taranaki and the New Plymouth coastline

The heir apparent to the title of NZ's best day walk, showcasing all the highlights of Mt Taranaki

Climb to the top of the slumbering 2518m volcano.

A kind-on-the-legs ascent through gorgeous forest to an alpine saddle and a hut with the eponymous sunrise views

Stay in scenic huts and admire views from an alpine ridge in Tararua Forest Park

Follow a deep valley between gravel cliffs to a badlands worth its place in the *Lord of the Rings* trilogy.

Treat yourself to beautiful coastal scenery and interesting accommodation options

Follow the deep-green pools of the Pelorus River, with an option to end at Nelson's outskirts over Dun Mountain

Loop out from the Pacific coast by day, and stay at farm properties by night

Explore a series of beautiful beaches and bays on this Great Walk

Follow in historic footsteps and enjoy a stunning variety of scenery on this Great Walk

Loop around the fascinating Mt Arthur Tableland, home to curious alpine plants, quizzical rock formations and deep, deep caves

Climb a challenging alpine pass, tempered by the beauty of Lake Angelus

Peer over lakes and mountains on this popular day walk, ascending through beech forest to the open tops of the range

Explore grassy river flats, beech forests, two alpine passes and the lake said to be the clearest in the world

TRACK	DURATION	DIFFICULTY	BEST TIME TO GO	GETTING THERE
CANTERBURY, ARTHUR'S PASS & AORAKI/MT COOK				
Banks Track (p191)	3 days	easy-moderate	Oct-Apr	shuttle bus
St James Walkway (p194)	5 days	easy-moderate	Nov-Apr	bus, shuttle bus
Avalanche Peak (p200)	6-8 hours	moderate	Nov-Mar	train, bus
Goat Pass Track (p202)	2 days	moderate	Nov-Mar	bus
Harper Pass (p204)	5 days	moderate	Nov-Mar	bus
Bealey Spur (p207)	4-6 hours	easy-moderate	Nov-Mar	bus
Mueller Hut Route (p210)	2 days	demanding	Nov-Mar	none
Hooker Valley Track (p212)	3 hours	easy	year-round	bus
WEST COAST				
Old Ghost Road (p221)	5 days	moderate	Nov-May	shuttle bus
Inland Pack Track (p226)	2 days	moderate	Dec-Mar	shuttle bus
Welcome Flat (p230)	2 days	easy-moderate	Nov-Apr	bus, shuttle bus
MT ASPIRING NATIONAL PARK & AROUND QUEENSTOWN				
Routeburn Track (p242)	3 days	moderate	Oct-Apr	shuttle bus
Greenstone Caples Track (p246)	3 days	moderate	Nov-Apr	shuttle bus
Rees-Dart Track (p250)	4 days	moderate–demanding	Dec-Apr	shuttle bus
Cascade Saddle (p253)	3 days	demanding	Dec-Mar	shuttle bus
Rob Roy Track (p256)	3-4 hours	easy-moderate	Dec-Mar	shuttle bus
Gillespie Pass Circuit (p257)	3 days	moderate–demanding	Dec-Mar	bus, jetboat, helicopter
Ben Lomond (p260)	6-8 hours	moderate	Nov-Apr	gondola
Roys Peak (p262)	5-6 hours	moderate	mid-Nov–Apr	shuttle bus
Diamond Lake & Rocky Mountain (p264)	2½-3 hours	easy-moderate	Oct-May	shuttle bus
FIORDLAND & STEWART ISLAND/RAKIURA				
Milford Track (p274)	4 days	moderate	Oct-Apr	shuttle bus, boat
Hollyford Track (p279)	5 days	moderate	Oct-May	shuttle bus, jetboat, plane
Kepler Track (p284)	4 days	moderate	Oct-Apr	shuttle bus, boat
Gertrude Saddle (p287)	4-6 hours	demanding	Dec-Apr	private
Hump Ridge Track (p289)	3 days	moderate	Nov-Apr	shuttle bus
Rakiura Track (p294)	3 days	moderate	Oct-Apr	plane, ferry

WHY GO?

Take in wonderful seascapes and wildlife on this private track

Cross two low passes while enjoying fine mountain scenery

Climb high above Arthur's Pass on the South Island's most scenic day tramp

Spend a night high above the bushline in Goat Pass Hut

Follow a historic gold-mining route over a low pass

One of Arthur's Pass's most gentle climbs doesn't skimp on views.

Climb steeply to spend a night among the spectacular peaks of Aoraki/Mt Cook National Park

See NZ's highest mountains and a pair of glaciers, while barely raising a sweat.

Rise high onto the Lyell Range through rainforest before squeezing through the stunning Mokihinui Gorge

Admire an unusual karst landscape and stay in one of NZ's largest rock bivvies

Follow the Karangarua River to spectacular hot springs

Explore one of NZ's best alpine crossings on this Great Walk

Loop through a pair of remote valleys, linked by an alpine crossing

Cross an alpine pass dividing two splendid valleys

Experience the lofty exposure of one of NZ's most scenic alpine passes

A short climb to a big scene dominated by a hanging glacier

Savour superb views and scenic beech-forested valleys

Begin near the centre of Queenstown and end up 1400m above

Watch Lake Wanaka shrink to a puddle as you ascend past the most famous high-mountain photo spot in NZ

Criss-crossing path around a low peak with a high lake and good views over Lake Wanaka

Experience lush rainforests, an alpine pass and high waterfalls along this Great Walk, the 'finest walk in the world'

Tramp to the rugged coast and explore the wildlife of Martins Bay

Spend a full day surrounded by alpine beauty on this Great Walk

Challenging alpine climb to a dramatic pass with an unforgettable view of Milford Sound

Explore a spectacular coast and intriguing logging relics

Follow this Great Walk to sheltered shores and beautiful beaches on NZ's third island

Plan Your Trip
Outdoor Pursuits

New Zealand is the outdoors burger with the lot – it'd be almost criminal to tramp here and not take to a trail on a bicycle, tackle some white water, or leap from something big and scary. Here we bring you a range of readily accessible outdoor activities that will complement your hikes and tramps.

Best Skydive Drop Zones

Queenstown

Fox & Franz Josef Glaciers

Taupo

Bay of Islands

Top White-Water Rafting Trips

Tongariro River, Taupo

Kaituna River, Rotorua

Shotover Canyon, Queenstown

Rangitikei River, Taihape

Buller Gorge, Murchison

Top Mountain-Biking Tracks

Redwoods Whakarewarewa Forest, Rotorua

Old Ghost Road, Westport

Queen Charlotte Track, Marlborough

West Coast Wilderness Trail, Hokitika

Alps 2 Ocean, South Canterbury

Bird-Watching

A diverse and fascinating array of birds may be seen in the wild, with many resident (or regularly returning) populations that are well protected and indeed promoted by high-profile visitor attractions. Examples include the Royal Albatross Centre on the Otago Peninsula; the godwits of Farewell Spit in Golden Bay; and the kotuku (white heron) sanctuary at Whataroa on the West Coast.

NZ does a great line in island sanctuaries and, increasingly, 'mainland islands' – reserves encircled by predator-proof fences. Such enclaves include Tiritiri Matangi island near Auckland, Ulva Island near Stewart Island, Kapiti Island near Wellington, and Motuara Island in the Marlborough Sounds. Visitor-friendly 'mainland islands' include Maungatautari near Hamilton, and Zealandia in Wellington.

Another opportunity to gain insight into NZ bird species and their conservation is at numerous captive-breeding facilities, including the West Coast Wildlife Centre in Franz Josef Glacier, where rowi – the rarest of all kiwi species – are hatched. Another such kiwi hatchery is Rainbow Springs, in Rotorua.

For a selection of some of the wonderful birds you may encounter on the tracks and elsewhere, refer to our bird-spotting guide (p34).

Fishing

Introduced in the 19th century, brown and rainbow trout have thrived in NZ's lakes and waterways and attract keen anglers from around the world. Many walking tracks follow rivers or skirt lakes, giving trampers ample opportunity to catch supper. Lake Waikaremoana and the Greenstone Caples Track are memorable places to try your luck. Licences (daily adult/youth $20/5, whole season adult/youth $163/25) are essential and can be bought at outdoor/fishing shops, visitor centres or online at Fish and Game New Zealand (www.fishandgame.org.nz), where you'll also find information on when, where and how to fish.

Sea-fishing options are bountiful too, whether casting off the beach or rocks, or reeling fish in from a kayak or chartered boat. Delicious snapper, cod, tarakihi and groper are all on the menu, but know your limits and release all undersize fish. Fishing rules and guidelines are available from www.fish.govt.nz, while www.fishing.net.nz can hook you up with charters and guides, as will i-SITE visitor centres nationwide.

Horse Trekking

Horse treks in NZ offer a chance to explore some remarkable landscapes – from farms to forests and along rivers and beaches. Rides range from one-hour jaunts (from around $60) to week-long, fully supported treks.

On the North Island, Taupo, the Coromandel Peninsula, Waitomo, Pakiri, Ninety Mile Beach, Rotorua, the Bay of Plenty and East Cape are top places for an equine encounter. There are plenty of options in the South Island, too, ranging from beachy trips in Golden Bay and adventures around mountain foothills near Mt Cook, Lake Tekapo, Queenstown and Glenorchy – as a bonus, you can canter through several *Lord of the Rings* filming locations. Spectacular treks are offered from Punakaiki into Paparoa National Park. For info and operator listings, check out True NZ Horse Trekking (www.truenz.co.nz/horsetrekking).

Sea Kayaking

Sea kayaking offers a wonderful perspective of the coastline and gets you close to marine wildlife you may otherwise never see. Meanwhile tandem kayaks, aka 'divorce boats', present a different kind of challenge.

There are ample places to get paddling. Hotspots include Waiheke and Great Barrier Islands, the Bay of Islands and Coromandel Peninsula, Marlborough Sounds (from Picton) and Abel Tasman National Park. Kaikoura is exceptional for wildlife spotting, and Fiordland for dazzling scenery. Wellington is noteworthy for offering the chance to paddle a traditional Māori *waka* (canoe).

Mountain Biking

Jaw-dropping mountains interlaced with farm tracks and old railway lines...it would be hard to design better mountain-biking terrain than NZ. The New Zealand Cycle Trail (www.nzcycletrail.com), some 2500km of tracks, helped mountain biking grow from a weekend sport to a national craze. Its popularity among outdoors enthusiasts of a certain age (and the potential for gear one-upmanship) has led mountain biking to be dubbed 'the new golf'. But no age group is immune, and the variety of trails in NZ brings a choice of gentle pootles in meadows to multiday cycle tours, half-day downhill-thrill rides to challenging week-long MTB adventures.

Mountain-bike parks – most with various trail grades and skills areas (and handy bike hire, usually) – are great for trying mountain biking NZ style. The most famous is Rotorua's Redwoods Whakarewarewa Forest, but among legions of others are Wellington's Makara Peak, Auckland's Woodhill Forest and Queenstown's downhill park, fed by the Skyline Gondola.

Classic trails include the 42 Traverse around Tongariro National Park, the Rameka on Takaka Hill and the trails around Christchurch's Port Hills – but this is just the tip of the iceberg. An increasing number of DOC hiking trails are being converted to dual use – such as the tricky but epic Heaphy Track and challenging, history-rich Old Ghost Road – but mountain biking is often restricted to low season due to hiker numbers. Track damage is also an issue, so check with DOC before starting out.

Your clue that there's some great biking around is the presence of bike-hire outfits. Bowl on up and pick their brains. Most likely cycle-obsessed themselves, they'll soon point you in the direction of a ride appropriate to your level. The go-to book is *Classic New Zealand Mountain Bike Rides* (from bookshops, bike shops and www. kennett.co.nz).

If cycle touring is more your pace, check out the *Pedallers' Paradise* booklets by Nigel Rushton (www.paradise-press.co.nz). Changeable weather and road conditions mean that cycle touring is less of a craze but there are remarkable road journeys, such as the Southern Scenic Route in the deep south.

The Southern Alps are studded with amazing climbs. The Aoraki/Mt Cook region is outstanding; but there are other zones extending throughout the spine of the South Island from the Kaikoura Ranges and the Nelson Lakes peaks all the way through to the hotbeds of Mt Aspiring National Park and Fiordland. Be warned, though: this is rugged and often remote stuff, and climber deaths are a regular occurrence. Even confident climbers are strongly advised to seek out a local guide, whatever the route.

The Christchurch-based New Zealand Alpine Club (www.alpineclub.org.nz) has background, news and useful links, and produces the annual *NZAC Alpine Journal* and quarterly *The Climber* magazine. It also has details on upcoming climbing courses.

Mountaineering

NZ has a proud mountaineering history – this was, after all, the home of Sir Edmund Hillary (1919–2008), who, along with Tenzing Norgay, was the first mountaineer confirmed to summit Mt Everest.

Rock Climbing

Time to chalk up your fingers and don some natty little rubber shoes. On the North Island, popular rock-climbing areas include Whanganui Bay, Kinloch,

TAKING THE LEAP

Bungy jumping was made famous by Kiwi AJ Hackett's 1987 plunge from the Eiffel Tower, after which he teamed up with champion NZ skier Henry van Asch to turn the endeavour into an accessible pursuit for anyone.

Today their original home base of Queenstown is a spiderweb of bungy cords, including the AJ Hackett's triad: the 134m Nevis Bungy (the highest in NZ); the 43m Kawarau Bungy (the original); and the Ledge Bungy (at the highest altitude – diving off a 400m-high platform). There's another scenic jump at Thrillseekers Canyon near Hanmer Springs. On the North Island, head to Taihape, Rotorua or Auckland, although the most scenic jump is over the Waikato River in Taupo. Huge rope swings offer variation on the theme; head to Queenstown's Shotover Canyon or Nevis Swing for that swooshy buzz.

With some of the most scenic skydiving jump zones in the world, New Zealand is a fantastic place to take a leap. First-time skydivers can knock off this bucket-list item with a tandem jump, strapped to a qualified instructor, experiencing up to 75 seconds of free fall before the chute opens. The thrill is worth every dollar, from $249 for a 9000ft jump to $559 for NZ's highest free-fall jump (a nerve-jangling 19,000ft, on offer in Franz Josef). Extra costs apply for a DVD or photographs capturing your mid-air terror/delight.

A surprisingly gentle but still thrilling way to take to the skies, paragliding involves setting sail from a hillside or clifftop under a parachute-like wing. Hang gliding is similar but with a smaller, rigid wing. Most flights are conducted in tandem with a master pilot, although it's also possible to get lessons to go it alone. To give it a whirl, try a tandem flight in Queenstown, Wanaka, Nelson, Motueka, Hawke's Bay, Christchurch or Auckland.

Kawakawa Bay and Motuoapa near Lake Taupo; Mangatepopo Valley and Whakapapa Gorge on the Central Plateau; Humphries Castle and Warwick Castle on Mt Taranaki; and Piarere and popular Wharepapa South in the Waikato.

On the South Island, try the Port Hills area above Christchurch or Castle Hill on the road to Arthur's Pass. West of Nelson, the marble and limestone mountains of Golden Bay and Takaka Hill provide prime climbing. Other options are Long Beach (north of Dunedin), and Mihiwaka and Lovers Leap on the Otago Peninsula.

Raining? You'll find indoor climbing walls all around the country, including at Rotorua, Whangarei, Auckland, Tauranga, Taupo, Wellington, Christchurch and Hamilton.

Climb New Zealand (www.climb.co.nz) has the low-down on the gnarliest overhangs around NZ, plus access and instruction info. Needless to say, instruction is a must for all but the most-seasoned climbing pros.

Rock climber, Whanganui Bay

Caving

Caving (aka spelunking) opportunities abound in NZ's honeycombed karst (limestone) regions. You'll find local clubs and organised tours around Auckland, Waitomo, Whangarei, Charleston and Karamea. Golden Bay also has some mammoth caves. Waitomo is home to 'black-water rafting': like white-water rafting but inside a pitch-black cave!

For comprehensive information including details of specific areas and clubs, see the website of the New Zealand Speleological Society (www.caves.org.nz).

Scuba Diving & Snorkelling

NZ is just as enchanting under the waves, with warm waters in the north, interesting sea life all over and some impressive shipwrecks. The flag-bearer is the Poor Knights Islands, where subtropical currents carry and encourage a vibrant mix of sea life. Also rich with marine life is the wreck of the Greenpeace flagship *Rainbow Warrior*, which slumbers beneath the Cavalli Islands (reached from Matauri Bay).

Other notable sites for scuba and snorkelling include the Bay of Islands, Hauraki Gulf, Goat Island and Gisborne's Te Tapuwae o Rongokako Marine Reserve. In the Marlborough Sounds, the MS *Mikhail Lermontov* is one of the world's largest diveable cruise-ship wrecks. In Fiordland, experienced divers can head for Dusky Sound, Milford Sound and Doubtful Sound, which have clear conditions and the occasional friendly fur seal or dolphin. Snorkellers should check out the reefs of Taputeranga Marine Reserve (Wellington) and wildlife-rich Waiheke Island.

Expect to pay anywhere from $160 for a short, introductory, pool-based scuba course, and around $600 for a four-day, PADI-approved, ocean-dive course. One-off organised boat- and land-based dives start at around $170.

Clean seas and diving-safety advocates **New Zealand Underwater Association** (www.nzunderwater.org.nz) website has safety info, diving tips, gear maintenance advice and more.

Snowboarder, Mt Ruapehu (p93)

Skiing & Snowboarding

New Zealand is a premier southern-hemisphere destination for snow bunnies, where wintry pursuits span all levels: family-friendly ski areas, cross-country (Nordic) skiing, daredevil snowboarding terrain and pulse-quickening heliskiing. The NZ ski season varies between areas but it's generally mid-June through September, though it can run as late as mid-October.

The variety of locations and conditions makes it difficult to rate NZ's ski fields in any particular order. Some people like to be near Queenstown's party scene or Mt Ruapehu's volcanic landscapes; others prefer the quality high-altitude runs on Mt Hutt, uncrowded Rainbow or less-stressed club skiing areas. Club areas are publicly accessible and usually less crowded and cheaper than commercial fields, even though nonmembers pay a higher fee.

New Zealand's commercial ski areas aren't generally set up as 'resorts' with chalets, lodges or hotels. Rather, accommodation and après-ski carousing are often in surrounding towns, connected with the slopes via daily shuttles. It's a bonus if you want to sample a few different ski areas, as you can base yourself in one town and day trip to a few different resorts. Many club areas have lodges where you can stay, subject to availability.

Visitor information centres in NZ, and Tourism New Zealand (www.newzealand.com) internationally, have info on the various ski areas and can make bookings and organise packages. Lift passes usually cost $65 to $120 per adult per day (half price for kids) but more for major resorts. Lesson-and-lift packages are available at most areas. Ski and snowboard equipment rental starts at around $50 a day (cheaper for multiday hire). Private/group lessons start at around $120/60 per hour (adult/child).

Surfing

Big swells, golden sand, uncrowded beaches...are you scrambling for a surf board yet? NZ's surf scene is world class, and the long coastline means there's heaps of variety for beginners and experienced surfers: point breaks, reefs, rocky shelves, hollow sandy beach breaks, and islands with swells from all points of the compass. If you're willing to travel off the beaten track, you can score waves all to yourself. A number of hostels and holiday parks double as surf schools and gear-rental outfits, making it easy to roll straight from bed to beach.

Regardless of the season, you'll need a wet suit and some weather research. Water temperatures and climate vary greatly from north to south. In summer on the North Island you can get away with a spring suit and boardies; on the South Island, a 2mm–3mm steamer. In winter on the North Island use a 2mm–3mm steamer, and on the South Island a 3mm–5mm with extras like a hood and booties. Be rip tide aware: don't fight strong currents that sweep you away from the shore and swim parallel to the beach to get beyond the rip's reach before making your way back to land.

Surfing New Zealand (www.surfingnz. co.nz) has a list of approved surf schools where you can learn to catch waves, along with a calendar of competitions and events where you can go slack-jawed at the pros.

White-Water Rafting, Canoeing & Kayaking

Epic mountain ranges and associated rainfall mean there's no shortage of great rivers to raft, nor any shortage of operators ready to get you into the rapids. Rivers are graded from I to VI (VI meaning they can't be safely rafted), with operators often running a couple of different trips to suit ability and age (rougher stretches are usually limited to rafters aged 13 or older).

Queenstown's Shotover and Kawarau Rivers are deservedly popular, but the Rangitata (Geraldine), Buller (Murchison)

and the Arnold and Waiho rate just as highly. For a multiday epic, check out the Landsborough. The central North Island dishes up plenty, including the popular Tongariro, Rangitikei, Mohaka and Wairoa. There are also the Kaituna Cascades near Rotorua, the highlight of which is the 7m drop at Okere Falls.

Kayaking and canoeing are rampant, particularly on friendly lake waters, although there are still plenty of places to paddle the rapids, including some relatively easy stuff on the Whanganui 'Great Walk'. The river conservation nonprofit New Zealand Rafting Association (www. nz-rafting.co.nz); provides river gradings and listings of rafting operators.

Jetboating

The jetboat was invented in NZ by an engineer from Fairlie – Bill Hamilton (1899–1978) – who wanted a boat that could navigate shallow, local rivers. He credited his eventual success to Archimedes, but as most jetboat drivers will inevitably tell you, Kiwi Bill is the hero of the jetboat story.

River jetboat tours can be found throughout NZ, and while much is made of the hair-raising 360-degree spins that see passengers drenched and grinning from ear to ear, they are really just a sideshow. Just as Bill would have it, jetboat journeys take you deep into wilderness you could otherwise never see, and as such they offer one of NZ's most rewarding tour experiences. In Haast and Whataroa, jetboat tours plunge visitors into pristine wilderness, aflutter with birds.

Big-ticket trips such as Queenstown's Shotover, Kawarau and Dart all live up to the hype. But the quieter achievers will blow your skirt up just as high. Check out the Buller and Wilkin in Mt Aspiring National Park, and the Whanganui – one of the most magical A-to-B jetboat trips of them all.

New Zealand's Birds

New Zealand may lack for mammals, but that's conversely created a unique population of birds - a number of species are flightless, having had no need to take to the air to avoid predators.
Check out the excellent Digital Encyclopedia of New Zealand Birds (www.nzbirdsonline.org.nz), and tune up on bird calls at the Department of Conservation website (www.doc.govt.nz/nature/native-animals/birds).

1. Silvereye/Tauhou
One of NZ's most prevalent birds, this small, agile creature is easily recognised by its white eye-ring and inclination to sing.

2. New Zealand pigeon/Kereru
If you hear heavy wingbeats overhead, it'll be the kereru. NZ's handsome native pigeon is widespread through the country and fond of powerlines and branches.

3. Bellbird/Korimako
Sounding less like a bell and more like Adele, this enchanting songbird sounds big but is a small, green slip of a thing, fond of nectar and found on both islands.

4. Fantail/Piwakawaka
This little charmer will entrance you up close, but in truth it cares not a jot about you, merely the insects you displace.

5. Grey Warbler/Riroriro
NZ's most widely distributed endemic bird species is also one of its smallest. Tending to hide in dense vegetation, the featherweight affirms its presence by warbling its jolly head off.

6. Woodhen/Weka
Often mistaken by visitors as a kiwi, this large flightless bird has a keen nose for lunch crumbs and will often appear at well-frequented picnic spots.

7. Pukeko
Looking like a smooth blue chicken with a red forehead, this bird is often seen pecking about in paddocks or crossing the road in front of high-speed traffic. It's territorial, highly social and easily recognised.

8. Paradise Shelduck
This colourful, conspicuous and honking waterfowl could be mistaken for a small goose as it hangs out in wild wetlands, river flats, sportsfields and other open grassed areas.

9. Rifleman/Tititipounamu
NZ's smallest bird, this hyperactive forest dweller produces a characteristic 'wing-flicking' while moving through the canopy and foraging up and down tree trunks.

10. Kiwi
A national icon with an onomatopoeic name, at least for the male, which cries 'kiwi!' The females make an ugly sound, a bit like someone with a sore throat. There are five different species.

11. Robin
Inhabiting forest and scrub, the distinct North Island and South Island robins stand leggy and erect, sing loud and long, and will often approach very closely.

2 TESSA PALMER/SHUTTERSTOCK ©

3 GRANT REABURN/GETTY IMAGES ©

5 MARTIN PELANEK/SHUTTERSTOCK ©

6 LAZINGBEE/GETTY IMAGES ©

8 MALGORZATA LITKOWSKA/SHUTTERSTOCK ©

9 MARTIN PELANEK/SHUTTERSTOCK ©

0 ROBIN BUSH/GETTY IMAGES ©

11 DAVID TIPLING/GETTY IMAGES ©

12. Tomtit/Miromiro

Widespread inhabitant of forest and shrubland, the tomtit is often reclusive and hard to see, but occasionally moves in for a closer look.

13. Kea

Resident only in the South Island, this is the world's only true alpine parrot. Kea appear innately curious, but this is simply a pretence to peck destructively at your possessions.

14. Falcon/Karearea

The NZ falcon is a magpie-sized bird of prey found in both forest and open habitats such as tussocklands and roughly grazed hill country.

15. Kaka

This screechy parrot flaps boldly across the sky and settles in a wide variety of native forest, including podocarp and beech forest.

16. Tui

Common throughout town and country, the 'parson bird' is metallic bluey-green with white throat tufts. Sometimes tuneful, and sometimes cacophonous, it is always an aerobatic flapper.

17. Morepork/Ruru

You may not see this small, nocturnal owl, but you'll probably hear its 'more-pork' call and peculiar screeches. If you're lucky it may eyeball you from a low branch in both native and exotic forests.

18. Blue Duck/Whio

Mostly confined to clear, fast-flowing rivers in the mountains, this darling little bird issues a shrill 'whio' whistle above the noise of turbulent waters.

19. Kakariki

Also known as the red- or yellow-crowned parakeet and now reasonably rare on the mainland, these birds will most likely be seen in tall forest.

Plan Your Trip
Safety in the Outdoors

While tramping has some inherent risks, it takes only a bit of planning and preparation, selecting tracks compatible with your ability and paying attention to the weather to significantly increase your chances of a successful adventure. Venturing into the wilderness shouldn't be taken lightly. It's extremely important to understand the risks involved, and to be prepared for them.

New Zealand Outdoor Safety Code

Plan Your Trip
Seek local knowledge and plan the route you will take and the amount of time you can reasonably expect it to take.

Tell Someone
Tell someone your plans and leave a date by which the alarm should be raised if you haven't returned.

Be Aware of the Weather
New Zealand's weather can be highly changeable. Check the forecast and expect weather changes.

Know Your Limits
Challenge yourself within your physical limits and experience.

Take Sufficient Supplies & Equipment
Make sure you have enough food, clothing, equipment and emergency rations for the worst-case scenario. Take an appropriate means of communication.

Trip Planning
Clothing, Equipment & Food

It's paramount to have the right kit (p47) for the job. Staying warm and dry is essential, so pack at least three clothing layers, including a spare set of dry clothes to change into in camp or huts. The rest of your kit will be dictated by your trip length and location, but always carry an emergency kit that includes first-aid supplies and a head torch, wet-weather gear, warm clothes (including a hat and gloves) and a means of communication.

You'll expend far more energy than normal when tramping. Fuelling up on the right types of food and staying hydrated will keep you rational, and smiling.

Intentions

Telling someone your plans, including setting a date and time for raising an alarm if you haven't returned, is an essential part of your pre-trip planning. There are several options available, and it's important you use a method that works for you and your trusted contact. This includes calling someone, leaving a written note, posting a personal message to someone on social media or using the outdoors intentions form at www.adventuresmart.org.

nz/outdoors-intentions. Just remember to inform your trusted contact that you've returned safely to prevent the possibility of an unnecessary search.

When you're on the track, write in the hut logbooks even if you're not staying there, as this acts like a breadcrumb trail and will help would-be rescuers locate and find you more quickly.

Get the Latest Information

Before you set off, make sure you get the latest weather and track information. Check in at the nearest DOC office for track and condition updates and visit the MetService website (www.metservice.com) for weather details.

Navigation
Stay on Track

With the exception of remote and lightly used backcountry routes, NZ's track network is very well signposted. The DOC tracks typically use orange triangles, most commonly found on a tree or pole, but you may also see round, coloured-metal discs, although these aren't common. On routes or tracks above the bushline you may also see orange marker poles or rock cairns (piles of rocks) that mark the route – pay particular attention when following cairns and don't move on until you can see the next one ahead of you.

In areas where pest eradication is taking place you may also notice blue or pink triangles, or coloured ribbons hanging from branches. Do not follow these as these mark bait/trap lines, not tracks.

A significant challenge to navigation is bad weather, when the risk of getting lost is heightened by poor visibility. The art of navigation is an essential tramping skill. Not only will it ensure that you know where you are and where you need to go, but reading a map and using a compass will help you see the bigger picture, including having an awareness of the surrounding area and possible exit routes, distances and types of terrain.

Maps

An up-to-date topographic map is recommended for all but the shortest of day

walks. The most commonly used maps are the NZTopo50 map series (1:50,000) produced by Land Information New Zealand (LINZ; www.linz.govt.nz), which cover the whole country. Hard copies are available from most outdoor gear shops, while digital maps can be viewed and downloaded from the LINZ website and www.topomap.co.nz.

A great alternative is the NewTopo map series (www.newtopo.co.nz), of varying scales, which logically cover popular tramping areas previously covered by multiple maps. Whichever hard-copy maps you use, they're best laminated or placed in a clear plastic sleeve to protect them from the elements.

With today's smartphones it's very easy and convenient to use maps loaded onto your device, but relying solely on this option can be very risky – batteries can go flat!

Navigation Equipment
Maps & Compass

Always carry a good topographical map and know how to read it properly. Before the tramp, ensure that you understand the contours and the map symbols, plus the main ridge and river systems in the area.

Familiarise yourself with the north–south bearings, and the general direction you're heading in. On the track, identify major landforms (mountain ranges, gorges etc) and find them on the map. This will give you a better understanding of the local geography.

Buy an adjustable-dial compass and learn how to use it. A compass in NZ will point towards magnetic north, so the needle needs to be specially weighted to keep it horizontal. Northern-hemisphere compasses should not be used in NZ. Magnetic north in NZ is between 18 and 25 degrees east of grid north; using a variation of 21 degrees is adequate for most tramping navigation around NZ, but check the map for local variation.

Using a Compass

A compass only has value if you know how to use it – an essential skill on any tramp. Learn to orient your map, take bearings and then be able to follow them. Once you've mastered the basics, practise on short walks.

GPS

Hand-held Global Positioning System (GPS) receivers are relatively cheap, compact, easy to use and, in the right conditions, able to identify your location to within around 20m. On many models you can input waypoints, mark your route, measure your altitude, record your progress and overlay maps. They are, however, no substitute for sound navigational skills and a compass and map. Batteries go flat, units get dropped and you can't always get a good satellite signal under forest canopies, below high cliffs or in snow or hail.

Watch the Weather

Crowded House probably put it best when they sang 'Four Seasons in One Day' – New Zealand is a couple of narrow islands in a big sea, so its weather is highly unpredictable, occasionally extreme and can change in a blink.

The prevailing weather pattern in NZ is a cycle of high-pressure systems (anticyclones or ridges) followed by low-pressure systems (troughs or depressions), travelling west to east. Anticyclones normally pass the northern portions of the country at intervals of three to seven days, bringing fine weather with light or moderate winds. In between are depressions of rain, strong winds and lower temperatures.

Because most of the country's mountain ranges run roughly north–south, they generate their own local weather conditions. It's not uncommon to have rain on the windward (western side) of a range, fine weather on the lee (eastern) side, and miserable conditions of heavy wind, rain and snow (even in summer!) along the ridge tops.

Check the Forecast

Always check the weather forecast before you set off. MetService (www.metservice. com) provides NZ's official weather forecasts, weather warnings and watches, and it has very handy national-park and mountain forecasts for specific areas of the country. Its range of apps also provide easy-to-use weather information that's handy to access when you're on the move.

The DOC and i-SITE visitors centres are a reliable source of short- and long-range forecasts, with the information they use also coming from MetService. You're also bound to get varying predictions from accommodation providers, shuttle-bus drivers and the lady at the pie shop. None of these are a substitute for official, up-to-date reports, but they may provide some local context.

If things are looking ordinary, delay your trip or seek advice from local experts on alternative routes or other options.

Read the Weather

Once on the track, keep an eye on the skies. Given sufficient warning you can put your foot on the gas to outpace an oncoming storm, choose to wait it out in a hut, or slow down to maximise a slot of sunshine. The key thing to remember, though, is that New Zealand's weather can change extremely quickly, especially in the mountains.

Two early signs of approaching bad weather are an increase in wind speed and the appearance of high cloud sheets. These sheets, often stacked on top of one another, or looking like flying saucers, are known as lenticular or hog's back clouds and are the outriders of northwesterly storms. As the depression moves onto the country, the wind alters direction, often quite suddenly, and a weather change results.

The wind is the key to reading the weather in the bush. As a general rule, northwesterlies bring wet weather and storms, while southerlies are a sign of a cool frontal change, often followed by cold and clear conditions. Northeasterlies may also signal good weather approaching, whereas southwesterlies are normally associated with cool, rain-laden winds.

The higher the altitude, the more severe the weather can be, with significantly lower temperatures, stronger winds and rain that can quickly turn to snow. Snowfall

Top: Lenticular clouds over Aoraki/Mt Cook National Park (p209)

Bottom: Hiker on the Kepler Track (p284)

NARUEDOM YAEMPONGSA/SHUTTERSTOCK ©

and blizzards can occur at any time of year in alpine areas, so you must be properly equipped.

If heavy storms move in once you're on the track, the best idea is to stay in a hut and take a day off, especially if you're in an alpine area. Be patient and don't worry about missing a bus or lift at the end of the tramp. There are more important things than schedules when conditions turn threatening. This is particular important if you need to cross a river to get out.

Extremes of Heat & Cold

Hypothermia

Hypothermia occurs when your body is unable to maintain its core temperature, leading to a loss of normal function and, in severe cases, possibly death. It's far less common these days, due largely to advances in clothing technology.

Avoiding getting cold is simple: wear the right fabrics. Clothing only retains the heat your body produces. Wear wool and synthetics, as they draw moisture away from the body and retain warmth. Avoid cotton clothing – it ceases to insulate you when it gets wet. The more layers you wear, the warmer you'll be. Take wind and rain protection. A good outer layer to protect you from rain and wind is essential. Put it on before you get wet or cold.

Eat nutritious food and staying hydrated. Food gives you the energy to keep your body warm. On cooler days you'll need more food. Drink regularly, including a hot beverage to start and end the day.

If anyone in your group starts to show signs of being cold, stop and find shelter. This can be as simple as getting everyone to huddle underneath a tent fly, or getting a couple of people inside a survival bag. Remove wet clothes and put on dry clothes. Get the cold person into a sleeping bag if they're still cold. If other people huddle with them, they'll warm up more quickly. Eat and have a warm, sweet drink.

Sunburn & Heatstroke

With long days in the sun, trampers are at high risk of sunburn, heat exhaustion, heatstroke and, in the long term, of developing skin cancer. Sunburn happens surprisingly quickly in New Zealand, with the ozone layer thinner here than in most other parts of the world.

Reduce the risk of sunburn by covering up, even when it's cloudy, and especially when you're at high altitude. Protect your eyes with good-quality sunglasses, particularly near water, sand or snow, and use SPF30+ sunscreen on exposed skin. A full-brimmed hat will keep the sun's rays (and – bonus prize! – some sandflies) at bay. Choose well-shaded spots for rest stops and lunch breaks.

Long, continuous periods of exposure to high temperatures and insufficient fluid intake can leave you vulnerable to heatstroke. Symptoms include nausea, minimal sweating and a high body temperature (above 39°C). In severe cases sweating may cease and the skin can become flushed. Headaches and a lack of coordination may also occur, and the patient may become

PLAN TO BE SAFE

If you're new to New Zealand, or if you'd like to plan your tramp the easy way, the Mountain Safety Council's online 'Plan My Trip' tool is an excellent resource. Through the MSC website (www.mountainsafety.org.nz), 'Plan My Trip' steps you through a few simple questions (activity type, intended location, length of trip, group size) before handing you any relevant warnings and notices for the trip. The tool can give you MetService weather warnings and watches, DOC alerts on huts, campsites and tracks and, if the area coincides with a forecast area, a NZ Avalanche Advisory forecast. It then pulls together all of the trip and alert information and adds an activity and seasonally specific packing list as well as trip recommendations into a shareable (via email/Facebook) and downloadable PDF.

It all takes just a few minutes and is a highly recommended mobile-friendly planning tool.

Hiker at Westland Tai Poutini National Park (p229)

confused or aggressive. Eventually the victim will become delirious and/or suffer convulsions. Evacuation to a hospital is essential for heatstroke sufferers. While waiting for evacuation get the patient out of the sun, remove his or her clothing, cover them with wet clothing or a wet sheet or towel, then fan them continuously. Also, administer fluids if they're conscious.

River Crossings

Crossing rivers while tramping in New Zealand presents one of the most significant hazards and doing so should not be taken lightly. Remember: if in doubt, stay out.

Most rivers and major streams along well-used tracks are bridged at key crossing points, while smaller streams that typically only require an ankle-deep wade to reach the other side are not bridged. However, it's not uncommon to come across a river crossing that isn't bridged.

During your trip planning it's important to identify if you have any river crossings. If you think there will be, make sure you have considered alternative options

should the weather be poor and you need to change your plans. One of the most important things when considering a river crossing is patience. Stop, take off your pack, spend time assessing the river before you consider crossing, and follow these essential steps.

➡ Is it safe to cross? Assess the river and consider its speed – if it's flowing faster than walking pace, don't cross. Assess the depth – if it's deeper than mid-thigh on the shortest person, you shouldn't cross. Look for colour and clarity – can you see the bottom of the river, or is it brown or murky water? If the latter, these are signs the river is in flood. Look for any debris being washed down the river; tree branches or the sound of rolling rocks are signs the river is unsafe.

➡ Where to cross? Look for easy entry and exit spots, avoiding steep banks, rapids (white water) and edges that are covered in tree roots or have branches in the water. Consider what's downriver and avoid areas just upstream of waterfalls, rapids and dead trees that could cause you problems.

During and immediately after moderate to heavy rain is a particularly dangerous time to cross a stream or river. It doesn't take long – sometimes less than an hour – to turn a mountain creek into an impassable torrent of white water.

If you're not certain you can cross a river or stream safely, check your map for a bridge that offers a safe alternate route, take shelter and wait, or head back to the last hut or camp and sit it out.

Remember, you don't have to cross that river: again, if in doubt, stay out. Streams and rivers rise quickly, but return to their normal levels almost as fast. If you wait a day, or even an afternoon, the water will often subside enough to be crossed safely.

How to Cross

If you decide that it's safe to cross, look for an area where the river is braided into several shallow channels, or where the water is flowing over an even river bed. Avoid crossing near large boulders and uneven areas of the river bed. Plan to cross the river at an angle, moving slightly downstream with the current as you make your way across.

The best method to use when tramping in a group is the mutual-support method, which maximises the group's ability to support each other. Ideal group sizes are two to five people – if you're in a larger group, you should split and cross as two smaller groups.

The mutual-support method requires a bit of practice, so if you know you're going to cross a river you can give it a go on land at the hut or campsite the night before, or on the river bank before you cross. Appoint a leader who can manage the crossing and communicate actions to the group.

The method works as follows:

➡ Line up shoulder to shoulder, with the strongest person at the upstream end and the whole group facing the river.

➡ Keep waist belts on your backpack done up, loosen the shoulder straps and undo chest straps.

➡ Insert your arms between your neighbour's pack and their back. Supporting each other, cross together in a line with the current flowing parallel to the group line.

Wear your pack when crossing rivers. It can act as a buoyancy aid, and if you get swept away you'll want your gear when you make it back to the bank. If you fall, manoeuvre yourself feet first, using your arms and feet

for control and to move yourself to the nearest bank, or float to a shallow area to exit.

If you're tramping alone, use a pole as a 'third leg' to ensure you always have two contact points with the river bed when moving.

Emergencies & Rescue

Things can go wrong for even the most well-prepared and experienced trampers. If you find yourself in an emergency, the STAR model will help you make the right decision:

Stop Take a breath, sit down and remain calm.

Think Look around you; listen and brainstorm options.

Assess Evaluate the options and their potential consequences.

Respond Make the best decision.

If someone in your group is injured or falls ill and can't move, you may decide to seek help. If you have a suitable communication device, you should be able to get a message out. If not, leave somebody with that person while another person or two (preferably) goes for help. If the only option is to leave the injured person while you go for help, leave them with as much warm clothing, food and water as it's sensible to spare, plus a whistle and torch, and make sure you know exactly where they are.

Help rescuers find you by marking your position with arrows or cairns built out of rocks and wood, laying out brightly coloured items or tying them to trees so they can be easily seen from the air, and by burning green wood and leaves to produce smoke. If you have a personal locator beacon (PLB), activate it so rescuers know you're in trouble and can pinpoint your location. This can save precious time, and lives.

In NZ, many search-and-rescue evacuations are done by helicopter. Make sure there are no loose items around the area where the helicopter will land. Never approach a helicopter unless directed to, and always approach from the front. Avoid high ground, keep low and follow the instructions of the pilot and crew.

Communication

There are a number of ways that tramp-ers can equip themselves to communicate with the outside world or Police Search and Rescue in an emergency. The main methods for two-way communications are mountain radios, satellite phones and sat-ellite messenger devices.

Mobile phones should be carried, but don't rely on them as there's very little cov-erage in NZ's backcountry. If you do have a signal and encounter an emergency, dial 111. Keep your phone switched off when you're not using it to save batteries, and always stow it in a waterproof bag.

When activated, personal locator bea-cons (PLBs) emit a radio distress signal that's picked up by satellite or aircraft and relayed to the Rescue Coordination Cen-tre of New Zealand. They're lightweight, require no set-up and could save your life. They're also cheap to hire (from $5 per day) and readily available from outdoor gear shops and some visitor centres and DOC offices. Only activate your PLB in life-threatening situations. PLBs don't provide two-way communications so they're only useful in an emergency situation. See www.beacons.org.nz for more details.

Satellite phones can be used anywhere there's line of sight to a satellite. They're expensive to buy and operate, but they can be hired from around $20 per day.

Satellite messenger devices, such as SPOT (www.findmespot.com) or Garmin inReach (www.garmin.com) allow you to send and receive messages and alert emer-gency services. These are becoming more popular and, unlike PLBs, provide an alter-native communication option that isn't just a distress call.

The Mountain Radio Service (www.mountainradio.co.nz) comprises volunteer organisations providing backcountry ra-dio communication for the South Island and Stewart Island, including regular updates from base control to relay weather forecasts, locations and intended routes. You can rent radio sets cheaply (from $5 per day) from the organisations and some outdoor gear shops. It's an excellent way of keeping in touch, and although not all areas are monitored 24/7, there's usually someone listening in on one of the fre-

WARNING: AVALANCHES

Avalanche conditions are most likely to occur between June and October (winter to spring), but avalanche paths can be active at any time of year if there are unseasonable snow-falls. If you're heading above the bushline or into alpine territory, you should check the Mountain Safety Council New Zealand Avalanche Advisory (www.avalanche.net.nz) for the latest avalanche forecasts. Lo-cal DOC offices also have the latest avalanche forecasts and condition updates, and can advise on the saf-est routes during avalanche season. If you visit avalanche-prone areas, don't tramp alone and make sure you stick to low-angle slopes to minimise risk, as avalanches occur most com-monly on slopes angled between 30 and 45 degrees.

quencies. Other similar services exist for the North Island, including Wellington Mountain Radio Service (www.wmrs.org.nz) and Central North Island Mountain Radio Service (www.cnimrs.org.nz).

If You Get Lost

If you do get lost, the last thing you want to do is wander hopelessly in the bush. If you are lost and can't help yourself, stop, stay where you are and use your communi-cation device to raise the alarm. Remem-ber the following rules:

➡ If you think you can retrace your route, do so, marking your starting spot (in case you have to start again) and your route as you move. Otherwise, stay put or move to an open area such as a clearing or river bank.

➡ If you have to spend a night in the open, find or make a shelter, put on extra clothes and build a fire.

➡ Help searchers find you by building arrows or cairns out of rocks and wood, laying out brightly coloured items that can be easily seen from the air, and by burning green wood and leaves to produce smoke.

INJURY PREVENTION

Falling is the most common reason for injuries, fatalities and the need for rescue while tramping in New Zealand. You can minimise the risks associated with falling by adhering to the following:

➡ Stay on marked tracks.

➡ Never venture too close to the edge of cliffs or bluffs (you can still get that photo by standing back a couple of metres).

➡ Pay particular attention and use careful foot placement on sections of tracks that have drops beside them.

The most common injuries sustained by trampers are to the lower body, primarily the ankles and knees. To avoid injuries:

➡ Use good-quality, sturdy footwear.

➡ Warm up at the start of the day by doing some light stretching before you set off and again at the end of the day to cool down.

➡ Use walking poles to minimise the impact on your joints.

➡ Pack your backpack appropriately to maximise comfort and to avoid placing unnecessary strain on your lower limbs.

First Aid

At least one person in your group should possess adequate first-aid knowledge and the skills to apply it. If possible, attend a course before heading into the outdoors or at least do some reading; the Mountain Safety Council's *New Zealand Outdoor First Aid* manual is comprehensive and can be purchased through their website (www.mountainsafety.org.nz), as is the St John online First Aid Library (www.stjohn.org.nz). A first-aid kit is a must for any tramp.

Drinking Water

As part of your trip planning think about access to drinking water. If you're staying at recognised huts or campsites, there will typically be a water supply nearby, but during the day you may not have easy access to drinking water, especially on alpine tramping sections above the bushline in summer. Plan to carry a minimum of 2L per person in these situations.

Tap water is clean and safe to drink in NZ. Water in lakes, rivers and streams will look clean and may be OK, but since the diarrhoea-causing *Giardia lamblia* parasite has been found in some waterways, water from any of these sources should be treated before drinking. The protozoan *cryptosporidium* (crypto) has also been found in some feral animals and livestock (mainly possums and cows). DOC can advise on the occurrence of giardia and crypto in national parks and forests, and along tracks it administers. Most huts are equipped with a rainwater tank that provides safe drinking water safe, but follow the advice of signs.

If you're unsure about the quality of water, treat it before drinking. Boiling is the simplest method. Water should be brought to a rolling boil for one minute. At altitudes above 2000m, you should boil water for three minutes. If boiling water isn't possible, a combination of filtration and chemical disinfection is the most effective pathogen reduction method in drinking water for backcountry use. Manufacturers' instructions must be followed. Note that disinfection with iodine or chlorine is not effective in killing *cryptosporidium*, while disinfection with chlorine dioxide has a low to moderate effectiveness in killing *cryptosporidium*. Disinfection with iodine or chlorine has a low to moderate effectiveness in killing giardia, while disinfection with chlorine dioxide has a high effectiveness in killing giardia. Filtration (without chemical disinfection) is not effective in removing viruses.

Filtering with a giardia-rated filter is a good and more rapid method for treating water. Filters are widely available from outdoor gear retailers, and they'll also remove crypto. Also available are compact battery-powered purifiers that kill most waterborne bacteria and viruses using UV light.

Plan Your Trip

Clothing, Equipment & Food

On a tramp, what you don't carry is just as important as what you do. Learn which items of clothing, equipment and food are indispensable and which are ballast. Test your pack-load before setting off, so that your back and shoulders can tell you if you really need those little extras.

Clothing

When buying clothes for tramping, consider their weight, warmth, fit, breathability and, for outer layers, their ability to keep you dry. Always be prepared for bad weather; carrying an extra midlayer just in case is a smart option.

Layering

The key to staying warm is layering your clothes, which traps air between layers (the best way to conserve body heat) and allows you to add or remove clothing to suit conditions. You should be able to wear all of your layers together if absolutely necessary.

Choose your base layer (closest to the skin) carefully as these items have to deal with sweat, which in cool conditions can reduce your ability to keep warm. Merino wool, polypropylene, polyester or merino-synthetic mixes are good options; cotton is not as it doesn't trap the air inside or keep any body warmth when wet. Ultrafine merino has become a bit of a staple base layer among trampers. It can be expensive, but it's soft and comfortable and won't smell even after a few days on the trail. Polypropylene and polyester are excellent

Tips for Packing Light

Take only the food and fuel you need, plus one or two days' spare in case you're delayed by bad weather, an impassable river or other mishaps.

Plan the amount of water you'll need to carry, accounting for availability en route.

Beyond a spare set of clothing for the evening, you need not take anything more than what you plan to hike in.

Don't take jeans or any cotton clothing: they're heavy, especially when wet, difficult to walk in and don't retain any heat.

Limit your toiletries (miniature travel packs are ideal); weight obsessives have even been known to snap their toothbrushes in half!

Repackage all foodstuffs into lightweight plastic. Avoid carrying tins of food – you'll have to carry the empty tins out.

Share gear – if you're tramping in a pair or a group, share your stove, food, toothpaste, first-aid kit...everything you can without leaving the essentials behind.

at wicking moisture away from the skin, but they do tend to retain odours.

An insulating midlayer provides essential additional warmth. Many trampers use a jersey or jacket of pile or fleece fabric, such as Polartec, or merino wool. Avoid cotton hooded sweatshirts, as they won't insulate when wet and take forever to dry. Also toss into your backpack some woollen mittens and a wool or fleece hat. The body loses most of its heat through its extremities, particularly the head.

A common and practical uniform for the track is thermal leggings under a pair of hiking shorts, giving maximum freedom of movement while providing protection from cold weather, light rain, excessive sun and bugs. If you prefer long trousers they should preferably be of stretch nylon, synthetic pile or light merino, never denim.

Waterproof Shell

Your jacket should be made of a breathable waterproof fabric, with generous pockets, a good-quality heavy-gauge zip protected by a storm flap, and a hood that's roomy enough to cover a cap or warm hat, but which still affords peripheral vision. Make sure the sleeves extend well down the wrist, and that the overall body length allows you to sit down without getting a wet, mossy bum. If your jacket is shorter and ends around your waist, pack waterproof overtrousers.

Overtrousers are essential if you're tramping in wet and cold conditions. Choose a style with slits for pocket access and long ankle zips so that you can pull them on and off over your boots.

Footwear

Many trampers now opt for lightweight nylon boots made by a number of sporting-shoe companies. Designed for trail hiking, easy terrain and carrying light loads, such boots are fine for well-maintained tracks such as the Kepler, Milford, Routeburn and Greenstone. A growing trend is towards hiking shoes, without the ankle support (and weight) of boots, though in New Zealand terrain and conditions they're not really suited to anything other than well-maintained easy tracks. Any overnight tramps will require a minimum of light-weight boots.

For more challenging tramps, which often use less-maintained tracks or routes covered in rocks, tree roots and loose gravel, sturdy hiking boots are a much wiser choice, offering more support, with a stiff leather upper, durable sole and protective shanks. Many also feature a high-tech waterproof lining.

Gaiters

Gaiters, which protect your lower legs and come in two lengths, are something of a Kiwi tramping institution, and for good reason. If you're likely to be tramping through snow, deep mud or scratchy scrub, consider using them to protect your lower legs, to keep unwanted stones out of your boots and to try to keep your socks dry. The best gaiters are made of strong synthetic fabric or canvas, have a hook to attach them to laces (to prevent them slipping up and down your legs), and an easy-to-undo method of securing them around feet.

Equipment

Backpack

For day tramps a 30L to 40L day-pack should suffice, but for multiday tramps you'll likely need a backpack of between 60L and 70L. The required capacity will depend on the destination, whether you plan to camp or stay in huts, the facilities provided and the duration of your tramp. Your pack should be roomy enough for your gear without the need to strap additional items to the outside.

Assemble everything you intend to take and try loading it into a pack to see if it's large enough. Keep in mind that as your pack's weight increases, your enjoyment and walking speed decreases, so think twice about taking unnecessary items.

A good backpack should have adjustable, well-padded shoulders straps and hip belt, and a chest strap to evenly distribute the weight between your shoulders and hips. External pockets are good for quick access to water bottles, snacks and maps.

Even if the manufacturer claims your pack is waterproof, it's not (nothing is in continuous NZ rain!). Use a heavy-duty interior plastic liner to ensure everything stays dry.

EQUIPMENT CHECKLIST

This is a general guide to the things you might take on a tramp. Your personal list will vary depending on the type and length of your tramp, whether you're camping or staying in huts and lodges, and on the terrain, weather conditions and time of year.

Clothing

☐ sturdy walking boots and spare laces
☐ gaiters
☐ warm hat or balaclava
☐ scarf or buff
☐ gloves/mittens
☐ waterproof overtrousers
☐ waterproof rain jacket with hood
☐ footwear for hut use: sandals or thongs (flip flops, jandals)
☐ shorts and trousers or skirt (quick-drying)
☐ socks (multiple pairs)
☐ underwear
☐ sunhat
☐ sunglasses
☐ sweater or fleece jacket
☐ thermal top and bottoms
☐ T-shirt and long-sleeved shirts (quick-drying)

Equipment

☐ backpack with waterproof liner
☐ first-aid kit
☐ food and snacks (high-energy) and emergency supplies for one or two days
☐ tent, pegs, poles and guy ropes (if not staying in huts)
☐ sleeping bag and bag liner/inner sheet
☐ sleeping mat (if not staying in huts)
☐ portable stove, fuel and pan(s)
☐ cooking, eating and drinking utensils
☐ insect repellent
☐ map (waterproof, or in clear plastic cover) and compass

☐ communication device (mobile phone and one of satellite phone/mountain radio/personal locator beacon)
☐ torch (flashlight) or headlamp, spare batteries and bulb
☐ water bottle or bladder (minimum 2L capacity)
☐ pocket knife
☐ sunscreen and lip balm
☐ survival bag or blanket
☐ toilet paper and trowel
☐ plastic bags (for carrying rubbish)
☐ whistle (for emergencies)
☐ dishwashing kit (pot scrubber and biodegradable detergent)
☐ matches and lighter
☐ sewing/repair kit
☐ spare cord
☐ toiletries
☐ small towel
☐ water purification tablets, iodine or filter

Optional Items

☐ GPS receiver
☐ duct tape
☐ book
☐ camera
☐ day-pack (for side trips)
☐ tent groundsheet
☐ swimming costume
☐ walking poles
☐ deck of cards

Sleeping Bag & Mat

Down sleeping bags are warm, lightweight and compact, but useless if they get wet. Synthetic bags are cheaper and more effective when wet, but are generally heavier and bulkier. Mummy-shaped designs prove best for weight and warmth, but can be a little more restrictive to sleep in.

A sleeping bag's rating (minus 5°C, for instance) is the coldest temperature at which a person should feel comfortable in the bag. For extra warmth, purchase a sleeping-bag liner, which will also protect the sleeping bag and add years to its life. Most huts have mattresses and are warm enough that a medium-weight bag of synthetic fibres is more than sufficient. Huts

Camping in Mt Aspiring National Park (p241)

don't have blankets, so you'll need to bring your sleeping gear with you everywhere you tramp.

Self-inflating sleeping mats provide comfort and insulation from the cold. Foam mats are cheap, but can be far less comfortable. If you're planning to stay in huts you most likely won't need a sleeping mat. However, if you're tramping a popular track during high season, the hut might be full when you arrive, in which case a sleeping mat will make a night on the floor much more pleasant.

Stove & Fuel

Before your trip, check whether the huts you intend to stay at have gas cookers. Even if they do, carrying your own stove means you won't have to fight for space on the hob, and you can prepare hot food or a cup of tea on the track, providing warm relief on wet and cold days, or if you're delayed and have to make camp unexpectedly.

When buying a stove, choose one that's lightweight and easy to operate. Isobutane canister stoves are the easiest to operate. Multifuel stoves are versatile but

need pumping, priming and lots of cleaning. In general, liquid fuels are efficient and cheap; look for high-performance, cleaner-burning fuel. Gas is more expensive, cleaner and a reasonable performer. When using gas canisters, be sure to sure to carry yours out at the end of a tramp. In New Zealand, fuel can be found at outdoor gear shops, hardware stores (white gas), some supermarkets and petrol stations.

Airlines prohibit flammable materials and may well reject empty liquid-fuel bottles, or even the stoves. Check with your airline for its rules before you fly.

Most huts have fireplaces, but these are designed as a heating source in poor weather, not a cooking facility. Don't plan to cook on them.

Tent

A tent is obviously a necessity on tracks without huts, such as the Te Paki Coastal Track, but they can also come in handy on popular tracks when huts might be full, snorers keep you awake, or you just want to enjoy the outdoors in solitude.

A three-season tent will suffice in most conditions. Because of the amount of climbing encountered on many New Zealand tracks, weight is a major issue, with most trampers selecting tents of around 2kg to 3kg that will sleep two or three people. The floor and the fly should be waterproof, have taped or sealed seams and covered zips to stop leaks. Dome- and tunnel-shaped tents handle blustery conditions better than flat-sided tents. Make sure you peg out all your guy lines as strong winds commonly blow tents over.

Walking Poles

It's become popular to tramp with walking poles, especially on tracks and routes above the bushline. A pair of lightweight telescopic poles will help you balance, give you an added push when climbing steep ridges and slopes, and ease the jarring on your knees during descents.

Buying & Hiring Locally

Most major towns in NZ will have at least one outdoor-gear shop. Stores to keep an eye out for include Bivouac Outdoor (www.bivouac.co.nz), Outside Sports (www.outsidesports.co.nz), Torpedo7 (www.torpedo7.co.nz), Macpac (www.macpac.co.nz) and Kathmandu (www.kathmandu.co.nz).

Outdoor-gear shops in popular tramping areas such as Queenstown, Te Anau and Nelson will often hire a variety of gear for a daily or weekly charge. Prices vary, but expect to pay around $10 a day for a sleeping bag, backpack and jacket, and about $5 for a stove. Overseas travellers who want to tramp more than one track should bring all their own gear, or at least the major items such as tent, boots, backpack, sleeping bag and stove.

Food

Having enough of the right food is a tramping essential and will enhance your trip substantially. A hearty and tasty meal at the end of the day, or a square of chocolate or delicious snack on the track, helps keep both energy levels and morale high.

Food should be lightweight and nutritious. A good overall ratio is 1:1:4 for proteins (meats, cheese, eggs, milk powder, nuts), fats (cheese, chocolates, cured meats) and carbohydrates (sugar, bread, rice, pasta, sweets, dried fruit). If it's a short tramp – two or three days – you can take fresh vegetables and even meat. For longer trips, save weight by taking more dehydrated foods and ready-made meals, which can be purchased at most outdoor gear shops and some supermarkets.

Always include extra meals for that unscheduled additional day on the track due to bad weather or an emergency.

Regions at a Glance

Northland, Auckland & Coromandel

Forests
Beaches
History

Green Giants

Explore extensive tracts of remnant native forest on a multitude of tracks in Northland, the Coromandel's Kauaeranga Valley and on Great Barrier Island. Stars of the show are the ancient kauri giants that can live for more than 2000 years.

Strands of Sand

With a subtropical climate that beckons a dip, this region rolls out beaches along the Te Paki Coastal Track, Cape Brett Track and Coromandel Walkway.

Tales of the Past

Wander through the golden glow of history in Karangahake Gorge, or find the ghosts of kauri past in the Kauaeranga Valley.

p52

Tongariro, Te Urewera & Central North Island

Volcanoes
Lakes
Outdoor action

Belching Peaks

The three steaming, smoking, occasionally erupting volcanoes at the heart of the North Island are the focus of both a Great Walk and a trail that many say is the greatest day walk of all.

Water Wonders

New Zealand's mightiest river is born from its greatest lake; Lake Taupo. Aquatic pursuits such as kayaking, sailing and fishing make it a great base between hikes. In remote Te Urewera, the magical, mystical Lake Waikaremoana waits to be explored.

Outdoor Action

Skydiving, bungy jumping, whitewater rafting, jetboating, mountain biking, wakeboarding, parasailing, skiing – you want thrills, you got 'em.

p90

Taranaki & Southern North Island

Nature Reserves
Coastal scenery
Capital city

Vintage Reserves

Mt Taranaki (Egmont National Park) is a classic volcano with fabulous tramping, while Ruahine and Tararua Forest Parks are surprisingly wild.

Shore Thing

On foot, the Putangirua Pinnacles unveil the wild southern tip of the North island, while Surf Hwy 45 south of New Plymouth has fine black-sand beaches and gnarly breaks.

City Calling

Compact, cool and creative, Wellington is home to Te Papa museum and the internationally flavoured City Gallery. It's also NZ's most hospitable city with scores of hip cafes and restaurants and a revolutionary craft-beer scene.

p110

Queen Charlotte & Marlborough

The Sounds
Wildlife
Wineries

Sounds Good

A popular playground for lovers of the sea and the great outdoors, these labyrinthine waterways can be explored by boat or on foot or bike on a network of trails, including the Queen Charlotte Track.

Animal Antics

The top of the South Island is home to myriad creatures, both in the water and on the wing. Motuara Island in the Sounds is a bird-spotting paradise, while Kaikoura's waters are like a festival ground for whales, dolphins and seals.

Grape Escapes

Bobbing in Marlborough's sea of sauvignon blanc are barrel-loads of quality cellar-door experiences and some fine regional food.

p138

Abel Tasman, Kahurangi & Nelson Lakes

National parks
Beaches
Geology

Park Perfect

The Nelson region has three national parks: Nelson Lakes, Kahurangi and Abel Tasman. Explore sun-kissed coastlines, remote river valleys and mountain ranges.

Sand Steps

Abel Tasman is lined with dozens of secluded golden beaches accessible only by boat, kayak or on foot. Kahurangi's roaring West Coast beaches are equally appealing for a walk on the wild side on the Heaphy Track.

Rock On

A smorgasbord of geological delights, from Abel Tasman's rocky granite outcrops, to karst landscapes etched with caves, arches and bluffs in Kahurangi, and the glaciated valleys and alpine basins of the Nelson Lakes.

p156

Canterbury, Arthur's Pass & Aoraki/ Mt Cook

Mountains
Night skies
History

Alpine Magic

Soaring Southern Alps peaks, glaciers, passes, the highest mountain in the land, and some of NZ's finest high-country tramps.

Stars of the Show

The night skies above this area are so clear and the stars so bright that part of it has been designated as the Aoraki Mackenzie International Dark Sky Reserve. Lay back on a hut deck and enjoy the show.

Historic Feats

Akaroa and the Banks Peninsula, home to the Banks Track, celebrate their French heritage, while Aoraki/ Mt Cook was where Sir Edmund Hillary learned the ropes.

p188

West Coast

Shared trails
Coast
Birds

Hike or Bike?

On old mining routes such as the Old Ghost Road and the emerging Paparoa Track, you can tramp through the mountains or speed things up on a mountain bike.

The Wild West

From Kohaihai at the end of the Heaphy Track, to Jackson Bay in the south, stretches around 600km of wild and woolly coastline, sculpted by the elements into crazy rock formations such as Punakaiki's Pancake Rocks.

All Atwitter

The West Coast is a haven for wildlife, especially birds. Highlights include a white heron sanctuary at Whataroa and cute kiwi chicks in Franz Josef's West Coast Wildlife Centre.

p218

Mt Aspiring National Park & Around Queenstown

Mountains
Lakes
Adrenaline

Soaring Summits

The big names and big views are here – Mt Aspiring, Roys Peak, Ben Lomond, the Remarkables – all given a mythological edge by the area's starring role in *Lord of the Rings* and *The Hobbit*.

Head of the Lake

Lakes Wakatipu and Wanaka are just the headliners (but what headliners!) – tramping here unveils other smaller water gems such as Diamond Lake.

The Queen of Adventures

Queenstown is no place to sit still – build in time and courage for bungy jumping, whitewater rafting, skydiving, mountain biking or seemingly several billion other adventures.

p238

Fiordland & Stewart Island/ Rakiura

National parks
Famous fiord
Bird life

Parks & Recreation

Rugged Fiordland National Park is the country's biggest – see it on the Milford or Kepler Tracks, or cross park boundaries into Mt Aspiring on the Routeburn. Smaller Rakiura National Park still takes up around 85% of Stewart Island.

Sound & Saddle

The jewel in the crown is remarkable Milford Sound, but take your time exploring the Eglinton Valley on your way to Milford, climbing to Gertrude Saddle for a rarely seen angle on the fiord.

Feather Your Nest

Stewart Island is home to a rich bird population boasting more than 100 species. It's also your best chance of seeing (or at least hearing) a kiwi.

p270

On the Track

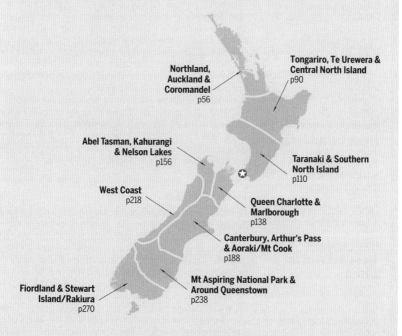

Northland, Auckland & Coromandel

Best Landforms

➡ Cape Reinga (p62)

➡ Cape Brett (p66)

➡ Rangitoto (p67)

➡ The Pinnacles (p81)

➡ Karangahake Gorge (p81)

Best Historic Sites

➡ Cape Reinga Lighthouse (p62)

➡ Cape Brett Lighthouse (p66)

➡ Kauaeranga Kauri Trail (p78)

➡ Karangahake Windows (p84)

Why Go?

Spiked with capes, peninsulas and bays, New Zealand's long northern arm sits far from any of the country's Great Walks, yet there's ample here to entice trampers.

The star natural feature is Cape Reinga, NZ's chosen northern point (even if that isn't really true), where two seas collide around one of the country's most sacred Māori sites. Te Paki Coastal Track affords an opportunity to cross the cape on foot, stringing together seven beaches, including the epic Ninety Mile Beach. Another cape crusade beckons in the Bay of Islands, where the rugged Cape Brett Track ends in sight of the famed Hole in the Rock.

Auckland provides a couple of fine tramping possibilities, while the Coromandel Peninsula is the veritable hiking burger with the lot. Tramps here provide fascinating glimpses into the history of NZ's kauri forests and a gold-giving gorge, while also showing off a coast that couldn't possibly feel this remote so close to Auckland...yet it does.

When to Go

The northernmost stretch of the North Island boasts a mild climate with long dry periods in summer. Temperatures range from almost tropical around the northern tip at Cape Reinga, to an average closer to 20°C around Auckland in summer. The islands northeast of Auckland are often a degree or two warmer, averaging 25°C from December to February and sometimes climbing to 30°C. Winters are moist, with most of the rain falling in June and July. Weather on the Coromandel Peninsula may differ between the east and west coasts due to the mountain range running through the interior. As a general rule, though, the weather during summer is good, with temperatures reaching as high as 31°C. Torrential rain, however, can occur at any time, especially during winter.

Background Reading

Discover the far north in detail in *A Field Guide to Auckland: Exploring the Region's Natural and Historic Heritage* (Ewen Cameron, ed). This worthy companion features more than 140 interesting sites, including the islands of Hauraki Gulf, and details their natural features, such as rock formations, plants and animals, as well as history. Keep an eye out in newsagents for *Wilderness* magazine, which includes features and tramp descriptions from across the country, including the far north.

DON'T MISS

You'll see great kauris, the most impressive of all NZ's trees, on the Aotea Track and Kauaeranga Kauri Trail, but to see the mightiest of them all you should head to Waipoua Forest, 60km north of Dargaville on Northland's west coast.

Near the park's northern end stands mighty **Tāne Mahuta**, named for the Māori forest god. The largest kauri alive, Tāne Mahuta stands at 51.5m, with a 13.8m girth and wood mass of 244.5 cu metres. He's reckoned to have been growing here for somewhere between 1200 and 2000 years.

The second-largest living kauri is just 1km down the road. **Te Matua Ngahere** (the Father of the Forest) is 30m in height, but a girth of 16.4m makes him the fattest living kauri. It's estimated that he could be up to 3000 years old. It's a 20-minute walk to Te Matua Ngahere past the Four Sisters, a graceful stand of four tall kauri trees fused together at the base.

DOC Visitor Centres

➡ DOC Auckland Visitor Centre (p86)

➡ DOC Kaitaia Area Office (p61)

➡ DOC Pēwhairangi/Bay of Islands Office (p65)

➡ DOC Whangarei Office (p89)

➡ DOC Kauaeranga Visitor Centre (p80)

➡ DOC Hauraki Office (p78)

GATEWAY TOWNS

➡ Auckland (p85)

➡ Kaitaia (p87)

➡ Russell (p87)

➡ Whangarei (p88)

➡ Thames (p89)

NORTHLAND, AUCKLAND & COROMANDEL

Fast Facts

➡ Ninety Mile Beach is a historical misnomer, thought to have been overestimated by missionaries travelling along the sand on horseback; its length is in fact just under 90km.

➡ Victoria Battery was the world's first stamper battery to use the cyanide process for extracting gold from crushed ore.

➡ Only 5% of the Coromandel's original kauri forests remain unlogged, mostly in the Manaia Forest Sanctuary.

Top Tip

Most of the tramps in this region can't be reached by public transport, but many have camping grounds near or at their trailheads. Hiring a campervan – a classic Kiwi travel experience – makes for easy access to the tracks.

Resources

➡ www.northlandnz.com

➡ www.aucklandnz.com

➡ www.thebarrier.co.nz

➡ www.thecoromandel.com

Northland, Auckland & Coromandel

$\hat{N}$ 0 ————— 40 km
0 ————— 20 miles

TE PAKI COASTAL TRACK
Round New Zealand's beach-lined northern tip. (p59)

SOUTH PACIFIC OCEAN

CAPE BRETT TRACK
High cliffs and a lighthouse-tipped cape. (p63)

COROMANDEL WALKWAY
Remote, rugged and raw. (p76)

AOTEA TRACK
Logging history and hot springs. (p70)

RANGITOTO ISLAND LOOP
Scale a volcanic island. (p66)

KAUAERANGA KAURI TRAIL
Sharp-tipped pinnacles and kauri logging relics. (p78)

KARANGAHAKE GORGE
Golden history in a deep gorge. (p82)

Te Paki
Te Kao
Pukenui
Mangonui
Awanui
Kaitaia
Kaeo
Ahipara
Herekino
Kerikeri
Russell
Kohukohu
Paihia
Cape Brett
Kaikohe
Russell Forest
Helena Bay
Opononi
Matapouri
Maunganui Bluff (460m)
Kaihu
Hikurangi
Tutukaka
Whangarei

Tasman Sea

Dargaville
Brynderwyn
Great Barrier Island
Matakohe
Mangawhai
Kaiwaka
Wellsford
Leigh
Warkworth
Puhoi
Waiwera
Mt Moehau (892m)
Port Charles
Colville
Coromandel Town
Kuaotunu
Muriwai Beach
Rangitoto Island
Oneroa
Whitianga
Te Henga (Bethells Beach)
Piha
Auckland
Clevedon
Hahei
Tapu
Coromandel Forest Park
Papakura
Te Puru
Kaiaua
Pukekohe
Thames
Maramarua
Bay of Plenty
Pukekawa
Waihi
Rangiriri
Tahuna
Waihi Beach
Huntly
Mt Te Aroha (952m)
Mt Maunganui
Tauranga
Raglan
Hamilton
Matamata
Te Awamutu
Tirau
Otorohanga
Waikato River
Tokoroa
Te Kuiti

Te Paki Coastal Track

Duration 3 days

Distance 42.5km (26.4 miles)

Difficulty Easy

Start Te Paki Stream (Kauaeparaoa)

End Kapowairua

Gateways Kaitaia (p87)

Transport Shuttle bus

Summary A scenic tramp along the sweeping Te Paki coastline, encompassing coastal forest, the sands of seven semitropical beaches and revered Cape Reinga (Te Rerenga Wairua).

The northern tip of NZ is a place pounded by the seas, whipped by winds and bathed in sunshine. It's a wild and powerful spot, where the strong and unforgiving currents of the Tasman Sea and Pacific Ocean sweep along the shorelines before meeting in a fury of foam just west of Cape Reinga.

Providing trampers with a front-row seat to nature's beauty and drama here is Te Paki Coastal Track, which meanders between spectacular beaches, coastal forest, wetlands and towering dunes. Once described as a 'desert coast', Ninety Mile Beach is one of NZ's longest beaches and is almost concrete-hard below the high-tide line – which makes for easy (if at times footsore) tramping – and is bordered much of the way by sand dunes up to 6km wide and rising in places to 143m in height. The tramp then climbs to Cape Reinga, site of the famous lighthouse, but also a sacred Māori site, before following cliff tops and descending to idyllic, sandy beaches.

DOC maintains four camping grounds along the track. The tramp can be extended by starting in Ahipara, 83km south of Te Paki Stream (Kauaeparaoa) at the southern end of Ninety Mile Beach, adding three or four days to the journey. You can also join it at Waipapakauri (69km south of Te Paki Stream), Hukatere (51km) or the Bluff (19km) – the 32km portion from Hukatere to the Bluff (a famous spot for surf fishing) is ruler-straight. Keep in mind, however, that you'll encounter cars and tour buses daily on Ninety Mile Beach until you pass Te Paki Stream.

History

Māori were already well established in NZ's far north by the time Europeans arrived, and Cape Reinga had long been regarded by Māori as the departure point of the spirit after death.

Only the village of Te Hapua remains from the once-thriving settlements. However, ancient *pā* (fortified villages), middens and relics of gardens and food-storage pits remain as reminders of a previous era in Te Paki's history.

In 1642 Dutch explorer Abel Tasman sailed past and named Cape Maria van Diemen, a point southwest of Cape Reinga. Captain James Cook also sailed by during his first visit to NZ in 1769, but arrived during a storm. He sat tight and refused to leave until he had recorded, with remarkable accuracy, the position of the cape. In 1941 a lighthouse was erected at Cape Reinga. Originally sited at nearby Motuopao Island, it was one of the first in the country to be automated by electric power provided by a diesel generator, and it shines a warning signal 49km out to sea.

Environment

Because of its isolation from mainland NZ for millions of years, Te Paki is described as an ecological treasure trove, with many plants and animals unique to the area. It's home to a large number of rare insects, plants and trees, including one of the world's rarest trees: the Rata Moehau or Bartlett's rata, which once numbered only five trees in the wild. There are impressive stands of native bush, containing giant kauri and pohutukawa trees, around Sandy Bay, Pandora and Tapotupotu Bay.

The wildlife most trampers will encounter includes coastal birds such as oyster catchers, NZ dotterels, pied stilts, terns, gulls and the occasional white-faced heron. Make sure to pack your snorkelling gear and take the plunge into crystal-clear, aquamarine water teeming with life.

ℹ Planning

WHEN TO TRAMP

This is a great tramp for any time of year. During summer the region gets long spells of dry weather, with temperatures warm enough to be considered almost tropical. Most of the rain comes during winter, with monthly averages of around 120mm at Cape Reinga – about double the rainfall of summer months.

The tramp involves estuary crossings, so check tide times in advance at **MetService** (www.metservice.com) and try to coordinate crossings with low tide.

WHAT TO BRING

As there are no huts on this tramp, a tent is essential. The track is exposed and the sun can be intense in summer, so ensure you have sunscreen, a wide-brimmed hat, a long-sleeved shirt and capacity to carry at least 2L of water per person.

Te Paki Coastal Track

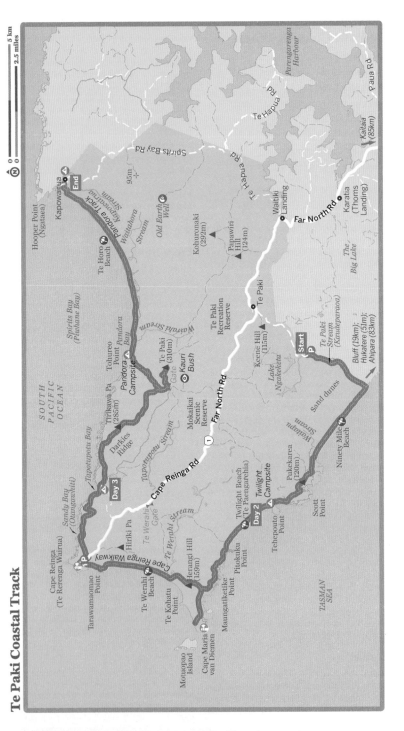

The extreme fire risk in summer means that open fires are prohibited, so pack a stove. All drinking water should be treated, so bring a filter (or boil the water).

MAPS

The track is covered by NewTopo's 1:40,000 *Cape Reinga Coastal Walkway* map and NZ Topo50's *AT24 (Cape Reinga)*.

CAMPING

There are no huts along this track. Basic (free) campsites are located at Pandora and Twilight Beach, both with toilets and fresh water. The Standard campsites at Kapowairua (Spirits Bay) and Tapotupotu (per person $8) also have cold showers.

INFORMATION

The **DOC Kaitaia Area Office** (☎ 09-408 6014; www.doc.govt.nz; 25 Matthews Ave; ⊙ 8am-4.30pm Mon-Fri) has all the necessary information for walking Te Paki Coastal Track.

ⓘ Getting to/from the Tramp

Kapowairua is around 110km from Kaitaia, but there's no public transport past Pukenui (65km from Kapowairua). **Olly Lancaster** (☎ 09-409 7500; return $20) offers shuttles to and from the track ($20 return) from his base in Paua, around 30km shy of the cape, storing your vehicle at his house (you can also camp there).

Harrisons Cape Runner (☎ 0800 227 373; www.harrisonscapereingatours.co.nz; adult/child $50/25) has scheduled daily tours departing at 9am from Kaitaia ($50) and is happy to drop trampers at Cape Reinga and pick up again from here.

🏃 The Tramp

Day 1: Te Paki Stream (Kauaeparaoa) to Twilight Beach

3½–4 HOURS / 12KM

Te Paki Stream (Kauaeparaoa) marks the southern border of Te Paki Recreation Reserve, but is more famous for being a 'quicksand stream'. If your bus drops you off at the Te Paki Stream Rd car park, rather than at the stream mouth, it's an additional 45 minutes of wet trekking through the stream.

From the end of the stream head northwest along the wide, flat expanse of **Ninety Mile Beach**, flanked by sand dunes on the east and the pounding surf of the Tasman Sea to the west. After an hour you come to Waitapu Stream, which may or may not be dry. The track then leaves the beach and begins a steep climb – on steps, thankfully – to the southern side of Scott Point. Cross a small gully then

resume climbing steeply before topping out to good views of Ninety Mile Beach below.

On **Scott Point** the track moves into scrub and then joins a track to arrive at a good area for backcountry camping. There are no facilities, but the grassy site sits high above the pounding surf. You can see over to Cape Maria van Diemen during the day, and the glow of its lighthouse is visible at night.

The track continues across Scott Point, well marked with orange posts to guide you through the maze. It takes 1½ hours to cross the point and descend onto Twilight Beach (Te Paengarehia), which is named after a schooner that sank here in 1871. **Twilight Campsite**, near the southern end of the beach, has composting toilets and water from a tank. All water from the tank should be boiled or treated.

Day 2: Twilight Beach to Tapotupotu Bay

6 HOURS / 13KM

It's a 45-minute walk to the northern end of the beach, where there's a small stream and a signposted route to the Te Werahi gate along Cape Reinga Rd, a 1½ hour walk away. Head left along an old 4WD track that skirts a swamp and then climbs a ridge that separates the wetland from the sea. Heading northwest through flax and manuka scrub, there are views of Cape Maria van Diemen and even a glimpse of the Cape Reinga Lighthouse.

Having left the ridge and headed into sand dunes, the track reaches a signposted junction one hour from Twilight Beach. Turn west (left) to head out onto **Cape Maria van Diemen**. This side trail follows the coast for 40 minutes, providing excellent views most of the way to this cape's lighthouse, which was built after the one on nearby Motuopao Island closed in 1941.

There are two ways to reach Te Werahi Beach from the end of Cape Maria van Diemen. Most trampers backtrack and head north (left) at the junction to follow the high-level track around **Herangi Hill** (159m). Going this way takes 45 minutes to one hour to walk to the southern end of Te Werahi Beach. At low tide, more adventurous souls can follow the rocky shoreline. If you have any concerns about the tide or your timing, take the high-level track. The tracks meet at Te Werahi Stream, which should be crossed near low tide.

From the stream it takes 45 minutes to one hour to tramp along the sweeping **Te Werahi Beach** to **Tarawamaomao Point** at the northern end. At high tide you'll get your boots wet, as the cliffs close in at the northern end before the track climbs sharply away from the beach. Continue along steep cliff tops where on a clear day you'll be rewarded with spectacular views of sandy beaches, Cape Maria van Diemen and Motuopao Island.

Within an hour of the ascent from Te Werahi Beach, the walkway emerges at Cape Reinga. The lighthouse is a 10-minute stroll away. Reinga means 'place of leaping' in Māori. On the headland, perched above a turbulent eddy of swirling kelp, is a solitary pohutukawa tree. Māori spirits were said to have descended to the underworld by sliding down a root into the sea, emerging on Ahau, the highest point of the Three Kings Islands – to bid farewell before returning to their ancestral homeland, Hawaiki. The Three Kings Islands are visible on a clear day. A nature reserve, they are home to a number of rare and endangered trees, as well as a rich abundance and variety of marine life.

Interpretive signage provides an insight into the natural and human history of this magnificent site, one of NZ's most photographed spots. The swirling seas where the Pacific Ocean and Tasman Sea meet is utterly mesmerising, and keeping an eye on the waters may reward you with sightings of the pods of dolphins that round the cape in feeding forays. There are flush toilets at the cape, which cater to the hordes of tourists who make the popular pilgrimage here.

The walkway resumes in the car park and heads east, sidling a hill, then descending to

---

TE PAKI IN A DAY

If you only have a day to walk near Cape Reinga, a recommended tramp is the Twilight–Te Werahi Loop Track, a 16km circuit that incorporates one of the best sections of Te Paki Coastal Track. From the Te Werahi Gate near Cape Reinga, a pair of trails head west to the coast. The Twilight Track will bring you to Twilight Beach within one to 1¼ hours, where you turn north to cross Cape Maria van Diemen – be sure to detour out to the point.

The loop turns back towards the gate along the Te Werahi Track, the junction for which is just north of the Te Werahi Stream crossing. If you have time you can also continue along Te Werahi Beach to Cape Reinga and the lighthouse.

Sandy Bay (Otangawhiti), a pretty spot with a freshwater stream and grassy flats beneath pohutukawa trees. It is reached 30 minutes from the lighthouse. On the other side of the small bay the track begins a steep climb to a coastal ridge, turns inland for a spell then returns to the cliff tops and good views, from where it descends sharply towards Tapotupotu Bay, 2½ hours from Cape Reinga.

Tapotupotu is one of the most scenic beaches in the far north, a horseshoe of white sand and light-green seas enclosed by forested cliffs. There's a freshwater stream here and a road-accessible and therefore well-populated DOC campsite with a shelter, cold showers, toilets and drinking water.

Day 3: Tapotupotu Bay to Kapowairua

7–8 HOURS / 17.5KM

Many trampers pass up this rewarding section of track due to the difficulty of arranging transport out of Kapowairua. This leg of the journey can be extended into two days by an overnight stop at tranquil Pandora Bay, where a small backcountry campsite nestles among burgeoning pohutukawa. The first part of the day is along old ridge-top farm tracks; the second is through stunning Pandora Bay and Te Horo Beach.

At Tapotupotu Bay, begin by walking to the end of the campsite and cross the stream on a boardwalk and small bridge. The track resumes at the end of the bridge and leads to a bush-clad hill, making a 200m climb to the top of the coastal ridge. For the next 40 minutes to one hour there are spectacular views of Tapotupotu Bay and all the way back to Cape Reinga, before the track descends inland.

You then climb over Tirikawa Pa (285m) and traverse Darkies Ridge to reach the Pandora Track, an old metalled road, at a signposted junction within two hours of the Tapotupotu Bay campsite. South along the Pandora Track, 15 minutes from the junction, is a side track to Te Paki (310m), the highest point in the area. Plan an hour for the return trip to the summit, where you can see the remains of a wartime radar station and a spectacular view of the coastline.

Turn left on Pandora Track, heading northeast and down to secluded Pandora Bay, reached one hour from the junction. Pandora Campsite, which has composting toilets and tank water, sits on the grassy flats alongside the beach, surrounded by fruit trees and the remains of an old tourist camp from the 1920s. It's the perfect spot to strip down to your nothings and jump into the sea. A snorkel and mask will prove welcome here.

If you hit the beach near low tide you can reach Spirits Bay by the seaward route, around the rocky shoreline. Otherwise, follow the orange posts that mark the high-tide route, as it climbs a pair of headlands divided by Wairahi Stream.

Once on the bay you can follow Te Horo Beach to Kapowairua at the eastern end of the beach, a three-hour (8.5km) trek from Pandora. After the rock-hard surface of Ninety Mile Beach, many trampers find the soft sand of Te Horo to be exhausting work. The alternative is to tramp behind the sand dunes along an old vehicle track marked by orange poles. The walking is easier and the wetlands you skirt are an interesting change from the pounding sea.

For either route you must first cross Waitahora Lagoon, which is where Waitahora Stream flows into the ocean. A boardwalk provides safe passage and a close-up experience of this dynamic wetland environment. Look out for flowering native hibiscus in the late summer.

Cape Brett Track

Duration 2 days

Distance 33km (20.5 miles)

Difficulty Moderate

Start/End Rawhiti

Gateways Russell (p87), Whangarei (p88)

Transport Water taxi

Summary Roll along the rugged tops and cliffs of Cape Brett to spend a night in a former lighthouse keepers' cottage, peering out at the famous Hole in the Rock.

A scenic underscore to the Bay of Islands, Cape Brett is a gossamer-thin strip of land that famously ends beside the Hole in the Rock, the most popular tourist attraction in the area.

But while boats and helicopters hurry to the Hole in the Rock, the Cape Brett Track winds slowly along the tops of the cape, always climbing or descending, and peeling open views of the Bay of Islands before coming to its moment of splendour – as you step through a small saddle just beyond the turn-off to Deep Water Cove, the land plummets away into the Pacific Ocean and the full cliff-lined drama of Cape Brett is revealed. It's a spectacular couple of days on foot, aided by the opportunity to stay a night inside a former lighthouse keepers' cottage, in one of the finest coastal regions in New Zealand.

Between Rawhiti and the Deep Water Cove junction, the track crosses private, Māori-owned land. To cover track maintenance along this section, a permit fee of $40 is charged to tramp the track. You'll pay the fee online when you book your stay at the Cape Brett Hut. Bookings and the permit payment can also be made in person at the Bay of Islands i-SITE (p65) in Paihia.

TE ARAROA – NEW ZEALAND'S TRAIL

In a nation filled with trampers, the idea of a track the length of the country – from Cape Reinga on the northern point of the North Island, to Bluff on the southern tip of the South Island – has always been an appealing one. The idea was first proposed in 1967 by the Federated Mountain Clubs (FMC), and was on the agenda in 1976 when the New Zealand Walkways Commission (NZWC) was established.

After putting in more than 100 small trails, the NZWC was dissolved in 1989, without having progressed the long-trail concept. That goal was revived in 1994 when journalist Geoff Chapple wrote a piece for the *Sunday Star-Times* urging the construction of Te Araroa – New Zealand's Trail. Support poured in, resulting in the establishment of the Te Araroa Trust (www.teararoa.org.nz), with Sir Edmund Hillary as a patron. The trust opened its first trail – a 22km section between Waitangi and Kerikeri in Northland – in 1995. From small acorns...

Launched in 2011, Te Araroa is a continuous trail from Cape Reinga to Bluff. It's 3000km in length, which is more than double the straight-line distance from NZ's top to tail. To walk it in one hit would take around five months, but sections can be sampled in a few hours, a few days, or more. It traverses many of NZ's most famous landscapes and trails, including the Tongariro Alpine Crossing (p95), Queen Charlotte Track (p141) and Harper Pass (p204).

Around 40% of the trail is through conservation land, with the remainder linking towns and cities across the map. The official guidebook, *Te Araroa: A Walking Guide to New Zealand's Long Trail,* by trail revivalist Geoff Chapple, provides the best coverage of the route. The trust's website is excellent for trip planning.

Cape Brett Track

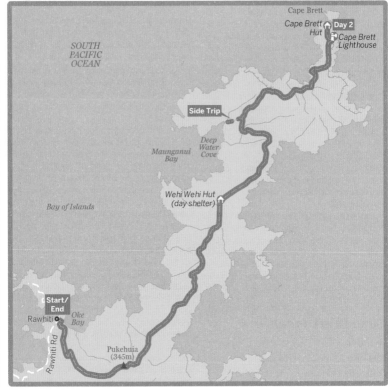

History

For many centuries before the construction of Cape Brett's lighthouse, the cape already served as a beacon for seafaring Māori, who used light reflecting from the crystalline rocks of its cliffs as a guide to landfall in NZ.

The 14m-high lighthouse was first lit in 1910. Across the 68 years of its staffed operation, it had more than 100 lighthouse keepers. It was decommissioned in 1978, when it was replaced by the automated light that continues to shine today.

ℹ️ Planning

WHEN TO TRAMP

Positioned at the coastal heart of the subtropical Northland region, Cape Brett provides good year-round tramping. After rain the track can become wet and quite slippery, so step carefully; winter (June to August) brings the most rain. Summer temperatures average around 24°C, which is

often moderated by the winds off the ocean and the prospect of a swim at Deep Water Cove.

WHAT TO BRING

Cape Brett Hut contains gas cookers, pots and all cutlery and crockery (and a guitar on our visit...), so you'll need only a sleeping bag for the night. In summer it's wise to bring enough drinking water for two days – the water tanks at the hut can be unreliable if there hasn't been recent rain.

MAPS & BROCHURES

NZTopo50 *AV30 (Cape Brett)* covers the entire track.

HUTS

The only overnight option on the track is DOC's Cape Brett Hut ($15). Hut tickets can't be used, and the hut must be booked online in advance. The hut is kept locked, so it's vital that you call the **DOC Pēwhairangi/Bay of Islands office** the day before you set out on the tramp to get the access code. The office is only open weekdays, so if you need the access code on a weekend or public holiday, phone the **Bay of Islands i-SITE**.

INFORMATION

The **DOC Pēwhairangi/Bay of Islands office** (☑ 09-407 0300; www.doc.govt.nz; 34 Landing Rd) in Kerikeri is the primary source of information about the track. The **Bay of Islands i-SITE** (☑ 09-402 7345; www.northlandnz.com; 69 Marsden Rd, Paihia; ⊘ 8am-5pm Mar-Dec, to 7pm Jan & Feb) in Paihia can also arrange the bookings for the Cape Brett Hut and the track permit.

ⓘ Getting to/from the Tramp

The tramp begins in Rawhiti, a small settlement without any services that's strung along the Bay of Islands shore. It's a 1½ hour drive north from Whangarei, or a winding 40-minute drive from Russell; there's no public transport. If you want to get started early on the track, you can camp ($10) behind the Kaingahoa *marae*, about 1km from the trailhead.

There's no parking at the trailhead, but off-street parking is offered at 253 Rawhiti Rd (Julie's Backpackers) for $5 a night.

If you don't want to walk the entire track, Rawhiti-based **WaiNot** (☑ 0800 924 668; www.wainot.co.nz; 199 Rawhiti Rd, Rawhiti) runs a water-taxi service that can whisk you out to Deep Water Cove ($40 per person, minimum $200) or Cape Brett ($50 per person, minimum $250). This gives you the option to walk the most rugged and spectacular section, from Deep Water Cove to Cape Brett, or to walk the track in just one direction (from Cape Brett to Rawhiti).

🏃 The Tramp

Day 1: Rawhiti to Cape Brett

7–8 HOURS / 16.5KM

If you've left your car at Julie's Backpackers, it's a 1km walk to the trailhead, turning right onto Rawhiti Rd as you leave Julie's and followed the road to Hauai Bay, where the track is clearly signposted.

The track begins under a Māori archway – the first 12km of the track is across Māori lands – and up a flight of steps. Within a couple of minutes you'll come to the first of the day's many views, down onto the perfect sands of Oke Bay. A short side trail detours down to the sands – you might think it too early for a stop, but you won't see sand again until you return here the next day.

At the head of the steps, turn right, heading up the ridge, with the wide track tunneling through bush as it climbs. Just beyond the 2km marker, the track rounds a knoll and begins the final ascent to Pukehuia (345m), the highest point of the tramp (1¼ hours from the start). The shelter here has a small rainwater

tank and views down to Oke Bay and across the Bay of Islands, with the namesake islands looking like pot plants strewn over the sea.

From here the track rolls along the top of the ridge pretty much all the way to Deep Water Cove. At times the ridge is very narrow, falling away either side of the track, but there's no real sense of exposure.

Around 10 minutes from Pukehuia, the track passes a junction to the former Whamgamumu whaling station. Continue straight ahead and in another 30 minutes you'll pass another track junction (with toilet) to Toroa Bay. Just beyond this is an electrified predator fence designed to keep possums out of the cape area. Be sure to close the gate.

The final climb before Deep Water Cove tops out at Wehi Wehi Hut, a day shelter with rainwater tank and toilet. From the grassy clearing in front of the shelter on a clear day, you'll be looking out south to the Poor Knights Islands, often rated as one of the world's best dive sites.

From the shelter the trail descends before climbing back onto the ridge and following it to the Deep Water Cove track junction, 45 minutes to an hour from Wehi Wehi Hut (12km from the trailhead). Just before the junction there's a steep dip in and out of a deep gully – this can get pretty slippery after rain. If the weather is warm, it's worth taking the 1.4km (45 minutes return) detour steeply down to Deep Water Cove, a small, stony notch in the cape that can provide a cooling swim.

Now the fun really begins. From the junction the track climbs for 30 minutes to a small saddle in the ridge, where you pop out at an extraordinary view. The Pacific Ocean churns 200m below and the rugged cliffs lead all the way to the tip of Cape Brett. The last bit of rock you can see beyond the cape is the famed Hole in the Rock, though the hole is hidden by the angle.

The views disappear for a while as the track heads back into bush, crossing a series of streams, including one that has you almost back down to sea level, before the inevitable climb back up. At the final saddle along the ridge, you peer across a narrow cove to high coastal cliffs. After heavy rain, these cliffs can turn suddenly and spectacularly into waterfalls.

The sense of exposure on the next section of climb is alleviated by the presence of a handrail as you pass under the branches of a pohutukawa tree and ascend steeply on to

NZ SHORT WALKS & DAY HIKES

The Great Walks have long been the backbone of New Zealand's multiday tramping track network, but they now have a day-walk equivalent, with DOC unveiling plans in late 2017 to promote a network of 19 'Short Walks and Day Hikes'.

Ranging from 20 minutes to eight hours in length, the walks are spread across the country and are existing DOC tracks perceived to provide the greatest beauty and experience, and the capacity to accommodate increased numbers of trampers.

Short Walks

Kura Tāwhiti Access Track (Canterbury, 20 minutes) Wander in to the jumble of limestone boulders at Kura Tāwhiti (Castle Hill), one of the most striking sights along SH73 and a favourite with boulderers.

Blue Lakes & Tasman Glacier Walks (Aoraki/Mt Cook National Park, 40 minutes) Stroll past the Blue Lakes to view NZ's longest glacier, Haupapa/Tasman Glacier.

Lake Gunn Nature Walk (Fiordland National Park, 45 minutes) A short loop through red beech forest on the shores of Lake Gunn along the highway into Milford Sound.

Devil's Punchbowl Walking Track (Arthur's Pass National Park, one hour) Walk 1km from SH73 to reach the foot of this powerful 131m-high waterfall pouring through the Southern Alps.

Fox Glacier/Te Ara o Tuawe Valley Walk (Westland Tai Poutini National Park, one hour) Walk up a valley to a lookout within 500m of the mighty Fox Glacier terminal face.

Blue Pools Track (Mt Aspiring National Park, one hour) Blue by name, blue by nature, this track passes through lush beech forest beneath Haast Pass to the transparent blue pools at the confluence of the Makarora and Blue Rivers.

Cape Foulwind Walkway (West Coast, 1¼ hours) A typically wild slice of West Coast shoreline, passing the Cape Foulwind Lighthouse and a breeding colony of New Zealand fur seals.

Wainui Falls Track (Abel Tasman National Park, one hour 20 minutes) Head upstream beneath ferns and nikau palms to the largest waterfall in the Golden Bay area.

Cathedral Cove Walk (Coromandel Peninsula, 1½ hours) A coastal walk to one of NZ's signature natural features: the gigantic limestone arch at Cathedral Cove.

reach the **Cape Brett Lighthouse**. Propped 150m above the sea, the evocative lighthouse was first lit in 1910 and staffed by three men (with enough kids to warrant the presence of a school here). Its light could be seen almost 50km out to sea. As an indicator of the harshness of the conditions, workers found 60 layers of paint when it was stripped for repainting in 2007.

Follow the poles as they head to the left, winding down the grassy slopes to **Cape Brett Hut** (23 bunks), a red-roofed building that was once the lighthouse keepers' cottage, perched on a ledge above the sea. It's worth exploring the surrounds, including the remnants of the tramway that was used to haul goods from boats to the lighthouse. Prior to the tramway's construction, it was the job of one horse to haul the goods. It's said that the horse became so weary of the climb that it took to hiding when it heard approaching boats.

Day 2: Cape Brett to Rawhiti

7–8 HOURS / 16.5KM

Retrace your outward steps from Day 1. If you don't fancy the tramp back, water-taxi pickup can be organised with WaiNot (p65).

Rangitoto Island Loop

Duration 4–5 hours

Distance 10km (6.2 miles)

Difficulty Easy

Start/End Rangitoto Wharf

Gateway Auckland (p85)

Transport Ferry

Summary Tramp to the summit of the Rangitoto volcano and then along the coast of the island it created 600 years ago. The views of Auckland are among the best you'll find.

Lake Matheson/Te Ara Kairaumati Walk (Westland Tai Poutini National Park, 1½ hours) Hike in to the famously reflective Lake Matheson/Te Ara Kairaumati, where at dawn and dusk Aoraki/Mt Cook and Mt Tasman are typically etched onto the lake surface.

Rangitoto Summit Track (p67; Rangitoto Island, two hours) Take the direct route to and from the tip of this volcanic island.

Mt Manaia (Northland, two to three hours) Climb to a summit along the lumpy Whangarei Heads for a view over the harbour entrance and the Hen and Chicken Islands.

Mangawhai Cliffs Walkway (Northland, two to three hours) A coastal walk located between Auckland and Whangarei that reveals ancient pohutukawa trees, curious rock formations and possibly whale sightings.

Charming Creek Walkway (West Coast, 2½ to three hours) Follow a former logging tramway through the lower Ngakawau Gorge and along Charming Creek, passing Mangatini Falls to an abandoned coal mine.

Day Hikes

Hooker Valley Track (p213; Aoraki/Mt Cook National Park, three hours) A short hike beneath a very big mountain, following a stunning valley to the glaciated foot of NZ's highest peak.

Cape Kidnapper's Walking Track (Hawke's Bay, five hours) Hike along a wild limestone coastline to the world's largest mainland gannet colony – it's spectacular real estate for birds.

Te Whara Track (Northland, five to six hours) Round the tip of dramatic Whangarei Heads, hiking through thick coastal forest to a vast view from Bream Head, which peers north to Cape Brett and out to sea to distant Great Barrier Island.

Roys Peak Track (p262; Wanaka, five to six hours) A long climb to one of the country's finest vantage points...even before you reach the summit.

Tongariro Alpine Crossing (p95; Tongariro National Park, seven to eight hours) A volcanic spectacular on a long day through a landscape of mind-boggling features and colours.

Even if you only have a day to spare in Auckland before moving on, seriously consider warming up your tramping legs with this easy yet fascinating walk on Rangitoto Island. Part of the Hauraki Gulf Marine Park, this 23-sq-km island is only 10km northeast of the city and features tramping tracks that wind through the island's black lava fields and around the summit crater of its volcano.

Rangitoto is connected to Motutapu Island by a causeway and, if you take a tent and sleeping bag, you can turn this tramp into a two-day adventure. At the head of Islington Bay pick up the Motutapu Walkway on the east side of the causeway, and follow it to the DOC camping ground at Home Bay, a 1½ hour walk across farmland and cliff tops. The next day it's a 2½ hour tramp back to Islington Bay along farm roads via Administration Bay.

History

Rangitoto is a relatively young volcano, having emerged from the sea in a series of fiery eruptions only 600 years ago. Māori were living on neighbouring Motutapu Island at the time of the eruptions and Rangitoto's sudden and dramatic appearance ensured it would always have an important place in their history and mythology. The island's name is derived from the Māori phrase 'Te Rangi totongia a Tama-te-kapua' (the day the blood of Tama-te-kapua was shed). Tama-tekapua was chief of one of the canoes that brought the early Polynesian settlers. He arrived about 1350 and then lost a major battle with Tainui at Islington Bay, which lies between Rangitoto and Motutapu Islands.

The Crown purchased Rangitoto in 1854 from Māori, and during the 1920s and 1930s prisoners built 19km of hard-packed roads and trails on the island, some of which are still in use. During WWII Rangitoto was used as a base for harbour defence and a radar station. A handful of the old cement huts and foundations can still be seen along the tracks. In 2014 legislation was passed returning the summit of Rangitoto – to be

Rangitoto Island Loop

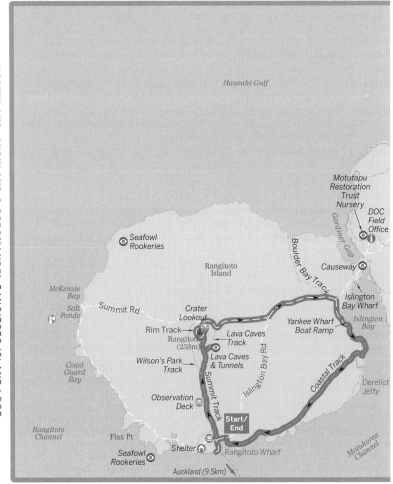

Hauraki Gulf

Motutapu
Restoration
Trust
Nursery

DOC
Field
Office

Seafowl
Rookeries

Rangitoto
Island

Gardiner Gap

Causeway

McKenzie
Bay

Salt
Ponds

Summit Rd

Boulder Bay Track

Islington
Bay Wharf

Islington
Bay

Crater
Lookout

Rim Track

Rangitoto
(259m)

Wilson's Park
Track

Lava Caves
Track

Lava Caves
& Tunnels

Yankee Wharf
Boat Ramp

Islington Bay Rd

Coast
Guard
Bay

Summit Track

Coastal Track

Derelict
Jetty

Observation
Deck

Rangitoto
Channel

Flax Pt

Start/
End

Seafowl
Rookeries

Shelter

Rangitoto Wharf

Motukorea
Channel

Auckland (9.5km)

named Ngā Pona-Toru-a-Peretu – to Ngā
Mana Whenua o Tamaki Makarau as part of
a Treaty of Waitangi settlement. The public
continues to have access to the summit.

Environment

Rangitoto is the largest of the 50 volcanic
cones and craters in the Auckland area, and
is the only one of its kind in NZ. The black
basaltic lava that erupted and now consti-
tutes much of the island makes Rangitoto
one of the few basalt shield volcanoes in the
world, and a miniature version of the great
volcanoes of Hawaii. Although Rangitoto is

thought to be extinct, the Auckland volcano
field is regarded as only dormant – that is,
'resting' but potentially active.

The lava rock is an inhospitable environment for plant life, as it is highly porous and
heats to very high temperatures. Still, plants
and bush are slowly covering the open lava
fields. Moss, lichen and algae were the first
plants to colonise, followed by pohutukawa
trees. Rangitoto now has the largest remaining pohutukawa forest in NZ. The island is
also home to more than 250 species of native trees and flowering plants, including 40
species of fern and several species of orchid.

The new forest does not support many land birds, but seabirds are common along the shoreline. The population includes a black-backed gull colony.

ⓘ Planning

WHEN TO TRAMP

You can tramp year-round on Rangitoto, though it can get very hot and dry during summer; often it's a degree or two warmer than Auckland. From December through February the temperature is usually around 25°C, and at times can reach 30°C. When the sun and heat reflect off the lava fields, it can feel as though you're tramping through an oven. Christmas and Easter holidays can be very busy on the island, and with so many people heading for the summit of Rangitoto, it becomes like a pilgrimage. Once you're away from the Summit Track, however, you will encounter far fewer trampers, and possibly none at all on the Coastal Track.

WHAT TO BRING

There are no supplies on Rangitoto, so you must bring everything with you. You'll need a full water bottle, food, sunscreen, a wide-brimmed hat and strong walking shoes, if not boots, as the ground is rocky and at times loose. If you plan to stretch the walk into a second day by staying at Home Bay, you'll need to be completely self-sufficient for camping. The camp does have a water supply.

MAPS

The track is covered by NewTopo's 1:42,000 *Walks on Rangitoto & Motutapu Islands* map, as well as NZTopo50 *BA32 (Auckland)*.

CAMPING

There are no huts or other accommodation on Rangitoto Island. On Motutapu Island there is a Standard campsite ($8) at Home Bay with a water supply. Bookings are essential.

INFORMATION

The **DOC Auckland Visitor Centre** (p86) supplies information and handles bookings for tracks nationwide. It has information about trails on Rangitoto and camping at Home Bay. There's a host of information about the island on the Rangitoto Island Historic Conservation Trust website (www.rangitoto.org).

ⓘ Getting to/from the Tramp

Fullers (☑ 09-367 9111; www.fullers.co.nz; adult/child return $33/16.50) has ferry services to Rangitoto from Auckland's Ferry Building (25 minutes). Ferries leave Auckland at 9.15am, 10.30am and 12.15pm daily, with a handy additional 7.30am departure on weekends. Return ferries depart Rangitoto at 12.45pm, 2.30pm and 3.30pm (4pm and 5pm rather than 3.30pm on weekends).

🏃 The Tramp

At the Rangitoto Wharf there are toilets and a large day shelter in which to escape the sun as you prepare for the tramp.

The Summit Track is well marked and heads north into bush, but within 10 minutes breaks out into a lava field that is a jumbled mass of black rocks. In the middle of it is an observation deck with interpretive displays. From here the track continues climbing at a very gentle rate, passing a signposted junction to Wilson's Park Track (left) before reaching the Lava Caves Track (right), 45 minutes from the wharf. Follow this side track for 15 minutes to a series of caves and tunnels, formed when the outer surface of the lava cooled after an eruption (when the liquid inner lava drained, the hardened outer shell remained as a cave).

Return to the Summit Track and continue climbing. The trail steepens for the final 15 minutes to the crater rim, but is never what anybody could consider strenuous. About 2km from the wharf you reach Crater Lookout, a large wooden deck peering into the Rangitoto crater, which is 60m deep and 200m wide. The inner edge is dotted with tall pohutukawa trees, while in the crater itself there's a thicket of manuka and kanuka.

Head west at the deck to follow the Rim Track, which immediately climbs a long stairway to the highest point on Rangitoto – the 259m summit is marked by a large trig on the edge of the crater. There are great views here, including a fine panorama of Auckland's city centre. Also located here is a cement hut that served as a fire command post during WWII.

Continue along the Rim Track to return to the Crater Lookout in 10 minutes. You never see into the crater from the trail, but a few minutes from the trig you pass a view of the west side of Rangitoto Island, taking in the lighthouse in McKenzie Bay. Just beyond it is another cement hut that served as a wireless radar room during WWII.

Back at Crater Lookout, follow the long set of stairs that descends to the northeast and ends at Summit Rd, which is used by Fullers to drive visitors up from McKenzie Bay. Head east on the narrow gravel road as it gently descends through more lava fields. Within 30 to 40 minutes of the stairs on Summit Rd, you'll arrive at a signposted intersection with Islington Bay Rd. Continue heading east towards Islington Bay, and in 30 minutes you'll reach a signposted junction with Boulder Bay Track (left). It's a 1½-hour return walk to Boulder Bay on the north side of the island. The bay was once used as a wrecking ground for old ships, and in its first cove are four wrecks, though none can be seen from the island.

Another 15 minutes from the Boulder Bay Track junction, or 5km from the wharf, you reach a signposted junction. The road to the left continues to Islington Bay Wharf and the causeway to Motutapu Island. Take the road to the right, marked as the Coastal Track, heading south along the shoreline of Islington Bay. If it's a holiday or weekend, the bay will be filled with boats at anchor.

The gravel road ends at the Yankee Wharf boat ramp, and from here the Coastal Track continues along the shoreline for another 10 minutes before heading inland. For the next 1½ hours the track stays away from the shore and it is a moderately difficult tramp over a path of loose lava rock. This can be a hot and tiring stretch, heading through bush with little to look at.

Eventually the track emerges at a large lava field, crossing it to return to the shoreline. The final 30 to 40 minutes to the Rangitoto Wharf is a well-beaten path along the shore, where you can search for seabirds or view Auckland on the horizon. The Coastal Track joins Islington Bay Rd just before you reach the day shelter at Rangitoto Wharf.

Aotea Track

Duration 3 days

Distance 27km (16.7 miles)

Difficulty Moderate

Start/End Whangaparapara Rd

Gateway Auckland (p85)

Transport Shuttle bus

Summary Explore the rugged interior of Great Barrier Island, climbing to the island's highest peak, with the reward of a soak in a natural hot spring.

The Aotea Track loops around Great Barrier Island's central mountainous area and is an easily manageable adventure for any reasonably fit tramper. It can be walked in either direction, and although the route described here starts and ends at Whangaparapa Rd, there are two other access points. From the east, it is possible to reach Mt Heale Hut (in three to 3½ hours) starting at Windy Canyon and tramping Palmers Track, which is accessed from Aotea Rd at the top of Okiwi Hill. This is a short and easy option with superb views at the start of the track. Trampers can also set off from Port FitzRoy, the island's other main harbour. One hour's drive from Tryphena, Port FitzRoy is serviced by ferries, has a store for provisions, and the Akapoua campsite lies to the south.

Great Barrier Island lies 88km northeast of Auckland, set within the Hauraki Gulf Marine Park. It's a place of unspoilt beaches, hot springs, old kauri dams, a forest sanctuary and a network of tramping tracks. Because

WAITĀKERE RANGES

This 160-sq-km wilderness west of Auckland was covered in kauri until the mid-19th century, when logging claimed most of the giant trees. A few stands of ancient kauri and other mature natives survive amid the dense bush of the regenerating rainforest, which is now protected inside the Waitākere Ranges Regional Park. Bordered to the west by wildly beautiful beaches on the Tasman Sea, the park's rugged terrain is a spectacular sight.

Sadly the forest is facing a new threat, with the fungal disease kauri dieback (p79) already affecting many trees in the regional park. To prevent its further spread, the Auckland Council made the decision to close all tracks through the forested section of the park, including the multiday Hillary Trail. However, you can still visit **Arataki** (☑ 09-817 0077; www.aucklandcouncil.govt.nz; 300 Scenic Dr; ⊙ 9am-5pm) 🌿 FREE, the park's impressive visitor centre, where staff can advise on any non-forested tracks that remain open. The Māori carvings at the entrance depict the ancestors of the local Kawerau *iwi* and there are expansive views over the rainforest from its rear deck. On the ground floor, the 12-minute *Dawn to Dusk* video offers an informative overview of the ranges.

there are no possums on the island, the native bush is exceptionally lush.

Named Aotea (meaning 'cloud') by the Māori, and Great Barrier (due to its position at the edge of the Hauraki Gulf) by James Cook, this rugged and exceptionally beautiful place is the fourth-largest NZ island (285 sq km), coming in behind South, North and Stewart Islands. It closely resembles the Coromandel Peninsula, to which it was once joined, and like the Coromandel it was once a mining, logging and whaling centre. Those industries have long gone and today two-thirds of the island is publicly owned and managed by DOC. In 2015 the Aotea Conservation Park, covering 43% of the island, was gazetted.

Despite its proximity to Auckland, Great Barrier seems a world – and a good many years – away. The island has no supermarket, no electricity supply (only private solar, wind and diesel generators) and no main drainage (only septic tanks). Many roads are unsealed and petrol costs are high. Mobile-phone reception is very limited and there are no banks, ATMs or street lights. It was also the third site in the world, and the first island, to be listed as a Dark Sky Sanctuary.

A network of tracks through wild bush combines with old logging roads to provide numerous tramping opportunities.

History

The Hauraki Gulf was one of the first places in NZ settled by Polynesians. Captain Cook sighted and named Great Barrier Island (it seemed to bar the entrance to the Hauraki Gulf) in 1769. It was Great Barrier Island's natural riches that led Europeans to settle here.

The first European settlement was a village established by Cornish miners in 1842 at Miners Cove in the island's northwest corner, and whalers often worked the waters offshore in the 1800s.

It was, however, the kauri tree and its natural by-product – gum – that was the most sought-after and longest-lasting resource. By the 1930s logging had devastated the land. Timber drives, using kauri dams and large amounts of water to flush the logs out to sea, had been especially destructive, and quickly eroded valleys and stream beds, leaving a broad silt flat at river mouths. In 1946 the New Zealand Forest Service began rehabilitating the forest and, in 1973, it was declared a forest recreation reserve. When DOC was established in 1987 it took over administration of the Crown land.

ℹ Planning

WHEN TO TRAMP

Tramping is possible year-round on the Aotea Track, though the wet winters can quickly turn the tracks to mud. The peak season is mid-December to mid-January. However, because of the cost of getting to Great Barrier Island, the tracks and huts, though busy, are not overrun. Elsewhere the island does fill up, so make sure you book transport and accommodation well in advance if planning to tramp at this time. Visitors begin thinning out after January, and the best time to explore the island is arguably March to May, when temperatures are still warm but the rainy season has yet to set in.

WHAT TO BRING

There is no reticulated water on the island, but fresh water is available from various sites. While most water is considered safe to drink, the parasite giardia may be present, so you'll

Aotea Track

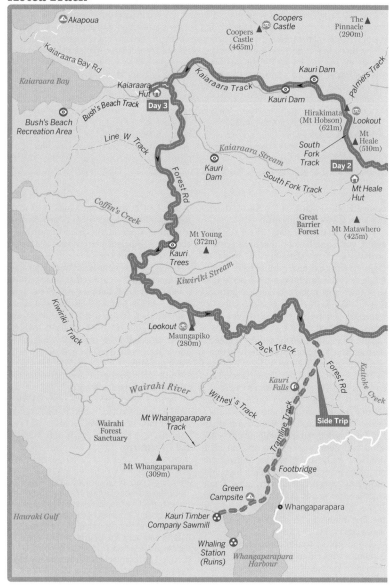

need to either boil water or bring a water purifier or other treatments. Fires are not permitted at any campsites, so bring a stove if you plan to camp.

There's also no mains power on the island and no streetlights, so bring a torch (flashlight). Food is available, but it is more expensive, and there's less choice, than on the mainland, so it's wise to bring all supplies from Auckland.

MAPS & BROCHURES

NZTopo50 map *AY34 (Claris)* covers this tramp, as does NewTopo's 1:45,000 *Aotea Great Barrier Island* map. DOC's *Aotea Track* and *Great Barrier Island Aotea* brochures are also helpful.

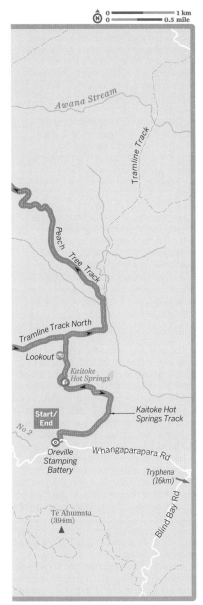

advance throughout the year. Bookings can be made on the DOC website (www.doc.govt.nz).

The **Green Campsite** (p76) can also be booked online, which is recommended as it's the smallest of the five DOC campsites on the island, with just 15 sites.

INFORMATION

For information before you set off from the mainland, call in at the **DOC Auckland Visitor Centre** (p86). On the island, there is a small information counter at the airport that's attended during the high season.
You can pick up leaflets and brochures about the track here. There is also a small visitor centre near the shop at Port FitzRoy, with limited opening hours. Call in for brochures, maps and weather information.

GETTING TO/FROM THE TRAMP

FlyMySky (☑ 09-256 7025, 0800 222 123; www.flymysky.co.nz; adult/child one way $109/79) and **Barrier Air** (☑ 0800 900 600, 09-275 9120; www.barrierair.kiwi; adult/child from $99/94) fly daily from Auckland to Claris on the island.

SeaLink (☑ 0800 732 546, 09-300 5900; www.sealink.co.nz; adult/child/car one way $84/61/290, return $106/84/359) runs car ferries four days a week from Wynyard Wharf in Auckland to Tryphena's Shoal Bay (4½ hours) and once a week to Port FitzRoy (five hours).

The Aotea Track begins and ends on the Kaitoke Hot Springs Track on Whangaparapara Rd, 4km west of Claris. There are a number of businesses that offer transport to the track. **Go Great Barrier Island** (☑ 0800 997 222; www.greatbarrierislandtourism.co.nz) offers transfers to the trailhead (one person from Claris $20, additional people $10 each), as well as rental cars and accommodation. **Great Barrier Wheels** (☑ 021 226 6055, 09-429 0062; www.greatbarrierwheels.co.nz; 67 Hector Sanderson Rd, Claris; ⊙ 8am-7pm Mon-Sat) offers on-demand shuttle services from Claris and Tryphena Wharf.

🏃 The Tramp

Day 1: Whangaparapara Road to Mt Heale Hut

3–4 HOURS / 8KM / 480M ASCENT

The trailhead is indicated at Whangaparapara Rd by a large display sign and a toilet. The first leg of the hike is along Kaitoke Hot Springs Track, which is easy and flat as it crosses Kaitoke Wetlands on boardwalks, where you should look out for birds. You may hear the rare fernbird around this area.

It takes around 40 minutes to reach Kaitoke Hot Springs, the best of which are half-hidden in a canopy of trees. You could

HUTS & CAMPING

There are two Serviced huts ($15) on the track (the only two DOC huts on the island), both of which have gas cookers. One of them, Kaiaraara Hut, also has a wood stove. Backcountry hut passes and tickets are not valid in these two huts, both of which need to booked in

ENVIRONMENT

Great Barrier Island is predominantly volcanic rock, the eroded remnants of a line of andesitic and rhyolitic volcanoes that erupted more than three million years ago. The result is a rugged landscape, and one of the last wilderness areas in the Auckland region.

The heart of the island is a regenerating 80-sq-km kauri forest, crowned by Hirakimata (Mt Hobson). These trees are threatened by a disease called kauri dieback, which kills kauri of all ages. It's caused by microscopic spores in soil. They infect a kauri's roots and destroy tissues carrying water and nutrients to the tree. As a result, the tree slowly starves to death. The spores can be spread in minute amounts of soil on a boot, which makes it essential that you thoroughly clean your boots before and after walking through a forest with kauri. It's also essential to stay on the track and never stand on a kauri's roots.

On the island's west coast, steep forested ridges extend to the sea, where they merge into a flooded coastal landscape and a maze of bays and harbours, making Great Barrier a popular destination for kayakers. The east coast is gentler, featuring sweeping white beaches and alluvial flats.

The island is a haven for a long list of rare and endangered birds. There are no possums, stoats, weasels, ferrets or hedgehogs on Great Barrier Island, all of which are major predators of eggs and chicks of native birds. More than 60% of NZ's entire pateke/brown teal population lives on Great Barrier, and they can often be seen in the Whangapoua and Okiwi Estuaries. The island also serves as a stronghold for the North Island kaka and banded rail. There are also some spotless crakes and fernbirds.

Great Barrier Island has one of the most diverse lizard populations in the country. The absence of hedgehogs, stoats, ferrets and weasels is also good news for the lizards. The 13 native lizard species recorded on the island include the large and rare chevron skink, which is found only on Great Barrier and Little Barrier Islands.

grab an early soak here, though you could also save it until Day 3, when you're on your way out again. Beware: not only are some of the pools too hot to get into, they may also contain amoebic parasites, so *do not immerse your head in the hot water*.

After a brief but steep climb, you reach Tramline Track North and turn right. Along this wide, old tramline are relics of the logging era, when the Kauri Timber Company used to haul kauri logs out of the forest.

Peach Tree Track soon appears on the left, which you should follow to climb steadily through the regenerating forest to **Mt Heale Hut** (20 bunks). There are spectacular views from here, especially on clear evenings when there are striking sunsets over Little Barrier Island (Hauturu).

Day 2: Mt Heale Hut to Kaiaraara Hut

3 HOURS / 6KM / 230M ASCENT, 630M DESCENT

From Mt Heale Hut, it's a steep 40-minute climb north along South Fork Track to the junction with Kaiaraara Track, which descends towards Kaiaraara Hut. Before starting the descent, however, be sure to take the five-minute side track to the summit of **Hirakimata** (Mt Hobson; 621m).

The peak has a wooden platform with a large trig and views of both sides of Great Barrier Island, as well as the outer islands in the Hauraki Gulf. You also stand a chance here of seeing several rare native birds, as it's a spot favoured by the tomtit, black petrel and recently reintroduced North Island robin. It's also frequented by kakariki and kaka. The beautiful endemic Great Barrier tree daisy and tiny sundews like it here as well.

You will encounter a mix of steep paths, stairways and bridges as you descend the west slope of the mountain, ending just before you arrive at the remnants of the upper **kauri dam**. All that remains of the dam is a stack of large logs and rusting cables, but the view of the sheer rock walls of the gorge below is stunning.

Around 40 minutes from the Hirakimata (Mt Hobson) summit you'll see a two-minute side track to the remnants of the **kauri driving dam**. This was built in the 1920s, along with six smaller dams upstream. Unfortunately the lower kauri dam was washed away by floodwaters in a major storm in 2014. The lower dam was once an impressive site: a massive, wooden structure held in place across the gorge by huge kauri logs. When this dam was tripped, the force of water sent the logs all the way to Kaiaraara Bay, where they were held in huge booms until being floated to sawmills in Auckland. These dams were constructed in 1926 and amazingly, after all the work to build them, were used for only three years.

The intriguing scenery continues just beyond the lower dam, when the track passes through a nikau grove that makes you feel as though you're in a true tropical wilderness. At this point the track improves remarkably, and within 15 minutes you cross a large suspension bridge and arrive at the junction with Coopers Castle Route (right) – it's a 45-minute climb along this track to a lookout, and if you keep going you'll eventually reach Port FitzRoy.

Kaiaraara Track (left) crosses a series of suspension bridges across this branch of Kaiaraara Stream. **Kaiaraara Hut** (28 bunks) is just to the right (1½ hours from the lower dam). Built in 1973 by the New Zealand Forest Service, it has been well cared for and is a pleasant place to spend an evening.

Day 3: Kaiaraara Hut to Whangaparapara Road

4 HOURS / 13KM

The final day of the tramp is an easy route, following Forest Rd, which was built in the 1950s to provide firefighters access to the island's rugged interior, though today it is closed to vehicles.

From Kaiaraara Hut, return to Forest Rd and head right. The road takes you on a gentle climb and within 15 minutes (1km) passes a signposted junction with South Fork Track (left). South Fork Track is an alternative route back to Mt Heale Hut. Continue climbing and soon you'll see an impressive kauri tree along the road and then, high above, the stone fortress that is the peak of Mt Young (372m).

In less than an hour you reach the signposted junction with Line W Track (right), which heads west to Kiwiriki Track (25 minutes). Forest Rd, however, descends to cross **Coffins Creek**, with a dark and lush **grotto** upstream, and then climbs to a signposted spur track leading to a pair of **kauri trees**, reached two hours (5km) from the hut. It's a short descent to these impressive giants, with one so large four people couldn't link arms around the trunk. It's hard to imagine that at one time most of Great Barrier Island was covered with trees like these.

The road descends to cross **Kiwiriki Stream** and then makes the longest climb of the day, a steady 30-minute (1.5km) march towards Maungapiko (280m). You top out near Kiwiriki Track (right) and a short spur track to **Maungapiko Lookout**. This rocky outcrop is a 20-minute side trip and rewards with fine views of the island's west coast. Forest Rd descends to reach a junction with Pack Track (right), 30 minutes from the lookout. (Pack Track remains closed after damage caused by the 2014 storm).

Continue along Forest Rd to the junction of the Tramline Track, which leads south to the Green Campsite, an hour or so away.

Should you decide to skip the side trip to the Green Campsite, continue on to Tramline Track North, heading towards Kaitoke Hot Springs Track. The wide track drops steeply through the rugged terrain to Kaitoke Creek No 2, ascends on the other side, and then descends again to a tributary of Kaitoke Creek No 1. It follows the stream, gradually dropping towards the eastern side of the island, until it arrives at a signposted junction for Kaitoke Hot Springs Track.

Head right (southeast) on Kaitoke Hot Springs Track, which immediately crosses Kaitoke Stream. It then climbs steadily to a ridge, where there are excellent views of Kaitoke Swamp, the surrounding ridges and the crashing surf of Kaitoke Beach to the east. You may want to stop at the **Kaitoke Hot Springs** now to soak away three days of effort.

Before long you will reach the Whangaparapara Rd trailhead, thus closing the loop. Before you go, be sure to check out the massive stone walls of the **Oreville Stamping Battery**, above and below Whangaparapara Rd. They are an impressive reminder of the mining period.

Side Trip: The Green Campsite

2–3 HOURS / 6KM RETURN

From the junction of Forest Rd and the Tramline Track, head south on the latter towards the Green Campsite. On the way, you can make a five-minute detour to **Kauri Falls**, where a 3m waterfall empties into a swimming hole.

Continue on the Tramline Track, crossing bridges over several small streams and passing signposted junctions with Withey's Track and the Mt Whangaparapara Track. Within 30 minutes you arrive at a fenced paddock. Step over the fence and arrive at a junction just before a footbridge.

To reach the secluded **Green Campsite** (☑ 09-379 6476; www.doc.govt.nz; Whangaparapara Harbour; sites per adult/child $13/6.50), on the western shore of the harbour, follow Old

NORTHLAND, AUCKLAND & COROMANDEL AOTEA TRACK

Mill Track, signposted at the junction. It's an easy 15-minute walk to the grassy meadow, where the DOC camping ground offers a view of the harbour, a shelter, sinks, display panels and toilets.

From the campsite, a rough track continues west, climbing steeply over two ridges to reach the site of the Kauri Timber Company sawmill, which was the largest in the southern hemisphere in 1910. Today, all that remains are the concrete foundations, some pilings and an old steam traction engine.

At low tide you can continue around the shore of a small bay for 30 minutes to the ruins of an old whaling station.

Coromandel Walkway

Duration 6–7 hours

Distance 20km (12.4 miles)

Difficulty Moderate

Start/End Stony Bay

Gateway Thames (p89)

Transport Shuttle bus

Summary A remote, wild coastal walk near the northern tip of the Coromandel Peninsula, combining thick forest, dramatic coastline and views of the Hauraki Gulf islands.

Despite being just 60 straight-line kilometres from Auckland, and 100km by road from Thames, there's a remoteness to the Coromandel Peninsula's northern tip that mere distances can't portray. Forming a boundary between the Pacific Ocean and Hauraki Gulf, there's a real sense of the wild as the sea storms ashore on Poley Bay, and Sugar Loaf and its entourage of rocks stand like petrified waves. With rugged coastline, unruly seas and gorgeous sections of bush, the Coromandel Walkway is a fitting crown for the peninsula, and if the stunning drive up the Coromandel to get here doesn't create expectation, you're not paying attention.

There are DOC campgrounds at both ends of the trail, so you may want to linger for a while either side of your tramp, or you can throw on the backpack and turn it into a two-day tramp, staying the night at Fletcher Bay.

The walkway can be tramped in either direction, but the dramatic surprise of rising to the main lookout point above Shag Bay is enhanced if you walk from Stony Bay, having not yet sighted the coast around Poley Bay and Sugar Loaf. If you're looking for a shorter tramp, the most spectacular section of the walkway is between Stony Bay and Poley Bay.

At a glance the Coromandel Peninsula looks almost too postcard-perfect to be such a dramatic tramping destination. Its east coast has some of the North Island's best white-sand beaches, and during summer it can seem as though half of Auckland decamps here. But step off the likes of Cathedral Cove or Hot Water Beach and you discover a mountainous spine criss-crossed with walking tracks, allowing trampers to explore large tracts of untamed bush where kauri trees once towered and are starting to do so again.

Add to this a walkway along the peninsula's rugged and remote northern tip, and a gorge where gold once flowed, and you have a very enticing tramping destination in easy reach of Auckland.

History

It is thought that the crews of canoes carrying early Polynesian settlers to NZ rested on the Coromandel Peninsula during their epic journey. In 1769 Captain James Cook sailed into a rugged little inlet on the eastern shore of the peninsula. He raised the British flag over NZ for the first time and named the spot Mercury Bay (after the planet that appeared in the sky that night). The peninsula, however, takes its name from the HMS *Coromandel*, which visited in 1820, bringing with it the missionary Samuel Marsden.

Full-scale kauri logging began on the peninsula in the mid-1850s, and ramped up with the Thames gold rush in the 1860s, due to the sudden demand for building materials in the booming towns. Gold mining declined from around WWI, though there remains a working open-pit mine in Waihi. Kauri logging ended in 1928, and the Coromandel Forest Park, which covers an area from Karangahake Gorge to Cape Colville, was declared in 1938, along with a program to re-establish the native bush.

Environment

Before it was logged, the Coromandel Peninsula had a rich variety of forest flora, which was unmatched by any other area of comparable size in the country. Now, much of the park is busy regenerating native bush, including kauri and rata – with the latter noted for its brilliant orange-red flowers. The interior ridges are covered with podocarps and hardwoods, a few scattered pockets of kauri, and areas of bracken, fern and scrub. The predominant species around here are rimu and tawa, but you can also find miro, matai and kahikatea.

Coromandel Walkway

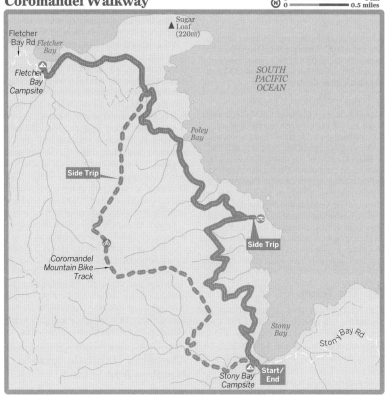

The peninsula's wildlife consists of many of the usual native NZ birds – tui, bellbirds, kiwi, kereru (NZ pigeon) and fantails – and introduced mammals, such as pigs, possums, goats, cats and mustelids (stoats, ferrets and weasels).

Various kinds of jaspers, petrified wood, rhodonite and agate are found in or near most streams, which makes this place an excellent source of rare rocks and gemstones. (Permits are not required for mineral collecting, but interested rock-hounds should make themselves aware of where the activity is allowed. No more than 2kg of rock can be removed per person, per day.)

🛈 Planning

GUIDED TRAMPS

Coromandel Town–based **Coromandel Adventures** (☎ 0800 462 676; www.coromandel adventures.co.nz; 90 Tiki Rd; tours adult/child from $75/45) runs a four-day Coromandel Ultimate Hikes trip ($650) that includes a day

tramping the Coromandel Walkway, and another day through the Kauaeranga Valley (p79) to the Pinnacles, as well as a day on the east coast at Cathedral Cove and Hot Water Beach.

WHEN TO TRAMP

The Coromandel's subtropical climate means that the walkway is a good option at any time of year. After heavy rain, the dirt roads into Stony Bay can be the greatest hazard. The campgrounds at the tramp's end points get pretty crowded during summer school holidays – avoid the Christmas period and January if you want solitude.

MAPS

The walkway is covered on NZTopo50 *AZ34 (Moehau)*. The Coromandel Walkway page on DOC's website (www.doc.govt.nz) includes a link to an elevation profile.

CAMPING

The walkway links two popular DOC campsites (per person $13, plus a $3 recycling and waste fee per site): Stony Bay and Fletcher Bay. They're both large affairs, with around 120 non-powered sites each. Bookings are required, and there's a minimum two-night stay over the New Year break.

INFORMATION

As you drive up the peninsula, stop for information at the **DOC Hauraki office** (Department of Conservation; ☑ 07-867 9180; www.doc.govt. nz; cnr Pahau & Kirkwood Sts) or the **DOC Kauaeranga Visitor Centre**.

GETTING TO/FROM THE TRAMP

Stony Bay is around 50km north of Coromandel Town, but the nature of the narrow, unsealed, winding road means that the drive takes around 1½ hours. If you're in a hire car, check with the rental agency about any restrictions on driving here – past Coromandel Town much of the road is the sort that agencies tend to frown upon.

If you're without wheels, or just keen not to walk the return leg, **Coromandel Discovery** (☑ 07-866 8175; www.coromandeldiscovery.co.nz; 39 Whangapoua Rd, Coromandel Town; adult/child $135/75) will drive you from Coromandel Town up to Fletcher Bay and pick you up from Stony Bay four hours later ($135 per adult, minimum $290). Pick-ups from Coromandel Town are at 8.30am.

 The Tramp

The walkway car park is inside Stony Bay Campsite, just before the Stony Bay Creek causeway. Walk across the causeway and follow the road through the Ailsa Heights section of the campsite. Turn right at the Henry's Hill sign (where there's a boot-wash station to help control the spread of kauri dieback disease), heading out along the coast.

The walkway traverses above Stony Bay's pohutukawa-lined beach, climbing slowly all the time as it rounds several deep gullies spiked with nikau palms.

On a spur above Shag Bay, the walkway cuts inland, winding across thickly forested slopes high above the bay. As it swings back to the coast and the forest begins to break open, you'll come to a marked turnoff (1¼ hours from Stony Bay) to a lookout, five minutes' walk away. The stunning view from the lookout provides a visual mud map of your day, looking back to Stony Bay and along the rugged black coastline to Poley Bay and round-shouldered Sugar Loaf, which falls just a few hundred metres shy of being the Coromandel's northern tip.

For the next 45 minutes the walkway winds across the slopes above the ocean, offering some fine views of Sugar Loaf and its attendant rocks, before curling steeply down towards Poley Bay. This grey pebbly beach, rimmed with pohutukawa trees, is reached on the shortest of side trails as the walkway bottoms out at a stream. There's a raw beauty to the bay, but swimming isn't recommended because of submerged rocks beneath the waves.

What goes down must come up, and it's a steep climb out from Poley Bay. Fifteen minutes from the bay, at about the top of the climb, the walkway crosses a stile and enters farmland, cutting across cleared slopes that provide excellent views of the coast. This section of track can get pretty chopped up (and sloppy) by livestock. Another 15 minutes from the stile, you'll pass a junction with the Coromandel Mountain Bike Track. Continue straight ahead, crossing another stile and beginning the descent towards Fletcher Bay. The view is now completely transformed, with grassy slopes stretching out ahead and Little Barrier Island balancing on the horizon.

From here, simply follow farm tracks down to the coast (look for walkway poles and markers). The main thing to note is that it doesn't drop down to the first beach that you see (by the stream outlet). Instead it stays along the fence line, crossing a stile and a headland before descending to Fletcher Bay (30 minutes from the mountain-bike track junction), with another large DOC campsite and grey beach. Retrace your steps to return to Stony Bay.

Alternative Finish: Coromandel Mountain Bike Track

2½–3 HOURS / 7.5KM

For a different perspective on the walk back to Stony Bay, turn right and uphill when you come to the Coromandel Mountain Bike Track junction. This shared path provides a more direct but steeper and hillier return, climbing to 540m above sea level – straight up – before descending into Stony Bay – straight down. From the top there are views of Fletcher Bay, adjoining Port Jackson and the Hauraki Gulf islands.

Kauaeranga Kauri Trail

Duration 2 days

Distance 14km (8.7 miles)

Difficulty Moderate

Start/End Kauaeranga Valley Rd

Gateway Thames (p89)

Transport Private

Summary A tramp up the popular Kauaeranga Valley, featuring historic logging

THE MIGHTY KAURI

The kauri (*Agathis australis*) is an outsize member of the conifer family and one of the world's most massive trees. It can live for more than 2000 years, reach 50m in height and boast an impressive girth of up to 16m.

When the first humans arrived in New Zealand, kauri forest covered large areas of Northland, the Coromandel and Great Barrier Island. The trees played an important role in many aspects of early Māori culture; they were integrated in creation mythology, rituals, war, art and everyday life. Some large trees were given names and revered as chiefs of the forest. On special occasions giant trunks were used to carve out large *waka taua* (sea/war canoes). Kauri gum had many valuable functions: burnt as an insecticide in kumara plots, wrapped in flax to make torches for night fishing, and used as chewing gum. Resin was also burnt and mixed with fat to create the ink for *moko* (facial tattooing).

It didn't take long for European settlers to cotton on. Prizing the excellent timber and useful gum, they went about decimating these magnificent forests. The first kauri stands to be felled were close to the sea, and on rolling country where bullock teams could easily haul logs out. But as demand for timber increased, it became necessary to log more rugged locations, such as the headwaters of the Kauaeranga Valley. The problem of transporting logs to mills was overcome by the creation of reusable kauri dams.

The first dams were built before the 1850s and they remained the main feature of logging until 1930. The massive wooden structures were built across the upper portions of streams to trap water. Trees were cut and positioned in the creek bed, either above or below the dam catchment, and when the water was high enough, a loose-plank gate in the middle of the dam was tripped. The sudden flood swept the timber through the steep and difficult terrain to the rivers below.

Of the 70 dams that were built in the Kauaeranga Valley, remnants of one-quarter of them can still be seen, including six on the Kauaeranga Kauri Trail, though most are now unrecognisable as dams. You can spot the odd giant kauri here, too.

Saved from the lumberjacks, the kauri are now under threat from a fungus-like disease known as kauri dieback, which has killed thousands of the trees. Visitors to areas where kauri grow need to do their bit to prevent the spread of spores, which infect the roots of the trees. Clean all your gear and stay on tracks. Keep well away from kauri tree roots. Any footwear or equipment that comes into contact with soil should be cleaned both before and after you leave the area. See www.kauridieback.co.nz for more information.

trails and regenerating forests. A side trip to the lofty Pinnacles gives spectacular views to both coasts.

The 719 sq km of rugged, forested reserves that make up the Coromandel Forest Park are spread across the Coromandel Peninsula. There are more than 30 tramps through the forest park, with the most popular area being the Kauaeranga Valley, which cuts into the Coromandel Range behind Thames.

A logging boom took place in the Coromandel Range during the late 19th century, when stands of massive kauri were extracted. Today, the Kauaeranga Valley is filled with remnants of its lumbering past: packhorse trails, tramway clearings and many old kauri dams. Dancing Camp Dam (close to Pinnacles Hut) has been partly restored, and is one of the few dams which are not now inaccessible and/or unrecognisable.

 Planning

WHEN TO TRAMP

Kauaeranga Valley is only a two-hour drive from Auckland, so it can be busy much of summer. On weekends, Pinnacles Hut and Crosbies Hut are usually full. The most popular tramping time is autumn. As many school and youth groups frequent the area, it will pay to phone the Kauaeranga Visitor Centre for information if you do not want to share the huts or campsites with these groups.

MAPS & BROCHURES

Most tramps in the Kauaeranga Valley are covered by NZTopo50 *BB35 (Hikuai)*, with *BB34 (Thames)* covering the western fringe. Download DOC's *Kauaeranga Valley & Broken Hills Recreation* brochure, which details all walks in the park.

HUTS & CAMPING

Pinnacles Hut ($15) must be booked in advance year-round; DOC hut passes and tickets are not valid. The hut has gas stoves, a solid fuel heater, running water, mattresses, a barbecue and

Kauaeranga Kauri Trail

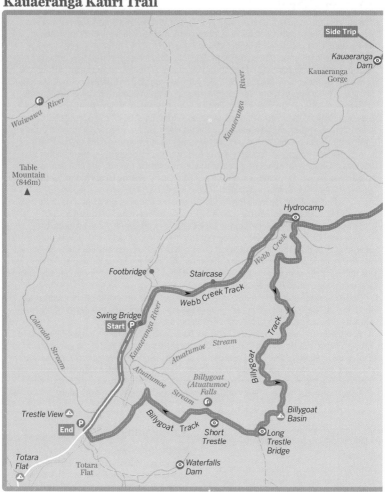

solar-powered lighting. The old hut is now used as a residence for a permanent hut warden.

There are eight self-registration Scenic campsites (per person $13) around the valley, all in appealing settings with water supply and toilets. There are also Backcountry campsites ($5) near Pinnacles Hut, at Billygoat Basin and Moss Creek.

INFORMATION

The **DOC Kauaeranga Visitor Centre** (Department of Conservation; ☑ 07-867 9080; www. doc.govt.nz; Kauaeranga Valley Rd; ⊘ 8.30am-4pm) is in the Kauaeranga Valley, 9km from the start of the tramp. It has interesting historical displays, dispenses maps, brochures and advice, and handles hut and campsite bookings.

ⓘ Getting to/from the Tramp

The DOC Kauaeranga Visitor Centre is 14km off SH25; it's a further 9km along a gravel road to the start of the trail. There's no public transport to the trail, but since it's little more than 20km from Thames, it's feasible to take a cab here from **Thames Taxis** (☑ 027 206 3887, 07-868 3100).

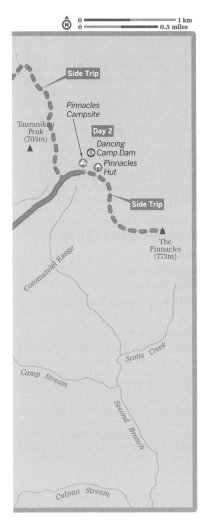

 The Tramp

Day 1: Kauaeranga Valley Road to Pinnacles Hut via Webb Creek Track

3 HOURS / 7KM / 380M ASCENT

The tramp begins at the far end of Kauaeranga Valley Rd (9km beyond the visitor centre), where you will see a large display sign offering directions. Follow the main track north, as it almost immediately crosses a swing bridge over the Kauaeranga River.

The main track then skirts the true left (east) bank of the river for 20 minutes, going through an impressive forest of rata, ferns and nikau palms. Just before Webb Creek is a signposted junction, with the left fork leading to Moss Creek. Take the right fork (the main track), heading east towards Hydrocamp. This historical packhorse route was used by kauri bushmen in the 1920s to reach logging sites further up the valley.

After crossing Webb Creek you will climb a staircase that was cut into rock to make the journey easier for the packhorses. Care is required in places as the rocks can be slippery.

At the top of the climb up Webb Creek, the remains of a skidded road are visible beside the track. Skidded roads were made from small logs laid lengthwise with cross pieces forming the 'skids'. Logs were pulled along the skids by teams of bullocks or steam haulers.

The Hydrocamp, reached 1½ to two hours from the trailhead, is a clearing built in the late 1940s by workers erecting power lines from Thames to Whitianga. It is also the major junction for those walking back to Kauaeranga Valley Rd via Billygoat Track.

Take the left fork towards Pinnacles Hut, heading along a continuation of the old packhorse track. It climbs onto an open ridge, where there are superb views of the Coromandel Peninsula's east coast and the rugged Kauaeranga Valley. The track remains on the ridge for 45 minutes and eventually you're rewarded with a view of the Pinnacles forming a jagged skyline straight ahead.

One hour beyond Hydrocamp you reach a signposted junction. Take the right fork east towards the Pinnacles to arrive at the huge Pinnacles Hut (80 bunks) in 10 minutes. Nearby, but out of view, are the warden's quarters and campsite.

From the hut it's a five-minute walk down a side trail to Dancing Camp Dam. This was the second-largest kauri dam in the valley when it was built in 1921. It's also one of the best preserved after it was partially restored in 1994 with kauri timber that had washed downriver in a flash flood the previous year.

Side Trip: The Pinnacles

1½–2 HOURS / 3KM RETURN

From the hut a track swings southeast, becomes a marked route and in 45 minutes reaches the jagged summit of the Pinnacles (773m). The route to the top is steep but well signposted, and has ladders bolted into the rock face in some sections to assist you. The views from the summit are among the best in the area; you can see the entire Coromandel Peninsula, from Mt Moehau in the north to Mt Te Aroha in the south.

Side Trip: Kauaeranga Gorge

1½–2 HOURS / 3KM RETURN

Another interesting side trip from Pinnacles Hut is to view Kauaeranga Gorge and Dam. To get there, head back to the Pinnacles Hut track junction on the main ridge track and head north. Within about 45 minutes you descend steeply into the Kauaeranga Valley and reach the river. When the river is low it's possible to hike down to Kauaeranga Gorge by departing from the track and heading past Kauaeranga Dam, 10 to 15 minutes downstream.

Built in 1912, the Kauaeranga was the largest dam constructed in the valley, but all that remains today is the floor and a few supporting beams. There are good swimming pools near the dam. Travel in the gorge should never be attempted when the river is swollen, and even at normal water levels it will involve tramping through waist-deep pools.

Day 2: Pinnacles Hut to Kauaeranga Valley Road via Billygoat Track

4 HOURS / 7KM / 380M DESCENT

Make a careful assessment of conditions before setting out this day. The Billygoat Track crosses the Kauaeranga River to reach the track end, and this can be extremely hazardous – and should not be attempted – in wet weather. If it is wet, return along the Webb Creek Track instead.

If taking the Billygoat Track, backtrack to Hydrocamp, an hour's tramp from Pinnacles Hut. At the signposted junction take the left fork to follow Billygoat Track, beginning with a 30-minute climb to a saddle, where there are excellent views down the Kauaeranga Valley to the Hauraki Plains.

A little further on, a knoll overlooks the Billygoat Basin. The first attempt to log this basin was made in the 1880s but was abandoned within a few years, as driving logs down Billygoat (Atuatumoe) Falls proved too destructive. The basin was successfully logged in the 1920s after the construction of the Billygoat incline to bypass the falls, and with the use of a steam hauler.

Drop down into Billygoat Basin and cross Billygoat Stream before passing through a clearing with basic camping facilities. A few minutes further on, a 50m side

track overlooks the collapsed remains of the Long Trestle bridge, which at one time was 160m long and 11m high.

The main track swings northwest and follows the route of the Billygoat tramway down past the Tarawaere Track junction and the remains of Short Trestle, a bridge built for the tramway. Near here you'll enjoy some spectacular views of Billygoat (Atuatumoe) Falls below you. Billygoat Track ends with a steep descent to the Kauaeranga River. The river must be crossed to reach Kauaeranga Valley Rd and the Tarawaere car park (three hours from Hydrocamp), about 1km down the valley from the end of the road. Turn right at the road and head back to the car park.

Karangahake Gorge

Duration 5–6 hours

Distance 16.5km (10.3 miles)

Difficulty Easy

Start/End Karangahake Hall

Gateway Thames (p89)

Transport Tourist train

Summary Combining natural and human history, this tramp through a former gold-rich gorge reveals dramatic views and a unique walk through mining remnants.

As SH2 journeys between Auckland and Tauranga it passes through the dramatic Karangahake Gorge, creating one of the most scenic short stretches of road on the North Island. Running along the opposite bank of the gorge, which is cut by the Ohinemuri River, is a network of walking trails that are even more beautiful.

This tramp follows a shared hiking/ cycling trail through the most beautiful stretch of the gorge, branching off onto hiking-only trails that explore the remnants of the gorge's gold-rush days, at one point even burrowing through tunnels carved by miners.

The tramp is a NZ rarity – predominantly flat – with a quirky cafe stop at the turn-around point. By tramping standards, this is about as civilised as it gets.

The most spectacular section is the lower gorge and Windows area, so if you only have half a day, walk the Railway Tunnel Loop, which passes through the lower gorge and back through the tunnel, taking in the Windows along the way. Note that the section of the Windows Walk through the lower Waitawheta Gorge can sometimes close due to rockfall or instability of the cliffs.

Karangahake Gorge

0 1 km
0 0.5 miles

Waikino Rd
Old Waitekauri Rd
SH 2
Waikino
Victoria St
Poland St
Abbott Rd
Waikino
Victoria Battery
Pukekauri Rd
Hollis Rd
Waitawheta Rd
Ohinemuri River
Waitawheta Rd
Owharoa Falls
Waitawheta Rd
Kennedy Rd
Swetman Rd
SH 2
Dickey Flat Rd
Karangahake Gorge
Waitawheta River
Rail Tunnel
Moresby St
Armstrong St
Woodstock Battery
Talisman Battery
Windows
Rahu Rd
SH 2
Ohinemuri River
River Rd
Albert St
County Rd
Start/End
Crown Battery
Crown Hill Rd

History

Māori have had a long connection to Karangahake Gorge, with the Ohinemuri River translating as 'the maiden left behind'. Legend tells that a *pā* (fortified village) here was attacked and taken by an invading tribe, who killed most of its residents and drove out the rest. The chief's daughter was away, later returning to find her people disappeared. She took refuge in a nearby cave until the chief returned, driving out the invaders.

Gold was discovered in the gorge in the 1880s, with mines and the township of Karangahake quickly springing up to make hay while the gold shone. At its peak there were around 2000 people living in the town, which had two pubs and a school. The cyanide process for extracting gold from crushed ore was pioneered here in the 1890s.

Plans to push SH2 through the gorge were also born in the 1880s, though it took until 1901 for the job to be completed. The North Island's main trunk railway was also finally completed through the gorge in 1904 after three years of work. This section of railway was closed in 1978 after the construction of a tunnel deviated the line. The course of the railway is now the guiding line for this tramp.

Gold mining remains a part of the local economy, with a large open-pit mine continuing to operate in Waihi, around 5km from Waikino. A walking trail runs around the pit rim if you want a view of the operation.

ℹ Planning

WHEN TO TRAMP

There are no real climatic limitations on this track – it can be tramped at any time of year. If it's raining just wait for another day.

WHAT TO BRING

A torch (flashlight) is recommended for exploring the Windows. It'll also be useful through the old rail tunnel, even if purely to alert cyclists to your presence.

MAPS & BROCHURES

The NZTop50 *BC35 (Paeroa)* map covers the route. DOC also produces a *Karangahake: New Zealand's Gorge of Gold* brochure that has comprehensive information on the gorge and its trails.

INFORMATION

The **DOC Hauraki office** (p78) in Thames can provide information about the gorge and walks, as can the **Paeroa Information Centre** (✆ 07-862 6999; www.paeroa.org.nz; Old Post Office Bldg, 101 Normanby Rd; ⊙ 9am-5pm Mon-Fri).

ℹ Getting to/from the Tramp

InterCity (p87) coaches running between Auckland and Mt Maunganui pass through Karangahake Gorge and stop at Paeroa and Waihi, though this leaves you at least 8km short of either end of the tramp. From Waihi, you can get to Waikino on the **Goldfields Railway** (✆ 07-863 8251; www.waihirail.co.nz; 30 Wrigley St, Waihi; adult/child return $20/12, bikes per route extra $2; ⊙ departs Waihi 10am, 11.45am & 1.45pm Sat, Sun & public holidays), a vintage tourist train that makes the scenic 30-minute journey to the Waikino railway station, the eastern end point of the tramp.

If you're driving, turn off SH2 onto Crown Hill Rd at the western edge of Karangahake village, and cross the metal bridge. There's parking by the hall, just a few metres past the bridge.

🏃 The Tramp

Cross the road from Karangahake Hall to the shelter at the entrance into Crown Battery, about 50m up the hill from the metal bridge, and head east along the signposted Karangahake Gorge Historic Walkway. Go straight ahead at the first junction heading along the true left (south) bank of the Ohinemuri River. Within minutes you'll come to a view along the river and gorge.

Opposite the main gorge car park, pass above the first suspension bridge (over the Ohinemuri River) and descend to cross the second suspension bridge over the Waitawheta River. The remains of the Woodstock Battery, a rock crusher used by the gold mines, sit at the end of the bridge.

Turn right here, heading into the lower Waitawheta Gorge, ascending on the Windows Walk. In just a few metres, turn left, heading up the steps towards Woodstock Tramway. At the head of the third lot of steps turn right, literally stepping through the Talisman Battery.

The tracks of the tramway lead to and through the Windows, a tunnel carved into the cliffs, with 'windows' cut through the rock so miners could toss waste rock into the Waitawheta River, flowing past below. You can now peer through the windows to the river and the cliffs and trail opposite. This tunnel is just a small part of 12km of mining tunnels that puncture the area. Things get pretty dark in the Windows tunnel; if you don't have a torch, you could be banging into walls.

At the end of the tunnel, descend the wooden steps, turn right and cross the wooden Crown Tramway Bridge over the

Waitawheta River. At the bridge's end you used to be able to detour left and burrow through the cliffs again to the Underground Pumphouse, but the unstable nature of the tunnel means that route has been permanently closed. Turn right instead, where the cliffs arch over the track, and follow the waterway back down to the Ohinemuri River.

Re-cross the suspension bridge to Woodstock Battery, turning left here this time to pass below the battery and begin along the bank of the Ohinemuri River. This well-benched trail follows the fast-flowing river, with SH2 on the opposite bank. At times you'll be among ferns and moss, while at other times the bank is devoid of vegetation, with the trail all but overhanging the river. Around 15 to 20 minutes from Woodstock Battery, the trail comes to a steel bridge popping out of an old rail tunnel. Turn right here, joining the Hauraki Rail Trail and continuing along the same bank. There's a blessed sense of removal as you follow the now-wide trail with SH2 traffic hurrying past across the river.

About 45 minutes from the rail tunnel bridge, cross Waitawheta Rd and the side trail to Owharoa Falls. Ignore the wooden Waikino Memorial Bridge over the river (unless a beer at the Waikino Tavern on the opposite bank is calling you) and in about 100m (10 minutes from Waitawheta Rd) the bush parts to reveal the concrete ruins of **Victoria Battery**, the most extensive of the gorge's gold-mining relics. Most prominent among the ruins are the circular cyanide tanks. If you're here on a Wednesday or Sunday, you might stumble into the scheduled tours and tramway rides around the battery site.

At the end of the battery, leave the rail trail to cross the Ohinemuri River on a footbridge. This leads immediately to an underpass beneath SH2, where you pop out beside the Waikino railway station and the **Waikino Station Cafe** (☑ 07-863 8640; www.facebook.com/waikinostationcafe; SH2; mains $10-20; ☺ 10am-3pm Mon-Fri, 9.30am-4pm Sat & Sun), noted for its home baking...always a tramper's best friend.

From the station, retrace your steps back along the rail trail to the bridge beside the rail tunnel. Cross the bridge this time and enter the tunnel. At 1100m in length, it's said to be the longest recreational-use tunnel in NZ. Exit the tunnel and cross the bridge high above SH2. Take the stairs to the left before the end of the bridge to return to Crown Battery and Karangahake Hall.

HAURAKI RAIL TRAIL

The most interesting way to access the Karangahake Gorge tramp is by bike, with the Hauraki Rail Trail cutting through the gorge and forming the spine of the tramp. This 58km trail from Thames to Waihi is one of the 22 trails that make up the Nga Haerenga/New Zealand Cycle Trail and is often called New Zealand's easiest cycling trail. From Thames, it's a 42km ride to Karangahake, while from Waihi it's about 9km to Waikino. If coming from Thames, the ideal way to structure the trip is to cycle to Paeroa or Karangahake, stay the night and tramp the next day.

Information about bike hire, luggage transfers and accommodation is available at https://haurakirailtrail.co.nz.

Side Trip: Owharoa Falls

10 MINUTES / 200M

At Waitawheta Rd, maps show a trail running up the true left (east) side of the tributary, but this is overgrown. Instead turn up Waitawheta Rd and in 50m duck down right onto the Owharoa Falls Track. It's 50m along this track to the base of the falls, which bounce over a lumpy ledge of rock. This is the lowest of the waterfall's three tiers. You can see another section higher up from the start of the falls track, or you can wander a couple of hundred metres further up Waitawheta Rd to where it crosses the stream just above the falls.

TOWNS & FACILITIES

Auckland

☑ 09 / POP 1.42 MILLION

New Zealand's largest city is a good spot to ready yourself for tramping adventures, or recover afterwards. Vibrant, cosmopolitan and crammed with multifarious supplies, Auckland is also lush, leafy and surrounded by ocean and islands.

🛏 Sleeping & Eating

Haka Lodge   HOSTEL $

(☑ 09-379 4556; www.hakalodge.com; 373 Karangahape Rd; dm $31-41, r with/without bathroom $139/109; ☎) 🖉 The transformation of one of Auckland's dodgiest old pubs into a bright and shiny hostel is a modern miracle. Dorms have custom-made wooden bunks with privacy curtains, lockers and their own power points – making them perhaps the most comfortable bunkrooms in Auckland. Wi-fi is free and unlimited. And it couldn't be better located for the bustling Karangahape Rd scene.

★**Hotel DeBrett**　　　BOUTIQUE HOTEL $$$
(☑09-925 9000; www.hoteldebrett.com; 2 High St; r from $370; 🛜) This hip historic hotel has been zhooshed up with stripy carpets and clever designer touches in every nook of the 25 extremely comfortable rooms. Prices include a continental breakfast, free unlimited wi-fi and a pre-dinner drink.

Sofitel Viaduct Harbour　　　HOTEL $$$
(☑09-909 9000; www.sofitel-auckland.com; 21 Viaduct Harbour Ave; d from $420; P🛜🏊) Auckland is one of the world's great harbour cities, so it makes perfect sense to stay beside the water. In close proximity to the restaurants and bars of Viaduct Harbour and the Wynyard Quarter, the Sofitel has classy rooms and suites arrayed around a central ornamental pool. Moored yachts bob nearby, and Auckland's 'City of Sails' moniker definitely rings true.

Atomic Roastery　　　CAFE $
(☑0800 286 642; www.atomiccoffee.co.nz; 420c New North Rd, Kingsland; snacks $9-11; ⊗8am-3pm) Follow your nose to one of the country's best-known coffee roasters. Tasty accompaniments include pies served in mini-frypans, bagels, salads and cakes.

Depot　　　MODERN NZ $$
(☑09-363 7048; www.eatatdepot.co.nz; 86 Federal St; dishes $16-38; ⊗7am-late) TV chef Al Brown's popular eatery offers first-rate comfort food in informal surrounds (communal tables, butcher tiles and a constant buzz). Dishes are designed to be shared, and a pair of clever shuckers serve up the city's freshest clams and oysters. It doesn't take bookings, so get there early or expect to wait.

★**Cassia**　　　INDIAN $$$
(☑09-379 9702; www.cassiarestaurant.co.nz; 5 Fort Lane; mains $32-40; ⊗noon-3pm Wed-Fri, 5.30pm-late Tue-Sat) Occupying a moodily lit basement, Cassia serves Indian food with punch and panache. Start with a *pani puri,* a bite-sized crispy shell bursting with flavour, before devouring a decadently rich curry. The Delhi duck is excellent, as is the Goan-style snapper. Artisan gins and craft beer are other highlights. Often judged Auckland's best restaurant.

🎒 Supplies & Equipment

For equipment or tramping clothing, the best option is to head to Queen St, which has a selection of outdoor specialists.

Bivouac　　　SPORTS & OUTDOORS
(☑09-366 1966; www.bivouac.co.nz; 210 Queen St; ⊗9am-6pm Mon-Fri, 10am-5pm Sat & Sun) Outdoorsy clothing, footwear and equipment.

New World　　　SUPERMARKET $
(☑09-307 8400; www.newworld.co.nz; 2 College Hill, Freemans Bay; ⊗7am-midnight) A large supermarket with long opening hours.

Countdown　　　SUPERMARKET $
(☑09-275 2567; www.countdown.co.nz; 76 Quay St; ⊗24hr) A large 24-hour supermarket.

ℹ️ Information

Princes Wharf i-SITE (☑09-365 9914; www.aucklandnz.com; Princes Wharf; ⊗9am-5pm) Auckland's main official information centre, incorporating the **DOC Auckland Visitor Centre** (☑09-379 6476; www.doc.govt.nz; ⊗9am-5pm Mon-Fri, extended hours Nov-Mar).

ℹ️ Getting There & Away

Auckland is the main international gateway to NZ, and a hub for domestic flights. **Auckland Airport** (AKL; ☑09-275 0789; www.aucklandairport.co.nz; Ray Emery Dr, Mangere) is 21km south of the city centre. It has separate international and domestic terminals, a 10-minute walk apart from each other via a signposted footpath; a free shuttle service operates every 15 minutes (5am to 10.30pm). Both terminals have left-luggage facilities, eateries, ATMs and car-rental desks.

Coaches depart from 172 Quay St, opposite the **Ferry Building** (99 Quay St), except for InterCity services, which depart from **SkyCity Coach Terminal** (102 Hobson St). Many southbound services also stop at the airport.

InterCity (☑09-583 5780; www.intercity.co.nz) has direct services to New Plymouth (from $35, 6¼ hours, daily), Taupo (from $25, five hours, five daily) and Wellington (from $29, 11 hours, four daily).

Naked Bus (www.nakedbus.com) travels along SH1 as far north as Paihia ($25, four hours) and as far south as Wellington (from $25, 11 hours), as well as heading to Rotorua ($18, 3¾ hours) and Napier (from $24, 12 hours).

Northern Explorer (☑0800 872 467; www.greatjourneysofnz.co.nz) trains leave from **Auckland Strand Station** (Ngaoho Pl) at 7.45am on Monday, Thursday and Saturday and arrive in Wellington at 6.25pm. Stops include Tongariro National Park (5½ hours) and Palmerston North (8½ hours). Standard fares to Wellington range from $119 to $219.

Kaitaia

📞 09 / POP 4890

Kaitaia is about 80km from the start of the Te Paki Coastal Track and serves as the main departure point for most trips and tours to Ninety Mile Beach and Cape Reinga.

🛏 Sleeping & Eating

Loredo Motel   MOTEL $$
(📞 09-408 3200; www.loredomotel.co.nz; 25 North Rd; units from $120; 🐾🖳) Opting for a breezy Spanish style, this tidy motel has well-kept units set among palm trees and lawns, with a pool.

Kaitaia Motor Lodge   MOTEL $$
(📞 09-408 1910; www.kaitaiamotorlodge.co.nz; 121 North Rd; units $130-150; 🐾) This old-style brick motel on the outskirts of town has clean and tidy units with full kitchens. There's also a barbecue area and swing set for the kids.

Gecko Cafe   CAFE $
(📞 09-408 1160; 71 Commerce St; mains $9-18; ⊙7am-3pm Mon-Fri, 8am-1.30pm Sat) Morning queues of locals attest to the Gecko having the best coffee in town (they roast their own), and the food's pretty good, too. Kick off another day on the road with mushrooms and chorizo, or grab a mussel-fritter burger for lunch.

Beachcomber   BISTRO $$
(📞 09-408 2010; www.beachcomber.net.nz; 222 Commerce St; mains lunch $19-36, dinner $25-38; ⊙11am-2.30pm Mon-Fri & 5-9pm Mon-Sat; 🖉🖳) This Pacific-themed family restaurant is easily the best dinner option in Kaitaia, with a wide range of seafood, meat and vegetarian fare, and a well-stocked salad bar. Save room for the pavlova of the day.

🔒 Supplies & Equipment

Hunting & Fishing   SPORTS & OUTDOORS
(📞 09-408 0906; www.huntingandfishing.co.nz; 147 Commerce St; ⊙8.30am-5pm Mon-Fri, to 3pm Sat) Kaitaia's biggest outdoor store, selling clothing, tents, fishing gear, freeze-dried meals and mozzie nets.

Riders Sports Depot   SPORTS & OUTDOORS
(📞 09-408 0240; www.fishingandshootingoutdoorsgroup.co.nz; 73 Commerce St; ⊙8.30am-5pm Mon-Fri, to 1pm Sat) A small independent store jam-packed with outdoor equipment, including tents, backpacks, snorkels and fishing gear.

Pak 'n Save   SUPERMARKET $
(📞 09-408 6222; www.paknsave.co.nz; 111 North Rd; ⊙7am-9pm) The biggest supermarket in town.

ℹ Information

Far North i-SITE (📞 09-408 9450; www.northlandnz.com; Te Ahu Centre, cnr Matthews Ave & South Rd; ⊙8.30am-5pm) An excellent information centre with advice for all of Northland.

ℹ Getting There & Away

InterCity (📞 09-583 5780; www.intercity.co.nz) links Kaitaia to Auckland, with stops en route and beyond. Buses depart from the **Te Ahu Centre** (📞 09-401 5200; www.kaitaianz.co.nz; Cnr South Rd & Matthews Ave) in Kaitaia.

Russell

📞 09 / POP 720

The closest town to the Cape Brett Track, Russell was once known as the hellhole of the Pacific. The orgies on the beach are long gone and it's now a historic town filled with gift shops and B&Bs.

🛏 Sleeping & Eating

Wainui   HOSTEL $
(📞 09-403 8278; www.wainuilodge-russell-nz.com; 92d Te Wahapu Rd; dm/s/d $29/54/68; 🐾) Hard to find but worth the effort, this modern bush retreat with direct beach access has only two rooms that share a pleasant communal space. It's 5km from Russell on the way to the car ferry; you wouldn't want to stay here without your own wheels. Take Te Wahapu Rd and then turn right into Waiaruhe Way.

Russell Top 10   HOLIDAY PARK $$
(📞 09-403 7826; www.russelltop10.co.nz; 1 James St; sites from $25, unit with/without bathroom from $150/100; 🖳🐾) This leafy and extremely well-maintained holiday park has a small store, good facilities, wonderful hydrangeas, tidy cabins and excellent self-contained units with decks, coffee machines and bay views.

★Arcadia Lodge   B&B $$$
(📞 09-403 7756; www.arcadialodge.co.nz; 10 Florance Ave; r/ste $220/330; ⊙Sep-Jun; 🐾) 🖉 The characterful rooms of this 1890 hillside house are kitted out with interesting antiques and fine linen, while the breakfast is probably the best you'll eat in town – complemented by spectacular views from the deck. Grab a book from the library and a drink from the honesty bar, and find a spot in the garden to relax in.

Hell Hole   CAFE $
(📞 022 175 7847; www.facebook.com/hellholecoffee; 19 York St; snacks $6-12; ⊙7am-5pm Jan & Feb, 8am-3pm Mar, Apr, Nov & Dec) Bagels, baguettes and croissants, along with the best coffee in town

at this compact spot, one block back from the waterfront. Beans are locally roasted, and organic soft drinks and artisan ice blocks all combine to make this a hugely popular place.

★ Gables   CONTEMPORARY $$

(☑ 09-403 7670; www.thegablesrestaurant.co.nz; 19 The Strand; mains lunch $22-28, dinner $27-35; ⊙ noon-3pm & 5.30-10pm Wed-Mon) The Gables occupies an 1847 building on the waterfront built using whale vertebrae for foundations. Ask for a table by the windows for maritime views and look forward to top-notch local produce, including oysters and cheese.

Hōne's Garden   PIZZA $$

(☑ 022 466 3710; www.facebook.com/hones garden; 10 York St; pizza $18-25; ⊙ noon-10pm Wed-Mon Nov-Apr) Head out to Hōne's pebbled courtyard for wood-fired pizza (with 11 different varieties), cold craft beer on tap and a thoroughly easy-going Kiwi vibe.

🛍 Supplies & Equipment

Pick up any outdoors needs long before you arrive in Russell.

Four Square   SUPERMARKET $

(☑ 09-403 7819; www.foursquare.co.nz; 27 The Strand; ⊙ 7.15am-9pm) The town's main grocery store occupies a prominent 19th-century trading store on the waterfront.

❶ Information

Russell Booking & Information Centre (☑ 09-403 8020; www.russellinfo.co.nz; Russell Wharf; ⊙ 8am-5pm, extended hours summer)

❶ Getting There & Away

The quickest way to reach Russell by car is via the car ferry (car/motorcycle/passenger $13/5.50/1), which runs every 10 minutes from Opua (5km from Paihia) to Okiato (8km from Russell), between 6.50am and 10pm. Buy your tickets on board. If you're travelling from the south, a scenic alternative is the coastal route via Russell Rd.

On foot, the easiest way to reach Russell is on a **passenger ferry** from Paihia (adult/child return $12/6). They run from 7am to 9pm (until 10pm October to May), generally every 30 minutes, but hourly in the evenings. Buy your tickets on board or at the **i-SITE** (p65) in Paihia.

Whangarei

☑ 09 / POP 56,400

Northland's only city is surrounded by natural beauty, and is a good base for the Cape Brett Track. There's a thriving artistic community, some good walks, and interesting cafes and bars.

🛏 Sleeping & Eating

Little Earth Lodge   HOSTEL $

(☑ 09-430 6562; www.littleearthlodge.co.nz; 85 Abbey Caves Rd; s/d/tr from $67/78/96; 🐾) Set on a farm 6km from town and right next to Abbey Caves, Little Earth makes most other hostels look downright shabby in comparison. Forget dorm rooms crammed with nasty, spongy bunks: settle down in a proper cosy bed with nice linen. Resident critters include miniature horses and alpacas, and there's a free-standing cabin available.

Whangarei Falls Holiday
Park & Backpackers   HOSTEL, HOLIDAY PARK $

(☑ 09-437 0609; www.whangareifalls.co.nz; 12 Ngunguru Rd, Glenbervie; sites/dm from $25/32, s/d $60/72; 🐾🏊) Located 5km from central Whangarei, but a short walk from Whangarei Falls, this holiday park has good-value cabins, some with small kitchenettes but none with private bathrooms. It's also part of the YHA network and has a 10-bed dorm with bunks, along with smaller backpackers rooms.

Lodge Bordeaux   MOTEL $$

(☑ 09-438 0404; www.lodgebordeaux.co.nz; 361 Western Hills Dr; apt from $195; 🅿🐾🏊) This European-styled motel has tasteful units with stellar kitchens and bathrooms (most with spa baths), private balconies on the upstairs rooms, and access to a barbecue, small swimming pool and excellent wine.

Quay   CAFE, BISTRO $$

(☑ 09-430 2628; www.thequaykitchen.co.nz; 31 Quayside, Town Basin; mains brunch $14-20, dinner $29-35, pizza $21-25; ⊙ 9am-10pm) Sit out on the wraparound veranda of this beautiful riverside villa or take a table in the stylish, hollowed-out interior. The menu shuffles from cooked breakfasts to pizza and bistro-style meals in the evening.

Fat Camel   ISRAELI $$

(☑ 09-438 0831; 12 Quality St; mains $10-25; ⊙ 9am-9pm) In a pedestrian laneway lined with ethnic eateries, this little Israeli cafe stands out for its pita pockets and platters laden with falafels, salads and grilled meat. For something a little different try the *malawach*, a Yemeni flaky pastry-like pancake served with salad and dips. The coffee's good, too.

TopSail   BISTRO $$$

(☑ 09-436 2985; www.topsail.co.nz; 206 Beach Rd, Onerahi; mains $40-44; ⊙ 6pm-late Wed-Sat)

Located upstairs in the Onerahi Yacht Club, around 10km from central Whangarei, serving French-style bistro classics, fresh Northland seafood and NZ produce such as Fiordland venison. Just a 15-minute taxi ride from town. Bookings are recommended.

Supplies & Equipment

Kathmandu SPORTS & OUTDOORS
(☑ 09-438 7193; www.kathmandu.co.nz; 22 James St; ☺ 9am-5.30pm Mon-Fri, 9am-4pm Sat, 10am-3pm Sun) Outdoor gear and travel clothing.

Whangarei Growers' Market MARKET
(www.facebook.com/thewhangareigrowersmarket; 17 Water St; ☺ 6am-10am Sat) Stock up on local produce at this farmers market.

ℹ Information

DOC Whangarei Office (☑ 09-470 3300; www.doc.govt.nz; 2 South End Ave, Raumanga; ☺ 8am-4.35pm Mon-Fri)

Whangarei i-SITE (☑ 09-438 1079; www.whangareinz.com; 92 Otaika Rd (SH1); ☺ 9am-5pm) Information, cafe, toilets and showers.

ℹ Getting There & Away

Whangarei Airport (WRE; ☑ 09-436 0047; www.whangareiairport.co.nz; Handforth St, Onerahi; ☎) is at Onerahi, 6km southeast of the city centre. **Air New Zealand** (☑ 0800 737 000; www.airnewzealand.co.nz) flies to/from Auckland. Taxis into town cost around $25.

Long distance coaches stop at the **Hub** (☑ 09-430 1188; www.whangareinz.com; 91 Dent St, ☺ 9am-5pm; ☎), in the Town Basin. **InterCity** (p87) has three or four buses a day to/from Auckland (from $31, three hours), Paihia (from $12, 1¼ hours) and Kerikeri (from $12, 1¾ hours).

Thames

☑ 07 / POP 7060

A former gold-rush town sprinkled with dinky wooden buildings, Thames serves as the Coromandel Peninsula's western gateway and the main service centre for the peninsula.

🛏 Sleeping & Eating

Sunkist Guesthouse B&B $
(☑ 07-868 8808; www.sunkistguesthouse.nz; 506 Brown St; s/d & tw $75/95; @☎) Formerly the Lady Bowen Hotel, this 1860s heritage building offers singles, twins and doubles, and a sunny garden. Breakfast is included and all rooms share bathrooms. The well-equipped kitchen is ideal for self-catering meals, and there's a pleasant barbecue area.

Grafton Cottage & Chalets CHALET $$
(☑ 07-868 9971; www.graftoncottage.co.nz; 304 Grafton Rd; units $140-220; @☎☒) Most of these attractive wooden chalets perched on a hill have decks with awesome views. Free internet access and breakfast are provided, as well as use of the pool, spa and barbecue areas.

Coastal Motor Lodge MOTEL $$
(☑ 07-868 6843; www.stayatcoastal.co.nz; 608 Tararu Rd; units $164-169; ☎) Motel and chalet-style accommodation is provided at this smart, welcoming place, 2km north of Thames. It overlooks the sea, making it a popular choice, especially in the summer months.

Wharf Coffee House & Bar CAFE $
(☑ 07-868 6828; www.facebook.com/thewharfcoffeehouseandbar; Shortland Wharf, Queen St; snacks & mains $10-18; ☺ 9am-3pm Mon & Tue, to 7pm Wed, Sat & Sun, to 9pm Thu & Fri) Perched beside the water, this rustic wood-lined pavilion does great fish and chips. Grab a table outside with a beer or a wine to understand why the Wharf is a firm local favourite.

Supplies & Equipment

Hunting & Fishing SPORTS & OUTDOORS
(☑ 07-868 8260; www.huntingandfishing.co.nz; 103 Kopu Rd, Kopu; ☺ 7am-5pm Mon-Fri, 6am-1pm Sat) Convenient shop for outdoor gear.

Pak'nSave SUPERMARKET $
(http://paknsave.co.nz/; 100 Mary St; ☺ 8am-9pm) Thames' best supermarket.

Thames Organic Shop MARKET $
(☑ 07-868 8797; organiccoop@clear.net.nz; 736 Pollen St; ☺ 9am-5pm Mon-Fri, to noon Sat; ☝) 🍃 A good source of vegetables, nuts, bread, eggs and meat. Good for vegan travellers.

ℹ Information

Thames i-SITE (☑ 07-868 7284; www.thecoromandel.com/thames; 200 Mary St; ☺ 9am-4pm Mon-Fri, to 1pm Sat & Sun) Excellent source of information for the entire Coromandel Peninsula.

ℹ Getting There & Away

InterCity (☑ 09-583 5780; www.intercity.co.nz) has bus services to Auckland ($22, 1½ hours). **Go Kiwi** (☑ 0800 446 549; www.go-kiwi.co.nz) also services Auckland ($49, 2¼ hours). A Monday to Friday shuttle from **Coromandel Adventures** (p77) links Coromandel Town and Rotorua with stops en route at Thames; from December to April this service runs daily.

Tongariro, Te Urewera & Central North Island

Best Sights

➡ Emerald Lakes (p97)

➡ Mt Ngauruhoe (p95)

➡ Tama Lakes (p101)

➡ Lake Waikaremoana (p103)

➡ Puketapu Trig (p105)

➡ Pukenui Trig (p105)

Best Huts

➡ Old Waihohonu Hut (p101)

➡ Oturere Hut (p100)

➡ Panekire Hut (p105)

Why Go?

Few regions offer such an overwhelming sense of raw wilderness as the North Island's central strip of volcanoes and dense forest. In one corner is the trio of volcanoes at the heart of Tongariro National Park, shielding what's often described as New Zealand's only desert; in the other is the vast and virgin forest of Te Urewera.

For trampers, Tongariro calls like a siren, drawing tens of thousands of people each year across the track that's almost universally acclaimed as the best day walk in the country. But beyond the Tongariro Alpine Crossing is a more in-depth audience with the volcanoes on the Tongariro Northern Circuit, a Great Walk that loops around the most striking of the peaks, Mt Ngauruhoe – Mt Doom, for *Lord of the Rings* fans.

Head east and the volcanic moonscape finds its counterpoint in the lush and misty Te Urewera, where one of NZ's lesser-known Great Walks runs along the bluff-lined shores of remote Lake Waikaremoana.

When to Go

With plenty of mountains in their midst, the tramping areas around Tongariro National Park and Te Urewera are prone to unpredictable weather patterns. What is predictable, however, is heavy rain appearing at some point or another, raising river levels and potentially making them impassable. The same weather patterns can leave alpine areas snowbound even through to the start of summer. The substantial alpine sections of Tongariro's Northern Circuit and Alpine Crossing mean the tramps are best attempted November to March. This is also the most pleasant time to be on other tracks in this region, though they can be tramped at any time of year in favourable conditions.

Background Reading

If you're tramping in Tongariro National Park you'll witness a host of volcanic features – vents, craters, lava bombs, fumaroles. To gain a full understanding of this geological gurgle, grab a copy of the *Encyclopedia of Volcanoes* by Haraldur Sigurdsson.

On the Tongariro Northern Circuit you'll pass NZ's oldest backcountry hut, Old Waihohonu, built in 1904. The story of the country's hut system, which now extends to almost 1000 huts, is detailed in *Shelter from the Storm*, an illustrated history of the huts and the people who built them, written by respected tramping authors Shaun Barnett, Rob Brown and Geoff Spearpoint.

DON'T MISS

If Tongariro has whet your volcanic appetite, take a walk on the even wilder side with a visit to Whakaari (White Island). New Zealand's most active volcano, Whakaari lies 49km off the coast from Whakatane and is part of the Taupo Volcanic Zone, the same geological feature that created the Tongariro volcanoes.

The island is dramatic, with hot water hissing and steaming from vents over most of the crater floor, which is dusted yellow with sulphur. Temperatures of 600°C to 800°C have been recorded. The atmosphere is so acidic it's been known to tarnish silver and affect dyes in clothing, while guides go through boots at a rapid rate as the soles get eaten away by the acid.

The island is privately owned so you can only visit it with a licensed tour operator. Scenic flights operate for an aerial perspective, but the only boat trip to the island is run by **White Island Tours** (☑ 0800 733 529; www.whiteisland.co.nz; 15 The Strand; 5½hr trips adult/child $219/130) 🖋. These trips include up to 1½ hours of walking around the island's fascinating and active volcanic features, including a visit to the century-old ruins of the sulphur-mining factory. The mine closed in 1914 after all 10 of its workers were killed in a lahar (volcanic mudflow).

Visitor Information Centres

➡ Tongariro National Park Visitor Centre (p95)

➡ Turangi i-SITE (p108)

➡ **DOC Murupara Office** (☑ 07-366 1080; www.doc.govt.nz; Main Rd, Murupara; ⊙ 9am-5pm Mon-Fri)

➡ Te Urewera Visitor Centre (p103)

GATEWAY TOWNS

➡ Taupo (p106)
➡ Turangi (p107)
➡ National Park Village (p108)
➡ Wairoa (p109)

Fast Facts

➡ Tongariro was NZ's first national park, and only the fourth in the world at the time, created in 1887.

➡ The Tongariro Alpine Crossing is NZ's most popular day walk, completed by up to 130,000 people each year.

➡ Te Urewera contains the largest untouched native forest on the North Island.

➡ Signs marking side tracks to Mts Ngauruhoe and Tongariro were removed in 2017 to discourage trampers from climbing the sacred volcanoes.

Top Tip

Changes to parking rules have made it impossible to park on Mangatepopo Rd and hike the Tongariro Alpine Crossing, so use one of the many shuttle services instead.

Resources

➡ www.greatlaketaupo.com
➡ www.nationalpark.co.nz
➡ www.tongarirocrossing.org.nz
➡ www.visitruapehu.com
➡ www.ngaituhoe.iwi.nz

TONGARIRO, TE UREWERA & CENTRAL NORTH ISLAND

Tongariro, Te Urewera & Central North Island

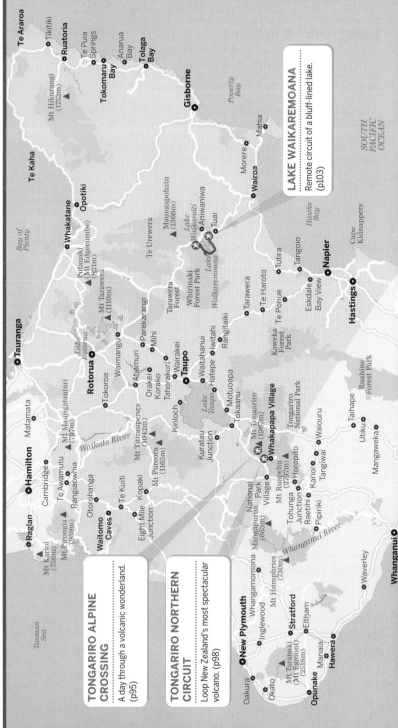

TONGARIRO ALPINE CROSSING
A day through a volcanic wonderland. (p95)

TONGARIRO NORTHERN CIRCUIT
Loop New Zealand's most spectacular volcano. (p98)

LAKE WAIKAREMOANA
Remote circuit of a bluff-lined lake. (p103)

50 miles
100 km

TONGARIRO NATIONAL PARK

Tongariro National Park (797 sq km) lies at the heart of the North Island. Its landmark features are its active volcanoes, in particular the trio of Ruapehu, Ngauruhoe and Tongariro.

These mountains are the southern end of a volcanic chain that extends northwest through the heart of the North Island, past Taupo and Rotorua, to finally reach Whakaari (White Island) in the Bay of Plenty. The volcanic nature of the region is responsible for Tongariro's hot springs, boiling mud pools, fumaroles and craters.

Ruapehu, at 2797m, is the highest mountain on the North Island and its snowfields are the only legitimate ski area north of Wellington. Northeast of Ruapehu is the almost symmetrical cone of Ngauruhoe (2287m) and then Tongariro (1967m), the lowest in height and northernmost of the three peaks.

Since its establishment in 1887, the park has been developed for recreational use. It now contains the famous Chateau Tongariro Hotel, a golf course, various ski fields and a network of tracks, many of which pass through bare lava fields and tussock, making Tongariro the best alpine tramping area in the North Island.

The variety of scenery and recreational activities make Tongariro one of the most popular national parks in NZ. Many people come to ski, but many thousands arrive each summer to tramp around the mountains – 130,000 alone to hike the Tongariro Alpine Crossing in the 2016/17 season. The park does get busy, most noticeably on the Alpine Crossing, but most visitors consider this a small price to pay for the chance to experience its volcanic wizardry.

The most popular tramps in the park are the Alpine Crossing and the Tongariro Northern Circuit, but there are plenty more besides. These range from excellent day walks to challenging multiday routes that should only be attempted by the fit, experienced and well equipped. One of these is the Round the Mountain Track, a remote 66km, four- to six-day tramp circuiting Mt Ruapehu.

History

It is the powerful Māori history of Tongariro that has earned the national park an unusual dual World Heritage status – it is cited on both natural and cultural grounds.

To the Māori the volcanoes of Tongariro were *tapu* (sacred) and they sought to prevent anybody from climbing them. They believed Ngatoro-i-rangi, high priest of the Ngati Tuwharetoa tribe of Lake Taupo, arrived in the Bay of Plenty and travelled south to claim the volcanic plateau for his people. He climbed Ngauruhoe to view the land but, upon reaching the top, suddenly found himself in the middle of a raging snowstorm. It was something the high priest had never experienced and he cried out to priestess sisters in the north to send him warmth.

The sisters responded by sending fire from the earth. It burst from the ground, creating the craters of Ngauruhoe and Tongariro, thus saving Ngatoro-i-rangi. He slew a female slave, then climbed to the newly formed crater and tossed the body in to give his prayer more strength, claiming the surrounding land for his people.

The volcanoes, especially Tongariro, have been sacred to Maori ever since. They often travelled to Ketetahi Hot Springs to bathe, but were forbidden to go any further. Europeans were also discouraged from visiting the area. In 1839 John Bidwill, a botanist and explorer, became the first Pākehā to scale Ngauruhoe.

For the next 12 years the local tribe was successful in keeping intruders from its sacred grounds. However, in 1851, Ruapehu fell to a climber's passion when Sir George Grey ascended one of the volcano's peaks and then hid from his Māori guides to avoid their discontent. In 1879 George Beetham and JP Maxwell became the first Europeans to scale Ruapehu and see Crater Lake.

During the mid- to late 1880s the local *iwi* (tribe) was under considerable pressure to relinquish the lands to farmers, loggers and rival tribes. Horonuku Te Heuheu Tukino IV, paramount chief of Ngāti Tūwharetoa, came up with a solution: on 23 September 1887 he gifted the sacred volcanoes of Tongariro, Ngauruhoe and Ruapehu to the people of NZ.

An Act of Parliament formally established Tongariro National Park in 1894 and it was gazetted as such in 1907. The original gift area of 23.6 sq km has been increased over the years by government purchase of surrounding land to create a national park of 797 sq km.

More recently, the park's fame has been bolstered by starring roles in Peter Jackson's *Lord of the Rings* and *The Hobbit* movies. Mt Ngauruhoe was most noticeably transformed into fiery Mt Doom of Mordor, while numerous locations around Ruapehu, including the Mangawhero Falls and River, make magical appearances.

In late 2017, track signs at side tracks to Mts Ngauruhoe and Tongariro were removed along the Alpine Crossing, with trampers requested to stay on the marked tracks and no longer climb the peaks as had previously been common.

Environment

Geologically speaking, the Tongariro volcanoes are relatively young. Both Ruapehu and Tongariro are less than 300,000 years old. They were shaped by a mixture of eruptions and glacial action, especially in the last ice age. At one time, glaciers extended down Ruapehu to below 1300m, leaving polished rock far below their present snouts.

Ngauruhoe is even younger. Its first eruptions are thought to have occurred 2500 years ago. Until 1975 Ngauruhoe had erupted at least every nine years, including a 1954 eruption that lasted 11 months and disgorged six million cubic metres of lava.

Ruapehu is one of the world's most active volcanoes. One eruption began in March 1945 and continued for almost a year, spreading lava over Crater Lake and sending huge dark clouds of ash as far away as Wellington. Ruapehu rumbled again in 1969 and 1973, but its worst disaster was on Christmas Eve 1953, when a crater lake lip collapsed. An enormous lahar (mud flow) swept down the mountainside, taking everything in its path, including a railway bridge. Moments later a crowded train plunged into the river, killing 151 people; it was one of NZ's worst tragedies.

Ruapehu hasn't let up, with significant eruptions occurring with suspicious frequency. In 2007 a primary school teacher had a lucky shave when a rock was propelled through the roof of Dome Shelter. He survived, but his leg was crushed. Ongoing rumbles are reminders that these volcanoes are very much in the land of the living.

The last major event was in 2012 when the Te Maari craters on Mt Tongariro gave a couple of good blasts from the northern craters – the first eruptions on this mountain for more than a century. It caused a nine-month partial closure of the famous Alpine Crossing track. In the first eruption, a rock spat from the crater crashed through the roof of Ketetahi Hut.

To see video of recent eruptions, visit www.doc.govt.nz/eruption.

THE BIRTH OF NZ'S FIRST NATIONAL PARK

After the New Zealand Wars (Land Wars), during which Ngāti Tūwharetoa chief Horonuku Te Heuheu Tukino IV aided the rebel Te Kooti, those tribes loyal to the Crown wanted the land around Tongariro redistributed. In 1886, at a schoolhouse in Taupo, the Native Land Court met to determine the ownership of land.

Horonuku pleaded passionately with the court to leave the area intact. At one point, he turned to the rival chiefs who were longing for the land and asked: 'Where is your fire, your *ahi kā*? You cannot show me for it does not exist. Now I shall show you mine. Look yonder. Behold my fire, my mountain Tongariro!'

The forcefulness of his speech dissuaded Māori from dividing up the sacred land, but Horonuku was equally worried about Pākehā, who were eyeing the area's tussock grassland for grazing. 'If our mountains of Tongariro are included in the blocks passed through the court in the ordinary way, what will become of them? They will be cut up and sold, a piece going to one Pākehā and a piece to another.'

The chief saw only one solution that would ensure the land's everlasting preservation. Before the Native Land Court, on 23 September 1887, Horonuku presented the area to the Crown for the purpose of a national park, the first in NZ and only the fourth in the world. With incredible vision, the chief realised that Tongariro's value lay in its priceless beauty and heritage, not as another sheep paddock.

An Act of Parliament created Tongariro National Park in 1894, but its development was slow. The main trunk railroad reached the region in 1909. By then there were huts at Waihohonu, in the east, with a track leading to them and to Ketetahi Hot Springs. The railroad brought a large number of tourists to the western side of the park, and by 1918 a track and hut were built at Mangatepopo for skiers on Ngauruhoe.

Development of the park mushroomed in the 1950s and 1960s as roads were sealed, tracks cut and more huts built. Nowadays the park receives more than 100,000 international visitors alone each year.

ℹ Planning

WHEN TO TRAMP

The safest and most popular time to tramp in the national park is December to March, when the tracks are normally clear of snow and the weather is most settled. In winter many of the tracks, including the Alpine Crossing, become full alpine adventures, requiring alpine experience and potentially an ice axe and crampons. If you're not experienced in these conditions, please consider using a guide who is trained in assessing avalanche risks, ice-axe rescues and crampon use.

WHAT TO BRING

This is a highly changeable alpine environment, so appropriate clothing is paramount. Think a merino (or equivalent) base layer, warm fleece and a waterproof jacket (and ideally waterproof trousers). Gloves and a warm hat are good too, even in summer. And don't even think about wearing anything other than sturdy boots – volcanic rocks are sharp and loose. Bring plenty of water and sunscreen, especially on hot days.

MAPS & BROCHURES

The best map for planning a tramp in Tongariro National Park is the 1:80,000 Parkmap *273-04 (Tongariro)*, which has inset 1:50,000 maps of Mt Ruapehu's summit area and the Tongariro Alpine Crossing. Tongariro is also covered by NZTopo50 *BH34 (Raurimu)*, *BH35 (Turangi)*, *BJ34 (Ruapehu)* and *BJ35 (Waiouru)*. NewTopo produces four maps of the national park: *Mount Ruapehu* (1:40,000), *Tongariro Northern Circuit* (1:60,000), *Tongariro Alpine Crossing* (1:30,000) and *Ruapehu Round the Mountain Track* (1:60,000).

DOC brochures covering the area include *Tongariro Northern Circuit* and *Tongariro Alpine Crossing*, as well as the extensive and helpful *Walks in and around Tongariro National Park*, which features more than 30 tramps. All the brochures can be downloaded at www.doc.govt.nz.

INFORMATION

The DOC information hub is **Tongariro National Park Visitor Centre** (Whakapapa Visitor Centre; ☑ 07-892 3729; www.doc.govt.nz/tongariro-visitorcentre; Bruce Rd; ☺ 8am-5pm daily last weekend Oct-Apr, 8.30am-4.30pm daily May-last Fri Oct), which has interesting exhibits and displays on the park's geological history – enough to keep you occupied for at least half a rainy day. The visitor centre also doubles as an i-SITE and can make bookings for tramping shuttles and other activities in the region.

The **Turangi i-SITE** (p108) is also a DOC agent and can therefore supply information and maps on Tongariro National Park.

> **WARNING: VOLCANIC ACTIVITY**
>
> This might be the only place you ever hike where it's best to not only check the weather forecast, but also the volcanic activity forecast. Alert levels for any volcanic activity around Tongariro National Park can be found online at www.geonet.org.nz/volcano/tongariro.

GUIDED TRAMPS

Walking Legends (☑ 021 545 068, 0800 925 569, 07-312 5297; www.walkinglegends.com) runs a small-group, fully catered three-day trip on the Tongariro Northern Circuit ($970) and a 3½-day Tongariro Hiking Tour ($1590) that includes the Alpine Crossing and Mt Ruapehu's Crater Lakes.

Adrift Guided Outdoor Adventures (☑ 07-892 2751; www.adriftnz.co.nz; 53 Carroll St; ☺ by appt) operates lots of different guided tramps in Tongariro National Park, including summer and winter trips on the Tongariro Alpine Crossing ($195 to $433) and three-day tramps on the Northern Circuit (from $950).

Adventure Outdoors (☑ 0800 386 925, 027 242 7209; www.adventureoutdoors.co.nz; 60 Carroll St; ☺ by appt) also guides trips on the Tongariro Alpine Crossing, including winter hikes ($185) and a sunrise tramp ($345) that sets out at 2.30am by torchlight.

Tongariro Alpine Crossing

Duration 7–8 hours

Distance 19.4km (12 miles)

Difficulty Moderate

Start Mangatepopo Rd

End Ketetahi Rd

Gateways Turangi (p107), Taupo (p106), National Park Village (p108)

Transport Shuttle bus

Summary A volcanic wonderland of gleaming lakes, steaming craters and ominous peaks on this highly scenic traverse between two of Tongariro's three major volcanoes.

You don't get to be routinely called the best day walk in New Zealand without being something pretty special. And the Tongariro Alpine Crossing is indeed that. This tramp is like a mobile field guide to volcanoes, threading between Mt Tongariro and the perfectly conical Mt Ngauruhoe,

Tongariro Alpine Crossing

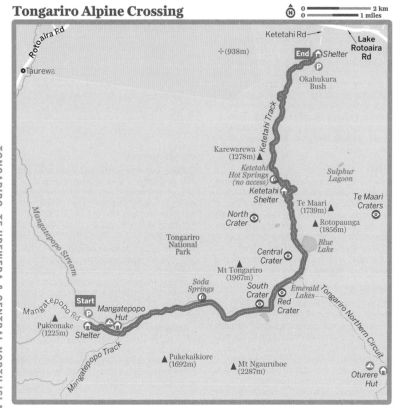

passing neon-bright lakes that contrast with the black earth, while vents steam, hiss and fart in sulphurous clouds, and rocks spat from the volcanoes take on crazy shapes.

With big reputations come big crowds. In the early 1990s the Crossing would attract around 20,000 trampers a year; today that number is up to around 130,000. On the busiest days there can be more than 2000 people on the track. It's these sorts of numbers that have led to recent changes on the Crossing. Parking restrictions at the trailhead now apply, making it all but compulsory to use the abundant shuttle services, while in late 2017 signs marking the side trails to Mts Tongariro and Ngauruhoe were taken down, with trampers requested not to climb them.

The crowds are the price of volcanic paradise, for the Alpine Crossing is truly something to behold. But don't let the big numbers fool you into thinking that the Alpine Crossing is a casual stroll. It's a long day – and fierce in bad weather – climbing 750m from its start to the top of Red Crater and then descending 700m to Ketetahi Rd.

ⓘ Planning

WHEN TO TRAMP

This is a fair-weather tramp. In poor conditions it's little more than an arduous up-and-down. Should strong winds be blowing on top, you'll be practically crawling along the ridge of Red Crater, the high point of the Crossing. On such days, the shuttles won't be running.

WHAT TO BRING

Don't be one of the ill-equipped trampers who are legendary on this route. Bring plenty of warm clothing and wet-weather gear. You'll also need plenty of water, as there is none along the way.

HUTS & CAMPING

If you want to get a jump on the crowds, you can try booking a night in Mangatepopo Hut ($36), but plan well ahead as the hut is part of the Tongariro Northern Circuit Great Walk hut network. The 20-bunk hut has gas cookers and a resident warden during the Great Walks season (late October to the end of April). In the winter season ($15), there are no cookers or warden, and bookings aren't required. There's a campsite next to the hut.

You can't spend the night at Ketetahi Shelter, which closed to overnight stays after a rock plummeted through its roof in the August 2012 Te Maari eruption. It now operates as a day shelter only.

ℹ️ Getting There & Away

Our best advice: leave the car behind. Parking is limited to four hours at the Mangatepopo Rd trailhead, making the plethora of shuttle buses the best way to access the Crossing.

Buses service both ends of the track, delivering trampers to Mangatepopo Rd in the morning and picking them up from the Ketetahi car park in the afternoon. Shuttles run from Taupo, Turangi, Whakapapa and National Park Village. Operators include the following:

Tongariro Expeditions (☑ 0800 828 763, 07-377 0435; www.tongariroexpeditions.com) Runs shuttles from Taupo ($65), Turangi ($50) and the Tongariro Base Camp (12km north of the Mangatepopo Rd corner; $35).

Turangi Alpine Shuttles (☑ 0272 322 135, 0508 427 677; www.alpineshuttles.co.nz) Shuttles from Turangi ($50).

Backyard Tours (☑ 022 314 2656, 07-386 5322; www.backyardtours.com) Shuttles from Turangi (from $50).

Roam (☑ 021 588 734, 0800 762 612; www. roam.net.nz; Whakapapa Holiday Park, Bruce Rd; adult/child $35/25) Shuttles from Whakapapa Village ($35).

Tongariro Crossing Shuttles (☑ 07-892 2993; www.tongarirocrossingshuttles.co.nz) Return service from National Park Village ($40).

🚶 The Tramp

From the Mangatepopo Rd car park, the track starts out fairly flat, heading east along a partly boardwalked section to the junction with the Mangatepopo Track, part of the Tongariro Northern Circuit route to Whakapapa. Take the left fork and you'll soon pass the short side trail to Mangatepopo Hut, 20 to 30 minutes from the trailhead.

It's an easy tramp up Mangatepopo Valley and over a succession of old lava flows. Within an hour you pass a spur track to Soda Springs (an easy 15-minute return trip), which, if the wind is right, might be smelt before they are seen. Look out for pretty yellow buttercups here.

The main track continues up the valley and quickly begins a well-marked climb to the saddle between Mts Ngauruhoe and Tongariro. The ascent among the lava rocks is steep, but well marked with stacks of steps and marker poles. After 45 minutes to one hour you reach the top.

Follow the poles as they continue past the junction and cross South Crater, an eerie place when the clouds are low, and a huge walled amphitheatre when the weather is clear. The walk through the crater is flat, with the slopes of Ngauruhoe to the right and the Tongariro summit to the left.

Once across the crater, the track – now a poled route – resumes climbing the ridge, and at the top you can see Oturere Valley and the Kaimanawa Range to the east.

Having slogged up the rocky ridge, you will find the gaping Red Crater to the right. You sidle around this to the highest point on the track (1886m). It's essential to have favourable weather when traversing this section, and if you're lucky enough to get a clear day you will enjoy stupendous views that might even include Taranaki to the west and Mt Tauhara, Mt Putauaki and Mt Tarawera to the north.

The track begins its descent along the side of Red Crater, where you will get your first view of the surreal Emerald Lakes. These three old explosion pits feature brilliant colouring, thanks to minerals washing down from Red Crater.

The track then drops steeply into Central Crater, passing the Tongariro Northern Circuit's departure into the Oturere Valley. Be careful along this stretch of track, which begins as loose scree but turns into a hard, packed surface with loose stones that act like marbles. Many trampers have injured themselves here.

The track climbs out of the crater to Blue Lake, aka Te Wai-whakaata-o-te-Rangihiroa (Rangihiroa's Mirror), a cold, acidic lake that's up to 16m deep. It's a sacred lake and you shouldn't stop to eat here. The track heads onward around the flanks of North Crater before beginning its descent towards Ketetahi Shelter, with views ahead over Pihanga and Lake Rotoaira to Lake Taupo. As you to and fro through the switchbacks just before the hut, notice the impact craters

TONGARIRO, TE UREWERA & CENTRAL NORTH ISLAND TONGARIRO ALPINE CROSSING

DAY WALKS IN TONGARIRO NATIONAL PARK

The overwhelming presence of the Tongariro Alpine Crossing makes it easy to overlook the fact that there's a range of day walks in Tongariro National Park. If you want a day out on foot that's not the Crossing, here are a few good options.

Tama Lakes (17km, five to six hours) Follow the Tongariro Northern Circuit east from Whakapapa, detouring up to the rim of an impact crater filled with Lower Tama Lake, which glows almost as brightly as the more famous Emerald Lakes on the Alpine Crossing. Continue up to get a look over Upper Tama Lake and fine views of Ruapehu and Ngauruhoe.

Taranaki Falls (6km, two hours) An abbreviated version of the Tama Lakes hike, this walk follows the Northern Circuit as far as 20m-high Taranaki Falls, which pour over an old lava flow, before circuiting back to Whakapapa.

Silica Rapids (7km, 2½ hours) Setting out 250m from the Tongariro National Park Visitor Centre, this loop track leads through beech forest and past seepage ponds home to freshwater crayfish to reach the white Silica Rapids, named for the silica mineral deposits formed there by rapids on the Waikare Stream.

Skyline Route (1½ to two hours) Take the high road on Ruapehu, setting out from the top of the Waterfall Express chairlift, 2000m above sea level, and following a poled summer route over rock and scree to the top of the ski field's Valley T-bar. There's no formed track, but a ridge beside the top of the T-bar has great views.

Waitonga Falls (4km, 1½ hours) The walk to Tongariro's highest waterfall (39m) passes an alpine bog that often provides good reflections of Mt Ruapehu.

and boulders plugged beside the track. These rocks were spat from the Te Maari craters during an eruption in August 2012. You'll see the craters steaming away just to the east and likely be thankful you weren't tramping that day.

Ketetahi Shelter, reached about an hour from Blue Lake, was once an overnight hut, but a boulder crashed through the roof during the 2012 eruption. Today it functions solely as a day shelter; you can peer into the bunk room to see where the rock came through. Just past the shelter, as you continue down, you'll see the steam of Ketetahi Hot Springs off to the left. These springs are sacred and on private land, and no access is allowed.

The track cuts across a ridge to the stream that flows down from Ketetahi Hot Springs, descending through tussock grasslands with fine views of the Te Maari craters. After so long above the bushline, it comes as a moment of high contrast to enter the podocarp forest that signals the approaching end of the track. Here you follow for a time beside a stream, but don't be tempted to drink from it – it's naturally polluted by the thermal activity higher up the slopes.

Tongariro Northern Circuit

Duration 4 days

Distance 50km (31 miles)

Difficulty Moderate

Start/End Whakapapa Village

Gateways Turangi (p107), Taupo (p106), National Park Village (p108)

Transport Shuttle bus

Summary This spectacular alpine Great Walk laps the multifeatured volcanic slopes of Mt Ngauruhoe, on the way taking in the famed Tongariro Alpine Crossing.

Circumnavigating Ngauruhoe, this track is a Great Walk for a number of good reasons. The route can be easily walked in four days, and though there is some moderate climbing, the track is well marked and well maintained, putting it within the ability of people of medium fitness and tramping experience. But most of all, the Northern Circuit includes spectacular and colourful volcanic areas that have helped earn the park its status as a Unesco World Heritage Site.

The traditional place to start and finish the tramp is Whakapapa Village, the

Tongariro Northern Circuit

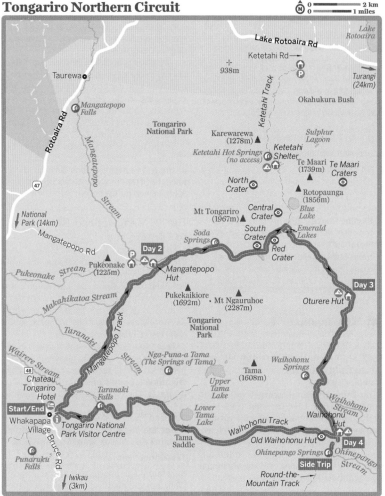

site of the park's visitor centre. However, many trampers begin at Mangatepopo Rd to ensure they have good weather for the tramp's most dramatic day – the Alpine Crossing section. This reduces it to a three-day tramp, with stays at Oturere and Waihohonu Huts, ending at Whakapapa Village. If doing this, note that you'll need to use one of the myriad shuttles (p97) that service the Alpine Crossing, since changes to parking regulations prevent trampers from parking for extended times at the Mangatepopo Rd car park.

🛈 Planning

HUTS & CAMPING

The Tongariro Northern Circuit is a Great Walk. Between mid-October and 30 April the three DOC huts – Mangatepopo, Oturere and Waihohonu – are designated Great Walk huts ($36). Each has gas cookers, heating, cold running water and good old long-drop loos, along with communal bunk rooms with mattresses.

Campsites are located next to the huts; the $14 fee (per person) allows campers use of the hut facilities.

Great Walk hut tickets must be obtained in advance. This can be done at the Tongariro National Park Visitor Centre (p95), online through **Great Walks Bookings** (☏ 0800 694 732; www.greatwalks.co.nz), or at DOC visitors centres nationwide. The circuit is popular, so it will pay to book early during the Great Walk season. In the off-season the huts become Standard huts (hut $15, camping per person $5), with the gas cookers removed. Fees in the off-season can be paid with backcountry hut passes and tickets.

ⓘ Getting There & Away

The Northern Circuit begins in Whakapapa Village. Trampers are able to park in the village; ask at the DOC visitors centre for a four-day car parking pass.

Turangi Alpine Shuttles (p97) can transfer you to Whakapapa from Turangi on its 7.30am Alpine Crossing shuttle (from $55). A return service operates from the Whakapapa visitor centre at 2.15pm.

If you're setting out from Mangatepopo Rd, changes to parking regulations in 2017 mean that there is a four-hour limit at the car park. If you're starting from here, book an Alpine Crossing shuttle (p97).

The Tramp

Day 1: Whakapapa Village to Mangatepopo Hut

3–5 HOURS / 8.5KM

Many trampers skip this first day of the circuit because the Mangatepopo Track once had a reputation for being uninteresting and extremely muddy. The scenery has not changed but the track has certainly improved over the years with the addition of boardwalk and bridges. That said, it may take a full five hours in bad weather.

From 100m below the Tongariro National Park Visitor Centre, head up Ngauruhoe Pl to the signposted Mangatepopo Track on your left. The tramp begins here, along a well-maintained track that wanders through tussock grass and a few stands of beech for 1.5km. At Wairere Stream it passes a signposted junction with a track that leads to Taranaki Falls, and eventually to the Tama Lakes.

Within 3km of the start are impressive views of the volcanic cones of Ngauruhoe and Pukekaikiore to the northeast. Straight ahead is the small cone of Pukeonake, formed by a continuous eruption of scoria – small pebbles of lava that have erupted from within.

After a few more stream crossings the track swings eastward around Pukekaikiore and you quickly climb a ridge from which you can see Mangatepopo Hut (20 bunks), 2km in the distance.

The hut sits at 1180m in a pleasant spot. On clear evenings you can enjoy fine sunsets over Mt Taranaki, around 140km away, and by looking in the other direction you can study the climb to South Crater, one of the first destinations for the next day. The campsite is situated next to the hut.

To the west of the hut is a track that after 30 minutes reaches the car park and shelter at the end of Mangatepopo Rd, which connects to SH47. This is where the Tongariro Alpine Crossing begins.

Day 2: Mangatepopo Hut to Oturere Hut

5–6 HOURS / 12.8KM / 700M ASCENT, 530M DESCENT

This is the day you complete the Tongariro Alpine Crossing (p95), a section of trail loudly hailed as the finest day hike in NZ. You can hurry through to Oturere Hut, but if the weather is clear plan on spending the whole day on and around the track to marvel at the amazing volcanic scenery.

Brace yourself for encounters with hordes of day hikers – there are days when 2000 people set out on the Alpine Crossing. They will start stampeding past the hut soon after daybreak. They will almost certainly want to cut a faster pace than you do, so take your time and let them steam on ahead.

For the section of the Tongariro Alpine Crossing starting at Mangatepopo Valley and ending at Central Crater, see p97.

From here, turn off at the junction signposted to Oturere Valley (the Ketetahi Track is the finish of the Alpine Crossing), where there are views of the Kaimanawa Ranges and Rangipo Desert. A barren landscape of reddish sand with small clumps of tussock, this unique desert landscape is the result of two million years of volcanic eruptions – especially the Taupo eruption about 2000 years ago, which coated the land with thick deposits of pumice and destroyed all vegetation.

The track weaves through a moonscape created by early eruptions from Red Crater. Oturere Hut (26 bunks) nestles on the eastern edge of these flows. Directly in front of the hut is an impressive waterfall that you should check out.

Day 3: Oturere Hut to Waihohonu Hut

3 HOURS / 7.5KM / 240M ASCENT, 400M DESCENT

This relatively short day's tramp will leave you plenty of time to take in a couple of leisurely side trips.

From Oturere Hut the track swings southwest through open, desertlike country as it skirts the eastern flanks of Ngauruhoe. It descends straight towards Ruapehu, working its way across numerous streams, before a lengthy 120m descent bottoms out at a bridge over the upper branch of Waihohonu Stream, 1½ to two hours from Oturere Hut.

On the other side, climb through a beech-clad valley, topping out on the 1269m crest of an open ridge before making a final descent to Waihohonu Hut (28 bunks) in the next valley. The hut, the third to be built in this area, is in a pocket of beech trees near a branch of the Waihohonu Stream. There are camping sites nearby.

The first of the Waihohonu huts is still standing and makes for an interesting side trip after you drop your pack. Another short side trip is to follow the Round-the-Mountain Track south to Ohinepango Springs, a 20-minute walk from Waihohonu Hut. The springs are cold and they bubble up from beneath an old lava flow. A huge volume of water discharges into the Ohinepango Stream.

Day 4: Waihohonu Hut to Whakapapa Village

5½–6 HOURS / 16KM

At the track junction with the Round-the-Mountain Track (which continues south along the slopes of Ruapehu) and the Waihohonu Track (which heads east towards Desert Rd, 1½ hours away), the Northern Circuit turns right, following the Waihohonu Track west. The track follows the upper branch of Waihohonu Stream, dropping and climbing out of several streams that have eroded the thin covering of tussock grass. The walking is tiresome at times, but beautiful if the weather is clear. Ngauruhoe's perfect cone is on one side and Ruapehu's snow-capped summit is on the other.

Eventually the track rises gently to Tama Saddle, between the two volcanoes, and in another 1.5km arrives at a junction to Tama Lakes. A view point over the lower lake is a short trip up the side track, but it's 45 minutes along an exposed ridge to the upper lake.

The main track continues west, working down and across another six streams until it descends to Wairere Stream where there are two routes returning to Whakapapa Village. The track to the right passes Taranaki Falls, where the Wairere Stream spills over a 20m rock face into a boulder-ringed pool, and then merges into Mangatepopo Track 1.5km from its start on Ngauruhoe Pl. The track to the left makes a steady descent to Whakapapa Village, passing through grasslands and small patches of beech forest. It's 30 to 45 minutes to the village along either route.

OLD WAIHOHONU HUT

Old Waihohonu Hut is NZ's oldest mountain hut, and it's certainly one of the most beloved among Kiwi trampers.

The hut was built in 1904 by the Tourist and Health Resorts Department as a stop-off for stagecoaches on the Grand Tourist Route from Wanganui to Taupo, through what is now Whanganui and Tongariro National Parks. After the main trunk railway was opened on the other side of the park in 1908, Waihohonu Hut became the base for the first recreational skiing in NZ in 1913. Later it served as shearers' quarters before becoming popular with trampers. The hut was finally retired in 1968, and was eventually declared a historical structure.

The fact that it has endured more than a century of extreme weather is testament to the Kiwi ingenuity of its builders. The hut was constructed from pit-sawn totara-wood beams, and clad with corrugated iron, with all materials being carried up by men or horses. Workers then filled the wall cavities with pumice stones to insulate the hut and protect it from fire. The hut is so well designed that it has survived the foul weather buffeting the slopes of Ruapehu, occasional trampers' mishaps with stoves, and even a few volcanic eruptions.

Today, the classic red structure, the oldest example of an early two-room alpine hut in the country, is a museum with an interesting series of displays of early equipment and photos.

TE UREWERA

Te Urewera is the North Island's largest tract of virgin rainforest, encompassing 2127 sq km cut with lakes and rivers. The highlight is Lake Waikaremoana (Sea of Rippling Waters), a deep, 55-sq-km crucible of water encircled by the Lake Waikaremoana track, one of NZ's Great Walks. Rugged bluffs drop away to reedy inlets, with the lake's mirror surface disturbed only by mountain zephyrs, waterbirds taking to the skies and the occasional pleasure boat.

It's remote, rugged and immense, so it's not surprising that Te Urewera became a stronghold for Māori. Te Urewera is the home of Ngāi Tūhoe (www.ngaituhoe.iwi.nz) and was formerly one of NZ's largest national parks. In 2014 its national park status was removed by an Act of Parliament – the Te Urewera Act 2014. This legislation provided a world-leading move that saw Te Urewera granted legal identity in and of itself, inspiring people to commit to its care. Today Ngāi Tūhoe resumes its responsibilities for Te Urewera, with the support of the Crown. Te Urewera is managed by the Te Urewera Board, and is encouraging and welcoming of visitors.

History

Te Urewera is the homeland and the heartland of the Tūhoe people, who say that the mountains, forests, lakes and valleys of Te Urewera express and energise Tūhoe identity, opportunity and way of life. Tūhoe are *na tamariki o te kohu*, the children of the mist, descendants of the mountains and the ever-present mist, with their origins lying in the land itself.

During the early decades of NZ's colonisation, Tūhoe encountered a foe from which even the mountains of Te Urewera couldn't protect them. In 1865 and 1866 government forces, pursuing other Māori accused of rebellion, invaded Tūhoe's northern lands around Ohiwa harbour and their southern lands at Waikaremoana. Tūhoe didn't engage in conflict but their northern and southern lands were still confiscated. In 1868 they agreed to provide sanctuary to Te Kooti Rikirani, a famed prophet and leader from Gisborne. In return Te Kooti fought alongside Tūhoe in a campaign of guerrilla warfare for their confiscated land. The government responded with a scorched-earth policy lasting three years, making Te Urewera uninhabitable and forcing Te Kooti and Tūhoe out of the mountains. Hundreds of Tūhoe died from fighting, illness and starvation.

When the fighting ended in 1871, Tūhoe agreed to a peace compact with the government, who withdrew and recognised Tūhoe's authority over Te Urewera. In 1896 the Urewera District Native Reserve Act was enacted to reaffirm this authority, while providing for Tūhoe self-government and limited land dealings. The government soon undermined the 1896 Act by illegally purchasing land interests and imposing high costs for land surveys and roads that were never built. By 1921 it held large shares and used these to push Tūhoe into the enclaves they retain today. Tūhoe remember this as Te Mowai: cutting the land adrift. This left most of Te Urewera in government hands, which it set aside as a national park in 1954.

Where visitors saw a misty mountain retreat of wild beauty and splendid isolation, Tūhoe saw a homeland over which their authority had been denied and replaced for more than 100 years. The Tūhoe Settlement Act and Te Urewera Act, both legislated in 2014, passed administration of Te Urewera to the Te Urewera Board. Under the Te Urewera Act, the area is no longer a national park.

Environment

Te Urewera contains the largest untouched native forest on the North Island. It is a rugged land that rises to 1400m and forms part of the mountainous spine stretching from the East Cape to Wellington. The forests form a blanket over the mountains so thick that barely a peak or ridge can be seen.

Lake Waikaremoana was formed by a landslide that dammed the Waikaretaheke River around 2200 years ago. The lake filled up to a maximum depth of 248m, but was lowered 5m in 1946 by a hydroelectric development.

There is a diverse selection of trees in Te Urewera's forests, ranging from tall and lush podocarp and tawa forests in the valleys, to stunted, moss-covered beech on the higher ranges. The major change in forest composition occurs at around 800m, where the bush of rimu, northern rata and tawa is replaced by beech and rimu. Above 900m only beech is usually found. It is estimated that 650 types of native plant are present in Te Urewera.

The area's remoteness has preserved much of its wildlife, with a full complement of North Island forest birds to be found within its confines. Te Urewera's rivers and lakes offer some of NZ's finest rainbow-trout fishing. There is good fly-fishing for brown trout from the shore on the Lake Waikaremoana tramp. Fishing with both fly and spinning gear is allowed in most areas.

❶ Planning

HUTS & CAMPING

There are more than 43 huts within Te Urewera. All of them are either Standard ($5) or Basic huts (free), with the exception of the huts along the Lake Waikaremoana Great Walk and Sandy Bay Hut, which is a Serviced hut ($15).

There are also numerous Backcountry campsites (free) and Standard campsites (per person $6) throughout Te Urewera. On Lake Waikaremoana, **Waikaremoana Holiday Park** (✆ 06-837 3826; www.doc.govt.nz/waikaremoana-holiday-park; 6249 Lake Rd/SH38; unpowered/powered campsites from $36/42, cabins/chalets d from $65/130) is a good tramping base for Te Urewera. It has chalets, cabins, campsites and a shop with the likes of hot pies, chocolates and a swarm of fishing flies. The holiday park can also hook you up with tramping supplies and fuel, and it offers gear and car storage.

Lake Waikaremoana Great Walk

Duration 4 days

Distance 46km (28.6 miles)

Difficulty Easy to moderate

Start Onepoto

End Hopuruahine Landing

Gateway Wairoa (p109)

Transport Shuttle bus, boat

Summary This Great Walk follows most of the bluff-lined shore of Lake Waikaremoana, the largest lake in Te Urewera.

Built in 1962 as a volunteer project by boys from 14 secondary schools, the Lake Waikaremoana Great Walk is indeed a great walk, with spectacular views from Panekiri Bluff, deep green forest, numerous beaches and swimming holes. Around 15,000 trampers tackle the walk annually.

The track, which is well benched and easy to follow, can be completed in either direction, although by starting from Onepoto you put the steep climb up spectacular Panekiri Bluff behind you in the first few hours. Walking in the opposite direction you'll need an extra hour from Waiopaoa Hut to Panekire Hut, but then it will take less time from Panekire Hut to the end of the trail at Onepoto.

❶ Planning

WHEN TO TRAMP

Because of the mountainous nature of the area, trampers can expect rain year-round, with the annual average rainfall of 2500mm swept in by prevailing northwesterly and southerly winds. This can fall as snow at any time of the year at the higher altitudes. That said, the track can be tramped throughout the year. It is particularly popular at Easter and during the summer school holidays from mid-December until the end of January. In summer, trampers can generally expect regular spells of fine, dry weather.

MAPS & BROCHURES

The tramp is covered by NZTopo50 *BG40 (Waikaremoana)* and *BG39 (Ruatahuna)*. The whole area is covered by NewTopo's 1:35,000 *Waikaremoana* map. The *Lake Waikaremoana* brochure, which can be downloaded from DOC's website (www.doc.govt.nz), includes an elevation profile for the track and a useful directory of local visitor services.

HUTS & CAMPING

Lake Waikaremoana has five Great Walk huts ($32) along the track: Panekire, Waiopaoa, Marauiti, Waiharuru and Whanganui. Each has a wood-burning heater, water supply, benches on which to cook, vault toilets and bunks with mattresses. There are no cooking facilities, so you need to bring a stove.

There are five designated Great Walk campsites (per person $14): one at Waiopaoa and Waiharuru Huts, as well as Korokoro, Maraunui and Tapuaenui. These have grassy sites, cooking shelters, water supply and vault toilets. Camping on the track is only permitted at these campsites.

Note that for both huts and campsites, water supply is rainfall dependent. It is also recommended that you boil or treat all drinking water.

As this is a Great Walk, you need to book your huts or campsite in advance through **Great Walks Bookings** (p100), or DOC visitors centres nationwide, including the one at Waikaremoana. Backcountry hut passes and hut tickets are not valid. This applies year-round.

INFORMATION

Situated in the hub of Waikaremoana, near the lakeshore, **Te Urewera Visitor Centre** (Te Kura Whenua Paradise; ✆ 06-837 3803; www.ngaituhoe.iwi.nz; 6249 Lake Rd; ⊙ 8.30am-4pm) has weather forecasts, and water taxi, shuttle and accommodation information. You can buy hut and camping passes here for the tramp.

GUIDED TRAMPS

Walking Legends (✆ 0800 925 569, 07-312 5297; www.walkinglegends.com; per person $1490-1590) runs a fully catered, four-day guided tramp (ex-Rotorua) that includes two days on the Lake Waikaremoana track as well

Lake Waikaremoana

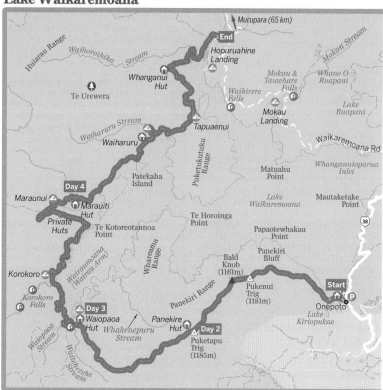

as a day around adjoining Lake Waikareiti and another in the Whirinaki Forest. **Te Urewera Treks** (☏ 07-929 9669; www.teureweratreks.co.nz/home; per person $1500) also offers small-group, guided four-day hikes along the length of the Lake Waikaremoana Great Walk. One- and three-day Te Urewera walks are also available, sometimes with tree-planting activities as part of the experience.

ℹ Getting There & Away

Waikaremoana can be approached from two directions via SH38, which links Wairoa and the east coast with the central North Island. The highway has a gravel surface for about 90km between Murupara and Waikaremoana. There are well-marked side roads to the main boat ramps, campsites and walk entrances.

Both ends of the track are easily accessible off SH38. The southern end is at Onepoto, 10km south of the visitor centre; the northern end is near Hopuruahine Landing, 19km northwest of the visitor centre.

Vehicle storage and water-taxi services are offered by **Big Bush Water Taxi** (☏ 0800 525 392, 06-837 3777; www.lakewaikaremoana.co.nz/water-taxi; per person one way $50-60), with hut-to-hut pack transfers for the less gung-ho. It also runs minibus shuttles to and from Wairoa (from $50 per person one way), which is on the **InterCity** (p137) bus route between Gisborne and Wellington. There are no scheduled transport options from Taupo or Rotorua.

🥾 The Tramp

Day 1: Onepoto to Panekire Hut

4–6 HOURS / 9KM / 530M ASCENT

The beginning of the track is signposted 500m from SH38, next to the day shelter (where there is track information). Before setting out, make sure you fill your water bottle – there is no water available along this first leg.

There is little time to warm up at this end of the track because it immediately begins a steep climb up the sandstone cliffs of Panekiri Bluff. Plan on 2½ to three hours to ascend 530m over 4km to Pukenui Trig, one of the highest points of the trip at 1181m. From there you begin the second half of the day's tramp, following the track along an undulating ridge of knobs and knolls, rewarded each time with spectacular views of Lake Waikaremoana, 600m below.

Continue along the ridge through mixed beech forest for almost 4km, until you suddenly break out at a sheer rock bluff that seems to bar the way. Closer inspection reveals a staircase up the bluff, where the bush has been cleared.

Panekiri Hut (36 bunks) is 100m further on, at Puketapu Trig (1185m). Only 10m from the edge of the bluff, this hut offers the tramp's best panorama, encompassing most of the lake, the Huiarau Range and some-

times even the coastal town of Wairoa. A rainwater tank is the sole water source at the hut.

Day 2: Panekire Hut to Waiopaoa Hut

3–4 HOURS / 8KM / 580M DESCENT

Continue southwest and follow the main ridge for 3km, gradually descending around bluffs and rock gullies until the track takes a sharp right swing to the northwest. If the weather is good there will be panoramas of the lake and forest. At this point the gradual descent becomes steep, with the track heading off the ridge towards Wairaumoana (the Wairau Arm of the lake). At one section it drops 250m in about 1km. Trampers are aided here by a staircase.

On the way down there is an interesting change in vegetation as the forest moves from the beech of the high country to tawa and podocarp, with a thick understorey of ferns. The grade becomes more gentle as you approach the Wairaumoana and, eventually, you arrive at Waiopaoa Hut (30 bunks) and campsite, near the shoreline. The hut is a short stroll from a sandy bay with good spots for fishing and swimming.

Day 3: Waiopaoa Hut to Marauiti Hut

4–5 HOURS / 12KM

Start the day early to take advantage of the many places where you can linger and while away the afternoon. The track turns inland from Waiopaoa Hut to cross Waitehetehe and Waiopaoa Streams, then follows the lakeshore across grassy flats and terraces of kanuka. In the first hour you'll encounter a number of streams that are bridged.

The signposted junction to Korokoro Falls is 3.5km from Waiopaoa Hut, a 1½ hour walk for most trampers, and makes for a scenic diversion. It's 15 minutes to the falls, which drop 20m over a sheer rock face in one of the most impressive displays of cascading water in the catchment. Korokoro Campsite is 200m past the swing bridge and is a very scenic place to pitch a tent.

The main track continues around the lake, rounding Te Kotoreotaunoa Point then dropping into Marauni Bay. It's 30 to 40 minutes along the southern shore of the bay, past a Māori reserve and private huts, to Te Wharau Stream, a popular fishing spot. Located at the stream, around 2½ hours from the Korokoro Falls junction, is Maraunui Campsite.

From here the track climbs over a low saddle in the Whakaneke Spur and, in 1.7km, dips to Marauiti Bay and the 200m side track to **Marauiti Hut** (26 bunks) on the lakeshore.

Day 4: Marauiti Hut to Hopuruahine Landing

4–5 HOURS / 14KM

Return to the main trail and immediately cross the stream at the head of Marauiti Bay. The track follows the northern side of the bay before swinging northeast to skirt Te Kopua Bay, 30 minutes from Marauiti Hut. This is one of the most isolated and beautiful bays on the lake.

The track leaves the bay, climbs to a low saddle in the Te Kopua headland and descends to Te Totara Bay. It then passes **Patekaha Island**, no longer a true island, and hugs the shoreline, which is dotted with a number of small sandy beaches. It's 1.5km from the island to **Waiharuru Hut** (40 bunks), a two-hour walk from Marauiti Hut. This is the largest hut on the track, and has a deck with lake views. Next to it is the Waiharuru Campsite.

The track swings inland to cross Waiharuru Stream then returns to the shoreline and climbs over a saddle, returning to the lakeshore at Tapuaenui Bay in the Whanganui Inlet, 1½ hours from Waiharuru Hut. **Tapuaenui Campsite** is located here. For the next hour follow the shoreline (with a short diversion up Tapuaenui Stream) until it reaches **Whanganui Hut** (18 bunks), on a grassy flat between two streams, close to a nice beach.

From Whanganui Hut, the track contours above the lakeshore before a climb up and over the ridgeline to Huiarau Stream. The track then follows the grassy Hopuruahine River flats to reach the Hopuruahine suspension bridge. Once across the bridge, the track continues up through the grassy flats on the northwestern side of the Hopuruahine Stream to a point opposite the access road. Thanks to a swing bridge, trampers no longer have to ford the river or endure an extra 30-minute walk to a road bridge on SH38.

Hopuruahine Stream and its mouth are popular fishing spots. It's 1km up the gravel access road to SH38 if you haven't arranged for a water-taxi pick-up from Whanganui Hut or shuttle collection from Hopuruahine Landing.

TOWNS & FACILITIES

Taupo

📞 07 / POP 32,900

With an abundance of adrenaline-pumping activities, thermally heated waters, lakeside strolls and some wonderful places to eat, Taupo now rivals Rotorua as the North Island's premier resort town. Beyond its lake, which is the size of Singapore, you can see the snow-capped peaks of Tongariro National Park

🛏 Sleeping & Eating

Finlay Jacks HOSTEL **$**

(☑ 07-378 9292; www.finlayjacks.co.nz; 20 Taniwha St; dm/s/d/f from $23/35/80/120; 🛜) Our pick of Taupo's hostels, Finlay Jacks has turned an ageing motel into a colourful hub for young people. The largest rooms are 12-bed dorms, but they feel less crowded, with bunks separated into lots of eight and four. Affordable private rooms with en suites have supercomfy beds. We love the pop-culture prints on the walls, patterned bed covers and grassy lawn.

Lake Motel MOTEL **$$**

(☑ 07-378 4222, 021 951 808; www.thelakeonline. co.nz; 63 Mere Rd; studio $125-175, 1-bdrm units $145-185; @🛜) A reminder that 1960s and '70s design wasn't all *Austin Powers*-style groovaliciousness, this boutique motel is crammed with furniture from the era's signature designers. The four one-bedroom units sleep between two to four people and have kitchenettes and living areas, and, along with the two studios (maximum two people), use of the garden. Look out for paintings of well-known musos by the owners' son.

Bikes available to borrow free of charge.

⭐ **Waitahanui Lodge** MOTEL **$$**

(☑ 0800 104 321, 07-378 7183; www.waitahanui lodge.co.nz; 116 SH1, Waitahanui; d $119-199; 🛜) Ten kilometres south of Taupo, these five beachfront, beach-hut-style units are ideally positioned for swimming, fishing and superb sunsets. Pick of the bunch are the two absolute-lakefront units, numbers three and four, but all have lake access, sociable communal areas plus free use of row boats and kayaks. The units are all self-contained with kitchenettes, or you can fire up the shared barbecue.

★ **Storehouse** CAFE $$

(☑07-378 8820; www.facebook.com/store housenz; 14 Runanga St; mains $13-18; ⊙7am-3.30pm Mon-Fri, 8am-3.30pm Sat, to 3pm Sun; ☜⋔) If you're looking for Taupo's coolest cafe, you've just found it. Setting the scene since 2013, Storehouse is located in an old plumbing store over two levels. Downstairs, indoor plants drape over warehouse beams, and upstairs a bike is inexplicably fastened to the wall. The breakfast salad bowl often sells out – guess that means we're having fried-chicken waffles.

Southern Meat Kitchen SOUTH AMERICAN $$

(SMK; ☑07-378 3582; www.facebook.com/ smktaupo; 40 Tuwharetoa St; mains $22-34; ⊙noon-midnight Wed-Sun, 4-11pm Mon & Tue) Calling all carnivores! SMK slow-cooks beef brisket, pulled pork and shredded chicken on an American wood-fire smoker – and you can order it by the half-pound (upgrade to a pound for $8). Arrives with mac 'n' cheese, slaw and rice. Save room for jalapeño-and-cheddar cornbread, served in a skillet with addictive honey butter. Beer-tasting paddles for $15.

Bistro MODERN NZ $$

(☑07-377 3111; www.thebistro.co.nz; 17 Tamamutu St; mains $26-39; ⊙5pm-midnight) Popular with locals – bookings are recommended – the Bistro focuses on doing the basics very, very well. That means harnessing local and seasonal produce for dishes such as bacon-wrapped Wharekauhau lamb, washed down with your pick from the small but thoughtful beer-and-wine list. Even the kids' menu is tempting.

🔒 Supplies & Equipment

Torpedo7 SPORTS & OUTDOORS

(☑07-376 0051; www.torpedo7.co.nz; 41 Tamamutu St; ⊙9am-5.30pm Mon-Fri, to 4pm Sat, 10am-4pm Sun) Ginormous sporting and equipment store selling everything you need for cycling, motorbiking, snow sports, camping, tramping and more.

❶ Information

Taupo i-SITE (☑07-376 0027, 0800 525 382; www.greatlaketaupo.com; 30 Tongariro St; ⊙9am-4.30pm May-Oct, 8.30am-5pm Nov-Apr) Handles bookings for accommodation, transport and activities; dispenses cheerful advice; and stocks DOC and town maps.

❶ Getting There & Away

Taupo Airport (☑07-378 7771; www.taupo airport.co.nz; Anzac Memorial Dr) is 8km south of town. Expect to pay about $25 for a 12-minute cab from the airport to the centre of town.

Air New Zealand (☑09-357 3000, 0800 737 000; www.airnz.co.nz) flies from Auckland to Taupo two to three times daily (50 minutes) and **Sounds Air** (☑03 520 3080, 0800 505 005; www.soundsair.com) flies between Wellington and Taupo at least once per day except Tuesday and Wednesday (one hour).

InterCity (☑07-348 0366; www.intercity coach.co.nz), **Mana Bus** (www.manabus.com) and **Naked Bus** (www.nakedbus.com/nz) services stop outside the Taupo i-SITE, where bookings can be made.

Turangi

☑07 / POP 3000

Once a service town for the nearby hydro-electric power station, sleepy Turangi's claim to fame nowadays is as the 'Trout Fishing Capital of the World' and as one of the country's premier white-water-rafting destinations. Set on the Tongariro River, the town is a short hop for Tongariro National Park trampers.

🛏 Sleeping & Eating

Riverstone Backpackers HOSTEL $

(☑07-386 7004; www.riverstonebackpackers. com; 222 Te Rangitautahanga Rd; dm $35, tw $76, d with/without bathroom $82/76; ☜) This homey backpackers' hostel resides in a refitted house close to the town centre. Along with an enviable kitchen and comfortable lounge, it sports a stylish landscaped yard with a large wooden deck and pizza oven.

★ **Braxmere** MOTEL $$

(☑07-386 6449; www.braxmere.co.nz; 88 Waihi Rd, Tokaanu; unit $180; ☜) Just 8km from Turangi on the southern fringes of Lake Taupo, Braxmere is a collection of 10 self-contained units with only a grassy lawn separating them from the lake. All are spacious one-bedroom numbers with decks and barbecues, the decor is maritime-chic and there's the added bonus of Lakeland House restaurant (p108) on-site. When we visited, there were plans for a private thermal pool.

Oreti Village APARTMENT $$$

(☑0800 574 413, 07-386 7070; www.oretivillage. com; Mission House Dr, Pukawa; apt $220-310; ☜≋) This enclave of smart, self-contained apartments sleeping between four and nine people sits high over the lake, surrounded by bird-filled native bush and landscaped with colourful rhododendrons. Ask about the walking track to the private black-sand beach, and be sure to buy a bottle of NZ wine from the fantastic restaurant to enjoy on the balcony – best views this side of Lake Taupo.

Take SH41 for 15km, heading northwest of Turangi, and turn right into Pukawa Rd.

★ **Cadillac Cafe**   CAFE $$

(☑ 07-386 0552; www.facebook.com/Thymefor foodcafe; 35 Turangi Town Centre; mains $9-20; ☺ 8.30am-3pm) Step back in time at Cadillac with its array of vintage chairs, posters and impressive toy collection from the '50s and '60s. Retro games are available while you wait for your massive burger, sticky ribs or fish and chips. Just try to resist the American cakes in the rotating cabinet. Kids' and gluten-free menus available. Lots of outdoor seating.

Lakeland House   INTERNATIONAL $$

(☑ 07-386 6442; www.braxmere.co.nz; 88 Waihi Rd, Tokaanu; mains lunch $20-40, dinner $27-40; ☺ 10am-3pm & 6pm-late) Destination dining with a view across Lake Taupo with generous pastas, salads and chowder dominating the daytime menu. Craft beer from Tuatara Brewing is on tap, and come evening diners can salivate over pan-fried snapper with hollandaise and cajun tiger prawns followed by sticky date pudding with maple-and-walnut ice cream. Six kilometres from Turangi, just off SH41.

🔒 Supplies & Equipment

It's best to pick up any necessary tramping equipment and supplies in Turangi, as National Park and Whakapapa Village have very limited offerings.

New World   SUPERMARKET $

(☑ 07-384 7570; www.newworld.co.nz; 19 Ohuanga Rd; ☺ 7am-8pm Sun-Thu, to 9pm Fri & Sat) Self-caterers should head to this big, centrally located supermarket.

Sporting Life   SPORTS & OUTDOORS

(☑ 07-386 8996; www.sportinglife-turangi.co.nz; The Mall, Town Centre; ☺ 8.30am-5.30pm Mon-Sat, 9.30am-5pm Sun) Sports store laden with fishing paraphernalia and basic tramping and camping gear. Check the website for the latest weather and fishing reports.

ℹ️ Information

Turangi i-SITE (☑ 07-386 8999, 0800 288 726; www.greatlaketaupo.com; 1 Ngawaka Pl; ☺ 9am-4.30pm summer, 8.30am-4pm winter; ☎) A good stop for information on Tongariro National Park, Kaimanawa Forest Park, trout fishing, and snow and road conditions. It issues DOC hut tickets, ski passes and fishing licences, and makes bookings for transport, accommodation and activities. Check out the Volcanic Activity Centre (www.volcanoes. co.nz; i-SITE, 1 Ngawaka Pl; adult/child $12/7; ☺ 9am-4pm) while you're here.

ℹ️ Getting There & Away

InterCity (p107) and **Naked Bus** (www.naked bus.com/nz) coaches **stop** (Ngawaka Pl) outside the Turangi i-SITE.

National Park Village

☑ 07 / POP 200

The small sprawl of National Park Village is the most convenient place to stay when tramping in Tongariro, with more accommodation and eating options than nearby Whakapapa. There is no visitor information centre, so visit www.nationalpark.co.nz and www.visitruapehu.com for info.

🛏️ Sleeping & Eating

Plateau Lodge   LODGE, HOSTEL $

(☑ 07-892 2993, 0800 861 861; www.plateaulodge. co.nz; 17 Carroll St; sites $40, dm $30, d $78-120, apt from $165; ☎) Family-friendly Plateau has cosy rooms, some with en suite and TV, as well as an attractive communal lounge and kitchen. The dorms don't get bigger than two sets of bunks, and there are also two- and three-bedroom apartments sleeping up to six. Campervan sites have the best access to the covered spa pool. Local shuttle services available.

Park Hotel   HOTEL $$

(☑ 07-892 2748, 0800 800 491; www.the-park. co.nz; 2/6 Millar St; d/tw/f from $115/115/125; ☎) Positioned on SH4, this is our pick when tackling Tongariro Crossing. Neat and super affordable, the twin, queen and family mezzanine rooms are quiet and comfortable. The B&B and two-night crossing packages are great value and once you've conquered the mountain, there are spa pools for soaking. Spiral Restaurant & Bar (mains $20 to $34) is a decent place to eat.

Tongariro Crossing Lodge LODGE $$
(☑07-892 2688; www.tongarirocrossinglodge.
com; 27 Carroll St; d $189-209; 🛜) This pretty
white weatherboard cottage is decorated
with a baby-blue trim and rambling blooms
in summer. The new owners have refreshed
the six, spacious rooms – most of which
have a living area. The two studios share a
kitchen, another two are self-contained and
the remainder are great for families. Dotted
with period furniture, there's a sunny deck
and barbecue area, too.

Station Cafe CAFE $$
(☑07-892 2881; www.stationcafe.co.nz; cnr Findlay
St & Station Rd; lunch $15-28, dinner $29-35; ⊗9am-
9pm) This cosy little restored railway station
is now one of the few places serving up half-
decent sustenance in National Park Village.
Eggy brunches, sandwiches, coffee and decadent cakes, plus a dinner menu that reads like
a neighbourhood gastropub (pork tenderloin,
sirloin steak, panko-crumbed chicken). Book
ahead for the Sunday-night roast ($20).

🔒Supplies & Equipment

Four Square SUPERMARKET $
(☑07-892 2879; www.foursquare.co.nz; cnr SH4 &
Waimarino–Takaanu Rd; ⊗7am-7pm) This shop-
cum-service station stocks groceries and
tramping food. Fill your backpack here before doing the Tongariro Alpine Crossing.

❶ Getting There & Away

The Village lies at the junction of SH4 and SH47
at 825m above sea level.

InterCity (☑09-583 5780; www.intercity.
co.nz) buses stop at National Park Station at
the **Station Cafe** (p109), where the *Northern
Explorer* train run by **KiwiRail Scenic** (☑04-495
0775, 0800 872 467; www.kiwirailscenic.co.nz)
also pulls up.

Wairoa
☑06 / POP 4260
At the intersection of SH2 and SH36, Wairoa
serves as the eastern gateway to Te Urewera.
This is your last decent opportunity to stock
up on supplies before you head there.

🛏 Sleeping & Eating

Riverside Motor Camp HOLIDAY PARK $
(☑06-838 6301; www.riversidemotorcamp.co.nz;
19 Marine Pde, Wairoa; powered sites per 2 people $36, dm/cabins from $25/60; @) Grassy
river-side camping and simple cabins; the
backpacker dorm assumes the shape of
a large room with bunks and a TV. The
cheapest beds for many a mile.

Three Oaks Motel MOTEL $$
(☑06-838 8204; www.threeoaksmotel.co.nz; cnr
Clyde Rd & Campbell St, Wairoa; d from $115, extra
person $10; 🛜🐾) A short walk from town,
this basic, old-fashioned motel will do the
trick if you're just looking for a bed.

Eastend Cafe CAFE $
(☑06-838 6070; eastendcafe@xtra.co.nz; 250
Marine Pde, Wairoa; meals $7-20; ⊗7am-3pm
Mon-Fri, 8am-4pm Sat & Sun) A surprisingly ex-
cellent little cafe on the river-side road in
Wairoa. Expect the likes of tarragon chicken
pie, pots of local honey for sale, local beers
and wines from the bar in the corner, and
occasional Friday night dinner-and-music
sessions.

Supplies & Equipment

New World SUPERMARKET $
(☑06-838 8019; www.newworld.co.nz; 41 Queen
St, Wairoa; ⊗7am-7pm) For self-caterers. Stock
up before you head to Lake Waikaremoana.

❶ Information

Wairoa i-SITE (☑06-838 7440; www.visit-
wairoa.co.nz; cnr SH2 & Queen St; ⊗8.30am-
5pm Mon-Fri, 10am-4pm Sat & Sun) The spot
for local info, including advice on Lake Waika-
remoana and accommodation around town.

❶ Getting There & Away

Wairoa is 98km southwest of Gisborne and
117km northeast of Napier. InterCity (www.
intercity.co.nz) buses trundle in from Gisborne
(1½ hours, from $10) and Napier (2¼ hours,
from $14).

TONGARIRO, TE UREWERA & CENTRAL NORTH ISLAND WAIROA

Taranaki & Southern North Island

Best Huts

➜ Pouakai Hut (p119)

➜ Sunrise Hut (p126)

➜ Jumbo Hut (p129)

Best Views

➜ Pouakai Tarns (p120)

➜ Mt Taranaki Summit (p123)

➜ Armstrong Saddle (p126)

➜ Mt Holdsworth (p129)

➜ Putangirua Pinnacles lookout (p131)

Why Go?

The southern half of the North Island might not zing with names like Milford, Abel Tasman and Tongariro, but it's here that some of the roots of New Zealand tramping lie. Egmont National Park was the country's second national park, created in 1900, and NZ's first tramping club was formed in Wellington in 1919.

Like the central North Island, tramping here is dominated by a volcano – Mt Taranaki – and a spectacular, perfectly conical one at that (think, Mt Fuji with a Kiwi accent). The mountain is laced with tramping routes, from a contender for the title of NZ's best day hike, to a lap around the volcano and a summit climb.

Elsewhere there's the chance for an easy introduction to the alpine world on the Sunrise Track, there's hoodoo heaven on a half-day wander into the Hollywood heavy hitter that is the Putangirua Pinnacles, as well as tracks into the rugged and raw terrain of the Tararua Forest Park.

When to Go

Weather conditions in the southern half of the North Island vary greatly, but one common trait across the region is the potential for it to get ugly. In the high-altitude areas of Egmont National Park, the Ruahines and the Tararuas the weather can change in a matter of hours, with blue skies obliterated by raging storms that can bring white-outs and freezing temperatures. If you want to explore high along the peaks, aim to visit between November and April, though come prepared for the possibility of bad weather at any time of year.

Background Reading

In *Ask That Mountain,* author Dick Scott vividly captures a seminal period in early Māori–Pākehā relations. Once named among the 10 most important NZ books, it tells the story of Parihaka, a small Māori settlement at the foot of Mt Taranaki, which from the mid-1860s became the centre of a peaceful resistance movement. In response to the surveying of confiscated tribal lands, Māori – led by Te Whiti-o-Rongomai and Tohu Kakahi and wearing the movement's emblematic white feather in their hair – obstructed development by ploughing troughs across roads, erecting random fences and pulling survey pegs. Despite many Māori being arrested and held without trial, the protests continued and intensified. Finally, in November 1881 the government sent a force of more than 1500 troops to Parihaka in a quest to quash the resistance.

DON'T MISS

Continue the wild journey past Putangirua Pinnacles for 25km and you'll come to Cape Palliser, the southernmost point of the North Island.

Staking the island into the sea here is the 18m-high, cast-iron Cape Palliser Lighthouse, its candy-striped figure having illuminated this windy and ruthless corner of the island since 1897. The 250-step climb to the base of the lighthouse rewards with a great view, and it's a good place to linger if the wind isn't blowing your eyeballs into the back of your head. The surrounding shoreline is home to the North Island's largest breeding area for seals. You can wander among the fur seals, but whatever you do, don't get between them and the sea: if you block their escape route they're likely to charge you – and they can move surprisingly fast.

Also just before Cape Palliser is the quirky fishing village of Ngawi, which claims to have more tractors per head of population than anywhere else in the world – they're used to haul fishing boats in and out of the waves.

DOC Visitor Centres

➡ Egmont National Park Visitor Centre (p114)

➡ Dawson Falls Visitor Centre (p114)

➡ DOC Wellington Visitor Centre (p128)

➡ DOC (Palmerston North Office) (p125)

➡ DOC Masterton Office (p128)

GATEWAY TOWNS

➡ New Plymouth (p132)

➡ Napier (p133)

➡ Palmerston North (p134)

➡ Masterton (p135)

➡ Wellington (p136)

Fast Facts

➡ At 2518m Mt Taranaki is the North Island's second-highest mountain.

➡ Tararua Forest Park is the largest DOC-managed conservation park on the North Island, covering an area larger than Hong Kong.

➡ Armstrong Saddle, at the top of the Sunrise Track, is named after a pilot who crashed a plane here in 1935. All that was found of him was shirt with a 'XXX' label – hence the name of nearby Triplex Hut.

Top Tip

This region has some rugged, wild and weather-whipped tracks. It's essential to obtain current forecasts from the MetService (www.metservice.com) and updates on conditions from DOC (www.doc.govt.nz). If the weather looks dicey, delay your tramp.

Resources

➡ http://visit.taranaki.info

➡ www.manawatunz.co.nz

➡ www.wairarapanz.com

➡ www.wellingtonnz.com

Taranaki & Southern North Island

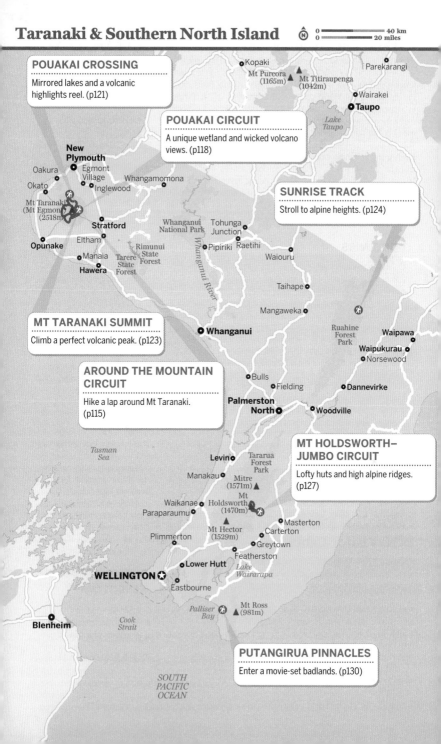

0 | 40 km
0 | 20 miles

POUAKAI CROSSING
Mirrored lakes and a volcanic highlights reel. (p121)

POUAKAI CIRCUIT
A unique wetland and wicked volcano views. (p118)

SUNRISE TRACK
Stroll to alpine heights. (p124)

MT TARANAKI SUMMIT
Climb a perfect volcanic peak. (p123)

AROUND THE MOUNTAIN CIRCUIT
Hike a lap around Mt Taranaki. (p115)

MT HOLDSWORTH–JUMBO CIRCUIT
Lofty huts and high alpine ridges. (p127)

PUTANGIRUA PINNACLES
Enter a movie-set badlands. (p130)

Kopaki
Mt Pureora (1165m)
Mt Titiraupenga (1042m)
Parekarangi
Wairakei
Taupo
Lake Taupo

New Plymouth
Oakura
Egmont Village
Okato
Inglewood
Whangamomona
Mt Taranaki (Mt Egmont) (2518m)
Stratford
Eltham
Whanganui National Park
Tohunga Junction
Pipiriki
Raetihi
Opunake
Manaia
Rimunui State Forest
Tarere State Forest
Hawera
Waiouru
Wairoua
Whanganui River
Taihape
Mangaweka
Ruahine Forest Park
Waipawa
Waipukurau
Norsewood
Whanganui
Bulls
Fielding
Dannevirke
Palmerston North
Woodville
Tasman Sea
Levin
Tararua Forest Park
Manakau
Mitre (1571m)
Waikanae
Mt Holdsworth (1470m)
Paraparaumu
Masterton
Carterton
Plimmerton
Mt Hector (1529m)
Greytown
Featherston
WELLINGTON
Lower Hutt
Lake Wairarapa
Eastbourne
Mt Ross (981m)
Palliser Bay
Blenheim
Cook Strait
SOUTH PACIFIC OCEAN

EGMONT NATIONAL PARK

Draw the classic conical shape of a volcano and you pretty much have the outline of Mt Taranaki, the 2518m-high peak that creates the large bulge in the North Island's west coast.

Taranaki's last significant eruption was over 350 years ago and experts say that the mountain is overdue for another blow. But don't let that put you off – geology goes by a different clock to humans, and this mountain is an absolute beauty. From its slopes and summit there are magnificent views of patchwork dairy farms, the stormy Tasman Sea and Taranaki's volcanic cousins, the Tongariro peaks, to the east.

The entire mountain along with the Kaitake and Pouakai Ranges lie inside Egmont National Park. The park includes 335 sq km of native forest and bush, more than 145km of tracks and routes, and scattered huts and shelters. There are three main roads into the park; two take motorists to 900m and the other up to 1140m.

History

Māori believe Taranaki once resided with the mountains of the central North Island. After a tiff with Mt Tongariro over the maiden Pihanga (a small volcano near Lake Taupo) he fled his ancestral home, gouging a wide scar in the earth (now the Whanganui River) on his journey to the west coast. He remains here in majestic isolation, hiding his face behind a cloud of tears.

Mt Taranaki is a sacred place to Māori – a place where the bones of chiefs are buried, and a place of refuge against marauding enemies. The legendary Tahurangi was said to be the first person to climb to the summit, where he lit a fire and claimed the surrounding land for his *iwi* (tribe).

Captain Cook named the peak Mt Egmont in order to flatter the second Earl of Egmont. Joseph Banks, the botanist on Cook's *Endeavour,* described it as 'the noblest hill I have ever seen'. Two years after Cook's visit, Mt Taranaki was the first thing French explorer Marion du Fresne saw of New Zealand. Both Cook and du Fresne recorded seeing the fires of Māori settlers, but never made contact with the people. Naturalist Ernest Dieffenbach did, however, in 1839. While working for the New Zealand Company, which had been awarded large tracts of land and was responsible for the

English settlement of them, Dieffenbach told the local Māori of his plans to climb to the summit. The Māori tried passionately to dissuade him, but Dieffenbach set off in early December. Although his first attempt was unsuccessful, the naturalist set out again on 23 December and, after bashing through thick bush, he finally reached the peak.

The volcano soon became a popular spot for trampers and adventurers. Fanny Fantham was the first woman to climb Panitahi (also known as Te Iringa and Rangitoto, depending on the *iwi*) – the cone on Mt Taranaki's southern side – in 1887, and it was quickly renamed Fanthams Peak in her honour. A year later the summit route from the plateau (Stratford Plateau) was developed. In 1901 Harry Skeet completed the task of surveying the area for the first topographical map. Tourism boomed.

To protect the forest and watershed from settlers seeking farmland, the Taranaki provincial government set aside an area of roughly 9.5km in radius from the summit. Egmont National Park was created in October 1900.

Mt Taranaki eventually reclaimed its name, although the name Egmont has stuck like, well, egg. If the mountain looks familiar – apart from that classic hands-in-prayer shape, of course – it starred as Mt Fuji in the 2003 movie *The Last Samurai.*

Environment

Volcanic activity began building Mt Taranaki around 130,000 years ago and it last erupted around two centuries ago. It's estimated that significant activity occurs approximately every 340 years, leading vulcanologists to conclude that, rather than Mt Taranaki being extinct, the near perfectly symmetrical cone you see today is a slumbering active volcano.

It won't be like this forever, though. Even if volcanic gurglings peter out to the odd puff of smoke and belch of ash, Taranaki will eventually be worn down by rain, wind and ice, as has happened to the deeply eroded stumps of the Kaitake and Pouakai volcanoes that now form the ranges to the northwest.

The very high rainfall and Taranaki's isolation from NZ's other mountainous regions have created a unique vegetation pattern. Species such as tussock grass, mountain daisy, harebell, koromiko and foxglove have developed local variations, and many common NZ mountain species are not found here. In particular, trampers will notice the complete absence of beech trees.

The lush rainforest that covers 90% of the park is predominantly made up of broadleaved podocarps. At lower altitudes you will find many large rimu and rata. Further up, around 900m, kamahi (often referred to as 'goblin forest' because of its tangled trunk and hanging moss) becomes dominant.

ℹ Planning

WHEN TO TRAMP

Mt Taranaki's high altitude means that trampers can be exposed to strong winds, low temperatures and foul weather at any time of year. Changes are often sudden. Most tracks in Egmont National Park should be walked during the traditional tramping season of October to May, with January to March the best time to climb to the Mt Taranaki summit.

Trampers must always be prepared for poor conditions, taking with them warm clothing, including a hat, gloves and good rain gear, no matter how things look when they set off. Be prepared, also, to turn around if bad weather sets in.

MAPS & BROCHURES

The park is covered by NZTopo50 *BJ29 (Egmont National Park)*, as well as NewTopo's 1:35,000 *Taranaki Mt Egmont* map. DOC produces a range of brochures covering tramps in the national park, including dedicated *Pouakai Circuit, Around the Mountain Circuit* and *Mt Taranaki Summit Climb* brochures.

ℹ EMERGENCY EXITS

Mt Taranaki is famous for its trickery, giving visitors a false sense of safety that results in numerous accidents each year. The high altitudes reached by roads put inexperienced trampers within easy reach of icy slopes and unpredictable conditions, including massive rain dumps and subsequent rising river levels. A good number of rivers and streams aren't bridged and may become impassable after heavy rain. Usually it's simply a case of waiting it out – once the rain stops, the rivers recede almost as quickly as they rise. From Kahui or Pouakai Huts it's possible to exit the park along tracks not requiring river crossings, such as the Kahui and Puniho Tracks from Kahui Hut, and the Mangorei Track from Pouakai Hut.

HUTS & LODGES

Six of the park's eight huts are Serviced huts ($15): Holly, Lake Dive, Maketawa, Pouakai, Waiaua Gorge and Waingongoro. They all have wood burners, unlike the two Standard huts ($5), Kahui and Syme. You'll need to carry a stove and fuel for all huts. Purchase hut tickets at the Egmont National Park Visitor Centre, Dawson Falls Visitor Centre and other DOC visitors centres nationwide. Hut tickets can also be bought at the region's i-SITES.

Behind the Egmont National Park Visitor Centre you'll find the **Camphouse** (☑ 06-756 0990; www.doc.govt.nz; Egmont Rd, North Egmont; per adult/child $25/10, exclusive use $600), a historic 32-bed bunkhouse complete with gun ports in the walls and endless horizon views from the porch. It's managed by DOC and advance bookings are required.

Further south, on the road up to the Stratford Plateau (the highest road in the park), is the **Ngāti Ruanui Stratford Mountain House** (☑ 06-765 6100, 027 588 0228; www.stratford mountainhouse.co.nz; Pembroke Rd; d/f from $155/195; 🛜), an upbeat lodge with motel-style rooms and an on-site cafe and restaurant.

Near the Dawson Falls Visitor Centre is the Swiss-style **Dawson Falls Mountain Lodge & Cafe** (☑ 06-765 5457; www.dawsonfallsmountain lodge.kiwi.nz; Manaia Rd; s/d/f incl breakfast from $125/190/200), which has meals available. Also nearby is **Konini Lodge** (☑ 06-756 0990; www. doc.govt.nz; Manaia Rd, Dawson Falls; dm adult/ child $25/10), a DOC-managed 38-bed bunk-room lodge with a full kitchen and good views of the mountain from an outdoor deck. Bookings are essential.

INFORMATION

DOC operates two visitor centres on the mountain, providing maps and other information, including the latest weather forecasts and track conditions. **Egmont National Park Visitor Centre** (☑ 06-756 0990; www.doc.govt.nz; Egmont Rd, North Egmont; ⊙ 8am-4pm, reduced winter hr) is the closest to New Plymouth, and the major departure point for trampers. The centre also houses displays and contains the **Kamahi Cafe** (☑ 06-756 0990; www.facebook.com/kamahicafe; Egmont Rd, North Egmont; meals $10-18; ⊙ 9am-4pm) for those end-of-tramp cold drinks and ice creams. On the southeastern side of the mountain is **Dawson Falls Visitor Centre** (☑ 06-443 0248; www.doc. govt.nz; Manaia Rd, Dawson Falls; ⊙ 9am-4pm Thu-Sun, daily school holidays).

GUIDED TRAMPS

Top Guides Taranaki (☑ 0800 448 433; www.topguides.co.nz; half-/full-day tramps per person from $99/299) runs a guided day walk along the Pouakai Crossing, as well as a couple of half-day tramps in the park.

ℹ Getting There & Away

Three roads – Egmont, Pembroke and Manaia – take you into the national park. Many trampers access the park at the end of Egmont Rd, because it's the closest entrance to New Plymouth – it turns off SH3 13km southeast of New Plymouth, from where it's another 16km to the Egmont National Park Visitor Centre.

Pembroke Rd extends for 18km from Stratford to the Plateau (1140m), on the eastern side of the volcano. Manaia Rd is 15km southwest of Stratford, on the Opunake Rd just north of Kaponga, and it runs for 8km to Dawson Falls.

There are no public buses to the national park, but there are a few shuttle/tour operators who will take you there for around $40/60 one way/return (usually cheaper for groups):

Eastern Taranaki Experience (✉ 06-765 7482, 027 4717136, 027 246 6383; www.eastern-taranaki.co.nz; 5 Verona Place, Stratford; per person incl lunch from $210) Shuttles from Stratford to any road end and trailhead in the national park.

Taranaki Tours (✉ 06-757 9888; www.taranakitours.com; per person from $145) Daily runs from New Plymouth to Egmont National Park Visitor Centre.

Top Guides Taranaki (p114) Transport to trailheads from New Plymouth.

Around the Mountain Circuit

Duration 5 days

Distance 49–53km (30.4–32.9 miles)

Difficulty Moderate to demanding

Start/End Egmont National Park Visitor Centre

Gateway New Plymouth (p132)

Transport Shuttle bus

Summary Circumnavigate Mt Taranaki and be spoilt for views up, down and around the mountain, with options for side trips to waterfalls, a historic hut and the 2518m summit itself.

The Around the Mountain Circuit (AMC) is exactly what the name on the tin suggests – a spectacular loop around Taranaki for experienced trampers, on a backcountry track through stunted subalpine forest and spectacular volcanic scenery.

The track can be started at either the Egmont National Park Visitor Centre or Dawson Falls. The tramp is described here in an anticlockwise direction beginning at the Egmont National Park Visitor Centre. Trampers start-

ing at Dawson Falls often travel clockwise and go directly to Waiaua Gorge Hut via the upper level tracks on the first day. Note that high- and low-level tracks exist for some sections of the track, giving you the chance to climb high in good weather, or stay low and safe in bad. It's important to remember that there are lots of rivers along the track, and not many bridges. Rivers can become dangerous to cross after heavy rain. If in doubt, wait it out.

🚶 The Tramp

Day 1: Egmont National Park Visitor Centre to Holly Hut

3–4 HOURS / 8KM / 340M ASCENT

Follow Day 1 of the Pouakai Circuit (p119) as far as Holly Hut.

Day 2: Holly Hut to Waiaua Gorge Hut

7–9 HOURS / 13KM

The track crosses Holly Flats then swings around the **Dome** (1052m) and steadily descends on steps to the Stony River. The 30-minute detour to view the spectacular **Bells Falls** is worthwhile.

Continue in a generally westerly direction beside (and sometimes along) the bed of **Stony River**, taking care as it is severely eroded. Look carefully for marker poles.

Around 4km from Holly Hut the entrance to the Kapoaiaia Track is on the true left of the river. Follow this track across two badly eroded stream beds to reach Puniho Track. From here there are two options, each going their own way for around two hours before meeting again. For the high track, turn left and follow Puniho Track uphill into subalpine forest and around to **Kahui Hut** (six bunks), then continue down Kahui Track to turn left at the Oaonui Track junction. For the low track, continue along Kapoaiaia Track through the forest, crossing many streams, to the junction with the Kahui and Oaonui Tracks.

Both options then follow the Oaonui Track for about two hours, climbing in and out of numerous gullies. Finally you meet Ihaia Track; turn left and follow it to **Waiaua Gorge Hut** (16 bunks), being careful to look for markers along the open river-bed section. You'll have to cross the unbridged Oaonui Stream before reaching the hut. Built in 1984, the hut is situated on the cliffs above the deep Waiaua Gorge and provides excellent views of Taranaki's western slopes.

Mt Taranaki Multiday Hikes

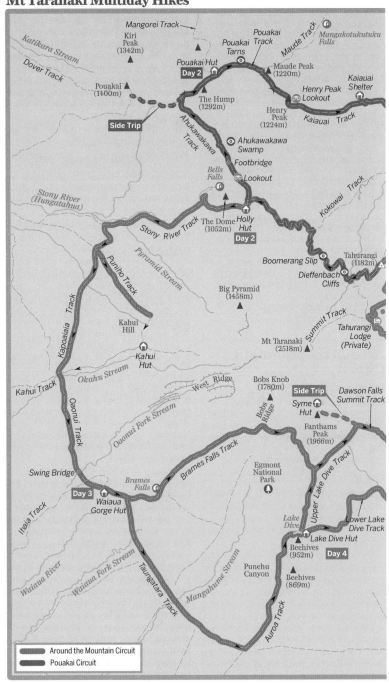

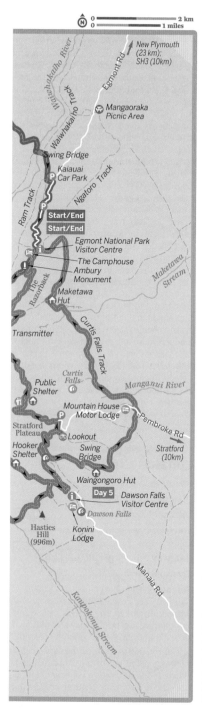

Day 3: Waiaua Gorge Hut to Lake Dive Hut

7–8 HOURS / 10KM / 340M ASCENT

Follow Brames Falls Track into the Waiaua Gorge via an aluminium ladder and a steep track, then cross the unbridged Waiaua River and climb out again to the Taungatara Track junction, which you will reach about 45 minutes from the hut. There are two options from here, both of which take around seven hours.

For the high track, continue up the Brames Falls Track, climbing steeply to the rock bluffs of Bobs Ridge. Carefully follow the poled route through eroded rocky sections and across tussock slopes before descending to the Lake Dive Track junction. Take the right fork for a 45-minute tramp down to Lake Dive Hut. The left fork leads directly to Dawson Falls (2½ hours), though this high track can be impassable due to snow in wintry conditions.

For the low track, turn right and follow the Taungatara Track approximately 6km through forest, until reaching the Auroa Track junction. Turn left and ascend along the Auroa Track to Lake Dive Hut. This track can be very muddy with lots of tree falls, and has many stream crossings.

Lake Dive Hut (16 bunks), built in 1980, is situated at the eastern end of the lake, and on a windless day a reflection of Fanthams Peak graces the water in front of it. If you're contemplating a swim after a hot day above the bushline, keep in mind that the water is very cold and the bottom very muddy.

Day 4: Lake Dive Hut to Dawson Falls

3–4 HOURS / 7KM

Although it is possible to tramp all the way to the Egmont National Park Visitor Centre in one day from Lake Dive Hut, splitting the distance into two days will allow sufficient time to take the rewarding side trip to Fanthams Peak, which can be reached by taking either the Upper Lake Dive Track, or the Lower.

The high track offers excellent views but is very exposed and requires mountaineering experience in winter conditions. It climbs steeply from the hut up Upper Lake Dive Track (retracing your steps from yesterday if you came this way) to the junction with the Brames Falls Track. Turn right to continue along the Upper Lake Dive Track, heading across tussock slopes to the Fanthams Peak Track junction. Turn right to

TARANAKI & SOUTHERN NORTH ISLAND AROUND THE MOUNTAIN CIRCUIT descend to Dawson Falls, or left for the side trip to Fanthams Peak and Syme Hut.

The low-level option follows Lower Lake Dive Track, undulating through forest, crossing many unbridged streams and dipping into gorges on its way to Dawson Falls. When the track eventually reaches the junction with the Fanthams Peak Track, turn right and descend through 'goblin forest' to Dawson Falls, where you can stay at either Konini Lodge (p114) (advance bookings required), or continue to Waingongoro Hut (16 bunks), 1½ hours from Dawson Falls.

Side Trip: Fanthams Peak

6–7 HOURS / 10KM RETURN / 1070M ASCENT

When the weather is kind this is a worthy side trip with splendid views that take in Taranaki and the coastline far below.

If taking the high route from Lake Dive Hut, turn left when you hit the Fanthams Peak Track. If coming up from the Dawson Falls direction on the low track, take the Fanthams Peak Track and follow it up past the Hooker Shelter before ascending a steep staircase to the junction with Upper Lake Dive Track.

From here it's around 1½ hours following a poled zigzagging route up precipitous scoria slopes to Syme Hut (10 bunks) and Fanthams Peak (1966m). The hut, at 1950m, is the second-highest on the North Island. Soak up the grand views before heading back down the same route you came up, or settle into the hut if you've been feeling fit enough to lug your pack up with you.

The track is very exposed along its upper parts and is best avoided in winter and or at any sign of bad weather, unless parties are appropriately experienced and equipped with ice axes and crampons.

Day 5: Dawson Falls to Egmont National Park Visitor Centre

HIGH TRACK 4–5 HOURS / 11KM / 610M ASCENT; LOW TRACK 7–8 HOURS / 14.5KM

Again, there are low- and high-track options for the day's tramp. The high track is the more direct route, and is achievable in fine weather. In bad weather it's very exposed, and may be impassable due to snow/ice in wintry conditions.

The high track follows the well-benched Wilkies Pools Track, which climbs northwest away from the car park. The tramp begins in forest, and within 30 minutes arrives at Wilkies Pools, an interesting series of small

pools and cascades gouged out of a lava flow by the stream.

From Wilkies Pools cross the river and continue until you reach a track junction; from here follow signs to Stratford Plateau. Once you reach the Stratford Plateau car park follow signs to the Manganui Ski Field. This track will take you through a small tunnel, and down into the Manganui Gorge before climbing to the ski-field area. Follow the markers across the tussock slope to continue on the track to privately owned Tahurangi Lodge, around 1½ hours from the Stratford Plateau. From the lodge turn downhill and follow the 4WD track to Egmont National Park Visitor Centre, passing the giant TV transmission tower on your descent.

For the low track from Dawson Falls, follow signs for Waingongoro Hut. Before reaching the hut, take the left at the track junction and cross the swing bridge before following the track to the Te Popo car park. The route continues across Pembroke Rd as Curtis Falls Track. It's a difficult three- to four-hour tramp to Maketawa Hut, and includes climbing in and out of five gorges and crossing many unbridged streams. Although most trampers push on to the Egmont National Park Visitor Centre, a nice option is to stay at Maketawa Hut (16 bunks), which includes a wood fire and an outdoor deck where you can sit and admire some final views of Mt Taranaki. This is also a great base if you want to climb to the summit. The final leg from the hut is a 1½-hour tramp along a forested track

Pouakai Circuit

Duration 2 days

Distance 25km (15.5 miles)

Difficulty Moderate

Start/End Egmont National Park Visitor Centre

Gateway New Plymouth (p132)

Transport Shuttle bus

Summary This short circuit is Egmont National Park's classic tramp, passing through diverse forest, tussock and swamp, and offering spectacular views of Mt Taranaki and the New Plymouth coastline.

The Pouakai Circuit features spectacular views from the top of the Pouakai Range, which at one time was a volcano of similar size to Mt Taranaki. Natural erosion has reduced it to a rugged area of high ridges and rolling hills of subalpine bush.

The track also passes through the mighty Ahukawakawa Swamp, a unique wetland formed around 3500 years ago. It is home to many plant species, some of which are found nowhere else on the planet. Sedges, sphagnum moss, herbs and red tussock are all common here, along with small orchids and other flowering plants.

This loop can be tramped in either direction, but trampers can also walk it in a day, leaving the route at Pouakai Hut and following the Mangorei Track (a two-hour tramp) to the end of Mangorei Rd – this is the Pouakai Crossing (p121). This road leads to New Plymouth, a mostly downhill walk of 15km (there's usually little traffic this far up).

 The Tramp

Day 1: Egmont National Park Visitor Centre to Pouakai Hut

5–6 HOURS / 12KM / 640M ASCENT

The tramp begins along Holly Hut Track, signposted near the Camphouse. The track climbs steadily up steps, gaining 240m and passing the Ambury Monument on the way to a trig on **Tahurangi** (1182m), where, if the day is clear, you're rewarded with spectacular views of Mt Taranaki and the valleys below. The track continues beyond the trig and up the narrow Razorback ridge, ascending another 100m, before leaving the lava flow and sidling around the slope. Within an hour (3km) of leaving the Camphouse you'll reach a signposted junction. The left turn takes you via the Around the Mountain Circuit to Stratford Plateau.

The Pouakai Circuit continues past the junction and follows the well-marked Holly Hut Track as it climbs around the headwaters of the Waiwhakaiho River and along the base of the **Dieffenbach Cliffs**, which rise above you. Enjoy views of New Plymouth while skirting the mountain's northern flanks for the next hour or so.

The track descends slightly to the headwaters of Kokowai Stream and cuts across **Boomerang Slip**. Extreme care must be used when tramping across this slide of loose rocks and dirt. From the slip the track works around the head of Kokowai Stream, and then gently climbs a prominent ridge to the junction with the signposted Kokowai Track. From this point you will be able to view Ahukawakawa Swamp and much of the track up the Pouakai Range.

Head left, following the track as it descends 244m over 2.5km to the junction with the Ahukawakawa Track (the right fork). Turn left if you want to reach **Holly Hut** (32 bunks), five minutes away across the unbridged Minarapa Stream. This is a popular place to spend a night, with Mt Taranaki looming behind and good views of the Pouakai Range from the veranda.

If you have time, consider going the extra distance from Holly Hut to the spectacular 31m-high **Bells Falls**, around 30 minutes away. The falls are signposted from the hut. The track heads across Holly Flats before swinging north around the Dome and descending towards the Stony River. At the signposted junction turn right and follow the track upstream to the base of the falls.

Trampers continuing to Pouakai Hut should follow the Ahukawakawa Track. Within 500m the track reaches an elaborate

TARANAKI & SOUTHERN NORTH ISLAND POUAKAI CIRCUIT

GREAT WALKS BECOME GREATER WALKS

When the Paparoa Track (p225) opens in 2019, it will grow New Zealand's Great Walks network to 10 tracks, but it won't linger on that number for long. In 2017 DOC invited proposals to nominate existing trails that should be upgraded to Great Walk status, with one or two to be selected. Given the high number of Great Walks on the South Island, DOC was hoping primarily for proposals for tracks on the North Island. By the time you read this, the new Great Walk(s) may well have been decided, with the final decision expected to have been made and announced by the end of 2018. Required track developments and upgrades are forecast to be completed in time for both tramps to commence as Great Walks by the start of the 2021 summer season.

Proposals were invited up until the end of November 2017, and by the time you read this the two new Great Walks may well have been decided, with the final decision expected to have been made and announced by the end of 2018. Required track developments and upgrades are forecast to be completed in time for both tramps to commence as Great Walks by the end of 2021.

viewing platform and then descends to the southwest end of Ahukawakawa Swamp. This remarkable sphagnum-moss swamp is crossed on 1km of boardwalks, with an unusual arched bridge over Stony River.

On the northern side of the swamp the track begins a long climb up a forested ridge. The 300m ascent to the junction with the Pouakai Track is a one- to 1½-hour effort, with the first 20 to 30 minutes the steepest part. The track then levels briefly, before continuing at a more gentle incline. If the day is nice, views of the swamp and Mt Taranaki rising above it are well worth the knee-bending effort. If it's raining, this can be a bit of a slog, even with all the steps that have been installed.

Two hours from Holly Hut you top out at a saddle that opens up to views of New Plymouth, and reach Pouakai Track at a signposted junction. Head right, as the track sidles around the north side of the Hump (1292m) and then makes a short descent to a signposted junction with Mangorei Track. Those with sharp eyes will see a corner of Pouakai Hut 15 to 20 minutes before reaching it.

Pouakai Hut (16 bunks) is just five minutes down Mangorei Track (left), about 2½ hours from Holly Hut. Nestled on the west side of the ridge, it has grand views from its veranda over the curved coastline and New Plymouth. The sunsets can be spectacular from this perch, followed by the city lights of New Plymouth gradually flickering on.

Mangorei Track is a good exit off the mountain in bad weather.

Side Trip: Pouakai

2 HOURS / 6KM RETURN / 200M ASCENT
Pouakai Hut is in such a scenic location that you may be tempted to spend a spare day here. If so, use part of it to climb to the summit of Pouakai (1400m) for even better views of the Taranaki region.

To get there, head back up to the Pouakai Track junction and turn right. It's a one-hour (3km) climb from here along a route that marches straight to the top of the peak.

Day 2: Pouakai Hut to Egmont National Park Visitor Centre

5–7 HOURS / 13KM / 740M ASCENT, 970M DESCENT
Keep your fingers crossed for clear weather as you traverse the backbone of the Pouakai Range because the views are superb.

Return to the Pouakai Track and head northeast (left) to follow the tussocky ridge for a level and scenic stretch, with New Plymouth on one side of you and Mt Taranaki on the other. Within 1km of setting out, you reach the Pouakai Tarns. On a clear and windless day, Mt Taranaki will be reflected in the surface of these two small pools, making for Taranaki's classic photograph.

The track sidles around Maude Peak (1220m) then drops into a low saddle at the base of Henry Peak, 45 minutes from Pouakai

---

WHANGANUI JOURNEY – THE GREAT WALK THAT ISN'T

One of NZ's Great Walks, the Whanganui Journey, is not a walk at all. This 145km route is a canoe or kayak trip along the Whanganui River from Taumarunui to Pipiriki, west of Tongariro National Park. The journey takes around five days and is one of NZ's great river adventures, wending from highlands to lowlands, through the heart of Whanganui National Park.

It's a journey of natural beauty, history and cultural interest. Along the way are two huts, a bunk house and 11 campsites. The level of effort and skill required is largely dictated by the river flows. When the river is running slow, be prepared to paddle for hours. Frequent rapids are generally gentle and fun, but you will need water confidence, paddling skills and good general fitness – this is, after all, a long journey through the middle of nowhere. The most beautiful stretch is arguably the Mangawaiiti section past John Coull Hut, where a deep gorge creates often mirror-perfect reflections. There are also chances to pull ashore and take short walks to see the likes of the accurately-named Bridge to Nowhere.

If you want to shorten the journey, a popular starting point is Whakahoro, from where it's an 87km paddle to Pipiriki. Local companies are well geared up to set you on your paddling way, and fully guided trips are available if you don't want to tackle it on your own.

For more information and bookings, which are essential during the Great Walks season (mid-October to the end of April), contact Great Walks Bookings (p100) or any DOC visitors centre. Bookings are not required at other times.

A good potted summary of the journey is also compiled in DOC's *Whanganui Journey* brochure, which can be downloaded from its website (www.doc.govt.nz).

Hut. The 150m climb to the top of Henry Peak (1224m) looks more daunting than it is, with most trampers reaching the viewing platform within 20 minutes. It's well worth the modest effort for the wraparound view.

From the peak the track begins a long, steady descent on a series of steps. Within an hour you emerge at the edge of Kai Auahi Stream, where you can peer into its gorge. The track skirts the gorge for another 30 minutes before arriving at Kaiauai Shelter. This three-sided shelter was built for trampers to wait in when the stream was too flooded to ford; now it's a good spot for a break before descending to cross the bridge across the stream.

For the next hour the track climbs in and out of a couple of small gorges and two major ones. Less than 1½ hours from the shelter you reach a signposted junction with Kokowai Track, which heads right up the mountain. Head left and in five minutes you'll arrive at a swing bridge across the Waiwhakaiho River.

On the other side is a junction with Waiwhakaiho Track (left fork), which heads downhill. You're now less than 30 minutes from Egmont Rd. Continue right on Kaiauai Track as it climbs out of the gorge, passes a signposted junction with Ram Track (right fork) and then breaks out on to asphalt at the Kaiauai car park.

The Egmont National Park Visitor Centre is 2km – a good 30-minute walk – up the road. The alternative is to follow Ram Track back to the centre, a two-hour walk from its junction with the Kaiauai Track. Most trampers take the road, knowing they're that much closer to a cold drink at the Kamahi Cafe.

Pouakai Crossing

Duration 7½–9½ hours

Distance 17km (10.6 miles)

Difficulty Moderate

Start Egmont National Park Visitor Centre

End Mangorei Rd

Gateway New Plymouth (p132)

Transport Shuttle bus

Summary Take in almost all of the major highlights of Egmont National Park along this stunning day tramp that rivals the Tongariro Alpine Crossing for volcanic spectacle.

If the Tongariro Alpine Crossing is widely regarded as the best day walk in New Zealand, the Pouakai Crossing is its heir apparent. This walk is another volcanic highlights reel, taking in spectacular cliffs, a waterfall, the primeval Ahukawakawa Swamp and the (hopefully) mirror-perfect Pouakai Tarns.

This walk packs plenty of panoramic punch without the need to lug a heavy pack filled with overnight gear. It's also a great option for those staying in New Plymouth, allowing you a grand day out with a debrief back among the bright lights of the city. Its relatively low altitude means it can also be walked much of the year, though it's worth checking in with Egmont National Park Visitor Centre before you leave to make sure the track's OK.

Starting at the visitor centre, the track follows the first day of the Pouakai Circuit as far as Pouakai Hut before heading down Mangorei Track to the road, where you can be collected by shuttle bus for the return trip to New Plymouth. It's a full-on day, but a hugely satisfying one.

🏃 The Tramp

Follow the route for Day 1 of the Pouakai Circuit (p119), from North Egmont to Pouakai Hut. If you're a steady tramper you should have no trouble factoring in the side trip to Bells Falls.

From Pouakai Hut there are other side trips that shouldn't be missed if you can help it: the two-hour return trip to Pouakai (1400m), and the track east to Pouakai Tarns, a pair of pools that provide one of NZ's great photo opportunities in the right conditions. You'll need to allow another hour if you want to head up and down Henry Peak (1224m) with its 360-degree views.

The way home is via Mangorei Track, which departs from above Pouakai Hut and heads steadily downhill on a stepped boardwalk for about two hours to reach the road's end. This track is very popular with locals due to its proximity to New Plymouth.

After a short downhill stretch through low shrub the track partially circumnavigates the knoll known to locals as Photographic Peak (1232m). Look out for the historical graffiti carved in rock on the left as you descend, and be sure to pause to appreciate the views of northern Taranaki and the coastline before you drop below the bushline.

The last area of low shrub is known as Graylings Clearing, where pioneering summit parties would graze their horses and

TARANAKI & SOUTHERN NORTH ISLAND POUAKAI CROSSING

Mt Taranaki Day Hikes

pick up a fresh mount. Growing in this area is the unusual parasitic plant *Dactylanthus taylorii*, otherwise known as wood rose.

From here the track continues its constant descent through rainforest broken only by one of the last stands of mature rimu and miro to escape the last eruption of Mt Taranaki. Around 30 minutes later you will emerge at a gravel road; follow it for five minutes to reach the road end and transport pick-up point.

Mt Taranaki Summit

Duration 8-10 hours

Distance 12.6km (7.8 miles)

Difficulty Moderate to demanding

Start/End Egmont National Park Visitor Centre

Gateway New Plymouth (p132)

Transport Shuttle bus

Summary A challenging and rewarding climb to the 2518m pinnacle of the slumbering Taranaki volcano.

The majestic Mt Taranaki, the central point of Egmont National Park, is approximately 130,000 years old. It's the park's most recent volcanic peak, last erupting around 200 years ago – the mountain has been quiet for a while but is not considered extinct.

It's said to be the most climbed mountain in New Zealand, and in ideal summer conditions most fit trampers can make it to the summit, but you need to be prepared – a long list of people have been killed on its slopes. It's an ascent of around 1570m – a big day out – so don't take it lightly whatever the conditions. You must check the forecast, and be prepared to turn tail and retreat if the weather deteriorates (check in with the Egmont National Park Visitor Centre before you set out for up-to-date information).

ℹ️ Planning

WHEN TO TRAMP

The best time of year for trampers to climb Mt Taranaki is from January to March, when the mountain is often clear of snow and ice, other than in the crater.

WHAT TO BRING

Sudden weather changes here mean you must have the right gear and supplies (including plenty of water as there are no streams). Good hiking boots, rain gear and warm clothing are essential. Walking poles might help alleviate the knee strain of the long descent, while it's wise to carry a torch (flashlight) in case you get caught out in the dark.

The Tramp

From the Egmont National Park Visitor Centre, follow the Summit Track signs and head up the 4WD Translator Rd. This 1½-hour walk is a good warm up, with one section aptly named 'the Puffer'. There's a small public day shelter under the privately owned Tahurangi Lodge, and public toilets just below the giant TV tower.

From the lodge a track continues to Hongi Valley then climbs up a heap of steps to 1950m, where you move onto the scree slope of North Ridge. Follow the poles as they zigzag up the loose gravel to the ridge known as the Lizard (2134m). Be mindful of falling rocks here.

The poles up the Lizard lead to the north, or summer, entrance of the crater, where you will encounter snowfields and icy rocks. Once in the crater, at 2450m, it's a walk across the ice and snow to the west rim and a clamber up rocks to the summit, around four hours from Tahurangi Lodge.

The summit area is sacred to Māori, and visitors are asked to respect the mountain by not standing directly on the summit peak, by not camping, toileting or cooking on or around the summit area and by removing all rubbish.

You return back along the ascent route. It will take around four hours to reach the Egmont National Park Visitor Centre, so allow yourself plenty of time to descend safely before nightfall.

RUAHINE FOREST PARK

Pinched between Palmerston North and Napier, Ruahine Forest Park spans 936 sq km, from the Manawatu Gorge in the south to the Taruarau and Ngaruroro Rivers, which form its northern boundary with Kaweka Forest Park. Ruahine is long (95km), narrow (only 8km wide at its southern end) and very rugged. It encompasses the main Ruahine Range, as well as the Mokai Patea, Hikurangi, Whanahuia and Ngamoko Ranges.

The park is laced with tracks and poled routes, and within its boundaries are 60 DOC and club huts available to trampers. East–west crossings over the Ruahines are popular, but the area is not well served by public transport, making it difficult for trampers to arrange a drop-off on one side of the mountains and a pickup on the other. If you're looking for an alpine adventure, where it's possible to spend an afternoon tramping alone along a ridge and through tussock, then the Ruahines are well worth the effort needed to reach the tracks.

History

There has been human activity in and around the park area for almost 1000 years, beginning with the Māori. In pre-European times the forests and streams were a good source of food for the descendants of the Rangitane, Ngāti Apa and Ngāti Kahungungu people.

The first European to explore the Ruahine Range was Reverend William Colenso. After arriving in NZ in 1834, Colenso became a travelling missionary and crossed the range seven times. He was a skilled botanist whose observations became the basis of the first botanical records of the area. Eventually the Māori track he used became known as Colenso's Track.

In the early 1900s the forests in the Ruahine foothills were cleared for farms and milling. Red deer were released in the mid-1920s for game hunting, but their numbers increased so rapidly their browsing caused extensive forest destruction. That resulted in the New Zealand Forest Service (NZFS) building many of the park's tracks and huts in the 1960s for deer cullers.

Ruahine's most famous hut, Rangiwahia, was originally a shepherd's shelter, built in 1930 just above the bushline on the western side of the range. It became the focal point of a ski hill in 1938, after a group of young men drinking pints in the Rangiwahia Hotel formed the Rangiwahia Ski Club – only the second ski club to be incorporated in NZ. The skiers winched a bulldozer up the valley to level out the slopes, built a towrope that used an engine from an Indian motorcycle and added a wing to the hut. The club's membership peaked with 80 skiers, but sadly it was disbanded during WWII and never reformed.

WARNING: NORTHWEST WINDS

Trampers should keep an eye on the weather and the possibility of strong winds when hiking in the Ruahines. The predominant northwest winds are the main ones you need to watch carefully. Often it can be sunny and calm on the surrounding plains, and even at trailheads, but by the time you reach the bushline on the Ruahines a northwesterly will be blowing across the ridges, exposing you to strong gusts and cold rain.

Environment

The Ruahine Range forms part of the North Island's main divide. The dividing range traps moisture carried by prevailing westerly winds, causing heavy rainfall and a damp climate on the west and a rain-shadow effect on the east, where there are drier conditions. The southern end of the range is generally lower than the northern end, which includes Mangaweka, the highest point in the park at 1733m. The range is geologically young and is still uplifting – combined with the dramatic weather this precipitates high rates of erosion. In general the terrain is steep and rugged, and features sharp-crested ridges.

The forests within the park extend to 1100m. Broadleaved podocarp is found on the lower slopes, while beech, kamahi and pahautea dominate higher altitudes. Above the forest, leatherwood and subalpine vegetation take over, giving way to tussock and alpine herb fields.

A number of common native birds can be found in the park, including the tui, korimako (bellbird), piwakawaka (fantail), popokotea (whiteheads), kereru, titipounamu (rifleman) and riroriro (grey warbler). If you're lucky you'll see kakariki (parakeets) and kararea (falcons) and hear kiwi and kaka.

Sunrise Track

Duration 4½–5½ hours

Distance 12km (7.5 miles)

Difficulty Easy to moderate

Start/End North Block Rd

Gateways Napier (p133), Palmerston North (p134)

Transport Private

Summary A gentle climb through gorgeous forest to a hut with high views and an easily attained alpine saddle.

This well-graded track is the perfect introduction to mountain tramping in New Zealand, rising slowly through changing forest to offer a glimpse of alpine country – if you're new to life above the bushline it could be love at first sight.

The gradient and changing scene make the Sunrise Track a good tramping option for families, but it's also more than just a taster of the mountains. The forest that drapes the slopes of the Ruahine Range is

Sunrise Track

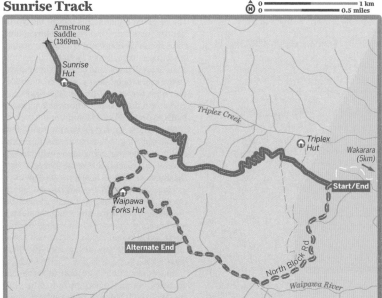

stunning, with the track setting out through red beech, rimu and kahikatea forest, and rising through mountain beech and mountain cedar (kaikawaka) to top out among subalpine herb fields.

If you want to personally discover the reason for the track's name, book a night at Sunrise Hut – if the morning dawns clear and fine, you'll be amply rewarded by the views.

ℹ Planning

WHEN TO TRAMP

Rain and strong winds often pummel the Ruahines, making summer the best time to undertake this tramp. If it is raining, or there are white-out conditions, consider giving Armstrong Saddle a miss – conditions at the saddle can be significantly more challenging than at Sunrise Hut, even though the hut is just below the saddle ridge line.

WHAT TO BRING

The Ruahine Range catches the cloud, producing five times the amount of rain as the east coast just below it – ergo, bring good wet-weather gear. It can get very cold and windy on the saddle, so pack plenty of warm clothing as well. If you're staying the night at Sunrise Hut, bring a stove and fuel as it has no cooking facilities.

MAPS

To get the full perspective on the tramp, you'll need two NZ Topo50 maps: *BK36 (Taoroa Junction)* and *BK37 (Tikokino)*.

HUTS

The tramp can be broken into two leisurely days by staying the night at Sunrise Hut ($15). This Serviced hut must be booked ahead from mid-November to the end of April.

INFORMATION

The **DOC office** (☑ 06-350 9700; www.doc. govt.nz; 28 North St; ⊙ 8am-4.30pm Mon-Fri) in Palmerston North is the primary source of information for the Ruahines. If you're coming from the north, you can also get advice and hut passes at the **DOC office** (☑ 06-834 3111; www. doc.govt.nz; 59 Marine Pde; ⊙ 9am-4.15pm Mon-Fri) in Napier.

ℹ Getting There & Away

The Sunrise Track car park is 30km from Tikokino (115km northeast of Palmerston North and 65km southwest of Napier), reached via Makaroro Rd, which is accessed off SH50. Once on Makaroro Rd, follow the signs to Ruahine Forest Park. The last few kilometres are through private farmland – be sure to close each gate as you pass through. There's a toilet and information boards at the car park. There's no public transport to the trail.

🥾 The Tramp

From the car park, cross the stile and begin along farm tracks, rising gently through farmland to enter Ruahine Forest Park in just a few minutes. About 100m on, turn left at the second junction, descending at first through a beautiful section of mossy red-beech forest to cross a wooden bridge over a stream. Just beyond the bridge, take the left fork (signed to Sunrise Hut), beginning the climb.

A series of switchbacks among tall kahikatea and rimu makes the going easy to begin, before the track contours across the slopes to a junction with the track to Waipawa Forks Hut (one hour from the car park). Continue straight ahead. Around the top of the first set of switchbacks past the junction, the forest begins to thin. For the next hour you'll climb through a gradually shrinking forest – the final layer of stunted beech, padded with moss, is particularly enchanting.

When you step out of the bushline you're immediately greeted by **Sunrise Hut** (spoiler alert: you're actually greeted first by its toilets). Sitting among tussocks at 1280m, the 20-bunk hut stares east over Hawke's Bay. The mezzanine bunks get the million-dollar views.

The track to Armstrong Saddle leaves from the right side of the hut and turns immediately right along a narrow ridge. The route simply follows this ridge north for 1km (20 to 30 minutes) to the saddle. Nearing the saddle – at about the point where the massive landslips fall away to the left – it becomes a poled route to assist when there's low visibility. From **Armstrong Saddle** (1369m), with its beautiful subalpine herb fields, there are views to Mt Ruapehu on a clear day. The saddle is named after a pilot, Hamish Armstrong, who crashed his Gypsy Moth plane here in 1935. Armstrong was never found.

Return to Sunrise Hut and retrace your steps back down the slopes to the North Block Rd car park.

Alternative End: Waipawa River

2 HOURS / 4KM

For variety you can turn down the track to Waipawa Forks Hut and return to North Block Rd along the bed of the Waipawa River. Note that you should avoid this route if there's been heavy rain or if river levels are high.

It's a steep descent to the Waipawa River from the track junction, with Waipawa Forks Hut (12 bunks) on the southern side of the river. From here it's an unmarked route along the river before climbing out to the end of North Block Rd.

TARARUA FOREST PARK

North of Wellington is a place where the wind whips along the sides of mountains and the fog creeps silently in the early morning. It's a place where gales blow through steep river gorges, snow falls on sharp, greywacke (grey sandstone) peaks and rain trickles down narrow ridges. This is Tararua Forest Park, the largest conservation park managed by DOC on the North Island.

The park is centred on the Tararua Range, which stretches 80km from the Rimutaka Saddle in the south to the Manawatu Gorge, a natural gap that separates the Tararuas from the Ruahine Range, in the north. The highest peak is Mitre (1571m), but there are many other peaks close to that height throughout the park. The ridges and spurs above the bushline are renowned for being narrow, steep and exposed.

Only 50km from Wellington, the park used to be popular largely with weekend trampers from the windy city. Today trampers from around the country are attracted to the Tararuas' broken terrain and sheer features, which present a challenge to even the most experienced hikers.

The park has an extensive network of tracks, routes and huts, most accessible from the main gateways of Otaki Forks in the west (off SH1), and Holdsworth and Waiohine Gorge on the eastern, Wairarapa side.

These tracks are not as well formed as those in most national parks, so it's easy to lose them. On the open ridge-tops there are rarely signposts or poles marking the routes, only the occasional cairn. The Mt Holdsworth-Jumbo Circuit is less demanding than most routes through the Tararuas, and is therefore undertaken by a greater number of trampers.

History

Although the range was probably too rugged for any permanent Māori settlements, the local Māori did establish several routes through it to the west coast. It was Māori guides who led JC Crawford to the top of Mt Dennan in 1863, the first recorded European ascent in the range. From the 1860s to the late 1880s, prospectors struggled over the ridges and peaks in search of gold, but little was ever found.

The Tararua Tramping Club, the first such club in NZ, was formed in 1919 by Wellington trampers keen to promote trips into the range. Independent trampers had been visiting the Tararuas since the 1880s.

When the New Zealand Forest Service was established in 1919, a move began to reserve a section of the Tararua Range, but it was not until 1952 that the government set aside the area as NZ's first forest park. It was gazetted in 1967 and now covers 1165 sq km.

Environment

The sediments that would later form the Tararua Range were laid in a deep-sea basin 200 million years ago. Earth movements along a series of faults that extended through the Upper Hutt Valley and the Wellington region then resulted in a complicated uplifted mass of folded and faulted rock. This mass was subsequently eroded by wind, rain and ice, resulting in the rugged Tararuas.

There's a good variety of plants in the park, and many species reach their southern limits here. Cover is predominantly verdant rainforest, and podocarp tawa and kamahi forest in the lowlands scattered with rimu and northern rata. Silver beech is the species along the bushline in the south, while above 1200m the forest gives way to open alpine tussock, snow grass and herb fields.

The Tararuas were one of the last known refuges of the huia, a now-extinct wattlebird, with the last official sighting recorded in 1903 on the Mt Holdsworth Track. Clearing of lowland forest habitats and predation by introduced pests have also meant the disappearance of whio, kiwi, North Island robin and kokako from the range. But there are still plenty of birds in the park – on the river flats you're likely to encounter honking paradise shelducks (look for the female with her brilliant white head) while in the forests there are riflemen, grey warblers, tomtits and whiteheads, which are all easier to hear than spot.

Mt Holdsworth–Jumbo Circuit

Duration 3 days

Distance 24km (14.9 miles)

Difficulty Moderate to demanding

Start/End Holdsworth Lodge

Gateway Masterton (p135)

Transport Private

Summary A long-time favourite of local trampers, this circuit includes nights at two scenic huts above the bushline, and a day following alpine ridges.

WARNING: WIND, FOG & STORMS

Wind, fog and rain are the trademarks of the Tararua Forest Park, with the Tararua Range exposed to westerly winds that funnel through the gap between the North and South Islands. The range is often the first thing the airstreams hit, which they do with full force, smacking against the high ridges and peaks. At times it's almost impossible to stand upright in the wind, especially with a backpack on. On average, the summits and peaks are fogbound two days out of three. Storms arrive with little warning and can dump more than 300mm of rain in a single day. Trampers must be prepared to spend an extra day in a hut if such storms blow in, because they quickly reduce visibility around the mountain tops and cause rivers to flood

This classic Tararua tramp climbs through beech forest to quickly ascend to the alpine tops of the range. Mt Holdsworth brings wraparound views, while the huts along the route also provide expansive panoramas, bringing a serene sense of removal as you look out to the lights of Masterton in the evening.

Although you can cover this tramp in two days, it's a better idea to schedule three in order to savour the alpine walking and to build in the possibility of losing a day to the bad weather which can easily force you to sit out a day in one of the alpine huts.

ℹ Planning

WHEN TO TRAMP
Attempting this tramp out of season is not recommended – the season is October through to May.

WHAT TO BRING
Given the Tararua Range's potential for wild weather, it's vital to come prepared for the worst – warm clothing for the trail and in the huts, and good-quality rain gear.

MAPS
The tramp is covered by NZTopo50 *BP33 (Featherston)* and *BP34 (Masterton)*. NewTopo's 1:55,000 *Tararua Tramps* map provides a wider overview of the Tararuas.

LODGES & HUTS
The tramp starts at **Holdsworth Lodge** (dm $25), a large, roomy lodge popular with school

Mt Holdsworth–Jumbo Circuit

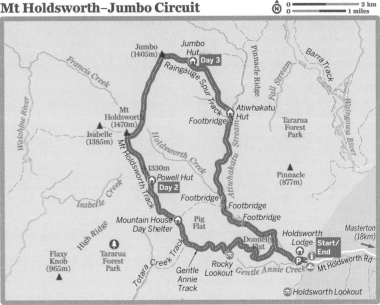

groups and tramping clubs but also available to individual trampers. You need to book in advance, which can be done online (via www. doc.govt.nz). There is a caretaker at the lodge, whose office of which serves as a visitor information centre. The extensive fields of the recreation area surrounding the lodge make for excellent camping (per person $12), and have toilets and water supply.

Powell and Jumbo Huts, the recommended stops, are both Serviced huts ($15). A third hut along the route, Atiwhakatu Hut, around one to 1½ hours' hike from Jumbo Hut, is a Standard hut ($5) with no stoves. All of the huts need to be booked online in advance from October to April. Outside of this period you can stay with hut tickets purchased from the **Masterton i-SITE** (p136), **DOC Masterton Office** (p128) or DOC centres nationwide.

INFORMATION

The **DOC Wellington Visitor Centre** (☎ 04-384 7770; www.doc.govt.nz; 18 Manners St; ☺ 9.30am-5pm Mon-Fri, 10am-3.30pm Sat) in the centre of Wellington handles bookings, passes and information for national and local parks and tracks. Closer to the park, the **DOC Masterton Office** (☎ 06-377 0700; www.doc. govt.nz; 220 South Rd, Masterton; ☺ 9am-4.30pm Mon-Fri) can provide detailed information on the Tararua Forest Park and sells hut tickets.

❶ Getting There & Away

Holdsworth Lodge is reached from SH2 by turning west onto Norfolk Rd, just south of Masterton. Norfolk Rd leads into Mt Holdsworth Rd, which ends at the recreation area, 15km from SH2. If you don't have your own vehicle, **Masterton Radio Taxis** (☎ 06-378 2555) charges around $60 for the 19km trip from Masterton.

🚶 The Tramp

Day 1: Holdsworth Lodge to Powell Hut

3–4 HOURS / 6KM / 880M ASCENT

The track departs the lodge heading west on a wide gravel path, and crossing a footbridge over Atiwhakatu Stream, which has some brisk but brilliant swimming holes. After 30 minutes you'll pass a track (left) to Holdsworth Lookout, then another junction 200m further ahead.

Follow the well-graded Gentle Annie Track southwest (left fork), climbing steadily towards Mountain House shelter. Approximately one hour from Holdsworth Lodge you reach Rocky Lookout, from where there are good views of Powell Hut and, for those with sharp eyes, the trig on Mt Holdsworth.

The track sidles around to the junction with Totara Creek Track, approximately 45 minutes from Rocky Lookout. Continue north (signposted to Pig Flat) and cross to a track leading to **Mountain House shelter**, which has historical displays and a long-drop toilet nearby.

Beyond the shelter, the well-marked track begins with a steep climb and in 45 minutes emerges from the bushline into subalpine scrub. Follow the track along the ridgeline up to **Powell Hut** (28 bunks).

Originally built in 1939, rebuilt in 1981 and then burnt to the ground in 1999, the hut was rebuilt again within a year because it is one of the most popular spots in the park to spend a night. The hut has gas stoves and excellent views of the surrounding mountains and valleys from its veranda. If the night is clear you can watch the lights of Masterton switch on after sunset.

Day 2: Powell Hut to Jumbo Hut

3½–4 HOURS / 7KM / 270M ASCENT, 260M DESCENT

The climb from Powell Hut to Mt Holdsworth has very few markers or cairns, but the trip is so popular that a track has been worn to the peak and most of the way to Jumbo Hut. Fill your water bottles before leaving Powell Hut, as there is little water along the ridge.

Heading northwest, climb steeply for 15 to 20 minutes until you reach a small **knoll** at 1330m with a battered sign on top. Looking back you'll see Powell Hut below, while in good weather you can see the trig on Mt Holdsworth above. It takes another 30 to 45 minutes of tramping along the ridge to reach the trig. From the summit of **Mt Holdsworth** (1470m) there are excellent views of Mt Hector, the main Tararua Range and the small towns along SH2.

Three ridges come together at Mt Holdsworth. The track from Powell Hut follows one ridge, while another is marked by an obvious route that heads first northwest, then west towards Mid Waiohine Hut (two hours). The track to Jumbo Hut is signposted, heading to the east. You almost have to backtrack a few steps from the trig to pick up the partially worn track that drops quickly to the ridge below.

Once on the ridge it takes 1½ to two hours to reach Jumbo Hut. The route climbs a number of knolls: the first is marked with a rock cairn near the top; the second involves working around some rock outcrops on the way up; and the third, **Jumbo** (1405m), is really a pair of knolls with several small tarns between them. As a side trip you can continue along the main ridge to Angle Knob, about 40 minutes away, for some good views.

Jumbo peak's southern knoll has a small cairn at one side, and a track running along the east-sloping ridge begins here. It's a steady 30-minute descent to Jumbo Hut. Within 20 minutes you come to a spot on the ridge where it's possible to see the hut far below. **Jumbo Hut** (20 bunks) sits in alpine terrain and has excellent views from its veranda. At night you can see the lights of Masterton, Carterton and Greytown, and if you get up early on a clear morning the sunrise is spectacular.

Given the reasonably short tramp from Powell Hut to Jumbo Hut, an enjoyable afternoon can be spent exploring the ridges to the north and viewing prominent features such as Broken Axe Pinnacles and the Three Kings.

Day 3: Jumbo Hut to Holdsworth Lodge

3–4 HOURS / 9KM / 890M DESCENT

Just south of Jumbo Hut is a benched track heading southeast. This is the beginning of the descent along **Raingauge Spur**. The track is well marked though steep and slippery, especially during wet weather. It should take about one hour to reach the valley and **Atiwhakatu Hut** (26 bunks).

The track from this hut to Holdsworth Lodge is well defined and level. Jumbo Creek and Holdsworth Creek used to pose problems in wet weather – in fact they were downright dangerous. Nowadays they are bridged, making for an all-weather track. Soon after the bridge across Holdsworth Creek, you come to a junction. The trail you can see climbing to the west (right) rises steeply to Mountain House shelter (one to 1½ hours).

Stay on the main track, which is well formed and runs along the stream, past a small gorge, to **Donnelly Flat**. This wooded area, with camping, is 1km from Holdsworth Lodge. A 15-minute loop track at the flat passes through tall stands of podocarp forest – rimu, matai and kahikatea. The walk from Donnelly Flat meets the outward route from Day 1 at the junction with Gentle Annie Track. From here it's about 15 minutes' walk to the lodge.

CAPE PALLISER

The southernmost tip of the North Island, Cape Palliser is a wild, remote and sparsely populated corner of the country. It's best known for its landmark lighthouse and the North Island's largest breeding area for seals, but it also offers a standout half-day tramp into a geological oddity that's had more than its 15 minutes of cinematic fame.

History

The Cape Palliser coast forms the fringe of the Wairarapa region. Māori settled here in the 14th century, and it was one of the earliest regions in the country to be settled by Europeans, in the 1840s. New Zealand's first sheep station was established here, south of Martinborough, not far from the Putangirua Pinnacles tramp. Farming has long been the area's lifeblood, though wine and olives have more recently come to feature among the produce. The candy-striped Cape Palliser Lighthouse was built in 1897.

In recent years the region has become something of a Hollywood star. Sir Peter Jackson filmed parts of *Lord of the Rings* trilogy (and one of his earlier movies) among the Putangirua Pinnacles, while Jackson and fellow director James Cameron have both put down roots around here.

Putangirua Pinnacles

Duration 3 hours

Distance 6.5km (4 miles)

Difficulty Easy to moderate

Start/End Putangirua Pinnacles Campsite
Gateway Wellington (p136)

Transport Private

Summary Delve into a badlands landscape of hoodoos and fast-eroding cliffs, climbing to high views of the wild Wairarapa coastline, the southernmost fringe of the North Island.

With their otherworldly appearance, the fragile and fluted cliffs and hoodoos of the Putangirua Pinnacles could easily inspire a sense of Middle-earth, which is exactly what they did for Sir Peter Jackson, who cast them as the Dimholt Road in *Lord of the Rings* (he also used them as a location for the opening sequence of his 1992 splatter-horror flick, *Braindead*).

The Pinnacles, as they're known locally, are cut into a wild section of coast near Cape Palliser. They've been formed due to the erosion of the soft earth by rain, creating a series of deep gullies. When boulders are exposed, they shed the rainwater, protecting the ground beneath from erosion and thus creating stone-capped hoodoos.

The Pinnacles present a raft of tramping options, none taking more than half a day (leaving time for a rehydrating pinot noir back in Martinborough, the centrepiece of the Wairarapa wine region, less than 45 minutes' drive away). You can walk to the Pinnacles' base along the stream bed, climb to a high lookout point along a ridge track, combine the two, or make a larger loop – as we've described – that also casts a wide eye along the entire Palliser Bay coast.

ⓘ Planning

WHEN TO TRAMP

This tramp can be undertaken at any time of year, but the stream route should be avoided after heavy rain or in high wind when rockfall is common from the loose and fragile gravel cliffs. The stream, which needs to be crossed on the low route, can also rise quickly after rain.

WHAT TO BRING

The water source at the Putangirua Pinnacles Campsite is unreliable, so bring in all the water you'll be needing. The ridge section beyond the Pinnacles is very exposed, so bring good-quality wind and rain gear.

MAPS

The tramp is covered by NZTopo50 *BQ33 (Lake Wairarapa)*.

CAMPING & COTTAGES

It's easy to do this tramp as a day outing from Martinborough or Wellington, but there's also a DOC campsite (per person $8) at the start of the trail. The camp has 50 sites strung along the bank of the Putangirua Stream. There's a water tap in the camp, but it shouldn't be relied on and all water should be treated.

A few minutes' walk from the campsite, and also on the tramp route, **Te Kopi** comprises a basic DOC cottage and cabins sleeping up to 10 people. It can only be booked for sole use ($200); bookings can be made on the DOC website (www.doc.govt.nz).

INFORMATION

The DOC Wellington Visitor Centre (p128) can help with information about the Pinnacles. The DOC Masterton Office (p128) can also provide detailed information.

ⓘ Getting There & Away

Metlink (p136) buses from Wellington can get you as close to the trail as Martinborough, 45km from the trailhead, but beyond there you'll need your own transport.

Putangirua Pinnacles

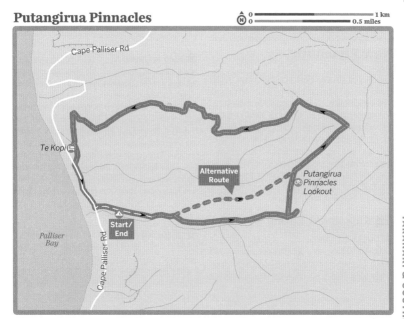

🏃 The Tramp

From the campsite, the track heads upstream along the true right (west) side of the stream, coming to a junction within 10 minutes.

The left fork heads onto the ridge track, climbing high through bush along an ever-narrowing ridge. The more interesting route (right fork) goes along the bed of the stream towards the base of the Pinnacles. If there's been heavy rain or if it's particularly windy, err on the side of caution and take the ridge track, as the stream can rise quickly and the risk of rockfall from the cliffs becomes higher in poor conditions.

If following the stream bed, you'll pass another track junction that heads steeply up to the lookout, but continue ahead to first explore beneath the **Pinnacles** (45 minutes from the campsite). Backtrack to the lookout track and make the steep climb to the **lookout**, a wooden tower, peering across to the fluted line of the Pinnacles, which appear to be part badlands and part Cappadocia.

If you've come along the high track, you'll reach a track junction around 45 minutes from the campsite. Take the right fork; the lookout tower is about 100m along this track.

To continue on the loop, head back up to the ridge track and turn right – there are a couple more glimpses of the Pinnacles before the track climbs into beech forest to meet a T-junction (10 to 15 minutes from the lookout). Take the left fork, and in another 10 minutes come to a junction with another wide track. Continue straight ahead along the ridge, where views now open out across the entire Palliser Bay – from along the coast towards Cape Palliser in the east to beyond Lake Onoke in the west.

Ignore a faint track to the right, continuing straight down on the vehicle track towards the coast. This track winds down the ridge towards a plateau of farmland.

On the plateau, as the track rounds the foot of the hills, look for a stile in the fence next to a dam to the left. Cross the stile and follow the orange markers around the patch of coastal forest to continue towards the coast; the stream will always be just on your left.

Beside the plateau edge, the now-faint path meets up with another vehicle track, which descends down the slopes to the DOC cottage **Te Kopi**. Turn left by the cottage's sheds to join Cape Palliser Rd, following it for 700m back to the campsite (around 1½ hours from the lookout).

TOWNS & FACILITIES

New Plymouth

📞 06 / POP 74,200

Dominated (in the best possible way) by Mt Taranaki and surrounded by lush farmland, New Plymouth is the only international deep-water port in this part of New Zealand. Like all port towns, the world washes in and out on the tide, leaving the locals buzzing with a global outlook. The city has a bubbling arts scene (with two superb free galleries), some fab cafes and a rootsy, outdoorsy focus. Surf beaches and Mt Taranaki (Egmont National Park) are just a short hop away.

🛏 Sleeping & Eating

★ **Ducks & Drakes**   HOSTEL, HOTEL **$**

(📞 06-758 0404; www.ducksanddrakes.co.nz; 48 Lemon St; hostel dm/s/d from $32/68/90, hotel r from $130; 🛜) The hostel here occupies a labyrinthine 1920s heritage building with bright feature walls and fancy timberwork brimming with character. Upstairs rooms are the pick: secluded, quiet and catching the morning sun. Next door is a pricier hotel wing with snazzy studios and one-bedroom suites, to which the owner escapes when his teenage daughter has friends over.

★ **One Burgess Hill**   MOTEL, APARTMENTS **$$**

(📞 06-757 2056; www.oneburgesshill.co.nz; 1 Burgess Hill Rd; d from $146, 1-/2-bedroom ste from $186/255; 🛜) Completely exceeding motel expectations, lovely One Burgess Hill is a complex of 15 stylish units on a green hillside, about 5km south of central New Plymouth (en route to Mt Taranaki). Slick interior design, nifty kitchens, wood heaters and private valley views offer a departure from the usual drive-in motels. Upstairs rooms have baths by the bed overlooking the Waiwhakaiho River.

★ **Monica's Eatery**   MODERN NZ **$$**

(📞 06-759 2038; www.monicaseatery.co.nz; cnr King & Queen Sts; breakfast $13-19, lunch $15-39, dinner $23-40; ⏰ 6.30am-late; 🛜 ✍) Beside the **Govett-Brewster Art Gallery** (📞 06-759 6060; www.govettbrewster.com; 42 Queen St; ⏰ 10am-5pm) FREE and **Len Lye Centre** (📞 06-759 6060; www.lenlyefoundation.com; 42 Queen St; ⏰ 10am-5pm; ✍) FREE, this all-day diner is homey despite its contemporary interior. Perhaps it's seeing handmade pappardelle lowered into bowls through the open kitchen, or the upbeat soundtrack that swings between Bill Withers and the Supremes. It's quite possibly the staff, who advise holding onto warm house focaccia for 'sauce mopping'. Whatever it is, we feel at home here.

★ **King & Queen**

Hotel Suites   BOUTIQUE HOTEL **$$$**

(📞 06-757 2999, 0800 574 683; www.kingandqueen.co.nz; cnr King & Queen Sts; d from $179, ste from $219-440; 🅿 @ 🛜) This regal hotel occupies the corner of King and Queen Sts (get it?) in the cool West End Precinct. Run by unerringly professional staff, each suite features antique Moroccan and Euro furnishings, lustrous black tiles, hip art, leather couches and touches of industrial chic. Guests can borrow free bikes, and there are chargeback facilities set up with some of New Plymouth's top cafes, bars and restaurants.

★ **Social Kitchen**   LATIN AMERICAN **$$**

(📞 06-757 2711; www.social-kitchen.co.nz; 40 Powderham St; share plates $30-55; ⏰ noon-late; 🛜) Inside what was once the Salvation Army Citadel, this trendy restaurant is filled with neon charm and taxidermy. Hanging meat and pigs' heads are displayed like art, but you can avoid them in the courtyard strung with colourful festoon lights. Arrive hungry and share flavour-packed Spanish sausage and Waitoa free-range chicken cooked in a Mibrasa charcoal oven.

Federal Store   CAFE **$$**

(📞 06-757 8147; www.thefederalstore.com; 440 Devon St E; mains $12-19; ⏰ 7am-4.30pm Mon-Fri, 8.30am-4.30pm Sat & Sun; ✍ 👶) Superpopular and crammed with retro furniture, Federal conjures up a 1950s corner-store vibe. Switched-on staff in dinky headscarves take your coffee requests at the counter as you queue beneath colourful bunting, keeping you buoyant until your southern-fried-chicken bagel, *shakshuka* or eggs Benedict arrives. Cakes, tarts and premade counter food are also available. Kid-friendly.

🔒 Supplies & Equipment

Macpac   SPORTS & OUTDOORS

(📞 0800 622 722, 06-758 7209; www.macpac.com.au; 28 Devon St W; ⏰ 9am-5.30pm Mon-Fri, to 5pm Sat, 10am-4pm Sun) Visit to start your Taranaki tramp prepared with camping and tramping gear galore.

Kathmandu   SPORTS & OUTDOORS

(📞 06-769 5581; www.kathmandu.com.au; 10 Gill St; ⏰ 9am-5.30pm Mon-Fri, to 5pm Sat, 10am-4pm Sun) From waterproof clothing and solid hiking shoes to sleeping bags and hiking accessories, you're probably already familiar with Kathmandu for good reason.

New World SUPERMARKET
(☑06-759 9052; www.newworld.co.nz; 78 Courtenay St; ☺7am-11pm) Self-catering supplies.

Pak 'n Save SUPERMARKET
(☑06-758 1594; www.paknsave.co.nz; 53 Leach St; ☺8am-10pm) Self-catering supplies, just east of downtown New Plymouth.

ⓘ Information

New Plymouth i-SITE (☑06-759 6060; www.taranaki.co.nz; Puke Ariki, 1 Ariki St; ☺9am-6pm Mon, Tue, Thu & Fri, to 9pm Wed, to 5pm Sat & Sun, closed public holidays) In the **Puke Ariki** (☑06-759 6060; www.pukeariki.com; 1 Ariki St; ☺9am-6pm Mon, Tue, Thu & Fri, to 9pm Wed, to 5pm Sat & Sun) building, with a fantastic interactive tourist-info database.

ⓘ Getting There & Away

New Plymouth Airport (☑0800 144 129; www.newplymouthairport.com; Airport Dr) is 11km east of the centre off SH3. **Scott's Airport Shuttle** (☑0800 373 001, 06-769 5974; www.npairportshuttle.co.nz; per person $18-28, per 2 people $22-32) operates a door-to-door shuttle to/from the airport. Airlines include:

Air New Zealand (☑06-357 3000, 0800 737 000; www.airnewzealand.co.nz) Daily direct flights to/from Auckland, Wellington and Christchurch, with onward connections.

Singapore Airlines (www.singaporeair.com) Flies between New Plymouth, Christchurch and Auckland.

Virgin Australia (www.virginaustralia.com) Flies the same routes as Air New Zealand.

Bus services run from the **Bus Centre** (cnr Egmont & Ariki Sts) in central New Plymouth. Standard fares (ie, no refund) are cheapest.

InterCity (www.intercity.co.nz) services include the following:

Destination	Fare	Time (hr)	Frequency (daily)
Auckland	from $43	6	2
Hamilton	from $33	3½-4	4
Palmerston North	from $28	4	1
Wellington	from $29	7	1
Whanganui	from $23	2½	1

Naked Bus (www.nakedbus.com) services ply similar routes and sometimes link up with other operators. Visit the website for routes and fares.

Napier

☑06 / POP 63,100

The Napier of today – a charismatic, sunny, composed city with the air of an affluent English seaside resort – is the silver lining of the dark cloud that was the deadly 1931 earthquake. Rebuilt in the popular architectural styles of the time, the city retains a unique concentration of art-deco buildings. Linger a while to discover some of regional New Zealand's best restaurants and also a few excellent wineries.

🛏 Sleeping & Eating

Napier YHA HOSTEL $
(☑06-835 7039; www.yha.co.nz; 277 Marine Pde; dm/s/d from $30/45/69; ☏) Napier's friendly YHA is housed in a lovely old timber beach-front villa with seemingly endless rooms. There's a fabulous reading nook and a sunny rear courtyard. It's the best of several hostels along Marine Pde. Bike hire $20 per day.

★**Kiwiesque** B&B $$$
(☑06-836 7216; www.kiwiesque.com; 347 SH 5, Eskdale; d $295-345; ☏) 🅿 Located in rural Eskdale, around 18km north of Napier, Kiwiesque offers accommodation right beside expansive vineyards. For independent travellers, the best options are the four suites in the property's modern woolshed-influenced building. Breakfast packed with seasonal produce is included, bathrooms are elegant, and outdoor decks offer vineyard views. Eco-aware design includes double glazing and sheep-wool insulation in the walls.

Navigate Seaside Hotel HOTEL, APARTMENT $$$
(☑06-831 0077; www.navigatenapier.co.nz; 18 Hardinge Rd, Ahuriri; d/f/2-bedroom apt from $199/255/315; ☏) Navigate yourself towards Navigate for 26 snazzy apartment-style units over three levels, with funky furnishings, nifty perforated-metal balconies and sea views from the best rooms. There's a large kids' playground across the street for the offspring. It opened in 2013, so everything is in good nick.

Cafe Ujazi CAFE $
(☑06-835 1490; www.facebook.com/ujazicafe; 28 Tennyson St; mains $10-22; ☺8am-5pm; ☏) The most bohemian of Napier's cafes, Ujazi folds back its windows and lets the alternative vibes spill out onto the pavement. It's a long-established, consistent performer offering blackboard meals and hearty counter food (vegetarian and vegan a speciality). Try

the classic *rewana* special – a big breakfast on traditional Māori bread. Oooh – homemade limeade!

⭐ **Mister D** MODERN NZ $$
(☑ 06-835 5022; www.misterd.co.nz; 47 Tennyson St; mains $25-36; ⊙ 7.30am-4pm Sun-Wed, to late Thu-Sat) This long, floorboarded room with its green-tiled bar is the pride of the Napier foodie scene. Hip and slick but not unaffordable, with quick-fire service delivering the likes of pulled pork with white polenta or roast-duck risotto. Addictive doughnuts are served with syringes full of chocolate, jam or custard (DIY injecting). Bookings essential.

⭐ **Bistronomy** MODERN NZ $$$
(☑ 06-834 4309; www.bistronomy.co.nz; 40 Hastings St; mains lunch $22-28, dinner six/nine courses $75/100; ⊙ noon-late Fri-Sun, from 5pm Wed & Thu; ☑) ✦ Bistronomy is proof that some of NZ's best food can be enjoyed outside the country's biggest cities. The finely judged seasonal tasting menus, which could include sumac-cured kingfish or chicken poached in kawakawa (a NZ forest herb), are highly recommended; they're great-value experiences you'll definitely talk about when you get back home. Lunch is slightly less formal, but equally excellent.

Supplies & Equipment

Kathmandu SPORTS & OUTDOORS
(☑ 06-835 5859; www.kathmandu.co.nz; cnr Dickens & Hastings Sts, West Point Plaza) Sells a good range of affordable tramping and outdoor gear.

Countdown SUPERMARKET $
(www.countdown.co.nz; cnr Munroe & Dickens Sts; ⊙ 7am-10pm) Centrally located supermarket.

ℹ Information

Napier i-SITE (☑ 06-834 1911; www.napiernz.com; 100 Marine Pde; ⊙ 9am-5pm, extended hours Dec-Feb; ☎) Central, helpful and right by the bay.

ℹ Getting There & Away

Hawke's Bay Airport (www.hawkesbay-airport.co.nz; SH2) is 8km north of the city.

Air New Zealand (☑ 0800 737 000; www.airnewzealand.co.nz) flies direct to/from Auckland, Wellington and Christchurch. Jetstar links Napier with Auckland, and Sounds Air has direct flights to Blenheim three times a week.

InterCity (www.intercity.co.nz) buses can be booked online or at the **i-SITE** (p134). **Naked Bus** (https://nakedbus.com) tickets are best booked online.

Both companies depart from **Clive Sq bus stop** (Clive Sq), with daily services (several daily for Hastings) to the following:

Destination	Company	Cost ($)	Time (hr)
Auckland	InterCity	50	7½
Auckland	Naked Bus	26	9
Palmerston North	InterCity	18	3
Taupo	InterCity	18	2
Taupo	Naked Bus	15	2
Wairoa	InterCity	14	2¼
Wellington	InterCity	33	5½
Wellington	Naked Bus	23	5

Palmerston North

☑ 06 / POP 80,080

Located on the banks of Manawatu River, and in the shadow of Wellington, Palmerston North can fulfil any tramper's needs before or after a walk.

🛏 Sleeping & Eating

Peppertree Hostel HOSTEL $
(☑ 06-355 4054; www.peppertreehostel.co.nz; 121 Grey St; dm/s/d/f $31/65/78/124; ☎) Inexplicably strewn with green-painted, succulent-filled boots, this endearing 100-year-old house is the best budget option in town. Mattresses are thick, the kitchen will never run out of spatulas and the piano and wood fire make things feel downright homey. Unisex bathrooms, but there is a gals-only dorm. Nine rooms and 35 beds.

Palmerston North Holiday Park HOLIDAY PARK $
(☑ 06-358 0349; www.palmerstonnorthholidaypark.co.nz; 133 Dittmer Dr; campsites/cabins from $35/50, d/f units $95/105; ☎) About 2km from the Square, off Ruha St, this shady park with daisy-speckled lawns is quiet, affordable and right beside Victoria Esplanade gardens. Trees and gardens add calm, until the kids take over the playground!

City Corporate Motor Inn MOTEL $$
(☑ 06-355 4522; www.citycorporate.co.nz; 209 Fitzherbert Ave; d $160-180, apt $240; 🅿 ❄ ☎) Not a motel person? This could be what turns you. These luxury rooms with oversized double spa baths beside the beds, roomy work stations and handsome leather and timber finishes are as good as it gets.

Home-baked goodies take it from corporate to comfort. Splurge on an apartment if you want to do your own cooking.

★**Saigon Corner** VIETNAMESE **$**
(☑06-355 4988; www.facebook.com/saigon-cornernz; 54 Princess St; mains $8.50-16; ☺11am-3pm & 5-8.30pm Tue-Sat, 11am-3pm Mon; 🥢) The pick of Palmy cheap eats, this cheerful, casual Vietnamese restaurant nails all the classics: *pho, banh mi*, rice-paper rolls, and noodle and rice dishes. Fresh and filled with locals, it's good to eat in or take away.

★**Local** CAFE **$**
(☑06-280 4821; www.cafelocal.co.nz; 240 Broadway Ave; dishes $10-15; ☺7am-3.30pm Mon-Wed, to 7pm Thu & Fri, 8am-4pm Sat; 🛜🚸) Brilliant Local specialises in build-your-own meals. For breakfast, that means eggs with additions like potato-herb hash and grilled salmon, and for lunch, wholesome bowls with your choice of protein on salad. Sharing the building with property brokers, Local scores top marks for the teal banquettes, tiled features and a roomy outdoor area. Try the curly fries.

★**Nero Restaurant** INTERNATIONAL **$$$**
(☑06-354 0312; www.nerorestaurant.co.nz; 36 Amesbury St; mains $39-44; ☺11am-3pm & 5pm-late Mon-Fri, 5pm-late Sat) Set in a refreshed 1918 Victorian with a manicured al fresco dining area, Nero is the peak of fine dining in Palmy. The chef and owner is an ambassador for Beef & Lamb New Zealand, but also serves dishes like sticky pork belly and cauliflower steak with flair. Look out for the dry-aged beef and say 'hi' to Truffles, the cat.

🛍 Supplies & Equipment

Bivouac Outdoor SPORTS & OUTDOORS
(☑06-359 2162; www.bivouac.co.nz; 99 The Square; ☺9am-5pm Mon-Fri, to 4pm Sat, 10am-4pm Sun) Outdoor gear and advice from local experts.

Pak 'n Save SUPERMARKET
(☑06-356 4043; www.paknsave.co.nz; 327 Ferguson St; ☺8am-10pm) Cheap and cheerful self-catering.

ⓘ Information

Palmerston North i-SITE (☑06-350 1922, 0800 6262 9288; www.manawatunz.co.nz; The Square; ☺9am-5.30pm Mon-Thu, to 7pm Fri & Sun, to 3pm Sat; 🛜) A superhelpful source of tourist information, now hiring out electric bikes (hourly/half day/full day $30/45/65). Love the A4 printed guides to local walks, parks, shopping and more.

ⓘ Getting There & Away

Palmerston North Airport (☑06-351 4415; www.pnairport.co.nz; Airport Dr) is 4km north of the town centre.

Air New Zealand (www.airnewzealand.co.nz) runs daily direct flights to Auckland, Christchurch and Wellington. **Jetstar** (www.jetstar.com) has flights to/from Auckland and Wellington. **Originair** (www.originair.nz) flies between Palmy and Nelson, down south.

InterCity (www.intercity.co.nz) buses operate from the **Main St bus terminus** on the east side of the Square; destinations include the following:

Destination	Cost	Time (hr)	Frequency (daily)
Auckland	from $42	9½	3
Napier	from $24	3½	3
Taupo	from $24	4	3
Wellington	from $22	2¼	9
Whanganui	from $18	1½	4

Naked Bus (www.nakedbus.com) services also depart the Main St bus terminus to most North Island hubs:

Destination	Cost	Time (hr)	Frequency (daily)
Auckland	from $28	10	2-4
Napier	from $22	2½	2-4
Taupo	from $15	4	2-3
Wellington	from $13	2½	2-4

KiwiRail Scenic Journeys (☑0800 872 467, 04-495 0775; www.kiwirailscenic.co.nz) runs long-distance trains between Wellington and Auckland, stopping at the retro-derelict **Palmerston North Train Station** (Mathews Ave), off Tremaine Ave about 2.5km north of the Square. From Palmy to Wellington, take the Northern Explorer ($69, 2½ hours) departing at 4.20pm Monday, Thursday and Saturday; or the Capital Connection ($35, two hours) departing Palmy at 6.15am Monday to Friday. To Auckland, the Northern Explorer ($179, nine hours) departs at 10am on Tuesday, Friday and Sunday. Buy tickets from KiwiRail Scenic Journeys directly, on the train and at the **i-Site** for the Capital Connection (no ticket sales at the station).

Masterton

☑06 / POP 23,400

The Wairarapa's main hub, Masterton (Whaka-oriori) is an unremarkable, unselfconscious little city getting on with the business of life. Of particular interest to trampers is the DOC-run **Pukaha Mt Bruce National Wildlife**

Centre ([☑]06-375 8004; www.pukaha.org.nz; 85379 SH2; adult/child $20/6, incl guided walk $45/25; ⊙9am-4.30pm) ⏸, 30km north, a 1000-hectare breeding ground for endangered birds.

🛏 Sleeping & Eating

Mawley Holiday Park   HOLIDAY PARK **$**
([☑]06-378 6454; www.mawleypark.co.nz; 5 Oxford St, Masterton; sites from $36, unit with/without bathroom from $100/70) ⏸ This amenable, clean camping ground is spread across the verdant banks of the Waipoua River, just north of the town centre. Units range from basic cabins (bring your own linen) to self-contained two-bedroom units.

Cornwall Park Motel   MOTEL **$$**
([☑]06-378 2939; www.cornwallparkmotel.co.nz; 119 Cornwall St, Masterton; unit from $120; 🛜⊕) Hide yourself away on the backstreets in this tidy motel. The neat brick units are warm and comfortable, set among manicured lawns centred on a large old elm tree.

★**Clareville Bakery**   CAFE **$**
([☑]06-379 5333; www.theclarevillebakery.co.nz; 3340 SH2, Clareville; mains $6-22; ⊙7.30am-4pm Mon-Sat; 👶) Located on SH2 immediately northeast of Carterton, this brilliant bakery-cafe is famous for its sourdough bread, lamb-cutlet pie, open steak sandwich and lavash-style crackers – but everything displayed on the counter is borderline irresistible. There's garden seating, a play area for the kids and regular live-music evenings.

Gladstone Inn   PUB FOOD **$$**
([☑]06-372 7866; www.gladstoneinn.co.nz; 571 Gladstone Rd, Gladstone; pizza $17-20, mains $27-32; ⊙11am-late Tue-Sun; 👶) Gladstone, 18km south of Masterton, is less a town, more a state of mind. There's very little here except a handful of vineyards and this classic old timber inn, haven to thirsty locals, bikers, Sunday drivers and lazy afternoon sippers who hog the tables in the glorious garden bar by the river. There's the odd crafty beer on tap, too.

🛍 Supplies & Equipment

Kathmandu   SPORTS & OUTDOORS
([☑]06-377 2953; www.kathmandu.co.nz; 211 Queen St; ⊙9am-5.30pm Mon-Fri, 10am-3pm Sat & Sun) Stockist of good-quality gear for the outdoors.

New World   SUPERMARKET **$**
([☑]06-370 0618; www.newworld.co.nz; cnr Queen & Bruce Sts, Masterton; ⊙7am-9pm) For self-caterers and tramping trip stock-ups.

🛈 Information

Masterton i-SITE ([☑]06-370 0900; www. wairarapanz.com; 6 Dixon St, Masterton; ⊙9.30am-4.30pm) Can sort you out with local information, including a copy of the *Wairarapa Visitor Guide,* and advice on accommodation.

🛈 Getting There & Away

Masterton is the terminus of the Wairarapa Line, receiving six **Metlink** ([☑]0800 801 700; www. metlink.org.nz) trains on weekdays (two on weekends) from Wellington ($18, 1¾ hours).

Tranzit also runs the **InterCity** (p137) service to Palmerston North ($21, two hours) five days a week (no Monday or Saturday buses but two on Friday).

Wellington

[☑]04 / POP 208.000

NZ's capital is windy, wonderfully arty and wall-to-wall with restaurants, cafes and bars. It's also green and hilly, which will be welcome news to visiting trampers, and is a major travel crossroads, being the northern port of interisland ferry services.

🛏 Sleeping & Eating

There's no shortage of good accommodation in the city centre, including at the budget end, where a few good hostels keep things keenly priced. There's plenty of great food, too – head to Cuba St and Courtenay Place for the highest density.

★**Dwellington**   HOSTEL **$**
([☑]04-550 9373; www.thedwellington.co.nz; 8 Halswell St, Thorndon; dm/r from $29/85; 🅿🛜) Two conjoined heritage houses have been reinvented to create this terrific modern hostel, sandwiched between the US and Chinese embassies. There are no en suites, but the rooms are clean, bright and comfortable, and there's free wi-fi and breakfast. The location is handy for the ferries, trains and inter-city buses, but a fair hike from the after-dark fun around Cuba St.

Gilmer Apartment Hotel   HOTEL **$$**
([☑]04-978 1400; www.10gilmer.co.nz; 10 Gilmer Tce; apt from $118; 🅿🛜) There's a hip, artsy vibe to this 62-unit inner-city apartment hotel. Sizes range from studios to two-bedroom apartments, and they all have their own kitchens and laundries. The nonrefundable advance-purchase rates are a steal for this part of town.

★ QT Museum Wellington
HOTEL $$$

(☑ 04-802 8900; www.qtwellington.com; 90 Cable St; r/apt from $215/296; ❊ 🌐 ❄) The hippopotamus themed decor says a lot about the quirkiness of this art-filled hotel. In the hotel wing, black lifts open on to darkened corridors leading to flamboyantly decorated rooms. The apartment wing is marginally more restrained but equally luxurious, and units have kitchenettes and laundry facilities.

★ Ohtel
BOUTIQUE HOTEL $$$

(☑ 04-803 0600; www.ohtel.nz; 66 Oriental Pde, Oriental Bay; r from $229; ❊ 🌐) 🅿 Ever feel like you've walked into a design magazine? This bijou hotel has 10 individually decorated rooms with immersive NZ scenes plastered above the bath-tubs and original, mid-century, Scandi-style furniture and ceramics, avidly collected by the architect-owner. The best rooms have decks and harbour views.

★ Loretta
CAFE $$

(☑ 04-384 2213; www.loretta.net.nz; 181 Cuba St; mains $13-28; ⊙ 9am-10pm Tue-Sun; 🖊) From breakfast through lunch and into dinner, Loretta has won leagues of fans with her classy, well-proportioned offerings served in bright surrounds. Try splitting a pizza and grain-filled salad between two. Bookings for lunch only.

Fidel's
CAFE $$

(☑ 04-801 6868; www.fidelscafe.com; 234 Cuba St; mains brunch $9-22, dinner $13-26; ⊙ 8am-10pm; 🖊) A Cuba St institution for caffeine-craving alternative types, Fidel's cranks out eggs any which way, pizza and super salads from its itsy kitchen, along with Welly's best milkshakes. Revolutionary memorabilia adorns the walls of the low-lit interior, and there's a small outdoor area and a street-facing booth for takeaway coffees.

★ Whitebait
SEAFOOD $$$

(☑ 04-385 8555; www.white-bait.nz; 1 Clyde Quay Wharf; mains $38; ⊙ 5.30pm-late year-round, plus noon-3pm Wed-Fri Nov-Mar) Neutral colours and gauzy screens set an upmarket tone for this top-rated seafood restaurant. All the fish is sustainably sourced and deftly prepared, with a scattering of quality non-fishy options. Early diners (before 6.30pm) can take advantage of a good-value set 'bistro' menu ($55 for an oyster, entree, main and petit four).

🔒 Supplies & Equipment

Bivouac Outdoor
SPORTS & OUTDOORS

(☑ 04-473 2587; www.bivouac.co.nz; 39 Mercer St; ⊙ 9am-5.30pm) The best of the outdoor shops around Wellington, staffed by people who know because they go.

New World
SUPERMARKET

(☑ 04-384 8054; www.newworld.co.nz; 279 Wakefield St; ⊙ 7am-11pm) Large downtown supermarket.

ℹ️ Information

Wellington i-SITE (☑ 04-802 4860; www.wellingtonnz.com; 111 Wakefield St; ⊙ 8.30am-5pm; 🌐) After an earthquake chased them out of their regular digs, the i-SITE has taken over the Michael Fowler Centre's old booking office. It looks like they'll be here for the foreseeable future, but check their website for the latest. Staff book almost everything here, and cheerfully distribute Wellington's *Official Visitor Guide*, along with other maps and helpful pamphlets.

ℹ️ Getting There & Away

Wellington Airport (WLG; ☑ 04-385 5100; www.wellingtonairport.co.nz; Stewart Duff Dr, Rongotai), 6km southeast of the city, is an international gateway to NZ and has domestic flights to destinations around the country.

Wellington is a major terminus for North Island bus serves.

InterCity (☑ 04-385 0520; www.intercity.co.nz) coaches depart from platform 9 at Wellington Railway Station. Destinations include Auckland (from $28, 11¼ hours, three daily), Rotorua (from $26, 7½ hours, three daily), Taupo (from $26, six hours, four daily), Napier (from $19, 5¼ hours, two daily) and Palmerston North (from $15, 2¼ hours, six daily).

Three days a week the **Northern Explorer** (www.greatjourneysofnz.co.nz) train heads to/from Palmerston North (from $59, two hours), National Park (from $79, 5¼ hours) and Auckland (from $139, 11 hours).

The daily Capital Connection train heads from Palmerston North ($35, two hours) to Wellington on weekday mornings, returning in the evening.

There are two ferry options between Wellington and Picton:

Bluebridge Ferries (☑ 04-471 6188; www.bluebridge.co.nz; 50 Waterloo Quay; adult/child/car/campervan/motorbike from $53/27/120/155/51; 🌐) Up to four sailings between Wellington and Picton daily (3½ hours).

Interislander (☑ 04-498 3302; www.interislander.co.nz; Aotea Quay; adult/child/car/campervan/motorbike from $56/28/149/181/84) Up to five sailings between Wellington and Picton daily; crossings take 3¼ to 3½ hours. A free shuttle bus heads from platform 9 at Wellington Railway Station to Aotea Quay, 50 minutes before every daytime sailing and returns 20 minutes after every arrival.

Queen Charlotte & Marlborough

Best Swimming

➜ Meretoto/Ship Cove
(p143)

➜ Mistletoe Bay (p146)

➜ Anakiwa (p146)

➜ Pelorus Bridge Scenic
Reserve (p149)

Best Views

➜ Eatwells Lookout (p145)

➜ Onahau Lookout (p146)

➜ Totara Saddle (p150)

➜ Dun Mountain (p150)

➜ Skull Peak (p153)

Why Go?

The Marlborough Sounds might be most typically a Baccha-nalian playground of water fun and wineries – NZ's larg-est wine region is here – but it's also home to one of the country's most famous tramps: the Queen Charlotte Track. Shared between trampers and mountain bikers, the track threads through the area's convoluted maze of waterways, revealing beaches, bays and water views.

There are more great water views in Kaikoura, a town shaken by a major earthquake in 2016, but determinedly recovering. Marine wildlife watching is the backbone of Kai-koura's tourism, and even trampers on the Kaikoura Coast Track might spot dolphins and basking seals – and the bur-ied remains of an 8000-year-old forest – as they walk across the long beach at the start of the track.

Inland, the less-known and less-trodden Mt Richmond Forest Park offers plenty of solitude and rivers that have drawn filmmakers. The park's signature tramp, the Pelorus Track, features deep-green river pools and rare lowland for-est.

When to Go

The forecast is good: the Marlborough region soaks up some of New Zealand's sunniest weather. January and February are the warmest months, with daytime temperatures aver-aging 22°C, but even in the middle of winter the daily aver-age is a relatively balmy 12°C.

These conditions make the tracks around the Marlbor-ough Sounds and Kaikoura year-round tramping options. If you're around the Sounds from Christmas to mid-February, however, be prepared to jostle with flocks of Kiwi holiday-makers on their summer holidays.

Rain is more limiting in the Mt Richmond Forest Park, which sees plenty of the wet stuff. The Pelorus Track here is best tramped from October to April.

Background Reading

In high summer you might easily think the Marlborough Sounds are very well populated, but for the most part the shores of these waterways are incredibly sleepy. And so it has always been. Such isolation, particularly in the outer reaches, breeds singular folk with strange stories to tell, such as those collected in books by Don Grady. Another local yarn-spinner is Heather Heberley, storyteller and bi-ographer, and kin to a prominent whaling family. Notable books in the same genre include *Tales of Kenepuru* (Helen Godsiff), *The Lighthouse Keeper's Wife* (Jeanette Aplin) and *Angelina* (Gerald Hindmarsh), the remarkable tale of a young Italian immigrant who finds herself living on remote D'Urville Island in the early part of the 20th century.

DON'T MISS: WILDLIFE WATCHING

Despite being well and truly shaken by an earthquake in November 2016, the Pacific coast town of Kaikoura re-mains a terrific spot for marine wildlife viewing. Whales, dolphins, NZ fur seals, penguins, shearwaters, petrels and wandering albatross are just some of the interesting creatures that stop in or call this place home.

A good place to get to grips with this lively, salty town is Point Kean, where seals laze around on a craggy reef – and sometimes in the car park. From there you can pick up the three- to four-hour Kaikoura Peninsula Walkway, along which you might see various soaring seabirds.

For a fully immersive experience, consider a swim with seals or dolphins – tours run from the town. The ultimate Kaikoura experience, however, is to go on a whale-watching boat trip with Whale Watch Kaikoura (0800 655 121, 03-319 6767; www.whalewatch.co.nz; Rail-way Station; 3½hr tours adult/child $150/60), on which you can get up close to a range of whales, including sperm, humpback and the largest of all creatures, the blue whale.

Visitor Information Centres

➡ Picton i-SITE (p154)

➡ DOC Nelson Visitor Centre (p185; inside Nelson i-SITE)

➡ Kaikoura i-SITE (p155)

GATEWAY TOWNS

➡ Picton (p154)

➡ Nelson (p184)

➡ Kaikoura (p155)

➡ Christchurch (p214)

Fast Facts

➡ Queen Charlotte Sound is a classic example of a drowned valley, caused by the tilting of the land 15 to 20 million years ago.

➡ Marlborough is NZ's vinous colossus, producing around three-quarters of the country's wine.

➡ The earthquake that shook Kaikoura in November 2016 was 7.8 in magnitude; the epicentre was around 60km from the town.

Top Tip

The Queen Charlotte and Kaikoura Coast Tracks both offer a great opportunity to undertake an overnight tramp without the burden of a heavy pack. Take ad-vantage of water taxis that will ferry your bags from lodge to lodge, or camp to camp, on the Queen Char-lotte. Luggage transfers are included in the fee on the Kaikoura Coast Track.

Resources

➡ https://marlboroughnz.com

➡ www.qctrack.co.nz

➡ www.kaikoura.co.nz

➡ http://kaikouratrack.co.nz

QUEEN CHARLOTTE & MARLBOROUGH

Queen Charlotte & Marlborough

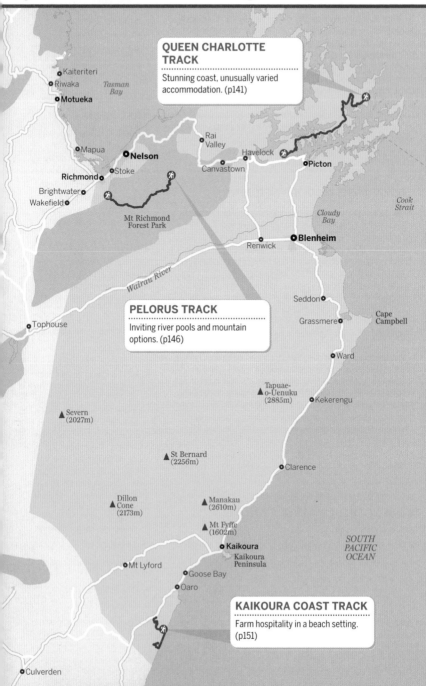

QUEEN CHARLOTTE TRACK

Stunning coast, unusually varied accommodation. (p141)

PELORUS TRACK

Inviting river pools and mountain options. (p146)

KAIKOURA COAST TRACK

Farm hospitality in a beach setting. (p151)

QUEEN CHARLOTTE & MARLBOROUGH TRAMPS

History

Māori knew the Marlborough area as Te TauIhu o Te Waka a Maui ('The Prow of Maui's Canoe'). The region's many archaeological sites have revealed that *pā* (fortified villages) and the sites surrounding them were not permanently occupied, and that the Māori were highly mobile, moving with the seasons to access different resources.

The first European to visit the Marlborough region was Abel Tasman, who spent five days sheltering off the east coast of D'Urville Island in 1642, but never landed. It was to be more than a century before the next European, James Cook, turned up, in January 1770. Cook stayed 23 days and made four more visits over the next seven years to Ship Cove and the stretch of water he named Queen Charlotte Sound. In 1827 the French navigator Jules Dumont d'Urville discovered the narrow strait now known as French Pass, and his officers named the island to the north in his honour. In the same year a whaling station was established at Te Awaiti in Tory Channel, which brought about the first permanent European settlement in the district.

In June 1840 Governor Hobson's envoy, Major Bunbury, arrived in the Marlborough Sounds on the HMS *Herald* to gather Māori signatures for the Treaty of Waitangi. It was on 17 June, on the Sounds' Horahora Kakahu Island, that Bunbury proclaimed British sovereignty over the South Island.

Environment

The Marlborough region is diverse. Great swaths of its plains have been given over to agriculture, including the growing of grapes for the wines for which it's renowned. It is also home to the fascinating Molesworth Station, NZ's largest farm, managed by DOC in line with its notable ecological values.

The east coast around Kaikoura is famous for wildlife. Indeed, there are few places in the world with so much visible marine wildlife: whales, dolphins, NZ fur seals, penguins, shearwaters, petrels and wandering albatross all stop by or call this area home. Marine animals are abundant here due to ocean-current and continental-shelf conditions: the seabed gradually slopes away from the land before plunging to more than 800m where the southerly current hits the continental shelf. This creates an upwelling, bringing nutrients up from the ocean floor into the feeding zone.

The Marlborough Sounds are a mixed bag of habitats, varying from farmland to commercial forestry, to regenerating native forest and some forest that has remained more or less undisturbed. The Queen Charlotte Track offers opportunities to experience this great diversity. The area through which the track passes is distinctly divided into three recognisable forest types, with coastal broadleaved forest at Ship Cove, regenerating forest from Kenepuru to Torea Saddles, and mature beech forest between Mistletoe Bay and Anakiwa.

Bird life is prolific. The birds of the forest include tui, bellbird, tomtit and silvereye. In summer you'll hear long-tailed and shining cuckoos, and at night, moreporks and weka. Waders are prominent in tidal estuaries.

Queen Charlotte Track

Duration 4 days

Distance 71km (44.1 miles)

Difficulty Moderate

Start Meretoto/Ship Cove

End Anakiwa

Gateway Picton (p154)

Transport Boat, shuttle bus

Summary Tramp around bays and along ridges that separate Queen Charlotte and Kenepuru Sounds, combining beautiful coastal scenery with accommodation in interesting lodges, hostels and resorts.

The hugely popular, meandering Queen Charlotte Track offers gorgeous coastal scenery on its way from historic Meretoto/Ship Cove to Anakiwa, passing through a mixture of privately owned land and DOC reserves. The coastal forest is lush, and from the ridges there are regular views into either Queen Charlotte or Kenepuru Sounds.

Queen Charlotte is a well-defined track, suitable for people of most fitness levels. It can be completed in three to five days, and can be walked in either direction, though Meretoto/Ship Cove is the usual (and recommended) starting point. This is mainly because it's easier to arrange a boat from Picton to Meretoto/Ship Cove than the reverse. It can also be walked in sections by hopping aboard numerous boat services. A good two-day tramp is from Meretoto/Ship Cove to Punga Cove (27km), while recommended day walks include the sections from Mistletoe Bay to Anakiwa (12.5km), or Meretoto/Ship Cove to Furneaux Lodge (15km).

Queen Charlotte Track

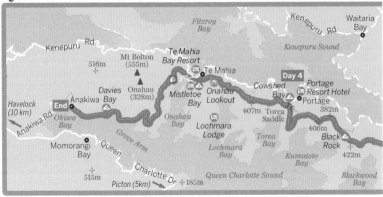

You can also turn the tramp into a multisport outing by combining sections of hiking with kayaking or mountain biking. In 2013 the track was opened to cyclists, though they're forbidden from riding the section between Meretoto/Ship Cove and Kenepuru Saddle from 1 December to the end of February.

Six DOC camping grounds are dotted along the route, while other accommodation ranges from old-fashioned home-stays to luxury waterfront lodges. This is one of the appeals of the track – the chance to spend the day tramping, then enjoy a hot shower and a cold beer at the end of it. Boat operators will also happily transport your pack along the track for you as a packhorse-type service. At first it seems decadent...then it just seems welcome.

The district council, DOC and private landowners manage the track as a partnership. The private landowners are members of the Queen Charlotte Track Land Cooperative (www.qctlc.com). They require each track user to purchase and display a pass for the private-land sections between Kenepuru Saddle and Bottle Bay (a one-day pass costs $10, while the $18 pass covers you for up to five consecutive days). Passes can be purchased from various accommodation providers and boat operators near the track, and from the Picton or Blenheim i-SITEs.

ⓘ Planning

WHEN TO TRAMP

The Queen Charlotte Track can be hiked year-round. The warmest weather coincides with the NZ school holidays in January, which means the best times to tramp are just outside of this: November, December and February through April.

WHAT TO BRING

There's little or no shade along some stretches of the track, so bring a wide-brimmed hat, potent sunscreen and a large-capacity water bottle. The sweet Sounds' forest is a hot spot for wasps, so bring antihistamines if you're allergic to stings.

MAPS & BROCHURES

The track is covered by NZTopo50 *BQ28 (Havelock), BQ29 (Waikawa)* and *BP29 (Endeavour Inlet)*. NewTopo's 1:40,000 *Queen Charlotte Track* covers the entire track in sufficient detail in just one map. Its 1:130,000 *Marlborough Sounds* map may even prove sufficient and is useful for planning. DOC's *Queen Charlotte Track* brochure is comprehensive, and includes details of transport operators and all accommodation options along the track. It can be downloaded from DOC's website (www.doc.govt.nz).

LODGES & CAMPING

There are no DOC huts along the Queen Charlotte Track, but there are six DOC campsites, many of them in spectacular settings: **Schoolhouse Bay** (www.doc.govt.nz; adult/child $6/3), **Bay of Many Coves** (www.doc.govt.nz; adult/child $6/3), **Black Rock** (www.doc.govt.nz; adult/child $6/3) and **Davies Bay** (www.doc.govt.nz; adult/child $6/3) are Backcountry campsites, **Camp Bay** (www.doc.govt.nz; adult/child $6/3) is a Standard campsite and **Cowshed Bay** (www.doc.govt.nz; adult/child $13/6.50) is a Scenic campsite. There are also a couple of private camping grounds, along with a variety of resorts, lodges, hostels and guesthouses.

Unless you're camping, it pays to book your track accommodation well in advance, especially in summer.

INFORMATION

Located 200m from the ferry terminal, **Picton i-SITE** (p154) is a one-stop shop for

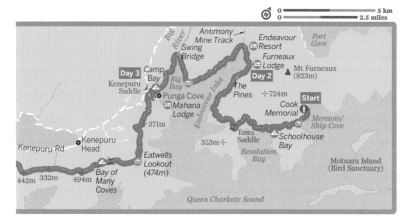

accommodation and transport bookings, maps, hut and campsite tickets and the Queen Charlotte Track Pass.

Picton's **DOC Sounds District Office** is largely a field office and offers only hut and camp tickets and local tramping information.

ℹ Getting There & Away

The only way to reach the start of the track at Meretoto/Ship Cove is by a 45-minute boat trip. Numerous operators ply this route, including **Arrow Water Taxis** (☏ 03-573 8229, 027 444 4689; www.arrowwatertaxis.co.nz; Town Wharf, Picton), **Beachcomber Cruises** (☏ 03-573 6175, 0800 624 526; www.beachcombercruises.co.nz; Town Wharf, Picton; mail runs $101, cruises from $85, track round trips $103) and **Cougar Line** (☏ 03-573 7925, 0800 504 090; www.cougarline.co.nz; Town Wharf, Picton; track round trips $105, cruises from $85). They can also drop you at various other spots along the track, and forward your luggage where possible. A track return trip with luggage transfers along the route will cost around $100. You'll find operators clustered at Picton's pleasant town wharf.

🥾 The Tramp

Day 1: Meretoto/Ship Cove to Furneaux Lodge

4–5 HOURS / 15KM

James Cook anchored at Meretoto/Ship Cove five times between 1770 and 1777, as commemorated by the memorial and interpretation on the grassed picnic area. If time allows, while away an hour or two at this beautiful spot where one of the first meetings of Māori and Europeans took place.

The track climbs quite steeply at first, through podocarp and broadleaved forest of kahikatea, rimu and kohekohe with an understorey of ferns and pigeonwood, and then into beech forest. After about an hour, you will reach the saddle at the top of the ridge where there's a lookout over bird-filled Motuara Island (www.doc.govt.nz; Queen Charlotte Sound) and outer Queen Charlotte Sound, as well as sweeping views down to Resolution Bay.

The track drops steeply to the bay and then sidles the hill until it comes to a signposted junction. The track to the Schoolhouse Bay Campsite is down the left fork, about 10 minutes along the coast. No fires are permitted at the campsite. Continue southwest (right fork), reaching Resolution Bay, two hours from Ship Cove.

The track climbs above Resolution Bay, and in 1½ hours reaches Tawa Saddle between the bay and Endeavour Inlet. There are toilets and benches here. A stop is obligatory, or at least that's what the cheeky weka seem to think as they inevitably pop out of the bush to see what's for lunch. Resist their scampering antics and admire the view.

There are plenty of views of Endeavour Inlet on the descent, before you bottom out and pass through a cluster of holiday homes and boat sheds known as the Pines. From here the track stays in the forest until it arrives at Furneaux Lodge, reached 25 minutes from the Pines, or 1½ hours from the saddle.

The lodge is a Sounds' stalwart, the highlights of which are the historic lodge building and epic lawns throughout the resort. This place welcomes pit-stopping trampers for coffee, beer, lunch etc, but there's also adequate accommodation to suit most budgets.

Day 2: Furneaux Lodge to Camp Bay

4 HOURS / 12KM

The track wanders through a regenerating forest and then, in 1km, emerges into an open area and passes **Endeavour Resort** (☑03-579 8381; www.endeavourresort.co.nz; Endeavour Inlet, Queen Charlotte Sound; dm $45, cabins & units $98-145), a retro board-and-batten-bach-style complex. It's a real Kiwi classic, with a communal building and basic units dotted throughout its hillside gardens.

About 10 minutes past the resort a swing bridge crosses a stream that empties into the inlet. On the other side is a signposted junction. To the north (right) is the **Antimony Mine Track**, a two-hour return walk to the narrow and dark remains of abandoned antimony mines. The Queen Charlotte Track continues south (left fork) as a grassy corridor that hugs the western side of the inlet.

The track soon climbs away from the shoreline, and for the next 8km passes through regenerating bush as it skirts the western slopes above Endeavour Inlet. The walking is easy, with only gentle climbs and descents.

Within 1½ hours of passing Endeavour Resort, the track rounds the ridge separating Endeavour Inlet from Big Bay and you arrive at a **view point** into Big Bay, the halfway point between Furneaux Lodge and Camp Bay. The track swings northwest and in 30 minutes you cross Big River on a swing bridge. **Camp Bay** is an hour away, and is reached after a bit of climbing. This section of the trail can be muddy after rain. Eventually you pass a signposted junction to Kenepuru Saddle. Turn left and follow a lower track, which breaks out of the bush at the **Camp Bay Campsite**.

It's about five minutes to **Punga Cove Resort** (☑03-579 8561; www.pungacove.co.nz; Endeavour Inlet; units $320-485; @ 🖥 🛜 🛏), a rustic but charming resort with a variety of accommodation, including basic dorm rooms. The views easily atone for any rough edges, as do ample facilities (including a pool and spa, and kayak and bike hire), plus a restaurant and boatshed bar-cafe serving decent local beers and pizza.

Around 10 minutes further along the bay is **Mahana Lodge** (☑03-579 8373; www.mahanalodge.co.nz; Camp Bay, Endeavour Inlet; d $250; ⊘closed Jun-Aug) 🍃. This idyllic waterside property has a purpose-built lodge with en suite doubles. Ecofriendly initiatives include bush regeneration, pest trapping and an organic vegie garden, and feel-good factors abound: free kayaks, home baking and a blooming conservatory where prearranged evening meals are served.

MOUNTAIN BIKING THE QUEEN CHARLOTTE TRACK

The Queen Charlotte Track is a dual-use trail, open to both trampers and mountain bikers. It's become one of the most popular overnight mountain-bike trips in New Zealand, and is one of the 22 trails in Nga Haerenga/New Zealand Cycle Trail (www.nzcycletrail.com).

Although the track features some good hills and a few other hazards, it's an achievable ride for a fit, competent cyclist. Bike rental is readily available in Picton, and most water taxis will transport the bike to the track for you. A way to really mix things up is with a three-day multisport Ultimate Sounds Adventure trip (from $820) offered by the **Marlborough Sounds Adventure Company** (☑03-573 6078, 0800 283 283; www.marlboroughsounds. co.nz; Town Wharf; half-/5-day guided packages $95/2420, kayak hire per half day from $40). It involves tramping from Meretoto/Ship Cove to Furneaux Lodge, a day of kayaking in Kenepuru Sound from the Portage Resort Hotel, then mountain biking to Anakiwa from Portage.

To keep both walkers and cyclists happy, an easy-to-follow code of conduct has been developed:

➡ Mountain bikers are allowed on the Kenepuru Saddle to Anakiwa section any time of the year, but can only cycle the section from Meretoto/Ship Cove to Kenepuru Saddle from March to November.

➡ Mountain bikers should give way to trampers, who have the right of way at all times.

➡ Cyclists need to avoid excessive braking as it can damage the track surface, especially after rain.

➡ Cyclists need to control their speed and not surprise trampers from behind; use a bell or give a yell.

➡ Trampers need to respect the bikers' right to be there, and share the track with them.

Day 3: Camp Bay to Portage

8 HOURS / 23KM

This is a tough day's walk, kicking off with a steep climb up to Akerbloms Rd, where signs will command you continue onward and upward. You'll have a good half-hour warm-up under your belt when you reach **Kenepuru Saddle**, at the intersection of Akerbloms and Titirangi Rds. Follow the signpost directing you south to the Bay of Many Coves.

The track sidles the ridge, and at first you're treated to views of Deep Bay to the east, but most of the time you're gazing down at the head of Kenepuru Sound to the west. Constant climbing and descending is rewarded with ever-changing panoramas of the inlets and sounds on both sides.

Two hours from the saddle you hit the longest and steepest climb of the day, which tops out at a signposted side track to **Eatwells Lookout**. This short track climbs steadily to 474m, one of the highest points along the Queen Charlotte Track. The climb is worth it. From the lookout you can see both Queen Charlotte and Kenepuru Sounds, while 1203m Mt Stokes, the highest mountain in the Marlborough Sounds, is to the north.

From the junction you begin a long descent that bottoms out at Bay of Many Coves Saddle, from where it's just another 15-minute climb to the **Bay of Many Coves Campsite**. Great views, a shelter, water and toilets make this a nice spot for morning tea or lunch. It's not the most sheltered spot for pitching a tent if the wind happens to be blowing.

From the shelter there's a gentle 40-minute climb to a high point, from where the track continues relatively level for an hour or so before some more uphill action is required. Around 1½ hours from the Bay of Many Coves Campsite, the track skirts the south side of the ridge, and for almost 1km you enjoy a continuous view of Blackwood Bay. The track then dips into the bush and emerges to more great views on the north side. Less than 30 minutes from reaching Black Rock you make a long descent, and then an equally long climb, until you top out at the **Black Rock Campsite**, which is a six-hour walk from Camp Bay and two hours from Portage. Situated on the south side of the ridge, the campsite shelter affords panoramic views, including a glimpse of Picton across Queen Charlotte Sound.

From Black Rock the track climbs gently before levelling out, providing great views for the next 30 minutes. You leave the crest of the ridge and descend into beech forest along the south side for the next hour, with the occasional glimpse of Queen Charlotte Sound. For the most part, this last stretch is a gentle and easy descent at the end of what will have been a long day.

Almost two hours from Black Rock you pop out at a war memorial on **Torea Saddle**. The road here crosses the same route used by Māori to haul their *waka* (canoes) from Queen Charlotte to Kenepuru Sound, thus saving a considerable sea journey. To the south, Torea Rd leads to a jetty on Torea Bay, where you can catch a water taxi to Picton.

Follow Torea Rd downhill to reach **Portage**, around 15 minutes away. This is where your pack will be if it is being transported for you. You can reach nearby **Cowshed Bay Campsite** by this route, too, or take the direct track as signposted (if you're carrying your own gear). It can be busy in summer here.

Portage is home to the renovated 1990s-era **Portage Resort Hotel** (☑ 03-573 4309; www.portage.co.nz; Kenepuru Rd, Portage; d $225-330; 🛜). Most rooms and suites have balconies – enjoying great views and extra comfort are the Kowhai Lodge suites – and the hotel's bar and two restaurants are all open to outside guests. A two-minute walk away is **Treetops** (☑ 03-573 4404; www.qctrack.co.nz; Kenepuru Rd, Portage; s with/without linen $50/45), a homely guesthouse framed by native bush. There is a fully equipped kitchen and rates include bag pick-up if needed.

Day 4: Portage to Anakiwa

7–8 HOURS / 21KM

Return to Torea Saddle and head west on the track. This section follows the ridge proper, and involves the ascent of two features that are each more than 400m in height. Within 1½ hours of leaving Torea Saddle you reach the fine **view point** at the top of a 407m knoll. A long descent follows before the track bottoms out in a pasture on private land. You continue on an old bridle trail that gently climbs to a view of Lochmara Bay, and then passes a side trail to **Lochmara Lodge** (☑ 03-573 4554, 0800 562 462; www.lochmaralodge.co.nz; Lochmara Bay; units $99-300; 🛜) 🖉 . Situated in lush surroundings, this arty, eco-retreat has en suite doubles, units and chalets, a fully licensed cafe and restaurant, plus a bathhouse where you can have those muscle knots kneaded away with a massage or spa.

You now begin the steady climb towards a 417m knoll, the highest point of the day. The track skirts its northern flank, begins descending and then comes to the Onahau Lookout (p146) track junction. The descent now steepens until you arrive at the junction with James Vogel Track. This is a challenging 20-minute descent to idyllic **Mistletoe Bay** (☑ 03-573 4048; www.mistletoebay.co.nz; Onahau Bay; campsites adult/child $16/10, dm/d $40/80, linen $7.50; ☏) ∥. Surrounded by bushy hills, this sweet spot has attractive camping, simple accommodation and communal facilities, and a jetty just perfect for leaping off. (For an easier descent into Mistletoe Bay, continue on the Queen Charlotte Track and follow the road down to the bay.) It's a 9km, four-hour walk from Torea Saddle to Mistletoe Bay, making the bay ideal for a lunch break or lazy afternoon.

Just beyond the junction with James Vogel Track, the Queen Charlotte Track arrives at Onahau Rd and Te Mahia Saddle, which heads south to provide vehicle access to Mistletoe Bay, and north to reach **Te Mahia Bay Resort** (☑ 03-573 4089; www.temahia.co.nz; 63 Te Mahia Rd; d $160-258; ☏). This pleasant, low-key resort has a range of delightful rooms with views. The on-site shop has precooked meals, pizza, cakes, coffee and camping supplies (wine!), plus there's kayak hire and massage.

Turn down Onahau Rd towards Mistletoe Bay for 500m, where you will see the sign back on to the Queen Charlotte Track. Past the road you follow old bridle paths above Onahau Bay, passing through regenerating forest and skirting grazing land for about 1½ hours before a long, gentle descent through beech forest above Bottle Bay. There are wonderful views on this section, with Queen Charlotte Sound visible to the Grove Arm.

From Bottle Bay there are views to the water, which sparkles through an understorey of ferns, pittosporums, five-finger, broadleaved rangiora and tawa. About 2½ to three hours from Mistletoe Bay, you reach the spacious camping area at **Davies Bay**.

The last hour of this day is one of the walk's finest parts. The track passes through **Iwituaroa Reserve** and its splendid stands of beech, before emerging at the **Anakiwa** car park where there is a shelter, toilets, and an ice-cream and coffee caravan if you time it right. The Outward Bound school has a jetty here where boat operators will pick you up for the trip back to Picton. The jetty's also a good launch pad for a refreshing dip after a sticky day's walking.

Anakiwa is a soothing spot to rest for the night if you want to stick around at the end of the tramp. It has a number of accommodation options, including **Anakiwa 401** (☑ 03-574 1388; www.anakiwa401.co.nz; 401 Anakiwa Rd; s/q $75/200, d $100-120; ☏) inside a former schoolhouse.

Side Trip: Onahau Lookout
1 HOUR / 150M ASCENT

The Onahau Lookout track is three hours from Torea Saddle. Follow the left fork as it climbs to the lookout, located between Lochmara and Onahau Bays. This is the best view point of the entire trip and a rewarding moment as you look back at the ridge you've traversed all the way from Camp Bay.

Pelorus Track

Duration 3 days

Distance 36km (22.4 miles)

Difficulty Moderate

Start Maungatapu Rd

End Hacket picnic area

Gateway Nelson (p184)

Transport Shuttle bus

Summary This track offers a remote forest experience up the Pelorus Valley at the edge of bustling Nelson. The Pelorus River is noted for its deep green pools, which are the delight of both trout and footsore trampers.

Often overlooked by trampers rushing off to Abel Tasman National Park, Mt Richmond Forest Park is right on the doorstep of Havelock, Picton, Blenheim and Nelson. The Richmond Range forms the backbone of the 1660-sq-km park, which covers most of the steep, bush-clad mountains between Blenheim and Nelson, reaching north to the Tasman Sea near Cape Soucis.

There are more than 250km of cut and marked tracks in the park, with about 30 huts scattered along them. The tracks range from challenging alpine routes to easy overnight walks suitable for families.

One of the most popular tramps is the Pelorus Track. The Pelorus is renowned for its large trout, which often use the river's deep pools as their hideaways. Trampers will find these pools a delight on hot days on the trail, though accessing them often involves a scurry off the track.

Officially the western end of the Pelorus Track is the Hacket picnic area, but it is difficult – although not impossible – to arrange transport from there to Nelson. For this reason, an alternative route into Nelson, the

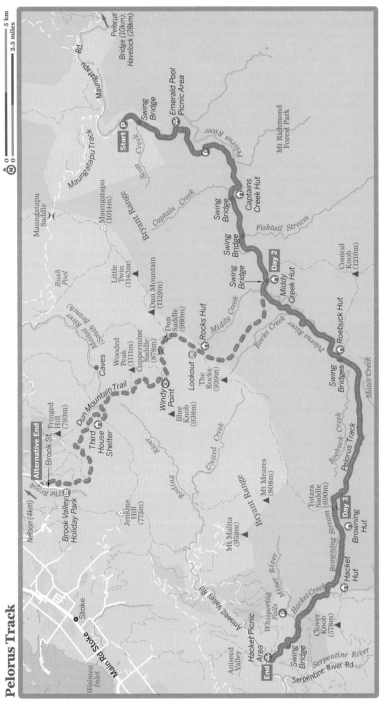

Pelorus Track

Dun Mountain Trail, has been included in our description. This track conveniently lands trampers on Brook St on the edge of Nelson, the more-popular finish. Trampers following this route hike directly from Middy Creek Hut to Nelson, a long seven- to eight-hour day.

A better alternative, especially if you get a late start on Day 1, is to stay the first night at Captains Creek Hut, and hike to Rocks Hut the second night. Rocks Hut, with its mountain views, offers much nicer accommodation than Middy Creek Hut.

There is plenty of other tramping to be had in the forest park, including the moderate two-day Wakamarina Track, following an old gold-miners' trail across the Richmond Range from the Wairau Valley to the Wakamarina River. Another worthwhile option for experienced alpine trampers is the Mt Richmond Alpine Route, a three- to four-day route along exposed ridges.

History

Māori had a number of argillite quarries in the Mt Richmond area, where they mined hard mudstone for weapons and tools. The first European visitors were also attracted by minerals – initially copper and chromium. There was a mining company on Dun Mountain as early as 1852, and Hacket Creek chromite was being removed from open shallow-cut mines by the 1860s. There are still parts of an old, benched bullock track – the Old Chrome Rd – near Hacket Creek, on the western side of the forest park.

Gold was discovered in the Wakamarina River in 1861, and within three years thousands of canvas tents had sprung up as miners flocked to the prosperous goldfield, which was one of the richest in the country. The township of Pinedale, in the Wakamarina Valley, 8km west of Havelock, earned the nickname Canvastown. However, the boom lasted only until 1865.

When most of the accessible alluvial gold had been mined, quartz reefs were developed. Companies operated in the Wakamarina Valley from 1874 until the 1920s.

Environment

The whole park is covered by forest, with the exception of small patches of alpine tussock around the summits of taller peaks. The bush includes all five species of beech, as well as the podocarp species of rimu, miro, totara, matai and kahikatea. Uncommon birds found in the park include the whio

(blue duck), the yellow-crowned parakeet, kaka and, occasionally, weka.

ℹ Planning

WHEN TO TRAMP

The Pelorus and Aniseed Valleys receive some of the highest rainfall in Mt Richmond Forest Park, and streams may become impassable in heavy rain. The track is therefore best tramped from October to April.

MAPS & BROCHURES

This track is covered by NZTopo50 *BQ26 (Nelson)* and *BQ27 (Rai Valley)*. The *Pelorus Track* brochure can be downloaded from DOC's website (www.doc.govt.nz).

HUTS & CAMPING

All huts in Mt Richmond Forest Park are graded as Standard ($5), including Captains Creek, Middy Creek, Rocks, Roebuck, Browning and Hacket. Te Araroa trail traverses the park, so the huts can become busy, but none require booking.

Near the Maungatapu Rd trailhead, camping can be found at Pelorus Bridge Campground (p149). At the trailhead for the Dun Mountain Trail is **Brook Valley Holiday Park** (✔ 03-548 0399; 600 Brook St; unpowered/powered sites per person $10/17), in a rural location around 4km from central Nelson. Its future existence seems to be in perpetual limbo, so check ahead.

INFORMATION

The DOC Nelson Visitor Centre is located within the **Nelson i-SITE** (p185) and, along with other local i-SITEs, is the best source of information for the tramp.

ℹ Getting There & Away

The start of the Pelorus Track is 13km up the Pelorus Valley from the Pelorus Bridge Scenic Reserve, at the end of Maungatapu Rd.

The western end of the track is at the Hacket picnic area, at the confluence of Hacket Creek and Roding River, in the Aniseed Valley. This picnic area is 29km from Nelson and is reached by driving 1.5km south of Hope on SH6 and turning east onto Aniseed Valley Rd. If you take the alternative finish to the Brook, which is by far the most popular option, you arrive 4km from the Nelson city centre, so transport will not be a problem; you can always just keep walking down into the town.

From Nelson, **Trek Express** (✔ 027 222 1872, 0800 128 735; www.trekexpress.co.nz) runs an on-demand shuttle-bus service to the Maungatapu Rd trailhead (per person $60). It will also pick you up at the Hacket picnic area, transporting you back to Nelson ($30). The services require a minimum of five people, but if you check the 'Existing Trips' link on the website, you may find a shuttle that's already booked on which you can travel.

PELORUS BRIDGE SCENIC RESERVE

A pocket of deep green forest tucked away among paddocks of bog-standard pasture, 18km west of Havelock, Pelorus Bridge Scenic Reserve contains one of the last stands of river-flat forest in Marlborough. It survived only because a town planned in 1865 didn't get off the ground by 1912, by which time obliterative logging made this little remnant look precious. The reserve was born, and now visitors can explore its many tracks and its towering trees, admire the historic bridge and take a dip in the limpid Pelorus River (beautiful enough to star in Peter Jackson's *The Hobbit*).

But wait, there's more. Nestled into the forest, 13km from the start of the Pelorus Track, where SH6 crosses the Pelorus River, **Pelorus Bridge Campground** (☑ 03-571 6019; www.doc.govt.nz; Pelorus Bridge, SH6; unpowered/powered sites per person $9/18) is a magical place to spend a night or two. It's a picturesque gem with hot showers, a smart kitchen and a large deck with river views. The nearby cafe has delightful home-baked pies, which you can walk off on a nearby trail before heading back in for cake.

Otherwise, passing bus companies will drop you off at Pelorus Bridge Scenic Reserve (13km from the start of the track), which is on the Picton–Nelson route. Your best bet is **InterCity** (☑ 03-548 1538; www.intercity.co.nz; Bridge St). Once at Pelorus Bridge, stop in at the cafe and ask about a lift to the trailhead. Often there is somebody who will provide transport for a small fee.

 The Tramp

Day 1: Maungatapu Road to Middy Creek Hut

5–6 HOURS / 14KM

The start of the track is just down the road from the car park at the end of Maungatapu Rd, and begins by descending towards the river. In 10 to 15 minutes you arrive at the first of many swing bridges, this one over Scott Creek, near where it empties into a deep pool of the **Pelorus River**. Continue following the true left (west) side of the river to enter the forest park. One hour (3km) from the start you'll arrive at **Emerald Pool**, where a picnic table will indicate that you have arrived at the popular day-walk destination – it's a great place for a dip if the sandflies aren't swarming.

At this point the track leaves the river and makes a steep 100m climb through a thick forest of rimu, tawa (quite rare in this park), matai and beech. Within 30 minutes you're sidling the river bluff and the walking is easier. Follow the river for one hour (3km), descending sharply twice on switchbacks, the second time right back to the edge of the Pelorus.

The track now swings to the west and in 30 minutes reaches the short side track to **Captains Creek Hut** (six bunks), located in a clearing just above the river. The hut is a three- to four-hour walk from the car park. It has no rainwater supply; there's a nice pool for swimming right in front of the hut. You may also see the occasional angler in these parts.

From here, the main track continues to follow the river and within 10 minutes crosses **Captain Creek**, a good-sized stream rushing out of the mountains, on a new cable bridge. In another five minutes the track arrives at a swing bridge that spans a tight, rocky gorge high above the Pelorus. If swing bridges make you uneasy, this one will have you gripping its cables all the way across.

Once on the true right side (south) of the Pelorus, you climb steeply out of the gorge and then sidle the bluffs until the track descends to a swing bridge across **Fishtail Stream**, reached one hour (3km) from Captains Creek Hut. From the creek you climb again and cross a bush-clad terrace where the Pelorus forms a wide loop. It's another 1km before you pop out at **Middy Creek Hut** (six bunks), a two-hour (6km) walk from Captain Creek, opposite the confluence of Middy Creek and the Pelorus River. Nearby is a signposted junction with a route that heads south to Conical Knob (1216m) and Mt Fell (1602m). The river is close at hand and there is a very deep pool under the nearby swing bridge. Beware of the ferocious sandflies.

Day 2: Middy Creek Hut to Browning Hut

7–8 HOURS / 16KM

About 150m west of Middy Creek Hut, a swing bridge crosses the Pelorus River to its true left side. From here you climb sharply to a junction with a track that continues up the spur to Rocks Hut and the Dun Mountain Trail. The Pelorus Track heads southwest (left fork), working its way to a saddle above Rocks Creek and then dropping steeply to the creek some distance upstream from the Pelorus River.

After crossing the creek the tramp becomes more challenging, starting with 4km of thick forest – a mixture of beech, rimu, tree ferns and horopito – with protruding tree roots ready to trip you up.

Eventually the track descends to Roebuck Creek and a pair of swing bridges. The first one crosses the creek; the second extends over the Pelorus River, 200m upriver. Roebuck Hut (six bunks), three to four hours from Middy Creek Hut, is on an open terrace directly across from the junction of the creek and the Pelorus, which at normal water levels can be forded here.

Return to the swing bridge over the Pelorus River, where on the true left side the track immediately climbs the ridge that separates Roebuck and Mates Creeks. It's a steep 30-minute climb for the first 150m of the ascent, and then the track begins to climb at a more gradual rate to Totara Saddle (690m). Before reaching the saddle the track works its way across the slopes of the Roebuck catchment, with good views of Mt Fell and Mt Richmond.

At the saddle there is a junction with a track heading northwards to Rocks Hut (four hours). The main track (left fork) heads west, dropping 180m in 1km. It traverses an open slip and goes through beech forest on the way to Browning Hut (eight bunks), situated in a large open area on the edge of Browning Stream.

Alternative End: The Brook via Dun Mountain Track

7–8 HOURS / 21KM / 800M ASCENT, 880M DESCENT

This is a long day that begins immediately with its longest climb. An early start is wise and, as water is scarce along this section, carry plenty with you and refill at Rocks Hut.

At the track junction, 20 minutes out from Middy Creek Hut, take the right fork and continue climbing. For the next 4km it's a steady 600m trudge uphill with a couple of major descents into the bargain. It's basically a three-hour climb with no views. As it climbs on, you pass moss-covered rock pinnacles and arrive at a signposted junction. The left fork is a ridge track that heads southwest to Totara Saddle and then Browning Hut.

The right fork quickly emerges from the bush into subalpine scrub and arrives at Rocks Hut (16 bunks), reached 6km (2½ to three hours) from Middy Creek Hut. This is a very appealing hut overlooking Mt Richmond and Mt Fell. There are few sandflies (if any) and there's a rainwater supply. If staying at the hut, follow the Browning Hut track for 30 minutes to check out a series of pinnacles known as The Rocks (939m).

From the hut the track heads northeast towards Dun Saddle and quickly passes a side track (10 minutes) to an open perch with a view to the west. Within 45 minutes you break out of the trees and stunted scrub for good, and then reach Dun Saddle (960m), one hour (2km) from Rocks Hut. It's usually too windy to hang around too long at this spot. Dun Mountain (1129m) is 45 minutes' walk away (1.5km) along a poled route that heads right. If the winds are light, consider a side trip to the mountain for excellent views of Nelson and the surrounding region.

From the junction head left along a barren route, which is not marked nearly as well as the previous section of track (keep an eye out for metal poles and orange triangles on the trees), but the views are great. You briefly re-enter the bush, but within 30 minutes of Dun Saddle you reach Coppermine Saddle (878m). This is the start of the old Dun Mountain Railway, NZ's first railway, which was constructed to enable horse-drawn carts to haul chromite ore from the mountain to Nelson. It's now the Dun Mountain Trail, one of NZ's listed Great Rides, so you can probably expect to see a few cyclists from here.

The track resumes by sidling a ridge off Wooded Peak, and in 30 minutes (two hours from Rocks Hut) arrives at Windy Point. This exposed tip of the ridge is signposted because the winds here are legendary – so much so that at times it can be hard to stand. Hang onto your hat...with both hands. Just as amazing, walk 15 minutes down the track and the roaring winds are often just steady breezes. Departing from near Windy Point is the poled Wells Ridge Route to Wooded Peak (1111m), 1½ hours away.

The Dun Mountain Trail continues to skirt Wooded Peak, and with every step looks more like the railroad bed that it is. The walking here is easy, making a pleasant end to a long day for many. You quickly re-enter the beech forest and 1½ hours from Windy Point you reach Third House Shelter. This is strictly a place for a break, as camping is not allowed and there is no water. At this point Brook St is two hours away along a well-signposted trail that still looks like a 4WD track. The final 30 minutes is a rapid descent, ending just north of the Brook Valley Holiday Park (p148), 4km from Nelson's city centre.

Day 3: Browning Hut to Hacket Picnic Area

2 HOURS / 6KM

The track immediately crosses to the true right (north) side of a tributary of Browning Stream. For the next hour it's easy walking through forest and across several eroded stream beds. During high water you can follow a steep, alternative track around these streams and slips. Shortly before crossing Browning Stream for the last time, you pass a side track that leads south (left fork) over a low saddle to **Hacket Hut** (six bunks). The main track crosses the stream after five minutes, near the confluence with Hacket Creek, which is forded immediately.

The other side of Hacket Creek is private farmland, but you don't need permission to walk through it. An easy, benched track follows the creek on its true left (west) side for an hour, almost to the Hacket picnic area. About 1km before the picnic area the track crosses a swing bridge over Hacket Creek, and then joins a 4WD track to a wooden footbridge over the Roding River.

Kaikoura Coast Track

Duration 2 days

Distance 26km (16.2 miles)

Difficulty Easy to moderate

Start/End Ngaroma

Gateways Kaikoura (p155), Christchurch (p214)

Transport Bus

Summary A private track that combines alpine views and a lengthy beach walk with gracious farm hospitality at night.

In 1994 adjoining farms along the Kaikoura coast were searching for a way to diversify their activities while preserving, even expanding, their large areas of native forest and bush. Taking a cue from the Banks Track (p191), the country's first private track, just down the coast, the farmers/landowners formed one of their own, opening up their farms and homes to a small number of trampers each day.

Kaikoura Coast Track is a two-day tramp that has you traversing tussock tops and skirting the Pacific Ocean, keeping an eye out for marine wildlife. A large part of the experience, however, is the farms themselves, Medina and Ngaroma – scattering sheep as you cut through a paddock, stopping to watch sheepdogs round up a flock, and sip-ping lemonade made from freshly squeezed home-grown lemons. It's a tramp through remote and rural NZ, with your hosts each night being the families who work the farms. For many that's as intriguing as the view from Skull Peak. The track fee includes both comfortable accommodation and the transport of your luggage and food. That means every night you can enjoy a hot shower and a soft bed, and pack along a few steaks and a bottle of good NZ wine. Without having to haul a backpack, the climbs are easily accomplished by most trampers, and you can then recover with a bit of luxury at night before setting out the next day.

The number of trampers on the track is limited to 10 per day, so bookings are essential if you have particular dates in mind. The cost is $200 per person (students $180), which includes transfers of luggage, accommodation and secured parking. Book through **Kaikoura Coast Track** (☑ 03-319 2715; www.kaikouratrack.co.nz; 356 Conway Flat Rd, Ngaroma; $200).

History & Environment

The Caverhill and Macfarlane families began farming Hawkswood in 1860, and at its peak the estate covered 245 sq km, including all the coastal land between the Conway River and Waiau Rivers. Today the two farms involved with the Kaikoura Coast Track combine for a total of 21.9 sq km, with the majority of the area being either tussock ridges or paddocks and farm blocks. Several gullies have been fenced off from livestock and turned into conservation areas. These pockets of native bush include ancient remnants of beech forest, giant podocarps such as kahikatea, matai and totara, and a variety of ferns. Don't know your native bush? Not to worry – the families have done an impressive job of labelling trees and plants along the track, and by the end of the tramp you will know the difference between lancewood and pigeonwood.

Most of the wildlife encountered will be a variety of birds in the forested areas, including riflemen, bellbirds, grey warblers, long-tailed and shining cuckoos, and possibly NZ harrier hawks and falcons on the tops. Along the beach, trampers have spotted Hector's and dusky dolphins playing in the surf, and occasionally seals basking on the sand.

ℹ Planning

WHEN TO TRAMP

The season for tramping this track is October to April, with the warmest months being December through March.

Kaikoura Coast Track

WHAT TO BRING

Sun protection (a wide-brimmed hat and sunscreen) is important. Many trampers will also use a chilly bin (cooler) to transport their meat and other perishable food between farms. Your hosts have chilly bins available for your use.

MAPS & BROCHURES

Every tramper is given a *Kaikoura Coast Track Guide Booklet*, which covers the natural highlights of each section of track and contains a map that is more than sufficient. For more detail, use NZTopo50 *BU26 (Parnassus)* and *BU27 (Oaro)*.

HUTS

Each farm provides accommodation for trampers along the track, with the first night spent at Ngaroma, and the second at Medina. The cost is included in the track booking fee.

Getting There & Away

The tramp begins and ends at Ngaroma, 7.5km off SH1, 150km north of Christchurch and 45km south of Kaikoura. InterCity buses (p215) will drop you off at the Conway River Bridge, where

you can be collected by the track operators with prior arrangement.

The Tramp

Day 1: Ngaroma to Medina

4–5 HOURS / 12KM

The first night is spent in the Beach House at **Ngaroma Farm**, which has great views of the Kaikoura Range. It's an easy stroll down to the Pacific Ocean from the accommodation, or you can wander around the farm and soak up the bucolic atmosphere.

The tramp begins the next morning. If you hustle, this section could easily take less than four hours, but why hurry? Linger on the beach, scan the ocean for marine life, look for shells in the cliffs and soak in the views.

To set off on the track, head to the beach following a gravel road east from the farmhouse and then cross a bridge and continue south. A track sign will divert you off the road to the greyish, gravelly beach. The darker the sand the better the footing, but overall this is something of a trudge. The scenery is amazing, however, and soon you're skirting the base of towering tan bluffs on one side, with the roar of the Pacific on the other. The endless crashing of waves onto the beach sets a tranquil tone for the rest of the morning.

About 1.8km from Ngaroma you reach the first stumps of the **Buried Forest** – matai, rimu and kanuka that were living trees 8000 years ago, but were eventually covered by sediment and preserved. Sea erosion has revealed these ancient trees in several locations along a 1km stretch of the beach to **Ploughman's Creek**, a wide gap in the bluffs where you can see a road bridge. Seal Gap and Doug's Gap follow, and one hour from Ngaroma (3.6km) you reach **Big Bush Beach**. Here the sand extends up into a huge gap to form a big beach.

The cliffs turn whitish and layers of shells are easily seen. You pass Dawn's Creek at 4.8km, and 1.2km later (two hours from Ngaroma) reach a track turning inland to **Circle Shelter**. This lunchtime shelter has loads of character, including a large and very comfortable bench seat, a 'loo with a view' and a fire pit where you can boil a billy for a cup of tea.

Within 1km of the shelter you reach **The Lookout**, where a bench allows you to enjoy a view of the coastline, with Kaikoura Peninsula 37km to the north and Banks Peninsula 145km to the south. The track then turns inland, cuts through a couple of paddocks and descends into the **Medina Conservation Area**. Protected from livestock grazing since

1984, this gully is rich in native plants and also features several ancient podocarps, including an 800-year-old kahikatea so large it takes four people to link their arms around it.

Eventually you climb out of the conservation area into open tussock, to reach the **Rest and Reflect Bench** (10.6km from Ngaroma) with its grand view of Medina Farm. From here it's less than 30 minutes to the farm's accommodation, **Medina**, where you will stay in either the Whare or the Garden Cottage. Both offer stunning views of the farm, its livestock and the mountains beyond. There's wine and beer in the refrigerator that can be enjoyed for a fair price.

Day 2: Medina to Ngaroma

4–6 HOURS / 12.3KM / 430M ASCENT, 450M DESCENT

The second morning begins with a short van ride taking trampers north on SH1 to the start of the day's track. The usual departure is 9am, but if it appears you're in for a hot and sunny day, you might consider an earlier start. All the uphill walking is completed in the first two hours, which is always easier in the cool of the morning.

From the trailhead you immediately climb through a pine plantation over a ridge, but within 1.5km you descend into **Buntings Bush Gully**. This conservation area is a rich forest compared to the farmed pines and features huge podocarps, including one totara big enough to be turned into a Māori war canoe. All too soon, however, you begin the long hike to the tussock tops. Within 3.5km (one hour) of setting out, you reach **Heather's Bench**, overlooking the Conway Valley, nd after another 1km you're out of the trees

for good, arriving at **Bruce's Bench** (the benches are named after two of your hosts). This bench, a huge split log overlooking a mountain panorama, almost commands you to take a break, even if you're not tired.

You're now ridge walking on the **Hawkswood Range**, by far the most scenic stretch of the day. With views all around, you reach a saddle and are greeted with the Kaikoura coast on the horizon, and then in another 500m you climb to **Skull Peak** (489m). At either point you can see the Pacific in one direction and inland mountains to the other.

From the peak you can also see the **Skull Peak shelter**, 1km and a tussock gully away. The final climb to this delightful lunch spot is gentle, and reached in two to three hours (7.5km) from SH1. Inside the small hut there is water, a gas cooker for tea and even a couple of mattresses for a post-lunch nap. Outside there are benches and stunning views.

The second half of the day is all downhill. You steeply descend along a 4WD track for more than 1km, losing much of the height you worked so hard to gain before lunch. You return to a walking track at the Back Paddock and, 2.5km from the shelter, re-enter native bush when you descend to Possum Dr, the reason there's a 'cow bar' across the track.

Over the final 2km of the day you cross a couple of bridges (one labelled 'Muddy Butt Bridge' because it's at the bottom of a long slippery slope) and cut through several paddocks complete with grazing sheep. Ngaroma Beach House, where you began your walk yesterday, is reached two hours (4.8km) from the Skull Peak shelter.

NO QUAKING IN YOUR BOOTS

On 14 November 2016 one of the largest earthquakes in New Zealand's recorded history – 7.8 in magnitude – rocked Kaikoura, causing massive damage. Its epicentre was just 60km from the town. Following the quake it's been business as usual on the Kaikoura Coast Track, but you will see signs of the natural disaster's destruction. The most obvious damage will be seen on the drive to Ngaroma from the Conway River Bridge. This road had to be rebuilt in many places, especially along its narrow sections between the cliff edges and the sea. At the time of writing, abseilers and machines were still working along these sections to stabilise the slopes. The homestead on Ngaroma Farm was also damaged beyond repair and needs to be rebuilt.

As you walk along the beach on the first day of the tramp, you'll see points where the cliffs collapsed in the earthquake. The ocean has now washed away most of the fallen material, but you'll still get a sense of just how much earth was moved in less than two minutes. The road in front of the Ngaroma Beach House accommodation is being barricaded with rocks to prevent further erosion by the waves. The main thing to be aware of is that the track and accommodation are totally safe.

TOWNS & FACILITIES

Picton

♩ 03 / POP 4360

Half asleep in winter, but hyperactive in summer, boaty Picton clusters around a deep gulch at the head of Queen Charlotte Sound. It's the main traveller port for the South Island, and the best place from which to explore the Marlborough Sounds and tackle the Queen Charlotte Track. There's ample accommodation, including lots of low-budget options. It's also a good spot for stocking up on provisions.

🛏 Sleeping & Eating

★ **Jugglers Rest**   HOSTEL $
(♩ 03-573 5570; www.jugglersrest.com; 8 Canterbury St; dm $33, d $75-85; ☺ closed Jun-Sep; @☻🐾) 🐾 Jocular hosts keep all their balls in the air at this well-run, ecofriendly, bunk-free backpackers. Peacefully located a 10-minute walk from town, or even less on a free bike. Cheery gardens are a good place to socialise with fellow travellers, especially during the occasional circus-skills shows.

Picton Top 10 Holiday Park   HOLIDAY PARK $
(♩ 03-573 7212, 0800 277 444; www.pictontop10.co.nz; 70 Waikawa Rd; sites from $48, units $78-165; @☻☀) About 500m from town, this compact, well-kept park has plenty of lawn and picnic benches, plus crowd-pleasing facilities including a playground, barbecue area and swimming pool.

Harbour View Motel   MOTEL $$
(♩ 03-573 6259, 0800 101 133; www.harbourviewpicton.co.nz; 30 Waikawa Rd; d $140-240; ☻) Its elevated position means this motel commands good views of Picton's mast-filled harbour from its smart, self-contained studios with timber decks.

Picton Village Bakkerij   BAKERY $
(♩ 03-573 7082; www.facebook.com/Picton VillageBakery; cnr Auckland & Dublin Sts; bakery items $2-8; ☺ 6am-4pm Mon-Fri, to 3.30pm Sat; 🐾) Dutch owners bake trays of European goodies here, including interesting breads, filled rolls, cakes and custardy, tarty treats. The savoury pies are great. An excellent stop before or after the ferry, or to stock a packed lunch.

Le Café   CAFE $$
(♩ 03-573 5588; www.lecafepicton.co.nz; London Quay; breakfast & lunch $14-25, dinner $24-30; ☺ 7.30am-8pm Sun-Thu, to late Fri & Sat; 🐾) Per-

ennially popular for its quayside location, dependable food and Havana coffee. The likes of salami sandwiches and sweets are in the cabinet, while a good antipasto platter, generous pasta dishes, local mussels, and lamb and fish dishes feature à la carte. The laid-back atmosphere, craft beer and occasional live gigs make this a good evening hang-out.

Supplies & Equipment

Picton Sportsworld   SPORTS & OUTDOORS
(♩ 03-573 6963; www.pictonsportsworld.com; 8 High St; ☺ 8.30am-5pm Mon-Fri, to 2.30pm Sat, 10am-2.30pm Sun) Good local sports shop stocking a selection of camping, hiking and fishing gear.

Fresh Choice Supermarket   SUPERMARKET $
(Mariners Mall, 100 High St; ☺ 7am-9pm) Pretty much the only supermarket choice, and fortunately a good one.

ℹ Information

Picton i-SITE (♩ 03-520 3113; www.marlboroughnz.com; foreshore; ☺ 8am-5pm) All vital tourist guff including maps, Queen Charlotte Track information, lockers and transport bookings. Dedicated Department of Conservation (DOC) counter.

ℹ Getting There & Away

Soundsair (♩ 03-520 3080, 0800 505 005; www.soundsair.co.nz; 10 London Quay; ☺ 7.30am-5.30pm Mon-Thu & Sat, to 7pm Fri, 9am-7pm Sun) flies between Picton and Wellington; a shuttle bus to/from the airstrip at Koromiko is available.

There are two ferry operators crossing Cook Strait between Picton and Wellington, and although all ferries leave from more or less the same place, each has its own terminal. The main transport hub (with car-rental depots) is at the **Interislander Terminal** (Auckland St). **Bluebridge Ferries** (♩ 0800 844 844, 04-471 6188; www.bluebridge.co.nz; adult/child to Wellington from $53/27; ☻) crossings take just over three hours, and the company has up to four sailings in each direction daily. Cars cost from $120 and campervans from $155. The sleeper service arrives in Picton at 6am. **Interislander** (♩ 0800 802 802; www.interislander.co.nz; Interislander Ferry Terminal, Auckland St; adult/child to Wellington from $52/32) crossings take just over three hours; there are up to six sailings in each direction daily. Cars are priced from $121, campervans (up to 5.5m) from $153, motorbikes $56, bicycles $15.

Buses serving Picton depart from the *Interislander* ferry terminal or the i-SITE. **InterCity** (♩ 03-365 1113; www.intercity.co.nz; outside Interislander Ferry Terminal, Auckland St) runs south to Christchurch twice daily ($56,

5½ hours) via Blenheim ($12, 30 minutes) and Kaikoura ($21, 2½ hours), with connections to Dunedin, Queenstown and Invercargill. Services also run to/from Nelson ($23, 2¼ hours), with connections to Motueka and the West Coast. At least one bus daily on each of these routes connects with a Wellington ferry service.

KiwiRail Scenic (☑ 0800 872 467; www. greatjourneysofnz.co.nz) runs the *Coastal Pacific* service daily each way between Picton and Christchurch via Blenheim and Kaikoura connecting with the Interislander ferry. Note this service was suspended following the November 2016 Kaikoura earthquake, but was planned to be back up and running in late 2018. Check KiwiRail's website (www.kiwirail.co.nz) for the latest update.

Kaikoura
☑ 03 / POP 2080

The whale-watching capital of NZ and a rewarding stop for lots of other salty activities, Kaikoura is a major tourism town and can cater to most tramping needs. Following the reestablishment of transport links that were badly damaged during the 2016 earthquake, the town is once again easily reached.

🛏 Sleeping & Eating

Albatross Backpacker Inn   HOSTEL $
(☑ 0800 222 247, 03-319 6090; www.albatross-kaikoura.co.nz; 1 Torquay St; dm $34-36, tw/d/tr $79/84/105; 🕸) 🧷 This arty backpackers resides in three sweet buildings, one a former post office. It's close to the beach but sheltered from the breeze. As well as a laid-back lounge with musical instruments for jamming, there are decks and verandas to chill out on.

★ Kaikoura Cottage Motels   MOTEL $$
(☑ 0800 526 882, 03-319 5599; www.kaikouracottagemotels.co.nz; cnr Old Beach & Mill Rds; d $140-200; 🕸) This enclave of eight modern tourist flats looks mighty fine, surrounded by attractive native plantings. Oriented for mountain views, the spick-and-span self-contained units sleep four between an open-plan studio-style living room and one private bedroom. Proud and lovely hosts seal the deal.

★ Lemon Tree Lodge   B&B $$$
(☑ 03-319 7464; www.lemontree.co.nz; 31 Adelphi Tce; s $280, d $280-320; 🕸) Enjoying superb ocean and mountain views, Lemon Tree Lodge combines four charming rooms in the main house with two quiet and secluded garden units. Our favourites are the Ocean View Suites with expansive windows and private balconies showcasing brilliant Pacific vistas. .

Hislops Wholefoods Cafe   CAFE $$
(☑ 03-319 6971; www.hislops-wholefoods.co.nz; 33 Beach Rd; breakfast & lunch mains $12-19, dinner mains $26-36; ⊙ 8.30am-8pm Wed-Sat, to 4pm Sun; 🅹) 🧷 Organic ingredients shine at this long-established eatery. Have breakfast on the shaded deck or book for dinner.

★ Green Dolphin   MODERN NZ $$$
(☑ 03-319 6666; www.greendolphinkaikoura.com; 12 Avoca St; mains $28-39; ⊙ 5pm-late) This top-ender dishes up high-quality local produce including seafood, beef, lamb and venison. There are also lovely homemade pasta dishes. Ask for a window table to experience a sunlit Kaikoura dusk. Booking recommended.

Supplies & Equipment

Coastal Sports   SPORTS & OUTDOORS
(☑ 03-319 5028; www.coastalsports.co.nz; 24 West End; ⊙ 9am-5.30pm Mon-Sat, 10am-5pm Sun, extended hours late Oct–Easter) Hire bikes (half/full day $30/40), surf gear (board and wetsuit per day $40) and get lots of local intel. There's also a good selection of hiking and outdoor gear.

New World Supermarket   SUPERMARKET $
(124 Beach Rd; ⊙ 8am-8pm) Ten-minutes' walk from the town centre.

❶ Information

Kaikoura i-SITE (☑ 03-319 5641; www.kaikoura.co.nz; West End; ⊙ 9am-5pm Mon-Fri, to 4pm Sat & Sun, extended hours Dec-Mar) Helpful staff make tour, accommodation and transport bookings, and help with DOC-related matters.

❶ Getting There & Away

InterCity (☑ 03-365 1113; www.intercity.co.nz) buses have traditionally run between Kaikoura and Nelson once daily (3¾ hours), and Picton (2¼ hours) and Christchurch (from $26, 2¼ hours) twice daily. The **bus stop** is next to the i-SITE (tickets and info inside). Note the service north to Picton was suspended post-earthquake, but normal schedules were expected to return following the full reopening of SH1 north to Picton in 2018. Check the website for the latest.

Kaikoura Express (☑ 0800 500 929; www.kaikouraexpress.co.nz; adult one way/return $35/60, child $30/50) (aka the 'Red Bus') runs a service (2¾ hours) linking Christchurch and Kaikoura that leaves from the i-SITE.

KiwiRail Scenic runs the daily *Coastal Pacific* service stopping at Kaikoura en route to Picton (2¼ hours), and Christchurch (2¾ hours) and vice versa. This service was suspended post-earthquake, but should be back by late 2018. Check www.kiwirail.co.nz for the latest update.

QUEEN CHARLOTTE & MARLBOROUGH KAIKOURA

Abel Tasman, Kahurangi & Nelson Lakes

Best Huts

➡ Angelus Hut (p179)

➡ James Mackay Hut (p170)

➡ Anchorage Hut (p163)

➡ Heaphy Hut (p171)

➡ Salisbury Lodge (p174)

Best Views

➡ St Arnaud Range (p180)

➡ Mt Arthur (p174)

➡ Blue Lake (p183)

➡ Separation Point (p165)

➡ Lake Angelus (p179)

Why Go?

Welcome to the sunny side. This corner of New Zealand is typically claimed as having more hours of sunshine than any other area in the country, which means long, sun-baked days for tramping. The region boasts three wonderful national parks – Abel Tasman, Kahurangi and Nelson Lakes – which combine to provide a remarkably diverse range of landscapes and experiences, from swimming in golden coves or quick plunges in frigid mountain streams, to tramping the sands of a wild West Coast beach, to exploring alpine peaks and passes, to wandering past the deepest caves in the southern hemisphere.

The sun will be welcome as you tramp the beaches on NZ's most popular Great Walk, the Abel Tasman Coast Track, while a second Great Walk, the Heaphy Track, threads through the mountains to the remote West Coast. Inland and upland, Nelson Lakes National Park seems all the better for being overshadowed by other alpine national parks such as Fiordland and Aoraki/Mt Cook.

When to Go

Sheltered by mountain ranges, Abel Tasman National Park basks in some of NZ's best weather. Particularly pleasant spells reliably occur through summer and autumn, but this park can happily be tramped year-round.

In contrast Kahurangi National Park cops the westerly winds that blow off the Tasman Sea, bringing substantial rainfall to mountain areas. This can quickly lead to river flooding. Snow is also possible at higher altitudes, but Kahurangi can be tramped year-round in favourable conditions.

Nelson Lakes National Park possesses a surprisingly moderate climate for an alpine region. Things can turn pearshaped very quickly though with the arrival of heavy rain or even a blizzard. The odds of good weather are considerably higher here from November to April.

Background Reading

Golden Bay writer Gerald Hindmarsh has produced several highly readable social-history books. In *Kahurangi Calling: Stories from the Backcountry of Northwest Nelson,* he describes many of the natural wonders found in Kahurangi and tells the stories of the fascinating characters who have lived there or travelled through, including explorers, miners, graziers, eelers, hermits and trampers. His 2013 book, *Outsiders: Stories from the Fringe of New Zealand Society,* continues in the same vein. Hindmarsh believes that a society is lucky to have people such as those he mentions in his book, and that these 'outsiders' offer 'an important counterbalance to the high-pressured, commercialised and urban world that most of us inhabit'.

DON'T MISS

Bleak, exposed and positively sci-fi, Farewell Spit is a wetland of international importance and a renowned bird sanctuary – its summer home of thousands of migratory waders, notably the bar-tailed godwit (which flies more than 12,000km to get there), Caspian terns and Australasian gannets. The spit, which is the northernmost point on the South Island, is 35km in length, and still growing, and features colossal, crescent-shaped dunes, from where panoramic views extend across Golden Bay and a vast low-tide salt marsh.

Walkers can explore the first section of the spit along a network of tracks that also venture along the coast to places such as Wharariki Beach, with its famously photogenic Archway Islands. To get towards the tip of the spit is possible only by tour. **Farewell Spit Eco Tours** (☑ 03-524 8257, 0800 808 257; www.farewellspit.com; 6 Tasman St, Collingwood; tours $130-165) ✐ runs trips ranging from two to 6½ hours, taking in the spit, lighthouse, gannets and godwits. Tours depart from Collingwood.

Visitor Information Centres

→ DOC Nelson Visitor Centre (p185; inside Nelson i-SITE)
→ Motueka i-SITE (p186)
→ Golden Bay Visitor Centre (p187)
→ Karamea Information & Resource Centre (p187)
→ DOC Nelson Lakes Visitor Centre (p178)

GATEWAY TOWNS

→ Nelson (p184)
→ Motueka (p185)
→ Takaka (p186)
→ Karamea (p187)

Fast Facts

→ Abel Tasman is NZ's smallest national park, covering 227 sq km. But small doesn't mean unpopular – around 43,000 people walk and kayak the Abel Tasman Coast Track every year, making it NZ's most popular Great Walk.

→ In contrast, Kahurangi is NZ's second-largest national park, at 4520 sq km, but only 6500 people a year complete its Great Walk, the Heaphy Track.

Top Tip

Mix things up by combining tramping with kayaking on the Abel Tasman Coast Track. Operators in Marahau and Kaiteriteri can sort out the ways to both paddle and walk in one trip.

Resources

→ www.nelsonnz.com
→ www.motuekaisite.co.nz
→ www.goldenbaynz.co.nz
→ http://heaphytrack.com
→ www.karameainfo.co.nz
→ www.starnaud.co.nz

ABEL TASMAN, KAHURANGI & NELSON LAKES

Abel Tasman, Kahurangi & Nelson Lakes

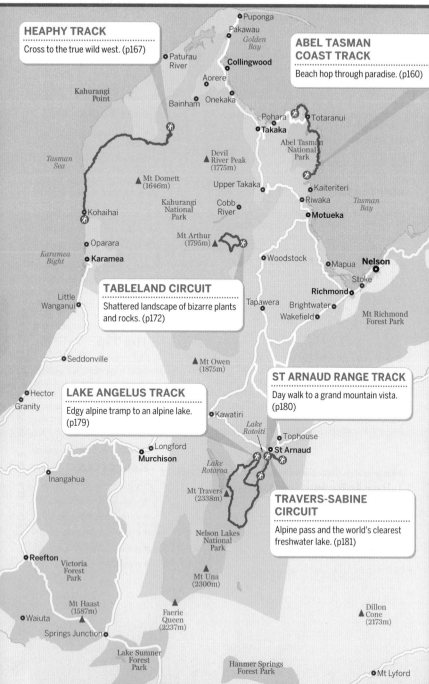

HEAPHY TRACK

Cross to the true wild west. (p167)

ABEL TASMAN COAST TRACK

Beach hop through paradise. (p160)

TABLELAND CIRCUIT

Shattered landscape of bizarre plants and rocks. (p172)

ST ARNAUD RANGE TRACK

Day walk to a grand mountain vista. (p180)

LAKE ANGELUS TRACK

Edgy alpine tramp to an alpine lake. (p179)

TRAVERS-SABINE CIRCUIT

Alpine pass and the world's clearest freshwater lake. (p181)

ABEL TASMAN NATIONAL PARK

Basking in sunshine at the top of the South Island, Abel Tasman National Park is renowned for its golden beaches, sculpted granite cliffs and world-famous Abel Tasman Coast Track, the most popular of all the Great Walks.

The park is named after the Dutch explorer Abel Janszoon Tasman, who ventured this way in 1642. Despite being NZ's smallest national park and with a high point of just 1156m, it contains a wealth of fascinating natural features – far more than just the familiar picture-postcard arcs of golden sand greeting seas of shimmering blue. Among its many other landmarks are limpid lagoons, marble gorges and a spectacular system of karst caves in its rugged interior.

Hugging the water's edge, the Abel Tasman Coast Track is by far the park's most popular trail, though in high summer there seems as much traffic on the water as off it. Come the Christmas school holidays an armada of NZ boaties make it one of the country's most popular ocean playgrounds.

History

Māori have lived along the shores of what is now the Abel Tasman National Park for at least 500 years. They had abundant sources of food from both the sea and the forest, and seasonally cultivated kumara (sweet potato).

Māori were in residence when, in 1642, Abel Tasman anchored his ships near Wainui. A skirmish ensued, the upshot of which was the death of four of Tasman's crew without any of the Europeans having ever set foot on land.

Captain Cook stopped here briefly in 1770, but recorded little about the coastal area and nothing of its inhabitants. It wasn't until Dumont D'Urville sailed into the area between Marahau and Torrent Bay in 1827 that Europeans met the Māori on peaceful terms. The French navigator made friends with the people, studied the wildlife, and charted the park's bays and shoreline.

European settlement of the area began around 1855. The new settlers ranged from farmers and fishers to shipwrights and loggers, but by far the most enterprising was William Gibbs. The farm and mansion he built at Totaranui, and the innovations he implemented – such as running water in every bedroom, a glasshouse that furnished grapes and a model dairy that used porcelain pans warmed by copper pipes to make cream rise – were ahead of their time.

The Abel Tasman National Park was declared in 1942. Much credit for its creation is due to Nelsonian Pérrine Moncrieff, the dedicated conservationist who wrote the first ornithological field guide, *New Zealand Birds and How to Identify Them*, in 1925. We thank you, Ms Moncrieff.

Environment

Nineteenth-century settlers embarked on their usual program of logging, quarrying and clearing forest to make way for pasture, and it was an ultimately successful campaign by conservationists that saw an original block of 150 sq km made into a national park in 1942. The varying vegetation cover of Abel Tasman reflects this history.

The moist, warm coastal areas are characterised by regenerating shrublands and lush coastal broadleaved forest, with vines, perching plants, tree ferns and an abundance of the country's national plant, the silver fern. On the drier ridges and throughout much of the park's interior, the bush is predominantly beech forest, with all five New Zealand species found within its confines.

The more common forest birds, such as tui and bellbird (korimako), can be seen, along with pukeko around the estuaries and wetlands. Oystercatchers (torea), shags (koau) and little blue penguins (korora) can be seen on the coast.

The park's boundaries formally exclude the estuaries, foreshore and seabed, though the estuaries and foreshore are now within the Tonga Island Marine Reserve, which was created along part of the Abel Tasman coast in 1993. All life in the marine reserve is protected. Native wildlife and natural, cultural and historical features are also protected within the park.

❶ Planning

WHEN TO TRAMP

The top of the South Island enjoys an enviable climate – Nelson is said to have more sunshine hours than any other place in New Zealand – making Abel Tasman a sparkling jewel at any time of year. Timing your visit for the shoulder season, or even winter, will avoid the crowds, as the Abel Tasman Coast Track can see more than 700 trampers a day in January. The best time to visit is from the end of February to May, when the crowds thin out but the weather is still pleasantly warm. Come August, you'll feel like you've got the whole track to yourself.

If you can't avoid January or February, you can keep out of people's way by skipping the huts and camping at smaller campsites. Avoid the main water-taxi and kayak drop-off and pick-up beaches between 9.30am and 10.30am, and 3.30pm and 5pm, when the coming and going of trampers is like rush-hour traffic in Auckland.

WHAT TO BRING

The main Abel Tasman tracks are so well graded that you needn't bring boots – a pair of runners is perfectly adequate. They're also easier to pull on and off again as you wade across tidal sections or paddle the shallows. Make sure you pack sunglasses, a swimsuit, a wide-brimmed hat, insect repellent and sunscreen. Bring a stove, as none of the huts have cooking facilities.

INFORMATION

Booking for the Great Walk huts and campsites on the Abel Tasman Coast Track can be done online at **Great Walks Bookings** (☎ 0800 694 732; www.doc.govt.nz). In recent years the popularity of the track has increased considerably and trampers coming in the peak season are advised to book well in advance. The DOC Nelson Visitor Centre, located within the **Nelson i-SITE** (p185), is the region's primary DOC centre and a good place to get advice, purchase hut tickets and maps, and help with bookings.

Information and bookings are also available at **Motueka i-SITE** (p186), and over the hill at the **Golden Bay Visitor Centre** (p187).

Abel Tasman Coast Track

Duration 5 days

Distance 60km (37.3 miles)

Difficulty Easy

Start Marahau

End Wainui car park

Gateways Motueka (p185), Nelson (p184)

Transport Bus, boat

Summary New Zealand's most popular multiday tramp, linking a series of beautiful and usually sun-filled beaches and bays.

Think of it as a beach holiday on foot. Arguably the most beautiful of the Great Walks, the Abel Tasman Coast Track is a seductive combination of reliably pleasant weather, sparkling seas, golden sand, quintessential NZ coastal forest and hidden surprises with intriguing names such as Cleopatra's Pool. We're pretty sure we have your attention now...

You're not alone. Such is the pulling power of this track that it now attracts more than 43,000 trampers and kayakers each year who stay at least one night in the park.

By way of comparison, the next most popular Great Walk is the Routeburn Track, which draws around 17,000.

Another attraction is the terrain, for this is not a typical, rugged New Zealand track. It is better serviced than any other track in the country: well cut, well graded and well marked. It's almost impossible to get lost and can be tramped in a pair of running shoes. Leaving the boots behind is a bonus, as you'll probably get your feet wet – indeed, you'll probably want to get your feet wet.

This is a track with long stretches of beach walking and crazy tides to work around. The tidal ranges in the park are among the greatest in the country – up to a staggering 6m. At Awaroa Bay you have no choice but to plan on crossing at low tide. Tide times are published on the the the DOC website (www.doc.govt.nz), and also displayed at DOC's Nelson Visitor Centre and regional i-SITEs. It's important to consult these at the time of planning your trip, as the times of the tides will affect the huts or campsites that you use and the direction in which you walk the track.

The tramp finishes at a car park near Wainui Bay, though most people extend their hike beyond Wainui by returning to Totaranui via the Gibbs Hill Track to pick up the water taxis back to Marahau or Kaiteriteri. You could always just stop at Totaranui the first time you walk through, but by continuing north you will discover the most dramatic view point (Separation Point), the least-crowded hut (Whariwharangi) and some of the best beaches (Anapai and Mutton Cove) in the park.

The entire tramp takes only three to five days, although with water-taxi transport you can convert it into an almost endless array of options, particularly if you combine it with a kayak leg (p162). Note, however, that kayaks aren't available from within the park and have to be brought in and out from Marahau/Kaiteriteri each day. If you plan to combine a tramp with kayaking, you should arrange the logistics with a kayak hire company before you book huts or campsites to ensure everything aligns.

If you can only spare a couple of days to tramp here, a deservedly popular option is the loop around the northern end of the park, hiking the Coast Track from Totaranui, passing Anapai and Mutton Cove, overnighting at Whariwharangi Hut then returning to Totaranui via the Gibbs Hill Track. This will give you a slice of the park's best features (beaches, seals, coastal scenery) and will be far less crowded than any other segment.

Abel Tasman Coast Track

N
0 — 5 km
0 — 2.5 miles

Whariwharangi Bay

Alternative Route

Separation Point

Taupo Hill (205m)

TASMAN SEA

Mutton Cove

Whariwharangi Hut

Anapai Bay Track

Motu Island

Abel Tasman Point

Abel Tasman Dr

Wainui Bay

Ngawhiti Island

Ligar Bay

Abel Tasman

Tarakohe

Takaka (9km)

End

P

Gibbs Hill Track

Gibbs Hill (405m)

Anapai Bay

Day 5

Totaranui

McShane Rd

Alternative End

Totaranui Campsite

Totaranui Rd

Pigeon Saddle

Awaroa Saddle

Goat Bay

P

Centre Peak (534m)

Inland Track

Wainui Falls

Awapoto Hut

Awaroa Rd

Pound Creek

Waiharakeke Bay

Awaroa Head

Awaroa Bay

Awaroa Lodge & Cafe

Tonga Island Marine Reserve

Inlet

Awapoto River

Waterfall Creek

Awaroa Hut

Day 4

Tonga Saddle (260m)

Onetahuti Beach

Caves

Wainui River

Stony Hill (394m)

Onetahuti Bay Campsite

Tonga Island

Camp Creek

Awaroa River

Tonga Quarry (disused)

Arch Point

Tonga Hill (458m)

Tonga Quarry Campsite

Murray Peak (1101m)

Jenkins Falls

Abel Tasman National Park

Alternative Route

Day 3

Foul Point

Wainui Hut

Table Creek

Bark Bay Hut

Bark Bay

Pisgah Hill (1096m)

Pages Saddle

Wainui Saddle

Bare Knob (314m)

Side Trip

Falls River Track

Falls River

Cascade Falls

Torrent Bay Village Campsite

Mt Evans (1156m)

Moa Park Shelter

Te Pukatea Bay Campsite

Torrent Bay

Canaan Saddle

Castle Rock Hut

Inland Track

Cleopatra's Pool

Torrent River

Day 2

Anchorage Hut

Holyoake Clearing Shelter

Observation Beach Camping Ground

Watering Cove Campsite

Akersten Bay Campsite

Adele Island

Marahau River

Tinline Campsite

Appletree Bay Campsite

Holyoake Stream

Start

P

Tinline Bay

Shelter

Coquille Bay

Fisherman Island

Ngaraua Caves

Marahau

Sandy Bay

60

Otuwheru Stream

Tokongawha Point

Ngaio Island

TASMAN SEA

Those wishing to explore the interior of the national park might like to consider the Inland Track, a tougher and much less frequented path taking three days. It can be combined with the Coast Track to form a five- to six-day loop.

ⓘ Planning

MAPS & BROCHURES

This track is so well trodden that a topographical map isn't essential for navigation. The map within DOC's free *Abel Tasman Coast Track* brochure and track guide provides sufficient detail. However, NewTopo's 1:40,000 *Abel Tasman* map and the Geographx 1:40,000 *Abel Tasman Track* map will give you the lie of the land.

HUTS & CAMPING

There are four huts on the Abel Tasman Coast Track: at Anchorage, Bark Bay, Awaroa and Whariwharangi. They are designated Great Walk huts (Great Walks season NZ local/foreigner $38/75, off-season $32), and have bunks, tables, benches, heating, flush toilets, and washbasins with cold water only. There are no cooking facilities or lighting (except at the Anchorage hut, which has solar lighting). There are also 19 designated Great Walk campsites (Great Walks season NZ local/foreigner $15/30, off-season $15).

The Abel Tasman Coast Track is a Great Walk, and all huts and campsites must be booked in advance year-round. Bookings can be made online through **Great Walks Bookings** (p160), or at any DOC visitor centre. DOC hut tickets and annual passes cannot be used on the track, and there is a two-night limit on staying in huts

---

KAYAKING THE ABEL TASMAN

The coastal beauty of Abel Tasman National Park makes it a seductive location for sea kayaking, an activity that can easily be combined with a tramp here.

A variety of kayaking operators will be able to float your boat, and the possibilities and permutations for guided or freedom trips are vast. You can kayak from half a day up to any number of days. You can even kayak one day, camp overnight then walk back, or walk further into the park and catch a water taxi back.

Most operators offer similar trips at similar prices. Marahau is the main base for operators, but trips also depart from Kaiteriteri. There are numerous day-trip options, including guided trips often departing Marahau and taking in bird-filled Adele Island. There are also various multiday guided trips, with three days a common option, costing anything from $260 to $750 depending on accommodation and other inclusions.

Freedom rentals (double-kayak and equipment hire) are around $80/135 per person for one/two days. Check the websites of operators for the various permutations on transport and walk options.

Instruction is given to everyone, and most tour companies have a minimum age of either eight or 14, depending on the trip. None allow solo hires. Camping gear is usually provided on overnight trips, and if you're disappearing into the park for a few days, most operators provide free car parking.

November to Easter is the busiest time, with December to February the absolute peak. You can, however, paddle all year-round, with winter offering its own rewards – the weather is surprisingly amenable, the seals are more playful and there's more bird life and less haze.

The following are the main players in this competitive market:

Abel Tasman Kayaks (☑ 0800 732 529, 03-527 8022; www.abeltasmankayaks.co.nz; Main Rd, Marahau; guided tours from $150)

Kahu Kayaks (☑ 0800 300 101, 03-527 8300; www.kahukayaks.co.nz; 11 Marahau Valley Rd; self-guided/guided tours from $75/215)

Kaiteriteri Kayaks (☑ 0800 252 925, 03-527 8383; www.seakayak.co.nz; Kaiteriteri Beach; ☺ adult/child from $80/60)

Marahau Sea Kayaks (☑ 0800 529 257, 03-527 8176; www.msk.co.nz; Abel Tasman Centre, Franklin St, Marahau; tours from $150)

R&R Kayaks (☑ 0508 223 224; www.rrkayaks.co.nz; 279 Sandy Bay-Marahau Rd; tours from $135)

Sea Kayak Company (☑ 0508 252 925, 03-528 7251; www.seakayaknz.co.nz; 506 High St, Motueka; tours from $85)

Wilsons Abel Tasman (p163)

or campsites. The exception is Totaranui, which has a one-night limit for trampers. Penalty fees will apply if you don't have a valid booking, and you may be required to leave the park.

Moored permanently in Anchorage Bay, **Aqua-packers** (☑ 0800 430 744; www.aquapackers. co.nz; Anchorage; dm/d $85/245; ☺ closed May-Sep) is a specially converted 13m catamaran providing unusual but buoyant backpacker accommodation for 22. Facilities are basic but decent, and prices include bedding, dinner and breakfast. Bookings are essential.

GUIDED TRAMPS

Kahurangi Guided Walks (☑ 03-391 4120; www.kahurangiwalks.co.nz) operates one- to five-day trips in Abel Tasman National Park ($250 to $1750). **Wilsons Abel Tasman** (☑ 03-528 2027, 0800 223 582; www.abeltasman. co.nz; 409 High St, Motueka; walk/kayak from $62/90) offers a wide range of combination tours (tramp, kayak, cruise) and owns beachfront lodges at Awaroa and Torrent Bay. **Abel Tasman Tours & Guided Walks** (☑ 03-528 9602; www.abeltasmantours.co.nz; Riwaka; tours from $295) runs day tramps ($295), that include a packed lunch and water taxis.

ⓘ Getting There & Away

The major gateway town to the Abel Tasman is Motueka, one hour's drive from Nelson. From here it's easy to get to the Coast Track's major entry points of Marahau (the southern access) and Totaranui to the north, accessible by driving over Takaka to Golden Bay. Wainui is the official northern trailhead, though it is more common to finish in Totaranui, either skipping the northernmost section of the track or looping back to Totaranui over Gibbs Hill Track. **Abel Tasman Coachlines** (p185) runs daily services from Nelson and Motueka to Marahau, while **Golden Bay Coachlines** (p185) has buses from Totaranui and Wainui to Nelson via Takaka and Motueka, though the service departs in the morning.

Trek Express (p148) runs services from Nelson to Marahau ($35) and Wainui ($55), and from Wainui back to Marahau or Nelson (both $55). It maintains a list of scheduled departures on its website, and also operates on demand.

Unless you wish to retrace your steps, your return transport options from Totaranui are a long drive over Takaka Hill or, much more easily, a water-taxi service that doubles as a scenic cruise (they will also most likely take you to see any seals or dolphins that are around). There are numerous and regular water-taxi services departing from either Marahau or Kaiteriteri up to Totaranui (to preserve the top end of the park as a more simple and natural experience, no services are permitted past that point), stopping off at Anchorage, Torrent Bay, Medlands Beach, Bark Bay, Tonga Quarry, Onetahuti and Awaroa along the way.

Note that the water taxis at Awaroa stop near the famous Awaroa Beach; there is then a walk of up to 1½ hours to get to Awaroa Hut and campsite from the drop-off point. One-way prices start from around $33 (Anchorage, Torrent Bay) and range up to around $46 for Totaranui. Water-taxi operators are very well versed in tailoring options to suit individual requirements, including kayak/walk packages for those who want to mix things up a bit. Key operators include **Abel Tasman Aqua Taxi** (☑ 03-527 8083, 0800 278 282; www.aquataxi. co.nz; Marahau-Sandy Bay Rd, Marahau), **Abel Tasman Sea Shuttle** (☑ 03-527 8688, 0800 732 748; www.abeltasmanseashuttles.co.nz; Kaiteriteri; cruises from $45), **Wilsons Abel Tasman** and **Marahau Water Taxis** (☑ 03-527 8176, 0800 808 018; www.marahauwatertaxis.co.nz; Abel Tasman Centre, Franklin St, Marahau).

 The Tramp

Day 1: Marahau to Anchorage

4 HOURS / 12.4KM

The track begins at a turn-off 1km north of Marahau, where there is a car park, information kiosk and shelter. From here it crosses the Marahau estuary on an all-tidal causeway, climbs gently to a clearing above Tinline Bay, and then passes Tinline Campsite, one hour (2.5km) from the car park. Just beyond the campsite a sign marks one end of the **Inland Track**.

The Coast Track continues northeast, skirting around dry ridges, hugging the coast and opening up to scenic views of Adele and Fisherman Islands, and Coquille and Appletree Bays. Signposts indicate side tracks leading down to the beaches where you can enjoy a refreshing swim in the surf. Trampers can pitch a tent at **Appletree Bay Campsite**, but be aware that this is a popular stop for kayakers.

After passing Yellow Point and its spur track, the trail turns inland, climbing in and out of gullies and along ridges lined with silver ferns. Eventually the trees thin out and you are rewarded with views of Torrent Bay. Here the track branches at a signposted junction. The main track heads east (right fork), passes a spur track (right), descends quickly to **Anchorage Beach** – 30 minutes away – and goes along the beach to the improved **Anchorage Hut** (34 bunks), constructed in 2014. Just beyond the hut is the Anchorage Campsite, a large and very popular spot in summer. The whole area becomes a makeshift marina at this time of year, with kayaks, water taxis and yachts coming and going, or sitting anchored offshore.

You can escape the crush of humanity around the hut by following the short side track at the eastern end of the beach to **Te Pukatea Bay Campsite**, or backtracking and taking the signposted spur track to **Watering Cove Campsite**.

Day 2: Anchorage to Bark Bay

4 HOURS / 11.5KM

This is a short day that could easily be combined with the next stage for a seven-hour walk to Awaroa...but then, why hurry when you could dally along the way, take the side trip along the Falls River Track, or hang out longer at Bark Bay?

From Anchorage Hut, head west along the beach and within 20 minutes climb an easy track over the headland into **Torrent Bay**. If the tide is right and the water low enough, you can zip straight across the bay; usually you have to be within two hours either side of low tide to cross. The recommended route, however, is to take the all-tide track at the junction above the tidal crossing on Torrent Bay. It takes around 1½ hours to walk the 3.5km track, which circles the bay through bush, arriving at the bach settlement of Torrent Bay. The main reason to come this way, even at low tide, is to take the 15-minute side track to beautiful **Cleopatra's Pool**, where the Torrent River gushes over smooth rocks. The cold, fresh water is invigorating after a day in the sun and sea.

Near **Torrent Bay Village Campsite** you skirt the lagoon in front of a string of beaches, then turn left up the beach and pass yet more without a pang of envy...or maybe just one. Keep going for 500m before the track heads away from the coast.

Once the main track moves inland it climbs 90m and sidles around Kilby Stream, before reaching a low saddle, where a side track takes you to a **lookout**. The Coast Track descends to a swing bridge over **Falls River** and then climbs to a spur track to a second **lookout**. Take a breather and enjoy the views of Bark Bay to the north and the coastline to the south. From the junction it's a 20-minute descent to **Bark Bay**.

This bay is now a major access point for the track, with passenger boats coming in and out several times a day. **Bark Bay Hut** (34 bunks) is on the edge of the lagoon, a short walk from the beach. Like the hut, Bark Bay Campsite is a large facility, so at times this snug little bay can be overflowing with trampers. If you don't mind all the people, however, it's a beautiful place to spend a night.

Side Trip: Falls River Track

3 HOURS / 6KM RETURN

Those who want to see the various falls and pools of Tregidga Creek and Falls River should look for the track heading northwest from Torrent Bay Village. An easy track follows Tregidga Creek to the modest **Cascade Falls** after one hour. Stay on this track to reach Falls River, 15 minutes downstream from its main falls. A boulder-hopping scramble, helped by an occasional marker, will bring you to the impressive **cascade**.

If you want to spice things up a little, you could also join a canyoning trip down Torrent Bay River and its beautiful granite-lined canyon – swimming, sliding, abseiling and leaping into jewel-like pools – with **Abel Tasman Canyons** (☑ 03-528 9800, 0800 863 472; www.abeltasmancanyons.co.nz; Motueka; full-day trips $269).

Day 3: Bark Bay to Awaroa Bay

4½ HOURS / 13.5KM

The coast along this section of track is classified as **Tonga Island Marine Reserve**, and is home to a seal colony and visiting dolphins. Tonga Island itself is the small island off Onetahuti Beach.

The track follows the spit to its northern end and traverses the tidal lagoon that can be crossed two hours either side of low tide. If you're here closer to high tide, the all-tide track takes an extra 10 minutes.

Beyond the lagoon the track enters the bush and immediately begins to climb steeply to a low saddle. You then wind over several inland ridges before dropping sharply to **Tonga Quarry**, 3.5km from Bark Bay. A metal plaque describes the quarry operations that took place here, and several large, squarish stones are nearby. What remains of the wharf can be seen in the sand. Located just off the beach is the **Tonga Quarry Campsite**.

The most interesting feature of the bay can only be reached 1½ hours either side of low tide. Follow the rocky shore south from the southern end of the beach, and after a 10-minute scramble you come to the sea arches of **Arch Point**, a set of impressive natural stone sculptures formed by the repeated pounding of the waves.

The Coast Track continues by climbing the headland that separates Tonga Quarry and **Onetahuti Beach**. After a 1km walk you come to a clearing overlooking the graceful curve of the long beach. This is another classic Abel Tasman National Park beach, and **Onetahuti Bay Campsite** is at the southern end. Near the campsite a sign points the way to delightfully cold and clear freshwater pools that lie beneath a small waterfall – ideal after a hot day.

The beach is more than 1km in length. Follow it to the northern end where a boardwalk and two bridges will keep your feet dry. The Coast Track leaves the beach by gently climbing above the swamp, providing a nice overview of the area. Within an hour the track climbs to **Tonga Saddle** (260m), giving you a quick glimpse ahead of the beaches in the distance. If you're heading for Awaroa Hut, take the north-west path (left fork). The track descends to a bridge over Venture Creek and large orange discs lead along the shore for 15 minutes to **Awaroa Hut** (26 bunks), on a small beach in Awaroa Inlet. Nearby is Awaroa campsite.

The right fork leads to **Awaroa Lodge**, where you will find a cafe offering civilised refreshment. From the lodge the path to Awaroa Hut passes an airstrip before reaching Venture Creek, which can only be crossed here two hours either side of low tide. Once across the creek follow the orange discs to Awaroa Hut.

To spend the night at Totaranui you need a tent – there are no huts or cabins – and there is a one-night limit for trampers. **Totaranui Campsite** (☑ 03-528 8083; www.doc.govt.nz; Oct-Apr $15, May-Sep $10) is an extremely popular facility with a splendid setting next to the beach backed by some of the best bush in the national park. It borders on being a metropolis (it has capacity for 850 campers), but still gets completely booked out between 22 December and 8 February each year as it's the prime spot in the park for holidaying Kiwi families. Bookings open in early August and all places go within hours. A staffed DOC office has interpretive displays, flush toilets, cold showers and a public phone.

Follow the tree-lined avenue in front of the office and turn north at the intersection, passing the education centre. At the end of the road the **Anapai Bay Track** begins, crossing Kaikau Stream and reaching a junction with the Headlands Track. Take the left fork, climbing to a low saddle and then descending along a forested stream to **Anapai Bay**, which is split in two by unusual rock outcrops. The **Anapai Bay Campsite** is one hour from Totaranui; it makes for a great place to spend a night, as the sites overlook the scenic beach.

Day 4: Awaroa Bay to Anapai Bay

3 HOURS / 9.1KM

Awaroa Inlet can only be crossed 1½ hours before and up to two hours after low tide. It is important that you check the tide times at the planning stage of your trip, before you start the tramp. If you get it wrong, you can be stranded here for 10 hours, with no alternatives. Note also that if you're not carrying a tent, you'll need to hike through to Whari-wharangi Bay (the only hut beyond Awaroa Bay on the Coast Track) on this day, making for a walk of around 4½ to five hours.

Cross the bay directly in front of the hut and follow the large orange discs that lead to Pound Gully. The track follows the creek until it passes a signposted junction to Awaroa Rd, then quickly arrives at **Waiharakeke Bay**, another beautiful beach. The Waiharakeke campsite is a great spot, only 30 to 40 minutes north of Awaroa.

The track climbs away from the beach, across a rocky ridge and then descends into **Goat Bay**. From Goat Bay it is a 45-minute steep climb over the hill to **Totaranui**, with stunning views of the settlement there as you descend.

Day 5: Anapai Bay to Wainui Car Park

4–4½ HOURS / 13.5KM

The Coast Track continues up the sandy beach, then heads inland. After 2km it reaches **Mutton Cove** and the Mutton Cove Campsite.

From the campsite, the track – an old farm road – heads inland over a low saddle, or you can take an interesting one-hour alternative route that takes in **Separation Point**, the granite headland separating Tasman Bay from Golden Bay. Pick up this track by continuing along the beach at Mutton Cove to the northern end of the second bay. This track climbs to the side trail from the Coast Track and eliminates any backtracking. The views are worth the walk – Farewell Spit is visible to the northwest, and on an exceptionally clear day so is the North Island. The point is also a favourite haunt of migrating fur seals, which are often spotted sunning themselves on the rocks or swimming offshore. Continue west along the side trail and within 30 minutes you return to the true Coast Track at the low saddle between Mutton Cove and Whariwharangi Bay.

From this saddle the track descends through regenerating scrubland. About 2km from Mutton Cove it reaches **Whariwharangi Bay**, another beautiful, curved beach. **Whariwharangi Hut** (20 bunks) is at the western end of the bay, 500m inland. This hut is unique, being a restored two-storey farmhouse built in 1897 that was last permanently occupied in 1926. Nearby is **Whariwharangi Campsite**.

Most trampers will want to loop back to Totaranui, since transport options are difficult from Wainui (there's only one bus a day from Wainui and it departs in the morning; if you miss the bus you'll be stranded some 20km from Takaka). To loop back, turn left at the **Gibbs Hill Track** (three hours) beyond Whariwharangi, climbing over Gibbs Hill and descending to Totaranui.

Otherwise, continue to **Wainui** by following the Coast Track, which climbs another low saddle capturing views of Wainui Inlet, before descending to the estuary and skirting the shore to reach the Wainui car park, 5.5km (about 1½ hours) from Whariwharangi Bay.

KAHURANGI NATIONAL PARK

Situated due west of Abel Tasman National Park, Kahurangi – 'Blue Skies' in one of several translations – is New Zealand's second-largest national park. Within its 4520 sq km lie the Tasman Mountains, a chain of steep and rugged ranges, with a pair of significant ranges (Arthur and Matiri) alongside. The park's highest point is Mt Owen (1875m), while deep beneath the ground are the karst crevices that make up the largest known cave systems in the southern hemisphere.

Five major river systems drain the park: Aorere and Takaka flow into Golden Bay, Motueka pours into Tasman Bay, and Karamea and Heaphy end their journeys in the Tasman Sea. The best-known walk in Kahurangi is the Heaphy Track, which stretches from the Aorere Valley, near Collingwood, to the West Coast north of Karamea. It's just part of a 650km network of tracks that also includes the more challenging and less frequented Wangapeka and remote Leslie-Karamea Tracks.

History

The legendary moa thrived in the northwest region of the South Island, and were an important food source for the early Māori

who settled here from the 14th century. As was so often the case on the South Island, routes through the area were frequently created in the quest for *pounamu* (greenstone), sourced from the West Coast.

In 1846 Charles Heaphy (a draftsman for the New Zealand Company) and Thomas Brunner became the first Europeans to walk up the West Coast to the Heaphy River. In 1860 James Mackay and John Clark completed the inland portion of the Heaphy Track while searching for pastoral land between Buller and Collingwood. A year later gold was discovered at Karamea, inspiring prospectors to struggle over the track in search of riches.

The Heaphy was improved when JB Saxon surveyed and graded the track in 1888 for the Collingwood County Council. Gold deposits were never found, though, and use of the Heaphy Track declined considerably in the early 1900s.

After the Northwest Nelson Forest Park (which was to become Kahurangi National Park) was established in 1970, the track was improved dramatically, and the New Zealand Forest Service began to bench the route and construct huts. The Heaphy Track did not become really popular, though, until plans for a road from Collingwood to Karamea were announced in the early 1970s. Conservationists, deeply concerned about the damage the road would do to the environment, in particular to the area's nikau palms, began an intensive campaign to stop the work going ahead, and to increase the popularity of the track.

Environment

Kahurangi is the most diverse of New Zealand's national parks, both in landforms and in the range of its flora and fauna. Its most eye-catching features are arguably its rock formations, ranging from windswept beaches and sea cliffs to earthquake-shattered slopes and moraine-dammed lakes, and the smooth, strange karst forms of the interior tableland.

There's plenty of room in between for bush to flourish. Around 85% of the park is forested, with beech prevalent, along with rimu and other podocarps, particularly on the lower slopes in the western fringes. These fringes have an understorey of broadleaved trees and ferns, climbers and perching plants. More than 50% of all NZ's plant species can be found in the park, including more than 80% of its alpine plant species.

The ecological wonderment is not just confined to plants, with 60 native bird species flitting about the park, including the great spotted kiwi (OK, ambling rather than flitting), kea, kaka and whio (blue duck). There are rather spooky cave weta sharing a home with various weird beetles and a huge, leggy spider, and a majestic and ancient snail known as Powelliphanta, which is something of a (slow) flag bearer for the park's animal kingdom.

If you like a tramp that's a virtual field trip filled with plenty of things new and strange, Kahurangi National Park is the place for you.

ℹ Planning

WHEN TO TRAMP

It's possible to tramp here year-round. Easter is traditionally the most popular time to hike the Heaphy Track, while late February through March is a particularly good time to tackle any of the tracks in the park.

INFORMATION

Bookings for the Great Walk huts and campsites on the Heaphy Track can be done online at **Great Walks Bookings** (☑ 0800 694 732; www.doc. govt.nz). The DOC Nelson Visitor Centre in the **Nelson i-SITE** (p185) is the region's primary DOC centre and a good place to get advice, purchase hut tickets and maps, and get help with bookings. Information and bookings are also available at **Motueka i-SITE** (p186), and over the hill at **Golden Bay Visitor Centre** (p187), which also hands out copies of its indispensable yellow tourist map.

At the West Coast end, your port of call should be **Karamea Information & Resource Centre** (p187), an excellent, community-owned centre with all the necessary track services (including hut tickets and bookings) and the general lowdown on all things local.

Heaphy Track

Duration 5 days

Distance 78.5km (48.8 miles)

Difficulty Moderate

Start Brown Hut

End Kohaihai

Gateways Karamea (p187), Takaka (p186)

Transport Shuttle bus, plane

Summary A historic and beautiful crossing from Golden Bay to the wild West Coast, offering one of the widest ranges of scenery on any of New Zealand's tramps.

The Heaphy Track is one of the most popular tramping routes in the country, and is a Great Walk in every sense. It traverses incredibly diverse terrain – dense native forest, the mystical Gouland Downs, secluded valleys, and beaches that are a haze of salt spray and fringed by nikau palms.

Although quite long, the Heaphy is well cut and benched, making it easier than any other extended tramp in Kahurangi National Park. That said, it can still be arduous, particularly in unfavourable weather, which is often the special of the day on the West Coast.

By walking from east to west (as we've described the tramp) most of the climbing is done on the first day, and the scenic beach walk is saved for the end, creating a fitting and energising grand finale. A strong tramper could walk the Heaphy in three days, but most people choose to take four or five.

If you're tramping here between May and November, be alert to the possible presence of bikes, with the track also open to mountain bikers (p171) across these months.

ℹ Planning

WHAT TO BRING

Note that not all huts have gas rings, so check the DOC website (www.doc.govt.nz), or ask for details when you make your booking. Pack plenty of insect repellent, otherwise the sandflies may end up eating more than you do.

MAPS & BROCHURES

This tramp is covered by NZTopo50 maps *BP23 (Gouland Downs)* and *BP22 (Heaphy Beach)*. It is also covered by NewTopo's 1:55,000 *Heaphy Track* map. DOC's free *Heaphy Track* brochure and guide may also prove helpful.

HUTS & CAMPING

Seven Great Walk huts ($34) lie along the Heaphy Track: Brown, Perry Saddle, Gouland Downs, Saxon, James Mackay, Lewis and Heaphy. They each have bunks and a kitchen area, heating, flush toilets and washbasins with cold water. All of these huts – except Brown and Gouland Downs – have gas stoves, and a couple have lighting.

There are also nine Great Walk campsites ($14) along the track. The two day shelters (Aorere and Katipo) are just that; overnight stays are not permitted.

The Heaphy is a Great Walk and all huts and campsites must be booked in advance year-round. Bookings can be made online through **Great Walks Bookings** (p100), or at any DOC visitors centre. DOC hut tickets and annual passes can't be used on the track, and there is a two-night limit on staying in huts or campsites.

ABEL TASMAN, KAHURANGI & NELSON LAKES HEAPHY TRACK

Heaphy Track (North)

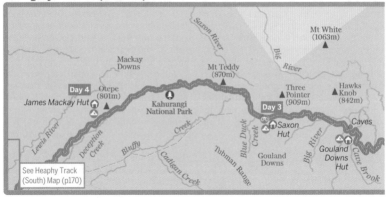

At the West Coast end of the track is the beachside **Kohaihai Campsite** (www.doc.govt. nz; per person $8), 15km north of Karamea.

GUIDED TRAMPS

Bush & Beyond (☑ 021 027 08209, 03-543 3742; www.heaphytrackguidedwalks.co.nz) offers a guided, fully catered six-day Heaphy Track package ($1900) as well as guided but self-catered five-day hike ($900 to $950). **Kahurangi Guided Walks** (p163) runs three guided Heaphy trips, ranging from four days ($1250) to six days ($2250).

❶ Getting There & Away

The two road ends of the Heaphy Track are an almost unfathomable distance apart – 463km to be precise – making this a through-hike on which you're unlikely to be leaving a vehicle at either end. By far the best way to close the loop is to fly back from Karamea by aeroplane or helicopter – the time saved and the aerial view go some considerable way to justifying the cost.

Aeroplane flights are run by **Adventure Flights Golden Bay** (☑ 0800 150 338, 03-525 6167; www.adventureflightsgoldenbay.co.nz; Takaka Airfield, SH60; from $40), which charges $185 per person for three to five people, or $200 per person for up to two people. The same company offers flights from Takaka to Brown Hut, saving an hour-long shuttle ride, combined with the flight back from Karamea ($240 to $265). **Golden Bay Air** (☑ 0800 588 885; www.golden bayair.co.nz) wings it over the same route ($149 to $179) and also offers shuttles from Takaka Airfield to Brown Hut ($65 per person for two people, or $45 per person for three or more) and car relocations back to the airfield from Brown

Hut ($80). **Helicopter Charter Karamea** (☑ 03-782 6111; www.helicharterkaramea.com; 78 Aerodrome Rd, Karamea) can carry up to three people for $750.

The Brown Hut trailhead is a one-hour drive from Takaka. **Golden Bay Coachlines** (p185) runs a daily 9.15am service (December to March) from Takaka ($35), which stops at Collingwood on the way.

Scheduled return-trip transport from Nelson (and stops in between) is offered from November to the end of April by **Heaphy Bus** (☑ 0800 128 735, 03-540 2042; www.theheaphybus. co.nz), servicing Brown Hut ($65) daily from December to mid-March and on Monday and Wednesday in November and from mid-March to April. It runs to and from Kohaihai ($115) twice weekly (Thursday and Sunday) from December to mid-March and on Sunday only in November and from mid-March to April. Out-of-season services are offered on demand through the same company in the guise of **Trek Express** (p148), running to Brown Hut for $65, and back from Kohaihai for $115; a minimum of five people is needed. It can also organise car relocations (Brown Hut to Kohaihai $375). **Heaphy Track Help** (☑ 03-525 9576; www. heaphytrackhelp.co.nz) also offers car relocations ($200 to $290 plus fuel, depending on the direction and time). The owner drives your car to the trail end and hikes the Heaphy Track back!

The Kohaihai trailhead is 15km from the small town of Karamea. **Karamea Connections** (☑ 03-782 6667; www.karameaconnections. co.nz) operates an on-demand shuttle service from Kohaihai to Karamea ($20 per person, minimum fare $40).

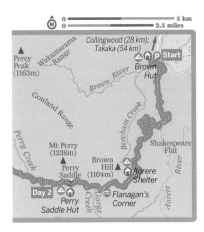

🏃 The Tramp

Day 1: Brown Hut to Perry Saddle Hut

5 HOURS / 17.5KM / 770M ASCENT

The car park at the Heaphy Track's eastern end is at Brown Hut (16 bunks), which was built to enable trampers to get an early start on the first leg of the journey – the climb to Perry Saddle. It has drinking water and flush toilets. Nearby is Brown Hut campsite.

From the hut the track follows Brown River for 200m before crossing it on a footbridge. On the other side you pass through pasture and then begin the long climb towards Gouland Downs. Beech forest with scattered podocarps and rata surrounds the wide track as it slowly climbs along monotonous switchbacks.

Within 1½ hours the track passes a junction with the Shakespeare Flat Track, a route that descends south (left fork) to the Aorere River.

The main track swings uphill and about three hours from Brown Hut, after 11km of climbing, reaches Aorere Shelter, an ideal spot for lunch or morning tea (depending how quickly you're moving), complete with a water supply. Nearby is Aorere Shelter campsite.

Beyond the shelter the track remains wide and continues to climb, but at a more gentle pace. Within one hour, or 3km, you reach Flanagan's Corner, the highest point of the tramp at 915m. A five-minute spur track (left) leads to a viewpoint that includes the surrounding ridges and 1238m Mt Perry.

From Flanagan's Corner it's another 40 minutes (2km) along a level track before you break out of the bush into the open tussock and patches of beech found on Perry Saddle. Five minutes away, at an elevation of 880m, Perry Saddle Hut (28 bunks) commands views of the Douglas Range across the Aorere Valley. Perry Saddle Campsite is also located here, and nearby is the deep Gorge Creek, a great spot to wash away the tramping day despite its rather shocking temperature.

Day 2: Perry Saddle Hut to Saxon Hut

3–4 HOURS / 12.5KM

A well-formed track enters the bush and remains in it for the next hour or so, crossing a handful of streams, three of them bridged. The third one is Sheep Creek, and from here the track opens into the bowl of Gouland Downs, a vast expanse of rolling tussock broken by patches of stunted silver beech and pygmy pine. You skirt the upper edge of this basin for more than 1km, and at one point you can look down and see Gouland Downs Hut. The track then begins a long descent, bottoming out at a bridge over Cave Brook. On the other side you quickly climb to Gouland Downs Hut (eight bunks) and Gouland Downs Campsite.

Although the small hut is old, it has a large fireplace and a cosy atmosphere. The fireplace is probably the only original part of the hut, which was built in 1932. Most trampers push on because the hut is only a two-hour (8km) walk from Perry Saddle.

Heading west you immediately enter a scene of eroded limestone caves and stone arches, covered by stunted beech and carpeted with thick moss. It's all rather fantastical. In a few minutes you emerge again onto the red-tussock downs and cross three streams in the next hour: Shiner Brook, Big River and Weka Creek.

From Weka Creek the track re-enters the bush and begins climbing. It's a gentle 20-minute climb before the track levels out and, in 10 minutes, reaches Saxon Hut (16 bunks) and Saxon Campsite, 1½ hours (5km) from Gouland Downs Hut. Located on the edge of the downs and with excellent views, Saxon is a very pleasant place to stay overnight, although many trampers push on another three hours and overnight at James Mackay Hut.

Heaphy Track (South)

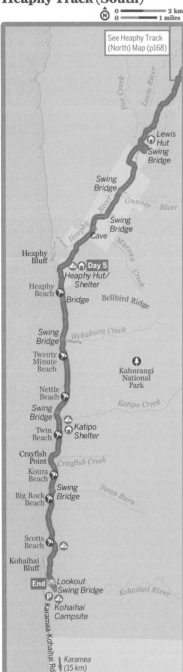

Day 3: Saxon Hut to James Mackay Hut

3 HOURS / 12KM

The day begins with 3km of level tramping, crossing **Saxon River** and **Blue Duck Creek** on bridges, and passing the signposted border between DOC's Tasman and Buller Districts. Welcome to the West Coast!

Eventually you enter the bush and begin the final climb to regain the height you lost in the descent to Gouland Downs. One hour from Saxon Hut you get your first glimpse of the Tasman Sea and the mouth of the Heaphy River.

The climb lasts for almost one hour, ascending 100m. When you finally top out, you emerge into the small patches of tussock that make up the **Mackay Downs**. It takes one hour to cross the southern end of the downs. Think of DOC fondly as you pass across the boardwalk, as this section used to be an absolute mudfest.

The track crosses several more streams and then **Deception Creek**, which is bridged and signposted. Within 15 minutes of crossing the river you arrive at **James Mackay Hut** (28 bunks). Located on the fringe of the bush, this hut has expansive views across the Tasman Sea and Gunner Downs. On a clear evening the sunsets are extraordinary, with the sun melting into a shimmering Tasman Sea. Nearby is the James Mackay Campsite.

Day 4: James Mackay Hut to Heaphy Hut

5–6 HOURS / 20.5KM / 710M DESCENT

The track heads southwest, and in 10 minutes passes a spur track that leads to one of the last views down the Heaphy Valley. From here you begin a steady descent towards the coast. Gradually the valley closes in, and within one hour you spy the Heaphy River below. In another two hours the 12km descent ends with the trail bottoming out beside your first nikau palms, three of them clustered 100m above the junction of the Lewis and Heaphy Rivers. In all you'll have dropped 600m in little more than two hours. **Lewis Hut** (20 bunks) is just five minutes away, down a short side trail.

The hut, a three-hour, 13.5km walk from James Mackay Hut, is perched on a terrace above the **Heaphy River**. From its veranda there is a nice view of the water. It would be an enjoyable place to sit and relax, if not for the sandflies, which are thick at times. You can stay here, but the popular Heaphy Hut, on the Tasman Sea, is just 2½ hours away.

Follow the track in front of Lewis Hut 100m upstream to the 150m-long **Heaphy River Bridge**. The track now follows the true left (south) bank of the Heaphy, and will remain on this side until it reaches the Tasman Sea. Limestone bluffs keep the track close to the river and occasionally you break out to a view of the water below. Most of the time you're in a rainforest so thick and lush, that its canopy forms a tunnel around the track.

Within 3km (one hour) of crossing the Heaphy you arrive at another bridge, over the **Gunner River**, and in another 30 minutes you cross the last swing bridge of the day, over **Murray Creek**. In the final hour the track remains close to the river until you skirt a steep bluff, looking at the Heaphy River below and the Tasman Sea just to the west. This is a scenic end to a fine day of tramping. You are now only about 15 minutes from the hut.

The spectacular **Heaphy Hut** (32 bunks), completed in 2013, is just up from the river in an open, grassy area enclosed by nikau palms and overlooking a lagoon in the Heaphy River where there is good swimming. However, swimming in the sea should be avoided as there are vicious undertows. Most trampers are simply content to stroll along the beach to witness its powerful surf and let the sea run through their toes. Having a beach like this in such a wilderness setting to yourself is worth every step it takes to reach it. Also near the hut is the Heaphy River Campsite and a shelter in a grassy clearing. This is the best campsite along the track, and the sandflies seem to agree.

Day 5: Heaphy Hut to Kohaihai Campsite

5 HOURS / 16KM

Unquestionably one of the most beautiful sections of track on the South Island, the final segment of the Heaphy Track meanders along the coast, sticking close to the pounding Tasman Sea. The track stays in the bush much of the way, but in many places well-worn paths show where trampers have decided to forgo the track and hike along the beach. Big seas and high tides have eroded short sections of the coastal track, and these are now marked with warning signs indicating that waves could break dangerously over the track. If in doubt, wait it out. Tide times are posted at Heaphy Hut (and also at Kohaihai Shelter).

The track departs from Heaphy Hut and, for the first time, heads south. It wends through a grove of nikau palms, which are occasionally alongside wetlands bordered by a forested bluff.

Within 1km you cross a bridge over Cold Creek and then break out to a view of **Heaphy Beach**. For the next hour you remain close to the shore, often in view of it. You cross **Wekakura Creek** on a swing bridge and then arrive at **Twenty Minute Beach**, where you have the opportunity to bypass the track and walk along the sand.

Orange markers lead you back onto the track and follow **Nettle Beach**, with the track staying well above the shoreline. At this point you head inland, into a grove of palms. Cross a long swing bridge over Katipo Creek and arrive at **Katipo Shelter**, the halfway point of the day, 2½ hours from Heaphy Hut. Also located here is Katipo Campsite.

To the south the track skirts **Twin Beach**, fords Crayfish Creek and then arrives at **Crayfish Point**. From the point, the track dips back into the bush and then climbs the bluff to skirt both **Koura Beach** and **Big Rock Beach**, allowing you to look down at the crashing surf. One hour (3km) from Crayfish Point you descend to **Scotts Beach Campsite**, where you may encounter day walkers who have come in from Kohaihai, just one hour away.

From **Scotts Beach** the Heaphy Track makes a steady but gentle climb to a saddle. You top out at a spur track to **Scotts**

ABEL TASMAN, KAHURANGI & NELSON LAKES HEAPHY TRACK

MOUNTAIN BIKING THE HEAPHY TRACK

The Heaphy Track is open to mountain bikers from 1 May to 30 November. Factoring in distance, remoteness and the possibility of bad weather, this epic bike journey is best suited to well-equipped cyclists with advanced riding skills. It takes most cyclists three days to complete. You can also just get a taster by zipping in from the West Coast for a day ride or spending a night at Heaphy Hut and then heading back out the next day. You can hire bikes in Takaka and Westport.

The DOC website (www.doc.govt.nz) has a page of information on mountain biking the Heaphy.

Hill Lookout – a 10-minute walk to a spectacular view of the coastline – and then descend. The track ends with a big swing bridge over the **Kohaihai River** that deposits you at Kohaihai, where there is a shelter and campsite (p168).

Tableland Circuit

Duration 3 days

Distance 28km (17.4 miles)

Difficulty Moderate

Start/End Flora car park

Gateways Nelson (p184), Motueka (p185)

Transport Shuttle bus

Summary This loop around the fascinating Mt Arthur Tableland packs in plenty of eye candy, from freaky alpine plants to twittering forest, odd rock forms and a grand peak, as well as wide-open views to lands far below.

The Arthur Range is one of three significant mountain ranges in Kahurangi National Park. Its highest peak is Mt Arthur (1795m), the summit of which can be reached by fit trampers without any special equipment in good weather, though snow can be present here at any time of year. To the west of the mountain is a great uplifted plateau known as the Mt Arthur Tableland, a fascinating area with strange and ancient rock formations, diverse plant life and relics from the pioneer era.

The tableland is also crossed by the long, remote and more demanding Leslie-Karamea Track, which heads southwest before connecting with the Wangapeka Track. It also lies adjacent to Cobb Valley, another great tramping area that is accessible from Golden Bay.

The gently rolling tableland is a remnant of a once-extensive sea-level plain that stretched across NZ more than 45 million years ago. As the land sank below sea level, thick quartz gravel and then limestone were deposited on the ancient plain. In the last 14 million years, the plain has been uplifted, mostly buckled and folded into mountains, with its limestones and quartz gravels eroded away. But here and there remnants have survived, and can be seen here.

There's something otherworldly – almost magical – about this place, and this three-day adventure is sure to leave you with indelible memories.

Planning

MAPS & BROCHURES

This tramp is covered by NZTopo50 maps *BP24 (Takaka)* and *BQ24 (Tapawera)*, as well as New-Topo's 1:55,000 *Mt Arthur and the Cobb Valley* map. DOC's excellent *Cobb Valley, Mt Arthur, Tableland* brochure details myriad walks in this area.

HUTS & CAMPING

There are four huts along this route. The recommended stops, Mt Arthur Hut and Salisbury Lodge, are both Serviced huts ($15), though only Salisbury has gas cookers, so be sure to carry a stove. There are numerous other huts on and around the tableland, ranging from Serviced to Basic, along with rock shelters, which are free. Only use the formal fireplaces inside the huts in this area.

Camping is also permitted and is free unless you wish to camp within 50m of a hut – in which case you will have to pay $5. Backcountry hut tickets or passes can be bought from any DOC visitors centre, and locally at the **Motueka i-SITE** (p186) and **Golden Bay Visitor Centre** (p187) in Takaka.

GUIDED TRAMPS

Kahurangi Guided Walks (p163) runs small-group tramps in Kahurangi National Park, including a day walk from Flora car park to the summit of Mt Arthur ($250). **Bush & Beyond** (p168) offers tailored trips of between two and six days around the tableland and Cobb Valley ($700 to $1700).

Getting There & Away

Flora car park is 75km from Nelson and 36km from Motueka, reached via the steep, winding and unsealed Graham Valley Rd, accessed off SH61 running up Motueka Valley. Follow signs from Ngatimoti, where a bridge crosses to Motueka River West Bank Rd. The road is steep and narrow and prone to slips; a 4WD is recommended during winter and after heavy rain. Flora car park has a toilet and an information kiosk.

Trek Express (p148) provides on-demand transport to Flora car park from Nelson ($45).

The Tramp

Day 1: Flora Car Park to Mt Arthur Hut

1½ HOURS / 3.6KM / 370M ASCENT

This is a short day's tramp, so those with energy, strength and good weather may consider combining it with the challenging but entirely possible climb to the summit of **Mt Arthur**, a three- to four-hour return trip from Mt Arthur Hut. With an early rise, it's also possible to bag

ABEL TASMAN, KAHURANGI & NELSON LAKES TABLELAND CIRCUIT

Tableland Circuit

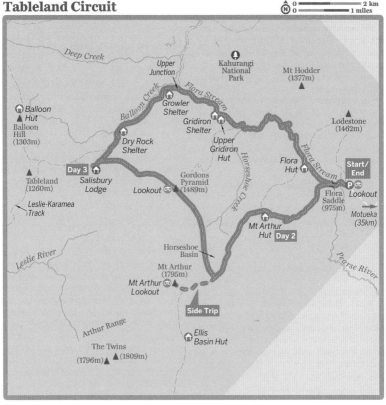

the peak on Day 2, which avoids some back-tracking, thus shaving off one to two hours.

Arriving at Flora car park deposits you at an elevation of 940m, where views of Mt Arthur can be had from a shelter with interpretive displays.

From the car park a wide gravel path, originally a miners' track, departs into the bush. Within 10 minutes you arrive at **Flora Saddle** (975m), where there is a signposted junction. Straight ahead lies the track to Flora Hut, on which you will return on Day 3, but for now you need to take the left fork towards Mt Arthur.

The well-graded track follows the ridge towards Mt Arthur, winding through beech forest and groves of shaggy mountain neinei, one of NZ's most peculiar-looking trees.

Mt Arthur Hut (eight bunks) sits on the bushline. It's a classic backcountry hut, with little room to swing a cat. It atones with a well-worn outdoor area. There are limited campsites around this hut. Weka are likely to pay you a visit. If you arrive looking to lap up some afternoon sun, it's worth heading up the track for five minutes or so, where the views open up even further.

Day 2: Mt Arthur Hut to Salisbury Lodge

4–5 HOURS / 10.4KM / 590M ASCENT, 770M DESCENT

This is a strenuous day's tramp across exposed terrain, even more so if you are factoring in the climb to the summit of Mt Arthur. Do not set off unless the weather is clear.

From Mt Arthur Hut, the track quickly emerges onto the open tops above the bushline. From here on in, it's nonstop views (except when you're watching your feet) for the best part of the day.

Follow the poled route as it winds first through rock gardens, where tufts of alpine plants spring out of the large cracks, then up and along a grassy ridge towards mountains looming large ahead.

A track junction marks the meeting of the **Mt Arthur Summit Track** (straight ahead), and a right fork to Salisbury Lodge via Gordons Pyramid. Those heading to the summit can leave their packs here, making the steep climb a bit easier.

To continue to Salisbury Lodge, take the right fork, which leads across **Horseshoe Basin**. There is considerable undulation, with some particularly steep and rocky bits – those tramping in groups may find it helpful to cooperate in hauling packs over the trickier sections.

It is a strenuous climb to the summit of **Gordons Pyramid** (1489m), but all will be forgiven as you take in the head-swivelling view, which includes the vast, partially forested tableland below.

This relief will be relatively short-lived though, as the apparently endless descent begins. Salisbury Lodge may seem close, but you will discover as the track drops into the forest that it's a lot further away than it looks. Those legs already severely punished by Mt Arthur and Gordons Pyramid may enter purgatory as they pick their way down through the forest of stunted beech trees festooned with lichen. The track is laden with tree roots that require careful placement of your feet.

Eventually you will emerge into the golden, tufty tussock lands known as **Salisbury's Open**. Cross the meadow to **Salisbury Lodge** (22 bunks), a relatively luxurious hut (well, there is solar lighting in the toilet) with views out over the golden meadows and the Arthur Range. The lodge is named after Thomas Salisbury, who stumbled across the tableland in 1865. Just east of the lodge is a small cave and some potholes that can be explored.

Side Trip: Mt Arthur

2–3 HOURS / 10KM RETURN / 250M ASCENT & DESCENT

The summit of Mt Arthur is a truly magnificent view point, taking in Tasman Bay, the Richmond Ranges, the nearby Twins, the Southern Alps and then some.

This track should only be attempted by experienced trampers with appropriate equipment and in favourable weather. A well-marked route ascends from Mt Arthur Hut, passing the junction to Gordons Pyramid, and continuing up an exposed ridge to the summit (1795m). Take care around the many bluffs, sinkholes and caves.

Day 3: Salisbury Lodge to Flora Car Park

4 HOURS / 14KM / 190M DESCENT

The last leg of the circuit is a relatively easy amble along a former stock route, passing a series of interesting landmarks along the way.

The track begins in front of Salisbury Lodge and heads north across open tussock lands towards Upper Junction and Flora Valley. Around 20 minutes into the day, a short side track leads to **Dry Rock Shelter**, an unusual rock bivvy.

The track continues its gentle descent, eventually dropping into the bush alongside Balloon Creek, and passing **Growler Shelter**, nestled into an overhang.

Heading east (the right fork) at Upper Junction, the Flora Track levels out and crosses Gridiron Creek. It then ambles through **Gridiron Gulch**, within which you will pass **Gridiron Shelter**, a rock bivvy burrowed under two mammoth rocks. Among its many admirable features is a sleeping loft.

Upper Gridiron Hut (three bunks) is a little further along, reached on a five-minute detour. This shelter is wedged under a huge rock overhang and features a swing seat.

Easy walking continues through the Flora Valley. Around two hours into the day you will pass beneath a wooden arch, the gateway to the gulch.

The track climbs gently towards Flora Saddle. Around 15 minutes from the saddle is historic **Flora Hut** (12 bunks). The grassy clearing it occupies was once the site of Edward's Store, from where provisions were supplied to gold diggers who, unfortunately, never dug up much at all. From here the track continues to **Flora Saddle** and the track junction, signalling that you have completed the loop. Continue along the main gravel path back down to Flora car park, 10 minutes away.

NELSON LAKES NATIONAL PARK

As the name suggests, Nelson Lakes National Park is framed around a pigeon pair of lakes: Rotoiti and Rotoroa. Beyond the lakes, however, its 1017 sq km cover the northern-most ranges of the Southern Alps. It's here that trampers will find their hiking inspiration, among the long, glaciated valleys, basins, tarns and craggy mountain ranges.

The park is home to numerous passes and routes that are not nearly as demanding as those found in other alpine national parks such as Arthur's Pass or Mt Aspiring. If you long to climb a mountain and stroll along an open ridge, Nelson Lakes is a good place to begin adventuring above the bushline. As it doesn't contain any of the big-name tramping routes, it also tends to get less crowded than many other alpine tramping areas.

The park is a mountainous region, with many peaks above 2000m, but lots of the tracks are benched and most routes are marked with cairns or poles.

A number of return trips are possible in the park, most requiring three to six days of tramping and the necessity of climbing over and along ridges and passes. A favourite tramp for hikers with limited alpine experience is the route along Robert Ridge to the grand Lake Angelus cirque basin. A more remote and challenging tramp is the Travers-Sabine Circuit, which includes hiking over Travers Saddle, which is not an easy climb but one that is well marked and, in good summer weather, within the capabilities of most fit trampers.

History

Although they rarely settled here, Māori did pass through this region along routes between Nelson, Marlborough, Canterbury and the West Coast in search of *pounamu* (greenstone). The lakes provided *kai* (food) in the form of eels, freshwater mussels and waterfowl.

The first European to visit the area was John Cotterell. In 1842 he and a Māori guide pushed their way through more than 300km of trackless terrain to the To-phouse, near St Arnaud, and then turned southeast to the Clarence River. The following January, Cotterell, with his friend Dick Peanter and a Māori guide, retraced the first leg of that earlier journey, but this time turned southwest. In doing so, Cotterell and Peanter became the first Europeans to see Lake Rotoiti.

Three years later, another Māori guide, by the name of Kehu, led William Fox, Charles Heaphy and Thomas Brunner on one of the best-recorded explorations on the South Is-land. With Heaphy keeping the diary and Fox painting the scenery as they went, the group struggled down to Rotoiti under heavy packs. From the lake, Kehu took the party up the Howard River, where they discovered Lake Rotoroa.

Camping by Lake Rotoiti was popular from the early 1900s, and before long holiday cottages were built and walkers began to explore the surrounding valleys and mountains.

The area's significant environmental and scenic worth was officially recognised in 1956 with the gazetting of the Nelson Lakes National Park, centred on the mountain catchments of the two main lakes, Rotoiti and Rotoroa. In 1983 the park significantly expanded, growing to its present size of 1017 sq km, with the addition of 430 sq km of beech forest in the Matakitaki and Glenroy Valleys to the southwest.

Environment

The landscape of Nelson Lakes was created by the Alpine Fault and carved by glaciers. The long, curved valleys that characterise the park were formed by a series of glaciers that waxed and waned with the onset of sequential ice-age periods that began two million years ago. When the glaciers finally retreated after the last ice age, 10,000 years ago, deep holes at the head of the Travers and Gowan Valleys were left, and these filled with water from the melting ice to become Lakes Rotoiti and Rotoroa.

The forests of Nelson Lakes are predominantly beech, with all five NZ beech species found here. In the lower valleys, where conditions are warmer and more fertile, you'll find red and silver beech interspersed with such species as kamahi and southern rata (which has a mass of bright flowers when in bloom). Mountain beech becomes dominant at altitudes above 1050m, or where there are poor soils in the lowlands.

The national park contains a rich diversity of bird life, particularly in the forests near St Arnaud, the site of the 50-sq-km Rotoiti Nature Recovery Project. More than 15 years of predator control has seen bird populations flourish, and it's not uncommon to see the raucous kaka, a large, native bush parrot. Melodious tui and bellbirds are abundant, and can often be heard calling on the forest tracks. If you keep alert you may also spot other birds such as tomtits, robins and NZ's tiniest feathered friend, the rifleman. Great spotted kiwi have been reintroduced and are

ABEL TASMAN, KAHURANGI & NELSON LAKES NELSON LAKES NP

Nelson Lakes National Park

Legend

- Lake Angelus Track
- St Arnaud Range Track
- Travers-Sabine Circuit

N

0 — 5 km
0 — 2.5 miles

Blenheim (95km)

63

Day Walk

Parachute Rocks

St Arnaud Range Track

Kerr Bay

Start/End

Start

Black Hill (946m)

St Arnaud

63

Murchison (57km)

Lake Rotoiti

Side Trip

Start End

Mt Robert Car Park

Mt Robert (1421m)

Relax Shelter

Paddy's Track

Bushline Hut

Lakehead Track

Lakeside Track

Coldwater Hut

Lakehead Hut

St Arnaud Range

Mt McRae (1878m)

Peanter Peak (1880m)

Pinchgut Track

Chandler Stream

Julius Summit (1794m)

Flagtop (1690m)

Speargrass Track

Robert Ridge Route

End

Hukere Stream

Swing Bridge

Maggie Creek

Maud Creek

Bad Weather Route

Speargrass Bridge

Speargrass Hut

Speargrass Creek Route

Bad Weather Route

Angelus Hut

Day 2

Lake Angelus

Mt Angelus (2075m)

Angelus Ridge

Hinapouri Tarn

Sunset Saddle

Hodgson Stream

Sabine-Speargrass Track

Cedric Stream

Mt Cedric (1552m)

Open Stream

Suspension Bridge

Stoempy Creek

Howard River

Howard Valley Rd

Howard Saddle

Muntz Range

Rotoroa Route

Lake Rotoroa

Sabine Hut

Sabine D'urville Track

D'urville Hut

Day 5

Rotoroa

Gowan Valley Rd

Mt Pickering (1241m)

Braeburn Track

Braeburn Range

Mt Hutton (1400m)

Tiraumea Track

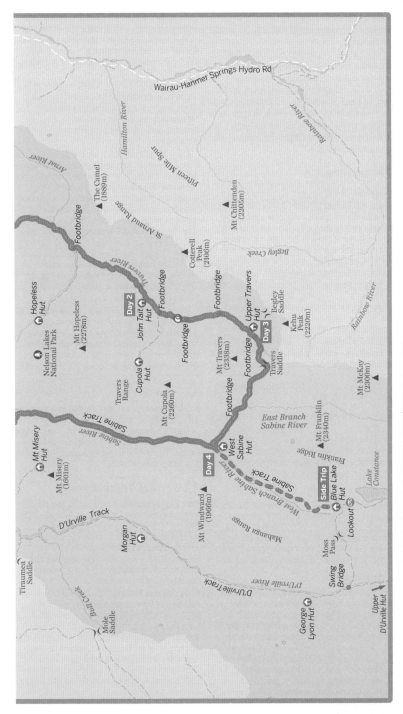

breeding quite successfully, although you're unlikely to encounter these shy, nocturnal creatures.

The native long-finned eel, some of which are more than 100 years of age, are found in large numbers around the jetties in both main lakes. They are fully protected, so fishing for them is not allowed. Brown trout is the predominant fish species caught here and can be found in both the lakes and the main rivers (Travers, D'Urville, Sabine, Matakitaki and Buller).

ℹ️ Planning

WHEN TO TRAMP

The overall climate of Nelson Lakes National Park is pleasantly moderate and is characterised in summer by long spells of settled, clear weather. Having said that, a warm, clear day on a mountain pass can become a white-out, with heavy rain or even a blizzard, in no time at all. Above the bushline, snow may fall throughout the year.

The Lake Angelus Track, St Arnaud Range Track and Travers-Sabine Circuit are in alpine environments that are best tramped from November to April, when weather and snow conditions are most favourable. January through March offers the most settled weather to tackle the tracks.

Many tracks in Nelson Lakes National Park can be safely navigated in winter, although the park is avalanche-prone during winter and spring; check conditions at the **DOC Rotoiti/Nelson Lakes Visitor Centre**.

WHAT TO BRING

It is vital that you come prepared for sudden weather changes, at any time of year. All trampers should carry warm clothing and good windproof and waterproof gear. Sandflies can be an itching nuisance, so bring insect repellent.

MAPS & BROCHURES

NZTopo50 maps *BR24 (Kawatiri)* and *BS24 (Mount Robert)* cover the tramps in detail. NewTopo also publishes a dedicated 1:35,000 *Travers-Sabine Circuit* map. Useful DOC brochures include *Angelus Hut Tracks and Routes, Travers-Sabine Circuit* and *Walks in Nelson Lakes National Park*.

HUTS & CAMPING

There are 24 huts within the national park, most dotted at convenient intervals along the main track network. Eight of these are Serviced huts ($15), equipped with mattresses, water supply, toilets, washbasins and heating, with fuel available. The rest are Standard huts ($5), Basic huts (free) or Bivvies (free). There are no cooking facilities in the huts, so all trampers should carry stoves. Hut tickets must be pre-purchased from the **DOC Rotoiti/Nelson Lakes Visitor Centre**.

Backcountry hut tickets and passes are valid at the park's huts, with the exception of the relatively luxurious Serviced Angelus Hut (28 bunks) from late November through to the end of April. During this peak period the hut ($20) and nearby campsites ($10) must be booked in advance online or through DOC visitors centres nationwide.

Camping is permitted throughout the park. There is a fee of one Backcountry hut ticket ($5) for camping close to Serviced huts. Camping around Standard/Basic huts and away from huts is free.

A short stroll from St Arnaud and a stone's throw from Lake Rotoiti, the lovely **Kerr Bay DOC Campsite** (www.doc.govt.nz; unpowered/powered sites per person $18/21) has bushy nooks for campervans and decent grass for tents. It also has hot showers, a cooking shelter and laundry facilities during summer. Further round the lake, the more basic **West Bay DOC Campsite** (☑ 03-521 1806; www.doc.govt.nz; adult/child $13/6.50; ☺ mid-Dec–Apr) is open mid-December to Easter. Both camps also have to be pre-booked during those months, from mid-December through to Easter. This can be done online or at the DOC Rotoiti/Nelson Lakes Visitor Centre.

About 2km west of St Arnaud, the **Teetotal DOC Campsite** (www.doc.govt.nz; per person $8) is a Standard campground, popular with mountain bikers, that has toilets and stream water. At the northern end of Lake Rotoroa, the **Lake Rotoroa DOC Campsite** (www.doc.govt.nz; per person $8) has toilets, water and ferocious sandflies.

INFORMATION

The **DOC Rotoiti/Nelson Lakes Visitor Centre** (☑ 03-521 1806; www.doc.govt.nz; View Rd; ☺ 8am-4.30pm, to 5pm Dec-Apr) is a five-minute walk from St Arnaud's centre and has park information, the latest weather forecasts, hut passes and interpretive displays.

ℹ️ Getting There & Away

Trek Express (p148) runs a scheduled service every Tuesday from Nelson to St Arnaud ($45) and the Mt Robert car park ($55) between December and February, working in cooperation with **Nelson Lakes Shuttles** (☑ 027 222 1872, 03-540 2042; www.nelsonlakesshuttles.co.nz). Both operators maintain a list of on-demand departures on their websites.

Rotoiti Water Taxis (☑ 021 702 278; www.rotoitiwatertaxis.co.nz; Kerr Bay) will ferry trampers between Kerr Bay and the head of Lake Rotoiti (up to three people $105, extra person $35). Many trampers use this as their starting point for the Travers-Sabine Circuit or to end the trip to Lake Angelus, as it shaves off 9km (three hours) of walking and provides the bonus of seeing the lake and mountains from a different perspective.

Lake Angelus Track

Duration 2 days

Distance 21.5km (13.4 miles)

Difficulty Moderate

Start Mt Robert car park

End Coldwater Hut

Gateway Nelson (p184)

Transport Shuttle bus, boat

Summary An epic ridge walk, with an alpine lake-filled basin and one of NZ's flashest mountain huts.

Despite its relatively short length, this tramp rates as one of the best in the country, showcasing all that's good about Nelson Lakes National Park. In fine weather, the walk along Robert Ridge is spectacular – seldom do tramps afford such an extended period across such open tops. The views will blow your socks off, as they will again as you descend into the extraordinary Lake Angelus basin (1650m) and Angelus Hut, which is a good base for short forays to the ridge above the lake and to Mt Angelus. A two-night stay at Angelus Hut is highly desirable.

Angelus Hut is an alpine hut and weather conditions can change rapidly. Snow, frost and freezing winds can occur even in midsummer, so visitors should be well equipped when attempting this tramp.

ℹ Getting There & Away

The start of the tramp is 7km from St Arnaud, and the Trek Express shuttle service to St Arnaud from Nelson continues on to the trailhead. Otherwise, the walk from St Arnaud will add around two hours and 165m of climbing.

From Coldwater Hut you can either catch a boat back across the lake – a nice way to finish – or tramp back to St Arnaud via the Lakeside Track (12km, four hours) or the Lakehead Track (9km, three hours), accessed from Lakehead Hut.

🏃 The Tramp

Day 1: Mt Robert Car Park to Angelus Hut

6 HOURS / 12KM / 770M ASCENT

Fill your water bottles before embarking on this day's tramp as there is no water along the way.

From the Mt Robert car park it's a steep, zigzagging climb up Pinchgut Track. After 30 minutes you'll come to the junction with

Paddy's Track, part of the **Mt Robert Circuit** – the most popular day walk in the park.

Keep walking beyond the junction and on to the poled route that wends steadily up into the distance. Follow this broad ridge past the second alpine basin, the site of an old ski field, and continue for 1.5km, ascending to **Flagtop** (1690m).

Along the tops, keep an eye out for the karearea (NZ falcon), squawky kea and elusive rock wren. If you don't spot any of these, console yourself by stroking the cushion-like vegetable sheep *(Raoulia eximia)*, a most peculiar plant that has found a foothold among the rocks.

The well-marked route continues climbing gently along **Robert Ridge** towards **Julius Summit** (1794m), with the third large tarn-filled basin to your left. Pass under the peak on its western side, then regain the ridge and follow it in a southwesterly direction. Take care along this sharp and rocky section.

When you reach the sign for Speargrass Hut on your right, you are only 30 minutes from Angelus Hut. Follow the track up on to the ridge where you will encounter views over **Angelus Basin**, then follow the poles down to the lakeside **Angelus Hut** (28 bunks), built in 2010. Perched on the edge of the lake, 1650m above sea level among golden tussock, this hut is as fine as they come – in 2017 it was even voted NZ's 'hut of the year' by readers of *Wilderness* magazine. It has insulated walls, a roomy common area and large sunny deck. From late November through to the end of April you will need to have booked a bed ahead, either online (www.doc.govt.nz) or through a DOC visitors centre.

Side Trip: Angelus Basin & Mt Angelus

2–3 HOURS RETURN

Angelus Hut is a fine place to spend a night, but it's even better if you stay two nights, taking a day to explore this beguiling alpine environment without having to carry a heavy, full pack. A good half-day option is to circumnavigate along the ridge around the cirque basin overlooking **Lake Angelus**. Gouged out by glaciers over a series of ice ages 10,000 to 20,000 years ago, the basin is made all the more impressive by the 100m-plus-high fans of scree and shattered greywacke peaks that almost encircle the lake. Earlier named Rangimarie ('peaceful') by an unknown European,

ABEL TASMAN, KAHURANGI & NELSON LAKES LAKE ANGELUS TRACK

Lake Angelus is known by Māori as Roto-maninitua (the 'glowing white lake', by our translation).

Mt Angelus (2075m) stands sentry to the south and, if it's free of snow, can be scaled with no special equipment or climbing experience required – just a good head for heights, a decent level of fitness and a love (or at least, acceptance) of scrambling up loose rock. It will take around three hours to the summit and back from Angelus Hut.

Day 2: Angelus Hut to Coldwater Hut

6 HOURS / 9.5KM / 1030M DESCENT

Return briefly back along the track behind Angelus Hut to the signposted junction where you can pick up Cascade Track. This is a steep and rocky, poled route down into the head of the Hukere Stream and alongside a series of dramatic cascades. Take your time and go easy on your knees during the upper section, where there are plenty of trip hazards and the additional danger of slipping when wet or icy. Once you hit the bushline, the track descends more gently through lush beech forest and past impressive rock chutes, before reaching the Travers Valley.

Once in the valley, take the bridge across Hukere Stream and then head north along the true left of the Travers River. If your knees are wobbling from the descent, they will welcome the easy walking along the valley flats, their golden meadows a stark contrast to the shadowy valley from which you have just emerged.

A pleasurable amble of around 1½ hours will see you reach Coldwater Hut

(12 bunks) at the head of Lake Rotoiti, an ideal spot for a post-tramp dip in the lake before your boat arrives to ferry you back to St Arnaud. Energetic and thrifty walkers can skip the boat and walk to St Arnaud via the Lakeside Track (12km, four hours), or the Lakehead Track (9km, three hours), accessed from Lakehead Hut (28 bunks).

St Arnaud Range Track

Duration 5 hours

Distance 11km (6.8 miles)

Difficulty Moderate

Start/End Kerr Bay

Gateway Nelson (p184)

Transport Bus

Summary This popular day walk features a steep ascent through beech forest and alpine terrain to the top of the range for a grand panorama of lakes and mountains.

This popular up-and-down day walk provides one of the best view points of Nelson Lakes National Park and beyond, surveyed from the top of the St Arnaud Range. It's around a 1000m ascent (and subsequent descent) from lake to ridge, but achy legs will be soothed by the splendour of beech forest – red, silver and mountain – that gradually changes with altitude.

Equally diverting is the chatter of native birds, the population of which is bolstered by the work of the Rotoiti Nature Recovery Project, through which this track passes.

Above the bushline (1400m) the views are worthy of a sit-down, but don't be content with gawping at the lake and Mt Robert from

---

ROBERT RIDGE BAD WEATHER ROUTE

The route along Robert Ridge is spectacular in good weather, requiring little more than a good head for heights and confidence walking over rough terrain as it winds its way along sharp ridges and through vertiginous scree slopes. However, the whole length of the ridge is exposed to winds from the southeast, with few places for shelter on the lee side. In bad weather, with low visibility, it is easy to become disoriented and wander off the route. Check with the DOC Rotoiti/Nelson Lakes Visitor Centre (p178) for the latest track and weather conditions before you set out, and do not attempt it if the weather is poor.

Should weather conditions prevent you attempting the Robert Ridge route, it may be possible to reach Angelus Hut safely along an alternative route. From Mt Robert car park, walk to Speargrass Hut (three hours) and then take the Speargrass Creek Route (three hours) up to the junction with Robert Ridge, 30 minutes shy of Angelus Hut. If the weather improves overnight, you can always return to St Arnaud along Robert Ridge, rather than taking the Cascade Track to Coldwater Hut.

Parachute Rocks, as many trampers are. Fuel up with some scroggin and conquer the final 30-minute climb through alpine tussock to the ridge (1650m). You won't be disappointed.

ℹ️ Getting There & Away

The trailhead at Kerr Bay is about a five-minute walk from the DOC visitors centre in St Arnaud; simply head down Kerr Bay Rd towards the lake.

🚶 The Tramp

You'll find the trailhead in the eastern corner of Kerr Bay, on the lake edge near the campsite toilet block.

To begin it follows three short walks through beech forest – **Bellbird Walk, Honeydew Walk** and **Loop Track** – which form part of the 50-sq-km Rotoiti Nature Recovery Project. Keep an eye and an ear out for nectarivorous tui and korimako (bellbird), and cute fantails, robins and tomtits that may flit around your feet as you kick up insects for them to feed on. Three species of beech mistletoe creep around tree trunks thanks to possum eradication programs, their yellow and red flowers resplendent in December and January.

Shortly after joining the Loop Track in the clockwise direction, the St Arnaud Range Track bears left and climbs steadily up and across moraine terraces deposited by glaciers. Divert your attention from the relentless climb by studying the trees as you ascend, noticing how they have adapted to the changing altitude and environment. At lower elevations red beech is dominant, while higher up silver beech is more apparent and then mountain beech after that. Nearing the bushline (1400m) the trees become more and more stunted.

Free of the forest, you can catch your breath on **Parachute Rocks**, aptly named after the canopy-shaped scree slope located to the north, and take in the spectacular views down to St Arnaud and across Lake Rotoiti to Mt Robert. From here the gradient doesn't let up, but the extra 30 minutes to the ridge through snow tussock and fields of alpine shrubs and herbs is certainly worth the effort. In late spring and early summer the herbs bloom in gloriously gold and white blankets across the steep slopes.

Atop the **ridge**, on a good day, the view is vast: west to Kahurangi National Park and the Buller Valley, north to Mt Richmond Forest Park, east down the Wairau Valley and south to the heart of the Nelson Lakes National Park. Those with energy to spare might like to explore southwest along the craggy ridge or scramble down to the tarn-filled basins on the eastern side.

Return to Kerr Bay on the same route that you came up, pausing as often as you can to savour the views before heading back into the forest.

Travers-Sabine Circuit

Duration 5 days

Distance 81km (50.3 miles)

Difficulty Moderate to demanding

Start Kerr Bay

End Mt Robert car park

Gateway Nelson (p184)

Transport Boat, bus

Summary Grassy river flats, beech forests, a high alpine saddle and a side trip to one of the world's clearest freshwater lakes are features of this circuit.

Like a wishbone, the Travers and Sabine Valleys combine to create a tramping route that could easily be a Great Walk in its own right. The Travers Valley provides easy tramping along good tracks with excellent alpine scenery, tranquil forest, plenty of huts and a bridge almost every time you need one. Combined with the track through the Sabine Valley, which is connected by Travers Saddle, the trip is ideal for those new to NZ's alpine areas. The pass is steep and shouldn't be taken lightly, but on a clear day – and there are usually many such days across summer and autumn – the views from the top are spectacular.

The tramp we describe is a five-day trip, but a different arrangement of legs (power legs or lazy legs) could spread it over anything from four to seven. The day-long side trip to enchanting Rotomairewhenua/Blue Lake is a must if you can afford the time. The tiny, colourful lake is a highlight of the park. More than a dozen huts on (or close to) the route facilitate extended missions.

ℹ️ Getting There & Away

Kerr Bay is about a five-minute walk from the DOC visitors centre in St Arnaud; simply head down Kerr Bay Rd towards the lake.

The tramp ends at the Mt Robert car park, from where a **Trek Express shuttle bus** (p148) departs for Nelson each Tuesday (December to February) at around noon.

🏃 The Tramp

Day 1: Kerr Bay to John Tait Hut

7–8 HOURS / 25KM / 180M ASCENT

Some trampers make Upper Travers Hut, rather than John Tait Hut, the destination for their first day. But even with boat transport to the head of Lake Rotoiti, this is still a long day (22km), leaving many with sore legs and feet on the eve of crossing Travers Saddle the following morning.

The trip begins on the **Lakehead Track**, running along the eastern shore of **Lake Rotoiti**. You can also take the Lakeside Track along the western shore, but this is a longer walk if you're beginning from St Arnaud.

The Lakehead Track is signposted from the Kerr Bay campsite. For the first 1km, to the junction of the Loop Track, the way is wide and level. Beyond the junction it more resembles a track, but remains an easy walk through forest at the edge of Lake Rotoiti. After 4km the track passes a gravel clearing, where there are good views of the northern half of the lake, including the peninsula between the bays. In another 2.5km it passes a second clearing, and this time the southern half of the lake can be seen.

Lakehead Hut (28 bunks) is reached around two to three hours (9km) from Kerr Bay and is on a grassy bank overlooking the mouth of the Travers River, where there is good trout fishing (fishing licence required). **Coldwater Hut** (12 bunks), which is smaller and older, is about 800m away, across the Travers River on the other side of the lake.

At Lakehead Hut, signposts direct you across **Travers River** and through a grassy flat to the walking track on the true left (west) side of the river. The alternative during high water is to follow the true right (east) side of the river for 5km, to a footbridge across the Travers. The true left side is more scenic because it swings close to the river in many places.

Once on the track on the true left side, head south and you soon pass a signposted junction for Cascade Track, which leads to Angelus Hut (4½ hours). The main track continues south, meandering between stands of beech and grassy flats until it reaches a swing bridge across the Travers. Stay on the true left side, following the river closely through the forest, to emerge after 3.5km onto another flat, where Mt Travers dominates the view.

Just beyond the end of the flat you arrive at a swing bridge over **Hopeless Creek**. On the other side is a signposted junction indicating the track to Hopeless Hut (2½ hours). The track now begins to climb gradually.

John Tait Hut (27 bunks) is less than two hours from the junction, and is in a small grassy clearing with good views of the peaks at the head of the valley. Its best feature is an enclosed veranda that allows you to enjoy the views but keeps the sandflies at bay.

Day 2: John Tait Hut to Upper Travers Hut

3 HOURS / 6KM / 510M ASCENT

This short day will freshen you up ready for the climb over the saddle on the following day.

The track sets off by continuing its climb up the valley. About 20 minutes (1km) from the hut it passes the track junction to Cupola Hut (2½ hours) before crossing a bridge over **Cupola Creek**. The climb steepens, and within another 1km the track enters a chasm and passes a side track to **Travers Falls**, a worthy three-minute detour to a 20m-high cascade that plunges into a sparkling, clear pool.

Back on the track, the gradient eases slightly and after crossing several scree slopes you walk over a bridge to the true right of the Travers River about 1½ hours from the falls. At this point you begin an even steeper climb to the bushline, passing three signposted avalanche paths along the way. At the edge of the bush, little more than 2km from the bridge, trampers are greeted with good views of the peaks of both the Travers Range and St Arnaud Range.

Upper Travers Hut (24 bunks) overlooks a tussocky flat before the last stand of mountain beech towards the saddle. At 1340m it's a beautiful spot, surrounded by gravel and scree slopes that can be easily climbed for better views, while looming overhead is the east face of Mt Travers.

Day 3: Upper Travers Hut to West Sabine Hut

6–8 HOURS / 8KM / 470M ASCENT, 1120M DESCENT

The route over Travers Saddle is well marked with snow poles, but is still a climb into the alpine zone. If the weather is foul, hold off and wait another day.

The track begins by crossing the river. After 30 minutes or so, the ascent is signalled when you emerge from the final stand of trees and head west into an area of tussock-covered slopes and large scattered boulders. From here you are technically following a route, but because of its popularity a track can be seen most of the way.

The route climbs gently towards the saddle for 1km, until you reach a signpost directing you up a steep scree slope. The zigzagging climb lasts several hundred metres; take your time and stop often to admire the fine views.

Once at the top of the slope, 450m above Upper Travers Hut, the final climb to the saddle is easy; you pass two tarns while the sharp-edged Mt Travers (2338m) towers overhead to the north. Travers Saddle (1787m) is reached 1½ hours from Upper Travers Hut and is marked by a huge rock cairn. It's a beautiful spot, but for a truly awe-inspiring outlook you should scramble to one of the nearby ridges.

From the saddle you begin descending the 1000m to Sabine Forks, passing first through tussock slopes then heading right over a rock slide before returning to grassland.

Around 1.5km from the saddle there is a superb view of the Mahanga Range, just before you descend into the bushline and return to the track. You remain in the stunted mountain beech only momentarily, because the track quickly swings into a scree-covered gully and embarks on a very rapid descent – 600m over just 3km. This is probably the hardest section of the day and care is required on the steep sections of loose rock. Halfway down, at the bushline, the track returns – with trail markers appearing on the left-hand side of the gully – and you follow it as it levels out next to the gorge of the East Branch Sabine River.

Shortly afterwards you cross a small bridge over the deep chasm. Although you won't actually see the water, you will certainly hear it roaring through the narrow rock walls. The best view is from the river bank upstream.

Once on the other side, the track follows the steep valley for 2km and in many places is a maze of tree roots. The final leg of this long day is a very steep drop down the East Branch of the Sabine. The track swings south to West Sabine Hut (30 bunks).

Side Trip: Blue Lake

6–7 HOURS RETURN / 14KM / 520M ASCENT & DESCENT

It's worth an extra day on the track to visit enchanting Rotomairewhenua/Blue Lake. Blue Lake Hut (16 bunks), set above the lake near the edge of the bushline, is a beautiful spot to spend the night if you don't want to return to West Sabine Hut the same day. It's a pretty steep climb to the lake though, and many trampers take the chance to visit Blue Lake as a return day trip from West Sabine Hut without their full packs.

From West Sabine Hut, cross the swing bridge to return to the true left (west) side of the West Branch Sabine River and continue south along the track. From the river fork, the track climbs over often-slippery beech tree roots, and after two hours the valley opens up at a large slip to a stunning view. In front of you is a theatre of mountains, with Moss Pass an obvious dip to the right. Turn around and you can look back down the valley or at Mt Cupola (2260m).

The track dips back into the bush and the climb becomes steeper as you traverse forest and scree slopes, many of them formed by avalanches. At one point you top out at a boardwalk and manicured track though a beautiful garden-like setting, with the river just to the left. Take a break and enjoy the beauty, because you still have one more steep, forested hillside to climb in the last 1km before Blue Lake finally comes into view.

Just before Blue Lake Hut is a spot where avalanches are funnelled down chutes and across the track from winter well into spring. Conditions are worst between May and November, but the avalanche paths can be active during unseasonable January snowfalls. Do not stop between the warning signs during periods prone to avalanches.

Blue Lake is thought to be the clearest natural freshwater lake in the world, with visibility of around 80m, so take care to avoid any contamination of the lake. If you take the track that climbs 1km south through one last stand of stunted beech you'll be rewarded with excellent views of both Lake Constance and Blue Lake. This is one of the most scenic spots in the national park.

Day 4: West Sabine Hut to Sabine Hut

5 HOURS / 15KM

Five minutes upriver from the hut is the swing bridge over the West Branch Sabine River. Cross to the true left (west) side, following the level route north. This is a very pleasant stretch as the track remains close to the water, and it's an easy start for those with achy legs from the climb over Travers Saddle. The track remains in the wooded fringe of the river for 7km before breaking out onto a grassy flat.

The track crosses the flat for 2km and climbs steeply at its northern end, only to descend onto another flat. At the northern end of this flat is a climb to a small knob that overlooks a deep gorge – this is the steepest ascent of a relatively easy day.

Once the track descends the other side, it follows the river to the junction with the track to D'Urville Hut (10 bunks). Cross the bridge over the impressive deep gorge. It's an easy scramble down to the water, and trampers have even been known to float through the gorge for a refreshing dip on a hot day.

From the bridge the track climbs out of the narrow valley, then spills onto a grassy flat. You are now less than 2km from Sabine Hut (32 bunks), reached along a wooded and level path. This hut has views of Lake Rotoroa and a spacious kitchen-common area. Despite the multitude of sandflies, you can enjoy excellent sunsets over the lake from the hut's jetty.

Day 5: Sabine Hut to Mt Robert Car Park

7½–9½ HOURS / 27KM

The final leg of the Travers-Sabine Circuit takes you to the Mt Robert car park via Speargrass Hut. However, if you're fit and the weather's fine, you can head up steep Mt Cedric Track to Lake Angelus and spend a night at the stunning Angelus Hut (28 bunks) before returning to St Arnaud via one of three tracks the following day. The different options are described in DOC's *Angelus Hut Tracks and Routes* brochure. Note, however, that advance bookings are required for Angelus Hut from late November to 30 April.

To get to Speargrass Hut from Sabine Hut, take the track north that skirts the shore of Lake Rotoroa before angling into beech forest and making a long climb to Howard Saddle. It takes one hour to climb the 350m to the saddle, which is dimpled by a series of small ponds. The track then swings more northeast and contours around the base of Robert Ridge.

Two hours from Sabine Hut is a suspension bridge over Cedric Stream. In the next hour you cross several streams, bridged where necessary. Now, only an hour from Speargrass Hut, the track vastly improves. It's well benched, and at one point follows more than 500m of boardwalk, complete with benches and a fine view of the Howard Valley. Botanists might admire the conical shape of the kaikawaka (NZ cedar), or search for the tiny sundew, a plant that survives the lack of nitrogen by catching and devouring insects on its sticky leaves.

Eventually the track makes a steep but short descent to Speargrass Hut (12 bunks), reached four to five hours from Sabine Hut. It is located in a small grassy meadow surrounded by mountains, and is a pleasant way to turn a long tramp into a couple of easy finishing days if you have time to spare.

From the hut the track crosses the flat and within five minutes arrives at a bridge over Speargrass Creek. On the other side is a signposted junction with the Speargrass Creek Route (right fork), which climbs to Lake Angelus (three hours).

Take the left fork along Speargrass Track, which begins with an hour-long descent, sidling the ridge until it bottoms out at Speargrass Creek. Follow the creek for 30 minutes and then begin the final leg, a steady but easy climb that lasts almost one hour and crosses bridges over two streams.

The day ends with a short descent to the Mt Robert car park, 2½ to three hours from Speargrass Hut. Unless you have transport, it's another 7km (1½ hours) of walking into St Arnaud.

TOWNS & FACILITIES

Nelson

☑ 03 / POP 46,440

Dishing up a winning combination of beautiful surroundings, sophisticated art and culinary scenes, and lashings of sunshine, Nelson is hailed as one of New Zealand's most 'liveable' cities. In summer it fills up with local and international visitors, who lap up its diverse offerings.

🛏 Sleeping & Eating

Nelson has a stack of hostels and other budget to midrange accommodation options. Its food scene is broad, and is particularly friendly to self-caterers.

Tasman Bay Backpackers   HOSTEL $

(☑0800 222 572, 03-548 7950; www.tasmanbay backpackers.co.nz; 10 Weka St; sites from $20, dm $28-30, d $76-88; @🛜) This well-designed, friendly hostel has airy communal spaces with a 100% Kiwi music soundtrack, hypercoloured rooms, a sunny outdoor deck and a well-used hammock. Good freebies: wi-fi, decent bikes, breakfast during winter, and chocolate pudding and ice cream year-round.

Sussex House   B&B $$
(☑ 03-548 9972; www.sussex.co.nz; 238 Bridge St; d $170-190, tr $180; ☞) In a relatively quiet riverside spot, only a five-minute walk to town, this creaky old lady dates back to around 1880. The five tastefully decorated rooms feature upmarket bedding, period-piece furniture and en suite bathrooms, except one room that has a private bathroom down the hall. Enjoy local fruit at breakfast in the grand dining room.

★ Cod & Lobster   SEAFOOD, BISTRO $$
(☑ 03-546 4300; www.codandlobster.com; 300 Trafalgar St; mains $22-36; ⊙ 11am-11pm) Stellar cocktails and NZ's biggest selection of gin make Cod & Lobster's corner bar an essential destination, but this heritage space also serves up excellent food. Unsurprisingly, seafood is the main focus, so enliven your palate with Bloody Mary oyster shooters before moving on to Louisiana-style prawns with spicy sausage or the good-value seafood platter ($40 for two people).

A concise selection of steak, chicken and vegetarian dishes is available, but it's the briny-fresh catch of the day you're really here for.

Urban Oyster   MODERN NZ $$
(☑ 03-546 7861; www.urbaneatery.co.nz; 278 Hardy St; dishes $11-27; ⊙ 4pm-late Mon, 11am-late Tue-Sat) Slurp oysters from the shell, or revitalise with sashimi and ceviche, then save your cravings with street-food dishes such as kung pao Sichuan fried chicken or smoked-pork empanadas with charcoal shrimp mayo. Black butchers' tiles, edgy artwork and a fine wine list all bolster this metropolitan experience, and craft beers come courtesy of Golden Bear Brewing in nearby Mapua.

🛒 Supplies & Equipment

Rollo's Outdoor Centre   SPORTS & OUTDOORS
(☑ 03-548 1975; www.rollos.co.nz; 12 Bridge St; ⊙ 9am-5.30am Mon-Fri, to 3pm Sat) Camping, tramping and kayak gear aplenty. Hire service too.

Fresh Choice   SUPERMARKET $
(69 Collingwood St; ⊙ 7am-9pm) Stock up on supplies.

ℹ Information

Nelson i-SITE (☑ 03-548 2304; www.nelsonnz.com; cnr Trafalgar & Halifax Sts; ⊙ 9am-5pm Mon-Fri, to 4pm Sat & Sun) A slick centre complete with DOC information desk for the low-down on national parks and tracks (including Abel Tasman and Heaphy). Pick up a copy of the *Nelson Tasman Visitor Guide*.

Nelson SBL Travel Centre (☑ 03-548 1539; www.nelsoncoachlines.co.nz; 27 Bridge St; ⊙ 7am-5.15pm Mon-Fri) You can book **Abel Tasman Coachlines** (☑ 03-548 0285; www.abeltasmantravel.co.nz), **InterCity** (p149) buses and Interisland ferry services here.

ℹ Getting There & Away

Nelson Airport is 5km southwest of town, near Tahunanui Beach. A taxi from there to town will cost around $30 or **Super Shuttle** (☑ 0800 748 885, 03-547 5782; www.supershuttle.co.nz) offers door-to-door service for around $20.

Abel Tasman Coachlines (p185) operates bus services to Motueka ($14, one hour), and Kaiteriteri and Marahau (both $21, two hours). These services also connect with **Golden Bay Coachlines** (☑ 03-525 8352; www.gbcoachlines.co.nz) services for Takaka and around. Transport to/from the three national parks is provided by **Trek Express** (p148).

InterCity (p149) runs from Nelson to most key South Island destinations including Picton ($23, two hours), Kaikoura ($52, 3½ hours) and Greymouth ($40, six hours).

Motueka

☑ 03 / POP 7600

Motueka (pronounced Mott-oo-ecka, meaning 'Island of Wekas') is a bustling town that trampers will find handy for stocking up en route to all three of the region's national parks.

🛏 Sleeping & Eating

Eden's Edge Lodge   HOSTEL $
(☑ 03-528 4242; www.edensedge.co.nz; 137 Lodder Lane, Riwaka; d/tw/tr with bathroom $120/120/150; ☞) 🅿 Surrounded by farmland 4km from Motueka, this lodge's facilities include smart rooms and relaxed communal areas. Breakfast is included – with organic eggs from the owners' hens – and there are fresh herbs aplenty in the garden for cooking up in the spotless kitchen. Hire a bike for nearby beer, ice-cream and coffee stops along the Great Taste Trail.

Resurgence
LODGE $$$

(☑ 03-528 4664; www.resurgence.co.nz; 574 Riwaka Valley Rd; d lodge from $695, chalets from $595; @ 🛜 🏊) 🏋 Choose a luxurious en-suite lodge room or a self-contained chalet at this magical green retreat. It's a 15-minute drive from Abel Tasman National Park, and a 30-minute walk from the picturesque source of the Riwaka River. Lodge rates include aperitifs and a four-course dinner as well as breakfast; chalet rates are for B&B, with dinner an extra $120. The lodge is 18km northwest of Motueka.

★ Toad Hall
CAFE $$

(☑ 03-528 6456; www.toadhallmotueka.co.nz; 502 High St; mains $16-23; ⊙ 8am-5pm Easter-Oct, 8am-6pm Mon & Tue, to 10pm Wed-Sun Oct-Easter) This fantastic cafe serves excellent breakfast and lunch dishes (think potato hashcakes and pork-belly burgers). Also on offer are smoothies, juices, baked goods, pies and selected groceries. Look forward to live music and pizza on Friday and Saturday nights in summer. Have a drink at its new tap room, with beers and ciders brewed on-site by **Townshend Brewery**.

Precinct Dining Co
CAFE $$

(☑ 03-528 5332; www.precinctdining.com; 108 High St; breakfast & lunch mains $10-18, dinner mains $24-30; ⊙ 9am-3pm Mon, 9am-late Tue-Sat) At the northern end of town, Precinct Dining Co is a relaxed and versatile slice of well-priced cosmopolitan cool. Kick off with eggs Benedict and pea-and-chorizo smash for brunch, before returning at dinner for fish with local Golden Bay clams or a rustic pumpkin risotto with toasted walnuts. Good coffee and a savvy drinks list seal the deal.

At the very least, stop in and buy one of its doughnuts. If you're lucky, you'll score one of the Tahitian vanilla and Nelson raspberry ones.

🛒 Supplies & Equipment

Coppins Great Outdoors Centre
SPORTS & OUTDOORS

(☑ 03-528 7296; www.facebook.com/CoppinsCycles; 255 High St; ⊙ 8.30am-5.30pm Mon-Fri, 9am-2pm Sat) Locally owned shop stocking sports, camping and hiking equipment. Also hires out and services bikes.

Countdown
SUPERMARKET $

(108 High St; ⊙ 7am-9pm) Centrally located supermarket.

ℹ️ Information

Motueka i-SITE (☑ 03-528 6543; www.motuekaisite.co.nz; 20 Wallace St; ⊙ 9am-4.30pm Mon-Fri, to 4pm Sat & Sun) An endlessly busy info centre with helpful staff handling bookings from Kaitaia to Bluff and providing local national-park expertise and necessaries. DOC information and bookings are also available.

ℹ️ Getting There & Away

Bus services depart from **Motueka i-SITE**, **Abel Tasman Coachlines** (p185) runs daily from Nelson to Motueka (one hour), Kaiteriteri (25 minutes) and Marahau (30 minutes). These services connect with **Golden Bay Coachlines** (p185) services to Takaka (1¼ hours). Note that from May to September all buses run less frequently.

Takaka

☑ 03 / POP 1240

Boasting New Zealand's highest concentration of yoga pants, dreadlocks and bare feet in the high street, Takaka is a lovable little town. Although the nearest town to the start of the Heaphy Track (Brown Hut) is actually Collingwood, regular transport services and a much wider range of supplies mean that Takaka is a preferable option.

🛏️ Sleeping & Eating

Kiwiana
HOSTEL $

(☑ 03-525 7676, 0800 805 494; www.kiwianabackpackers.co.nz; 73 Motupipi St; tent sites per person $24, dm/s/d $30/55/70; @ 🛜) Beyond the welcoming garden is a cute cottage where rooms are named after classic Kiwiana (the jandal, Buzzy Bee...). The garage has been converted into a convivial lounge, with wood-fired stove, table tennis, pool table, music, books and games; free bikes for guest use.

★ Adrift
COTTAGE $$$

(☑ 03-525 8353; www.adrift.co.nz; 53 Tukurua Rd, Tukurua; d $378-585; 🛜) 🏋 Adrift on a bed of beachside bliss is what you'll be in one of these five cottages dotted within landscaped grounds, right on the beach. Tuck into your breakfast hamper, then self-cater in the fully equipped kitchen, dine on the sunny deck, or soak in the spa bath. A minimum two-night stay usually applies. Also available is a stylish studio.

Top Shop CAFE $
(4 Willow St; snacks $2-9; ⊙6am-6.30pm) A dairy, tearoom and takeaway at the entrance to town with high-rating pies.

Dangerous Kitchen CAFE $$
(☑03-525 8686; www.thedangerouskitchen.co.nz; 46a Commercial St; mains $13-30; ⊙9am-8.30pm Mon-Sat; 🍴) 🍃 This cafe serves largely healthy, good-value fare such as felafel, pizza, bean burritos, pasta, great baking and juices, as well as local wines and craft beer. It's mellow and musical, with a sunny courtyard out the back and people-watching out the front. Check out the quirky, Instagramworthy mural near the entrance, and ask about occasional live music.

Supplies & Equipment

Fresh Choice SUPERMARKET $
(13 Willow St; ⊙8am-7pm) Stock up here while you can.

ⓘ Information

Golden Bay Visitor Centre (☑03-525 9136; www.goldenbaynz.co.nz; Willow St; ⊙10am-3pm Mon-Fri, to 2pm Sat) A friendly little centre with all the necessary information, including the indispensable official tourist map. Bookings and DOC passes.

ⓘ Getting There & Away

Golden Bay Air (☑03-525 8725, 0800 588 885; www.goldenbayair.co.nz; Takaka Airfield, SH60) flies at least once and up to four times daily between Wellington and Takaka (one way adult/child from $169/129).

Golden Bay Coachlines (p185) departs from Takaka and runs through to Totaranui ($24, one hour), and over the hill to Motueka ($28, 1¼ hours) and Nelson ($38, 2¼ hours).

Karamea

☑03 / POP 575
Friendly tramping hub Karamea is colourful, pint-sized, and perched by the enticing wilderness of Kahurangi National Park.

🛏 Sleeping & Eating

Last Resort LODGE $$
(☑0800 505 042, 03-782 6617; www.lastresort karamea.co.nz; 71 Waverley St, Karamea; dm $37, r for 2/3/4 guests with private bathroom $107/127/147, studio from $130; 🛜) Enclosed by greenery some 600m west of Market Cross, this rambling resort suits most budgets, with a choice of rooms with and without private bath-

rooms. At the posher end of the price range are self-contained two-bedroom cottages (from $155) complete with spa tub. Bonus points for laundry facilities and a comfy communal lounge with TV and tea-making.

Rongo Dinner, Bed & Breakfast B&B $$
(☑03-782 6667; http://rongo.nz; 130 Waverley St, Karamea; half board s/d $90/180; 🛜) 🍃 Rongo's rainbow-coloured exterior draws you in, while its free-spirited vibe lengthens your stay. Formerly a backpacker hostel, Rongo retains a slouchy, neo-hippie ethos but these days wows guests with zero-kilometre cuisine whipped up by a French chef (breakfasts and dinners included in the price).

Last Resort Cafe & Bar CAFE $
(☑03-782 6617; www.lastresortkaramea.co.nz; 71 Waverley St, Karamea; snacks from $4, mains $15-30; ⊙7.30am-11pm) Attached to the eponymous resort, this bright and breezy cafe is a sweet stop for pies and cakes as well as more inventive meals (salmon roulade on pineapple salsa, anyone?).

Karamea Village Hotel PUB FOOD $$
(☑03-782 6800; www.karameahotel.co.nz; cnr Waverley St & Wharf Rd, Karamea; meals $15-34; ⊙11am-11pm) Here lie simple pleasures and warm hospitality: a game of pool, a pint of ale, and a choice of roast dinners, nachos and beer-battered whitebait, to a soundtrack of local gossip and dinging pokie machines.

🛒 Supplies & Equipment

Four Square SUPERMARKET $
(☑03-782 6701; 103 Bridge St, Karamea; ⊙8.30am-6pm Mon-Sat, to 5pm Sun) This place will suffice for basic groceries, including camping food.

ⓘ Information

Karamea Information & Resource Centre (☑03-782 6652; www.karameainfo.co.nz; Market Cross; ⊙9am-5pm Mon-Fri, 10am-1pm Sat & Sun, shorter hours May-Dec) This excellent, community-owned centre has the local low-down, internet access, maps and DOC hut tickets. It also doubles as the petrol station.

ⓘ Getting There & Away

Karamea Express (☑03-782 6757; info@ karamea-express.co.nz) links Karamea and Westport ($35, two hours, Monday to Friday May to September, plus Saturdays from October to April). On Mondays and Saturdays, this service connects to a shuttle to Kohaihai ($20). Bookings essential – services are by demand outside peak season.

Canterbury, Arthur's Pass & Aoraki/Mt Cook

Best Huts

➡ Mueller Hut (p212)

➡ Stony Bay (p193)

➡ Goat Pass Hut (p203)

➡ Ada Pass Hut (p196)

Best Views

➡ Avalanche Peak (p202)

➡ Mueller Hut (p212)

➡ Hut Spur (p208)

➡ Hooker Lake (p214)

➡ Ada Valley (p197)

Why Go?

New Zealand's largest region, Canterbury is a tale of two landscapes: vast agricultural plains and towering Southern Alps peaks, including the country's highest mountain. For trampers, Canterbury is all about the mountains, be it the tightly packed peaks of Arthur's Pass National Park or the valleys and view points that unveil 3724m Aoraki/Mt Cook. There are steep climbs to the likes of Avalanche Peak and Mueller Hut that seem to reveal the world, but there are also gentler walks to a historic mustering hut on Bealey Spur, or into the broad and flat Hooker Valley at the foot of Aoraki/ Mt Cook, that are just as generous with views.

Away from the mountains and almost in sight of Christchurch, the privately operated Banks Track combines a dramatic volcanic coastline with chances to spy little blue penguins and fur seals.

Whether you're looking over a vast ocean horizon, or across waves of snow-tipped mountains, Canterbury is a diverse tramping delight.

When to Go

The Canterbury Plains are among the driest and flattest areas of NZ. The moisture-laden westerlies from the Tasman Sea hit the Southern Alps and dump their rainfall on the West Coast before reaching Canterbury, which collects a comparative dribble – 750mm or so.

For the most part though, you'll be tramping in the mountains, which when they're not attracting bad weather, are creating it. The Southern Alps have a volatile climate, where you can expect to encounter cold, wind and rain at any time of year. The optimum time to tramp here is December through April.

Background Reading

Get enthralled by Aoraki/Mt Cook with *The Conquest of Mount Cook and Other Climbs: An Account of Four Seasons' Mountaineering on the Southern Alps of New Zealand,* a memoir from Freda du Faur, the first woman to summit on Aoraki/Mt Cook. *The Spirit of Mountaineering* by Mary Hobbs tells the story of Jack Absalom, the first NZ-born mountain guide. It's the first of four planned volumes about mountain guides in the Aoraki/Mt Cook region.

The southern hemisphere's only Dark Sky Reserve is located around Tekapo and Aoraki/Mt Cook. To navigate your way across these clear skies, seek out astronomer Richard Hall's *How to Gaze at the Southern Stars.* This illuminating little book is packed with fascinating stories of the constellations, their origins and their role in the survival of humankind.

DON'T MISS

Inland SH8 between Christchurch and Aoraki/Mt Cook National Park is one of NZ's great scenic drives, the highlight of which is Lake Tekapo, an intensely turquoise lake with a backdrop of the Southern Alps. The town's lakeside Church of the Good Shepherd is one of NZ's obligatory photo stops, but it blinds visitors to the presence of Tekapo's finest landmark, Mt John, one of the country's best lookout points.

The best way to appreciate this 1031m mountain (which is actually more of a hill) is to hike to its summit (around three hours return from the town). Conveniently located at the top is the delightful **Astro Café** (Mt John University Observatory; mains $6-14; ⊙ 9am-6pm Oct-Apr, 10am-5pm May-Sep, weather dependent), a glass-walled pavilion with 360-degree views across the entire Mackenzie Basin.

The view, however, is equally dazzling at night. Thanks to clear skies and an absence of light pollution, the area is known as one of the finest spots on the planet to view the heavens. To unravel the mysteries of the southern hemisphere sky, take a stargazing tour with **Earth & Sky** (☎ 03-680 6960; www.earthandsky.co.nz; SH8) 🔗, based at Mt John Observatory.

Visitor Information Centres

➡ Christchurch DOC Visitor Centre (p196)
➡ DOC Arthur's Pass Visitor Centre (p200)
➡ Hanmer Springs i-SITE (p216)
➡ Aoraki/Mt Cook National Park Visitor Centre (p210)

CANTERBURY, ARTHUR'S PASS & AORAKI/MT COOK

Fast Facts

➡ In 2014 the height of Aoraki/Mt Cook was downgraded from 3764m to 3724m, owing to a summit avalanche in 1991 and subsequent erosion.

➡ The quickest runners in the now-defunct Avalanche Peak Challenge completed the 16km event in around 70 minutes. Fit trampers climb up and back in about six hours.

➡ Thanks to around half a century of possum-eradication efforts, the Otira Valley, north of Arthur's Pass, puts on possibly the South Island's best display of blooming rata every summer.

Top Tip

There's a good reason why tramping times here seem so long for such short distances. The steep, mountainous terrain usually means gruelling climbs and knee-crunching descents. Set off early and stop often to soak in the views and refuel on trail snacks.

Resources

➡ www.christchurchnz.com
➡ http://akaroa.com
➡ www.bankstrack.co.nz
➡ https://visithurunui.co.nz
➡ www.arthurspass.com
➡ https://mackenziezn.com

Canterbury, Arthur's Pass & Aoraki/Mt Cook

$\hat{\mathbb{N}}$

0   50 km

0   20 miles

ST JAMES WALKWAY
Low passes among high mountains. (p194)

HARPER PASS
Links two major South Island passes. (p204)

BANKS TRACK
Wildlife galore, with seascapes to boot. (p191)

HOOKER VALLEY TRACK
Low on effort, high on views. (p212)

MUELLER HUT ROUTE
Lofty perch to view Aoraki/Mt Cook. (p210)

GOATS PASS TRACK
Pass crossing to a fantastic hut. (p202)

AVALANCHE PEAK
The South Island's best mountain day walk. (p200)

BEALEY SPUR
Mild climb with wild views. (p207)

SOUTH PACIFIC OCEAN

Banks Track

Duration 3 days

Distance 29km (18 miles)

Difficulty Easy to moderate

Start Onuku Farm

End Akaroa

Gateways Akaroa (p215), Christchurch (p214)

Transport Shuttle bus

Summary This tramp takes you through the spectacular coastal scenery of the Banks Peninsula, which abounds with wildlife and is resplendent with remnant tracts of native forest and farmland.

Bulging from the coast beside Christchurch, beautiful Banks Peninsula is the eroded remains of two old volcanic craters, standing in high relief against the flat Canterbury Plains. Reached from nearby Christchurch via a long and winding road, the main township of Akaroa and its idyllic harbour lure in hordes of holidaymakers and cruise-ship passengers, most of whom avail themselves of the town's wine, food and waterside attractions. Relatively few, however, venture on foot into the hills and down into the many tiny bays. This is a fascinating landscape to explore, but most of it lies hidden beyond the fences of the peninsula's many farms.

The first private walk established in NZ, the Banks Track takes you across private farmland and forest and along the peninsula's remote outer bays. The route takes in a spectacular volcanic coastline, native bush, waterfalls and sandy beaches, with two crossings of the crater rim high above Akaroa Harbour.

Other than two steep climbs of nearly 700m each, this is a relatively leisurely tramp, which allows plenty of time to take in the marvellous scenery. For the more energetic, cutting the tramp to two days is an option.

Bookings are essential and should be made through Banks Track (p192). Tramper numbers are limited to just 16 setting out each day, so book early for peak summer and NZ holiday periods. The three-day package ($260) includes transport from Akaroa to Onuku, three nights' accommodation, landowners' fees, track registration and a copy of *Banks Peninsula Track: A Guide to the Route, Natural Features and Human History*. The two-day package ($195) covers the same route, but just the one night on the track, staying at Stony Bay (plus the night before the tramp at Onuku).

History

Māori have occupied the Banks Peninsula for centuries. First came the moa hunters, followed by the Waitaha and then the Ngati Mamoe from the North Island. In the 17th century the Ngāi Tahu landed at Parakakariki, near Otanerito Bay, and overcame the Ngati Mamoe.

Captain Cook sighted the peninsula in 1770. He named it after naturalist Sir Joseph Banks. Close European contact began in the 1820s, when traders arrived searching for dressed flax, which was used to make sails and rope. In 1836 the British established a whaling station at Peraki. Two years later French captain Jean Langlois chose the attractive site of Akaroa as a likely spot for French settlement.

In 1840 a group of 63 French and six German colonists set out from Rochefort, France, for NZ in the *Comte de Paris*. In 1849 the French land claim was sold to the New Zealand Company and the following year the French were joined by a large group of British settlers. However, the small group of French colonists clearly stamped their mark on this place – Akaroa strives to recreate the feel of a French provincial village, down to the names of its streets and houses.

Environment

Banks Peninsula is composed of the remnants of huge twin volcanoes, now attached to the South Island mainland by gravel pushed down from the eroding Southern Alps. It is believed to have once been an island, and was surrounded by a 15km band of swamps and reeds only 150 years ago. The Lyttelton volcano was already extinct when the Akaroa volcano began to erupt around nine million years ago. Both volcanoes were once much higher, with Akaroa estimated to have peaked at around 1370m.

During ice ages, when the sea level was considerably lower, valleys were gouged into the slopes of the volcanoes. When the sea rose, the valleys drowned and the peninsula took its present form, with rugged sea cliffs and skylines studded with basalt plugs. Once heavily forested, the land has been cleared for timber and farming, making this one of the few areas where trampers pass through paddocks filled with grazing sheep. There remains, however, plenty of interesting wildlife to be seen, such as penguins, fur seals and Hector's dolphins.

Birds of the bush include riflemen, bellbirds, kereru, fantails, tomtits and paradise shelducks. Shore and sea birds are prolific

Banks Track

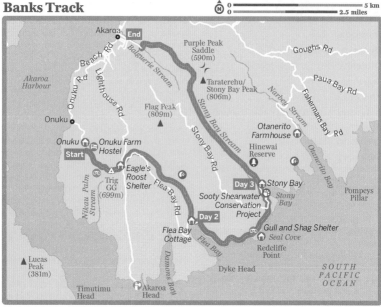

and include spotted shags, little shags, gulls, terns, oystercatchers, sooty shearwaters and petrels.

❶ Planning

WHEN TO TRAMP

The season for the track is October to April. The warmest months are December through March, with average temperatures of around 21°C maximum and 11°C minimum. The wildlife is most active in October and November, making this a great time on the track for nature lovers and photographers.

WHAT TO BRING

A broad-brimmed hat and sunscreen are essential for blue-sky days as it can get very toasty indeed.

MAPS & BROCHURES

As the track is very well signposted, a topographical map is not required. The booklet you're given as part of the track booking fee should keep you on course. To get a handle on the entire peninsula, grab NewTopo's 1:65,000 *Banks Peninsula* map.

HUTS

The beauty of this track is that all your accommodation and transport is included in the package. Accommodation is provided at Onuku Trampers Hut the night before you set out walking, followed by nights at Flea Bay Cottage and

track huts at Stony Bay. Drinks and chocolates are available for sale at Flea Bay Cottage, while Stony Bay has a small shop selling meal and snack items. Cash only.

A sleeping bag can be hired for $30, or private rooms booked ($225/150 for the three-/two-day tramp). There are also options to have your pack transported for you ($25 per pack, minimum $50) on Days 1 and 3 (the days with the longest climbs), or full pack cartage (three-day tramp $100 per pack, with a minimum of $400; two-day tramp $60, minimum $240).

INFORMATION

Bookings are essential and should be made through **Banks Track** (☑ 03-304 7612; www. bankstrack.co.nz; 2-/3-days from $195/260; ☺ Oct-Apr).

❶ Getting There & Away

Akaroa French Connection (☑ 0800 800 575; www.akaroabus.co.nz; adult/child return $50/35) and **Akaroa Shuttle** (☑ 0800 500 929; www.akaroashuttle.co.nz; adult/child one way $35/30, return $50/40; ☺ Oct-Apr) run bus services from Christchurch to Akaroa ($50 return, 1½ to two hours). Trampers are picked up from Akaroa's old post office at 5.30pm by the Banks Track bus. A free car park is provided at Mt Vernon Lodge, but you should allow 30 minutes for the walk to the post office from the lodge.

The Tramp

Day 1: Onuku Farm to Flea Bay

4–6 HOURS / 11KM

After spending a night at Onuku, you'll start the day near the farm gate, where there is a sign indicating the Banks Track. The marked track rises steeply through sheep paddocks, swings east, sidles around a rocky promontory on a ridge and traverses a patch of bush to reach the site of Paradise Farm; stockyards and exotic trees are all that remain of the farm. From the track there are great views of the harbour and Onuku Farm.

The track swings east, and about 45 minutes from the Onuku Farm gate you come to a prominent track junction on a ridge. To the west is a marked track to a lookout and an alternative route back to Onuku. The main track heads uphill and to the east. Keep following this track until you come to some park benches overlooking Akaroa Head. There is a side trip from here to a rock-studded knoll on the ridge.

The main track switches back from the benches, crosses an electric fence and aims for the highest point in the area, Trig GG (699m). Observe how the wind has shaped the vegetation here. If you're lucky you may also see Aoraki/Mt Cook 230km away to the west. From the Onuku Farm gate to this point is a solid two-hour climb.

From Trig GG it's a canter down to Eagle's Roost Shelter. The track leads from here to a road junction; Lighthouse Rd goes north to Akaroa, and south to the lighthouse near Akaroa Head. Ignore the road, follow signs to Flea Bay Rd and take that downhill for just over 1km. Watch out for the turn-off (a sharp left fork) to the track, which passes through the Tutakakahikura Scenic Reserve. This patch of remnant red beech has survived the once-extensive logging on this part of the peninsula. Climb the stile where it is signposted and follow the track down a serene gully, eventually joining the main stream, which drains into Flea Bay.

There are a number of signposted cascades and waterfalls along this stretch, all shrouded in tree ferns. About one hour after entering the gully, the track emerges into an open area and drops steeply. Park your backpack here and head off to do some exploring. There is a waterfall that you can walk behind.

The track soon passes through a grove of tree ferns and nikau palms at their southernmost natural limit. Beyond the palms the track follows the stream on its true left (east) bank for about 1.5km. The track crosses the stream a couple of times before arriving at Flea Bay Cottage, situated within the boundaries of New Zealand's largest mainland colony of little blue penguins. From October to January, there are free tours of the penguin colony available; check the information inside the cottage for details.

Day 2: Flea Bay to Stony Bay

2½–4 HOURS / 8KM

Head to the beach then take the road east through the gate and follow the markers up to a stile. Having elegantly negotiated it, you will find yourself heading uphill to circumvent high cliffs on the eastern side of Flea Bay. If you're very lucky you may see Hector's dolphins (one of the world's rarest and smallest) in the waters below.

The track heads southeast to the tip of the headland, rounds it and then heads northeast to the gully above Island Nook. The remarkable transitions of the tramp now become apparent: one moment there are sheep paddocks, the next ancient forest and then, suddenly, cliffs that seem to mark the edge of the world – indeed, the next landfall across the Pacific is South America.

From Island Nook the track sidles along the cliffs to Redcliffe Point, stained by iron oxide. The track heads northeast and crosses a stream before dropping to Seal Cove, about two hours from Flea Bay. The Gull and Shag Shelter here is a good lunch stop with a fantastic view of the great cliff formations and a soundtrack of squealing seabirds and barking fur seals, which lumber around the rocks or lie curled asleep in the cave.

It's quite a steep climb out of Seal Cove to the intersecting ridge between the cave and Stony Bay. From the top of the ridge there are great views across to Pompeys Pillar on the northern side of Otanerito Bay.

The track passes the Sooty Shearwater Conservation Project, protected by a predator-proof fence. This is the last mainland colony of muttonbirds (or titi, as they are known in Māori) in Canterbury; an interpretive display tells the story of the reserve.

The track continues past the colony and winds its way steeply down into Stony Bay, through coastal scrub. The idyllic Stony Bay track huts boast many welcome features, including two outdoor wood-heated baths, a swing, fresh produce, good hosts and the odd penguin nest. It's a very special spot to spend a night.

Day 3: Stony Bay to Akaroa

4–6 HOURS / 10KM

At Stony Bay the track turns inland, with the **Stony Bay Stream** as its guiding line for the first 4.5km of the day. After about 30 minutes the track enters the **Hinewai Reserve**, a 12.5-sq-km area managed privately for the protection and restoration of native vegetation and wildlife. There are more than 30 waterfalls in the reserve's valleys.

The final 1km along the stream steepens considerably, rising through red beech forest before emerging out of the trees into snow tussock shrubland and suddenly wide-open views. The route joins Tara Track and then Paripai Track, with views down from the crater rim into Akaroa Harbour, now around 700m below you, with Taraterehu/Stony Bay Peak rising above to your right.

Paripai Track descends in a series of switchbacks to meet Purple Peak Track and the final 3km descent into Akaroa, with the town in view much of the way.

St James Walkway

Duration 5 days

Distance 65km (40.4 miles)

Difficulty Easy to moderate

Start Lewis Pass

End Boyl

Gateways Hanmer Springs (p216), Christchurch (p214)

Transport Bus, shuttle bus

Summary The first walkway to be established in a subalpine area, this tramp features open valleys, two passes and great mountain scenery.

Built in 1981, the St James Walkway begins in the Lewis Pass National Reserve, traverses the western side of the St James Conservation Area, and ends in the Lake Sumner Forest Park. Despite taking in two mountain passes – Ada Pass (1008m) and Anne Saddle (1136m) – it's not particularly challenging, though there is one 17km day and some stream crossings. The climbs are not steep, and the rest of the walk is spent tramping through open valleys and beech forests.

The walkway follows historic pack tracks, is well benched and has an excellent series of serviced huts. The heart of the track, from Ada River along Anne River to upper Boyle River, runs through the St James Conservation Area. Vegetation within this area includes red, mountain and silver beech forests, manuka/kanuka and matagouri scrublands, numerous alpine species, at least five species of tussock and a vast expanse of valley-floor native grasslands. It is also home to around 430 indigenous species of flora and 30 native bird species.

History

Although this region was only sparsely settled, Māori did pass along part of the St James Walkway en route from the West Coast to Canterbury. Ngati Tumatakokiri, the most powerful tribe to use the route, were constantly warring with a rival tribe, Ngāi Tahu. This peaked in a particularly nasty manner when Ngati Tumatakokiri trapped and massacred a Ngāi Tahu party in a Maruia River gorge, now known as Cannibal Gorge.

Opened in November 1981, the St James became the first walkway to be established in a subalpine area. It's named after the historic sheep station through which it runs. Dating back to 1862, St James Station was one of NZ's largest sheep and cattle stations. It was purchased by the government in 2008 to protect its natural, physical and cultural value, and to open it up for recreation. With the exception of a breeding herd of wild horses, all livestock have since been removed.

Environment

St James Walkway passes through a mix of flats, forests and subalpine regions. At times you'll be passing through the grassy meadows and rocky paddocks of some of the most remote high-country stations in NZ.

Much of the tramp, however, will be spent in beech forest. Silver and red beech are common up to 950m, and mountain beech, found on higher slopes, is dominant in dry country such as Ada Pass.

The upper Ada Valley is particularly interesting, as it features flats, forests and subalpine areas, all within a few kilometres. These in turn support numerous species of birds. The area is known for its thriving population of South Island robins. Trampers may also spot paradise ducks, tomtits, pipits, long-tailed cuckoos and possibly even kea, among other birds.

ⓘ Planning

WHEN TO TRAMP

The St James Walkway traverses a subalpine area on the main divide of the Southern Alps,

St James Walkway

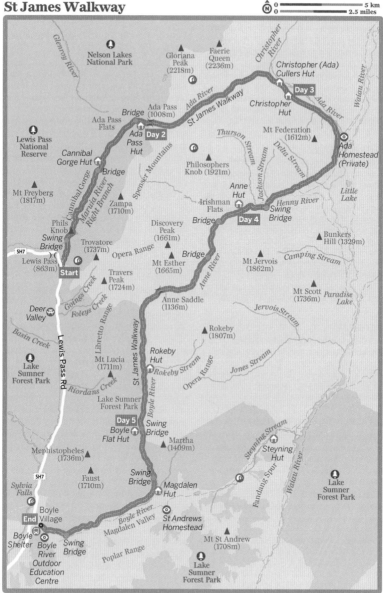

making it prone to extremely changeable weather, flooding and avalanches. Heavy rain and even snow can occur at almost any time of the year, even in the middle of summer.

The best time to tramp the St James is November to April, with the warmest times being January and February, and the most settled weather coming from late February through March.

WHAT TO BRING

Through summer be sure to bring a wide-brimmed hat and sunscreen, as the track is very exposed in places. Insect repellent to thwart the ferocious sandflies is highly recommended.

MAPS & BROCHURES

The most detailed coverage for this track is provided by NZTopo50 maps *BT23 (Lewis), BT24 (Ada Flat)* and *BU23 (Boyle Village)*. The tramp is also covered in its entirety by NewTopo's 1:40,000 *St James Walkway* map.

The *St James Conservation Area* brochure, which includes coverage and a map of the walkway, is available from visitor centres and the DOC website (www.doc.govt.nz). An elevation profile of St James Walkway is also available from the DOC website.

HUTS & CAMPING

The walkway has five Serviced huts ($15): Cannibal Gorge, Ada Pass, Christopher, Anne and Boyle Flat. Magdalen is a Standard hut ($5) and Rokeby and Christopher (Ada) Cullers are Basic huts (free). During peak holiday periods you might want to carry a tent, in case the huts are full. Hut tickets can be obtained from the **Hanmer Springs i-SITE** (p216), DOC visitors centres and the **Boyle River Outdoor Education Centre** (p198), which sometimes has backpacker accommodation available ($40).

DOC's Boyle Campsite ($8 per person) at the end of the walkway has parking for up to six campervans as well as 12 tent sites.

INFORMATION

The **Christchurch DOC Visitor Centre** (✏ 03-379 4082; www.doc.govt.nz; Arts Centre, 28 Worcester Blvd; ⊙ 9am-4.45pm) shares space with the Christchurch i-SITE and offers all necessary DOC services and resources, including hut tickets, maps and advice.

❶ Getting There & Away

Both ends of the walkway are located off SH7, which crosses Lewis Pass from North Canterbury to the West Coast. It's a 15-minute drive (and a far less appealing three-hour walk) between the ends of the track.

East West Coaches (✏ 03-789 6251; www.eastwestcoaches.co.nz) stops at both the track start and finish on its Westport–Christchurch route. It has a daily service from Sunday to Friday.

Hanmer Springs Adventure Centre (✏ 0800 368 7386, 03-315 7233; www.hanmeradventure.co.nz; 20 Conical Hill Rd; ⊙ 9am-5pm) runs shuttles to the start and end points of the tramp. It requires a minimum of two people ($125/150 to Boyle/Lewis Pass for two people, each additional person $50).

Trampers with their own vehicles can avail themselves of the services of **Boyle River Outdoor Education Centre** (p198), near the end of the track. A staff member will drop you off in your car at Lewis Pass ($30), then return your vehicle to Boyle, where it is stored until your return ($10 per night). This service must be booked in advance.

🚶 The Tramp

Day 1: Lewis Pass to Ada Pass Hut

5 HOURS / 10KM

Follow the Tarn Nature Walk from the Lewis Pass car park, passing a beautiful **tarn** that, on a still day, reflects the surrounding mountains. The nature walk leads you right onto the **St James Walkway**, which heads northeast. You begin with a climb into beech forest, followed by a steep descent that drops 170m. After 30 minutes you reach a swing bridge over the Maruia River Right Branch. From the middle of the bridge you can peer into the start of **Cannibal Gorge**.

On the true right (west) bank of the gorge the track begins the longest climb of the day, topping out in 30 minutes at **Phils Knob**, where you can enjoy a sweeping view of the rugged valley below. The track continues to sidle the side of the gorge, climbing in and out of numerous gullies, some posted as avalanche chutes.

Eventually you descend to a footbridge across the river, three hours (6km) from the car park, with **Cannibal Gorge Hut** (20 bunks) just another 15 to 20 minutes away. The hut is a nice facility on the edge of a grassy meadow and is a good choice if you set out late from Lewis Pass.

Beyond the hut the track follows the Maruia River, and in 20 to 30 minutes you're rewarded with your first alpine scene when you emerge from the beech forest into a meadow dominated to the north by Gloriana Peak (2218m). To the south you can see much of the valley you just passed through.

The track climbs a bush-clad terrace and stays above the Maruia River – now a rushing stream – for 30 minutes before descending into **Ada Pass Flats**, with peaks above it and a bridge at its end.

Cross the stream and within five minutes (1½ hours from Cannibal Gorge Hut) you'll arrive at **Ada Pass Hut** (14 bunks). This hut is not quite as roomy as Cannibal Gorge Hut, but the mountain views from its porch and windows are much better.

Day 2: Ada Pass Hut to Christopher Hut

4–5 HOURS / 10.5KM

This is an easy and short day, but don't rush it. Linger if the weather is fine, for the alpine scenery is the best of any along the walkway.

The track departs from the eastern side of the hut, and after around 10 to 15 minutes it begins a gentle ascent to **Ada Pass** (1008m), fording the Maruia River Right Branch (by now, little more than a creek) along the way. The bush-clad pass is recognisable by the large sign announcing that the saddle is 998m – despite what maps list – and it marks the border between Lewis Pass National Reserve and St James Conservation Area.

The walkway then proceeds to descend into **Ada Valley** along the true right (south) side of the Ada River, and within one hour breaks out into a large tussock grassland crowned by the craggy peak of Faerie Queen (2236m), which is often accented with fresh snow. It is but one highlight of this valley track that affords breathtaking views as it passes in and out of the forest.

Orange-tipped poles lead you almost 2km across the grassland to where the track resumes in beech forest. You stay in the forest for one hour (3.5km) but three times break out into small meadows; the second time providing a view up rugged Camera Gully to the north. Two hours from Ada Pass the track emerges from beech forest to reach the wide expanse of the St James Conservation Area. The flats (and track) swing southeast at the confluence of the Ada and Christopher Rivers.

For the rest of the day the track switches between crossing grassy river flats and climbing onto the forested ridge to avoid slips along the river. If the day is nice and the water levels normal, you can simply follow the flats, crossing the river at will until you spot Christopher Hut.

About 1km (15 minutes) before reaching that hut, the track passes **Christopher (Ada) Cullers Hut** (four bunks), which is maintained as a historic hut. Built in 1956 for deer hunters, it's now more a monument to the old New Zealand Forest Service than a place to stay. The roomier **Christopher Hut** (14 bunks) has good views of the mountains surrounding the Waiau Valley. You may see a herd of wild horses grazing here.

Day 3: Christopher Hut to Anne Hut

4–5 HOURS / 13KM

This day is spent almost entirely on open river flats, which means lots of sun and very little shade in summer.

Leaving Christopher Hut, you cut across grassy flats along the true right bank of the Ada River for almost 2km, without getting close to any trees. Moving into some scrub you follow the river closely around Federation Corner as it heads for its confluence with the

Waiau River. It takes 1½ hours (4km) to round the corner. Much of the time you're skirting the base of Mt Federation (1612m), occasionally climbing into bush to avoid slips and steep drop-offs. Halfway around you can see the complex of the privately owned **Ada Homestead** on the opposite side of the river. This used to be St James Station's operational base.

Once in Henry Valley, you cross grassy terraces for 4km, at times following a 4WD track. The track keeps to the lower slopes of Mt Federation, through matagouri thickets, and eventually sidles up a bush-clad terrace before descending to a long swing bridge across the **Henry River**. Once on the true right (south) bank, the track merges again with the 4WD track and gently climbs to Irishman Flats, a long grassy terrace and the site of **Anne Hut** (20 bunks). From the flats, there are excellent views up the Henry Valley and into an amphitheatre in the Spenser Mountains. The best viewing spot is the top of a grassy knoll, which the track passes five minutes beyond the hut. Another herd of wild horses is often present in this area.

Day 4: Anne Hut to Boyle Flat Hut

7–8 HOURS / 17KM

The longest day of the walkway is split between tramping over grassy flats and climbing through beech forest. The day begins with a descent along a 4WD track to a footbridge across **Anne River**. Crossing grassy flats, the track climbs a bush-clad spur to a second footbridge across Anne River, 4km from the hut. On the true right (east) side you return to more grassy meadows and follow the valley as it swings west towards Anne Saddle.

The climb to the saddle is remarkably mild, with only a steep pinch through the forest at the very end. Two to three hours (8km) from Anne Hut you reach **Anne Saddle** (1136m), which, despite being the highest point of the tramp, has no views.

The 30-minute descent from the saddle is steep, dropping 210m over almost 2km. You bottom out by the **Boyle River** in a steep wooded valley. Follow Boyle River for the next 3.5km, remaining on its true left (east) side. At several points the track climbs high above the river to avoid flood conditions. If the water level is normal, it is far easier and quicker to ford the river and continue along its banks.

At one point, 6km from the saddle, you pass a 'Flood Track' sign that leads you up a steep embankment to a scenic grassy terrace and **Rokeby Hut** (three bunks). This hut is in the best shape of all the old ones, and has canvas cots. It would be a great place to stay if you're not in a hurry to get out the next day.

Near the hut a bridge leads over Rokeby Stream, from where the flood track keeps you in the forest a bit longer before you descend to the grassy valley floor. You remain in open terrain for the final hour (3.5km), which ends with a swing-bridge crossing over the Boyle River, with **Boyle Flat Hut** (14 bunks) on the true right (west) side of an area that isn't actually that flat.

Day 5: Boyle Flat Hut to Boyle

4–5 HOURS / 14.5KM

This final section is along a well-benched track and is listed by DOC as 14.5km, though it seems much shorter.

Even though there is a bit more climbing, the start of this day is a refreshing change from walking across the river flats. After recrossing the swing bridge you quickly enter cool forest and find yourself on the edge of the steep **Boyle River Gorge**, well above the river. Signposted **Dead Horse Gully** is reached within 15 minutes, where a peek over the edge justifies its name.

It takes one hour (3km) to traverse the gorge and descend to the river's edge at a swing bridge. If you ignore the bridge and continue along the true left (east) side of the river, a track leads to **Magdalen Hut** (six bunks), 1km away (20 minutes).

Cross the bridge instead, and follow the track on the true right (west) side into Magdalen Valley. Within 1km you enter the valley to see the open pastoral land of Glenhope Station, and the **St Andrews Homestead** on the opposite side of the Boyle River. The next 8km stretch stays on the northern side of the Boyle, passing through patches of bush and climbing around a number of small gorges and slips. The walking is easy and fast, and eventually the track descends to a swing bridge.

From the other side of the bridge you have 2.5km to walk, starting with the day's longest climb. The track ends at a DOC car park and the Boyle campsite, where there are toilets. A gravel road leads past the **Boyle River Outdoor Education Centre** (☑ 03-315 7082; www.boyle.org.nz; 16 Magdalen Valley Rd; ◷ 9-11am & 1-5pm). Just beyond the centre is SH7, with Boyle Shelter for those waiting for a bus.

ARTHUR'S PASS NATIONAL PARK

Arthur's Pass National Park lies around 150km northwest of Christchurch, straddling both sides of the Southern Alps, which are known to Māori as Ka Tiritiri o te Moana (Steep Peak of Glistening White). Of its 1148 sq km, two-thirds lie on the Canterbury side of the Main Divide and the rest is in Westland. It is a rugged, mountainous area, cut by deep valleys and ranging in altitude from 245m at the Taramakau River to 2408m at Mt Murchison.

There are plenty of well-marked and popular day walks, especially around Arthur's Pass village. Longer trips, however, are largely confined to valley routes with saddle climbs in between. Cut tracks are usually provided only when necessary and much of the time they require boulder hopping along, or in, river beds. Most streams are unbridged and the weather is changeable, so common sense is an essential companion in this territory.

The park's most famous one-day tramp, Avalanche Peak, offers views so staggering (on a clear day, that is) that the track seriously challenges the Tongariro Alpine Crossing as NZ's greatest day walk. Bealey Spur Hut provides another good day walk away from the village. Goat Pass Track is a good choice for trampers new to pass-hopping and following routes, while Harper Pass is an easier multi-day tramp at the edge of the national park.

History

Māori often made their way through this mountain pass on the way to mine the highly prized *pounamu* (greenstone) of the West Coast. On the return journey, however, they preferred alternative passes as they provided easier ascents and more favourably positioned food sources.

In September 1857 Edward Dobson travelled up the Hurunui River as far as Harper Pass, and possibly into the Taramakau Valley, before turning back. But it was 20-year-old Leonard Harper who, in the same year, became the first European to cross the swampy saddle and descend the Taramakau River to reach the West Coast.

Edward Dobson didn't get a pass named after him, but his son, Arthur, did. In March 1864 23-year-old Arthur and his 18-year-old brother Edward journeyed up the Bealey Valley, crossed what is now Arthur's Pass, and descended a short distance into Otira Gorge. Another of Arthur's brothers, George, was later commissioned to find the best route from Canterbury to the West Coast goldfields, and it was George who first referred to the pass as 'Arthur's Pass'.

After gold was gleaned from the West Coast, a rush saw around 4000 people pour over Harper Pass between February and April in 1865. However, the poor condition of the pass intensified the efforts of Christchurch citizens to build a dray road through the mountains. Work began on the Arthur's Pass road, and by 1866 the first coach drove from one side of the South Island to the other.

The Otira rail tunnel was completed in 1923. The next year alpine train excursions began, and became so popular that 1600 day trippers from Christchurch poured into tiny Arthur's Pass village in a single day. Alarmed at visitors removing plants and cutting trees for firewood, residents began petitioning the government to turn the area into a national park. In 1929 Arthur's Pass became NZ's third national park, behind Tongariro and Egmont.

Environment

The Main Divide marks a sharp contrast in the park's ecology. The western side is very wet, with Otira averaging 5000mm of rain a year. Bealey Spur, on the eastern side, averages about 1500mm.

As to be expected, this has quite an effect on the park's flora. The Westland slopes, with their higher rainfall and milder temperatures, are covered with lush forests of tall podocarp and, higher up, kamahi, rata and totara. On the eastern side is mountain beech forest with less understorey and drier conditions on the forest floor. The thick bush on the park's western side also contains more bird life; commonly seen are tui, bellbird, tomtit, rifleman and grey warbler.

The bird to watch out for, literally, is the kea. This highly intelligent and naturally inquisitive alpine parrot searches huts for food, or just for amusement. Its most notorious traits are stealing food or shiny objects (including knives and car keys), dissecting boots and backpacks, and airing sleeping bags with its strong, curved bill. It's an entertaining bird, however, sighted often above the tree line and frequently in the village itself. Tempting as it may be, do not feed keas, as it encourages them to try new foods, often with fatal consequences.

ⓘ Planning

WHEN TO TRAMP

The mountains around Arthur's Pass not only attract bad weather, but also create it, so expect to encounter conditions that are colder, windier and wetter than the lowlands either side. The most unsettled weather occurs in spring and autumn. Heavy rain is common in November and early December, resulting in impassable rivers. All but low-level tramps should be avoided in winter.

All the tramps in the area are best undertaken from November to March, with the best weather generally encountered in February and March. Note, though, that it's never going to get that hot, with an average maximum for Arthur's Pass in February of 17.5°C.

Be very wary of setting off before, after or during heavy rain, and in strong winds or when low cloud is hanging around. Check in at the **DOC Arthur's Pass National Park Visitor Centre** (p200) to get the latest forecast and track conditions.

WHAT TO BRING

Pack rain gear and warm clothing whenever you embark on a tramp in the park, especially if you're heading above the bushline. The saddles and ridges will likely be cold and windy no matter how blue and appealing the sky.

COAST TO COAST

Spend any time on NZ's trails and you'll almost certainly bump into trail runners speeding along the path, an indication of this nation's fondness for doing things the long and hard way in the mountains. This is something that's perhaps most apparent in the annual Coast to Coast (www.coasttocoast.co.nz), the most coveted one-day multisport race in the country (there's also a two-day format), held in mid-February.

It starts in the wee hours of the morning at Kumara Beach, 25km south of Greymouth, with a gentle 2.2km run, followed by a 55km cycle. The literal high point of the race is through Arthur's Pass National Park, where there's a 30.5km run over Goat Pass (p202) – and you know any pass named after a goat isn't going to be flat. From there all there is to do is ride your bike another 15km, paddle your kayak 70km down the Waimakariri River and get back on the bike for the final 70km to Christchurch.

The strong, the brave and the totally knackered will cross the finish line to much fanfare. The course is 243km long and the top competitors will dust it off in about 11 hours – with slowpokes taking almost twice that.

MAPS & BROCHURES

With broad coverage and sufficient detail, NZ-Topo50 *BV20 (Otira)* is ideal for trip planning and navigation. You can purchase this map at the DOC Arthur's Pass National Park Visitor Centre. NewTopo also publishes a 1:55,000 *Arthur's Pass* map. DOC's *Discover Arthur's Pass* brochure is an excellent and comprehensive guide to the park.

INFORMATION

The **DOC Arthur's Pass National Park Visitor Centre** (☑ 03-318 9211; www.doc.govt.nz; 80 Main Rd; ☺ 8.30am-4.30pm) houses the DOC field centre. It can advise on all tramps in the park, sells maps and hut tickets, hires out locator beacons and issues updates on the savagely changeable weather. It doesn't make onward bookings or reservations, but can help with local accommodation and transport. There are interesting information displays, including a 17-minute video on the history of the area.

If you're coming from Christchurch, the **Christchurch DOC Visitor Centre** (p196) also offers all necessary DOC services and resources, including hut tickets, maps and advice.

Avalanche Peak

Duration 6–8 hours

Distance 7km (4.3 miles)

Difficulty Moderate

Start/End Arthur's Pass

Gateway Christchurch (p214)

Transport Train, bus

Summary This popular loop track clambers to the 1833m summit of Avalanche Peak, which dramatically looms over Arthur's Pass village. On a clear day the views of the surrounding peaks, valleys and hanging glaciers are wonderful.

In this park of peaks, Avalanche Peak is without question the most popular one to climb and is the only mountain marked with a poled route to the summit. Its location is ideal, looming directly above Arthur's Pass village and just south of Mt Rolleston.

The alpine world experienced during this tramp is stunning on a clear day. Many experienced trampers will claim that this is in fact NZ's best day tramp, outshining the Tongariro Alpine Crossing.

Unequivocal is the fact that Avalanche Peak is an alpine climb that should only be attempted by the fleet of foot in good conditions. The total climb and descent is 1100m, and although the route is clearly marked and well trodden, it's still an arduous climb with a climax of 200m of narrow, crumbly

ridge. People have died on Avalanche Peak when they failed to heed weather warnings.

Two routes, Avalanche Peak Track and Scotts Track, depart from SH73 and lead towards the peak, merging just before reaching it. Avalanche Peak Track is a much steeper climb, and at times you need to scramble up rock faces. Scotts Track is a more gradual and easier route. It's best to use Avalanche Peak Track to reach the summit and Scotts Track for the return, when your legs will be tired. Of course, the easiest return route to the peak is to simply use Scotts Track both ways, but that's not as much fun or as varied.

ⓘ Planning

MAPS

The best map for this tramp is NZTopo50 *BV20 (Otira)*.

ⓘ Getting There & Away

Getting to the start of this tramp is simplicity itself – it begins and ends right in Arthur's Pass village, eliminating any need for extra transport.

🚶 The Tramp

First things first: make sure your water bottles are full before you set off as there is virtually no water to be found en route. That task complete, you'll find the Avalanche Peak Track signposted at Arthur's Pass Chapel.

The track sets off along a gravel path that soon passes a waterfall-viewing site (it's well worth taking the very short detour up to the lookout, which peers along Avalanche Creek to the high falls pouring down through the forest) and then crosses over Avalanche Creek on historic Glasgow Bridge. Just beyond the bridge you begin climbing, and keep climbing. Within 10 minutes you're looking down at Arthur's Pass village, having already scrambled up your first rock face.

The climb is unrelenting – the only time it levels out is just before you break out of the bushline, 1½ hours and 400m above the chapel. Yellow markers and a worn path replace the track here, and lead up the ridge that rises between the Avalanche Creek and Rough Creek catchments.

The climbing continues once you reach the tussock grass, and it takes one to 1½ hours to follow this ridge to the base of Avalanche Peak. During the first half the route skirts a large slip that leads down to the Rough Creek catchment; at times you're treading right on its edge. This would be a deathtrap in high winds and poor visibility.

Avalanche Peak & Goat Pass Track

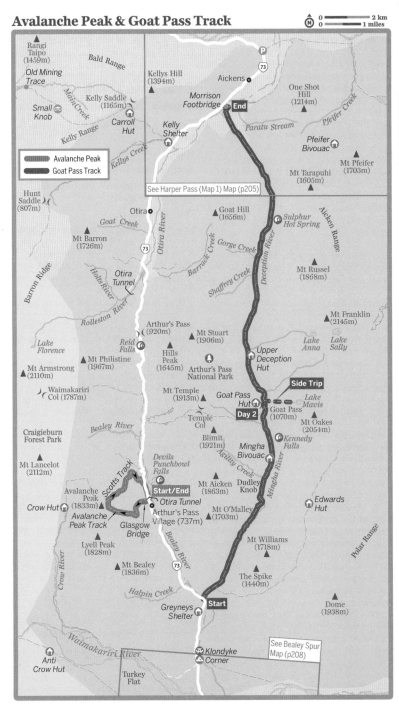

After passing a pair of large cairns the climbing eases a bit and the views improve tremendously. Mt Rolleston (2275m) lies straight ahead, while to the east the Punchbowl Falls come into view. Should the TranzAlpine train pass through the valley below, it's like watching a toy train.

At the northern end of the ridge, yellow markers lead you along its east side and around the tail of some rock scree. You then begin the final ascent to the prominent ridge that leads to Avalanche Peak. The ridge looks formidable, but the markers show a zigzag route up the side for an easier climb.

At the top, the yellow markers from Avalanche Peak Track merge with the orange markers from Scotts Track in a flat spot at 1680m; here you're 10 to 15 minutes from the summit.

The final leg is well poled, but you have to be careful. The ridge is narrow, falling sharply away to the McGrath Stream catchment at times, and the rock is loose. Avalanche Peak (1833m) is a rounded summit with enough space for about six people to sit comfortably and admire the views in every direction. The most impressive view is to the north, looking over towards Mt Rolleston with the icefall of Crow Glacier right below it.

If the wind is gentle and the sun is out you could spend much of the afternoon up here, enjoying the world at your feet. If you do stay a while, eventually a kea or two will arrive – do not feed them, and do not leave your day-pack or anything else unattended.

The return trip begins by backtracking to the junction of Avalanche Peak Track and Scotts Track. Whereas the yellow markers descend the ridge south, this time you stay with the orange markers as they continue along the crest of the ridge to the east.

In the beginning, Scotts Track will also have some narrow areas with steep drop-offs towards the McGrath Stream catchment, but 30 minutes from the summit the ridge eases up and the descent becomes a wonderful stroll through tussock. The bushline is reached in one to 1½ hours at a spot where the track is well marked among the stunted mountain beech.

It's a 300m descent from here to SH73, along a track that is not nearly as steep or rugged as Avalanche Peak Track. You will also enjoy great views on the way down, as you constantly pass small openings in the trees. Most of the views are dominated by Devil's Punchbowl Falls leaping 131m out of a cleft in the mountains. It takes most people at least one hour to descend through the bush, longer if their legs are tired. Eventually you arrive at SH73, just north of Arthur's Pass village. Follow the road 200m south back into the village.

Goat Pass Track

Duration 2 days

Distance 25km (15.5 miles)

Difficulty Moderate

Start Greyneys Shelter

End Morrison Footbridge

Gateways Arthur's Pass (p217), Christchurch (p214)

Transport Bus

Summary This popular tramp takes you over the 1070m Goat Pass and along much of the easy-to-follow route that snakes beside the Mingha and Deception Rivers. The highlight is a night spent at Goat Pass Hut above the bushline.

Goat Pass Track, also referred to as the Mingha-Deception Route (the two rivers the route follows), is an excellent introduction to tramping in Arthur's Pass. It is also one of the least complicated routes in the park, as long as the rivers run in your favour. Typical of the Southern Alps, the Bealey, Mingha and Deception Rivers can be very dangerous when in flood, and the Deception alone requires up to 30 compulsory crossings. This tramp should therefore not be attempted during periods of rain. Should the crossings start to look too difficult, backtrack or stay put – attempting a dicey crossing just isn't worth the risk.

This track forms the running leg of the Coast to Coast (p199), NZ's most famous multisport race. On your travels, you may come across some competitors training for the event. With luck you'll also encounter whio, the nationally vulnerable and very cute blue duck.

The Goat Pass Track can be tramped in either direction, but the Mingha-Deception direction allows for a shorter day first up.

ℹ Planning

MAPS

The best map for this tramp is NZ Topo50 *BV20 (Otira)*.

HUTS

Goat Pass is a Standard hut ($5), while Upper Deception Hut and Mingha Bivouac are Basic huts (free). Note that Mingha Bivouac is located in a known avalanche path and should not be used during or following heavy snowfall. There are no cooking facilities in any of the huts.

ℹ Getting There & Away

The southern end of the track is at the confluence of the Bealey and Mingha Rivers, near Greyneys Shelter, 5km south of Arthur's Pass on SH73. The northern end is at the Morrison Footbridge at the confluence of the Otira and Deception Rivers, 19km north of Arthur's Pass on SH73.

You can be dropped off and collected by various passing bus services by prior arrangement. Try **Atomic Travel** (☏ 03-349 0697; www.atomic travel.co.nz) and **West Coast Shuttle** (☏ 03-768 0028; www.westcoastshuttle.co.nz).

🏃 The Tramp

Day 1: Greyneys Shelter to Goat Pass Hut

4–5 HOURS / 9.5KM / 390M ASCENT

From Greyneys Shelter it's a 10-minute walk north along the road to the confluence of the Bealey River and Mingha River, which is easily spotted from SH73 as a huge gravel plain. Ford the Bealey at the safest-looking point, an instruction that applies throughout this tramp as the rivers are constantly changing course around here.

Once across, round the bend into the Mingha Valley and follow the river bed, crossing the river as necessary. About 1½ hours from the shelter the bush comes down to meet the river. Rock cairns mark both sides of the river here, indicating a ford back to the true right (west) side. Follow the Mingha along this side and across a huge rocky fan.

Continue following the river flat after the rock fan to quickly arrive at a track signposted with an orange marker on the edge of the beech forest. At first the track runs level with the river but then it makes a steep ascent to the top of Dudley Knob. It's a good climb and once on top you'll be able to see both sides of the river valley. The track descends the knob a short way and then begins a gentle climb towards Goat Pass. This stretch used to be very boggy, but has been extensively planked. A little more than 2km from the knob the track passes Mingha Bivouac (two bunks).

For the next 1.5km you follow the track, fording the river at a sharp bend, where there is a large orange triangle marker on the true left (east) bank. This marks the final climb. The track passes the impressive bowl of Mt Temple (1913m) then follows the gorge to Goat Pass (1070m), although you rarely see it. This tussock slope is quite wet and boggy in places, with long sections of board-walk. The climb is easy though, and from the pass you can look down on its northern side and spot the hut below.

Goat Pass Hut (20 bunks) is a great place to spend a night or two. It's roomy, with a radio link to the DOC Arthur's Pass National Park Visitor Centre that can be used to receive the latest weather report. There is no fireplace in the hut because of the lack of available wood, and it can get chilly on cold nights – you'll need that fleece and down jacket!

Side Trip: Lake Mavis

2 HOURS / 2KM RETURN / 500M ASCENT

Those with time to spare would do well to make the worthwhile climb to Lake Mavis, the national park's most accessible alpine lake. Ascend the spur about 350m south of Goat Pass Hut, following the vaguely cairned ridge route.

Day 2: Goat Pass Hut to Morrison Footbridge

7–9 HOURS / 15.5KM / 770M DESCENT

The day begins at the stream behind the hut, where a couple of snow poles have been placed. Follow the small stream, stepping from boulder to boulder, and you'll soon emerge at Deception River. A huge rock cairn and a large pole alert trampers heading up towards the pass to leave the river and avoid the gorge ahead.

Those heading down the valley continue boulder-hopping along the river, on the true right (east) side most of the time, although a series of cairns indicate when you should cross to the other bank. There are also short sections of unmarked track that can be used if found. After about 2km you pass Upper Deception Hut (six bunks), on the true right (east) bank, just before Good Luck Creek; look for it carefully because it's easy to miss.

Less than 2km from Upper Deception Hut you break out into a wide section of the valley. The walking becomes considerably easier and most of the track encountered will be on the true left (west) side of the Deception. Two hours from Upper Deception Hut you enter a gorge. Pass the junction of Gorge Creek at the gorge's northern end and, after another 2km, enter another small gorge.

Between the two gorges lies a sulphur hot spring. It is located on the true right (east) side of the river, 350m down the valley from Spray Creek. It is easier to smell the

CANTERBURY, ARTHUR'S PASS & AORAKI/MT COOK GOAT PASS TRACK

sulphur than it is to find the spring, which emerges from a rock bank and forms a small, two-person pool of 38°C water.

At the end of the second gorge, 10km from Goat Pass, the Deception Valley swings to the northwest and begins to widen. It's about 5.5km from here to SH73, with the final 2km passing through open flats.

Eventually the Deception River meets the Otira River, which can be crossed on Morrison Footbridge, just north of the confluence, on the true right side of Deception River.

Harper Pass

Duration 5 days

Distance 77km (47.8 miles)

Difficulty Moderate

Start Aickens car park

End Windy Point

Gateways Arthur's Pass (p217), Christchurch (p214)

Transport Bus

Summary A historic route followed by both early Māori and miners during the gold rushes, this track extends from Arthur's Pass National Park into Lake Sumner Forest Park, passing through beech forest and along wide river flats.

Māori often travelled over Harper Pass as they crossed to the West Coast in search of *pounamu* (greenstone), and it was that knowledge and experience that would eventually see them lead the first Europeans through the area in 1857. Two guides, Wereta Tainui and Terapuhi, took Leonard Harper across the pass that now bears his name. By 1862, just three years after the first bridle paths were surveyed, the route was serving as the main gateway to the West Coast goldfields, with stores and liquor shops along the way. When the gold rush ended, however, the track fell into disrepair, until its reinvention as a tramping trail.

Today it is one of NZ's classic tramps, connecting Arthur's Pass to Lewis Pass, and is part of the country-length Te Araroa route (p63). The track crosses the Main Divide over Harper Pass, a low saddle at just 963m above sea level. The segment in Arthur's Pass National Park is a valley route along the Taramakau River, but in Lake Sumner Forest Park the track is well cut and marked.

Be cautious with the Taramakau. It is a large and unruly river in a high-rainfall area,

making it prone to sudden flooding. The track can be walked in either direction, but a west-to-east crossing is recommended as you can be surer of good conditions as you cross the Otira, Otehake and Taramakau rivers, all of which are prone to flooding during rain. On the eastern side, the track is well defined along the Hurunui and Hope Rivers, and bridged at all major crossings.

ℹ Planning

MAPS

This tramp is covered by NZTopo50 maps *BU20 (Moana), BU21 (Haupiri), BU22 (Lake Sumner)* and *BU23 (Boyle)*.

HUTS

There are eight huts along the track, providing plenty of options. Only Hope Kiwi Lodge is a Serviced hut ($15). Locke Stream, Hurunui No 3 and Hurunui are Standard huts ($5), and Kiwi, Harper Pass Bivouac, Camerons and Hope Shelter are Basic huts (free).

ℹ Getting There & Away

The western end of the track is at Aickens on SH73, 21km north of Arthur's Pass village. You can arrange to be dropped off by various passing bus services, including **Atomic Travel** (p203) and **West Coast Shuttle** (☎ 03-768 0028; www. westcoastshuttle.co.nz; Lichfield St).

The eastern end of the track is Windy Point, on SH7, 7km west of the Hope Bridge and almost halfway between Maruia Springs and the turn-off to Hanmer Springs. **East West Coaches** (p234) provides drop-offs at both the track start and finish on its Westport–Christchurch route, with services running Sunday to Friday and dependent on demand (so book to create the demand!).

Trampers with their own vehicles can avail themselves of the services of **Boyle River Outdoor Education Centre** (p198), near the southern end of the track. They will drop you off in your car at the start of the track ($25), then return your car to Boyle where it is stored until your return ($10 per day).

The last day's walk takes most trampers five hours, so an early start is necessary if you hope to catch one of the buses. It is best to be at the highway, ready to flag down the bus, 30 minutes before it is due to arrive.

The Tramp

Day 1: Aickens Car Park to Locke Stream Hut

6 HOURS / 18KM

From the car park, follow the paddock fence to the Otira River. Check its water level

Harper Pass (Map 1)

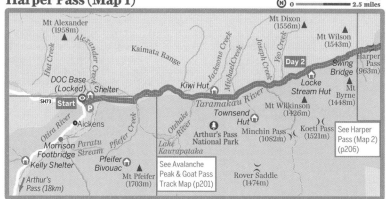

carefully – if it can't be forded, you should postpone your trip, because you won't be able to cross the Taramakau later in the day.

Crossing the Otira River, head for the orange triangle marker in the gap in the trees on the other side. A track leads through scrubby bush to grassy flats, which provide an easy walk to **Pfeifer Creek**. Near the creek is a junction with a track that leads south (right fork) to Lake Kaurapataka. The main route continues northeast, crossing first the **Otehake River**, followed by the **Taramakau River** to the true right (north) bank.

Continue along the true right for about 1km past the Otehake River, where a sign will indicate the short side track to **Kiwi Hut** (eight bunks), about 6km from Pfeifer Creek.

Above the hut, pick your own route, crossing and recrossing the river to take advantage of stable mossy flats. Towards Locke Stream the river bed begins to narrow and eroded banks on the true right become steeper. Cross to the true left and continue on as far as Locke Stream, about 9km from Kiwi Hut. A short track (around 10 minutes) leads up through the bush to **Locke Stream Hut** (18 bunks).

Day 2: Locke Stream Hut to Hurunui No 3 Hut

6–7 HOURS / 15KM / 280M ASCENT

Above Locke Stream the valley continues to narrow and the Taramakau appears more like a mountain stream. Ongoing slips may slow your progress through this section.

From the hut, the track winds in and out of the forest as it climbs towards Harper Pass. Keep your eye on the markers as you go. This section is challenging, but within 1½ hours (3km from Locke Stream) you should reach a

swing bridge. Cross to the true right (north) side and follow the Taramakau (rarely seen through the bush) to its headwater gorges. Here the track begins a steep and sometimes rough 280m ascent through forest to **Harper Pass** (963m), marked by a sign, around three hours into the day's journey.

The track drops quickly on the eastern side to the headwaters of the **Hurunui River**. Within 30 minutes you arrive at **Harper Pass Bivouac** (two bunks), located in a grove of ribbonwood above the stream on the true right (south) side.

Below the bivouac, walking becomes a lot easier as the track drops down through beech forest. It's a steady 6.5km, two-hour descent from the bivouac to the first substantial flat, where you will find **Camerons Hut** (four bunks) on the edge of the forest. At Cameron Stream there's an emergency walkwire 100m up from the Hurunui river bed. From here the track stays on the fringes of the forest for the next 1.5km until it opens onto a flat. Here you will find **Hurunui No 3 Hut** (16 bunks), which looks just like a deserted schoolhouse, standing in the middle of the grassy clearing. The old, two-roomed building has a large wooden porch and a wood stove.

Day 3: Huruni No 3 Hut to Hurunui Hut

3–4 HOURS / 10KM

From the hut, most of the tramping along the Hurunui Valley floor is through grassy flats. A 4WD track departs from the hut and crosses the flats, reaching a signposted junction after 1km. The main walking track veers to the southeast (right fork) and stays on the

Harper Pass (Map 2)

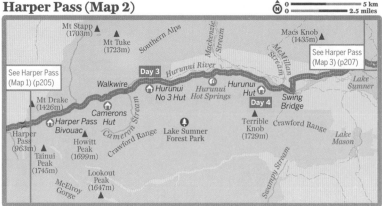

true right (south) side of the Hurunui River for the entire day.

The track undulates as it bypasses steep embankments cut into the hillsides. If you want flat and easy travel, veer north (left fork) at the junction and follow the 4WD vehicle track all the way along the true left (north) side. If you plan to stay at Hurunui Hut it's best to stick to the walking track.

From the junction the walking track is marked by a series of poles as it crosses the flats and enters forest. Sidle up and down along the forested hillsides for 2km, cross another flat and then make a long descent to the **Hurunui Hot Springs**, two hours from Hurunui No 3 Hut. Keep an eye out for the side trail to the springs as it is easy to miss. The sulphurous thermal water emerges from rock 30m above the Hurunui and forms a cascade of hot water to the river bed below. Depending on water levels it's possible for three or four people to soak chest deep in the pool.

The track leaves the hot springs and returns to the forest for 1km, before emerging onto a flat. Cut across the flat, return to manuka forest and, 1½ hours from the hot springs, arrive at **Hurunui Hut** (14 bunks).

Day 4: Hurunui Hut to Hope Kiwi Lodge

5–6 HOURS / 19KM

The track continues along the Hurunui River, and 1km below the confluence with **McMillan Stream** (about 30 minutes) it arrives at a swing bridge. Cross over, and follow the vehicle track to where it swings sharply to the west. Here, a marked route heads east (right fork) and crosses the valley along the edge of the forest. To avoid some cliffs the

track dips into the bush once before reaching the head of **Lake Sumner**.

On the northern side of the lake, the track enters forest again for an easy climb to **Three Mile Stream**, crossed by a swing bridge. There's a junction here, with one track heading north towards Three Mile Stream Hut and another south to Charley's Point, on the lake. The main track departs east across the stream and begins the day's steepest climb, gaining 150m before levelling off and finally reaching bush-clad **Kiwi Saddle** (677m). Just before the saddle there is a short track to a **lookout**, which has a fine view across Lake Sumner.

From the saddle descend to the swampy grasslands of **Kiwi Valley**. Follow the track on your left to avoid the bogs and then pick up a 4WD track along the true right (east) side of the river. It's a one-hour walk through the cattle flats to **Hope Kiwi Lodge** (20 bunks), near the western edge of the forest. This hut is large, with five rooms and a wood stove.

Day 5: Hope Kiwi Lodge to Windy Point

5–6 HOURS / 15KM

Follow the poled route from the hut through beech forest and grassy flats, and in around 30 minutes you will reach the **Hope River** swing bridge. On the true left (north) side of the river, the track immediately enters a large, open flat, and it's an easy walk for the next hour as you follow poles for 4km, until a bend in the river forces you to climb into the forest.

The track sidles between bush and more flats, and in 2km arrives at **Hope Shelter** (six bunks), marking the halfway point of

Harper Pass (Map 3)

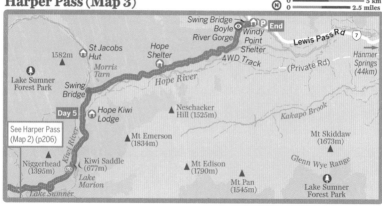

the day. Little more than 7km of the journey remains.

The track stays in beech forest for the next two hours, until it breaks out onto a series of grassy terraces and crosses farmland for 2km to a swing bridge over the **Boyle River gorge**. On the other side the track leads past an outdoor education centre to a picnic area and a small shelter. An unsealed road covers the remaining 500m to Windy Point Shelter on SH7, the Lewis Pass Hwy.

Bealey Spur

Duration 4–6 hours

Distance 13.5km (8.4 miles)

Difficulty Easy to moderate

Start/End Cloudesley Rd

Gateways Arthur's Pass (p217), Christchurch (p214)

Transport Bus

Summary A relatively gentle climb leads to a historic hut and grand views over the Waimakariri Valley and the surrounding peaks of Arthur's Pass National Park.

To climb almost anything in Arthur's Pass National Park is to submit to steep ground. Bealey Spur is a rare exception, climbing steadily but not steeply to a historic hut at around 1230m above sea level. Add to this the fact that the tramp doesn't climb above the bushline, and that it sits east of the Main Divide, making it often drier than other park tracks even when northwesterly winds are bringing rain to Arthur's Pass, and it's a comfort hike of sorts.

It's also a tramp where the rewards far exceed the effort, with expansive views over the national park and the valleys that cut so deeply into it. Though it's not steep, the tramp does climb around 600m from SH73 to Bealey Spur Hut.

ⓘ Planning

WHAT TO BRING

There's a small water tank at Bealey Spur Hut, but it shouldn't be relied upon – carry all the drinking water you need. There's no phone reception along the track to call for assistance, so be sure to pack for every eventuality.

MAPS

The tramp is covered on the NZTopo50 *BV20 (Otira)* map.

HUTS

If you plan to stretch the tramp into two days, Bealey Spur Hut is a Basic hut (free) with six bunks. It has an open fire but no other facilities (or even windows). Bookings are not required.

ⓘ Getting There & Away

The track begins on Cloudesley Rd at Bealey Spur village, 14km south of Arthur's Pass. Turn onto Cloudesley Rd from SH73 and then immediately right. The car park is 200m down this gravel track. Trampers can be dropped off at the top of Cloudesley Rd, but you can't park here.

You can be dropped off and collected by various passing bus services with prior arrangement. Try **Atomic Shuttles** (p215) and **West Coast Shuttle** (p204). If you can only be dropped at the Bealey Hotel, it's just a 1km walk east along the highway to the trailhead.

Bealey Spur

🥾 The Tramp

Walk along the gravel track and turn right on Cloudesley Rd, which climbs through a cluster of holiday homes to the trailhead proper, 500m along the road. The trail begins climbing through sparse beech forest before quickly swinging west, climbing parallel to the **Waimakariri River** and SH73. It's a gentle climb, at times even flat, along the top of the broad, moss-covered spur. After about 30 minutes the trail breaks out of the beech forest, opening up views to Mt Bruce across the deep gouge of **Bruce Stream**. For a time the track skims along the edge of the spur, with a steep drop-off into Bruce Stream.

As Bruce Stream bends into the mountains, the track continues straight ahead, becoming a little steeper. About one to 1½ hours from the trailhead, the track rises to a **knoll** with wrap-around views along the Waimakariri and Bealey Valleys and across to Mt Bealey on the opposite side of the braided streams of the Waimakariri.

From here the track dips in and out of beech forest again and across a shelf of small tarns before ending as you started – ascending through sparse beech forest draped across the spur. **Bealey Spur Hut** (six bunks) sits at the edge of the beech forest, about 45 minutes to an hour from the knoll.

The mint-green, corrugated-iron hut was built by a pair of local station owners in 1925 and originally used as a shelter for the stations' annual sheep muster. It was used for this purpose until 1978, when it became part of Arthur's Pass National Park. If you plan to spend a night here, note that even one of its early owners considered the bunks most uncomfortable.

Return back down the spur on the same track, or continue ahead on the side trip to Hut Spur.

Side Trip: Hut Spur

1¼–1½ HOURS / 2.5KM / 310M ASCENT & DESCENT

Bealey Spur Hut stares out across a snow clearing to Hut Spur, which sits like a cap atop Bealey Spur. From the hut, a faint track crosses the clearing, veering left to cut through beech forest before arriving at the base of the bald summit. Continue up on the still faint track, which beelines directly up the slopes to the main ridge line.

Here you feel truly at the heart of the Southern Alps, while the view behind you shows Bealey Spur Hut as a bright spot on the spur, with the Waimakariri Valley yawning open behind. You can continue along the ridge as far as time and effort allows, though there are excellent views from the point marked as 1545m on maps.

AORAKI/MT COOK NATIONAL PARK

The spectacular 707-sq-km Aoraki/Mt Cook National Park is part of Te Wāhipounamu (South West New Zealand) World Heritage Area, which extends from Westland's Cook River down to Fiordland. Fenced in by the Southern Alps and the Two Thumb, Liebig and Ben Ohau Ranges, more than a third of the park has a blanket of permanent snow and glacial ice.

Of the 23 NZ mountains over 3000m, 19 are in this park. The highest is the mighty Aoraki/Mt Cook – at 3724m it's the tallest peak in Australasia. Known to Māori as Aoraki, after an ancestral deity in Māori mythology, the mountain was named after James Cook by Captain Stokes of the survey ship HMS *Acheron*.

It's not surprising that, with so much rock and ice, this national park is not typically a natural fit for trampers. Although the scenery is phenomenal and the day walks to view points are numerous, this is really a haven for climbers. Most valleys west of the divide are extremely rugged, with steep gorges and thick bush, while to the east they inevitably lead to glaciers requiring extensive experience and special equipment to traverse. Crossing the passes between the valleys is a major climbing feat.

Unsurprisingly for a place of such grandeur, the Aoraki/Mt Cook area has long been a magnet for visitors. The area around Aoraki/Mt Cook Village was set aside as a recreation reserve in the 1880s, with the national park formally gazetted in 1953. Aoraki/Mt Cook and Mt Sefton dominate the skyline around the village, with the Hooker and Tasman Glaciers also easily viewed. Satisfying short walks abound, frequented by hordes of visitors, though it's not unusual to have to wait for days on end for Aoraki/Mt Cook to emerge from the cloud.

History

The first European to mention Aoraki/Mt Cook was Charles Heaphy. Travelling with Thomas Brunner along the West Coast in 1846, Heaphy made sketches of the mountain after learning about it from his Māori guides. In 1862 Julius von Haast and Arthur Dobson spent four months exploring the rivers, valleys and glaciers of what is now the park. Haast prepared a colourful account of their findings for the Canterbury Provincial Government, describing the incomparable scenery.

In the early 1890s exploration of the area began in earnest when the Canterbury Provincial Government sent surveyors to explore passages through the Main Divide. In 1892 surveyor Charles Douglas ventured from the West Coast up the Copland Valley and explored several passes, finally deciding that Copland Pass offered the best possibilities.

Two years later, climbers Tom Fyfe, George Graham and Jack Clarke had their day in the sun when they finally summited Aoraki/Mt Cook. In doing so they pipped English climber Edward Fitzgerald and his Italian guide, Mattias Zurbriggen, at the post. As a consolation, however, the European duo recorded the first east–west crossing in 1895, when they climbed what is now Fitzgerald Pass. They then spent three arduous days without supplies trying to find a way down the Copland Valley. Construction of the existing Copland Track began in 1910.

Environment

With only small patches of silver beech/tawhai left after early burn-offs, most of the native flora is found in the alpine shrublands and tussock grasslands. Over 300 species of plants are found in the park. Among the most spectacular are the daisy/tikumu (Celmisia), and the famed Mt Cook lily, which is the largest buttercup in the world.

CASS-LAGOON SADDLES TRACK

If the Bealey Spur tramp stirs a fondness for this section of the national park, you can extend things with a two-day tramp on the Cass-Lagoon Saddles Track, which can be seen cutting across the slopes of Mt Bruce from the Bealey Spur Track.

The track begins at **Cass**, a stop on the TranzAlpine railway, heading up the Cass River to cross 1326m **Cass Saddle**. It swings back north just past Hamilton Hut, rising over **Lagoon Saddle** (1173m), which, as the name suggests, has a tarn right in its centre. From here it heads back to SH73 at **Cora Lynn Homestead**, just down the highway from the Bealey Spur trailhead.

There are options aplenty for nights along the track, which is dotted with four DOC huts.

THE CONQUEST OF AORAKI/MT COOK

Inspired by photographs of Aoraki/Mt Cook viewed in a London exhibition, Irish parson William Spotswood Green mounted an expedition to summit the faraway mountain, accompanied by Swiss alpinists Emil Boss and Ulrich Kaufmann. In March 1882, having overcome numerous challenges en route, such as treacherous river crossings and a fierce storm, they picked their way along Haast Ridge on the mountain's northern side. Just a few hundred metres shy of the top they were halted by conditions and spent the night clinging to a narrow rock ledge at 3050m, listening to the boom of avalanches around them. The next morning they descended, having failed to reach the summit.

The gauntlet was picked up by local climbers Tom Fyfe, George Graham and Jack Clarke, who reached the summit proper on Christmas Day 1894. At one point expedition leader Fyfe (who would later become chief guide at the Hermitage in Aoraki/Mt Cook Village) dangled without footholds over the yawning abyss.

In 1913 Australian climber Freda du Faur became the first woman to reach the summit, much to the disdain of society ladies who considered such activity damaging to her 'reputation'. A lady in trousers? Out adventuring with the menfolk? Good grief!

In 1948 a young Auckland beekeeper named Edmund Hillary joined legendary local guide Harry Ayers in a party climbing the hitherto unconquered south ridge. Ayers would consider this climb his best-ever feat, while Hillary lauded his craft and experience. Just five years later Hillary and Tenzing Norgay would become the first to summit the world's highest peak, Mt Everest.

About 40 species of birds are found in the park, including the kea, a mischievous mountain parrot. Lucky bird spotters may spy the native falcon (karearea). There are plenty of invertebrates, including large dragonflies, grasshoppers and butterflies. The rare jewelled gecko lives in the region but is very secretive. You may also see introduced mammals such as thar and chamois.

❶ Planning

WHEN TO TRAMP

Aoraki/Mt Cook National Park does experience spells of fine weather, but it is long periods of foul weather for which it's most noted. The annual rainfall in Aoraki/Mt Cook Village is 4000mm and it rains an average of 160 days a year. The short tracks around the village, including the Hooker Valley Track, can be walked at any time of year, when conditions allow. The Mueller Hut Route, as with any alpine tramp, should be tramped during the traditional Aoraki/Mt Cook climbing season, from mid-November to late March, although trampers should closely monitor current conditions and heed forecasts.

MAPS & BROCHURES

The park is covered by NewTopo's 1:65,00 *Aoraki Mt Cook* map, which will prove helpful for trip planning. Numerous short walks from the village, including Mueller Hut and the Hooker Valley, are covered in DOC's *Walking Tracks in Aoraki/Mount Cook National Park* brochure.

INFORMATION

The **Aoraki/Mt Cook National Park Visitor Centre** (☑ 03-435 1186; www.doc.govt.nz; 1 Larch Grove; ☉ 8.30am-5pm Oct-Apr, to 4.30pm May-Sep) is first class. In addition to weather updates, hut bookings and personal advice, there are excellent displays on the natural and mountaineering history of the park. It's a fantastic place to while away a day of bad weather.

Mueller Hut Route

Duration 2 days

Distance 10km (6.2 miles)

Difficulty Demanding

Start/End Aoraki/Mt Cook Village

Gateway Aoraki/Mt Cook Village

Transport Bus

Summary This route offers a quintessential Southern Alps experience, with the chance to sleep in sight of NZ's highest mountains.

This route passes through a dynamic landscape, simultaneously uplifted and eroded in the never-ending battle between powerful natural forces. Rock beds of schist, sandstone, siltstone and greywacke have been carved out by glaciation, dramatically illustrated on the climb to Mueller Hut. Hanging glaciers, moraines and U-shaped valleys are all classic landmarks of icy geological transformation. Populating this

Mueller Hut Route

inhospitable environment are alpine flowers and herb fields, of which there are many to see during the 1000m climb to the rocky ridge and hut atop it.

Mueller Glacier was named by Julius Haast in 1862, after the Danish explorer and writer Ferdinand von Mueller. A series of Mueller Huts have perched above it since the first one was built between 1914 and 1915. The second, which replaced it in 1950, lasted only four months before being wiped out by an avalanche in its first winter. The scattered debris from the hut was hauled back up from the glacier and used to piece together temporary quarters (Mueller Hut the third) until a totally new hut could be constructed in 1953. Mueller Hut IV was located higher on the Sealy Range and was the first alpine hut in NZ built with materials air-dropped onto the site, rather than carried in.

Number five came alive in 2003, 300m southwest of its predecessor, and required 130 helicopter loads of building materials.

❶ Planning

WHAT TO BRING

Come prepared for strong winds, heavy rain and even snow in any season (then rejoice if the sky is clear and Aoraki/Mt Cook comes into view!). Some trampers take an ice axe on this route, though crampons and rope are usually unnecessary during summer. Trekking poles are recommended and can be hired from **Alpine Guides** (☑ 03-435 1834; www.alpineguides. co.nz; 98 Bowen Dr; beginners climbing course from $2350) in Aoraki/Mt Cook Village.

MAPS & BROCHURES

The map covering the Mueller Hut route is NZ-Topo50 *BX15 (Fox Glacier)*.

HUTS

For overnight stays in Mueller Hut ($36) you need to use the DOC (www.doc.govt.nz) online booking and payment system between mid-November and the end of April. You then need to sign in at the Aoraki/Mt Cook National Park Visitor Centre and sign out at the end of the trip.

For the rest of the year bookings aren't required, but you still need to sign in at the visitor centre and sign out at the end of the trip.

There are gas cookers in the hut throughout the year, as well as solar lighting.

 The Tramp

Day 1: Aoraki/Mt Cook Village to Mueller Hut

4–5 HOURS / 5KM / 1040M ASCENT

The tramp begins at the Hermitage Hotel, on Kea Point Track, a very level and well-maintained path that heads up the open scrub of Hooker Valley towards White Horse Hill. Within 30 minutes you pass Foliage Hill; you'll see two lodges and the campsite shelter near the base of White Horse Hill. The track begins to climb gently, moves into bush and comes to a signposted junction with Sealy Tarns Track. Kea Point is to the north (right fork), a 15-minute walk away. The side trip is worthwhile because the view point is on a moraine above Mueller Glacier, with Mt Sefton looming overhead.

The route to Mueller Hut heads west (left fork) on the Sealy Tarns Track. It's a steep two-hour climb to the tarns, but as soon as you begin climbing you are greeted with excellent views of the lower Hooker Valley to the south, including Aoraki/Mt Cook Village. Higher still, there are views of the upper portions of the valley and Mueller Glacier. Sealy Tarns, a series of small pools, make a natural rest stop as they're on the ridge in a narrow meadow of alpine shrubs, grasses and herbs. They are also the only sight of water you are likely to pass during the climb.

Just south of the tarns, look for a huge rock cairn that marks the continuation to

Mueller Hut. It begins as a well-worn track in tussock that involves a lot of scrambling, then eventually fades out altogether in a large boulder field. Follow the orange markers (every 200m) through the boulders, and finally up a steep and loose scree slope to the ridge. Take your time hopping from one boulder to the next to avoid any mishap.

The ridge line is marked by a large orange and black pole – impossible to miss on a clear day – and once you reach it there are views of the upper portion of Mueller Glacier as it flows past smaller hanging glaciers, with the peaks of the Main Divide in the background. Simply magnificent.

At this point, the route turns south and follows the ridge for 20 minutes to Mueller Hut (28 bunks), a bright red and orange structure, 1800m above sea level, that's easy to spot on a fine day. The boulder-and-scree slope here is very steep and is often covered by snow all the way to the hut. This is where an ice axe may be useful, but whether or not you have one, extreme care is required.

Mueller Hut is big and roomy, with viewing decks and benches looking out towards the mountainous scenery. During summer a warden is stationed here, and at 7pm each night there's a radio call, with a ranger providing weather and avalanche forecasts, and asking for the names of all the parties in the hut.

Needless to say, the views from the hut are excellent, including of the namesake glacier below and, if you're blessed with clear weather, the peaks of the Main Divide, crowned by Aoraki/Mt Cook.

Day 2: Mueller Hut to Aoraki/Mt Cook Village

3 HOURS / 5KM / 1040M DESCENT

Retrace your steps from Day 1. This is the unsung joy of the return tramp – everything looks different in the other direction!

SIR EDMUND'S BIG DAY OUT

Rising immediately behind Mueller Hut is 1933m Mt Ollivier. In 1939 a 20-year-old beekeeper from Auckland named Edmund Hillary was guided to this summit – it was the first real mountain he ever climbed and an experience he would describe as 'the happiest day I had ever spent'. Fourteen years later, he would summit Mt Everest.

If you want to emulate Sir Edmund, it's about a 30-minute rock scramble along the obvious ridge behind Mueller Hut to the summit, which is marked by a large cairn.

Hooker Valley Track

Duration 3 hours

Distance 10km (6.2 miles)

Difficulty Easy

Start/End White Horse Hill Campsite

Gateways Aoraki/Mt Cook Village (p217)

Transport Bus

Summary Few tramps reward so easily as this short journey along a wide and flat valley into the orbit of NZ's highest mountain. Along the way you'll pass glaciers and glacial lakes, while Aoraki/ Mt Cook rises dramatically ahead much of the way.

Aoraki/Mt Cook National Park's signature tramp, the Hooker Valley Track, is a visual extravaganza to the base of NZ's highest mountain. A journey on foot into a glacial valley where moraines, glacial lakes and the glaciers themselves stand front and centre, it culminates just 10 straight-line kilometres from the summit of Aoraki/Mt Cook, on the shores of iceberg-laden Hooker Lake. And once you're standing beside the lake, the mountain actually looks even closer than that.

The tramp follows a wide and remarkably flat track (given its proximity to a 3724m-high mountain) through the stunning valley, making this a simple wander into mountain magnificence. All of which adds up to one small price to pay – popularity – with more than 80,000 people hiking through the Hooker Valley each year. Beat the crowds by setting out early in the blue light of dawn, or take the chance to spread out along the shore of Hooker Lake, claiming a private audience with the grandest NZ mountain of all.

ⓘ Planning

MAPS

A map won't be necessary for navigation in the Hooker Valley, but will help bring the surrounding mountains and features into context; NZ-Topo50 *BX15 (Fox Glacier)* will do the trick.

ⓘ Getting There & Away

The tramp begins at White Horse Hill Campsite, around a 3km drive up the Hooker Valley from Aoraki/Mt Cook Village. If you don't have your own wheels to get up the valley from the village, you can start from beside the Hermitage, where a signed track sets out through the broad valley to the campsite. It's about 30 to 45 minutes' walk to White Horse Hill.

🚶 The Tramp

From the public shelter and toilet block at White Horse Hill Campsite the track heads east, crossing a wooden bridge just a few metres on and turning left. In a couple of minutes the track burrows through a section of bush and then passes Freda's Rock, about 20m off the track to the left. Australian Freda du Faur was the first woman to climb Aoraki/Mt Cook, on 3 December 1910, and a famous photo of her was taken by this rock on her return from the summit.

Hooker Valley Track

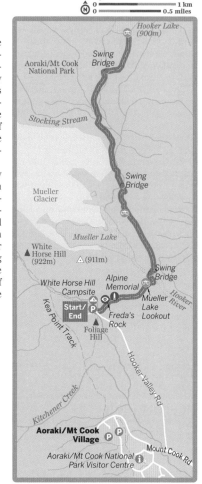

The track begins to round the base of White Horse Hill, coming quickly to a short spur trail that turns up to the left. Atop the rise is the Alpine Memorial, studded with memorial plaques to climbers who've been killed in the national park. It also provides the first view – a taster of what's to come – through the Hooker Valley to Aoraki/Mt Cook.

The track continues to cut across the valley to the Mueller Lake Lookout, perched atop an old moraine wall and peering along the Hooker River to the mud-brown Mueller Lake and the Mueller Glacier that feeds it.

Descend and cross the Hooker River on a long swing bridge, where you turn up the valley, winding now through a landscape shaped and kneaded by glacial activity. Keep an eye out along here for the white flowers of the Mt Cook buttercup/kōpukupuku, the world's largest buttercup. After about 15 minutes a short set of wooden steps leads up to another **lookout** over Mueller Lake and back to Aoraki/Mt Cook Village.

Cross a second swing bridge and continue up beside the rushing Hooker River. Almost immediately Aoraki/Mt Cook returns into full view. A small wooden bridge crosses **Stocking Stream** (there are toilets off to the right just across the bridge), from where an elevated boardwalk climbs gently through tussock lands to the final swing bridge. Just past the bridge, a short signposted side track dips down to an alpine **tarn**.

From here it's a 10-minute climb over a moraine to the **Hooker Lake view point**. A trail ducks down to the left of the lookout, heading to the shores of the lake, which is typically afloat with icebergs calved from Hooker Glacier, which you can see at the head of the lake, tucked into the base of Aoraki/Mt Cook.

Follow the shores around as far as the river outlet, where the water begins its journey towards the Pacific Ocean, then retrace your steps back to White Horse Hill Campsite.

TOWNS & FACILITIES

Christchurch

📞 03 / POP 375,000

Welcome to a vibrant city in transition, coping creatively with the aftermath of NZ's second-worst natural disaster. Traditionally the most English of NZ cities, Christchurch's heritage heart was all but hollowed out following the 2010 and 2011 earthquakes that left 186 people dead.

Today Christchurch is in the midst of an epic rebuild that has completely reconstructed the city centre, where over 80% of buildings needed to be demolished after the quake. Exciting new buildings are opening at an astonishing pace, and most sights are open for business.

🛏 Sleeping & Eating

There is a wide variety of accommodation available in Christchurch, from luxury hotels to a plethora of backpacker beds. As the rebuild progresses, more and more beds are becoming available in the city centre and its inner fringes.

⭐ **Jailhouse**   HOSTEL $

(📞 03-982 7777, 0800 524 546; www.jail.co.nz; 338 Lincoln Rd, Addington; dm $30-39, s/d $85/89; @🛜) From 1874 to 1999 this was Addington Prison; it's now one of Christchurch's most appealing and friendly hostels. Private rooms are a bit on the small side – they don't call them cells for nothing – but there are plenty of communal spaces to relax outside of your room. Perks include a TV room, unlimited free wi-fi and bikes for rent.

⭐ **Eco Villa**   GUESTHOUSE $$

(📞 03-595 1364; www.ecovilla.co.nz; 251 Hereford St; d $116-270, without bathroom $95-150; 🅿🛜) 🖊 There are only eight rooms in this beautifully renovated villa, each individually decorated with luxe fittings and muted colours. The lovely shared lounge, kitchen and dining room all emphasise the focus on sustainable, ecofriendly design, as does the lush edible garden (with twin outdoor bathtubs!). Be sure to try the delicious vegan breakfasts ($20 per person).

George   HOTEL $$$

(📞 03-379 4560; www.thegeorge.com; 50 Park Tce; r $490-525, ste $795-1050; 🅿@🛜) 🖊 The George has 53 luxe rooms in a defiantly 1970s-looking building on the fringe of Hagley Park. Discreet staff attend to every whim, and ritzy extras include huge TVs, luxury toiletries and two highly rated in-house restaurants – Pescatore and 50 Bistro.

Supreme Supreme   CAFE $

(📞 03-365 0445; www.supremesupreme.co.nz; 10 Welles St; mains breakfast $7-20, lunch $12-22; ⊙ 7am-3pm Mon-Fri, 8am-3pm Sat & Sun; 🖊) With so much to love, where to start? Perhaps with a cherry and pomegranate smoothie, a chocolate-fish milkshake or maybe just an exceptional espresso, alongside a fresh bagel, a goji bowl or even pulled corn-beef hash. One of NZ's original and best coffee roasters comes to the party with a right-now cafe of splendid style, form and function.

⭐ **Little High Eatery**   FOOD HALL $$

(www.littlehigh.co.nz; 255 St Asaph St; dishes $5-20; ⊙ 7am-10pm Mon-Wed, 8am-midnight Thu-Sat, 8am-10pm Sun; 🛜) Can't decide whether you want sushi, pizza or Thai for dinner? At Little High, you won't have to choose – this stylish new food hall is home to eight different gourmet businesses, offering everything from dumplings to burgers. Stop in for your morning coffee or swing by for a late-night mojito in the beautifully outfitted space.

Twenty Seven Steps   MODERN NZ **$$$**
(⌨ 03-366 2727; www.twentysevensteps.co.nz; 16
New Regent St; mains $34-40; ⊙ 5pm-late) 🍴
Overlooking the pastel-coloured New Regent St strip, this elegant restaurant showcases locally sourced seasonal ingredients. Mainstays include modern renditions of lamb, beef, venison and seafood, as well as outstanding risotto. Delectable desserts and friendly waitstaff seal the deal; reservations are advised.

🔒 Supplies & Equipment

Addington's Tower Junction Mega Centre has several shops stocking outdoor adventure gear, including the tramper's friend **Bivouac Outdoor** (⌨ 03-341 8062; www.bivouac.co.nz; 81 Clarence St, Tower Junction; ⊙ 9am-6pm Mon-Fri, to 5pm Sat, 10am-5pm Sun).

New World   SUPERMARKET **$**
(⌨ 03-377 6778; www.newworld.co.nz; 555 Colombo St; ⊙ 7.30am-9pm) Stock up on supplies.

🛈 Information

Christchurch i-SITE (⌨ 03-379 9629; www.christchurchnz.com; Arts Centre, 28 Worcester Blvd; ⊙ 8.30am-5pm)

🛈 Getting There & Away

Christchurch Airport (CHC; ⌨ 03-358 5029; www.christchurchairport.co.nz; 30 Durey Rd) is the South Island's main international gateway, with regular flights to Australia, China, Fiji and Singapore. Facilities include baggage storage, car-rental counters, ATMs, foreign-exchange offices and an **i-SITE** (⌨ 03-741 3980; www.christchurchnz.com; International Arrivals Hall; ⊙ 8am-6pm).

Tourist-oriented bus services generally stop outside the Canterbury Museum on Rolleston Ave; local and some long-distance services depart from the inner-city **Bus Interchange** (cnr Lichfield & Colombo Sts) on the corner of Lichfield and Colombo Sts.

Akaroa French Connection (⌨ 0800 800 575; www.akaroabus.co.nz; Rolleston Ave; return $50) Daily service to Akaroa.

Akaroa Shuttle (⌨ 0800 500 929; www.akaroashuttle.co.nz; Rolleston Ave; one way/return $35/50) Daily service to Akaroa.

Atomic Shuttles (⌨ 03-349 0697; www.atomictravel.co.nz; Lichfield St) Destinations include Picton ($40, 5¼ hours), Greymouth ($50, 3¾ hours), Dunedin ($35, 5¾ hours) and Queenstown ($55, seven hours).

Hanmer Connection (⌨ 0800 242 663; www.hanmerconnection.co.nz; Rolleston Ave; one way/return $30/50) Daily coach to/from Hanmer Springs.

InterCity (⌨ 03-365 1113; www.intercity.co.nz; Lichfield St) Coaches head to Dunedin (from $21, six hours), Queenstown (from $47, eight to 11 hours), Te Anau (from $63, 10¾ hours) and Picton (from $26, 5¼ hours) at least daily.

West Coast Shuttle (p204) Daily bus to/from the West Coast stopping at Arthur's Pass ($42, 2¾ hours) and Greymouth ($55, four hours).

Christchurch Railway Station (www.greatjourneysofnz.co.nz; Troup Dr, Addington; ⊙ ticket office 6.30am-3pm) is the terminus for two highly scenic train journeys, the hero of which is the **TranzAlpine** (⌨ 03-341 2588, 0800 872 467; www.kiwirailscenic.co.nz; one way from $119) between Christchurch and Greymouth, passing through Arthur's Pass National Park. The other, the *Coastal Pacific*, runs along the east coast from Christchurch to Picton, stopping at Kaikoura. The service was not operating at the time of research due to damage sustained in the 2016 quake, but was expected to recommence in late-2018. Contact **Great Journeys of New Zealand** (⌨ 0800 872 467; www.greatjourneysofnz.co.nz) for updates.

Akaroa
⌨ 03 / POP 624

Akaroa ('Long Harbour' in Māori) was the site of the country's first French settlement and descendants of the original French pioneers still reside here. It's a charming town that strives to recreate the feel of a French provincial village, down to the names of its streets and houses. It doubles as the pick-up point for the Banks Track.

🛏 Sleeping & Eating

Chez la Mer   HOSTEL **$**
(⌨ 03-304 7024; www.chezlamer.co.nz; 50 Rue Lavaud; dm $34, d $76, with bathroom $86; 🖥) Pretty in pink, this historic building houses a friendly backpackers with well-kept rooms and a shaded garden, complete with fish pond, hammocks and barbecue. There's also a cosy lounge and kitchen, and free bikes for loan.

★ Beaufort House   B&B **$$$**
(⌨ 03-304 7517; www.beauforthouse.co.nz; 42 Rue Grehan; r $395; ⊙ closed Jun-Aug; P🖥) Tucked away on a quiet street behind gorgeous gardens, this lovely 1878 house is adorned with covetable artwork and antiques. Of the five individually decorated rooms only one is without an en suite, compensated by a large private bathroom with a claw-foot tub just across the hall. A lovely breakfast is included.

Peninsula General Store CAFE, DELI **$**
(☑ 03-304 8800; www.peninsulageneralstore.co.nz;
40 Rue Lavaud; ☺ 9am-4pm Thu-Mon) Ⓝ Not only
does this darling little corner shop sell fresh
bread, organic local produce and groceries, it
also does the best espresso in the village.

Akaroa Fish & Chips FISH & CHIPS **$**
(59 Beach Rd; meals $10-20; ☺ 11am-7.30pm) This
is a suitably salty seaside location for tuck-
ing into blue cod, scallops, oysters and other
deep-fried goodies. You can eat in or take your
prize across the road to the harbour's edge.

🛒 Supplies & Equipment

There's not much in the way of camping
gear, but you'll find some food supplies
between Akaroa Boucherie & Deli (67 Rue
Lavaud; ☺ 10am-5.30pm Mon-Fri, 9am-4pm Sat)
and the Peninsula General Store (p216).

❶ Information

Akaroa i-SITE & Adventure Centre (☑ 03-
304 7784; www.akaroa.com; 74a Rue Lavaud;
☺ 9am-5pm) A helpful hub offering free maps,
info and bookings for activities, transport etc.
Doubles as the post office.

❶ Getting There & Away

From October to April the **Akaroa Shuttle** (p192)
runs daily services from Christchurch to Akaroa
(departs 8.30am), returning to Christchurch at
3.45pm. Check the website for Christchurch pick-
up options. Scenic tours from Christchurch exploring Banks Peninsula are also available.

  French Connection (p192) has a year-round
daily departure from Christchurch at 9am, returning from Akaroa at 4pm.

Hanmer Springs

☑ 03 / POP 840

The main thermal resort on the South Island,
Hanmer Springs is 10km off SH7, and 57km
southeast of Boyle, the end of the St James
Walkway. This makes the town an ideal place
to pick up supplies before the tramp and to
soak away those sore muscles afterwards.
Head directly to Hanmer Springs Thermal
Pools (☑ 03-315 0000; www.hanmersprings.co.nz;
42 Amuri Ave; adult/child $24/12, locker per 2hr $2;
☺ 10am-9pm; 🚼) Ⓝ for well-deserved bliss.

🛏 Sleeping & Eating

Kakapo Lodge HOSTEL **$**
(☑ 03-315 7472; www.kakapolodge.co.nz; 14 Amuri
Ave; dm $33, d $76, with bathroom $95; Ⓟ 🛜) The
YHA-affiliated Kakapo has a cheery owner,

a roomy kitchen and lounge, chill-busting
underfloor heating and a 1st-floor sundeck.
Bunk-free dorms (some with bathrooms)
and spotless double rooms are available.

★**Woodbank Park Cottages** COTTAGE **$$**
(☑ 03-315 5075; www.woodbankcottages.co.nz; 381
Woodbank Rd; d $190-225; Ⓟ ❄) Nestled among
the trees, these two plush cottages are a
six-minute drive from Hanmer but feel a mil-
lion miles away. Decor is crisp and modern,
with wrap-around wooden decks that come
equipped with gas barbecues and rural views.
Log-burning fireplaces and well-stocked
kitchens seal the deal.

Powerhouse Cafe CAFE **$$**
(☑ 03-315 5252; www.powerhousecafe.co.nz; 8
Jacks Pass Rd; brunch mains $15-24; ☺ 7.30am-
3pm) Delicious cakes and good-quality coffee are on the menu at this local favourite,
tucked away off the main street. Power up
with a huge High Country breakfast or try
the Highland Fling – caramelised, whisky-
sodden porridge topped with banana. Lunch
offerings are equally palatable.

Coriander's INDIAN **$$**
(☑ 03-315 7616; www.corianders.co.nz; Chisholm
Cres; mains $16-22; ☺ noon-2pm & 5-10pm Tue-
Sun, 5-10pm Mon; 🌱) Spice up your life at this
brightly painted North Indian restaurant
complete with *bhangra*-beats soundtrack.
There are plenty of tasty lamb, chicken and
seafood dishes to choose from, plus a fine
vegetarian selection.

🛒 Supplies & Equipment

Four Square SUPERMARKET **$**
(☑ 03-315 7190; 12 Conical Hill Rd; ☺ 8am-7pm Sat-
Thu, to 8pm Fri) The town's only supermarket,
this is the place for self-caterers and camp-
ers to stock up on essentials.

❶ Information

Hanmer Springs i-SITE (☑ 03-315 0020,
0800 442 663; www.visithanmersprings.co.nz;
40 Amuri Ave; ☺ 10am-5pm) Books transport,
accommodation and activities.

❶ Getting There & Away

The **main bus stop** is near the corner of Amuri
Ave and Jacks Pass Rd. **Hanmer Connection**
(☑ 03-382 2952, 0800 242 663; www.hanmer
connection.co.nz; adult/child one way $30/20,
return $50/30) has a daily bus to/from
Christchurch, departing Christchurch at 9am
and Hanmer Springs at 4.30pm. **Hanmer Tours
& Shuttle** (☑ 03-315 7418; www.hanmertours.

co.nz) runs daily buses to/from Christchurch city centre ($35, two hours) and Christchurch Airport ($45, two hours).

Arthur's Pass

03 / POP 30

New Zealand's highest settlement is a tiny place, but it still serves as the main centre for its namesake national park.

Sleeping & Eating

Mountain House YHA HOSTEL $
(03-318 9258; www.trampers.co.nz; 83 Main Rd; dm/d $33/92, motel units $165; P) Spread around the village, this excellent suite of accommodation includes a well-kept hostel, two upmarket motel units and two three-bedroom cottages with log fires ($340, for up to eight people).

Wilderness Lodge LODGE $$$
(03-318 9246; www.wildernesslodge.co.nz; Cora Lynn Rd, Bealey; half board s $569-770, d $938-1240; P) This midsize alpine lodge, tucked into beech forest just off the highway, is a class act. Two daily guided activities (such as tramping and kayaking) are included in the tariff, along with gourmet breakfast and dinner.

Arthur's Pass Store & Cafe CAFE $
(85 Main Rd; breakfast & lunch $7-24; 8am-5pm;) If you want to stock up on supplies, this is your best chance, with odds-on for egg sandwiches, hot chips, decent coffee, basic groceries and petrol.

Wobbly Kea CAFE $$
(www.wobblykea.co.nz; 108 Main Rd; breakfast $10-17, mains $24-26; 9am-8pm) Don your big-eatin' pants for brunch, lunch or dinner at the Wobbly Kea, which offers a short menu of simple but tasty home-cooked meals, such as meaty stew and curry. Pricey pizza ($33) is available to take away, as are fish and chips.

Supplies & Equipment

There are basic groceries only at the Arthur's Pass Store & Cafe.

Information

The online directory at www.softrock.co.nz is a mine of useful local information.

Getting There & Away

Buses depart from various stops all a stone's throw from the store. **Atomic Shuttles** (03-349 0697; www.atomictravel.co.nz) head to/from Christchurch ($40, 2¼ hours) and Greymouth ($40, 1¼ hours). **West Coast Shuttle** (p203) head to/from Christchurch ($42, 2¾ hours) and Greymouth ($32, 1¾ hours).

The **TranzAlpine** (04-495 0775, 0800 872 467; www.greatjourneysofnz.co.nz/tranzalpine; fares from $119) train stops here daily in each direction, heading to/from Christchurch (2½ hours) or Greymouth (two hours).

Mt Cook Village

03 / POP 200

This small tourist village is the access point for the bulk of visitors to Aoraki/Mt Cook National Park. Most accommodation is expensive due to limited availability.

Sleeping & Eating

Mt Cook YHA HOSTEL $
(03-435 1820; www.yha.co.nz; 1 Bowen Dr; dm/d $40/140; P) Handsomely decked out in pine, this excellent hostel has a free sauna, a drying room, log fires, a large kitchen and friendly, helpful staff. Rooms are clean and warm, although some are a tight squeeze (particularly the twin bunk rooms).

★**Aoraki/Mt Cook Alpine Lodge** LODGE $$
(03-435 1860; www.aorakialpinelodge.co.nz; Bowen Dr; d $169-240; P) This lovely family-run lodge has en suite rooms, including some suitable for families and two with kitchenettes; most have views. The huge lounge and kitchen area also has a superb mountain outlook, as does the barbecue area.

Old Mountaineers' Cafe CAFE $$
(www.mtcook.com; Bowen Dr; mains breakfast $9-15, lunch $14-26, dinner $24-35; 10am-9pm;) The village's best eatery also supports local and organic suppliers via an all-day menu offering salmon and bacon pies, cooked breakfasts, burgers and pizza.

Supplies & Equipment

There are no food or gear stores here; the nearest supermarket is in Twizel, 65km away.

Getting There & Away

Cook Connection (0800 266 526; www.cookconnect.co.nz) runs shuttle services to Lake Tekapo ($40, 1½ hours) and Twizel ($28, 45 minutes). **InterCity** (03-365 1113; www.intercity.co.nz) coaches stop at the Hermitage; however, they are operated as part of a 'tour' and can be pricey – you might be better off catching a shuttle back to Twizel and picking up an InterCity connection from there.

West Coast

Best Sleeps

➡ Ghost Lake Hut (p223)

➡ Ballroom Overhang (p229)

➡ Welcome Flat Hut (p232)

Best Views

➡ Rocky Tor (p223)

➡ Mokihinui Gorge (p224)

➡ Douglas Rock Hut (p232)

➡ Dilemma Gorge (p228)

➡ Ghost Lake Hut (p223)

Why Go?

Take a walk on the wild side, literally. The West Coast echoes with memories of lawless gold rushes, and its weather often appears equally lawless – locals say that if you can't see the mountains here then it's raining, and if you can see them it's about to rain. And yet the West Coast is one of the most dynamic tramping regions in New Zealand, with an emerging network of tracks that seems destined to elevate it to a position alongside the likes of Fiordland and Abel Tasman National Parks in the minds of trampers.

Leading the charge is the Old Ghost Road, opened at the end of 2015, soon to be followed by NZ's newest Great Walk, the Paparoa Track, slated to open in 2019. Or you can shun these lofty blow-ins and instead tramp a long-time, perpetual favourite, heading up the Copland Valley to the soothing hot springs of Welcome Flat.

When to Go

The West Coast is synonymous with rain – Cropp River, inland from Hokitika Gorge, is the country's wettest spot (in 2016 it had almost 12,000mm of rain). The average rainfall in the lowlands is between 2000mm and 3000mm, while it reaches 5000mm at the foot of the Southern Alps. Much of the rain falls in late winter and spring. Flooded and impassable rivers, however, should be expected at any time of year.

Warm ocean currents sweep along the coast, resulting in a surprisingly mild climate. Midsummer to autumn can be brilliantly sunny, with long spells of settled weather. Westport and Punakaiki average almost 2000 hours of sunshine annually.

Background Reading

Settlement of the West Coast was driven originally by the gold rushes, a time that was evocatively captured in Eleanor Catton's novel *The Luminaries*, which won the 2013 Man Booker Prize. The epic-length book was set around Hokitika, Kaniere and the Arahura Valley, which you're likely to pass through as you head between tramps on the West Coast.

Also passing through is the West Coast Wilderness Trail, one of several cycling trails – including the Old Ghost Road (p221) – on the West Coast. To get acquainted with the region's cycling trails, look for *Classic New Zealand Cycle Trails* by the Kennett Brothers, or *Mountain Biking South* by Dave Mitchell.

DON'T MISS

The undoubted natural stars of the West Coast are a twinset of glaciers, Franz Josef and Fox, that leak from the Southern Alps towards the Tasman Sea. The areas around both glaciers offer a range of tramping opportunities (including the famously reflective Lake Matheson, near Fox Glacier), but you can also get onto the ice itself with a guided helihike. These trips whisk you high up onto the glacier in a helicopter before you set out walking over the ice for about three hours. The walks are run by **Franz Josef Glacier Guides** (📞 03-752 0763, 0800 484 337; www.franzjosefglacier.com; 63 Cron St) and Fox Glacier Guiding (p236).

While at Franz Josef Glacier, also be sure to check out the **West Coast Wildlife Centre** (📞 03-752 0600; www.wildkiwi.co.nz; cnr Cron & Cowan Sts; day pass adult/child/family $38/20/85, incl backstage pass $58/35/145; ⊙ 8am-5pm) 🐾, which breeds two of the rarest kiwi – the rowi and the Haast tokoeka. A 'backstage' pass to the incubator and chick-rearing area is a rare opportunity to see fluffy kiwi chicks and learn how a species can be brought back from the brink of extinction.

DOC Visitor Centres

➡ **DOC Westport Office** (📞 03-788 8008; www.doc.govt.nz; 72 Russell St, Westport; ⊙ 8-11am & 2-4.30pm Mon-Fri)

➡ Paparoa National Park Visitor Centre (p226)

➡ Westland Tai Poutini National Park Visitor Centre (p230)

➡ DOC South Westland Weheka Area Office (p230)

GATEWAY TOWNS

➡ Westport (p233)

➡ Greymouth (p234)

➡ Punakaiki (p235)

➡ Fox Glacier (p236)

➡ Franz Josef Glacier (p237)

WEST COAST

Fast Facts

➡ The West Coast is NZ's most sparsely populated region. Its 32,150 residents make up less than 1% of NZ's population, spread throughout a disproportionate 9% of the country's area.

➡ It has been estimated that by the end of the 21st century, Fox Glacier will have retreated by up to 5km, losing around 40% of its mass.

Top Tip

Encountering the infamous West Coast sandfly is a certainty. Keep them at bay by covering up when they are at their most active (dawn and dusk) and coating any exposed skin with a citronella-based repellent.

Resources

➡ www.westcoast.co.nz

➡ http://westport.nz

➡ www.punakaiki.co.nz

➡ www.glaciercountry.co.nz

West Coast

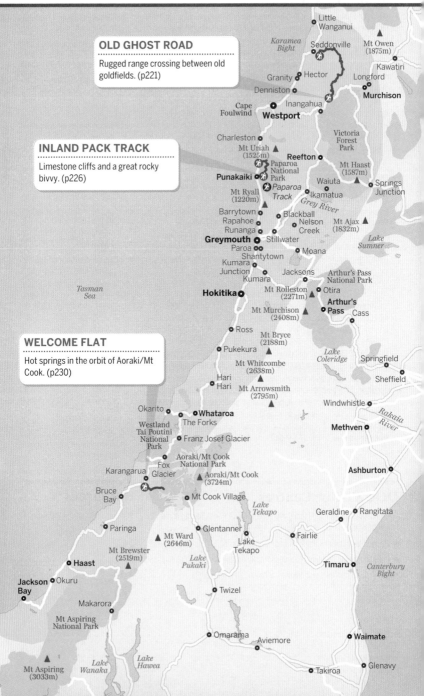

OLD GHOST ROAD

Rugged range crossing between old goldfields. (p221)

INLAND PACK TRACK

Limestone cliffs and a great rocky bivvy. (p226)

WELCOME FLAT

Hot springs in the orbit of Aoraki/Mt Cook. (p230)

0 — 40 km
0 — 20 miles

Little Wanganui
Karamea Bight
Seddonville
Mt Owen (1875m)
Kawatiri
Granity
Hector
Longford
Denniston
Murchison
Cape Foulwind
Inangahua
Westport
Victoria Forest Park
Charleston
Mt Uriah (1525m)
Reefton
Mt Haast (1587m)
Paparoa National Park
Punakaiki
Waiuta
Springs Junction
Paparoa Track
Ikamatua
Mt Ryall (1220m)
Grey River
Barrytown
Blackball
Rapahoe
Nelson Creek
Mt Ajax (1832m)
Runanga
Greymouth
Stillwater
Lake Sumner
Paroa
Moana
Shantytown
Kumara Junction
Jacksons
Arthur's Pass National Park
Kumara
Mt Rolleston (2271m)
Otira
Hokitika
Arthur's Pass
Mt Murchison (2408m)
Cass
Ross
Mt Bryce (2188m)
Lake Coleridge
Springfield
Pukekura
Sheffield
Mt Whitcombe (2638m)
Hari Hari
Mt Arrowsmith (2795m)
Windwhistle
Rakaia River
Okarito
Whataroa
The Forks
Methven
Westland Tai Poutini National Park
Franz Josef Glacier
Aoraki/Mt Cook National Park
Fox Glacier
Ashburton
Karangarua
Aoraki/Mt Cook (3724m)
Bruce Bay
Mt Cook Village
Lake Tekapo
Paringa
Glentanner
Geraldine
Rangitata
Mt Ward (2646m)
Fairlie
Mt Brewster (2519m)
Lake Tekapo
Haast
Lake Pukaki
Timaru
Canterbury Bight
Jackson Bay
Okuru
Makarora
Twizel
Mt Aspiring National Park
Waimate
Omarama
Aviemore
Mt Aspiring (3033m)
Lake Wanaka
Lake Hawea
Takiroa
Glenavy
Tasman Sea

Old Ghost Road

Duration 5 days

Distance 85km (52.8 miles)

Difficulty Moderate

Start Lyell Campsite

End Mokihinui Rd, Seddonville

Gateway Westport (p233)

Transport Shuttle bus

Summary A dramatic tramp into history, it follows an old gold-mining trail that was never completed, crossing the Lyell Range through beech forest, tussock tops, river flats and the magnificent Mokihinui Gorge.

A shared tramping and mountain-biking track – indeed, the longest stretch of continuous singletrack in the country for mountain bikes – the Old Ghost Road opened in December 2015, but had effectively been in the making for 140 years. The track is the completion of a path that was intended to link goldfields in Buller Gorge and along the Mokihinui River in the 1870s, though the attempt was defeated, in part by the rugged nature of the terrain in between.

The tramp begins in the Buller Gorge and climbs over, along and then off the Lyell Range, finishing in style through the deep and narrow Mokihinui Gorge. While the gold-mining heritage – the 'ghosts' of the title – is fascinating, the flinty spirit of the pioneers is only part of the track's appeal. The alpine section takes in truly spectacular panoramas, but the valley along the Mokihinui is just as captivating. The Mokihinui River is the third-largest on the West Coast, draining no fewer than five mountain ranges as it pours through ancient forest on its way to the Tasman Sea. It's a rich habitat, home to numerous threatened species, including great spotted kiwi, whio (blue duck), longfin eels and the carnivorous snail called Powelliphanta.

The tramp can be completed in either direction, perhaps best determined by the weather forecast to maximise views on the southern, alpine end between Lyell Saddle Hut and Ghost Lake Hut. We describe the tramp over five days, allowing a short second day to Ghost Lake Hut across the most exhilarating section of the Old Ghost Road. The presence of six huts along the journey, however, allows you to break things up in any way you choose.

History

In 1862 two Māori prospectors discovered gold in the Buller Gorge, at what is now Lyell Reserve, the starting point for the Old Ghost Road. The inevitable gold rush that ensued saw a town arise at Lyell with a population at one point of 2000 and the requisite oversupply of pubs – six hotels in all.

Meanwhile, on the other side of the Lyell Range, gold was soon found in the Mokihinui River, where another set of goldfields was staked. As the kea flies, the two gold areas were no more than 30km apart, but with a whole lot of difficult mountain terrain in between.

In the 1870s work began on cutting a track through the mountains to connect Lyell to the Mokihinui goldfields, but the mountains won. With the gold proving scarcer than the miners had hoped, the track was abandoned. And so it sat for more than a century until an old map was unearthed in 2007 showing the proposed course of the track. In true Kiwi style it was decided that it'd make a hell of a recreational trail. Years of ingenious construction later, the Old Ghost Road opened in December 2015, completing the miners' vision.

ⓘ Planning

WHEN TO TRAMP

Around a quarter of the Old Ghost Road is above 1000m, where snow may fall at any time, but particularly from May to November, and bad weather can blow in at any time of year. In favourable weather, however, it's possible to tramp this track year-round. The best time is November through May.

MAPS

The best map is NewTopo's tailor-made 1:40,000 *Old Ghost Road* map, which can be purchased through the Old Ghost Road website (https://oldghostroad.org.nz). The Mokihinui-Lyell Backcountry Trust also produces an excellent map, useful for planning. It shows an elevation profile and spots of mobile-phone coverage along the track. It can be downloaded or printed from the Old Ghost Road website.

HUTS & CAMPING

There are six huts along the Old Ghost Road, one of which – Goat Creek – is a Basic hut (free). The other five huts – Lyell Saddle, Ghost Lake, Stern Valley, Mokihinui Forks and Specimen Point – are managed by the Mokihinui-Lyell Backcountry Trust (https://oldghostroad.org.nz) and must be booked in advance through its online booking system. Four of these Trust

Old Ghost Road

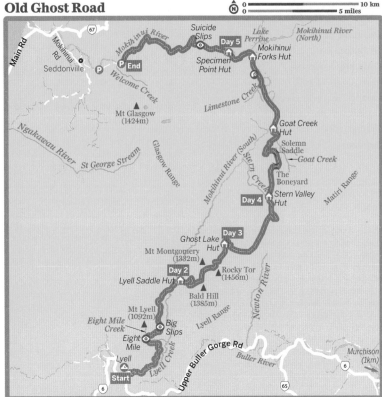

huts (Mokihinui Forks excluded) have two four-person sleep-outs suitable for families and those seeking privacy. Mokihinui Hut has only bunks with no sleep-out. All huts have bunks, mattresses, toilets and rainwater supply, and all but Mokihinui Forks have gas cooking facilities.

Camping is catered for at Lyell Saddle, Ghost Lake, Stern Valley and Specimen Point Huts by way of purpose-built campsites. These must also be booked through https://oldghostroad. org.nz. Camping is also permitted at the Lyell Reserve, where there is a Basic DOC campsite (free) right on SH6.

There's also pleasant camping at **Seddonville Holiday Park** (☑ 03-782 1314; www.seddon villepark.co.nz; 108 Gladstone St, Seddonville; powered sites $17-25, dm $15-20, s/d/f with shared bathroom from $20/30/45; 🛜), 3km from the trail's end, which makes excellent use of an old schoolhouse and grounds.

INFORMATION

The Old Ghost Road is managed by the Mokihinui-Lyell Backcountry Trust. All available information (and hut bookings) is on the track website (https://oldghostroad.org.nz).

ⓘ Getting There & Away

Lyell Reserve is 50 minutes' drive (62km) east of Westport, right on SH6 along the scenic Buller Gorge. Seddonville, at the northern end of the track, is 45 minutes' drive (50km) north of Westport.

Numerous companies run shuttles to and from the Old Ghost Road. Out of Westport, **Hike n Bike Shuttle** (☑ 027 446 7876; www.hikenbikeshuttle. co.nz; shuttle from $40) services both ends of the trail (Lyell/Seddonville $50/40) and can also organise a vehicle transfer, delivering your car from one end of the trail to the other (from $175). **Trek Express** (p148) runs to the Old Ghost Road from Nelson (Lyell/Seddonville $60/100).

The Tramp

Day 1: Lyell Campsite to Lyell Saddle Hut

4–6 HOURS / 18KM / 760M ASCENT

Located right on SH6 in the scenic Buller Gorge, the Lyell campsite is a popular stop with both day visitors and overnighters attracted by its historical interest, in particular the gold-mining relics and the overgrown **Lyell Cemetery**, secreted in the bush, 10 minutes' walk from the campsite.

The Old Ghost Road is well signposted at the far end of the campsite, and the wooden archway is pretty much a compulsory photo stop. Cross the bridge over **Lyell Creek** and follow the track as it begins its steady climb up what has long been a popular walkway, following the original miners' dray road – one of the sections of track they did complete. Beech forest dominates as you head up the Lyell Valley. Around 45 minutes into the tramp you will reach the site of **Gibbstown**, where side tracks lead down to the site of the old alpine battery. It will take around an hour (3km) to reach **Eight Mile** from Gibbstown, but it is only the odd rusty relic, stranded in the undergrowth, that betrays the existence of these settlements. Insightful interpretive displays will stir the imagination.

As you wind your way further up the valley, other interesting features come into view, such as the earthquake slips caused by the 1929 Murchison and 1968 Inangahua earthquakes. The damage is clearly visible in a series of gouges, still largely bald except for the odd tree clinging precariously to the loose, rocky slopes. The most ominous of them, the **Big Slips**, are crossed around 2½ hours into the journey. Entire slopes here sheared away in the 1929 earthquake, leaving a massive scar. Gate signs indicate that cyclists must dismount as they cross the slips, and they're sure not a spot to stop and linger for photos.

The track continues winding up the valley to Lyell Saddle, where a short spur track leads to **Lyell Saddle Hut** (11 bunks), perched on a ridge overlooking the Mokihinui South Branch and the Glasgow Range.

Day 2: Lyell Saddle Hut to Ghost Lake Hut

3–5 HOURS / 12KM / 460M ASCENT

From Lyell Saddle Hut the track climbs steadily but gently towards the tops, with the occasional view point out over the Glasgow Range and yonder as you wind hither and thither through the beech forest. The trees thin and become progressively stunted as you approach the bushline.

Around two hours (6km) from the hut you emerge onto the open tops of the **Lyell Range**, meandering along a benched track cut through the thick, golden tussock. Sweeping views take in an endless sea of peaks, all the way through to the area around Ghost Lake Hut, around two hours (6km) away along the tops of the range. If you have plenty of time to dawdle, this is the spot to do it. Be sure to check out the 'ghost phone' as you stand looking out towards Rocky Tor.

The trail remains more or less level as it continues up towards **Mt Montgomery** (1332m), sidling across its slopes before passing beneath **Rocky Tor** (1456m), the highest peak along the route. From here it is another hour of precipitous meandering along the ridge and side slopes before you reach **Ghost Lake Hut** (12 bunks), 1200m above sea level. Views abound in every direction, including down to its namesake lake, ringed with beech, and across the squiggly lines of the track as it descends then climbs over Skyline Ridge – your route tomorrow. It's the most spectacularly positioned of the Old Ghost Road's huts, but be sure to stay on the boardwalk if you go to explore the lake as it is a fragile environment.

Day 3: Ghost Lake Hut to Stern Valley Hut

4–5 HOURS / 13KM / 800M DESCENT

It's mostly downhill from here – 800m over 13km, to be precise. Fortunately the gradient is mostly gentle, which means it's not as hard on the knees as some descents can be.

From Ghost Lake Hut, the route wiggles and winds its way through gorgeous meadows and scrub back down into mature bush. The track then climbs onto **Skyline Ridge**, a floss-thin ridge with wrap-around views of the Matiri Range to the east and the forested slopes of the Lyell Range to the west.

At the end of the ridge, the track descends on stairs back into beech forest – goodbye alpine section. These stairs were a concession to the terrain, with the trail builders unable to find a way to construct a track that could be cycled here. Be grateful that you're carrying just a backpack down the steps, and not a laden bike.

Around three hours from Ghost Lake Hut, you enter **Stern Valley**. There are two bridged crossings before you arrive in the valley meadows, with **Stern Valley Hut** (10 bunks) alongside the creek.

Day 4: Stern Valley Hut to Specimen Point Hut

7–10 HOURS / 25KM

The trail begins by meandering up through the north branch valley of Stern Creek, across strange but beautiful meadows. At the twins lakes known as **Lake Grim** and **Lake Cheerful** – pick your favourite according to your mood – the route switches back into climbing mode for a short, sharp ascent through a rock-strewn landscape known as the **Boneyard**, before one last sidle to reach **Solemn Saddle** and the start of the descent into the catchment of Goat Creek. Once over the saddle it's just over one hour to **Goat Creek Hut** (four bunks), which has been restored to its original 1958 design. It will take around four to five hours to cover the 14km from Stern Valley to Goat Creek Hut, which means you're just over halfway through the day's journey.

The hut sits near the confluence of Goat Creek and the **Mokihinui River South Branch**, which is then followed in the direction of Mokihinui Forks. The south branch of the Mokihinui River is crossed on the longest suspension bridge (90m) on the track. As the track follows the river downstream, it passes through the magnificent podocarp **Mokihinui Forest**, in which reside whio, the karearea (NZ falcon) and pekapeka (native bats). Along the way you will also pass the **Resurgence**, a large spring that breaks the surface in a magical bubbling pool. It is thought to be the single largest freshwater spring in the southern hemisphere.

It's around two to three hours (8km) from Goat Creek to Mokihinui Forks, where the South Branch meets the Mokihinui River North Branch. The historic **Mokihinui Forks Hut** (10 bunks) is located here.

Turning left at the forks, the trail continues for another 3km (less than an hour) to the head of the Mokihinui River Gorge and **Specimen Point Hut** (14 bunks). This hut sits atop a bluff over the Mokihinui with spectacular views down the river.

Day 5: Specimen Point Hut to Mokihinui Road

4–6 HOURS / 17KM

From Specimen Point, the **Mokihinui Gorge** leads the way as you follow the old miners' road for the largely flat walk out to Seddonville.

The Mokihinui River was the focus of a significant environmental stoush, when a government-owned electricity company was granted consent to dam the river and build a hydroelectric power station just upstream from Seddonville in 2010. DOC, backed by other ardent conservationists Forest & Bird, lodged an appeal with the Environment Court and in 2012 the project was abandoned.

This section of track passes through old gold workings, with remnants to view along the way including a pelton wheel, drill rods, a stamping battery and, most significantly, the track itself, which at times is carved into the cliffs. It also crosses three airy suspension bridges spanning the infamous **Suicide Slips**. These slips were formed by the 1968 Inangahua earthquake and have posed a physical challenge to anyone wishing to travel up beyond the gorge.

About 45 minutes past the Suicide Slips the track reaches the site of yet another mining ghost town – **Seatonville**. The clearing here is an excellent lunch spot. Another hour on is a striking **lookout point** to Rough and Tumble Creek. The old iron bridge lying collapsed in the river is a hint that the track for the remainder of your journey was once the only land route to the northern town of Karamea.

With 2km to go, the track momentarily broadens into a 4WD road before re-entering bush and singletrack for the last 1km. The trail ends at a car park with a roofed shelter (and hungry sandflies), immediately adjacent to the Rough & Tumble Lodge (p233).

PAPAROA NATIONAL PARK

the first explorers 170-odd years before them, most tourists travelling along the isolated West Coast between Westport and Greymouth are totally enthralled by the rugged seascape. Most famous are the Pancake Rocks, the curious limestone stacks at Dolomite Point that are battered by huge ocean swells and punched through by blowholes.

Inland are the rugged granite peaks of the Paparoa Range, lined by tramps rich with natural wonders and gold-mining history. Not until the creation and development of Paparoa National Park in 1987 did tracks such

PAPAROA TRACK

For as long as most trampers care to remember, there have been nine Great Walks in New Zealand. That's about to change, with the creation of the **Paparoa Track Great Walk,** which, at the time of research, was forecast to open in 2019. Linking two existing tramps, the Croesus Track and the Inland Pack Track (p226), the Paparoa Track will be a three-day, 55km tramp that crosses the West Coast's Paparoa Range to end beside the coast at Punakaiki.

The shared-use track (for trampers and mountain bikers) begins near **Blackball**, about 45 minutes' drive from Greymouth, setting out along the Croesus Track. This track begins along Blackall Creek, passing the site of two gold-rush-era hotels – the second hotel site opens up grand views of the Paparoa Range, which you soon begin to climb. Emerging into alpine tussocks, there are wide views to the Tasman Sea. The first night is spent at **Moonlight Tops Hut** (19.9km from the trailhead), with views that stretch north into Paparoa National Park.

Early on Day 2, the track passes a junction with the **Pike29 Memorial Track**, which is also being created as part of the Great Walk project. This 10.8km (one-way) spur track descends into the **Pike Valley**, first through stunted alpine forest and then podocarp and red beech forest. It ends at the **Pike River Mine**, a former coal mine where 29 miners (hence the track's name) were killed in 2010 following a series of explosions.

Past the Pike29 Memorial Track junction, the Paparoa Track rolls along the top of the Paparoa Range escarpment, where both the views and the drop are extensive. Halfway to the night's stop at **Pororari Hut**, the track dips below the escarpment and into podocarp forest beneath cliffs, following the **Tindale Ridge** to Pororari Hut (16.4km from Moonlight Tops Hut).

It's a downhill run from Pororari Hut, heading through the upper Pororari Valley, then along an old pack track before meeting up with the **Inland Pack Track**. Mountain bikers will exit through the Punakaiki Valley, but trampers will continue ahead between the limestone walls of the lower gorge of the Pororari River to arrive in **Punakaiki.**

You can monitor the progress of the trail by subscribing to updates through the DOC website (www.doc.govt.nz).

as the Inland Pack Track catch the attention of trampers, and the park's tracks will get a further boost in 2019 when NZ's 10th Great Walk, the **Paparoa Track**, opens here.

History

Middens (mounds of discarded shells and bone fragments) have been recorded at Barrytown, suggesting that Māori must have made many seasonal excursions to the nearby bays and rivers to gather food. The rugged coastline was a trade route for Māori carrying *pounamu* (greenstone) north from the Arahura River.

The first European explorers through the area were probably Charles Heaphy and Thomas Brunner, who were led by Māori guide Kehu on a five-month journey down the coast in 1846. They passed a group of Māori heading north, but the first settlement seen was Kararoa, 20km south of Punakaiki.

Heaphy was greatly impressed by the Paparoa region, devoting 12 pages of his diary to it. He also wrote about incessant rain, delays caused by swollen rivers, and of climbing rotting rata and flax ladders up the steep cliffs of Perpendicular Point. Later that year Brunner and Kehu returned to the area. It was an epic journey, lasting 18 months, in which they completely circumnavigated the Paparoa Range, traced the Buller River from source to mouth and travelled as far south as Paringa.

Gold was discovered on the West Coast as early as 1864, but the hunt for the precious metal only really gained momentum two years later when famed prospector William Fox chartered the *SS Woodpecker* and landed it on the lee side of Seal Island. The area just south of where the Fox River empties into the Tasman Sea became known as Woodpecker Bay, and miners by their thousands stampeded to this stretch of coast.

Reaching the areas along the 'beach highway' was extremely challenging for miners. Despite the Nelson Provincial Government replacing the Māori flax ladders at Perpendicular Point with chains, miners still looked inland for a safer route. In 1866 work began on the Inland Pack Track, which avoided the hazardous Perpendicular Point. It was cut through the western lowlands of the Paparoa Range, and in 1868 was used to extend the Christchurch–Greymouth telegraph line north to Westport.

After the miners left, tourism became the region's main activity. A coastal track being cut by the early 1900s eventually became SH6.

The Paparoa Range and lowlands were thrust into the consciousness of the nation in the 1970s, when there was interest in logging the area. This sparked a heated conservation campaign that led to the establishment, in 1987, of the 430-sq-km national park.

Environment

The Paparoa Range is composed mainly of granite and gneiss peaks, which have been carved by glaciers and weathered by rain, snow and wind into a craggy chain of pinnacles and spires. It is a low but very rugged range, between 1200m and 1500m in height, offering a true wilderness encounter suitable only for experienced trampers with strong mental fortitude. Cloud and rain feature regularly in Paparoa's midst.

Between the mountains and the coast are the western lowlands, which are totally different in character. This is a karst landscape – a limestone region where the soft rock has been eroded by rivers and underground drainage. What remains are deep canyons and gorges, with limestone walls that rise up to 200m above the rivers. There are blind valleys, sinkholes, cliffs, overhangs, numerous caves and streams that disappear underground.

The nikau palms that line the coast and highway also extend inland. They combine with a profusion of black mamaku tree ferns, smaller ferns and supplejack vines to form a jungle-like canopy. Still further inland, the lowland forest becomes a mixture of podocarp, beech and broad-leaved trees, with rimu and red beech often the most dominant species.

The size of the forest, and the fact that it's been left relatively untouched by humans, has led to the park's profusion of bird life. Commonly spotted along the tracks are bellbirds, tomtits, fantails, grey warblers, kereru (NZ pigeons), tui and the tiny rifleman. One of the favourites encountered is the western weka, a brown flightless bird often spotted in the Fossil Creek area along the Inland Pack Track, as well as in many other areas of the park. There are also many great spotted kiwi, but

you'll hear them at night more often than you'll see them.

Planning

INFORMATION

Paparoa National Park Visitor Centre (✉ 03-731 1895; www.doc.govt.nz; SH6, Punakaiki; ◷ 9am-5pm Oct-Nov, to 6pm Dec-Mar, to 4.30pm Apr-Sep), opposite the entrance to the Pancake Rocks, is a helpful centre, selling maps, hut tickets and Great Walk passes. As the track involves many river crossings, be sure to check in here for the latest weather and track conditions.

Inland Pack Track

Duration 2 days

Distance 25km (15.5 miles)

Difficulty Moderate

Start Punakaiki

End Fox River bridge

Gateways Punakaiki (p235), Greymouth (p234)

Transport Shuttle bus

Summary This historic track, carved by gold miners in 1866 to bypass the rugged coast, features an unusual landscape of steep gorges and interesting caves, as well as one of NZ's largest rock bivvies.

This track explores Paparoa National Park's otherwise hidden treasures, including valleys lined with nikau palms and spectacular limestone formations. A major highlight is spending a night at the Ballroom Overhang, one of the largest rock bivvies in NZ.

While there are no alpine passes to negotiate, nor any excruciating climbs above the bushline, the tramp is no easy stroll. There is plenty of mud to contend with, and numerous river crossings. It is suitable for well-equipped trampers with solid route-finding skills.

Dilemma Creek flows through a gorge so steep and narrow that trampers just walk down the middle of it. Occasionally you can follow a gravel bank, but much of the tramp involves sloshing from one pool to the next. When water levels are normal the stream rarely rises above your knees, and if it's a hot, sunny day this can be the most pleasant segment of the trip, but during heavy rain and flooding you should avoid this track at all costs. If the forecast is poor, wait another day or move down the coast to find another

Inland Pack Track

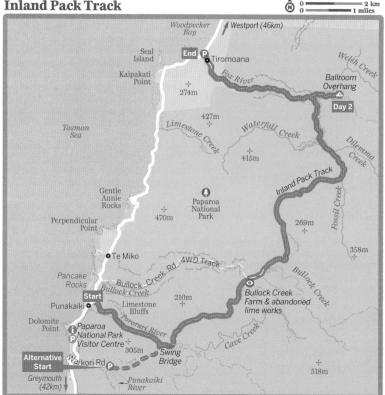

tramp. To be trapped by rising rivers with no tent makes for a very long night.

The track can be tramped in either direction, but starting at Punakaiki makes navigating the Fox River bed much easier.

ℹ Planning

WHEN TO TRAMP

The Inland Pack Track is best tramped from December through March, when the rivers are usually at their lowest. It's also often good in autumn. River levels can be high in spring, when rainfall is typically high, so check at the DOC visitors centre in Punakaiki about conditions if planning to tramp then.

WHAT TO BRING

To stay overnight you'll need a tent, as there are no huts along the track. No fires are permitted at the Ballroom Overhang, so take a camp stove.

MAPS & BROCHURES

This tramp is covered by NZTopo50 map *BS19 (Punakaiki)* and *BS20 (Charleston)*. It's also shown in full on NewTopo's 1:35,000 *Punakaiki and the Inland Pack Track* map.

DOC's *Paparoa National Park* brochure details tramps of varying lengths around the Punakaiki area, including the Inland Pack Track.

CAMPING

There are no huts on this tramp. The bivvy known as the Ballroom Overhang is the site of the only designated campsite.

ℹ Getting There & Away

There are two places to start the tramp, both within a 15-minute walk of the Paparoa National Park Visitor Centre in Punakaiki. The more scenic start is from the Pororari River bridge, north of Punakaiki on SH6. The alternative is off Waikori Rd, along the Punakaiki River, south of Punakaiki on SH6.

ⓘ WARNING: HEAVY RAINFALL

It cannot be stressed enough that the Inland Pack Track should not be attempted during or after periods of heavy rain. There are numerous river crossings and the route from Fossil Creek to Fox River–Dilemma Creek junction involves walking alongside and through the creek. These rivers and creeks can rise very quickly following rainfall – a swollen river should never be crossed.

Before departing, check conditions with the **Paparoa National Park Visitor Centre** (p226), which posts daily weather forecasts. If heavy rain is forecast do not attempt the track.

The finish is at Fox River on SH6, 12km north of Punakaiki. **Punakaiki Beach Camp** (p235) runs on-demand tramper shuttles to Fox River ($20 per person, minimum two people). It can also drop your car at Fox River for you to pick up at the tramp's end for $50.

🥾 The Tramp

Day 1: Punakaiki to Ballroom Overhang

7–8 HOURS / 19KM

The track starts from the car park at the Pororari River bridge on SH6. It follows the river closely along its true left (south) bank, through a spectacular landscape of towering limestone bluffs graced by nikau palms and tree ferns. Keep an eye on the river's deep green pools: you may spot trout or eels in the morning, or perhaps you might feel inclined to take a dip...

After 3.5km the track comes to a junction, with the right fork leading back to Punakaiki River and SH6 – a popular three-hour loop walk for day trampers. Continue on the main track, which in 300m reaches a swing bridge across the **Pororari River**.

Heading northwards, the next 4km stretch works its way through silver beech forest. The track can become muddy in places, with fairly consistent scenery of thick bush and an occasional signposted sinkhole, but it is easy to follow.

After 1½ hours you enter a clearing where views of the Paparoas come into frame. Here you join a 4WD track across **Bullock Creek Farm**. The route passes the shacks of an abandoned lime works and a junction, the left fork of which leads back to SH6. Continue onwards to **Bullock Creek**, where large orange markers indicate the best place to ford.

Once across the creek, the track follows a farm road for almost 1km and then re-enters the bush. The track stays in beech and rimu forest, but sidles an open area and passes some immense stands of flax. After 2km the track begins ascending to a low saddle (200m) on the main ridge dividing Bullock Creek and the catchment formed by Fox River. There's lots of mud here but the climb is easy, and views of Mt Fleming and flat-topped Mt Euclid are possible on a clear day. The descent on the other side is rapid.

The track remains fairly level until it emerges at **Fossil Creek**, 2½ hours from Bullock Creek, marked by a large rock cairn and a small sign. There is no track at this point – you simply follow the creek downstream for 1km or so, walking under a thick canopy of trees. The pools will be easy to wade through in normal conditions, though Fossil Creek regularly jams up with trees that came down in Cyclone Ita in 2014 and are now washing downstream. This might continue for several years yet!

It takes 30 minutes to reach the confluence with **Dilemma Creek**, marked by another rock cairn and a small sign. This section of track, following **Dilemma Gorge** downstream, is the most spectacular part of the trip. Hemmed in by massive limestone walls, you will constantly ford the river, avoiding deep pools and following gravel bars. Keep in mind that if the first ford is a problem, the rest will be even more difficult. Fox River can be reached in well under an hour, but most trampers, revelling in the stunning scenery, take 1½ to two hours to cover this short stretch through the gorge.

A signpost on the true left side of Dilemma Creek, just before the confluence with **Fox River**, indicates where the track resumes. The confluence is easy to recognise because a sharp rock bluff separates the two gorges.

If you are heading to the Ballroom Overhang you need to assess the river levels carefully – do not assume that Fox River is safe to cross. There are deep pools at the confluence, and during high water this is not a good place to ford. If you follow the track west (left) for 400m you come to a signposted junction for an alternative river crossing. This track drops to Fox River at a place where it may be forded. Again, assess your crossing carefully.

To reach the Ballroom Overhang, you will need to walk approximately 30 minutes upstream from the confluence along the Fox River. There is no formed track – you simply follow the river bed, crossing the river numerous times. The **Ballroom Overhang** is located on the true right (north) side of the river.

The rock overhang is appropriately named. It's about 100m long, with a cavern and a towering arched ceiling, which is 20m high in the middle. The roof is a hanging garden of sorts, with grass, vines, rows of ferns and even small trees growing from it. There is plenty of sheltered space in which to pitch your tent; note that lighting fires is not permitted. You can freshen up in the Fox River, but remember: no soap!

Alternative Start: Punakaiki River Track

2 HOURS / 4KM

Purists who want to complete the whole, historic track should head south from Punakaiki on SH6, and turn down Waikori Rd (east). This short gravel road (1.5km) leads to a parking area just before a suspension bridge over the Punakaiki River.

After crossing the bridge, head northeast, following the large orange track markers. The track passes through logged swamps to the base of the hill that separates the Punakaiki River from the Pororari. A well-benched track climbs to a low saddle and then drops gently 80m to the Pororari. It levels off as it approaches the signposted branch track down the Pororari, one hour from the saddle. Head upstream to cross the swing bridge over the Pororari River, around 300m away.

Day 2: Ballroom Overhang to Fox River Bridge

2–2½ HOURS / 6KM

Return to the track on the true left (south) side of Fox River. A benched track here follows the river west. It's a pleasant walk along the gorge, high above the river, and you pass scattered nikau palms and tangled kiekie. The track follows the valley for 3km before dropping to Fox River, where a wide ford to the true right (north) bank is marked.

On the other side is a junction. The track heading east (right) used to access **Fox River Caves**, but at the time of research it had been closed due to a slip at the entrance to the caves. It's not expected to be reopened any time soon.

Stay on the true right (north) side and follow the track west along the river, crossing numerous gravel bars and following the large orange trail markers designed to keep wandering trampers on course. This section takes about 45 minutes. You emerge at the car park off SH6 at Fox River.

WESTLAND TAI POUTINI NATIONAL PARK

Around halfway down the West Coast, the 117-sq-km Westland Tai Poutini National Park extends from the highest peaks of the Southern Alps to the rugged and remote beaches of the wild West Coast. It is an area of magnificent primeval vistas – snow-capped mountains, glaciers, forests, tussock grasslands, lakes, rivers, wetlands and beaches. This magnificent landscape forms part of Te Wahipounamu–South West New Zealand World Heritage Area and is a treasure trove of amazing geology, rare flora and fauna and wonderful history.

The park is split by the Alpine Fault, creating a place of dramatic contrasts. East of the fault, mountains rise suddenly, and steep forested slopes are cut deeply with impassable gorges. High above, permanent snowfields feed myriad glaciers, including Fox Glacier (Te Moeka o Tuawe) and Franz Josef Glacier (Ka Roimata o Hine Hukatere), which descend right down to the lowlands.

On the west side are ancient rainforests – rata high up and a profusion of ferns, shrubs and trees lower down. There are many lakes to explore on the narrow coastal plain, and the soaring ice-covered mountains provide a dramatic backdrop.

History

Early Māori settlements were situated near Westland Tai Poutini's lakes and lagoons, where food was plentiful. However, as they moved up and down the coast in their pursuit of *pounamu* (greenstone), it is evident that they travelled widely through the forests and up into alpine areas.

It was gold, once again, that lured larger populations to the area. Indeed, in the year straddling 1864–65 at least 16,000 miners came to the rain-soaked wilderness in the hope of filling their pockets with the shiny stuff. The first prospectors headed for the rivers, but in the spring of 1865 gold was found glittering in the black-sand beaches.

Townships sprung up, but the rushes didn't last. Just 18 months after their incredibly rapid emergence, the seaside settlements of Okarito, Five Mile and Gillespies were virtual ghost towns.

However, word soon spread of the stunning landscape – Fox and Franz Josef Glaciers, in particular. Determined visitors ventured to the remote coast to check it out for themselves, and by the start of the 1900s demand was such that the government was allocating funds for tracks and huts. Parties were guided on to the ice and into the mountains by the Graham brothers, Peter and Alec, forerunners of the guiding enterprises that thrive to this day.

Suggestions that the snowfields and glaciers of the region should be added to Aoraki/Mt Cook National Park united West Coast support for its own national park. Westland Tai Poutini National Park was subsequently gazetted on 29 March 1960.

During the 1970s the focus of conservation shifted to the lowland forests of the West Coast, resulting in the 1982 addition of the southern part of Okarito State Forest and Waikukupa State Forest. The park was further extended in 1983 to incorporate the complete catchment of the Upper Karangarua Valley, thus establishing more natural boundaries and securing an area with distinctive ecological and scenic values. Other additions were made to the park in 2002, namely North Okarito and Saltwater State Forests, with another 44 sq km added in 2010.

Environment

Westland Tai Poutini has a very wet climate, with the prevailing westerly pushing storms laden with huge amounts of moisture across the Tasman Sea. When they hit the high peaks of the Southern Alps the resulting storms and rainfall can be impressive, and as a consequence there's plenty of snow and ice near the tops. In all, the park contains 60 named glaciers, two of which – Franz Josef and Fox – are among the West Coast's best-known tourist attractions.

The lowlands are covered in dense rainforest, while nearer the coast are scenic lakes, wetlands and wide river mouths. Wading birds and other water-loving creatures thrive among the wetlands. The threatened kamana (crested grebe) can be found on Lake Mapourika, and Okarito Lagoon is famous for the stunning kotuku (white heron).

In the heart of the lowland forest lives the only population of the endangered rowi – NZ's rarest kiwi. Kea are common throughout the park, and the forest is filled with bird life.

Planning

INFORMATION
The national park has two DOC offices, the biggest of which is the **Westland Tai Poutini National Park Visitor Centre** (☑ 03-752 0360; www.doc.govt.nz; 69 Cron St; ☺ 8.30am-6pm Dec-Feb, to 5pm Mar-Nov), located in Franz Josef, the larger of the two glacier towns. The other is the **DOC South Westland Weheka Area Office** (☑ 03-751 0807; SH6; ☺ 10am-2pm Mon-Fri) in Fox Glacier. Both stock maps and brochures, assist with hut bookings and hold current weather forecasts. The former doubles as an i-SITE, and so offers a broader range of general travel services.

Welcome Flat

Duration 2 days

Distance 36km (22.4 miles)

Difficulty Easy to moderate

Start/End Karangarua River bridge

Gateways Fox Glacier (p236), Franz Josef Glacier (p237)

Transport Bus, shuttle bus

Summary This tramp heads along the Karangarua and Copland Rivers to open alpine areas with grand mountain scenery, plus a soothing soak in the Welcome Flat hot springs.

This tramp up the Copland Valley to Welcome Flat Hut is a popular overnight return trip for visitors to the Glacier Region. It offers a window into Westland Tai Poutini's spectacular forest, river and mountain scenery, while natural hot pools at Welcome Flat are an added attraction for foot-weary adventurers.

> ### ⓘ LANDSLIDE WARNING
>
> There are two active landslide areas to be crossed on the track to Welcome Flat Hut. The landslide areas are approximately 30 minutes upstream of Architect Creek, and on the true left of Shiels Creek. Both are signposted. Due to unstable slopes, care is required during and just after heavy rain.

Welcome Flat

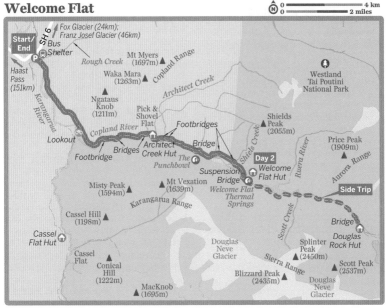

The forests of the Copland Valley are visually dominated by a healthy canopy of southern rata, which makes for a spectacular sight during the summer flowering season. The forest gives way at higher altitudes to the upper montane vegetation of tree daisies and *Dracophyllums*, which in turn give way to the truly alpine habitats of tussock grasslands and native herbs.

Regular possum control has been undertaken since the mid-1980s and as a result the forest damage is significantly less than in the neighbouring Karangarua Valley, which has extensive canopy dieback. The only real drawback of this tramp is that you must eventually turn around and backtrack to SH6.

❶ Planning

WHEN TO TRAMP

The tramp along the Copland Track to Welcome Flat can be undertaken year-round if the creeks are fordable. The high season is from November through April. Bookings are required at Welcome Flat Hut year-round.

MAPS

This tramp is covered by NZTopo50 maps *BX14 (Gillespies Beach)* and *BX15 (Fox Glacier)*.

HUTS & CAMPING

The recommended overnight stop for this tramp is Welcome Flat, a Serviced hut ($15), though it doesn't have cookers – you'll need to bring your own stove and fuel. The adjacent Sierra Room is a self-contained space (the old warden's quarters) with a gas cooker, cooking utensils and a hot shower ($100 per night). There are also two Standard huts ($5) along this route, Architect Creek and Douglas Rock, also without cookers.

Welcome Flat has become an extremely popular tramp, so huts and campsites must be booked year-round, either online (www.doc.govt.nz) or in person at DOC visitors centres and local i-SITEs.

❶ Getting There & Away

The start of the track, Karangarua River bridge, is right on SH6, 48km from Franz Josef Glacier and 26km from Fox Glacier. A car park is about 150m down a dirt road on the north side of the bridge.

There's a bus stop at the northern end of the bridge, from where you can flag down (or book ahead) the passing daily **InterCity bus** (p217), which heads past going south to Haast at around 9.10am, and north to Fox and Franz at around 2.55pm. **Glacier Shuttles & Charters Franz Josef** (☑ 0800 999 739) runs shuttles to the trailhead from Franz Josef and Fox; contact them for prices, which vary according to passenger numbers.

ℹ WEATHER WARNING

Heed the weather warnings before departing on a tramp to Welcome Flat! Although the track is well benched, with flood bridges at major crossings, even small streams can become raging torrents during and after heavy rain – a common occurrence on the West Coast. Be sure to check the latest weather forecast at the DOC offices in either Franz Josef Glacier or Fox Glacier, and leave your tramp intentions at **Adventuresmart** (www.adventuresmart.org.nz).

 The Tramp

Day 1: Karangarua River Bridge to Welcome Flat Hut

7 HOURS / 18KM

From the bus shelter, just northeast of the bridge on SH6, a vehicle track leads 150m to Rough Creek and a car park. The tramp begins by fording **Rough Creek** – a swing bridge 30 minutes' walk upstream is only needed during floods. You can usually rock-hop across the creek without getting your feet wet. Remember that if you need to use the flood bridge, you're going to encounter impassable rivers further up the valley and should not continue.

Beyond Rough Creek the track stays in the bush along the **Karangarua River**, although the track is out of view of the river most of the time until it breaks out onto an open river flat within 1km. Orange triangle markers lead you across the flat and back into the totara and rimu bush. About 4km from the car park the track passes the confluence of the Karangarua and Copland Rivers, where there is a five-minute side track (right) to a **lookout** over the rivers.

The track then swings almost due east to head up the Copland Valley. Eventually you descend to the water and begin boulder-hopping along the banks of the **Copland River**. Trail markers direct you back into the forest to cross a bridge over an unnamed stream, which drains the Copland Range to the north. Within 2km you cross another bridge over McPhee Creek and pass **Architect Creek Hut** (two bunks) before arriving at the long bridge over **Architect Creek**, the halfway point to Welcome Flat Hut.

At Architect Creek you begin an ascent (totalling 300m) to the hut. About 30 minutes beyond the creek is a landslide area. If conditions are wet, use caution and care when traversing these unstable slopes. At first the climb is gradual, and within 2km you reach the flood bridge over **Palaver Creek**. After **Open Creek** the track steepens until you cross Shiels Creek and reach the day's high point (500m). You're now 1km from the hot springs, with most of the tramp a descent through ribbonwood forest.

Welcome Flat thermal springs were first noted by Charles Douglas in 1896. The water emerges from the ground at around 60°C and flows through a series of three shallow pools towards Copland River. The hottest pool – knee-deep and the size of a tennis court – is still 55°C, so most bathers prefer the second pool. Sandflies can be thick here in the day, but a midnight soak on a clear evening is a trip highlight; lie back in the warm water and count the falling stars.

The excellent **Welcome Flat Hut** (31 bunks) is a short stroll from the pools and has a potbelly fireplace and coal. A warden is usually stationed here, and when there's no warden the hut has a radio.

Side Trip: Douglas Rock Hut

5 HOURS / 14KM

Despite being on a rougher track than that to Welcome Flat, the route to Douglas Rock Hut makes an ideal day trip from Welcome Flat, especially without the burden of a heavy backpack.

From Welcome Flat Hut, cross the suspension bridge to the south side of Copland River. Head east along the river, and after 30 minutes you break out at the open tussock lands of **Welcome Flat**. This pleasant area along the river is surrounded by peaks and snowfields, including Mt Sefton (3151m), the Footstool (2764m) and Scott Peak (2537m). The flats are marked with rock cairns that lead more than 2km to **Scott Creek** at their eastern end. Scott Creek is not bridged, but under normal conditions is easy to ford. In bad weather it is extremely hazardous.

From Scott Creek the track climbs out of the flats and sidles above the **Copland River Gorge**, crossing two major stream washouts. The well-defined track can be slippery, so be careful if it's wet. The track crosses a suspension bridge over **Tekano Creek**, 1½ hours from Scott Creek, then immediately arrives at **Douglas Rock Hut** (eight beds) in the first patch of forest below the bushline, at 700m.

Built in 1931–32, this hut originally had two rooms (one for men, one for women). In 1979 it was modified to one room, and platforms replaced the bunks. The only shelter between Copland Pass and Welcome Flat, the hut has a radio link to the DOC offices in Fox Glacier and Haast, providing weather reports at the times notified inside the hut.

Mt Sefton towers over Douglas Rock Hut, and beyond the hut a marked route continues towards Copland Pass. Marked by cairns and poles, the route ascends through subalpine vegetation with improving views of the high mountain peaks. The route ends at the alpine basin. Do not attempt to go further unless you have a high level of mountaineering experience and appropriate equipment.

Return to Welcome Flat Hut, reversing the day's route.

Day 2: Welcome Flat Hut to Karangarua River Bridge

7 HOURS / 18KM

Retrace your Day 1 steps to the Karangarua River bridge on SH6.

TOWNS & FACILITIES

Westport

☑ 03 / POP 4035

The 'capital' of the northern West Coast is Westport. The town's fortunes have waxed and waned on coal mining, but in the current climate it sits quietly stoked up on various industries, including dairy and, increasingly, tourism. It boasts respectable hospitality and visitor services, and makes a good base for the Heaphy Track and Old Ghost Road.

🛏 Sleeping & Eating

★ Bazil's Hostel   HOSTEL $

(☑ 03-789 6410; www.bazils.com; 54 Russell St, Westport; dm $32, d with/without bathroom $110/72; 🐕) Mural-painted Bazil's has homey, well-maintained dorm and private rooms in a sociable setting. It's managed by worldly types who offer surfing lessons (three hours $80; board and suit hire per day $45), rainforest stand-up paddle-boarding (SUP) trips, and social activities aplenty. So do you want the yoga class ($8), something from the pizza oven ($10), or a little of both?

Westport Kiwi Holiday Park   HOLIDAY PARK $

(☑ 03-789 7043; www.westportholidaypark.co.nz; 37 Domett St, Westport; sites from $36, d $70-150; @🐕) Though it's more gravel than grass, this chipper holiday park has family-friendly perks including a playground, little aviary and a minigolf course (adult/child $5/3) out the front. From campsites to affordable A-frame units and communal facilities, everything's in top working order. Fifteen minutes' walk to town.

★ Rough & Tumble Lodge   LODGE $$$

(☑ 03-782 1337; www.roughandtumble.co.nz; Mokihinui Rd, Seddonville; d incl continental breakfast $210, extra person $50; 🐕) 🖉 With invigorating views of river and bush, this luxe tramping lodge sits at the West Coast end of the Old Ghost Road, at a bend in the Mokihinui River. Its five split-level quad rooms have silver birch banisters, posh bathrooms and verdant views. Bonus: profits are poured back into the maintenance of the walking track.

In the attached cafe and bar, a French chef whipping up two-course dinners ($40) and superb pizzas ($20) provides an extra incentive to stick around, as does the selection of locally sourced beers.

PR's Cafe   CAFE $

(☑ 03-789 7779; 124 Palmerston St, Westport; mains $10-20; ⊗7am-4.30pm Mon-Fri, to 3pm Sat & Sun; 🐕) Westport's sharpest cafe has a cabinet full of sandwiches and pastries, and a counter groaning under the weight of cakes (Dutch apple, banoffee pie) and cookies. An all-day menu delivers carefully composed meals such as salmon omelette oozing with dill aioli, spanakopita, and fish and chips.

Tommyknockers   BISTRO $

(☑ 03-782 8664; www.minersonsea.co.nz; 117 Torea St (SH6), Granity; snacks from $4, mains $18-39; ⊗11am-8pm) With the only bottleshop in town, Tommyknockers was always going to be popular. But this bar and bistro pushes the boat out with great grab-and-go snacks (from homemade savoury pies to Dutch apple cake) alongside a menu of swankier-than-average meals: pork belly with polenta, beef en croute and a host of good-looking salads. It closes earlier in winter.

🛍 Supplies & Equipment

New World SUPERMARKET $
(☑03-789 7669; 244 Palmerston St, Westport; ⏰8am-8.30pm) The best supermarket for miles is located on the main road. Try the bakery's apple turnovers.

ℹ Information

Westport i-SITE (☑03-789 6658; www.buller. co.nz; 123 Palmerston St, Westport; ⏰9am-5pm Mon-Fri, 10am-4pm Sat & Sun; 🛜) Information on local tracks, walkways, tours, accommodation and transport. Self-help terminal for DOC information and hut and track bookings.

ℹ Getting There & Away

Sounds Air (☑0800 505 005, 03-520 3080; www.soundsair.com) has two to three flights daily to/from Wellington.

InterCity (☑03-365 1113; www.intercity. co.nz) buses reach Nelson (from $36, 3½ hours) and Greymouth (from $21, 2¼ hours). Change in Greymouth for Franz Josef or Fox Glacier (from $39, six hours). Similar prices on the same routes are available through **Naked Bus** (☑09-979 1616; https://nakedbus.com). Buses leave from the **i-SITE**.

East West Coaches (☑03-789 6251; www. eastwestcoaches.co.nz) Operates a service through to Christchurch, via Reefton and the Lewis Pass, every day except Saturday, departing from the Caltex petrol station.

Karamea Express (p187) links Westport and Karamea ($35, two hours, Monday to Friday May to September, plus Saturdays from October to April). It also services Kohaihai twice daily during peak summer, and other times on demand.

Trek Express (☑027 222 1872, 0800 128 735; www.trekexpress.co.nz) passes through Westport on its frequent high-season tramper transport link between Nelson and the Wangapeka/Heaphy Tracks.

Greymouth

☑03 / POP 13,371 (DISTRICT)

Greymouth is the the largest town on the West Coast. For locals it's a refuelling and shopping pit stop; for travellers it's a noteworthy portal to tramping trails. Arriving on a dreary day, it's no mystery why Greymouth, crouched at the mouth of the imaginatively named Grey River, is sometimes the butt of jokes. But with gold-mining history, a scattering of jade shops, and worthy walks in its surrounds, it pays to look beyond the grey.

🛏 Sleeping & Eating

⭐ **Global Village** HOSTEL $
(☑03-768 7272; www.globalvillagebackpackers. co.nz; 42 Cowper St; dm/d $32/80; @🛜) There's collages of African and Asian art on its walls, and a passionate traveller vibe at its core. Global Village also has free kayaks – the Lake Karoro wetlands reserve is a short walk away – and mountain bikes for guests, and relaxation comes easily with a spa, sauna, barbecue and fire pit.

Greymouth Seaside
Top 10 Holiday Park HOLIDAY PARK, MOTEL $
(☑0800 867 104, 03-768 6618; www.top10grey mouth.co.nz; 2 Chesterfield St; sites $40-46, cabins $60-125, motel r $110-374; 🛜) Well positioned for walks on the adjacent beach and 2.5km south of the town centre, this large park has various tent and campervan sites, simple cabins and deluxe sea-view motels. A playground and TV room keep kids entertained on rainy days, and there's a full quota of amenities like laundry, plus unexpected comforts like underfloor heating in the communal showers.

Paroa Hotel HOTEL $$
(☑0800 762 6860, 03-762 6860; www.paroa.co.nz; 508 Main South Rd, Paroa; units $149-300; 🛜) A family affair since 1954, from kitchen to reception the venerable Paroa has benefitted from a makeover. Sizeable units with great beds are decorated in fetching monochrome and share a garden. The hotel's warm service continues inside the noteworthy bar and restaurant. It's opposite the Shantytown turn-off.

The bar-restaurant (mains $18 to $35) has a pleasing menu of mostly meaty mains (try the 'oinkadoodledoo').

Recreation Hotel BISTRO $$
(☑03-768 5154; www.rechotel.co.nz; 68 High St; mains $17-26; ⏰11am-late) A strong local following fronts up to 'the Rec' for its smart public bar serving good pub grub, such as a daily roast, burgers and local fish and chips amid pool tables and the TAB.

Out the back, Buccleugh's dining room (evenings only) offers fancier fare such as venison backstrap, scallops accented with bacon and a dessert risotto (mains $18 to $34).

🛍 Supplies & Equipment

Greymouth Warehouse SPORTS & OUTDOORS
(☑03-768 9051; www.thewarehouse.co.nz; Mawhera Quay; ⏰7am-9pm) Camping equipment, fishing gear and sportswear are among the many products on sale in Greymouth's superstore.

ℹ Information

Greymouth i-SITE (☑ 03-768 7080, 0800 767 080; www.westcoasttravel.co.nz; 164 Mackay St, Greymouth Train Station; ☉ 9am-5pm Mon-Fri, 10am-4pm Sat & Sun; ☎) The helpful crew at the train station can assist with all manner of advice and bookings, including those for DOC huts and walks.

ℹ Getting There & Away

All buses stop outside the train station. **Inter-City** has daily buses north to Westport (from $21, 2¼ hours) and Nelson (from $40, six hours), and south to Franz Josef and Fox Glaciers (around $30, 3½ hours). **Naked Bus** runs the same route. Both companies offer connections to destinations further afield.

Atomic Travel (p203) runs daily between Greymouth and Christchurch, as does **West Coast Shuttle** (☑ 027 492 7000, 03-768 0028; www.westcoastshuttle.co.nz) – the fare is around $50.

Combined with the **i-SITE** in the train station, the **West Coast Travel Centre** (☑ 03-768 7080; www.westcoasttravel.co.nz; 164 Mackay St, Greymouth Train Station; ☉ 9am-5pm Mon-Fri, 10am-4pm Sat & Sun; ☎) books local and national transport, and offers luggage storage.

View-laden train connection to Christchurch **TranzAlpine** (☑ 04-495 0775, 0800 872 467; www.greatjourneysofnz.co.nz; one way adult/child from $119/83) leaves Greymouth daily at 2.05pm.

Punakaiki

☑ 03 / POP 70

Located midway between Westport and Greymouth is Punakaiki, a small settlement beside the rugged 38,000-hectare Paparoa National Park. Most visitors come for a quick squiz at the Pancake Rocks, layers of limestone that resemble stacked crepes. Get town information at the Paparoa National Park Visitor Centre (p226).

🛏 Sleeping & Eating

★**Punakaiki Beach Hostel**   HOSTEL $
(☑ 03-731 1852; www.punakaikibeachhostel.co.nz; 4 Webb St; sites per person $22, dm/d $32/89; ☎) The ambience is laid-back but Punakaiki Beach is efficiently run. This spick-and-span 24-bed hostel has all the amenities a traveller could need, from laundry and a shared kitchen to staff who smile because they mean it. Comfy dorm rooms aside, the en suite bus ($140) is the most novel stay, but cutesy Sunset Cottage ($150) is also worth a splurge.

There's a sea-view verandah to kick back in, and it's a about 1km north of Pancake Rocks.

Punakaiki Beach Camp   HOLIDAY PARK $
(☑ 03-731 1894; www.punakaikibeachcamp.co.nz; 5 Owen St; powered/unpowered sites per person $20/17, d $68-98; ☎) A classic Kiwi coastal camping ground five to 10 minutes' walk from Pancake Rocks, this salty, beachside park has good grass studded with clean, old-style cabins and amenities. Linen costs $5 extra per person.

There's a small grocery shop on-site (the only one in Punakaiki) that follows reception hours, roughly 8am to 8pm.

Hydrangea Cottages   COTTAGE $$$
(☑ 03-731 1839; www.pancake-rocks.co.nz; SH6; cottages $245-485; ☎) On a hillside overlooking the Tasman, these six stand-alone and mostly self-contained cottages are built from salvaged timber and stone. Each is distinct, like 'Miro' with splashes of colour and bright tiles, and two-storey 'Nikau' with a private, sea-facing deck. Occasional quirks like outdoor bathtubs add to the charm. It's 800m south of Pancake Rocks and the visitor centre.

At the top of the price range is an extremely chic self-contained cottage that sleeps up to 12 people (two-night minimum stay). Across the highway from the other cottages, it has a secluded feel and looks right onto the beach.

The owners also run **Punakaiki Horse Treks** (☑ 03-731 1839, 021 264 2600; www.pancake-rocks.co.nz; SH6, Punakaiki; 2½hr ride $180; ☉ mid-Oct–early May).

Pancake Rocks Cafe   CAFE $$
(☑ 03-731 1122; www.pancakerockscafe.com; 4300 Coast Rd (SH6), Punakaiki; mains $10-26; ☉ 8am-5pm, to 10pm Dec-Feb; ✍) Almost inevitably, pancakes are the pride of the cafe opposite the Pancake Rocks trail, heaped with bacon, berries, cream and other tasty toppings. Even better are the pizzas, from whitebait to four cheese (with a few good veggie options too). Time a visit for summer open-mic nights from 6pm on Fridays.

There are few food choices in Punakaiki, but fortunately Pancake Rocks Cafe delivers all-hours sustenance. Before 11am they serve good breakfasts ($10 to $24) ranging from bagels to German sausage fry-ups, and the conservatory area – all wooden benches and fairy lights – is a pleasant spot for a drink around sundown.

Punakaiki Tavern   PUB FOOD $$
(☑ 03-731 1188; SH6; breakfasts $6-26, mains $20-40; ☉ 8am-late; ☎) Expect good banter and big meals at this busy pub, which serves

food throughout the day. Corn fritter stacks, rib-eye steaks and pub mainstays like fish and chips feature on the menu, while a pool table and mixed cast of locals and tourists keep the ambience lively.

Heading north out of Punakaiki, the tavern's on the left before you cross the Porari River. Buy wi-fi vouchers from the bar.

⊕ Getting There & Away

InterCity and **Naked Bus** services travel daily north to Westport (from $16, one hour), and south to Greymouth (from $11, 45 minutes) and Fox Glacier (from $37, 5½ hours). Buses stop long enough for passengers to admire the Pancake Rocks.

Fox Glacier
☑ 03 / POP 400

Fox Glacier is 23km from Franz Josef Glacier, around halfway between Franz and the trailhead for the Welcome Flat track. It is the quieter of the two glacier towns, and a gateway to the extremely photogenic **Lake Matheson** (www.doc.govt.nz), with its gorgeous walkway and delightful cafe.

For non-DOC related information, including transport bookings, visit the folks at **Fox Glacier Guiding** (☑ 03-751 0825, 0800 111 600; www.foxguides.co.nz; 44 Main Rd).

🛌 Sleeping & Eating

★**Fox Glacier**

Top 10 Holiday Park   HOLIDAY PARK **$**
(☑ 0800 154 366, 03-751 0821; www.fghp.co.nz; Kerr Rd; sites $45-52, cabins from $75, units $144-280; 🛜) Inspiring mountain views and ample amenities lift this reliable chain holiday park above its local competition. Grassy tent and hard campervan sites include access to a quality communal kitchen and dining room, and trim cabins (no private bathroom) and upmarket self-contained units offer extra comfort. A spa pool, playground with trampoline and double-seater fun bikes pile on the family-fun factor.

Ivory Towers   HOSTEL **$**
(☑ 03-751 0838; http://ivorytowers.co.nz; 33-35 Sullivan Rd; dm $31-31, s/d without bathroom from $65/72, d/q with bathroom from $83/166; @🛜) Warren-like Ivory Towers has mixed and women-only dorms, along with plain, private rooms with flatscreen TVs (and some with balconies). There are plenty of nooks and crannies to hide in, a TV room,

three communal kitchens and a wee infra-red sauna (free).

Reflection Lodge   B&B **$$$**
(☑ 03-751 0707; www.reflectionlodge.co.nz; 141 Cook Flat Rd; d incl breakfast $230; 🛜) The gregarious hosts of this ski-lodge-style B&B go the extra mile to make your stay a memorable one. Blooming gardens complete with alpine views and a Monet-like pond seal the deal.

★**Lake Matheson Cafe**   MODERN NZ **$$**
(☑ 03-751 0878; www.lakematheson.com; Lake Matheson Rd; breakfast & lunch $10-21, dinner $29-35; ☺8am-late Nov-Mar, to 3pm Apr-Oct) Next to Lake Matheson, this cafe does everything right: sharp architecture that maximises inspiring mountain views, strong coffee, craft beers and upmarket fare. Bratwurst breakfasts are a good prelude to rambling the lake, the pizzas are heaped with seasonal ingredients, and seafood risotto is topped with salmon sourced down the road in Paringa.

Part of the complex is the **ReflectioNZ Gallery** next door, stocking quality, primarily NZ-made art, jewellery and souvenirs.

Last Kitchen   CAFE **$$**
(☑ 03-751 0058; cnr Sullivan Rd & SH6; mains $25-35; ☺4-9.30pm) Making the most of its sunny corner location with outside tables, the Last Kitchen serves locally sourced produce sprinkled with European flavour: creamy chicken Alfredo, heavily topped burgers and ginger lamb bulk out the mainly carnivorous menu.

🛒 Supplies & Equipment

Fox Glacier General Store   SUPERMARKET **$**
(☑ 03-751 0829; SH6; ☺8am-7.30pm) Fox's village store provides all the basics, including some fresh produce and ample frozen goods.

⊕ Getting There & Away

Direct **InterCity** (p234) and **Naked Bus** (p234) services along SH6 trundle through Fox Glacier once a day, heading south to Haast (from $20, 2½ hours) and north to Greymouth ($61, 4½ hours), stopping at Franz Josef ($10, 40 minutes) on the way. Book ahead for fares as low as $1. A direct daily bus also reaches Queenstown (from $59, 7¾ hours). For Nelson or Christchurch, transfer in Greymouth.

Most buses stop outside the Fox Glacier Guiding building.

Franz Josef Glacier

📞 03 / POP 441

Franz Josef Glacier is more action-packed than Fox Glacier, but heavy tourist traffic often swamps both towns from December to February.

🍴 Sleeping & Eating

Rainforest Retreat   HOSTEL, HOLIDAY PARK $$
(📞 0800 873 346, 03-752 0220; www.rainforest retreat.co.nz; 46 Cron St; sites $39-48, dm $30-39, d $69-220; 📶) Options abound in these forested grounds: en suite doubles, self-contained units and dorm rooms that sleep between four and six (four-bed 'flashpacker' rooms are worth the higher rate). Campervan sites are nestled in native bush, the backpacker lodge brims with tour-bus custom, and you may have to fight for a spot in the gigantic hot tub, touted as NZ's largest.

'Retreat' apartments ($300 to $650) suit luxury-leaning travellers, with underfloor heating, rain showers and large private decks to relax on.

Stop by the lively on-site **Monsoon** (📞 03-752 0220; www.monsoonbar.co.nz; 46 Cron St; mains $15-33; ⏲ 11am-11pm) for drinks in the sunshine or within the lively, chalet-style bar.

★ **Te Waonui Forest Retreat**   HOTEL $$$
(📞 0800 696 963, 03-752 0555; www.tewaonui. co.nz; 3 Wallace St; d incl breakfast & dinner from $749; ⏲ Sep-Apr; @ 📶) 🌿 Luxurious Te Waonui is filled with design flourishes that evoke the land: twinkly lights suggest glowworms, coal-black walls nod to the mining past, and local stone provides an earthy backdrop. Beyond the gorgeous, greenery-facing rooms, the prime draws are the five-course degustation dinner (included in the price) and the nightly Māori cultural show.

Top-notch green credentials include thoughtful use of natural light and building materials that are either recycled or sustainably sourced. Reuse your towels and the owners donate $5 to a kiwi conservation charity.

Glenfern Villas   APARTMENT $$$
(📞 0800 453 633, 03-752 0054; www.glenfern. co.nz; SH6; d $265-299; 📶) Forming something of a tiny, elite village 3km north of town, Glenfern's one- and two-bedroom villas are equipped with every comfort from quality beds to plump couches, gleaming kitchenettes and private decks where you can listen to birdsong. Book well ahead.

★ **Snake Bite Brewery**   ASIAN, FUSION $$
(📞 03-752 0234; www.snakebite.co.nz; 28 Main Rd; mains $18-25; ⏲ 7.30am-10.30pm) Snake Bite's motley Asian meals awaken taste buds after their long slumber through the West Coast's lamb-and-whitebait menus. Choices include nasi goreng (fried rice), Thai- and Malaysian-style curries, and salads of calamari and carrot that zing with fresh lime. Try the mussel fritters with wasabi mayo. Between courses, glug craft beers on tap or 'snakebite' (a mix of cider and beer). Happy hour is between 3pm and 5pm.

Alice May   MODERN NZ $$
(📞 03-752 0740; www.facebook.com/alicemay-franzjosef; cnr Cowan & Cron Sts; mains $22-33; ⏲ 4pm-late) Piling on the charm with its faux-Tudor decor, Alice May is the classiest restaurant in town. Sure, the menu includes meaty NZ favourites, but they usually come with a gourmet twist, like pork roasted in wine and star anise, brie-topped chicken or rosemary and pumpkin risotto. Try to snag an outdoor or window table for sigh-worthy mountain views. Happy hour (from 4.30 to 6.30pm) trims the drinks bill.

🛒 Supplies & Equipment

Four Square   SUPERMARKET $
(📞 03-752 0177; 24 Main Rd; ⏲ 7.45am-8.30pm) It's not as though you have options, so this mid-sized supermarket does the trick for self-catering and picnicking needs.

ℹ Information

Franz Josef i-SITE (📞 0800 354 748; www. glaciercountry.co.nz; 63 Cron St; ⏲ 8.30am-6pm) Helpful local centre offering advice and booking service for activities, accommodation and transport in the local area and beyond.

ℹ Getting There & Away

Direct InterCity (p234) and Naked Bus (p234) services along SH6 pass through once daily, northwards to Hokitika ($29, 2½ hours) and Greymouth (around $29, four hours) and south to Haast (from $23, 3¼ hours), stopping at Fox Glacier ($10, 40 minutes) on the way. Book ahead for fares as low as $1. A direct daily bus also reaches Queenstown (from $62, 8½ hours). For Nelson or Christchurch, change services in Greymouth.

The bus stop is opposite the Four Square supermarket.

After hours, there's a 24 hour petrol pump at **Glacier Motors** (📞 03-752 0725; Main Rd; ⏲ 8am-7.30pm).

WEST COAST FRANZ JOSEF GLACIER

Mt Aspiring National Park & Around Queenstown

Best Huts

➡ Routeburn Falls Hut (p245)

➡ Greenstone Hut (p249)

➡ Aspiring Hut (p255)

➡ Siberia Hut (p260)

Best Views

➡ Harris Saddle (p245)

➡ Key Summit (p246)

➡ Cascade Saddle (p256)

➡ Roys Peak (p263)

➡ Ben Lomond (p262)

➡ Rob Roy upper lookout (p257)

Why Go?

Few places ignite a sense of adventure quite like Queenstown, Wanaka and Mt Aspiring National Park – even the sedentary get drawn into hitherto unconsidered activities here. But not everything here involves falling from a plane or a bridge. Head to Glenorchy, at the quiet end of Lake Wakatipu, and some of New Zealand's finest mountain country awaits, including the Routeburn Track, the tramp many believe to be the greatest Great Walk of all. Just as enticing is the Matukituki Valley further north, providing a jaw-dropping gateway to hanging glaciers and airy passes.

For all that, you barely need leave Queenstown or Wanaka to get an eyeful of mountains as you tramp. Set out from near the centre of Queenstown and you can rise to lofty Ben Lomond, while Roys Peak, with its photo-perfect perch over Lake Wanaka, is Wanaka's tramp of the day every day.

When to Go

The weather varies greatly across this region, with the mountains dictating the terms. Glenorchy is relatively dry, notching up around 1140mm of rain each year, with the lower Rees, Matukituki and Wilkin valleys not much wetter at around 1500mm. Head into the Route Burn and Dart valleys, and the western half of the Greenstone and Caples, and you can multiply that by around five. Snow can fall above 1000m in almost any month, and late winter and spring are high-risk times for avalanches.

The weather is generally settled from late December to March, with February often considered the best for tramping. However, when an alpine region you must be prepared for sudden changes in weather and unexpected storms at any time of year.

Background Reading

Although much of the Queenstown area was originally settled in the quest for gold, this enterprise was quickly usurped by farming, with high-country stations scattered throughout the region. Many of today's tramping tracks, such as the Greenstone and Caples, pass through them and follow old stock-droving routes along the valleys. *High Country Legacy* by Alex Hedley recalls the life and times of four generations of farmers at Mt Aspiring Station, while Iris Scott's *High Country Woman* is the autobiographical tale of a widow (with three children) running the 1800-sq-km Rees Valley Station near Glenorchy. A read of these will certainly put the odd blister and sandfly bite into perspective.

DON'T MISS

Name your poison...in Queenstown, the so-called 'adventure capital of the world', you can pretty much set a flow meter on adrenaline. It was here that bungy jumping was famously pioneered by **AJ Hackett Bungy** (0800 286 4958, 03-450 1300; www.bungy.co.nz; The Station, cnr Camp & Shotover Sts), and today there are three jump sites around the town. When you're done bouncing around on the end of a rubber band, there's always skydiving, jetboating, river surfing (think rafting, but on a glorified boogie board), a high-powered 'shark' that leaps about the lake, heliskiing, paragliding and a more leisurely luge. A short stroll down Shotover St will lay it all out for you like an adventure buffet. Or you can simply slow down and ponder life and more mountains from the shores of Lake Wakatipu, where the view from Queenstown takes in the Remarkables, Cecil Peak and Walter Peak in one of the most beautiful mountain scenes in the country.

Evenings in Queenstown are just as promising, with its restaurants turning out an enticing range of international cuisines, often driven by local produce. Complementing them is a selection of speciality bars focusing on the likes of craft beer, rum and fine wine.

DOC Visitor Centres

→ DOC Visitor Centre (Queenstown) (p243)
→ Tititea/Mt Aspiring National Park Visitor Centre (p254)
→ Fiordland National Park Visitor Centre (p274)

GATEWAY TOWNS

→ Queenstown (p266)
→ Wanaka (p267)
→ Glenorchy (p269)
→ Te Anau (p297)

Fast Facts

→ Dominating the skyline is Tititea/Mt Aspiring (3033m), the highest peak in the country outside of the Aoraki/Mt Cook area.

→ Queenstown and Wanaka lie on NZ's third- and fourth-largest lakes, respectively. Lake Wakatipu is 283 sq km, and Lake Wanaka is 192 sq km.

→ The 32km Routeburn Track, NZ's second-most-popular Great Walk, is normally walked in three days. The 2017 winner of the Routeburn Classic race ran it in just over 2½ hours.

Top Tip

Queenstown is a honeypot for travellers, but Glenorchy and Wanaka make equally good (and quieter) bases for most of the tramps in the area.

Resources

→ www.queenstownnz.co.nz
→ www.lakewanaka.co.nz
→ www.glenorchyinfocentre.co.nz
→ www.makarora.co.nz

Mt Aspiring National Park & Around Queenstown

GILLESPIE PASS CIRCUIT
Remote and rugged, with a jetboat finish. (p257)

CASCADE SADDLE
Heady pass amid a mountain spectacular. (p253)

ROB ROY TRACK
Beech forest parts to reveal stunning glacier. (p256)

DIAMOND LAKE & ROCKY MOUNTAIN
Low peak hole-punched with a gorgeous lake. (p264)

ROYS PEAK
Perhaps the most photographed mountain perch in NZ. (p262)

REES-DART TRACK
Glaciated valleys split by a high saddle. (p250)

ROUTEBURN TRACK
Mountain magnificence on this alpine crossing. (p242)

GREENSTONE CAPLES TRACK
Trout-rich rivers and an alpine crossing. (p246)

BEN LOMOND
Queenstown one moment, mountaintop the next. (p260)

Tasman Sea

Rangitata

Temuka

Waimate

Oamaru

Maheno
Waianakarua
Moeraki

Palmerston

SOUTH PACIFIC OCEAN

Makarora

Lake Hawea

Lake Hawea

Hawea

Tarras

Dunback

Karitane

Pukerangi
Waitati
Mosgiel
Dunedin
Outram
Waihola
Taieri Mouth

Tititea/Mt Aspiring (3033m)

Lake Wanaka

Wanaka

Mt Cardrona (1936m)

Mt Pisa (1964m)

Cromwell

Omakau
Bannockburn

Alexandra

Clyde

Kyeburn

Mt Aspiring National Park

Treble Cone (2058m)

Centaur Peaks (2525m)

Coronet Peak (1649m)

Cardrona (1748m)

Lawrence

Waitahuna
Clarksville

Balclutha

Mt Tutoko (2723m)

Ben Lomond

Queenstown

Double Cone (2319m)

Lake Wakatipu

Kingston

Raes Junction

Clutha River

Clinton

West Arm

Walter Peak (1815m)
Cecil Peak (1978m)

Jane Peak (2035m)

Mavora Lakes

Five Rivers

Tapanui

Gore

Mataura

The Key

Manapouri

Lumsden

Winton

Wreys Bush

Otautau

Ohai

Clifden

N

0 ____ 40 km
0 ____ 20 miles

MT ASPIRING NATIONAL PARK

Mt Aspiring National Park is a fitting end to the Southern Alps. It has wide valleys with secluded flats, more than 100 glaciers, and stark mountain ranges topped by 3033m Tititea/Mt Aspiring, NZ's tallest mountain outside Aoraki/Mt Cook National Park.

The park stretches from the Haast River in the north to the Humboldt Mountains in the south, where it borders Fiordland National Park. The park is part of the Te-Wahipounamu–South West New Zealand World Heritage Area, which includes Aoraki/Mt Cook, Westland Tai Poutini and Fiordland National Parks.

At 3562 sq km, Aspiring is the country's third-largest national park, with the majority of tramping activity taking place around Glenorchy, where trailheads for the famous Routeburn, Rees-Dart and Greenstone Caples tracks can be found. The tramping territory to the north, through the Matukituki and Wilkin-Young valleys, provides more mountain solitude.

History

Although there are traces of early settlement in this area, it's thought that Māori primarily passed through on their way between Central Otago and South Westland where they sourced *pounamu* (greenstone), highly valued for its use in tools, weapons and *taonga* (treasure). Māori expeditions in search of *pounamu* are said to have been conducted as late as 1850 – about the same time the first Europeans began exploring the region.

In 1861 David McKellar and George Gunn, part explorers and part pastoralists, shed some light on the Greenstone Valley when they struggled up the river and climbed one of the peaks near Lake Howden. What they saw was the entire Hollyford Valley, which they mistakenly identified as George Sound in central Fiordland. The great Otago gold rush began later that year, and by 1862 miners were digging around the lower regions of the Dart and Rees Rivers, as well as in the Route Burn Valley.

A prospector called Patrick Caples made a solo journey up the Route Burn from Lake Wakatipu in 1863 and discovered Harris Saddle. He then descended into the Hollyford Valley and Martins Bay. Caples returned through the valley that now bears his name, ending a three-month odyssey in which he became the first European to reach the Tasman Sea from Wakatipu.

It was not until late in the 19th century that the first European crossed the Barrier Range from Cattle Flat on the Dart River to a tributary of the Arawata River. William O'Leary, an Irish prospector better known as Arawata Bill, roamed the mountains and valleys of this area and much of the Hollyford Valley for 50 years, searching out various metals and enjoying the solitude of these open, desolate places.

Mountaineering and a thriving local tourist trade began developing in the 1890s, and by the early 1900s it was booming, even by today's standards. Hotels sprang up in Glenorchy, along with guiding companies that advertised horse-and-buggy trips up the Rees Valley. Sir Thomas Mackenzie, Minister of Tourism, pushed for the construction of the Routeburn Track and hired Harry Birley of Glenorchy to establish a route. In 1912 Birley 'discovered' Lake Mackenzie and the next year began cutting a track.

The famous track had reached Lake Howden by the outbreak of WWI, but the final portion wasn't completed until the road from Te Anau to Milford Sound was built by relief workers during the Depression – until then a tramp on the Routeburn meant returning on the Greenstone Track.

The first move to make Mt Aspiring a national park came in 1935, but for all its beauty and popularity with trampers and tourists, the park wasn't officially gazetted until 1964. Its legendary beauty landed the park and surrounds starring roles in *The Lord of the Rings* trilogy. The Mavora Lakes area, in particular, stole the limelight, being the scene of Silverlode and Anduin Rivers, Nen Hithoel, the edge of Fangorn Forest and south of Rivendell.

Environment

The landscape of Mt Aspiring National Park is largely glacial in origin. During the ice ages, massive glaciers carved into the metamorphic and sedimentary rock. As they retreated they left a sculpted landscape of U-shaped valleys, small hanging valleys and rounded cirques and ridges. The park still contains more than 100 glaciers, ranging from the large Bonar Glacier on the flank of Tititea/Mt Aspiring to the smaller ones that hang from the sides of the Matukituki Valley.

Beech forest dominates below the bushline, with each beech species favouring different growing conditions. The red beech thriving in the sunny valleys makes for semi-open forests and easy tramping, unlike the Fiordland forests with their dense, close understorey. Look out for ribbonwoods, one of NZ's few deciduous trees. These are the first to colonise open areas caused by slips and avalanches. At higher altitudes you will find silver or mountain beech, while west of the Divide there's rainforest of rimu, matai, miro and kahikatea.

In between the valleys are blooming mountain meadows that support one of the greatest ranges of alpine plants in the world. In alpine areas there are beautiful clusters of snow berry and coprosma in subalpine turf. In the Route Burn Valley, look for mountain daisies, snow grasses and veronica. Another beautiful plant of this region is the NZ edelweiss.

The forests are alive with native birds, including fantail, rifleman, bellbird, pigeon and cute South Island robin and tomtits. Along the rivers you may see whio (blue ducks) and paradise shelducks, and towards evening, moreporks and native bats, which are NZ's only native land mammal. In alpine areas look out for the threatened rock wren and unmistakable kea.

Introduced animals include whitetail and red deer in lower areas and chamois about the mountaintops. Unfortunately, possums, rats and stoats are widespread. Introduced brown and rainbow trout are found in the lower Route Burn and brown trout are present in Lake Howden.

Routeburn Track

Duration 3 days

Distance 32km (19.9 miles)

Difficulty Moderate

Start Routeburn Shelter

End The Divide

Gateways Queenstown (p266), Glenorchy (p269), Te Anau (p297)

Transport Shuttle bus

Summary This most famous of alpine crossings is a best-of mountain compilation, and includes a breathtaking day above the bushline as you cross Harris Saddle.

The Routeburn is one of New Zealand's best-known tracks, taking trampers over the Southern Alps' Main Divide as it links Mt Aspiring and Fiordland National Parks. Much of it is through thick rainforest, where red, mountain and silver beech form the canopy, and ferns, mosses and fungi cover everything below like wall-to-wall shagpile carpet. It's the alpine sections, however, that appeal most to trampers. Views from Harris Saddle (1255m) and the top of nearby Conical Hill take in waves breaking far below in Martins Bay, while from Key Summit there are expansive views of the Hollyford, Eglinton and Greenstone Valleys.

The tranquillity of the forest and meadows and the dramatic views of entire valleys and mountain ranges provide ample reward for the steep climbs and frequent encounters with other trampers. Indeed, the track's overwhelming popularity resulted in the introduction of one of the first booking systems in New Zealand, in 1995. Independent walkers need to reserve their spot on the track before setting out – do so through **Great Walks Bookings** (☑0800 694 732; www.greatwalks.co.nz), or in person at DOC visitors centres nationwide. You must pick up your tickets at the Queenstown or Te Anau DOC visitors centres before heading out on the track.

In summer be prepared for huts that are full, a constant flow of foot traffic and a small gathering of people admiring the views at Harris Saddle. The large number of people is more than offset by the mountain scenery, which is truly exceptional.

The considerable amount of climbing is tempered by the well-benched and graded track. A strong tramper could walk the track in less than three days, but considering the beauty of everything around you, why would you want to?

The track can be hiked in either direction, but most trampers begin on the Glenorchy side and end at the Divide. The trip can be made into a virtual circuit by turning at Lake Howden and joining either the Greenstone or Caples Tracks.

ℹ Planning

WHEN TO TRAMP

The four huts on the Routeburn Track are well serviced from late October to late April. Outside this period the track is a winter crossing that should only be attempted by experienced trampers.

MAPS & BROCHURES

There are many maps for the Routeburn, but the best is the NZTopo50 *CB09 (Hollyford)*. The track is also covered by NewTopo's 1:40,000 *Routeburn, Greenstone & Caples Tracks* map. DOC's *Routeburn Track* brochure includes a useful directory of transport operators and local businesses.

Routeburn Track

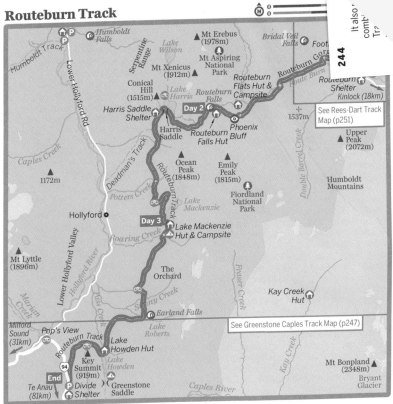

HUTS & CAMPING

All accommodation at huts and campsites must be booked in advance for any tramp from late October to late April. You must then stay on the nights booked, with rangers on duty to check that you've done so.

There are four huts on the Routeburn Track – Routeburn Flats, Routeburn Falls, Lake Mackenzie and Lake Howden – the most popular of which are Routeburn Falls and Lake Mackenzie, both near the bushline. All have gas rings for cooking.

During the Great Walks season, a night in a hut costs NZ locals/foreigners $65/130. Outside of the season, bookings are not required and the huts ($15) have limited facilities.

Camping (NZ local/foreigner $20/40) is permitted at Routeburn Flats and Lake Mackenzie, and at Greenstone Saddle (20 minutes from Lake Howden Hut), where it's free.

Overnight use of Harris Shelter and the track-end shelters is not permitted.

INFORMATION

The **DOC Visitor Centre** (☎ 03-442 7935; www.doc.govt.nz; 50 Stanley St; ◷ 8.30am-4.30pm) in Queenstown is the place to arrange logistics, obtain maps, passes and track updates and hire personal locator beacons. The Fiordland National Park Visitor Centre (p274) is close to the shores of Lake Te Anau and has friendly staff who can help with tramping arrangements, weather forecasts and info on track conditions. If you've booked online, you can pick up your hut or camping tickets at either office.

GUIDED TRAMPS

Ultimate Hikes (☎ 03-450 1940; www.ultimate hikes.co.nz; The Station, Duke St entrance; ◷ Nov-Apr) runs guided tramps on the Routeburn Track. Its three-day tramp features comfortable lodge accommodation, meals and expert interpretation. The trip starts from $1520 in high season (December to March) and $1375 in the low season (November and the first three weeks of April).

...ıns 'Grand Traverse' trips, a six-day ...ıation of the Greenstone and Routeburn ...ks (high/low season from $2049/1810), ...ıth smaller groups and more rustic accommodation, but including a welcome rest day at Lake McKellar to soak up the wilderness atmosphere.

If you want an informed opinion for the great Milford-versus-Routeburn debate, Ultimate Hikes also operates 'The Classic' (high/low season from $3815/3505), tramping both tracks with a rest day between in Te Anau.

ⓘ Getting There & Away

Transport options are plentiful and varied for the Routeburn.

Glenorchy Journeys (📞 03-409 0800; www.glenorchyjourneys.co.nz) runs shuttles to the Routeburn Shelter from Queenstown ($45) and Glenorchy ($25). Buses leave Queenstown at 8.15am, 11.30am and 1.45pm, returning from the Routeburn Shelter at 10am, noon and 4pm. Bookings required.

Info & Track (📞 03-442 9708; www.infotrack.co.nz; 37 Shotover St; ⏰7.30am-9pm) has three daily shuttles to the Routeburn Shelter from Queenstown ($49) and Glenorchy ($22). Its shuttle from the Divide to Queenstown ($81) departs at 10.10am and 3.15pm – you can throw in a Milford Sound cruise for an extra $78.

Buckley Track Transport (📞 03-442 8215; www.buckleytracktransport.nz) has an 8am and 11am shuttle from Queenstown to the Routeburn Shelter ($45). A return shuttle from the Divide ($80) leaves for Queenstown at 2pm.

Tracknet (📞 0800 483 262; www.tracknet.net), based in Te Anau, runs frequent services from the Divide to Te Anau ($41), continuing on to Queenstown ($81).

Trackhopper (📞 021 187 7732; www.trackhopper.co.nz) provides a handy car-relocation service, driving you to the Routeburn Shelter and then shifting your car to the Divide ($270 plus fuel).

ROUTEBURN CLASSIC

If you're short on time but not fitness, you could always consider the annual Routeburn Classic (race details are at http://goodtimesevents.net). Run (literally) in late April, the event sees the Routeburn Track turn into a running track, with athletes racing from the Divide to the Routeburn Shelter. The race has been held every year since 2001, and entries are limited to 350. As you set out walking on your third day along the Routeburn Track, consider this...the race record over the 32km is just a bit over 2½ hours.

EasyHike (📞 027 370 7019; www.easyhike.co.nz) also offers a car-relocation service (from $225). It can also kit you out for the tramp, offering a range of packages up to a 'Premium' service ($935) that includes booking your hut tickets, track transport, backpack, food, rain gear, cooking pots and first-aid kit.

Kiwi Discovery (📞 03-442 7340; www.kiwidiscovery.com; 37 Camp St) services the Routeburn Track and has a range of options starting from $47 out of Queenstown. It also offers a five-night package (from $720) that includes transport to the track, hut booking, pre-tramp briefing, a cruise on Milford Sound at the end and accommodation in Queenstown the night before and after your hike.

The Tramp

Day 1: Routeburn Shelter to Routeburn Falls Hut

4 HOURS / 8.8KM / 560M ASCENT

The track begins with a crossing of **Route Burn** on a swing bridge to its true left (north) bank, before winding for 1km through a forest of red, silver and mountain beech to a footbridge over **Sugar Loaf Stream**. The forest here is magnificent, with red beech trees towering overhead. Once across the stream the track climbs gently for 20 minutes until it reaches a swing bridge over the small gorge carved by Bridal Veil Falls. More impressive rock scenery follows as the track sidles **Routeburn Gorge**, providing ample opportunities to peer into the deep pools at the bottom. The dramatic views end at **Forge Flats**, a gravel bar along a sharp bend in the Route Burn and a popular place to linger in the sun.

Just beyond the flats, the track uses a long swing bridge to cross to the true right (south) side of the Route Burn and heads back into bush, where it skirts the grassy flats. It's an easy 30-minute stroll along a level track through the bush to a signposted junction, where the right fork leads to **Routeburn Flats Hut** (20 bunks), five minutes away. The hut overlooks the river, the wide grassy flats and the mountains to the north. Around 200m on is Routeburn Flats campsite.

The main track (left fork) begins a steady ascent towards Routeburn Falls Hut. The track climbs 270m over 3km (about 1½ hours) before reaching the hut above the bushline. **Emily Creek footbridge** is the halfway point of the climb, and just beyond it the track sidles a steep rock face called **Phoenix Bluff**. The track soon crosses a huge slip, where a massive 1994 flood sent trees crashing towards the flats below. The resultant forest clearing affords magnificent views of the valley and surrounding peaks.

From the slip you resume the steady but rocky climb to **Routeburn Falls Hut** (48 bunks), the scene of many comings and goings. The hut is right at the tree line (1005m) and its long veranda offers views of the flats and the surrounding Humboldt Mountains. Right behind the hut is a private lodge for guided trampers. There's no camping around this hut and wardens are strict about enforcing this rule.

Day 2: Routeburn Falls Hut to Lake Mackenzie

4–6 HOURS / 11.3KM / 215M ASCENT, 355M DESCENT

From the hut it's a short climb to the impressive **Routeburn Falls**, which tumble down a series of rock ledges. Once on top of the falls the track cuts across an alpine basin towards the outlet of Lake Harris. The walk is fairly level at first, crossing a couple of bridges and then beginning a steady climb. You pass beneath a pair of leaning boulders, ascend more sharply and then arrive at **Lake Harris**. Sore legs and aching muscles are quickly forgotten as the stunning view of the lake materialises, especially on a clear day, when the water reflects everything around it. Carved by a glacier, Lake Harris is 800m long and 500m wide. In winter it freezes over and chunks of ice are often seen floating on the lake when the Routeburn Track opens for the season in October.

The track works its way around the lake along bluffs and moraines. You get a second jolt 1½ to two hours from the hut, when entering the grassy meadows of **Harris Saddle**. From this 1255m vantage point, part of the Hollyford Valley comes into view, almost to Martins Bay if the weather is clear. If you are blessed with such weather, drop your packs and climb the steep side track to **Conical Hill** (1½ hours return). The 360-degree view from the 1515m peak includes the Darran Mountains, Richardson Range (in Otago) and the entire Hollyford Valley.

Positioned on the boundary between Mt Aspiring and Fiordland National Parks, the **Harris Saddle emergency shelter** is a popular stopping place. The track begins its descent towards the Hollyford Valley on wooden steps and then turns sharply south. For the most part the track here is narrow but level, clinging to the Hollyford face of the ridge, high above the bushline. A strong

tramper could probably walk [...] dle to Lake Mackenzie in less t[...] but why rush? This is the b[...] trip, a stretch where you nee[...] and soak up the incredible alp[...]

After 30 minutes the tra[...] a signposted junction with [...]**Deadman's Track**, an extremely steep route to the floor of the Hollyford Valley (five hours). The immense views continue, and 2km from the junction with Deadman's Track the route crosses a swing bridge over **Potters Creek**. In another 30 minutes you can see the cabins of Gunn's Camp at the bottom of the Hollyford Valley, directly below you.

Two hours from the saddle the track rounds a spur to the east side of the ridge and **Lake Mackenzie** comes into sight. The lake is a jewel set in a small, green mountain valley, and the hut is clearly visible on the far shore. The track zigzags down to the lake, dropping sharply for the final 300m. It then skirts the bush and arrives at **Lake Mackenzie Hut** (50 bunks), a two-storey building overlooking the southern end of the lake. There are bunks on the 2nd floor of the hut, and additional beds in a separate bunk room. Because of the fragile nature of the lakeshore and the alpine plants, the Lake Mackenzie campsite is a small facility, but it does have toilets, a water supply and a cooking shelter. The lake doesn't have a conventional outlet, so don't wash or bathe in it.

Day 3: Lake Mackenzie to the Divide

4–5 HOURS / 12KM / 380M DESCENT

The track begins in front of the hut, passes the lodge for guided trampers and enters the bush. You begin with a level walk, crossing several swing bridges over branches of **Roaring Creek**, and within 15 minutes begin climbing. The climb regains the height lost in the descent to Lake Mackenzie, and is steady but not steep.

About 40 minutes to one hour from the hut, the track breaks out at a natural clearing, known as the **Orchard**, where a handful of ribbonwoods resemble fruit trees. The view of the Darran Mountains is excellent.

More alpine views are enjoyed for the next hour or so, as the track passes through several avalanche clearings in the forest. Eventually you descend to **Earland Falls**, a thundering cascade that leaps 174m out of the mountains. On a hot day this is an ideal spot for an extended break, as the spray ckly cool you off. If it's raining the ...ill be twice as powerful and you might ...ve to use the flood route, which is sign-posted along the main track.

The track steadily descends and after 3km emerges at Lake Howden. This is a major track junction and during the peak season it resembles Piccadilly Circus, with trampers and guided walkers going every which way: the Routeburn Track is the right fork (west); the Greenstone Track is the left fork (south). If you're planning to spend an extra night on the track, you can either stay at Lake Howden Hut (28 bunks) on the shores of the beautiful lake, or camp near the south end of the lake by following the Greenstone Track for 20 minutes to Greenstone Saddle.

The Routeburn Track swings past the flanks of Key Summit and in 15 minutes comes to a junction. If you're not racing to catch a bus, the 30-minute side trip (left fork) to the top is worth it on a clear day – from the 919m summit you can see the Hollyford, Greenstone and Eglinton Valleys, and there are some crazy stunted beech trees and sphagnum bogs to marvel at.

From the junction the Routeburn Track descends steadily to the bushline, where thick rainforest resumes, before reaching the Divide, the lowest east–west crossing in the Southern Alps. It's 3km (one hour) from Lake Howden to the Divide, where there is a huge shelter with toilets and a car park. Buses and vans are constantly pulling in here on their way to either Milford Sound or Te Anau. Welcome back to civilisation.

Greenstone Caples Track

Duration 4 days

Distance 61km (37.9 miles)

Difficulty Moderate

Start/End Greenstone car park

Gateways Queenstown (p266), Glenorchy (p269)

Transport Shuttle bus

Summary These connecting tracks loop through a pair of valleys between Lake Wakatipu and the Divide, providing a glimpse of World Heritage–listed wilderness between Queenstown and the Routeburn Track.

From the shores of large Lake Wakatipu, this scenic tramp circuits through the Caples and Greenstone Valleys, crossing the subalpine McKellar Saddle, where it almost intersects with the Routeburn Track (p242).

The name of the Greenstone Valley hints at this valley's ancient use as a route for Māori to access the Dart Valley to collect highly prized *pounamu* (greenstone), though no Māori archaeological sites have been found in the Greenstone and Caples Valleys themselves. Europeans would later traverse the valleys in search of grazing sites, with farming commencing in the Caples in 1880. The Greenstone and Pass Burn were utilised as stock routes.

The Greenstone Valley is wide and open with tussock flats and beech forest. The Caples is narrower and more heavily forested, interspersed with grassy clearings. Many trampers consider the Caples, with its parklike appearance, to be the more beautiful of the two.

The two tracks link at McKellar Saddle and again near Greenstone car park, where the road links to Glenorchy and on to Queenstown. Trampers can choose to walk just one track in one direction (joining the end of the Routeburn Track down to the Divide), or traverse both as a there-and-back journey of four days. Routeburn trampers planning to continue on the Greenstone can easily walk from Lake Mackenzie Hut to McKellar Hut, which takes around five to seven hours.

ⓘ Planning

WHEN TO TRAMP

The Greenstone Track is a low-level route and can be tramped year-round. The Caples, however, climbs over the subalpine McKellar Saddle (945m) and therefore should be avoided in winter, except by those with experience and equipment for cold, snow and ice. The ideal time to tramp this route is November to April.

MAPS & BROCHURES

Maps required for the entire loop are NZTopo50 *CB9 (Hollyford)*, *CB10 (Glenorchy)* and *CC9 (North Mavora Lake)*. The track is also covered by NewTopo's 1:40,000 *Routeburn, Greenstone and Caples Tracks*.

DOC's brochure for the tramp is *Greenstone Caples Track*.

HUTS & CAMPING

There are three Serviced huts ($15) between the two tracks: Mid Caples, McKellar and Greenstone. They all have heating, but no stoves, and rangers are likely to be in the vicinity from late October until mid-April. Obtain hut tickets from DOC visitors centres nationwide.

Greenstone Caples Track

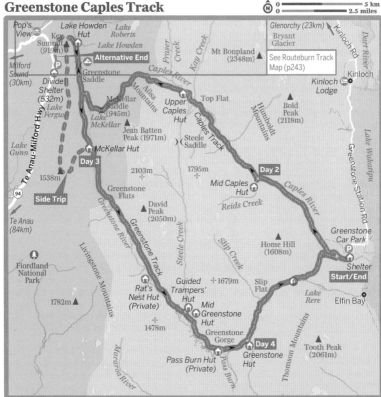

Camping is permitted next to the huts ($5) and along the bush edge through the valleys, though you must be at least 50m from the track. Camping isn't permitted on McKellar Saddle or in open areas along the valleys.

Upper Caples Hut ($25), once managed by DOC, is now owned and managed by the NZ Deerstalkers Association (http://southern lakesnzda.org.nz/huts). Trampers can stay here, but need to book ahead through their website.

INFORMATION

The **DOC Visitor Centre** (p243) in Queenstown is the place to arrange logistics, obtain maps, hut tickets and track updates, and hire personal locator beacons. The **Fiordland National Park Visitor Centre** (p274) is close to the shores of Lake Te Anau and can help with all tramping arrangements, weather forecasts and info on track conditions.

GUIDED TRAMPS

Ultimate Hikes (p243) runs a six-day 'Grand Traverse' tramp (from $1810) along the Greenstone Track and across the Routeburn Track.

ⓘ Getting There & Away

Glenorchy Journeys (p244) offers daily scheduled shuttle services to Greenstone car park from Queenstown ($55, 8.15am, 11.30am and 1.45pm) and Glenorchy ($35, 7am, 9am and 12.30pm). Shuttles return from the Greenstone car park at 10am, noon and 4pm. Bookings are essential.

Info & Track (p244) runs shuttles to Greenstone car park from Queenstown ($54, 8am) and Glenorchy ($37, 9.15am). The return shuttle departs from Greenstone at noon. **Buckley Track Transport** (p244) has an 8am shuttle from Queenstown to Greenstone car park ($55), with return shuttles departing for Queenstown at noon.

If you're tramping the Greenstone or Caples and exiting at the Divide, **Trackhopper** (p244) provides a handy car-relocation service, driving you to the Greenstone car park and then shifting your car to the Divide ($285). There are also shuttle-bus services to the Divide (p244).

🚶 The Tramp

Day 1: Greenstone Car Park to Mid Caples Hut

2½ HOURS / 9KM

The track departs the car park and in a few minutes passes a junction where the left fork leads to a bridge across the **Greenstone River**. Don't cross the bridge – remain on the true left (north) side of the Greenstone River, pass the confluence with the Caples River and, 30 minutes from the car park, you'll arrive at a signposted junction. Here the Greenstone Track heads southwest, quickly crossing a swing bridge over the Caples.

The **Caples Track** continues along the true left side of the Caples River, but stays in beech forest above the valley to avoid crossing Greenstone Station. At one point the woolshed of an old homestead may be spotted on the far bank.

It's about 2½ hours along the east bank before the well-marked track descends past an impressive **gorge** and crosses a bridge over the Caples to **Mid Caples Hut** (24 bunks) on an open terrace above the river.

Day 2: Mid Caples Hut to McKellar Hut

6–7 HOURS / 22KM

From Mid Caples Hut the track remains on the true right (west) side of the river and crosses open grassy flats for the first hour. You then ascend into beech forest to round a small gorge before quickly returning to the flats.

Eventually the track turns into bush before it emerges at the southern end of **Top Flat**. It takes about 25 minutes to cross the flat and cut through more beech forest. Just before Upper Caples Hut is a signposted junction with the Steele Saddle route south to the Greenstone Track, an extremely difficult tramp (10 to 12 hours).

> ### ⓘ WARNING: HEAVY RAIN
>
> The upper Caples River can rise extremely fast during periods of heavy rain. You'll cross a number of unbridged side streams along the track between the Upper Caples Hut and the junction with the Greenstone Track, and caution should be used when tramping this stretch during foul weather.

Upper Caples Hut (1½ to 2½ hours from Mid Caples Hut) is on a grassy flat where the valley begins to narrow. It has a beautiful setting, with the Ailsa Mountains rising directly behind the hut. The hut is owned by the NZ Deerstalkers Association (p246), and if you wanted to spend the night here, it can be booked ahead through them.

Past the hut, the track leaves the valley floor and climbs towards McKellar Saddle. At first the track is quite rough, with exposed tree roots and rocks, but becomes easier after an hour as it sidles up towards the bush edge.

Two hours from the hut it reaches **McKellar Saddle** (945m), an extremely wet and boggy area crossed by boardwalks built to protect the fragile subalpine vegetation. The views are good from the saddle – on a clear day the peaks and hanging valleys of Fiordland can be seen to the west.

Leaving the saddle, the track descends at an easy grade to a point where you break out of the bush near the head of **Lake McKellar**. Here, the track swings north to bypass swampy lowlands, then crosses a bridge to meet up with the **Greenstone Track**.

The Greenstone Track heads south (left) and crosses the grassy flat, where you're treated to views of Lake McKellar. It then gently climbs the forested edges of the lake, a couple of times dipping close enough for you to scout for cruising trout, but mostly skirting the hillsides, where views are limited to keyhole glimpses through the trees. **McKellar Hut** (24 bunks) sits in a small clearing next to the Greenstone River, with the rocky face of Jean Batten Peak (1971m) looming overhead.

Alternative Finish: Lake McKellar to the Divide

2–3 HOURS / 6.5KM

If you're not completing the loop on the Greenstone Track, your cue to head to the Divide comes when the Caples Track meets with the Greenstone Track by Lake McKellar. Take the right fork, heading north. After 45 minutes to one hour, you'll reach beautiful **Lake Howden** then **Lake Howden Hut** (28 bunks). At the hut you'll see a major track junction. Turn left (west) along the Routeburn Track, passing the flanks of Key Summit and another trail junction. The 30-minute side trip (left) to the top of **Key Summit** is worthwhile on clear days – from the 919m summit, you should be able to see the Hollyford, Greenstone and Eglinton Valleys.

From the Key Summit junction, the Routeburn Track descends steadily through bush and thick rainforest, before reaching the **Divide**, the lowest east–west crossing in the Southern Alps. It's 3km (one hour) from Lake Howden Hut to the Divide, where there's a car park and a shelter with toilets and water.

Side Trip: Peak 1538

6–8 HOURS / 17KM / 920M ASCENT

If you have a spare day at McKellar Hut, an interesting day walk is to climb Peak 1538 just southwest of the hut. Departing from the 'McKellar Hut' sign on the way towards Lake Howden Hut, is an unmarked track that climbs to the bushline. From there it's a steep climb through the alpine tussock to the top of **Peak 1538**. You can then follow the ridge to Key Summit (919m), descend to Lake Howden Hut and follow the first leg of the Greenstone Track back to McKellar Hut.

Day 3: McKellar Hut to Greenstone Hut

4½–6½ HOURS / 18KM

This day is spent tramping through the heart of the Greenstone Valley, where you'll see lots of cattle and, if you're wearing polarised sunglasses, a few of the river's famous trout (p250).

The track immediately crosses the **Greenstone River** on a bridge in front of the hut to the true left (east) side. The trail cut through beech forest for 30 minutes (1.5km), emerging at the northern end of **Greenstone Flats**, which are dominated by Jean Batten Peak.

The track cuts across bulrush grass and then returns to bush for almost 2km, skirting the Greenstone River, which boasts many beautiful pools. After crossing a large grassy flat, the track moves higher onto the forested bluffs.

For the next three hours the track stays predominantly in bush above the open valley. There's an occasional stretch of rocks and roots, but for the most part the track is a straightforward tramp with little climbing. When you emerge onto a large open flat you'll soon spot private **Rat's Nest Hut** on the opposite bank of the river.

You remain in grassy flats until the track ascends around a **gorge**. Short side trails

allow you to peer down between the rock walls at the roaring Greenstone River, before the track descends to **Steele Creek** and a major swing bridge. Just before the bridge is a signposted junction with a track heading north (left fork) to Steele Saddle and Upper Caples Hut, a demanding tramp of 10 to 12 hours. On the other side you break out of the trees and cross a grassy terrace to a signposted junction. The left fork heads off to a private hut for guided trampers. Right above you is the **Mid Greenstone Hut**, another club hut for the NZ Deerstalkers Association.

The right-hand fork descends to open flats for the next 3km. Re-enter the bush across from the confluence of the Greenstone River and Pass Burn; the hut on the other side of the river is private. The track now begins to skirt around **Greenstone Gorge** and, after 2km, comes to a junction with a track to Greenstone Hut. It's a five-minute descent to the bridge across the Greenstone River, from where there's a good view of the narrow rock walls of the gorge. Another 10 minutes from the swing bridge is **Greenstone Hut** (20 bunks) and the northern end of the Mavora–Greenstone Walkway. This is a great hut with a huge kitchen and wrap-around deck that peers out onto the surrounding mountains.

Day 4: Greenstone Hut to Greenstone Car Park

3–5 HOURS / 12KM

Begin the day by recrossing the bridge over the gorge and returning to the Greenstone Track. Head right on the main track as it continues on the true left (north) side of the river. You climb high above the gorge, and then swing left with the valley before crossing **Slip Creek** on a bridge and entering the western end of **Slip Flat**, 40 minutes to one hour from Greenstone Hut.

It's 1km across the flats before you re-enter the bush close to the river. After 20 to 30 minutes the track crosses a stream and comes to a signposted junction. The track to the east (right) stays close to the river before crossing a stock bridge and heading for **Lake Rere** (one hour). Take the main track to the north (left) instead, which remains on the true left (north) side of the river and climbs through the rest of the gorge.

About 1½ to two hours from the gorge, the track reaches a swing bridge over the

GREENSTONE & TROUT

Early European settlers to New Zealand, wishing to improve the country's farming, hunting and fishing opportunities, were responsible for the introduction of such ghastly wreckers as possums and rabbits. One of their more successful introductions was that of trout – brown and rainbow – released into NZ rivers in the second half of the 19th century.

Today they're much prized by anglers, whom you may stumble across, thigh-deep in limpid rivers or on the edge of deep green pools, flicking their flies. It's a pastime that, to its participants, often borders on obsession.

The Greenstone River is one of NZ's most-lauded trout fisheries. Accessible only on foot along the Greenstone Track (or by helicopter), the luminous green river boasts plentiful fish (both brown and rainbow trout) of legendary size, averaging between 1.5kg and 3kg. As you tramp alongside the river, keep an eye on the pools because you may well spot a few trout seemingly suspended in the clear water.

Trout fishing is highly regulated, with licences required to fish anywhere in NZ. Licences and information can be obtained from Fish and Game New Zealand (www.fishandgame.org.nz). If you're new to the sport, your best bet will be to go with a local guide; i-SITEs can help you find one. Otherwise, peruse the helpful online guide NZ Fishing (www.nzfishing.com).

Caples River, after which you will see a signposted junction.

Take the right fork (if you started this walk at the Divide, take the left fork onto the Caples Track to complete the loop) and follow the track along the true left bank of the Greenstone River. It will take 30 minutes to reach the trailhead at the Greenstone car park.

Rees-Dart Track

Duration 4 days

Distance 63km (39.1 miles)

Difficulty Moderate to demanding

Start Muddy Creek car park

End Chinamans Flat

Gateway Glenorchy (p269), Queenstown (p266)

Transport Shuttle bus

Summary Alpine scenery, wild rivers and a possible day trip to Dart Glacier have made the Rees-Dart one of the most popular tracks in Mt Aspiring National Park.

The Rees-Dart Track connects two splendid schist-lined valleys shaped by glaciation. The relatively small Dart Glacier was once part of an enormous system that terminated at Kingston, 135km away at the southern end of Lake Wakatipu.

As this tramp winds up one valley and back down the other, it takes in a variety of scenery, such as meadows of flowering herbs and mighty bluffs and moraine walls.

Pinched between the Routeburn Track and Cascade Saddle, the Rees-Dart has be-

come a popular tramp, but it is longer and definitely more challenging than either the Routeburn or Greenstone Caples, and has several stream crossings, which can be hazardous in heavy rain or snowmelt.

The most common approach to the tramp is to head up the Rees Valley and return down the Dart – this is the easiest direction in which to climb Rees Saddle and the way we describe the tramp. Plan an extra night at Dart Hut if you want to include a day trip to Dart Glacier or even on to Cascade Saddle (p253).

ⓘ Planning

WHEN TO TRAMP

The best time to tramp the Rees-Dart is December to April. From late winter through to early summer, the high sections of the route are subject to avalanches, with snow often lingering as late as December.

MAPS & BROCHURES

This tramp is covered by NZTopo50 maps CA10 (Lake Williamson) and CB10 (Glenorchy), as well as NewTopo's 1:40,000 Rees-Dart Track. Pick up DOC's The Rees-Dart Track brochure.

HUTS & CAMPING

There are three Serviced huts ($15) on this tramp: Shelter Rock, Dart and Daleys Flat. Each has a solid-fuel fire and water but no cooking facilities, so it's essential that you carry a stove.

You can camp next to the huts for $5, and elsewhere on the route with the exception of the fragile alpine and subalpine areas between Shelter Rock and Dart Huts.

Be sure to purchase your hut tickets in advance from any DOC visitors centre.

Rees-Dart Track

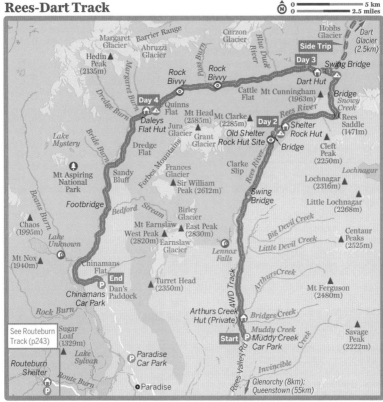

INFORMATION

The DOC Visitor Centre (p243) in Queenstown is the place to arrange logistics, obtain maps, hut tickets and track updates, and hire personal locator beacons.

ⓘ Getting There & Away

Glenorchy Journeys (p244) offers daily shuttle services to Muddy Creek from Queenstown ($55, 8.15am, 11.30am and 1.45pm) and Glenorchy ($35, 7am and 9am). Shuttles return from Chinamans Flat at 2pm and 4pm. Bookings are essential.

Info & Track (p244) runs shuttles to Muddy Creek from Queenstown ($54, 8am) and Glenorchy ($37, 9.15am). The return shuttle departs from Chinamans Flat at 2pm.

Trackhopper (p244) will drive you to Muddy Creek and deliver your car to Chinamans Flat, ready for you at the end of the tramp, for $160.

It used to be common to end this tramp with a jetboat pick-up as high up the river as Sandy Bluff, but changes to the river after the 2014 slip here have now made this impossible.

🥾 The Tramp

Day 1: Muddy Creek Car Park to Shelter Rock Hut

6–8 HOURS / 19KM

From Muddy Creek car park, ford the creek and head across the private farmland of Rees Valley Station for 2km, reaching the private **Arthurs Creek Hut** just beyond Bridges Creek. Grassy flats lie beyond, and it's one hour (4km) of open travel on the true left (east) side of **Rees River** until the track crosses a bridge over **Twenty Five Mile Creek**; poles mark the route.

The route continues along open river flats for another 1½ hours and can be extremely muddy at times – almost knee-deep in spots if it's been raining. Eventually you reach a track marked by a park boundary sign, and enter the bush. Within 500m the track crosses a swing bridge to the true right (west) side of **Rees River**. The track continues on this side of the river, passes through **Clarke Slip**, over grassy flats, and then begins a climb through beech forest. Within 2km the track passes the site of the **old Shelter Rock Hut**, now used occasionally as a campsite. From here it's 1km along the true right (west) bank of the Rees, through stands of stunted beech, before the track crosses a swing bridge back to the true left (east) bank to arrive at **Shelter Rock Hut** (22 bunks).

Day 2: Shelter Rock Hut to Dart Hut

4–6 HOURS / 10KM / 490M ASCENT

The climb over alpine Rees Saddle begins by following the river on the true left (east) side for a short time, picking up a well-marked track that rises through alpine scrub. The track gradually sidles up the valley until it reaches a tussock basin below the saddle, about 4km from the hut.

Rees Saddle is the obvious low point to the northeast. You keep to the stream bed before climbing up the steep slope to the top. The final ascent is marked with orange poles and a well-beaten path, but is still a steep climb. As you would expect of a 1471m-high pass, **Rees Saddle** provides great views of the surrounding peaks and valleys, making it the natural place for lunch if the weather is clear.

Follow the orange poles from the saddle towards Dart Hut. You quickly descend 90m to a terrace and a group of tarns above Snowy Creek. The track traverses steep, snow-grass slopes, which can be dangerous when wet or covered with snow.

The route stays on the true left (west) of **Snowy Creek**, then drops suddenly to a footbridge and crossing to the true right (east) side. This steep-sided creek fills with so much snow during the winter that DOC must remove the bridge in advance, or risk losing it to an avalanche. The track climbs above the bridge, passes some good views of the upper Dart Valley, and descends across broken slopes of rock and shrub.

Dart Hut is visible on the true left (south) bank of the Dart River during the final descent, which ends at a swing bridge across Snowy Creek. The camping spots just before the bridge signal that the hut is five minutes away.

Many trampers spend two nights at **Dart Hut** (32 bunks) so they can hike to view Dart Glacier. This has the tendency to create a bottleneck at the hut at the height of the tramping season.

Side Trip: Dart Glacier

4–6 HOURS RETURN, 14KM

The popular and rewarding hike to view Dart Glacier is strenuous and challenging and should only be attempted in good weather, and only by those confident navigating unmarked routes over steep terrain.

Cross the Snowy Creek bridge and follow the poles and rock cairns along the Dart River and the edge of Dart Glacier. After about three hours you will begin to climb moraine and tussock slopes with increasingly impressive views of the glacier and the Snowdrift Range to the west.

If conditions are ideal, and you have the energy, you can push on to Cascade Saddle (eight to 10 hours return from Dart Hut, 20km).

Day 3: Dart Hut to Daleys Flat Hut

5–7 HOURS / 18KM

The track climbs west, away from the hut and along a bluff above the **Dart River**, offering an occasional view of the rushing water below or the valley in front as it passes through thick forest.

Around 6km into the day, the track climbs sharply, but then drops into a rocky stream clearing near the eastern end of **Cattle Flat**. The track quickly emerges from forest onto the flat, a seemingly endless grassy area where the trail appears as a path of trampled grass marked occasionally by a rock cairn. The Dart River is seen as you cross the flat, as is a portion of Curzon Glacier, high in the mountains across the river. The track follows the middle of the flat and in 3km passes a sign to a **rock bivvy**. The bivvy, a three-minute walk up a side track, is a huge overhanging rock that can easily hold at least six people. If it's raining this is an excellent place for lunch.

The track continues across Cattle Flat for another 1.5km and finally returns to the bush. From here it's another 1½ to two hours to Daleys Flat Hut. You begin with a steady drop towards the river, reaching the banks of the Dart in 2.5km. Along the way you pass another rock bivvy, much smaller than the one at Cattle Flat. Eventually the track breaks out at **Quinns Flat**, a beautiful stretch of golden grass surrounded by mountains, and then returns to the bush.

The track crosses a few more streams and, in 30 minutes, arrives at Daleys Flat. Follow the trampled grass across the flat to reach **Daleys Flat Hut** (20 bunks).

Day 4: Daleys Flat Hut to Chinamans Flat

5½–7½ HOURS / 16KM

From the hut, the track heads through beech forest over a recently formed, 3km-long lake over **Dredge Flat**. This lake was created in 2014 after a massive landslide poured down into the valley. The track was closed for three years, but reopened in March 2017, with almost 3km of the route realigned.

From the lake, the new track heads up high above the Dart River on sections of track that are narrow and sometimes steep, adding about 1½ hours to the walk as it previously existed.

Eventually the track enters an open flat, with Chinamans Bluff straight ahead and an impressive waterfall from Lake Unknown visible high in the mountains across the Dart River.

The track skirts the bluff and descends onto **Chinamans Flat**. Skirt yet another bluff, this one along a segment of track that provides access around a washed-out area to the start of a 4WD track where you'll find a shelter, toilets and an information panel. If you haven't arranged a pick-up, it's still another 6km to the end of Glenorchy Paradise Rd – a good two-hour tramp along the 4WD track through Dan's Paddock.

Cascade Saddle

Duration 3 days

Distance 30km (18.6miles

Difficulty Demanding

Start/End Raspberry Creek car park

Gateway Wanaka (p267)

Transport Shuttle bus

Summary Climb to one of the most scenic alpine passes in the country for stunning views of Tititea/Mt Aspiring and the Dart Glacier, and to test your head for heights.

Cascade Saddle is one of the most beautiful and dramatic of all the passes that trampers can reach in NZ. Pinched between the West Matukituki and Dart Valleys, it's a very steep and demanding climb. On a fine day, the rewards are as numerous as the mountains you can see from atop the alpine pass, including a stunning view of Tititea/Mt Aspiring.

Cascade Saddle can also be reached from Dart Hut (p252) on the Rees-Dart Track, providing an enticing opportunity for a four-day tramp, crossing the pass from the West Matukituki Valley and exiting along the Dart Valley. The easiest approach is from the West Matukituki, as described here.

The West Matukituki is tramping royalty in the South Island, and it's worth building in a couple of extra days to explore upstream to Liverpool Hut, and take a detour out to Rob Roy Glacier. You could easily while away a decent week based at Aspiring Hut, branching out on day walks and soaking up the spectacular mountain scenes.

Be warned: Cascade Saddle is a difficult climb, partially smothered in super-slippery snow grass, and trampers have fallen to their deaths here. It should not be attempted by inexperienced trampers, or in adverse conditions. If you have any doubts, seek advice from the warden in Aspiring Hut, who will have current weather forecasts on hand.

ℹ Planning

WHEN TO TRAMP

Though you can hike through the West Matukituki Valley pretty much all year in favourable conditions, Cascade Saddle is a high alpine pass and should only be attempted when it's free of snow, normally from December to March. Even then, sudden cold fronts can sweep through and bring snow and fierce conditions at any time. It's also infamous for cloud, which can create white-out conditions for trampers.

MAPS & BROCHURES

The tramp is covered by NZTopo50 *CA11 (Aspiring Flats)* and *CA10 (Lake Williamson)*. DOC's *Cascade Saddle Route* brochure gives an overview of the tramp, though it's not as comprehensive as brochures for some other trails.

HUTS & CAMPING

Aspiring Hut (members/non-members $15/30) is a New Zealand Alpine Club (NZAC) hut that's managed by DOC. Fees can be paid at the Tititea/Mt Aspiring National Park Visitor Centre in

Cascade Saddle

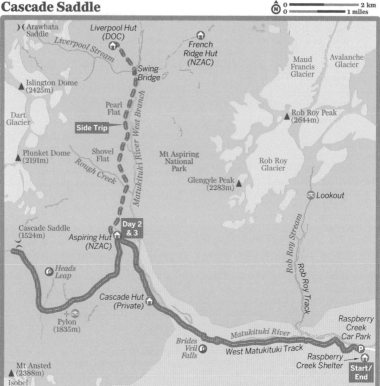

Wanaka, or online via the NZAC website (https:// alpineclub.org.nz).

There's a designated camping area ($5) adjacent to Aspiring Hut that's equipped with a shelter and toilet for campers – people choosing to camp can't use the hut facilities. Camping fees can only be paid at the Tititea/Mt Aspiring National Park Visitor Centre; the hut warden is likely to check for your receipt.

Note that there were plans to close Aspiring Hut for an indefinite time in 2018 for earthquake-strengthening work, so check ahead on its status through the NZAC website before setting out. The tiny Liverpool Hut is a Serviced hut ($15).

INFORMATION

DOC's **Tititea/Mt Aspiring National Park Visitor Centre** (☑ 03-443 7660; www.doc. govt.nz; cnr Ardmore St & Ballantyne Rd; ⊙ 8.30am-5pm daily Nov-Apr, Mon-Sat May-Oct) in Wanaka can provide full information

and take hut bookings. It also has museum-style displays on local geology, flora and fauna.

GUIDED TRAMPS

Wild Walks (☑ 03-443 9422; www.wildwalks. co.nz; 58 McDougall St) runs a unique two-day assisted tramp to Cascade Saddle. On this trip (from $355), you're guided to the saddle and to the beginning of the descent to the Dart Valley, where the guide leaves you on your own to tramp out.

ⓘ Getting There & Away

The tramp begins at a car park at Raspberry Creek, 50km from Wanaka. If you're coming in a rental car, check that you're covered for the drive – most of it is unsealed, with a series of creek fords along the way.

Ritchies (p269) runs shuttles from Wanaka to Raspberry Creek ($40) at 8.45am and 1.30pm, returning at 10am and 2.45pm.

🚶 **The Tramp**

Day 1: Raspberry Creek Car Park to Aspiring Hut

2–2½ HOURS / 9KM

Cross the bridge over Raspberry Creek to a 4WD track, which cuts across the open valley of grassy flats on the true right (south) bank of the **Matukituki River West Branch**. The scenery up the river includes Shotover Saddle and Mt Tyndall to the left (south), Cascade Saddle straight ahead (west), and grazing sheep and cattle. Within 2km the track passes the swing bridge that provides access across the river to the Rob Roy Track (p256).

The 4WD track continues up the valley on the true right (south) side of the river. At one point, near **Wilsons Camp**, the track climbs to the left to bypass a small bluff hidden in a clump of beech trees. Less than 4km from the bridge the track climbs away from the river again, passing **Brides Veil Falls**. The private Cascade Hut can be seen from the ridge. At this point the track swings northwest, passes Cascade Hut, and in another 30 minutes reaches **Aspiring Hut** (38 bunks).

Built by the NZAC in 1949, this stone-and-wood hut is a classic climbers' lodge, with an atmosphere of high adventure. The views are impressive, especially of the mountains at the head of the valley, including Tititea/Mt Aspiring (3033m) – try to nab a bunk under the big windows. The hut has gas cookers (only between late October and mid-April; bring your own stove at other times), wood stove, flush toilets and a water tank. A warden is stationed here in summer to collect fees and to relay weather reports.

Side Trip: Liverpool Hut

5–7 HOURS / 12KM / 630M ASCENT

For a grand day walk out from Aspiring Hut (or an overnight excursion), continue north along the Matukituki Valley on a track that's rated moderate during good conditions, though the tussocky tops can be treacherous and slippery when covered in snow.

From Aspiring Hut, follow the well-signposted track up the valley. After 10 minutes a bridge crosses **Cascade Creek**, and a 1km bush section emerges at an open terrace leading to **Shovel Flat**. From the head of Shovel Flat there's 400m of bush before you reach **Pearl Flat**, around 1½ hours from Aspiring Hut. If the climb to Liverpool Hut has you psyched out, you can continue up

ℹ️ **AVALANCHE WARNING**

The route to Cascade Saddle from Aspiring Hut is prone to avalanches, primarily between May and October, when the track should not be attempted. Before setting out, check the New Zealand Avalanche Advisory website (www.avalanche.net.nz) to get an idea of conditions.

to the head of the valley, another two hours (3.2km) ahead.

To reach Liverpool Hut, cross the swing bridge at **Liverpool Stream** and prepare yourself for a climb of a couple of hours or so. It's steep, and slippery, particularly below the bushline, so expect to put your arms into action as you pull yourself up and onward.

Above the bush the track initially leads across steep exposed shingle, rock and tussock terrain before reaching easier tussock-covered ground and a knoll overlooking the hut. When the hut is first sighted, do not sidle across to it below this knoll. With a 1100m perch, **Liverpool Hut** (10 bunks) enjoys stunning views of Tititea/Mt Aspiring and surrounding peaks. If you're planning to stick around for the night, the hut has mattresses and a water tank, but no heating or stoves.

Day 2: Aspiring Hut to Cascade Saddle Return

6–8 HOURS / 12KM / 1370M ASCENT & DESCENT

The track to Cascade Saddle is signposted behind the hut and heads southwest into mixed beech forest. Within an hour there are views of Tititea/Mt Aspiring to the north, and the rest of the valley to the east.

The track makes a steady ascent, and two to three hours from the hut it breaks out above the bushline. It's a glorious moment if the day is clear, as you're greeted by stunning views the minute you leave the last few stunted beech trees.

Savour the view, for the next section is very difficult. The route is marked by snow poles and follows a steep snow-grass and tussock ridge upwards. Sometimes you'll be on all fours working from one pole to the next, because the route sidles a few ledges and rocky outcrops, and at times becomes very steep. From the bushline it's a good two hours before the track swings to the left and then, veering right again, climbs an easy slope to the **Pylon**, the marker at 1835m. Take a break here – the views are wonderful.

From the marker, the track skirts the ridge to the south and then descends steadily through rock and scree to Cascade Creek. The route crosses the stream and climbs some easy slopes towards **Cascade Saddle** to the north. The route to the Rees-Dart Track veers left just before the saddle, but you can continue to the low point (at 1524m), where you can look from its edge straight down a sheer 1000m rock face to a small valley below – but be careful! It's an incredible feeling looking at so many landforms, with Tititea/Mt Aspiring to one side and the Dart Glacier to the other.

The return to Aspiring Hut is along the same route, so if the weather is fine, stick around a while and enjoy the lofty moments. The descent would provide an entirely different perspective were it not for the fact that you'll be looking at your feet the entire time. The tramp back down is interminable!

Day 3: Aspiring Hut to Raspberry Creek Car Park

2–2½ HOURS / 9KM

Follow the Day 1 route back to Raspberry Creek.

Rob Roy Track

Duration 3–4 hours

Distance 10km (6.2 miles)

Difficulty Easy to moderate

Start/End Raspberry Creek car park

Gateway Wanaka (p267)

Transport Shuttle bus

Summary A short, sharp climb through a beech-lined gorge takes you to the head of a stunning, sanctuary-like valley dwarfed by the hanging Rob Roy Glacier.

It's not uncommon to hear this short tramp, into a side pocket of the Matukituki Valley, described as the finest day walk in the South Island, and it's not difficult to see why. Few tracks provide such large-scale mountain scenery in such a short time frame, with the tramp beginning along the Matukituki Valley before climbing 400m through beech forest into a high and dramatic enclosure of mountains and glaciers.

The mix of beech forest and the clear blue water of Rob Roy Stream creates a bit of a fantasyland, before it all peels back to reveal the sort of mountain scene you might normally expect to find only after days of wilderness tramping.

Pay careful heed to the avalanche advisories if you're tramping in winter or spring, as the track beyond the lower lookout is susceptible to avalanches from the sheer-sided walls of the valley.

ℹ Planning

WHEN TO TRAMP

The best time for this tramp is through summer and autumn. The upper section of the track, beyond the lower lookout, is crossed by avalanche paths, and is at risk of avalanches from around May to November, particularly after recent snowfall. Check the ratings for the area on the New Zealand Avalanche Advisory website (http://www.avalanche.net.nz) before setting out, and be certain to call in to the **Tititea/Mt Aspiring National Park Visitor Centre** (p254) for advice.

MAPS & BROCHURES

The NZTopo50 *CA11 (Aspiring Flats)* map covers the entire tramp. DOC produces a dedicated *Rob Roy Valley Track* brochure that can be downloaded online (www.doc.govt.nz) or purchased at the Tititea/Mt Aspiring National Park Visitor Centre. If you want to link to other tramps around the Matukituki Valley area, also pick up DOC's *Matukituki Valley Tracks* brochure.

HUTS & CAMPING

If you fancy a night in the Matukituki Valley at the end of the tramp, it's feasible to turn up the valley on your return and hike to the NZAC's Aspiring Hut (members/non-members $15/30), following the Day 1 route of the Cascade Saddle tramp (p255). From the swing bridge over the Matukituki River, it's about a two-hour hike to Aspiring Hut. There's a camping area adjacent to the hut.

INFORMATION

Track conditions and any information regarding the Rob Roy Track are available from the A-framed **Tititea/Mt Aspiring National Park Visitor Centre** (p254) in Wanaka.

GUIDED TRAMPS

Eco Wanaka Adventures (☎ 03-443 2869; www.ecowanaka.co.nz) operates a guided day walk along the length of the Rob Roy Track ($295), departing from Wanaka. The hike runs year-round, depending on weather conditions.

ℹ Getting There & Away

The tramp begins at the Raspberry Creek car park, an hour's drive from Wanaka. If you're coming in a rental car, check that you're covered for the drive – most of it is unsealed, with a series of creek fords along the way.

Ritchies (p269) runs shuttles from Wanaka to Raspberry Creek ($40) at 8.45am and 1.30pm, returning at 10am and 2.45pm.

Rob Roy Track

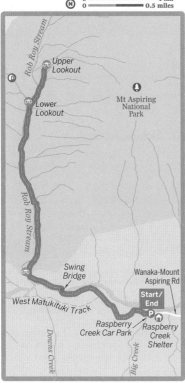

🥾 The Tramp

From the car park, follow a vehicle track straight up the valley on the true right (south) side of the Matukituki River, with the sharp line of Cascade Saddle visible straight ahead. The trail is wide and well formed as it passes through open farmland. In 15 to 20 minutes you'll come to a swing bridge, where you leave the Matukituki Valley trail, crossing the river and continuing upstream through beech forest on the opposite bank.

In a few minutes the track emerges from the forest again, where there's a seat with a perfect view up the Matukituki Valley. Here the track turns away from the valley, heading up into beech forest beside **Rob Roy Stream**. The stream quickly turns into a gorge, and there are early glimpses through the crack of the gorge to a stunning glaciated mountainscape ahead – it's a preview of things to come.

The track follows the line of the boulder-choked gorge, staying high on its bank. The beech forest gets mossier and more primeval as you ascend, with the stream below occasionally slowing into deeper, bluer pools.

One hour from the swing bridge, the track comes to a break in the forest that forms the **lower lookout**, unveiling a dramatic scene. A pair of waterfalls pour down from high above, and glaciers are scraped across the mountains like icing. On the opposite bank, the beech forest is strung with lichen.

Continue climbing along the bank through beech forest. At a large bend in the stream, the track turns up a tributary (beside a toilet), soon popping out from the bushline and into a maze of boulders. Among the boulders is the **upper lookout** (30 minutes from the lower lookout), with a series of interpretive signs sitting immediately below Rob Roy Peak and, most noticeably, Rob Roy Glacier, hanging precariously from its slopes. The waterfalls you spied from the lower lookout now sit almost directly across the stream, tumbling nearly 300m over the cliffs.

Mountains wrap right around the lookout, and it's well worth taking some time to simply hang about here for a while – it's quite likely that you'll get to witness bits of the glacier breaking away and avalanching down the mountain.

Gillespie Pass Circuit

Duration 3 days

Distance 58km (36 miles)

Difficulty Moderate to demanding

Start/End Makarora

Gateway Wanaka (p267)

Transport Bus, jetboat, helicopter

Summary This semi-circuit passes through scenic beech-forested valleys and is crowned by a superb view from an alpine pass at 1600m.

Located in the northern reaches of Mt Aspiring National Park, this popular tramp offers outstanding mountain scenery – some would say it rivals both the Matukituki and Glenorchy area tramps.

There is plenty to see and enjoy along this route, including valleys filled with silver beech (tawhai), and alpine tussock fields alive with grasshoppers, black butterflies, buttercups and mountain daisies. The bird life you might encounter includes the fantail, tomtit and

Gillespie Pass Circuit

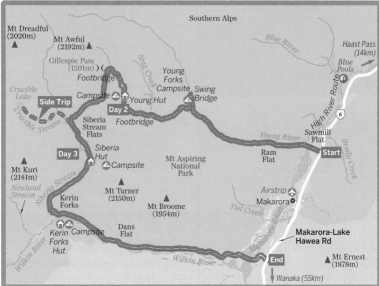

rifleman, as well as the mohua (yellowhead) and the parakeet known as the kakariki.

The tramp, which should only be undertaken by experienced parties, is described here from the Young Valley to the Wilkin Valley, the easiest way to cross Gillespie Pass. This also makes for a thrilling finish if you choose, as many do, to eschew the final four to five hours' walking in favour of a jetboat ride.

It is recommended that you carry a tent, as huts are often overcrowded in summer.

ℹ Planning

WHEN TO TRAMP
The track should be avoided in winter and spring as part of the route is snow-covered and/or exposed to avalanches. Summer is the best (and therefore busiest) time to walk the track.

MAPS & BROCHURES
NZTopo50 *BZ12 (Makarora)* and NewTopo's 1:40,000 *Wilkin Valley* map both cover the circuit. DOC's *Gillespie Pass, Wilkin valley tracks* brochure includes descriptions of the trail and an elevation profile.

HUTS & CAMPING
All three huts along the circuit are Serviced huts ($15) and have mattresses and multifuel burners for heating. Siberia Hut may need to be booked in advance in summer – check with the **Tititea/Mt**

Aspiring National Park Visitor Centre (p254). Otherwise, huts don't need to be booked.

Camping is permitted, but as this is a high-rainfall area you should choose your site with care. A $5 fee is payable if you use hut facilities.

INFORMATION
The DOC Makarora Visitor Centre, just north of the Makarora Tourist Centre, is now unstaffed and only offers display information. In Wanaka, the larger **Tititea/Mt Aspiring National Park Visitor Centre** (p254), in an A-framed building on the edge of the town centre, provides all the usual information and services as well as museum-style displays on local geology, flora and fauna.

GUIDED TRAMPS
Wild Walks (p254) offers a four-day Gillespie Pass Circuit walk (from $1715) that ends with a jetboat ride back to Makarora.

ℹ Getting There & Away

InterCity (☎ 03-442 4922; www.intercity.co.nz) has daily coaches to Makarora from Queenstown, Cromwell, Wanaka, Lake Hawea and Franz Josef. From the Makarora Tourist Centre, where they stop, it's about a 3km walk along SH6 to the mouth of the Young River. At the tramp's end, the mouth of the Wilkin is around 6km south of the tourist centre. If you need to spend a night in Makarora before setting out, the **Makarora Tourist Centre** (☎ 03-443 8372;

www.makarora.co.nz; 5944 Haast Pass-Makarora Rd/SH6; ☺ summer 8am-late, winter 9am-5.30pm; 🛖) is a large all-in-one complex incorporating a cafe, bar, shop, information centre, campsite (unpowered/powered sites $15/17), dorms ($30), cabins with kitchenettes ($85) and self-contained chalets (from $128).

Wilkin River Jets (📞 03-443 8351; www.wilkin riverjets.co.nz; Haast Pass-Makarora Rd/SH6; adult/child $120/69) offers jetboat transport on the Wilkin River. Many trampers choose this option as an exciting way to finish the tramp, and it can also be useful if you are short on time or if the river is swollen – the ford of the Makarora River near its confluence with the Wilkin is challenging enough at any time. The jetboat picks up trampers from Kerin Forks and travels back to Makarora ($110). The jetboat can also drop trampers at the mouth of the Young River ($25, minimum three people). IThe company can also provide helicopter transfers to/from the likes of Young Forks and Kerin Forks. Its office is beside the Makarora Tourist Centre.

 The Tramp

Day 1: Makarora to Young Hut

6–7 HOURS / 20KM

The **Makarora River** is generally forded at Sawmill Flat, about 3km north of Makarora village, on SH6. Study the Makarora carefully then choose the best ford between its confluence with Young River and Brady Creek. The crossing here is within the ability of most trampers when the water level is normal. A high-river option is available 5km to the north by taking the short (and very beautiful) **Blue Pools Walk** then following the link track along the bank of the Makarora River to the mouth of the Young River. It adds about 7km and two to three hours to the day.

Once on the true right (west) side of the Makarora, you round the corner into the Young Valley, where you will find a good track leading up the true left (north) bank of the **Young River**.

The track remains close to the river. Within three or four hours you enter the flats below the junction of the North and South Branches of Young River. Continue to just above the confluence, where a swing bridge allows you to safely cross the North Branch. A track here also leads up the North Branch to the **Young Forks Campsite**, 200m from the confluence.

On the other side of the bridge a track crosses a small grassy flat and then enters the bush to continue on the true left (north) side of the South Branch. Ten minutes from the bridge the track crosses a large, unsta-

ble slip – it is well marked with rock cairns, but exercise caution and remain at the same height above the river while crossing it. You then re-enter the bush and climb steeply for 100m before sidling a series of unstable slips, reaching a bridge over **Stag Creek** two to three hours after crossing the North Branch.

From here the track makes a steady climb to the bushline, reaching it within two hours of the bridge. The original Young Hut was another 1km up the valley, but in 2006 a new and larger **Young Hut** (20 bunks) was built within the bush to protect it from the avalanches that often occur here during winter.

Day 2: Young Hut to Siberia Hut

6–8 HOURS / 12KM / 520M ASCENT, 860M DESCENT

Leave the bush and continue up the valley, using a bridge to cross to the true right (south) side of the South Branch within 1km of Young Hut. Stay on this side of the river for the next 30 minutes, enjoying views of Mt Awful (2192m) framed by the valley walls, before reaching the start of the track to Gillespie Pass on your left. A large rock cairn and signs mark the start of the route, up a northeasterly facing slope of scrub and tussock. Make sure you fill your water bottles, as this is the last place for water until well over the pass.

It's a steep climb of 400m up the slope, alongside a rock bluff and then along the crest of a spur, where orange snow poles mark most of the route through snow grass. Just before reaching the **pass**, the route swings left up a small gully and climbs to a height of 1600m. It takes three to four hours to reach this point, and for many trampers the alpine setting is a good spot for an extended break or lunch, with Mt Alba (2360m) dominating the skyline.

You leave the pass by following the orange snow poles southeast along a ridge for 1km, until the route swings southwest. At times you are wandering down through snow-grass basins, which are very slippery when wet, so exercise caution. The track enters the forest on a small prominent spur and leads down to **Gillespie Stream**, a good spot for a rest. You continue down through forest, sidling above Gillespie Stream on its true left (south) bank, before descending steeply along a series of switchbacks to **Siberia Stream** and the track up to Crucible Lake (p260).

Continue southeast beside Siberia Stream. The walk through **Siberia Stream Flats** is easy and the mountain scenery is spectacular.

It takes about one hour to cross the grassy flats to Siberia Hut (20 bunks), on the true left (east) side of Siberia Stream. Plan on three to 3½ hours to reach the hut from the top of the pass. This part of the track has been marked with poles to keep trampers to a set path and minimise damage to the vegetation.

Side Trip: Crucible Lake

6–8 HOURS / 14KM RETURN / 530M ASCENT & DESCENT

There's no better reason to spend an extra night at Siberia Hut than to take a day tramp up to Crucible Lake, a true alpine lake nestled beneath Mt Alba. It takes three to four hours to get there from the hut, and about the same to return. To reach the lake, backtrack through Siberia Stream Flats to Crucible Stream, where a track enters the forest on the true left (north) side of the stream. The track climbs steeply up a narrow spur to a hanging valley filled with boulders and snow grass (be sure to turn around and admire the framed views of Siberia Valley and ranges beyond), before climbing a rock moraine to the spectacular shore of Crucible Lake.

Day 3: Siberia Hut to Makarora

7–8 HOURS / 26KM

Head for about 30 minutes to the southern end of Siberia Stream Flats to reach a marked track that enters the forest. The track remains on the true left (east) bank of Siberia Stream and gradually descends away from the flats through bush. It sidles around a shoulder then follows a series of switchbacks over the final 450m to Wilkin River, a short distance upstream from Kerin Forks.

Kerin Forks Hut (10 bunks) is on grassy flats 400m downstream from the confluence of Siberia Stream and Wilkin River, on the true right (south) bank of the Wilkin; the river must be crossed to reach it. From Siberia Hut it takes two to three hours to reach the Wilkin River, where many trampers will have arranged to be picked up by jetboat.

To continue down the river, follow the marked track along the true left (north) bank. The walk is easy and within four to five hours you come to the confluence with the Makarora River. Caution has to be used when fording this river, which is normally best done upstream (north) from its junction with the Wilkin. This is a challenging river crossing that should only be attempted by experienced parties in good weather. Do not try to cross after heavy rain or any time the river is running high.

QUEENSTOWN & WANAKA

Queenstown is where New Zealand's adventurous heart beats fastest, a place where you can throw yourself from bridges, planes or mountain tops, and skim through river canyons in jetboats or atop river boards. The town oozes adrenaline but, together with sister lake town Wanaka, it also provides a host of good mountain tramping at the edge of Mt Aspiring National Park.

Ben Lomond

Duration 6–8 hours

Distance 15.5km (9.6 miles)

Difficulty Moderate

Start/End Skyline Gondola base station

Gateway Queenstown (p266)

Transport Gondola

Summary Climb high above Queenstown on a popular ridge-top hike with ever-widening views over Lake Wakatipu, Queenstown and finally Mt Aspiring.

If you stand in Queenstown, it might be the Remarkables that dominate the scene, but if you're on the opposite shore, looking across the lake towards Queenstown, it is the pyramidal figure of Ben Lomond, standing tall directly behind the town, that crowns the view. For hikers it's the peak that also dominates thoughts of Queenstown.

Most of the tramp is above the bushline, providing superb views of Ben Lomond itself and the Remarkables rising like the spine of a sea monster from Lake Wakatipu.

For such an imposing-looking mountain, Ben Lomond provides a surprisingly straightforward climb, complicated only by weather and the endurance of your own legs – from Queenstown it's a climb of around 1400m to the summit. If time or energy is short you can ride the gondola to the top station, cutting out 2.5km of the approach walk and 400m of climbing.

Note that things steepen and the terrain gets more tricky beyond Ben Lomond Saddle, so if you're feeling the pinch at the saddle, or you struggle with heights, it's a good turnaround point that still affords terrific views. DOC recommends that children under 10 years of age don't climb past the saddle.

Ben Lomond

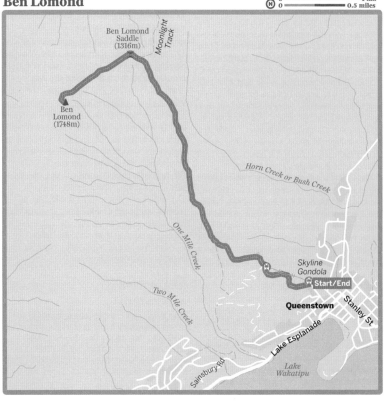

ⓘ Planning

WHEN TO TRAMP

The best time on the mountain is around November to April when the summit is likely to be free of snow. Between April and November there's the possibility of snow and ice on the mountain, so be sure to check at the DOC visitors centre in Queenstown if you're planning to climb during that time.

If it's windy by the shores of Lake Wakatipu, you can expect it to be even more blowy on the summit, so assess the conditions carefully.

WHAT TO BRING

Beyond the top gondola station, the trail does not pass any streams or other water sources, so carry all the drinking water you need.

MAPS

The Ben Lomond Track is covered by the NZ-Topo50 *CC11 (Queenstown)* map.

INFORMATION

Ben Lomond is the big-ticket walk in town, so Queenstown's DOC Visitor Centre (p243) is flush with information about the track and weather conditions. You can also pick up maps here.

ⓘ Getting There & Away

One of the great joys of this tramp is its accessibility, with the Tiki Trail beginning directly beside the base station for the **Skyline Gondola** (☏ 03-441 0101; www.skyline.co.nz; Brecon St; adult/child return $35/22; ⊙ 9am-9pm), around a 400m walk north of Queenstown's centre. The gondola offers the temptation of shortening the tramp, either taking out the steep climb on the Tiki Trail or floating you back down into town after a tiring day out...or both.

🥾 The Tramp

The ascent to Ben Lomond begins on the **Tiki Trail**, which sets out from beside the base station for the Skyline Gondola, heading up beside a mountain-bike trail. Cross the bike trail after about 100m, from where the Tiki Trail coils steeply and tightly up the slopes through Douglas fir forest, passing platforms for the Ziptrek zip-line tours through the forest.

Across the Skyline vehicle track, the Tiki Trail enters mountain beech forest and the gradient eases slightly as the track cuts across the slopes. At the next point that you meet the vehicle track you cross swords again with the mountain-bike trail. Bikes go straight across; you continue walking along the vehicle track. Stay on the vehicle track at the next bike-trail crossing, back now in Douglas fir forest as you continue to intersect with the mountain-bike park and the Ziptrek lines – it's a window into Queenstown's massive adventure industry. Past the Ziptrek office, you'll emerge into a clearing, one hour from the base station, and arrive at the **gondola's top station**.

Pass through the station complex (take a moment to enjoy the scene from the viewing deck) to the **Market Kitchen corner**, where the Ben Lomond Track sets out beside the luge chairlift. The blue Ben Lomond Track signs will guide you out of the hubbub of people and the luge, and back into dark Douglas fir forest. Within 10 minutes the track emerges from the forest to a view of Ben Lomond straight ahead.

Traverse beneath the ridge line, passing through a strip of beech forest before skirting the next, larger stand of beech, filling a deep gully, to rise to a saddle (1049m) in the ridge through tussocks and low subalpine scrub. From here the track simply follows the ridge line, keeping left at the Moonlight Track junction and rising to **Ben Lomond Saddle**, about 1½ hours from the top gondola station. Here you're greeted by an array of distant peaks, with a seat on which to sit and ponder the rest of the climb.

The track now steepens as it rises up the neck of the mountain, typically following the line of the ridge or just to its northern side. It continues to steepen as it rises, winding through bouldery schist and onto the **summit**, reached around one hour from the saddle. The summit has an unbroken view over one of the most spectacular mountain regions in the country, including the Remarkables and a distant Tititea/Mt Aspiring.

Return to Queenstown the same way. And if fatigue has set in, there's always the gondola...

Roys Peak

Duration 5–6 hours

Distance 16km (9.9 miles)

Difficulty Moderate

Start/End Wanaka–Mt Aspiring Rd

Gateway Wanaka (p267)

Transport Shuttle bus

Summary A long climb to a long view, this tramp ascends to the summit of a 1578m peak along the rim of Lake Wanaka, passing one of the country's most popular mountain photo stops along the way.

If you've seen any one photo of Lake Wanaka (other than of *that* tree), it's likely to have been taken from the Roys Peak Track, which provides one of the most photogenic vantage points in NZ. In the kindest of descriptions, the climb to Roys Peak is a grind, ascending 1220m from near the lakeshore to the antenna-tipped summit, but oh, those views...it's truly a spectacular tramp.

Those very views have made this an extremely popular track, though many hikers aspire only to reach the ridge, about three-quarters of the way up, from where the famous 'selfie with Lake Wanaka' moment bombards Instagram.

❶ Planning

WHEN TO TRAMP

Roys Peak Track crosses private farmland and closes for lambing from the start of October to 10 November each year. Winter typically brings snow over the mountain and the risk of avalanches, making the ideal time for this tramp around mid-November to April.

MAPS

For the best perspective, pick up NZTopo50 maps CA12 (Minaret Bay) and CB12 (Cardrona).

INFORMATION

In an A-framed building on the edge of Wanaka's town centre, the Tititea/Mt Aspiring National Park Visitor Centre (p254) offers advice on all tracks and conditions in the area. It also has a small display on the area's natural history.

❶ Getting There & Away

The trailhead is around 6km from Wanaka, on the road to Mt Aspiring National Park along the western shore of Roys Bay on Lake Wanaka. A new and larger car park was constructed at the trailhead in late 2017, but in summer it's still wise to walk or cycle from town along the lakeside Glendhu Bay Track as the car park gets pretty choked. A link trail between the Glendhu Bay Track and the Roys Peak car park was being constructed at the time of research.

Ritchies (p269) runs a shuttle-bus service from Wanaka to Mt Aspiring National Park that makes a stop at the Roys Peak trailhead (one way/return $15/20). The bus departs from the log cabin on Wanaka's lakeshore at 8.45am and 1.30pm.

Roys Peak

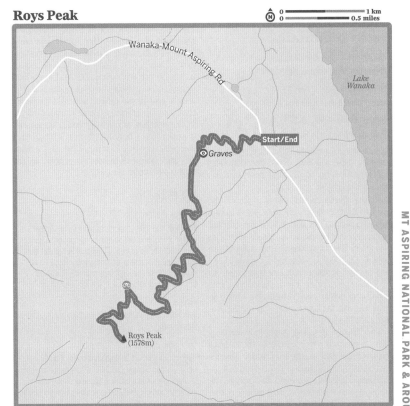

🏃 The Tramp

From the car park the Rob Roy Track begins as it intends to continue – climbing. Get used to that sting in your legs because it'll be steeply up most of the way, at first through wide switchbacks.

About 30 minutes from the trailhead, the track crosses a fence on a stile as the switchbacks continue. The cars in the car park will already look like toys below. Some 10 to 15 minutes on, as the switchbacks uncoil, you'll come to three **graves** beside a pine tree, including one of Willis Scaife (1887–1965), the one-time owner of Glendhu Station. There are a couple of picnic tables here also, so take a break and lap up the view of Lake Wanaka.

The gradient eases now as the track contours across the slopes for the next 20 minutes before the climb ramps up again, switchbacking through tussocky farmland, with Roys Peak now in view above you (if

you've picked the right day). One to 1½ hours from the graves, you'll cross a stile and enter the **Stack Conservation Area**.

After another lengthy traverse, the track rises to the crest of the ridge (45 minutes from the stile). Just below the track to the right is the **knoll lookout** where all those Roys Peak photos are snapped. The track turns up to the left from here, zigzagging up once again before crossing to the back of the ridge. After one final switchback the track follows the summit ridge to the antenna-topped tip of **Roys Peak**, around 30 to 45 minutes from the knoll lookout. If you've come on a good day, the view is stunning – down onto Lake Wanaka and across to Tititea/Mt Aspiring.

The Skyline Track continues along the ridge from here, but it's a challenging and long route that ends on Cardrona Rd, far from where you started, so follow your ascent route back down to the car park.

Diamond Lake & Rocky Mountain

Duration 2½–3 hours

Distance 7km (4.3 miles)

Difficulty Easy to moderate

Start/End Diamond Lake car park

Gateway Wanaka (p267)

Transport Shuttle bus

Summary A low-level hill climb past a beautiful lake to views over Lake Wanaka, the mouth of the Matukituki River and a distant Tititea/Mt Aspiring.

As the hiking crowds sweat it out on the track to Roys Peak (p262), there are wizened old trampers in Wanaka who'll secretly tell you that those people have missed Wanaka's best hike. Sitting across Glendhu Bay from Roys Peak, the trails around Diamond Lake and Rocky Mountain are less trafficked but no less spectacular than their big-name neighbour, while also sitting at a lower elevation, with far less ascent – around 450m compared to 1220m.

The tramp detailed here is effectively three conjoined loops taking in the bulk of the trail network on the mountain. Though we've outlined the tramp in an overall anticlockwise direction, you can take any of the loops in either direction. If there's any distinction, heading to the Lake Wanaka viewpoint first, as described here, provides the most gentle ascent.

History

Though Waitaha and Kai Tahu people occupied the area around Wanaka, there was no Māori presence when the first Europeans arrived here in 1853. The large Wanaka Station was established in 1859, and later divided into smaller runs, including Glendhu Station, which incorporated Rocky Mountain and Diamond Lake, in 1897.

Recreational use of the area began with the Wanaka Winter Sports Club, which used the frozen Diamond Lake for ice skating from the 1950s. In the 1990s a local man, Stuart Landsborough, came up with an idea to carve a walking track to the summit of Rocky Mountain, which he constructed with the support of the Glendhu Station landowners. For 13 years Landsborough maintained the trail himself, until the 106-hectare Diamond Lake Conservation Area was created in 2005.

Environment

The landscape you see at Rocky Mountain, including the hollow that holds Diamond Lake, was shaped by ice-age glaciers. A staircase of cliffs and bluffs shields pockets of native forest with New Zealand broadleaf (kapuka), wineberry (makomako), kohuhu and a few black pines (matai). The reeds that ring Diamond Lake are raupo. Bird life in the patches of forest includes the fantail (piwakawaka), bellbird (korimako) and grey warbler (riroriro). You may also see the New Zealand falcon (kārearea) overhead, as the bird is known to nest nearby.

ℹ Planning

WHEN TO TRAMP

Parts of the lower sections of the trail are shaded by bluffs and are prone to ice cover in winter, so avoid walking then. The track is a good option for the rest of the year and, unlike Roys Peak, doesn't close for lambing, making it a good springtime alternative when Roys is off limits.

MAPS

The NZTopo50 *CA12 (Minaret Bay)* map covers the tramp.

INFORMATION

Pay a visit to the Tititea/Mt Aspiring National Park Visitor Centre (p254), at the eastern edge of Wanaka's town centre, for any additional information on the Diamond Lake Conservation Area and track conditions.

ℹ Getting There & Away

The large car park at the start of the tramp is on the Wanaka–Mt Aspiring Rd, 18km from Wanaka. The road is sealed all the way.

Ritchies (p269) runs a shuttle-bus service from Wanaka to Mt Aspiring National Park that makes a stop at the Diamond Lake car park (one way/return $15/20). The bus departs from the log cabin on Wanaka's lakeshore at 8.45am and 1.30pm.

🥾 The Tramp

Cross the stile at the end of the car park and enter the Diamond Lake Conservation Area. The 4WD track climbs quickly to a plateau that's seemingly steamrolled flat into the mountain, crossing it to a track junction just past a large willow tree. Veer left to arrive at the willow-ringed shores of Diamond Lake, which you round clockwise. As you arrive beneath the cliffs, you'll come to another track junction. Continue straight ahead, signed to Rocky Mountain, rising to the base of the cliffs and then up a long flight of steps

Diamond Lake & Rocky Mountain

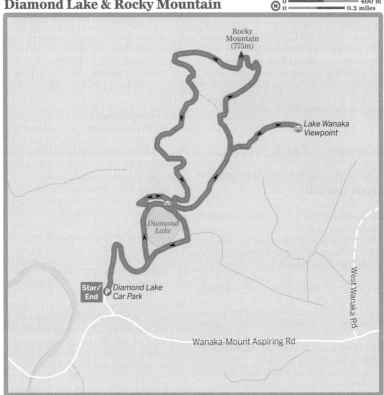

to a wooden lookout platform (30 minutes from the car park) directly above Diamond Lake, which now looks like a sinkhole below. Beyond the lake to the right, across the valley, you'll see Twin Falls, deeply gouged into the lower slopes of Treble Cone. The slope of exposed rock seen directly ahead over the lake is Hospital Flat, Wanaka's prime rock-climbing site.

The track continues to climb. At the next junction, a couple of minutes past the lookout, keep right, following the path signed to Lake Wanaka Viewpoint. In another 10 to 15 minutes, detour right, heading out to the Lake Wanaka Viewpoint, where a seat at the mountain's edge stares out over the lake to Albert Town and across Glendhu Bay to Roys Peak.

Return to the main track and turn right. Within 100m the track swings left, zigzagging steeply up the slopes, crossing a gully and then climbing just as steeply on a more rugged section of track. The going quickly flattens out as

you reach another high plateau. In a few steps, turn right onto the 'eastern track', climbing through the final rack of bluffs towards the summit. There are fine views of Lake Wanaka and the mouth of the Matukituki River as the trail creeps along the mountain's edge, but the grandstand view comes at the summit (1½ hours from the car park), as the scene peels open to reveal a cavalcade of features: Lake Wanaka, Treble Cone, Twin Falls and ahead, through the Matukituki Valley, the serrated summit of Tititea/Mt Aspiring.

Instead of returning on the same track, continue ahead onto the 'western track', which is marked on the summit by an orange pole. This track descends gently off the summit, rounds a couple of notches in the cliffs and then curls down to the high plateau. At the junction here, turn right (signed as 'western track'), heading to the western edge of the mountain, where you'll get an eyeball-to-eyeball view of Twin Falls.

The track descends through a damp gully – notice the sudden change in the vegetation – cutting at times beneath overhanging cliffs. A steep set of tight switchbacks delivers you back to the track junction just above the Diamond Lake lookout platform. Turn right, passing the lookout, and return to the lakeshore. Unless you're in a screaming hurry, turn left here, completing the lake loop before returning to the car park.

TOWNS & FACILITIES

Queenstown

🖊 03 / POP 12,500

Queenstown is as much a verb as a noun, a place of doing that likes to spruik itself as the 'adventure capital of the world'. It's famously the birthplace of bungy jumping, and the list of adventures you can throw yourself into here is encyclopedic – alpine heliskiing to zip lining. It's rare that a visitor leaves without having tried something that ups their heart rate, but to pigeonhole Queenstown as just a playground is to overlook its cosmopolitan dining and arts scene, its fine vineyards, and the diverse range of bars that can make evenings as fun-filled as the days.

Expect big crowds, especially in summer and winter, but also big experiences.

🛏 Sleeping & Eating

Choice abounds, but be sure to book your accommodation in advance from December to February, or when the ski season's in full flight from June to September.

★ **YHA Queenstown Lakefront**   HOSTEL $

(🖊 03-442 8413; www.yha.co.nz; 88-90 Lake Esplanade; dm/s/d without bathroom from $30/80/102; 🅿🛜) 🏊 This large lakefront hostel, fresh from a refit in 2017, has basic but neat-as-a-pin bunkrooms and an industrial-sized kitchen with window benches to absorb the view. The TV room is filled with beanbags and there are even a couple of massage chairs in the lounge. Lakeview suites get a shared balcony (and some traffic noise).

★ **Little Paradise Lodge**   LODGE $$

(🖊 03-442 6196; www.littleparadise.co.nz; Glenorchy–Queenstown Rd, Mt Creighton; s/d $90/140, units $180; 🅿) This isolated and peaceful lodge, almost midway between Queenstown and Glenorchy, is a whimsical gem. From the toilet-cistern aquariums (complete with fish) to the huge garden with 3000 roses, monkey puzzle trees and the Swiss owner's own sculptural work, you won't have seen a place like it. There are two rooms in the main house and a unit out the back.

If you're not staying, you can still wander the gardens ($15), which straddle the 45th parallel.

Creeksyde Queenstown Holiday Park & Motels   HOLIDAY PARK $$

(🖊 03-442 9447; www.camp.co.nz; 54 Robins Rd; sites from $55, d without bathroom from $83, units from $139; 🅿🛜) 🏊 In a garden setting, this pretty and extremely well-kept holiday park has accommodation ranging from small tent sites along the creek to fully self-contained motel units. It claims to be the 'world's first environmentally certified holiday park' and a number of the powered sites were switched to solar power in 2017.

There are quirky sculptures throughout and an ablutions block disguised as a medieval oast house (hop kiln).

★ **Hidden Lodge**   B&B $$$

(🖊 03-442 6636; www.hiddenlodgequeenstown.co.nz; 28 Evergreen Pl, Sunshine Bay; r from $395; 🅿@🛜) The well-named Hidden Lodge is literally the last place west in Queenstown. Tucked away in Sunshine Bay, it has enormous rooms, unfettered lake and mountain views, complimentary beer and wine, and a new outdoor hot tub. A quiet escape that is indeed a hidden gem.

★ **Public Kitchen & Bar**   MODERN NZ $$

(🖊 03-442 5969; www.publickitchen.co.nz; Steamer Wharf, Beach St; dishes $12-46; ⏰11am-late; 🛜) You can't eat closer to the water than at this excellent lakefront eatery where local is law: Cardrona lamb, Fiordland wild venison, Geraldine pork, South Island fish. Grab a group and order a selection of plates of varying sizes from the menu. The meaty dishes, in particular, are excellent.

Bespoke Kitchen   CAFE $$

(🖊 03-409 0552; www.bespokekitchen.co.nz; 9 Isle St; mains $11-19; ⏰8am-5pm; 🛜) Occupying a light-filled corner site near the gondola, Bespoke delivers everything you'd expect of a smart Kiwi cafe. It has a good selection of counter food, beautifully presented cooked options, a range of outside seating in sight of the mountains and, of course, great coffee. In 2015, within six months of opening, it was named NZ's cafe of the year.

Blue Kanu MODERN NZ $$
(☑ 03-442 6060; www.bluekanu.co.nz; 16 Church St; mains $28-38; ☻4pm-late) Disproving the rule that all tiki houses are inherently tacky, Blue Kanu serves up a food style it calls 'Polynasian' – *bibimbap* in one hand, fried chicken pineapple buns in the other. It's relaxed and personable, capable of making you feel like a regular in minutes. The marriage of the Polynesian decor and the chopsticks sounds impossible to pull off, but it works.

Fergburger BURGERS $$
(☑ 03-441 1232; www.fergburger.com; 42 Shotover St; burgers $12-19; ☻8am-5am) Who knew a burger joint could ever be a destination restaurant? Such are the queues at Fergburger that it often looks like an All Blacks scrum out the front. The burgers are as tasty and satisfying as ever, but the wait can be horrendous and the menu has more choices than the place has seats.

🛍 Supplies & Equipment

Small Planet Outdoors SPORTS & OUTDOORS
(☑ 03-442 5397; www.smallplanetsports.com; 15-17 Shotover St; ☻9am-7pm Oct-May, 8am-9pm Jun-Sep) This warren-like store is something of a bazaar of outdoors gear, with everything you might need for backcountry skiing, climbing, snowboarding or tramping.

Outside Sports MOUNTAIN BIKING
(☑ 03-441 0074; www.outsidesports.co.nz; 9 Shotover St; ☻8.30am-8pm) Has a good range of mountain bikes (from $39/59 per half/full day) and ski equipment ($25 to $59 per day) for hire, as well as outdoor gear for sale.

Alpine Supermarket SUPERMARKET $
(☑ 03-442 8961; cnr Shotover & Stanley Sts; ☻7am-10pm Mon-Sat, 9am-10pm Sun) Central supermarket if you're self-catering or stocking up for a tramp.

ℹ Information

Queenstown i-SITE (☑ 03-442 4100; www. queenstownisite.co.nz; cnr Shotover & Camp Sts; ☻8.30am-8pm) Friendly and informative despite being perpetually frantic, the saintly staff here can help with bookings and information on Queenstown, Gibbston, Arrowtown and Glenorchy.

ℹ Getting There & Away

Air New Zealand (☑ 0800 737 000; www.air-newzealand.co.nz) flies direct to Queenstown from Auckland, Wellington and Christchurch.

Jetstar (☑ 0800 800 995; www.jetstar.com) also flies the Auckland route.

Various airlines offer direct flights to Queenstown from Sydney, Melbourne, Brisbane and the Gold Coast in Australia.

Most buses and shuttles stop on Athol St or opposite the i-SITE; check when you book.

Atomic Travel (☑ 03-349 0697; www.atomictravel.co.nz) Daily (except Tuesday) bus to and from Twizel ($30, 3¼ hours), Tekapo ($45, four hours) and Christchurch ($55, 7¼ hours).

Catch-a-Bus South (☑ 03-479 9960; www. catchabussouth.co.nz) Door-to-door daily bus from Invercargill ($60, 3¼ hours) and Bluff ($75, 3¾ hours), heading via Gore ($61, 2½ hours) three times a week.

InterCity (☑ 03-442 4922; www.intercity.co.nz) Daily coaches to/from Wanaka (from $17, 1¾ hours), Franz Josef (from $62, eight hours), Dunedin (from $26, 4¼ hours), Invercargill (from $49, 2½ hours) and Christchurch (from $55, 8½ to 11½ hours).

Naked Bus (https://nakedbus.com) Buses daily to Wanaka (from $17, 1¾ hours), Te Anau (from $10, 2½ hours), Franz Josef (from $62, eight hours) and Christchurch (from $55, 8½ hours).

Ritchies (☑ 03-443 9120; www.alpineconnexions.co.nz) Daily buses to/from Dunedin ($50, 4½ hours).

Ritchies Connectabus Wanaka (☑ 0800 405 066; www.connectabus.com; ☎) Heads to/from Wanaka five times daily ($35, two hours). Does hotel pick-ups and has free wi-fi on board.

Wanaka

☑ 03 / POP 6480

So long described as Queenstown's smaller and more demure sibling, Wanaka now feels grown up enough to have asserted its own identity. What it does share with Queenstown is the fact that they're both lake and mountain towns bristling with outdoor and adventure opportunities. Despite constant growth in both size and costs, Wanaka retains a fairly laid-back, small-town atmosphere.

🛏 Sleeping & Eating

⭐**Wanaka Bakpaka** HOSTEL $
(☑ 03-443 7837; www.wanakabakpaka.co.nz; 117 Lakeside Rd; dm $31, d with/without bathroom $92/74; ℗@☎) The only lakeside hostel in town delivers million-dollar views at backpacker prices. Amenities are top-shelf and it's worth paying a bit extra for the en suite double with the gorgeous views, though you can also just lap it all up from the wide lounge windows. There are bikes for hire and the hot-water bottles come free.

YHA Wanaka
HOSTEL **$**

(📞 03-443 1880; www.yha.co.nz; 94 Brownston St; dm $30-38, d with/without bathroom from $108/93; @ 🛜) 🅿 This stalwart is older than many of its guests, and it's mellowed comfortably with age. It has a mix of dorms and private rooms, but best of all are the large lounge, with commanding lake and mountain views, and the quiet reading room. The giant topo map in the lounge is great for planning tramps.

Wanaka Kiwi Holiday Park & Motels
HOLIDAY PARK **$**

(📞 03-443 7766; www.wanakakiwiholidaypark.nz; 263 Studholme Rd North; campsites $25-27, units with/without bathroom from $124/80; 🅿🛜) This charming and relaxing campground is tucked under Roys Peak, with grassy terraced sites for tents and campervans, lots of trees and pretty views. Facilities include a barbecue area with heaters, and free unlimited wi-fi, plus spa pool and sauna ($5). Older-style motel units have all been renovated, and the newest budget cabins are warm and cosy with wooden floors. There's a courtesy van for runs into (but not back from) town.

★ Lakeside
APARTMENT **$$$**

(📞 03-443 0188; www.lakesidewanaka.co.nz; 9 Lakeside Rd; apt from $295; 🛜🏊) Luxuriate in a modern apartment in a prime position overlooking the lake, right by the town centre. All 23 apartments have three bedrooms, but can be rented with only one or two bedrooms open. The swimming pool is a relative rarity in these parts, and if you hire ski gear through the website it can be delivered to your door.

★ Kai Whakapai
CAFE **$$**

(📞 03-443 7795; cnr Helwick & Ardmore Sts; mains $19-26; ⏱ 7am-11pm; 🚲) As Wanaka as *that* tree, this local institution is where the town seems to congregate on a sunny evening for a liquid sundowner over excellent pizza or salad. Locally brewed craft beers are on tap and there are Central Otago wines as well.

Francesca's Italian Kitchen
ITALIAN **$$**

(📞 03-443 5599; www.fransitalian.co.nz; 93 Ardmore St; mains $20-32; ⏱ noon-3pm & 5pm-late) Pretty much the matriarch of Wanaka eateries, the perennially busy and cavernous Francesca's has the big flavours and easy conviviality of an authentic Italian family trattoria. Even simple things such as pizza, pasta and polenta chips are exceptional. It also runs a pizza food truck (📞 0800 4647 4992; www.francescaspizzas.com; pizza $10-20; ⏱ 4-9pm) on Brownston St.

Federal Diner
CAFE **$$**

(📞 03-443 5152; www.federaldiner.co.nz; 47 Helwick St; breakfast $10-19, mains $22-40; ⏱ 7am-4pm Mon & Tue, to 9pm Wed-Sun; 🛜) When it's this hidden away and still this popular, you know to expect good things. This cosmopolitan cafe delivers robust breakfasts, excellent coffee, legendary scones, gourmet sandwiches and salads. In the evenings the menu shifts to substantial dishes such as baked gnocchi and slow-roasted lamb shoulder.

★ Kika
TAPAS **$$$**

(📞 03-443 6535; http://kika.nz; 2 Dunmore St; plates $12-55; ⏱ 5.30pm-late) The baby sister to Francesca's has grown up fast, vaulting within just a year of opening to become the only Wanaka eatery named among New Zealand's top 100 restaurants in 2017. It's a Mediterranean mix of modern Italian food, served tapas-style in a casual dining space.

🎒 Supplies & Equipment

MT Outdoors
SPORTS & OUTDOORS

(📞 03-443 2888; www.mtoutdoors.co.nz; 17 Dunmore St; ⏱ 9am-6pm Sep-Jun, 8am-7pm Jul & Aug) Sells camping and tramping gear, and also sells and rents out ski equipment.

New World
SUPERMARKET **$**

(📞 03-443 0048; www.newworld.co.nz; 20 Dunmore St; ⏱ 7am-9pm) Stocks everything you need to self-cater or hit the trails.

Mediterranean Market
SUPERMARKET **$**

(📞 03-443 0118; 20 Ardmore St; ⏱ 8am-6.30pm Mon-Fri, 9am-4pm Sat & Sun) Grab a few of the finer things for your backpack or that picnic stash at this *buono* grocery store.

ℹ Information

Wanaka i-SITE (📞 03-443 1233; www.lakewanaka.co.nz; 103 Ardmore St; ⏱ 8am-7pm summer, to 5pm winter) Extremely helpful but always busy.

ℹ Getting There & Away

Queenstown is Wanaka's main transport link to the outside world, but bus services do range out from here to Dunedin and up the West Coast.

InterCity (📞 03-442 4922; www.intercity.co.nz) Coaches depart from outside the Log Cabin on the lakefront, with daily services to Queenstown (from $17, two hours), Makarora (from $12, 1½ hours) and Franz Josef (from $43, six hours).

Naked Bus (https://nakedbus.com) Services to Queenstown (from $17, two hours) and Franz Josef (from $43, six hours).

Ritchies (☑ 03-443 9120; www.alpinecoach-lines.co.nz) Links Wanaka with Dunedin ($50, four hours), transferring to an InterCity coach at Cromwell.

Ritchies Connectabus Wanaka (☑ 0800 405 066; www.connectabus.com) Heads to/from Queenstown five times daily ($35, two hours) via Queenstown airport. Free wi-fi on board. Call ahead for a hotel pick-up.

Glenorchy

☑ 03 / POP 360

Perhaps best known as the gateway to the Routeburn Track, Glenorchy sits on a rare shelf of flat land at the head of Lake Wakatipu. The small town is a great option if you want to be beside the lake and the mountains but prefer to stay away from the bustle and bluster of Queenstown. The tramping is sensational, and the town is also a base for horse treks, jetboat rides, helicopter flights and skydives.

🛏 Sleeping & Eating

Glenorchy Motel   MOTEL $$
(☑ 0274 368 531; www.glenorchymotels.co.nz; 87 Oban St; r from $150; 🛜) Given the full nip and tuck by new owners in 2017, the eight rooms here have some design savvy, an outdoor hot tub has been added, and there's a wood sauna out the back if you need to thaw some limbs after a day on the trails.

★**EcoScapes**   CABIN $$$
(☑ 03-442 4900; http://ecoscapes.nz; Kinloch Rd, Kinloch; r $395; 🛜) 🅿 Opened in 2017, these twin contemporary cabins are in utter contrast to the historic Kinloch Lodge next door. Built using passive design, they feature blonde woods, ultra-modern furnishings and feel almost like a city apartment plonked into the wilderness. The view from the bed across the lake is better than TV, but if you really must watch something else, the electronic blinds whirr down to become a screen for a data projector with Apple TV and Netflix.

Glenorchy Lake House   B&B $$$
(☑ 03-442 4900; www.glenorchylakehouse.co.nz; Mull St; r $295, house from $495; 🛜) 🅿 The well-named Lake House (it's the closest place in town to the lake) is a boutique B&B attached to the excellent Trading Post cafe. The two guest bedrooms are decked out with Egyptian cotton sheets and flat-screen TVs and there's an outdoor spa in which to soak away the rigours of a day's tramping. Rent the whole house (sleeping up to nine people) and you get the cute attic bedroom.

Queenie's Dumplings   DUMPLINGS $
(☑ 03-442 6070; http://queeniesdumplings.wixsite.com/queeniesdumplings; 27 Mull St; 9 dumplings $13.50, noodle soup $15; ⊙11am-4pm) Where else would you expect to find an authentic little dumpling joint than far-flung, rural Glenorchy? Choose from seven types of dumplings, or a handful of noodle soups.

Glenorchy Cafe   CAFE $$
(GYC; ☑ 03-442 9978; 25 Mull St; mains $12-20; ⊙10am-4.30pm Sun-Fri, to 1.30am Sat) Grab a sunny table out the back of this cute little cottage and tuck into cooked breakfasts, sandwiches and soup. Head inside on Saturday night to partake in pizza and beer underneath the oddball light fixtures.

Glenorchy Hotel   PUB FOOD $$
(☑ 03-409 2049; www.glenorchy-nz.co.nz; 42-50 Mull St; mains $19-32; ⊙8.30am-9pm; 🅿🛜) The front garden of this pub isn't a bad spot for a beer or a filling meal. It also has basic rooms (from $130/95 with/without bathroom) in a separate wing from the bar. It offers free parking while you're out tramping, and self-contained campervans can park up overnight.

🛍 Supplies & Equipment

Mrs Woolly's General Store   SUPERMARKET, CAFE $
(64 Oban St; ⊙10am-5.30pm) Mrs Woolly's has a small gourmet-grocery section that could fuel a few days of tramping – fresh fruit and vegetables, rice, pasta, chocolate, dehydrated hiking meals and handy ziplock bags of muesli. There's a campground (sites $35) out the back (you can even order breakfast and coffee delivered to your tent) and bikes for hire.

❶ Information

Glenorchy Information Centre & Store (☑ 03-409 2049; www.glenorchy-nz.co.nz; 42-50 Mull St; ⊙8.30am-9pm) Attached to the Glenorchy Hotel, this little shop is a good source of weather and track information. Fishing rods and mountain bikes can be hired, and it sells tramping supplies, including gas canisters and a good selection of maps. It also has a bottle shop, bless it.

❶ Getting There & Away

Glenorchy lies at the head of Lake Wakatipu, a scenic 40-minute (46km) drive northwest from Queenstown, winding around bluffs and coves with sweeping views over the lake and its frame of mountains. There are no bus services, but there are trampers' shuttles during the Great Walks season (late October to April). Shuttles pick up from the Glenorchy Hotel, which offers free parking to trampers.

Fiordland & Stewart Island/Rakiura

Best Huts

➡ Luxmore Hut (p286)

➡ Martins Bay Hut (p284)

➡ Okaka Lodge (p292)

➡ Hidden Falls Hut (p281)

Best Views

➡ Mackinnon Pass (p279)

➡ Sutherland Falls (p279)

➡ Mt Luxmore (p286)

➡ Martins Bay (p284)

➡ Trig F (p292)

Why Go?

Fiordland National Park is almost a byword for New Zealand tramping. Here you'll find the track once billed as the 'finest walk in the world' and the greatest representation of Great Walks in the country, with four of them, the Milford, Routeburn (p242), Kepler and Rakiura Tracks, found in Fiordland and Stewart Island.

Milford Sound is the region's headline act, and the Milford Track ends its journey on its shores, having crossed the wild Mackinnon Pass and passed the lofty Sutherland Falls (once erroneously believed to be the world's highest) along the way. The Kepler Track provides a stunning alpine crossing in easy reach of Te Anau, and the Rakiura Track is a remote glimpse into the island south of the South Island.

This is the deep-green deep south, a still-untamed outdoor treasure that's anchored by NZ's largest national park, where the only really feasible way to see beyond the road and the waters of Milford Sound is to set out on foot.

When to Go

In a word, Fiordland is damp: waterfalls, lakes, fiords... and rain. Prevailing winds from the Tasman Sea dump up to 8000mm annually around the park's western parts, although Te Anau, sheltered by mountains, averages just 1200mm. Overall the park averages 200 rainy days annually, with lowland summer temperatures of around 18°C.

Similarly Stewart Island's rainfall has been known to wreak tramping havoc. The annual measure at Halfmoon Bay may be a relatively low 1600mm, but it occurs over 275 days of the year. At higher altitudes and along the south and west coasts, the gauge fills with a snorkel-worthy 5000mm. Considering the latitude, though, the overall climate is surprisingly mild, with reasonable temperatures most of the year.

Background Reading

Tear your eyes from the attention-grabbing mountains and you'll find Fiordland stories dominated by pioneer history – much of it involving isolation, deprivation and occasional insanity. Two books that well illustrate this are *The Land of Doing Without: Davey Gunn of the Hollyford* by Julia Bradshaw, which brings to life the legendary backcountry hero (p280); and *Pioneers of Martins Bay,* which is Alice McKenzie's memoir of growing up in a wild and remote extremity of Fiordland.

DON'T MISS

There's no getting around it: a visit to Fiordland is not complete without a trip to Milford Sound (Piopiotahi). Like the Taj Mahal and Uluru, it's one of those places that lives up to, and even exceeds, the massive expectation. Sheer rocky cliffs rise from still, dark waters, while forests clinging to the slopes sometimes relinquish their hold, causing 'tree avalanches' into the waters. The spectacular, photogenic 1692m-high Mitre Peak rises dead ahead. A postcard will never do it justice and a big downpour will only add to the drama. The average annual rainfall of 7000mm is more than enough to fuel cascading waterfalls and add a shimmering, moody mist to the scene.

A cruise on Milford Sound is Fiordland's most accessible experience, complete with seals and dolphins. These cruises are incredibly popular, and you will encounter busloads of other visitors. But out on the water all this humanity seems tiny compared to nature's vastness. If you do want something a little more intimate, a couple of operators also run kayaking trips on the fiord.

Even without the gobsmacking fiord, the drive here alone is worth the journey, especially if you have your own transport, allowing you to stop at every DOC signpost you see. The 119km Te Anau–Milford Hwy (SH94) is a veritable dot-to-dot of short nature walks and lookout points. DOC's *Fiordland Day Walks* brochure will set you on your way.

DOC Visitor Centres

➡ Fiordland National Park Visitor Centre (p274)

➡ Tuatapere Hump Ridge Track Information Centre (p291)

➡ Rakiura National Park Visitor Centre (p295)

GATEWAY TOWNS

➡ Te Anau (p297)

➡ Invercargill (p298)

➡ Queenstown (p266)

Fast Facts

➡ Fiordland is NZ's largest national park, covering almost 5% of the country. The next-largest national park is less than half the size.

➡ Rudyard Kipling once described Milford Sound as the eighth wonder of the world.

➡ With a population of around 15,000, kiwi outnumber humans on Stewart Island by almost 40 to one.

Top Tip

Dodge the Milford and Kepler Track crowds (and save some cash) by tramping just outside of the Great Walks season – May and early October can be excellent times on the tracks.

Resources

➡ www.fiordland.org.nz

➡ https://southlandnz.com

➡ www.humpridgetrack.co.nz

➡ www.stewartisland.co.nz

FIORDLAND & STEWART ISLAND/RAKIURA

Fiordland & Stewart Island/Rakiura

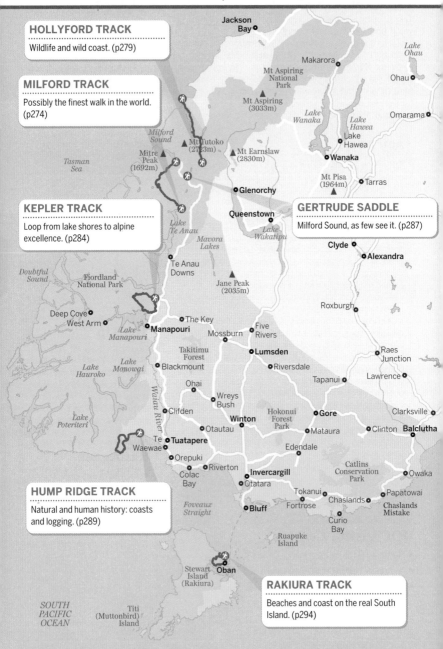

40 km
20 miles

HOLLYFORD TRACK
Wildlife and wild coast. (p279)

MILFORD TRACK
Possibly the finest walk in the world. (p274)

KEPLER TRACK
Loop from lake shores to alpine excellence. (p284)

GERTRUDE SADDLE
Milford Sound, as few see it. (p287)

HUMP RIDGE TRACK
Natural and human history: coasts and logging. (p289)

RAKIURA TRACK
Beaches and coast on the real South Island. (p294)

Jackson Bay

Makarora

Lake Ohau

Ohau

Mt Aspiring National Park

Mt Aspiring (3033m)

Omarama

Lake Wanaka

Lake Hawea

Lake Hawea

Milford Sound

Mt Tutoko (2723m)

Mitre Peak (1692m)

Mt Earnslaw (2830m)

Wanaka

Mt Pisa (1964m)

Tarras

Tasman Sea

Glenorchy

Queenstown

Clyde

Alexandra

Lake Te Anau

Mavora Lakes

Lake Wakatipu

Doubtful Sound

Fiordland National Park

Te Anau Downs

Jane Peak (2035m)

Roxburgh

Deep Cove

West Arm

Lake Manapouri

The Key

Manapouri

Mossburn

Five Rivers

Raes Junction

Lawrence

Takitimu Forest

Lumsden

Lake Hauroko

Lake Monowai

Blackmount

Riversdale

Tapanui

Clarksville

Ohai

Wreys Bush

Hokonui Forest Park

Gore

Clinton

Balclutha

Lake Poteriteri

Clifden

Otautau

Winton

Mataura

Waiau River

Te Waewae

Tuatapere

Edendale

Catlins Conservation Park

Owaka

Orepuki

Riverton

Invercargill

Papatowai

Colac Bay

Otatara

Tokanui

Chaslands

Chaslands Mistake

Foveaux Straight

Bluff

Fortrose

Curio Bay

Ruapuke Island

Stewart Island (Rakiura)

Oban

SOUTH PACIFIC OCEAN

Titi (Muttonbird) Island

FIORDLAND NATIONAL PARK

New Zealand's largest national park is a truly great wilderness, and you don't have to look too hard to see why it buddies up with Egypt's pyramids and the Grand Canyon in the list of Unesco World Heritage sites. It is jagged and mountainous, densely forested and cut through by numerous deeply recessed sounds (technically fiords) that reach inland like crooked fingers from the Tasman Sea.

It remains formidable and remote, with the rugged terrain, rainforest-like bush and abundant waterways having kept progress and people out of much of the park. The fringes of Fiordland are easily visited, but most of the park is impenetrable to all but the hardiest trampers, making it a true wilderness in every sense. The most intimate way to experience Fiordland is unquestionably on foot.

It is not the only way, though, as more than 500,000 annual visitors to Milford Sound (Piopiotahi) can tell you. Of that number – many of whom flock in during the peak months of January and February – some 14,000 arrive at the sound on foot via the Milford Track. This isn't just Fiordland's most famous track; it was once labelled the 'finest walk in the world' by a London newspaper, and the title seems to have stuck like a tattoo. But the rest of Milford Sound's visitors arrive along the 119km Te Anau–Milford Hwy (SH94), an intensely scenic road that passes through the beautiful, sheer-sided Eglinton Valley and crosses the Divide, the lowest east–west pass in the Southern Alps. The Divide is also the start or end point of the Routeburn Track, the tramp many think rivals the Milford as best walk in the country. Prepare to be amazed.

One of the first impressions trampers gain of the park is of the almost overpowering steepness of the mountains, an impression accentuated by the fact that they are usually separated only by narrow valleys. The rocks and peaks of Fiordland are very hard and have eroded slowly, compared to the mountains of Mt Aspiring and Arthur's Pass, which are softer. Gentle topography this is not. It is raw and hardcore all the way.

History

In comparison with other regions, little is known of the pre-European history of the Māori in Fiordland. There is evidence of a permanent settlement at Martins Bay, and possibly of summer villages throughout Fiordland that were used for seasonal hunting expeditions. The most significant archaeological find in the region was made in 1967, when mid-17th-century burial remains were discovered in a cave in Lake Hauroko.

In 1770 Captain Cook worked his way up the west coast in the *Endeavour*, but was unsuccessful in landing: it was too dusky in one instance, and doubtful in another... ergo the names of two of the region's sounds. He returned three years later, bringing the *Resolution* into Dusky Sound, where the crew recuperated after three months at sea. Recorded in his log in 1773 was probably the first written – and very accurate – description of sandflies: 'most mischievous animals...that cause a swelling, and such an intolerable itching, that it is not possible to refrain from scratching'.

In 1792 a 12-strong sealing gang arrived. Left in the sound for 10 months, they reaped a harvest of 4500 skins and constructed one of NZ's first European-style buildings. By 1795 there were 250 settlers in Dusky Sound.

Whaling briefly followed sealing, with the first significant shore-based South Island whaling station built in 1829 at Preservation Inlet. The industries devastated seal and whale populations, but encouraged exploration of the coast. In 1823, Welsh sealing captain John Grono was the first to record sailing into Milford Sound, naming it after his home town of Milford Haven.

Fiordland was explored from the sea until 1852, when a party reached Te Anau from the Waiau Valley. Nine years later two cattle drivers, David McKellar and George Gunn, climbed to the top of Key Summit and became the first Europeans to view the Hollyford Valley. This set off more explorations, resulting in myriad firsts, commemorated in the names of major landmarks.

As usual, it was gold mining that encouraged deeper delving into the wilderness. In 1868 the Otago Provincial Government attempted to stimulate growth by starting a settlement at Martins Bay. Some lots at Jamestown (as it was known) were sold, but the settlers who moved there found life hard and lonely. By 1870 there were only eight houses in Jamestown. Nine years later the settlement was deserted, leaving only a handful of people living at Martins Bay.

A couple of legendary hermits settled in Fiordland around this time, one of whom was Donald Sutherland, a colourful character who sailed single-handedly from Dunedin into Milford Sound in 1877 and became known as the 'Hermit of Milford'. In 1880 Sutherland and John Mackay struggled up the Arthur Valley from Milford Sound in search of precious minerals. The fine waterfall they found was named after Mackay when he won a coin toss for the honour. After several more days of bush-bashing they sighted a magnificent three-leap, 580m-high waterfall, which was equitably named after Sutherland.

After stumbling on to Mackinnon Pass and viewing the Clinton River, the pair returned to Milford Sound, where word soon got out about the mighty Sutherland Falls. Erroneously proclaimed the highest in the world, the falls soon had adventurers lined up to see them. The pressure was on to build a track to the Milford area, and in 1888 Quintin Mackinnon and Ernest Mitchell were commissioned by the government to cut a route along the Clinton River.

At the same time, a survey party from Otago was moving up through the Arthur Valley. Hearing of this development, Mackinnon and Mitchell stopped track-cutting, scrambled over the pass and made their way past the present site of Quintin Hut to meet the party. A rough trail was thus established, a few flimsy huts thrown up, and by the end of the year tourists were already using the route, with Mackinnon as guide. Seeking to exploit this opportunity, the Government Tourist Department began to take over all of the track's facilities in 1901.

Fiordland National Park was officially gazetted in 1952, preserving 10,000 sq km of land and protecting the route to Milford Sound. Fiordland National Park was rounded out to its present size – more than 12,000 sq km – in 1999 when the 22-sq-km Waitutu Forest was added.

Environment

The most important contributors to Fiordland's majestic mountain scenery are the glacial periods of the last ice age. The glaciers shaped the hard granite peaks, gouged the fiords and lakes, and scooped out rounded valleys. Evidence of the ice floes can be found almost everywhere, from the moraine terraces behind Te Anau and in Eglinton's U-shaped valley to the pointed peaks of Milford Sound.

One result of the glaciers is Fiordland's trademark lakes, such as Te Anau. At 66km in length, with 500km of shoreline and a surface area of 342 sq km, it is the largest lake on the South Island and the second-largest in the country.

The sheerness of the mountain walls and fiords (some sea cliffs rise 1.5km out of the water) allow plenty of scope for waterfalls. They can be seen all over the place – cascading, tumbling, roaring or simply dribbling down a green mossy bluff. All this moisture means lush vegetation. On the eastern side, forests of red, silver and mountain beech fill the valleys and cling to the steep faces. In the northern and western coastal sections, impressive podocarp forests of matai, rimu, southern rata and totara can be found.

Much of the forest grows on a surface of rock covered by only a thin layer of rich humus and moss, a natural retainer for the large amounts of rain. It is this peaty carpet that allows thick ground flora to thrive under towering canopies, and sets western Fiordland bush apart from that of the rest of the country.

Fiordland is well known to birdwatchers as the home of the endangered takahe. The birds trampers will probably spot are the usual kereru (NZ pigeons), riflemen, tomtits, fantails, bush robins, tui, bellbirds and kaka. In alpine regions you may see kea and rock wrens.

ⓘ Planning

INFORMATION

DOC's **Fiordland National Park Visitor Centre** (☑ 03-249 7924; www.doc.govt.nz; cnr Lakefront Dr & Te Anau–Manapouri Rd; ☺ 8.30am-4.30pm), located right on the lakeside at Te Anau, is a substantial visitor centre with a small museum and audiovisual theatre. It offers an array of advice, information, books and maps, as well as regional track information, daily weather reports and bookings for various huts and Great Walks.

Milford Track

Duration 4 days

Distance 53.5km (33.2 miles)

Difficulty Moderate

Start Glade Wharf

End Sandfly Point

Gateway Te Anau (p297)

Transport Shuttle bus, boat

Summary New Zealand's most famous track has towering peaks, deep glaciated valleys, rainforests, alpine meadows and spectacular waterfalls.

The Milford Track is popular, but don't let that have you believing that it's overrun. Despite an annual click-rate of more than 7000 independent trampers, things are controlled by a regulation system that, while keeping people moving through in significant volume, still ensures some level of tranquillity.

During the Great Walks season, the track can only be walked in one direction, starting from Glade Wharf. You must stay at Clinton Hut the first night, despite it being only one hour from the start of the track, and you must complete the trip in the prescribed three nights and four days. This is perfectly acceptable if the weather is kind, but if it goes sour you'll still have to push on across the alpine Mackinnon Pass and may miss some rather spectacular views. It's all down to the luck of the weather draw.

During the Great Walk season, the track is also frequented by guided tramping parties, who stay at cosy, private lodges with hot showers and proper food. Unsurprisingly such trips are in hot demand among trampers who want to carry less and eat and drink more.

The reason that everyone is here is obvious. The tramp enters along one gorgeous valley cut by a gin-clear river, climbs to a wild alpine pass and exits out another valley that's a shagpile carpet of moss and greenery, with one of the most spectacular waterfalls in the world pouring down beside it. The fact that you have to share all this with others is barely a detraction. The Milford Track is one of the greatest and most accessible of NZ's wilderness adventures.

ⓘ Planning

WHEN TO TRAMP

The Great Walks season for the Milford Track is late October to the end of April. Outside this period there is limited transport to and from the track, some avalanche-prone bridges are removed and hut facilities are reduced. A winter or spring crossing should only be attempted after careful consideration of weather, track and avalanche conditions by experienced, well-equipped trampers. New Zealanders, inclined to complain about how busy and expensive it is, commonly embark on the Milford Track just before or just after the Great Walks season, when both prices and numbers of trampers drop.

WHAT TO BRING

Pack insect repellent. You will encounter sandflies along most of the trail; depending on the time of year and weather conditions they will range from mildly bothersome to horrible.

The Milford area has one of the highest average rainfalls in NZ, so come with good wet-weather gear packed at the top of your backpack.

The huts have gas cookers, but some trampers still take their own stoves so they can enjoy hot soup for lunch and not wait in the evening until a stove is available. You will also need your own stove in the off-season, when the gas cookers are removed.

MAPS & BROCHURES

The track is covered by NewTopo's 1:38,000 *Milford Track* map and NZTopo50 *CB08 (Homer Saddle)*. DOC's *Milford Track* brochure has a route description and elevation profile.

HUTS

The Milford Track is a Great Walk and between late October and the end of April you'll need to book all three huts – Clinton, Mintaro and Dumpling – to hike the track ($240 for three nights). Each hut has gas cookers, cold running water and heating in the main kitchen/dining hut, plus communal bunk rooms with mattresses. Ablution blocks have flush toilets and washbasins, though in the off-season facilities are reduced to a long-drop toilet and tap only. In season, a DOC ranger is in residence at each hut and is able to pass on information about the environment and weather, or help you should an emergency arise.

Huts must be booked in advance during the Great Walks season, and we can't stress enough that you should book early for this popular track. You must begin the track on the day for which your booking is made, and you must walk the track in the prescribed four days. Bookings can usually be made from May for the following season.

Bookings can be made through **Great Walks Bookings** (☑ 0800 694 732; www.greatwalks.co.nz), or at any DOC visitors centre. If you are alone or in a pair and can wait a few days, there is a slight possibility of spaces becoming available late due to cancellations.

In the off-season there is no requirement to tramp the track with prescribed stops, and the huts revert to Serviced huts ($15). They don't need to be booked outside of the Great Walks season.

Camping is not permitted on the Milford Track.

GUIDED TRAMPS

Ultimate Hikes (☑ 03-450 1940, 0800 659 255; www.ultimatehikes.co.nz; 5-day tramps incl food dm/s/d $2295/3330/5390; ☺ Nov–mid-Apr) is the only operator permitted to run guided tramps of the Milford Track. Its five-day tramp includes comfortable private-lodge accommodation, meals and guided interpretation. The trip is priced from $2130, depending on sleeping configuration, which ranges from shared rooms to en suite single and queen rooms. Trips begin and end in Queenstown. You're best to book early, but it isn't always necessary.

Milford Track

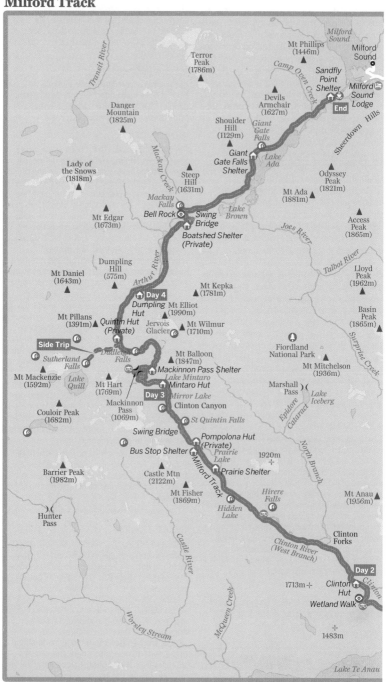

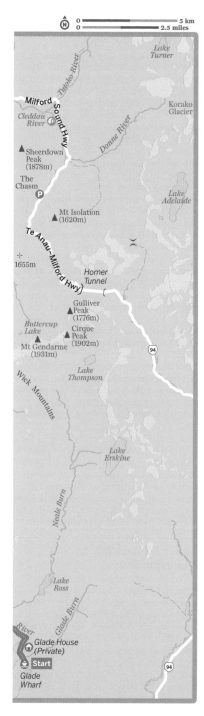

❶ Getting There & Aw

TO THE START

The track starts at Glade Wharf, wh
the head of Lake Te Anau and is acc
scheduled, thrice-daily, 1½-hour boa
Te Anau Downs. Te Anau Downs is 27 ... ..o...
Te Anau on the road to Milford Sound and has a
car-parking area if you wish to leave your vehicle.

Scheduled bus services from Te Anau to Te
Anau Downs ($28), coinciding with boat depar-
tures, are run by **Tracknet** (p244), which offers
a return-trip bus–boat–bus transfer leaving Te
Anau at 9.45am, 12.15pm and 1.30pm. It is based
at Te Anau Lakeview Kiwi Holiday Park & Motels
(p297), where there is secure parking.

Other bus companies with services that pass
through Te Anau Downs on the way to Milford
Sound are InterCity (p298) and Kiwi Discovery
(p244).

The boat service from Te Anau Downs to Glade
Wharf is run by **Real Journeys** (☑ 0800 656
501; www.realjourneys.co.nz; 85 Lakefront Dr;
⊙7.30am-8.30pm Sep-May, 8am-7pm Jun-Aug)
or **Fiordland Outdoors Company** (☑ 0800 347
4538; www.fiordlandoutdoors.co.nz). The Real
Journeys boats leave Te Anau Downs at 10.30am
and 1pm; the Fiordland Outdoors Company boat
departs at 2pm. Both charge $88.

Transport can be booked at the Fiordland
National Park Visitor Centre, or online when you
book your place on the track.

Another way to reach the start of the track from
Te Anau is with **Wings & Water** (☑ 03-249 7405;
www.wingsandwater.co.nz; Lakefront Dr), which
will fly you to Glade Wharf in a floatplane that
holds four passengers plus gear. It costs $828 per
flight from Te Anau, or $552 from Te Anau Downs.

FROM THE END

The Milford Track finishes at Sandfly Point, a
15-minute boat trip from Milford Sound village.
The boat departs at 2pm, 3pm and 4pm and
is usually booked as part of a track transport
package.

From Milford Sound, there are daily bus services to the Divide (the start of the Routeburn
Track; 45 minutes), Te Anau Downs (two hours),
Te Anau (2½ hours) and Queenstown (five
hours). You will be given options to book the
connecting transport online at the same time as
you book your hut tickets.

🥾 The Tramp

Day 1: Glade Wharf to Clinton Hut

1–1½ HOURS / 5KM

The track from Glade Wharf is a wide trail
once used by packhorses to carry supplies to the huts. In 15 minutes it passes

FIORDLAND & STEWART ISLAND/RAKIURA MILFORD TRACK

House, the official start of the Milford Track. The track crosses the **Clinton
River** on a large swing bridge, and continues
along the river's true right (west) side as a
gentle, well-trodden path.

At one point the track offers an impressive view of the peaks next to Dore Pass to
the east, but most of the tramp along the
river is through beech forest. Look out for
the short side track leading to the **wetland
boardwalk** that takes you into a fascinating
sphagnum moss swamp, home to all sorts of
unusual plant life.

Clinton Hut (40 bunks), the first hut for independent trampers, is situated in a clearing
alongside a wetland. The facility is actually
three huts, built after the Clinton Forks Hut
was removed in 1997 after the river threatened
to carry it away. There are now two sleeping
huts with 20 beds each, and a communal dining room, all facing onto a large deck.

Once you've offloaded your packs and had
a refreshing cuppa, stroll down to the river
to catch some sunshine. It's a beautiful spot
to reflect.

Warden talks at this (and every) Milford
Track hut during the Great Walk season are
given at 7.30pm. They include a weather
forecast and track condition update, and
are a great opportunity to ask questions and
share a few yarns.

Day 2: Clinton Hut to Mintaro Hut

5–6 HOURS / 16.5KM
This day is another easy, level walk, until the final two hours, when you climb to Mintaro Hut
– the first step in crossing Mackinnon Pass.

The track continues beside the Clinton
River to **Clinton Forks**. Keep an eye out
for whio (blue ducks) around this stretch of
river. Endemic to NZ, the whio has no close
relatives anywhere in the world. It is in fact
bluish-grey, with a pale pink bill and a red-
dish-brown spotted breast. The males whistle
and the females produce a guttural rattle-like
call. In 2004 a whio recovery program saw
ducklings released back into the wild at the
headwaters of the Clinton River. They are
sometimes seen in the Arthur River too.

Beyond Clinton Forks the track heads up
the **Clinton River West Branch**. A couple
of kilometres past Clinton Forks the track
climbs over debris left from a major land-
slip in 1982. The avalanche blocked the river
and created the lake to the right of the track,
with dead trees emerging from the water.
Wispy waterfalls feather down on both sides

of the valley and a short walk to the left
leads to views of the cascades. **Hirere Falls**
are about 1km further along the track.

About 4km past Clinton Forks the valley
becomes noticeably narrower, with granite
walls closing in on both sides. Mackinnon
Pass, further up the valley, comes into view
for the first time, and a short side track
curves west to **Hidden Lake**, which features
a towering waterfall on its far side.

The track remains in beech forest until
it comes to the prairies, the first grassy flat.
Prairie Lake, at the start of this stretch, is
a good place for a swim, since the water is
marginally warmer than other lakes in the
valley. There are good views from here towards Mt Fisher (1869m) to the west, and
Mackinnon Pass to the northwest. A **shelter**
(with toilet) is at the top end of the prairie
and makes a nice lunch stop.

The track re-enters bush and begins a
rocky climb to **Bus Stop Shelter**, a gloomy
lunch stop 9km from Clinton Forks, and
then to the deluxe Pompolona Hut, the second night's stop for guided trampers.

The track crosses **Pompolona Creek** on
an impressive swing bridge and continues its
course through low scrub. There are many
frame bridges along this stretch, before the
track ascends more steeply as it passes a side
track to **St Quintin Falls**, eventually working
its way to Lake Mintaro and **Mintaro Hut**
(40 bunks), 3.5km from Pompolona Hut.

If the weather is clear you might want to
stash your backpack at the hut and make a
foray to Mackinnon Pass to be assured of seeing the impressive views without obstruction
from clouds or rain. The pass is a 1½- to two-
hour climb from the hut and offers a spectacular view at sunset on clear evenings. If
you're planning to catch a sunset, make sure
you have a powerful head torch (with fresh
batteries) for a safe return to the hut.

Day 3: Mintaro Hut to
Dumpling Hut

6–7 HOURS / 14KM / 490M ASCENT, 970M DESCENT
This is the track's standout day, so allow
plenty of time to enjoy.

The track leaves the hut, swings west with
the valley and resumes its climb to Mackinnon Pass. Crossing the Clinton River for a second time, it follows a series of almost a dozen
switchbacks out of the bush and into alpine
territory. This is a stiff climb at a knee-bending angle, but after 4km the track reaches the
large **memorial cairn** that honours the dis-

covery of this scenic spot by Quintin Mackinnon and Ernest Mitchell in 1888.

The track then levels out and crosses **Mackinnon Pass** (1069m), with impressive views all around the Clinton and Arthur Valleys and several nearby peaks. The two most prominent peaks from the pass are Mt Hart (1769m) and Mt Balloon (1847m). If the weather is fair, you'll want to spend some extra time at the pass; if it isn't, you won't be able to get off it fast enough. The track passes several tarns, ascends to the highest point of the tramp at 1154m, and reaches **Mackinnon Pass Shelter** – a good place for a restorative break on cold days – before swinging north for the descent.

From the pass to Dumpling Hut the track drops 870m in 7km. Soon after leaving the pass, it arrives at **Roaring Burn**, crosses it and re-enters the bush. This stream, with its many beautiful waterfalls and rapids, is an impressive sight, but the long series of wooden and pierced-metal stairways and lookout platforms that trips down the valley beside it is almost as eye-catching. There are fine views of **Dudleigh Falls** on Roaring Burn shortly before Quintin Hut. Quintin is actually a series of lodge buildings for guided trampers, but there's also a day-use shelter for independent trampers. Nearby is historic **Beech Hut**, a reconstruction of a primitive hut from the early days of the Milford Track.

The awesome **Sutherland Falls** can be reached from Quintin Hut shelter, where you can leave your pack before following the spur track. It's well worth making the 1½-hour return trip. Dropping a total of 580m in three spectacular leaps, this is one of the loftiest waterfalls in the world.

The Milford Track leaves Quintin Hut and descends **Gentle Annie Hill**, re-entering thick forest, which is often slippery and wet underfoot. Within 3km (one hour) of Quintin Hut, the track arrives at **Dumpling Hut** (40 bunks), a welcome sight after a long day over the pass.

Day 4: Dumpling Hut to Sandfly Point

5½–6 HOURS / 18KM

The track descends back into bush and soon the roar of Arthur River is heard as the trail closely follows the true right (east) bank. About two hours (6km) from the hut, the track reaches the private Boatshed Shelter (a morning-tea stop for guided trampers) and crosses Arthur River on a large swing bridge.

Just beyond the bridge the track crosses another bridge over Mackay Creek, and comes to a very short side track to **Mackay Falls** and **Bell Rock**. This is your cue to lift the weight off your back for a bit while you take a gander at these amazing natural wonders. It's well worth the scramble into the tiny cave under Bell Rock, where the water has eroded a space large enough to stand in.

The track begins to climb a rock shoulder of the valley, laboriously cut with pickaxes about a century ago, above **Lake Ada**. At one point there is a view of the lake all the way to Joes Valley. From here the track descends to **Giant Gate Falls**, passing them on a swing bridge before continuing along the lakeshore. The shelter just before Giant Gate Falls is a popular lunch stop.

It takes about one hour to follow the lake past Doughboy Shelter (a private hut for guided trampers) through wide, open flats at the end of the valley to the Sandfly Point Shelter, the end of the tramp.

Hollyford Track

Duration 5 days

Distance 56.8km (35.3 miles)

Difficulty Moderate

Start Lower Hollyford Rd

End Martins Bay

Gateway Te Anau (p297)

Transport Shuttle bus, plane, jetboat

Summary This low-level tramp to isolated and historic Martins Bay has no alpine crossings but some excellent mountain scenery and the chance to see Fiordland-crested penguins/tawaki and one of NZ's largest seal colonies.

The Hollyford is the longest valley in Fiordland National Park, stretching 80km from the Darran Mountains to remote Martins Bay. The upper portions of the valley are accessible on Lower Hollyford Rd, which extends 18km from near the Divide on the Te Anau–Milford Hwy to the start of the track.

It's a track that rewards with lush rainforest, extensive bird life and distinctive marine fauna at Martins Bay. The track averages about 4000 trampers a year – taking in both guided parties and independent trampers – which is far less than the numbers using the Routeburn or Milford Tracks.

One reason the Hollyford will always lag behind its two famous counterparts is its length. The track is basically a one-way tramp, unless you continue from Martins Bay on the Pyke-Big Bay Route. This challenging and strenuous route loops from Martins Bay along the coast to Big Bay, heads inland to Pyke River, and then goes down the shore of Lake Alabaster to return to the Hollyford at Lake Alabaster Hut. A strong, experienced tramper could cover the walk from Martins Bay to Lake Alabaster along this route in three days, with nights spent at Big Bay and Olivine Huts. The second day, however, would be a nine- to 12-hour tramp. Contact DOC's Fiordland National Park Visitor Centre (p274) if you want to investigate this possibility.

The majority of trampers turn tail at Martins Bay and retrace their steps to Lower Hollyford Rd, or arrange to be flown out. If possible, allow an extra day by the bay. It offers superb coastal scenery and saltwater fishing, as well as good views of a seal colony and Fiordland-crested penguins/tawaki. But be prepared for the attentions of the even more prolific sandflies and mosquitoes – they will quickly introduce themselves.

ℹ️ Planning

WHEN TO TRAMP

The Hollyford is Fiordland's only major low-level track and can be tramped year-round. Summer is the most popular season.

WHAT TO BRING

Pack a stove and fuel; there are no stoves in the huts along the track.

MAPS & BROCHURES

The best maps for this tramp are NZTopo50 CB09 (Hollyford), CA09 (Alabaster) and CA08 (Milford Sound). DOC produces a Hollyford Track brochure that includes route descriptions and an elevation profile.

HUTS & CAMPING

Six DOC huts line the track. Hidden Falls, Lake Alabaster, Demon Trail, Hokuri and Martins Bay are Serviced huts ($15), with mattresses, heating, water and toilet facilities. McKerrow Island is a Standard hut ($5). Camping ($5) is permitted next to the huts, although the sandflies will prevent this from being even remotely enjoyable.

Bookings aren't required for the huts, but hut passes should be obtained from a DOC office before you set out.

To reach the trailhead, trampers will pass **Gunn's Camp** (www.gunnscamp.org.nz; Hollyford Rd; unpowered tent/campervan sites per person from $15, cabins $70, bed linen extra $7.50), a good place to head out from, especially if you've just completed the Milford or Routeburn Tracks. A small store stocks tramping food, but the highlight of the camp is undoubtedly the small museum dedicated to Davey Gunn and the history of the valley.

THE LAND OF DOING WITHOUT

Davey Gunn is one of the great legends of the NZ wilderness. The son of a shepherd, he was born in 1887 in Waimate, Canterbury. Gunn was a chip off the old block from the get-go, working as a stock agent and farmer, and then in 1926 buying the McKenzie family farm in remote Martins Bay. He eventually held the lease for more than 25,000 acres in the Hollyford Valley.

It was here that legend was born, as Gunn became the ultimate bushman. From his base at Deadmans Hut on the banks of the Hollyford River, Gunn lived on the sniff of an oily rag, calling the Hollyford 'The Land of Doing Without'. He set to improving the stock-driving track to facilitate his annual four-month-long, 175-mile cattle drive to the Invercargill saleyard. Talk about a hard row to hoe! It's not surprising then that Gunn looked for alternative sources of income.

Having constructed huts through the valley, he gradually went from running cattle to guiding tourists, beginning in 1936. This was to be the year of Gunn's greatest achievement: the emergency dash he undertook to get help for victims of an aircraft crash in Big Bay. Gunn tramped from Big Bay to Lake McKerrow, rowed up the lake and then rode his horse more than 40km to a construction camp, where he telephoned for help. The trip would take an experienced tramper three days – Gunn did it in 21 hours. And that's how you become a legend.

After slipping over a bluff in 1950, at the age of 63, Gunn began to lose much of his strength and vigour. On Christmas Day in 1955, as he was attempting to cross the Hollyford River with a 12-year-old boy in the saddle behind him, his horse stumbled and fell. Both Gunn and the boy were swept to their deaths; Gunn's body was never found.

GUIDED TRAMPS

The Ngāi Tahu–owned **Hollyford Track** (☏ 03-442 3000; www.hollyfordtrack.com; adult/child from $1895/1495; ☉ late Oct-late Apr) runs three-day guided trips ($1895 to $2095) on the track, staying at private huts/lodges. The journey is shortened with a jetboat trip down the river and Lake McKerrow on Day 2, and it ends with a scenic flight to Milford Sound.

ℹ Getting There & Away

Tracknet buses (p244) run to the trailhead on Lower Hollyford Rd on Monday, Wednesday and Friday, departing Queenstown at 6.55am and Te Anau at 11am. From October to April, **Trips & Tramps** (☏ 03-249 7081, 0800 305 807; www.tripsandtramps.com) offers a couple of transport packages for the track. You can travel by bus from Te Anau to Milford Sound, from where you fly to Martins Bay. You'll then be picked up by bus when you finish at Lower Hollyford Rd and returned to Te Anau ($305). If you have your own car, you can park at Lower Hollyford Rd, walk the track and be flown out from Martins Bay to Milford Sound, with bus transport back to your car ($245). Gunn's Camp (p280) can also transport you from the camp to the trailhead ($30 for up to four people), with car parking available ($2 a day).

If you want to simply fly in or out, **Fly Fiordland** (☏ 0800 359 346; www.flyfiordland.com; 52 Town Centre; up to 4 passengers $620) wings it to Martins Bay from Milford Sound for $185 per person, or you can fly out from Martins Bay to Glenorchy ($620 for up to four passengers) or Gunn's Camp ($750).

Hollyford Track (p281) also runs a jetboat along Lake McKerrow, between the Pyke confluence near McKerrow Island Hut and Martins Bay ($130), that's available to independent trampers. The boat runs every second day from October to April. It saves a day and eliminates walking the Demon Trail, by far the most arduous portion of the track. This service must be booked in advance.

🚶 The Tramp

Day 1: Lower Hollyford Road to Hidden Falls Hut

2–3 HOURS / 9KM

After floods washed out a road bridge in 1994, the Hollyford became 1km longer and it now begins at a swing bridge over Humboldt Creek. Within 1km, the track sidles along a rock bluff on a raised boardwalk that clings to the bluff's face and then descends to cross a swing bridge over Eel Creek.

Less than one hour from the car park you reach a bridge over Swamp Creek. The force of the 1994 floods is clearly seen here, with one side of the stream completely cleared of bush and trees.

The track remains level and dry, skirting Swamp Creek for a spell before emerging at the banks of the Hollyford River for the first time. At this point the track closely follows the true right (east) bank of the river and offers an occasional view of the snow-capped Darran Mountains to the west. It's about 4.5km from Swamp Creek to a point where the track emerges onto the open flat of Hidden Falls Creek, quickly passing a signposted junction to Sunshine Hut, a private shelter for guided trampers.

Just beyond the hut, a side track leads to Hidden Falls, two minutes upstream from the swing bridge. The waterfall is stunning and aptly named, as a rock cleft partially blocks the view. You can boulder hop along the stream to get a better view of the cascade.

Hidden Falls Hut (12 bunks) is 15 to 20 minutes away, on the northern side of the swing bridge, along the edge of a large river flat. There is a fine view of Mt Madeline (2536m) to the west.

Day 2: Hidden Falls Hut to Lake Alabaster Hut

3–4 HOURS / 10.5KM

The track departs from behind the hut and passes through a forest of ribbonwood and podocarps for 2km before beginning its climb to Little Homer Saddle (168m). It's about a 30- to 45-minute climb through beech forest to reach the saddle. The march up is steady but not steep, and along the way there are views through the trees of Mt Madeline and Mt Tutoko (2723m) – Fiordland's highest mountain and one of NZ's most inaccessible peaks – to the west.

The descent is noticeably steeper than the climb, and it includes a short series of switchbacks before finally reaching a swing bridge across Homer Creek. From the middle of this bridge you get a good view of Little Homer Falls thundering 60m into a pool in the stream. The track remains level until, after around 30 minutes, it swings back to the Hollyford and crosses a swing bridge over Rainbow Creek.

The track stays with the Hollyford for 2km before it meets the Pyke River. You never really see the confluence of the rivers, but you'll know you've reached the Pyke when the water

FIORDLAND & STEWART ISLAND/RAKIURA HOLLYFORD TRACK

Hollyford Track (South)

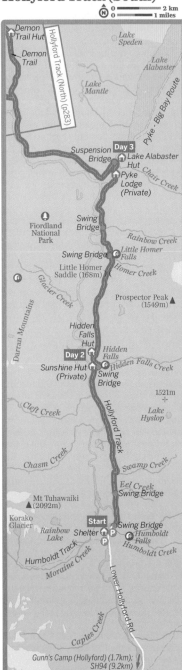

flows in the opposite direction to the Hollyford. The track passes Pyke Lodge, which serves as accommodation for guided trampers. After crossing **Chair Creek** you come to a suspension bridge over the Pyke River.

If you're planning to stop at **Lake Alabaster Hut** (26 bunks) for the night, skip the Pyke bridge and continue up the true left (east) side of the river for 20 minutes to the hut. It's on the shore of scenic **Lake Alabaster**, where a skinny dip could be had if you move like lightning to outwit the sandflies – watch where you get those bites! The track continuing northeast along the shore of Lake Alabaster is part of the Pyke-Big Bay Route.

Day 3: Lake Alabaster Hut to McKerrow Island Hut

3–4 HOURS / 10.5KM

Backtrack for 20 minutes to the suspension bridge over Pyke River and, after crossing it, continue beneath the rocky bluffs along the lower section of the river. Here the track enters a lush podocarp forest and all sights and sounds of the two great rivers are lost in the thick canopy of trees. The stretch of track from Pyke Bridge to the south end of Lake McKerrow can be rough, uneven and very muddy at times of wet weather.

The track works its way through the bush for two hours before breaking out into a clearing next to Hollyford River, now twice as powerful as it was above the Pyke River junction.

Before reaching **Lake McKerrow** the river swings west around **McKerrow Island**; another channel (usually dry) rounds the island to the east. Near the dry river bed there is a sign pointing up the main track to **Demon Trail Hut**. This is also the start of a marked route across the eastern channel to a track on McKerrow Island. Follow this track around the northern side of the island to reach **McKerrow Island Hut** (12 bunks), pleasantly situated near the mouth of the main channel and partially hidden by bush.

If there's been heavy rain it may be impossible to cross the eastern river bed, in which case you can continue on the Demon Trail, and in about 1½ hours reach Demon Trail Hut (12 bunks). If you're at McKerrow Island Hut when it rains, there's little you can do but wait until the channel can be safely forded.

The mouth of the main channel is popular for trout fishing, although in recent years the growing seal colony at Martins Bay has been venturing further and further into Lake McKerrow to feast on trout, much to the dismay of anglers. Seals have even been spotted as far inland as Pyke Lodge.

Day 4: McKerrow Island Hut to Hokuri Hut

6½–7½ HOURS / 13.8KM

From the signpost back on the main track it's a 20-minute tramp to the start of the **Demon Trail**, which begins in a clearing that was once a hut site. This leg used to have a reputation as one of the most exhausting nonalpine tracks in NZ, and though it's been upgraded in recent years it is still demanding, especially in the wet. Spare a thought for the Martins Bay settlers who built it in the 1880s as a cattle track – if they hadn't, it's likely the Hollyford Track wouldn't exist.

It's 3km (one hour) from the start of the trail to **Demon Trail Hut**, which sits in a pleasant spot overlooking Lake McKerrow.

At **Slip Creek**, considered the halfway point for the day, a nearby rock bivvy will shelter six people in inclement weather. But most trampers try to cover the section from McKerrow Island to Hokuri Hut as quickly as possible. **Hokuri Hut** (12 bunks) is on the shore of Lake McKerrow at Gravel Cove and was rebuilt in 2005.

Day 5: Hokuri Hut to Martins Bay

4–5 HOURS / 13KM

It's about a 10-minute walk beyond the hut to **Hokuri Creek**, which can usually be forded near its mouth on Gravel Cove; if it can't be crossed here, there is a three-wire bridge 20 minutes upstream. From the other side of the creek begins one of the most scenic stretches of the tramp, following the gravel lakeshore for almost two hours, providing views of the lake and the surrounding mountains on a clear day.

The track dips into a small bay, where a sign announces a short spur track leading to the site of the historic township of **Jamestown**. A plaque marks the spot, but all that remains of the settlement are apple trees planted by the early settlers.

Less than one hour from Jamestown you reach a signposted turn-off, where the track leaves the lake for good and heads inland. Here the track cuts through a lush podocarp forest with many impressive kahikatea trees. About 3km (one hour) from the lakeshore you break out into the grassy clearing of the **Hollyford Valley airstrip**. A sign points to

Hollyford Track (North)

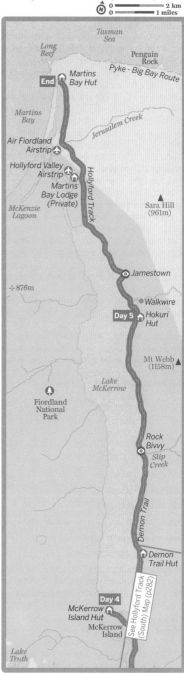

Martins Bay Lodge, which provides accommodation for guided walkers, while poles lead across the clearing and around one end of the airstrip. The track re-enters the bush of tall tutu and scrub and, just before emerging at Jerusalem Creek, passes a signposted junction to the Air Fiordland airstrip.

After the Jerusalem Creek ford (normally easy) the track continues through forest and climbs a bluff. Within 45 minutes you pass a sign for the Lower Hollyford boat launch, and just beyond that the track breaks out to a view of the river near its mouth. Martins Bay Hut (24 bunks) is a few minutes up the track (2½ hours from the shoreline of Lake McKerrow), overlooking the river mouth. This hut is an excellent place to while away an extra day, viewing the seal colony or looking for Fiordland-crested penguins/tawaki.

The seals use the large boulders of Long Reef for basking during the day. It's a 30-minute walk from the hut, beginning with a track that skirts the bluffs around the mouth of the river. After passing a sign for the Pyke-Big Bay Route, the track breaks out at the rocky shore. Boulder hop across the shore towards Long Reef seal colony, which is one of the largest in NZ. There are usually seals on both sides of the point. They are used to trampers, but do not approach too closely; adults will chase you away from their pups and it's amazing how fast they can move across the rocks. There is fascinating rock-pool examination to be had here, too.

An old cattle track continues north then east of Long Reef; this is the track to Big Bay and the circular route to Lake Alabaster.

Kepler Track

Duration 4 days

Distance 60.1km (37.3 miles)

Difficulty Moderate

Start/End Lake Te Anau control gates

Gateway Te Anau (p297)

Transport Shuttle bus, boat

Summary Built in 1988 to reduce the pressure on the Milford and Routeburn Tracks, this tramp rivals both for alpine scenery.

The Kepler Track was first conceived in 1986 and opened in 1988, during NZ's centennial celebration of its national park system. It's one of the best-planned tracks in NZ: a loop beginning and ending near the control gates where the Waiau River empties into the southern end of Lake Te Anau. DOC staff can actually show you the start of the track from a window inside the Fiordland National Park Visitor Centre.

Like the Routeburn, the Kepler is an alpine crossing and includes an all-day tramp across the tops, taking in incredible panoramas of Lake Te Anau, its South Fiord arm, the Jackson Peaks and the Kepler Mountains. Along the way it traverses rocky ridges, tussock lands and peaceful beech forest. It's quickly apparent why the Kepler has become one of the most popular tracks in NZ.

The route can be covered in four days, spending a night at each of the three huts. It is also possible to reduce the tramp to three days by continuing past Moturau Hut and leaving the track at Rainbow Reach swing bridge. However, spending a night at Moturau Hut on the shore of Lake Manapouri is an ideal way to end this tramp. The track can be walked in either direction, although the most popular is the anticlockwise option we've described.

ℹ Planning

WHEN TO TRAMP

The Great Walks season is from late October to the end of April. The track can be walked out of season, but should only be attempted by experienced and well-equipped trampers. There are nine avalanche paths along the track that can pose a risk in the winter season.

WHAT TO BRING

If hiking outside of the Great Walks season, note that the gas cookers are removed from the huts, so you'll need to carry your own stove and fuel.

MAPS & BROCHURES

The 1:60,000 Parkmap *335-09 (Kepler Track)* is sufficient for this track. NewTopo's 1:55,000 *Kepler Track* map also covers the hike in its entirety.

HUTS & CAMPING

The Kepler Track is a Great Walk and between late October and the end of April you need to book your space in advance in the three DOC huts (NZ local/foreigner $65/130 per night) – Luxmore, Iris Burn and Moturau. Each hut has gas cookers, cold running water and heating in the main kitchen/dining hut, plus communal bunk rooms with mattresses. Ablution blocks have flush toilets and washbasins. In season a DOC ranger is in residence at each hut and is able to relay information about the environment and weather, or help you should an emergency arise.

It pays to book early. Bookings for the following season usually open between February and May. Hut bookings can be made through Great Walks Bookings (p275), or at any DOC visitors centre.

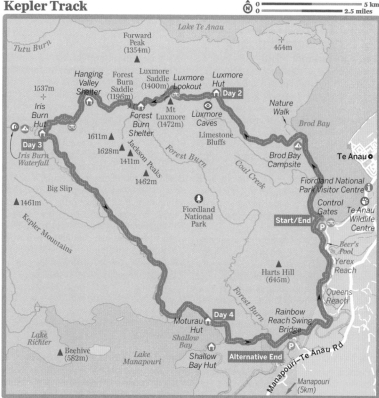

At Brod Bay and near Iris Burn Hut you will find Serviced campsites (NZ local/foreigner $20/40) with cooking shelters.

In the off-season, the huts revert to backcountry Serviced huts ($15), with facilities reduced to a long-drop toilet and limited water supplies (sometimes you may need to melt snow or obtain water from a nearby stream).

ⓘ Getting There & Away

The start of the track is 4km (a one-hour walk) from the DOC Fiordland National Park Visitor Centre (p274) along the Lakeside Track. This track skirts the southern end of Lake Te Anau and passes through the interesting Te Anau Wildlife Centre before reaching the control gates, where the Kepler Track begins.

If you are driving to the track, follow Manapouri–Te Anau Rd (SH95) south from the park visitor centre and take the first right turn, which is clearly marked by a yellow AA sign. Continue past the golf course and take another right-hand turn to a car park.

Tracknet (p244) operates the Kepler Track Shuttle from Te Anau Lakeview Kiwi Holiday Park & Motels (p297), where there is secure parking. It also does free pick-up and drop-off to/from all accommodation places in Te Anau. During the Great Walks season the shuttle departs for the control gates ($8) at 8.30am, 9.30am, 11.10am and 2.30pm, and picks up from the Rainbow Reach swing bridge ($14) at 10am, 3pm, 4pm and 5pm, stopping at the control gates 10 minutes later if you've completed the full circuit. Booked together, the return service is $18.

Topline Tours (☑ 03-249 8059; www.topline-tours.co.nz; 32 Caswell Rd) also runs a bus to the Kepler, departing Te Anau at 9am for the control gates ($5), and from the park visitor centre at 10.30am and 2.15pm for the swing bridge ($8). It returns from the swing bridge to Te Anau ($8) at 11am, 2.30pm and 4.30pm. Its services run on demand only in the off-season ($10 each trip).

Kepler Water Taxi (☑ 027 249 8365, 03-249 8364; www.keplerwatertaxi.co.nz; one way $25) offers a boat service across Lake Te Anau to Brod Bay ($25), slicing 1½ hours off the first day's tramp. The service runs daily at 8.30am and 9.30am.

🥾 The Tramp

Day 1: Lake Te Anau Control Gates to Luxmore Hut

5–6 HOURS / 13.8KM / 880M ASCENT

The track begins by skirting the lake to Dock Bay, following the fringe of a beech forest. Within 30 minutes it begins to wind through an impressive growth of tree ferns, with crown ferns carpeting the forest floor. The track continues to skirt the lake's western shore and crosses a footbridge over Coal Creek.

After a further 3km the track crosses another stream and arrives at Brod Bay, a beautiful sandy beach on the lake. There are toilets, a table and a barbecue here, and for those who started late and have a tent it's a scenic campsite.

The track to Mt Luxmore is signposted near the beach and you now begin the steepest climb of the tramp. The track ascends steadily and in 3km (two hours) reaches a set of towering limestone bluffs, an ideal lunch spot. At the bluffs the track swings due west, skirts the rock, then turns north and resumes climbing through stunted mountain beech.

Within 1km the track breaks out of the bush and you get the tramp's first glorious panorama, of Lake Te Anau, Lake Manapouri and the Takitimu, Snowdon and Earl Mountains. The track climbs a couple of small rises, and within one hour of leaving the bush skirts a small bluff. On the other side, at a commanding elevation of 1085m, is Luxmore Hut (55 bunks), with its namesake peak behind it. This hut, like all huts on the track, was built in 1987 and then quickly enlarged. It now features two levels and has great views from the common room. The warden receives a weather report every morning at around 8.30am.

Mt Luxmore (1472m) can be easily climbed without backpacks (two to three hours return), although you can also save this mission for the following day and instead venture out to Luxmore Caves. The short track leads to one of about 30 caves in the area, where you can step inside and, with the aid of a torch, view stalactites and stalagmites.

Day 2: Luxmore Hut to Iris Burn Hut

5–6 HOURS / 14.6KM / 590M DESCENT

Wait for the weather report from the warden in the morning to be sure of good conditions for the alpine crossing. Carry plenty of water as there are no streams along the way.

The track climbs the ridge towards the unnamed peak east of Mt Luxmore, but ends up sidling along its northern slopes, with Mt Luxmore looming overhead. Around 3km from the hut the track swings north.

For those interested in climbing to the summit of Mt Luxmore, easily distinguished by its large trig, it's best to follow the track to Luxmore Saddle (1400m) and drop your backpacks. From here it's an easy 15- to 20-minute climb along a rocky ridge to the top. If the weather is clear, the view is perhaps the finest of the tramp – a 360-degree panorama that includes the Darran Mountains, 70km to the north.

After crossing the ridge to the north of Mt Luxmore, the track skirts a bluff on steep-sided slopes for 3km, until it reaches a high point on the ridge beyond Luxmore Saddle. Here, the track swings away from the ridge and sidles along the slopes before descending to Forest Burn Shelter. This is close to Forest Burn Saddle, which is reached two hours from Luxmore Hut. Beware of strong wind gusts when crossing the saddle.

From the shelter the track skirts the bluffed end of a ridge, with great views of Lake Te Anau's South Fiord. About 3.5km from the shelter, the track rounds the bluffs onto a ridge crest and the tramp becomes considerably easier.

Follow the ridge, skirt two knobs and then climb another one. Once on this high point you can see Hanging Valley Shelter. The shelter sits on a ridge at 1390m and is usually reached two hours from Forest Burn Shelter. The views are great, so spend some extra time here if your day allows. It takes most trampers less than two hours to reach Iris Burn Hut from here, and because most of the tramp is through bush, this view is much more inspiring than anything else to come this day.

The track leaves the shelter and follows a ridge to the south for 2km. The ridge crest is sharp, and at times you feel as though you're on a tightrope. Eventually the track drops off the ridge with a sharp turn to the west and descends into the bush. The descent is a quick one, down a seemingly endless series of switchbacks, and the track drops 390m before crossing a branch of Iris Burn.

The track levels out as it skirts the side of this hanging valley, at one point becoming a boardwalk across the steep face. The views of Iris Burn are excellent, and there's even a seat, so lean back and take it all in.

The final segment of the day is over more switchbacks, with the track dropping 450m. Just when it levels out, Iris Burn Hut (50 bunks) comes into view – a welcome sight.

For a pleasant evening walk, head up the valley for 20 minutes to view the impressive Iris Burn waterfall.

Day 3: Iris Burn Hut to Moturau Hut

5–6 HOURS / 16.2KM

The main track begins behind the hut with a short climb, before levelling out in beech forest. Within 3km it crosses a branch of the Iris Burn and breaks out into a wide, open area. Evidence of the cause of this clearing – a huge 1984 landslide called the Big Slip – is to your right, where piles of rocks, now covered in regenerating vegetation, and fallen trees can be seen everywhere. The track returns to the bush across the clearing and continues down the valley, at times following the river.

The track crosses several branches of Iris Burn, and remains almost entirely in the bush (one section is through an incredibly moss-laden stand of trees) until it reaches a rocky clearing called Rocky Point, where some of the boulders are bright orange (the result of a healthy growth of red algae). At this point, 11km from Iris Burn Hut, the track climbs over Heartbreak Hill.

Having passed a view of Lake Manapouri at the mouth of Iris Burn, the track swings east, and in 1km comes within sight of the lake again. On its final leg the track skirts the shore of Shallow Bay until it arrives at Moturau Hut (40 bunks). This is a pleasant hut with a view of Lake Manapouri from the kitchen.

Day 4: Moturau Hut to Lake Te Anau Control Gates

4½–5 HOURS / 15.5KM

For the first 2km, the track heads southeast through bush until it reaches a junction with a short track to Shallow Bay Hut (six bunks). The main track heads east (left fork) and within 1km comes to a wetland known as Amoeboid Mire. This wetland is crossed on a boardwalk, which includes a viewing platform. After skirting the southern side of the grassy swamp, the track reaches an old river terrace that overlooks Balloon Loop, which is 5km from Moturau Hut.

A swing bridge crosses Forest Burn, which meanders confusingly before emptying into Balloon Loop. From here it's 30 minutes along the river terrace to the swing bridge at Rainbow Reach, 1½ hours from the hut. There is an option to leave the track here, and catch a shuttle back to Te Anau.

It's three hours (11km) from Rainbow Reach to the control gates, with the track continuing in an easterly direction. Within one hour it swings due north to pass Queens Reach, climbing onto a river terrace. There are views through the trees of a set of rapids, before the track moves into an area of manuka scrub. At Yerex Reach, two hours from the Rainbow Reach swing bridge, the track passes a few old posts and a quiet segment of the river known as Beer's Pool. At this point you're only 30 to 45 minutes from the control gates.

Gertrude Saddle

Duration 4–6 hours

Distance 7km (4.3 miles)

Difficulty Demanding

Start/End Te Anau–Milford Hwy

Gateway Te Anau (p297)

Transport Private

Summary A challenging but highly rewarding climb to a vertiginous mountain pass with stunning views into Milford Sound.

There are many ways to view Milford Sound, but few include the solitude and sense of achievement that comes with standing atop Gertrude Saddle after a tough climb from the Gertrude Valley. This route in the Darran Mountains, held by climbers to be the most rugged and difficult range in NZ, provides a high sense of mountain drama, heading up beside an alpine lake to a pass that falls away 800m into the Gulliver Valley, which drains away into Milford Sound.

The tramp follows a marked track through the Gertrude Valley, but the unmarked ascent to the saddle from the valley's head is challenging, scrambly and tricky. It pushes through bouldery terrain, with a couple of chain-assisted sections, so should only be attempted by experienced and confident trampers. If you're feeling uncertain, the tramp through just the valley to the base of the climb will itself provide plenty of memorable mountain scenes.

FIORDLAND & STEWART ISLAND/RAKIURA GERTRUDE SADDLE

Gertrude Saddle

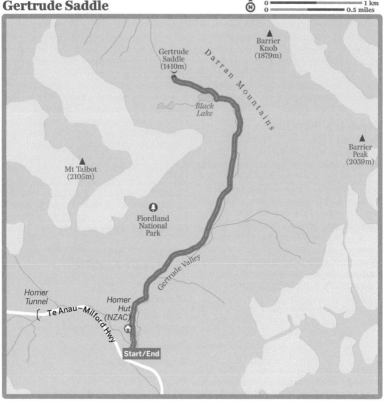

ℹ Planning

WHEN TO TRAMP

Summer and autumn are the best times to tramp to Gertrude Saddle. The steep walls of the U-shaped Gertrude Valley are prone to avalanches in winter and spring – there are six avalanche paths along the valley route – while the climb to the saddle is likely to be covered in snow and ice until well into spring, putting it out of condition as a tramping route. There are some steep rock slabs on the climb that can be treacherous when wet, so avoid rainy days – alas, a common sort of day here.

It's worth checking the condition of the route at any time with the Fiordland National Park Visitor Centre (p274).

MAPS & BROCHURES

The route is covered by the NZTopo50 CB09 (Hollyford) map, though it's also worth carrying CB08 (Homer Saddle) if you want a perspective on the view from the saddle. DOC's Fiordland

Day Walks brochure contains details of more than 30 day walks in the national park, including Gertrude Saddle.

HUTS & CAMPING

Just 200m from the trailhead is the New Zealand Alpine Club's Homer Hut (members/non-members \$20/35), which has 30 bunks, gas stoves and solar lighting. Only members can camp (\$15 per person) beside the hut, where there's space for six tents. Payment can be made to the hut warden.

There are also nine DOC campsites (\$13/6.50 per adult/child) along the Te Anau–Milford Hwy through the Eglinton Valley. All are scenic, but popular with sandflies.

INFORMATION

The only reliable source for current information on the Gertrude Saddle tramp is the Fiordland National Park Visitor Centre (p274), which has the bonus of a natural history display, and a shop stocking tramping supplies and topographic maps. Be sure to check in here about track and weather conditions, whatever the season.

ℹ Getting There & Away

The trailhead is 98km from Te Anau along the Te Anau–Milford Hwy, just 2km before the Homer Tunnel. Fleets of tourist buses roll along the highway to Milford Sound every morning from Te Anau and Queenstown, returning in the afternoon. You may be able to arrange for one to drop you off at the trail, but you'll also need to carefully time your finish to coincide with the bus's return.

🥾 The Tramp

From the car park you'll be looking straight up the Gertrude Valley to the imposing wall of Barrier Peak – the saddle is tucked away in an unseen gap to the left of the wall, behind Mt Talbot, which rises directly along the left side of the valley.

Cross the stream bed (usually dry), where the track begins, passing **Homer Hut** to the left and heading up the valley. The stony trail follows the true right bank up the valley, skirts a stand of beech forest and crosses the bouldery stream bed. On the opposite bank it briefly cuts through forest, thick with moss, before emerging back into the open and continuing up the valley. The track here stays close to the stream bed, and sometimes is in it, following orange-tipped poles.

As the track nears the head of the valley with its enormous wall of rock, it swings left, turning towards the obvious notch that will be your path up to the saddle. Here, one hour from the car park, the poled route ends and a faint track continues, heading up to the left of the waterfall face (look for the cairns), beginning the 500m ascent to the saddle.

The route crosses the first braid of the falls then continues ascending a small ridge pinched between streams. After 15 minutes you'll come to a large rock wall, where the track swings right, crossing the main stream. Gertrude Saddle now becomes prominent above, with the track leading up to the shores of **Black Lake** and then directly up to the saddle. There are chains to assist on the ascent immediately below the lake and on the first bit of the climb just after it. It's fractured, bouldery terrain, requiring careful steps.

As you rise to **Gertrude Saddle** (1410m), shaped a little like a sagging rope strung between Barrier Knob and Mt Talbot, an extraordinary view awaits. The Darran Mountains rise like broken fingers, while it's difficult not to get excited by the glistening sight of Milford Sound pooled between a wide gap in the mountains. You can probably expect a visit from a kea on the saddle.

Return to the car park along the same route, stepping carefully over the rocks on the descent.

Hump Ridge Track

Duration 3 days
Distance 62km (38.5 miles)
Difficulty Moderate
Start/End Rarakau car park
Gateways Invercargill (p298), Queenstown (p266)
Transport Shuttle bus
Summary Climbing over the crest of Hump Ridge, this community-run track is rich in natural and cultural history, from spectacular coastal and alpine scenery to the intriguing relics of a historic timber town.

Tuatapere Hump Ridge Track, although not classified as a Great Walk, has all the qualities of one. The track winds across some of NZ's wildest land – both public and private – leading trampers through parts of Fiordland National Park, along an alpine ridge, through ancient forest, across Māori land and beside the south coast.

Unlike almost all major NZ tracks, this one doesn't fall within DOC's remit. It was conceived and built by the local community, under the umbrella of the Tuatapere Hump Ridge Track Charitable Trust, formed in 1995. Not only did this community group need to raise $3.5 million for the project, but it also needed to secure the cooperation and permission of private landowners. An amazing effort on all fronts saw the track open in 2001, as NZ's first and only privately operated independent tramp on public land.

If you want to complete the entire circuit and stay in both lodges, the track must be tramped anticlockwise, with the first night at Okaka Lodge. If you aren't keen to climb Hump Ridge, a night at Port Craig Village makes for a wonderful and easy coastal walk.

The Hump Ridge Track is a tramp that can be done with a touch of style. In the lodges you can upgrade to a private room with single or double beds, linen and hot showers. The lodges are also licensed, with beer, wine and soft drinks sold.

History

The Waitutu, on the south coast between Fiordland and Tuatapere, was first visited by early Māori in their search for food, and

Hump Ridge Track

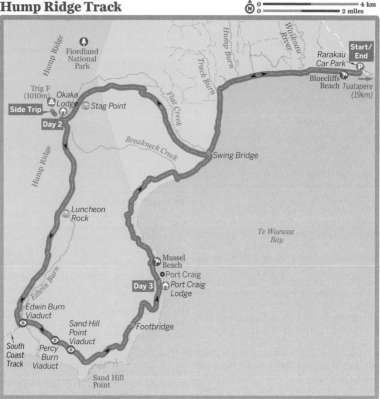

then later by Captain Cook. In 1770, while anchored off the mouth of the Waiau River, Cook wrote in his log: 'The face of the country bears a very rugged aspect, being full of high craggy hills'. This was the first recorded description of Fiordland, and it is thought that Cook was observing the Hump Ridge.

The first coastal track was cut by the government in 1868 to provide an alternative to the unreliable shipping service to the gold-rush towns in Preservation Inlet. In 1910 John Craig and Daniel Reese of the Marlborough Timber Company walked the area, assessing the forest for its commercial timber viability. The volumes were staggering, estimated at more than 152 million cu metres. The question was: how to get the timber out? It was decided that a mill, wharf and tramway system at Mussel Point (Port Craig) should be built to extract and ship the timber. Although Craig drowned in 1917, the new mill was built and was in operation three years later. At the time it was the largest in the country. The

mill was closed for the first time in 1929, a result of the Depression, and then permanently closed in 1932. It was dismantled during WWII, along with the wharf, by the NZ Navy, which feared a Japanese invasion.

With much of the Waitutu forest still uncut and its logging rights up for grabs, the area became the object of one of NZ's greatest environmental campaigns. In 1938 the Royal Forest and Bird Protection Society was the first group to push for the land to be added to the adjacent Fiordland National Park. In 1972 the Nature Conservation Council was successful in removing the Waitutu State Forest from a logging proposal for the area, and in 1981 the former National Parks and Reserves Authority again urged the government to add the forest to the national park.

After reaching a settlement on compensation for Māori land claims in the area, the Waitutu State Forest – comprising 460 sq km of virgin forest – was added to NZ's largest national park in 1998.

ℹ️ Planning

WHEN TO TRAMP

This tramp is possible year-round, but operates in three seasonal modes. During the shoulder (early November to mid-December) and high (mid-December to early April) seasons, the lodges are fully serviced and a manager is in residence. In winter (mid-April to late October), limited facilities are available – water pipes are disconnected and gas is removed, with the lodges operating as backcountry huts.

WHAT TO BRING

Good rain gear is a necessity, and gaiters may also prove useful. Along with gas cookers, all cooking equipment, crockery and cutlery are provided in the huts during the summer season. The bunk bedding includes a mattress, pillow, pillowcase and sheet. Sleeping bags can be hired when you book.

MAPS

Maps with track descriptions are handed out to trampers at the briefing before you set out. If you want to supplement that, the most detailed map is the NZTopo50 *CG07 (Sand Hill Point)*. DOC also produces a map for the coastal track, which you can purchase from the **Tuatapere Hump Ridge Track Information Centre**.

LODGES

The track is managed by the Tuatapere Hump Ridge Track Charitable Trust in similar style to a Great Walk: advance bookings are essential and you must pick up accommodation passes before commencing the tramp.

Independent walking (billed as the Freedom Walk) costs $175 and includes two nights on the trail, staying at Okaka Lodge and Port Craig Lodge. These huts are very well serviced in the main season, with heating, gas cookers, running water, flush toilets and a drying room. Hot showers can be purchased, with a towel, soap and shampoo included. Also included in the cost is hot porridge for breakfast.

A Prime Package ($450) is also available, which includes a night's accommodation in Tuatapere before the tramp, a pack transfer for the first day, bedding/linen, showers (with towel) and a freeze-dried evening meal. There are also 'heli-packing' options, transferring your bag between lodges, and even yourself to Okaka Lodge if you don't fancy the big hill.

INFORMATION

Bookings should be made through **Tuatapere Hump Ridge Track Information Centre** (☑ 0800 486 774, 03-226 6739; www.hump ridgetrack.co.nz; 31 Orawia Rd; ⊘ 7.30am-6pm Nov-Mar, limited hours Apr-Oct), which is also the prime source of information about the track.

GUIDED TRAMPS

The track trust offers guided tramps that include a night of accommodation in Tuatapere before the tramp, a helicopter flight that reduces the first day on the track by 10km, all meals, heli-packing service for your backpack on Day 1 (up the big hill; you must carry your pack on Days 2 and 3) and a choice of shared accommodation (from $1645) or private room (from $1845).

ℹ️ Getting There & Away

The trailhead is at Rarakau, 19km from Tuatapere. The track trust operates its own transport, available every day during high season, on scheduled days during the shoulder season and on demand during winter. Shuttles ($45 return) depart Tuatapere at 8am, returning from Rarakau at 2.30pm. Buses to and from Te Anau and Invercargill can also be arranged.

If you have your own vehicle, you can leave it at the Rarakau car park. It's on private land, is fenced and is overlooked by the farmhouse. A $5 donation is appreciated.

🥾 The Tramp

Day 1: Rarakau Car Park to Okaka Lodge

8–9 HOURS / 21KM / 940M ASCENT

From the car park, follow the signs to the beginning of the track, which leads you through the forest, away from the stony beach and within 2km descends to the Waikoau River footbridge. Nearby is a cluster of private holiday homes or, as they are known in Southland, cribs. Once across the Waikoau River, the next hour is a walk along a beautiful beach to **Hump Burn**. Keep an eye on the surf – you may see Hector's dolphins frolicking in small groups.

From the beach you enter forest and follow a former logging road, passing some old logging equipment along the way and two more cribs nestled in the forest. The one nearest the bridge at **Track Burn** kindly offers shelter and water, making it an ideal place for a break when it's raining.

The logging road ends at the Track Burn bridge, and on the other side is a well-graded, benched track that takes you high above the rocky shore. About 2.5km from the bridge (two to three hours from the car park) you reach a swing bridge in the **Flat Creek** ravine. On the other side is a signposted junction – the left fork is the walk to Port Craig Village and the right fork leads to Okaka Lodge, 10km away on Hump Ridge.

FIORDLAND & STEWART ISLAND/RAKIURA HUMP RIDGE TRACK

Heading right (west), the first 4.5km is easy, as you make your way up and over high river terraces and through mixed podocarp and beech forest. The track then crosses a steep-sided stream and begins the climb up a long spur. In places the ascent is quite strenuous. Eventually you come to **Stag Point**, a narrow, steep-sided ridge with a view to the east. It's another hour, and more steady climbing, until you reach a trail junction.

At the signposted junction, head right and follow the boardwalk through stunted silver beech forest and open alpine clearings to **Okaka Lodge** (32 bunks, plus 12 private beds). Built in 2001, the hut is magnificently located on the side of a glacial cirque, overlooking Te Waewae Bay and the Waiau basin, and the Takitimu Mountains to the north.

Side Trip: Trig F

30 MINUTES / 1KM RETURN / 50M ASCENT

It is well worth the extra effort to climb Hump Ridge itself and explore the alpine wonderland. The track to the crest of the ridge is a boardwalk that forms a loop around **Trig F**, a 1010m high point.

Hump Ridge consists of sandstones, mudstones and conglomerated rocks of the Tertiary period. A striking series of rock towers among the tussock, herb fields and alpine tarns have been left after years of weathering.

From Trig F the views to the west take in the rugged mountains of Fiordland National Park, Lake Hauroko and Lake Poteriteri. To the south you can see Solander Island in Foveaux Strait and Stewart Island.

JETBOATING THE HUMP RIDGE TRACK

For a different spin on the Hump Ridge Track, you can combine it with a jetboat exit. Trips operated by **Wairaurahiri Wilderness Jet** (☑ 0800 270 556; www. river-jet.co.nz; 17 Main Street, Otautau; day tours from $230) begin with a day of walking the coast from Rarakau to Port Craig Village, staying here the night. On the second day you tramp past the trio of viaducts, turning off the Hump Ridge Track to follow the South Coast Track to the Wairaurahiri River. From here, you skim upstream in a jetboat to Lake Hauroko – rapids along the river range up to Grade III. From Lake Hauroko, you're transported by road back to Rarakau. Trips cost $225.

Day 2: Okaka Lodge to Port Craig Lodge

7–9 HOURS / 21KM / 920M DESCENT

Be sure to check the weather forecast, and fill your water bottles before heading out; this day is along an exposed section of track and should be treated with respect.

Return to the main loop at the junction, and turn right, heading south towards Luncheon Rock. For the next 4.5km the track traverses the subalpine crest of Hump Ridge. For the most part it is an undulating tramp along the top of the ridge. On a nice day this is a section to be savoured for its spectacular views and interesting subalpine flora. A boardwalk is provided to protect the delicate plant life.

Within two hours you reach **Luncheon Rock**, site of a toilet, water and the last good views before the descent to the coast. For the next 2½ hours the track descends steeply to the coastal marine terraces, passing some interesting, ghostly rock outcrops. Once you bottom out it is 2km to the Edwin Burn Viaduct, with the track passing through the Rowallan Māori Lands. In 1906 this land was given to the southern Māori in compensation for land taken in Otago and Canterbury by the government in the 1840s. All trampers should respect the access given by the owners and keep to the track.

At the **Edwin Burn Viaduct** the trail emerges at the original South Coast Track, an old logging road. Edwin Burn is the first of three viaducts crossed or viewed on the way to Port Craig Village. Constructed from Australian hardwood, they were built to carry tramlines across the deep ravines.

The track follows the tramway all the way to Port Craig, and within 30 minutes the second and largest of the viaducts is reached. At 36m in height and 124m in length, the **Percy Burn Viaduct** is thought to be the largest wooden viaduct still standing in the world. The best point to view this immense structure is from the track below it.

From here it is 7km (two hours) to Port Craig Village, crossing the **Sand Hill Point Viaduct** along the way. Sand Hill Point is one Fiordland's most historic places, as it was used for centuries as a resting spot for Māori hunting parties. Unfortunately, a side trip to the point is strictly prohibited.

The monotony of the tramway is suddenly broken when you arrive at the open grassy area where **Port Craig Lodge** (32 bunks plus 12 private beds) is located. The old logging wharf at Port Craig – or what's left of it – makes for an interesting walk, with machinery and other relics still lying about. Also keep your eyes peeled for dolphins and possibly even a whale in Te Waewae Bay.

Day 3: Port Craig Lodge to Rarakau Car Park

6–8 HOURS / 20KM

After leaving the lodge the track enters the bush near the old school, before winding through large stands of podocarp forest and over a series of bluffs. It used to be possible to follow the coast around this section, but what the sea wants the sea shall have, and coastal erosion now makes this route impassable, even at very low tide.

After about 1¾ hours, the track emerges onto the coastline at **Breakneck Creek**. From here it climbs over the headland before dropping back to the coast again at **Blowholes Beach**.

At the end of the beach a post marked with a fishing buoy indicates the track over another headland to the next beach. The track leaves this beach and enters one final small cove before climbing back up onto the coastal terrace and past the junction of the track to Okaka Lodge. Continue to the swing bridge over Flat Creek and retrace your steps from Day 1 back to Track Burn and on to Rarakau car park. It's about two hours to the car park from Track Burn.

STEWART ISLAND/ RAKIURA

New Zealand's 'third' island, Stewart Island/ Rakiura is a remote place, comprising vast tracts of wilderness and populated by fewer than 400 people and a lot of birds, including the national icon, the kiwi.

Around 85% of the 1722-sq-km island was gazetted as Rakiura National Park in 2002. It is framed by 755km of coastline, punctuated by long beaches, sand dunes and crystal-clear bays fringed by lush rainforest. The interior is mostly bush, broken up by steep gullies and ridges, several of which emerge above the bushline. The highest point on Stewart Island – Mt Anglem/Hananui – is only 980m and sees the occasional dusting of snow.

Add a fascinating human history to this unique edge-of-the-world island and you've got a fine prospect for trampers. There are more than 280km of tracks, and while much

of it is quite challenging – with indecisive weather and widespread mud being notable features – the birds, views and serenity are ample rewards.

History

Rakiura, the Māori name for Stewart Island, means 'land of the glowing sky', referring perhaps to the aurora australis (Southern Lights), often seen here in the southern sky, or maybe to the spectacular blood-red sunrises and sunsets.

Excavations in the area provide evidence that, as early as the 13th century, tribes of Polynesian origin migrated to the island to hunt moa. However, Māori settlements were thin and scattered, because the people were unable to grow kumara (sweet potato), the staple food of settlements to the north. They did make annual migrations to the outer islands to seek muttonbird (titi), a favourite food, and to the main island to search for eel, shellfish and certain birds.

The first European visitor was Captain Cook, who sailed around the eastern, southern and western coasts in 1770 but couldn't figure out if it was an island or a peninsula. Deciding it was attached to the South Island, he called it South Cape. In 1809 the sealing vessel *Pegasus* circumnavigated Rakiura and named it after its first officer, William Stewart. Stewart charted large sections of the coast during a sealing trip in 1809, and drafted the first detailed map of the island.

Sealing ended by the late 1820s, to be replaced temporarily by whaling, but the small whaling bases on the island were never profitable. Other early industries were timber milling, fish curing and shipbuilding. A short-lived gold rush towards the end of the 19th century brought a sufficient influx of miners to warrant building a hotel and a post office.

The only enterprise that has endured is fishing. Initially those doing the fishing were few in number, but when a steamer service from Bluff began in 1885 the industry expanded, resulting in the construction of cleaning sheds on Ruapuke Island and a refrigerating plant in the North Arm of Port Pegasus.

Today, tourism and, to a much lesser extent, fishing are the occupations of most of the island's 370 or so residents.

Environment

Birds previously hunted, or at least taken for granted, by humans are now conserved and treasured, and Rakiura is establishing

NORTH WEST CIRCUIT

For a few hardy trampers, the Rakiura Track is just the warm-up for an epic 125km tramp around Stewart Island's northern half.

The North West Circuit loops out from Oban, beginning on the Rakiura Track but then venturing far from the world, taking in the island's wild west coast, where spectacular sand dunes stand braced against wild seas. It's a serious mission – 11 sizeable days through tough terrain and long, soupy sections of thick and deep mud – that's best attempted by experienced, fit and well-equipped trampers. If you're lucky you may see kiwis, penguins and seals.

Still not enough? Super-eager, experienced trampers can consider adding the Southern Circuit, a challenging 56km route that branches off the North West Circuit between Mason Bay and Freshwater Hut. DOC's *North West and Southern Circuit Tracks* brochure can be downloaded from its website (www.doc.govt.nz).

itself as a bird haven of international repute. With an absence of mustelids (ferrets, stoats and weasels) and with large areas of intact forest, Stewart Island has one of the largest and most diverse bird populations of any area in NZ, and offers more opportunities to spot kiwi in the wild. The Rakiura tokoeka (local brown kiwi) population is estimated to be around 15,000, though numbers are in decline.

A great place to see lots of birds in one place is Ulva Island/Te Wharawhara, a quick water-taxi ride from Oban. Established as a bird sanctuary in 1922, it remains one of Rakiura's wildest corners. As the result of an extensive eradication program, the island was declared rat-free in 1997 and three years later was chosen as the site to release endangered South Island saddlebacks.

There are also plenty of seabirds, including blue penguins, shags, prions, petrels and albatrosses, as well as sooty shearwaters, which are seen in large numbers during breeding season.

Exotic animals include two species of deer, the red and the Virginia (whitetail), which were introduced in the early 20th century, as were brush-tailed possums, which are now numerous across the island and destructive to the native bush. Rakiura also has NZ fur seals, NZ sea lions, elephant seals and, occasionally, leopard seals that visit the beaches and rocky shores.

Beech, the tree that dominates much of NZ, is absent from Rakiura. The predominant lowland bush is podocarp forest, with exceptionally tall rimu, miro, totara and kamahi forming the canopy. Because of mild winters, frequent rainfall and porous soil, most of the island is a lush forest, thick with vines and carpeted in deep-green ferns and moss.

Rakiura Track

Duration 3 days

Distance 39km (24.2 miles)

Difficulty Moderate

Start/End Oban

Gateway Invercargill (p298)

Transport Plane, ferry

Summary This Great Walk loop features the sheltered shores of Paterson Inlet and beautiful beaches on the way to Port William.

The Rakiura Track is a peaceful and leisurely loop offering a rewarding combination of coastal scenery, native forest, historical interest and diverse bird life, including forest songbirds, soaring seabirds and beaky waders.

The track is actually only 32km long, but adding the road sections at either end bumps it up to 39km, conveniently forming a circuit from Oban. As it provides the only short loop in Rakiura National Park (all the other possible loops require seven to 10 days), the track is the most popular Stewart Island tramp, with around 6500 people walking it annually. As a Great Walk, it has also been constructed so as to eliminate most of the mud for which the island is infamous.

This tramp is described here crossing from Port William to North Arm, which is the easiest direction to walk it, especially if starting later in the day.

ⓘ Planning

WHEN TO TRAMP

It is possible to tramp year-round on the Rakiura Track. At the summer solstice there are 17 hours of daylight; in winter this decreases to about nine. The best time on the track is from October to April.

Rakiura Track

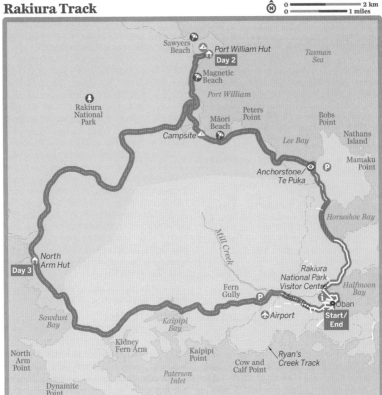

0 ———— 2 km
0 ———— 1 miles

Sawyers Beach
Port William Hut
Day 2
Magnetic Beach
Tasman Sea
Port William
Rakiura National Park
Peters Point
Māori Beach
Bobs Point
Nathans Island
Campsite
Lee Bay
Mamaku Point
Anchorstone/ Te Puka
Horseshoe Bay
North Arm Hut
Day 3
Mill Creek
Rakiura National Park Visitor Centre
Halfmoon Bay
Fern Gully
Oban
Sawdust Bay
Kaipipi Bay
Airport
Start/ End
North Arm Point
Kidney Fern Arm
Kaipipi Point
Cow and Calf Point
Ryan's Creek Track
Dynamite Point
Paterson Inlet

WHAT TO BRING

You can stock up well enough for the tramp on the island, but if you have specific food tastes or needs, it might be best to bring these items with you. Pack a stove for use in the huts. Mobile-phone coverage fades beyond Oban, so carrying a personal locator beacon is a good idea. Beacons can be hired from the Rakiura National Park Visitor Centre.

MAPS & BROCHURES

The Rakiura Track falls along the join of three NZTopo50 maps – CH09 (*Mount Anglem/ Hananui*), CH10 (*Foveaux Strait*) and CJ09 (*Mount Allen*). The single option is NewTopo's 1:45,000 *Rakiura Track* map.

As well as DOC's *Rakiura Track* brochure, get the excellent *Stewart Island/Rakiura Short Walks* brochure, which details 13 shorter hikes you might like to fit in around longer tramps. It can be downloaded from DOC's website (www. doc.govt.nz).

HUTS & CAMPING

As this is a Great Walk, all huts and campsites need to be booked in advance, either online or

in person at the **Rakiura National Park Visitor Centre** in Oban. Make sure you print the booking confirmation letter and carry it with you.

There are two Great Walk huts ($24), one at Port William and one at North Arm, which have wood stoves for heat (firewood provided) but no gas rings for cooking, so pack a stove and fuel. There's a limit of two consecutive nights in each of the huts and pre-booking ensures that you have a bunk for the night. Note that Standard hut tickets and Backcountry Hut Passes cannot be used on the Rakiura Track.

There are Standard campsites ($6) in the vicinity of both huts, along with another one at Maori Beach. Camping is not permitted elsewhere along the track.

INFORMATION

Rakiura National Park Visitor Centre (☎ 03-219 0009; www.doc.govt.nz; 15 Main Rd, Oban; ⊙ 8am-5pm Dec-Mar, 8.30am-4.30pm Mon-Fri, 9am-4pm Apr-May & Oct-Nov, 8.30am-4.30pm Mon-Fri, 10am-2pm Sat & Sun Jun-Sep) has useful information on the island and good displays on flora and fauna. You can book for the tramp here and also store gear while you're tramping (small/large locker $10/20).

ⓘ Getting There & Away

The tramp, as we describe it, begins and ends in Oban, the main settlement on the island.

Stewart Island Flights (☏ 03-218 9129; www.stewartislandflights.co.nz; Elgin Tce, Oban; adult/child one way $215/80, return $215/130) wings between Oban and Invercargill (20 minutes) three times daily. Fares include transfers between the island airport and the airline's office on the Oban waterfront.

Stewart Island Experience (☏ 0800 000 511, 03-212 7660; www.stewartislandexperience.co.nz; Main Wharf, Oban; adult/child one way $79/40, return $139/40) operates a passenger-only ferry between Bluff and Oban up to four times daily (reduced service in winter). Book a few days ahead in summer. The crossing takes one hour and can be a rough ride. Vehicles can be stored in a secure car park at Bluff for an additional cost.

🥾 The Tramp

Day 1: Oban to Port William Hut

4–5 HOURS / 13KM

Leave the Rakiura National Park Visitor Centre and turn right to walk down Main Rd. Turn left into Elgin Tce past the Ship to Shore store, and head up the hill. Follow this main coast road over a series of hills to **Horseshoe Bay** then on to **Lee Bay**, the official entrance to Rakiura National Park.

At beautiful Lee Bay, walk through the **Anchorstone/Te Puka**, a giant chain-link sculpture symbolising what the Māori believe was a spiritual connection between Stewart Island/Rakiura (the anchor) and Bluff/Motu Pohue (the stern post of the South Island, which is the canoe).

The track enters the bush and crosses a bridge over Little River to skirt the coast. You then follow the coast around **Peters Point** towards Maori Beach. Within 2km the track descends onto the southern end of **Maori Beach**, where you immediately come to a creek that can easily be waded at low tide. If the tide is in, stay on the track to quickly reach a footbridge inland. North of the creek is a campsite with a toilet and shelter, in a grassy clearing near the beach.

A sawmill began operating at Maori Beach in 1913, and at one time a large wharf, a second sawmill and a network of tramways were constructed to extract rimu. By 1920 there were enough families living here to warrant opening a school. The onset of the Depression led to the closure of the last mill in 1931, but a rusting **steam boiler** from that logging era can still be seen down a short track near the footbridge.

Continue north along the smooth sand of Maori Beach to reach a bridge at the far end, one hour from Little River. The track then climbs a small hill and continues to the intersection with the track to North Arm. To reach Port William, turn right and you will gradually drop to the Port William Campsite, nestled just above the shores of **Magnetic Beach**.

Just a few minutes beyond the campsite, at the beach's northern end, you'll find **Port William Hut** (24 bunks). In 1876 the government had grand plans for a settlement here, offering 50 families free land to develop the timber resources and offshore fisheries. The settlement was a dismal failure, as the utopia the government had hoped to foster was plagued by isolation and loneliness. All that remains of the settlement are the large gum trees next to the hut.

Day 2: Port William Hut to North Arm Hut

6 HOURS / 13KM

It will take around 45 minutes to backtrack to the turn-off on the hill between Port William and Maori Hill. Turn right, following the Rakiura Track as it heads inland, saying farewell to the east coast as you make your way through beautiful regenerating podocarp forest, as well as lush and dense virgin forest. Take a breather at the **log haulers**, massive machines that were used to drag forest giants from the depths of the gullies.

The walk settles into a pattern of climbing over a number of hills as it heads south, passing through a variety of vegetation, including previously milled and virgin podocarp forest.

The track descends to **North Arm**, which was an important food-gathering site for early Māori, on the shore of Paterson Inlet/Whaka a Te Wera.

The track leads you to **North Arm Hut** (24 bunks) and campsite. The hut is nestled above the shores of **Paterson Inlet**, and there are two short trails leading down to the shoreline, where you can enjoy fine sunsets.

Day 3: North Arm Hut to Oban

4–5 HOURS / 13KM

The track heads south then southeast, sidling around the headland from North Arm. A moderate and undulating walk takes you through kamahi and rimu, with stunning vistas across the inlet. It then follows the coast down to secluded bays and is interspersed with historic mill sites. **Sawdust Bay** has tidal mudflats, making it a great spot to watch wading birds feeding at low tide.

From Sawdust Bay the track swings in a more easterly direction, and after 1km reaches the shores of **Kidney Fern Arm**. You climb through kamahi and rimu forest over another peninsula ridge, this time descending to the tidal headwaters of **Kaipipi Bay**, and cross the sluggish river on the longest bridge of the track. After a short climb you arrive at a marked junction to the sheltered bay, which is only two minutes down a side trail. In the 1860s, two sawmills at this bay employed more than 100 people.

The track between Kaipipi Bay and Oban is the former **Kaipipi Rd**, which was once the best-maintained and most heavily used road on the island. The old logging road makes for quick tramping, and in 2.5km you arrive at a junction with Ryan's Creek Track. If you head south on this track, it's a scenic two-hour detour into Oban.

The main track continues east past the junction as an old road, and in 10 minutes you reach a signposted junction to Fern Gully car park. From the junction, follow the track southeast, soon arriving at a car park at the end of Main Rd. From here it's 2km to Oban.

TOWNS & FACILITIES

Te Anau

☑ 03 / POP 1911

Picturesque Te Anau is the main gateway to Milford Sound and three Great Walks: the Milford, Kepler and Routeburn Tracks. The township borders Lake Te Anau, New Zealand's second-largest lake, whose glacier-gouged fiords wind into secluded forest on its western shore.

🛏 Sleeping & Eating

This is a trampers' town and the accommodation options reflect that. Book early from late December to early February.

★**Te Anau Lakefront Backpackers** HOSTEL $
(☑ 03-249 7713, 0800 200 074; www.teanaubackpackers.co.nz; 48-50 Lakefront Dr; tent sites $20, dm $35, d with/without bathroom from $98/88; 🛜) Tidy dorm and private rooms with a lakefront location hoist this backpackers to the top spot among Te Anau's budget beds. Gaze at the lake through huge windows, let the staff fill your brain with local tips, or snooze in a game- and book-filled lounge with Dexter, the adopted house cat.

Te Anau Lakeview Kiwi Holiday Park & Motels HOLIDAY PARK $
(☑ 03-249 7457, 0800 483 262; www.teanauholidaypark.co.nz; 77 Te Anau–Manapouri Rd; unpowered/powered sites $23/24, dm/s/d without bathroom $35/40/80, units $125-306; @ 🛜) This 9-hectare grassy lakeside holiday park has plenty of space to pitch your tent or park your van. It also has a wide range of accommodation from basic dorms through to tidy cabins and the rather swanky Marakura two-bedroom motel units with enviable lake and mountain views.

Te Anau Lodge B&B $$$
(☑ 03-249 7477; www.teanaulodge.com; 52 Howden St; with breakfast s $225-350, d $250-375, tr $300-400; 🛜) In a sea of functional but fusty motels, Te Anau's former Sisters of Mercy Convent distinguishes itself with unique history. Each chamber carries a whisper of its previous function, from the elegant 'Music Room' to the lavish 'Mother Superior'. Sip complimentary wine in a fireside Chesterfield, collapse on a king-size bed, then awaken to an ample continental breakfast.

★**Kepler's** SOUTH AMERICAN $$$
(☑ 03-249 7909; 90 Town Centre; mains $29-40; ⊙ 5-9pm) Mountains of crayfish, mouth-watering ceviche and perfectly seared steaks are whisked to tables at this efficient but friendly family-run place. South American flair permeates the menu (quinoa-crusted orange roughy, Chilean malbec); we suggest the whopping roast lamb with a generous pour of merlot.

Sandfly Cafe CAFE $
(☑ 03-249 9529; 9 The Lane; mains $7-20; ⊙ 7am-4.30pm; 🛜) As popular with locals as travellers, Sandfly serves the town's best espresso alongside breakfasts, light meals of pasta or club sandwiches, and an impressive rack of sweet treats from caramel slices to berry friands (almond-flour cakes). Sun yourself on the lawn, or try to get maximum mileage out of the free 15 minutes of wi-fi.

Supplies & Equipment

Outside Sports SPORTS & OUTDOORS
(☑ 03-249 8195; www.outsidesports.co.nz; 38 Town Centre; ⊙ 9am-6pm) Tramping and camping equipment for sale or hire, plus bike rental (half/full day $30/50).

FIORDLAND & STEWART ISLAND/RAKIURA TE ANAU

Bev's Tramping Gear Hire SPORTS & OUTDOORS
(☑ 027 249 7389, 03-249 7389; www.bevs-hire.co.nz;
16 Homer St; ☺ 9am-noon & 6-7pm Mon-Fri Oct-Apr)
Bev hires out tramping and camping equipment, and sells dehydrated meals. She opens the shop outside of hours by prior arrangement, and is flexible when organising pick-up or drop-off of gear.

Fresh Choice Supermarket SUPERMARKET $
(☑ 03-249 9330; www.freshchoice.co.nz; 5 Milford Cres; ☺ 7am-9pm) A decent-sized supermarket right in the middle of town.

❶ Information

Fiordland i-SITE (☑ 03-249 8900; www.fiord land.org.nz; 19 Town Centre; ☺ 8.30am-8pm Dec-Mar, to 5.30pm Apr-Nov) Activity, accommodation and transport bookings.

❶ Getting There & Away

InterCity (☑ 03-442 4922; www.intercity.co.nz; Miro St) Services to Milford Sound ($22 to $44, three hours, two to three daily) and Queenstown ($21 $49, 3¼ hours, four daily), and daily morning buses to Dunedin ($25 to $49, 4½ hours) and Christchurch ($31 to $81, 11 hours). Buses depart from a stop on Miro St, at the town centre end.

Naked Bus (https://nakedbus.com) Daily bus services to Queenstown (from $30, 2¾ hours) and one daily morning bus to Milford Sound (from $32, 2¼ hours). Services depart from Te Anau Lakeview Kiwi Holiday Park (p297).

Invercargill

☑ 03 / POP 51,700

Any trip to Stewart Island/Rakiura inevitably includes a stopover in Invercargill, the southernmost city in NZ. Stock up on supplies here before heading to Rakiura.

⬛ Sleeping & Eating

★**Southern Comfort Backpackers** HOSTEL $
(☑ 03-2183838; www.southerncomfortbackpackers. com; 30 Thomson St, Avenal; dm/d from $32/72; ☎) A mix of snug and swish, this large Victorian house has a lounge with fireplace, fully equipped kitchen and peaceful gardens. Adding to the perks are the use of two free bikes, laundry and a herb garden.

Tower Lodge Motel MOTEL $$
(☑ 03-217 6729; www.towerlodgemotel.co.nz; 119 Queens Dr; units from $130; ☎) ✍ Units at this motel have nicely modernised kitchens and bathrooms, and two-thirds of them have a spa bath. Two-bedroom units also feature roomy dining areas.

★**Louie's** MODERN NZ $$
(☑ 03-214 2913; www.facebook.com/pg/LouiesRestaurant; 142 Dee St; tapas $13-16, mains $29-32; ☺ 5.30pm-late Wed-Sat) Part tapas and cocktail bar, part chic fusion eatery, Louie's is a great place to while away an evening snuggled into a sofa or fireside nook. The seasonally changing menu veers from creative tapas to more substantial mains such as slow-cooked pork, locally sourced blue cod and magnificent steaks..

★**Batch** CAFE $$
(☑ 03-214 6357; 173 Spey St; mains $13-20; ☺ 7am-4pm Mon-Fri, from 8am Sat & Sun; ☎✍) Large shared tables, a relaxed beachy ambience, and top-notch coffee and smoothies give this cafe its reputation as Southland's best..

Supplies & Equipment

Southern Adventure SPORTS & OUTDOORS
(☑ 03-218 3239; www.southernadventure.co.nz; 31 Tay St; ☺ 8.30am-5.30pm Mon-Fri, 10am-3pm Sat) Sells everything from maps and boots to sleeping bags and dried food.

Pak 'n Save SUPERMARKET $
(www.paknsave.co.nz; 95 Tay St; ☺ 8am-9pm) A large, centrally located supermarket.

❶ Information

The **Invercargill i-SITE** (☑ 03-211 0895; www. invercargillnz.com; Queens Park, 108 Gala St; ☺ 8.30am-5pm Mon-Fri, to 4pm Sat & Sun) can help with general enquiries and is a godsend for Stewart Island/Rakiura accommodation options.

❶ Getting There & Away

Air New Zealand (www.airnewzealand.com) Flights link Invercargill to Christchurch (from $159) and Wellington (from $208) multiple times per day.

Stewart Island Flights (☑ 03-218 9129; www. stewartislandflights.com) Connects Invercargill to Stewart Island/Rakiura three times a day year-round.

Buses leave from the **Invercargill i-SITE**.**Catch-a-Bus South** (☑ 03-214 4014, 24hr 027 449 7994; www.catchabussouth.co.nz) has scheduled services at least daily to Queenstown and Queenstown Airport ($60, 3 to 3¼ hours) and Dunedin ($57 to $60, 3½ hours). Bookings essential; reserve by 4pm the day before you travel. **InterCity** (☑ Dunedin 03-471 7143; www.intercity.co.nz) has direct daily coaches to and from Queenstown Airport ($49, 3½ hours) and Queenstown (from $38, 3¾ hours). **Naked Bus** (https://nakedbus.com) runs twice daily to and from Queenstown (from $35, 3¾ hours).

Understand New Zealand

New Zealand Today

Despite a decade marred by disasters, including devastating earthquakes and mining and helicopter tragedies, New Zealand never loses its nerve. The country remains a titan on both the silver screen and the sports field, and change is coming in the world of politics...

Best on Film

Lord of the Rings trilogy (2001–03) Hobbits, dragons and magical rings – Tolkien's vision comes to life.

The Piano (1993) A piano and its owners arrive on a mid-19th-century West Coast beach.

Whale Rider (2002) Magical tale of family and heritage on the East Coast.

Once Were Warriors (1994) Brutal relationship dysfunction in South Auckland.

Boy (2010) Taika Waititi's bitter-sweet coming-of-age drama set in the Bay of Plenty.

Best in Print

The Luminaries (Eleanor Catton; 2013) Man Booker Prize winner: crime and intrigue on West Coast goldfields.

Mister Pip (Lloyd Jones; 2006) Tumult on Bougainville Island, intertwined with Dickens' *Great Expectations*.

Live Bodies (Maurice Gee; 1998) Post-WWII loss and redemption in NZ.

The 10pm Question (Kate de Goldi; 2009) Twelve-year-old Frankie grapples with life's big anxieties.

The Collected Stories of Katherine Mansfield (2006) Kathy's greatest hits.

The Wish Child (Catherine Chidgey; 2016) Harrowing, heartbreaking WWII novel; NZ Book Awards winner.

Jacinda-Mania

In 2010 she was NZ's youngest sitting MP, by 2017 she was running the country. The swift rise of Jacinda Ardern has been touted as part of a global political shift. Ardern became the youngest ever Labour Party leader in 2017, only a few weeks ahead of the election that propelled her to the role of prime minister at the age of 37 – making her NZ's youngest PM for 150 years. Passionate about climate change, unabashedly feminist and an ardent supporter of gay rights, Ardern's ability to win support with her energetic style was dubbed 'Jacinda-mania'. The final polls gave Labour a less-than-maniacal 37% of the vote, but resulted in a coalition government led by Labour. Ardern's articulacy and verve have seen her aligned with other youthful, socially progressive world leaders like Justin Trudeau and Emmanuel Macron, part of a youth-powered political sea change. But Ardern's style remains quintessentially Kiwi: unpretentious and accessible.

In June 2018, Arden gave birth to her first Child, and made history by being only the second leader of a country to have a baby while in office, plus being the first premier in NZ's history to take maternity leave. She continues to be symbol of progress , returning to work after just six weeks' maternity leave, while her husband remains the stay-at-home-parent.

Cultural and Sporting Colossus

Cementing NZ's reputation as a primo movie set, movie director James Cameron has been working out of Wellington on his long-awaited four *Avatar* sequels. They're slated for staggered release between 2020 and 2025. Meanwhile, director Taika Waititi has been enjoying a wave of global adulation. His works *Boy* (2010) and *Hunt for the Wilderpeople* (2016) broke records in NZ, and vampire flat-sharing mockumentary *What We Do in the Shadows* (2014) ensnared a cult following. But Waititi went stratospheric as the director of *Thor: Ragnarok*

(2017), injecting distinctly Kiwi humour into a Marvel franchise that had lost its zest.

In the world of sport, NZ remains a force to be reckoned with. Following the All Blacks' success at the 2011 Rugby World Cup at home, the beloved national team beat arch-rivals Australia in 2015, becoming the first country ever to win back-to-back Rugby World Cups. The pressure is on for the 2019 World Cup. After the Black Caps made the final of the Cricket World Cup for the first time in 2015, they were deprived of glory in a stinging loss to their trans-Tasman rivals Australia. The 2019 World Cup is their chance to seize victory. Out on the water, Emirates Team New Zealand scored a victory in 2017 at venerable sailing race the America's Cup. Auckland 2021, anyone?

Big Issues
Being a dream destination isn't all it's cracked up to be, especially when tourist numbers boom and property investors swoop in. Aussie and Asian buyers are increasingly wise to NZ property: cue a spiralling housing crisis, and the IMF ranking NZ's housing as the most unaffordable in the OECD in 2016. With Auckland's population expected to increase by one million in the next 30 years, the fixes can't come swiftly enough.

The issue of managing NZ's increasing number of visitors – now an annual 3.54 million – is also high on the agenda. In response to the enormous popularity of the Tongariro Alpine Crossing, the DOC has placed a time limit at the car park at the beginning of the track, forcing tourists to use traffic-reducing shuttle services. Meanwhile tourism hubs like Te Anau, gateway to world-famous Milford Sound, are seeing their peak season start ever earlier. A country beloved for being wild, green and beautiful faces the challenge of keeping it that way, in the face of a tourism stampede.

Never Forget
Kiwi battler spirit has been repeatedly pushed to its limits over the past decade. Christchurch's recovery from the 2010 and 2011 earthquakes suffered a setback when another quake hit in 2016, while earthquakes in Kaikoura in November 2016 rattled road and rail access until repairs were finished at the end of 2017. But NZ doesn't just rebuild, it reinvents: pop-up cafes and restaurants and a shipping-container mall showed how fast Christchurch could dust itself off after disaster. Ensuing years have allowed the bigger post-earthquake projects to take shape, including the Canterbury Earthquake National Memorial, unveiled in 2017.

Another notable memorial remembers the Pike River Disaster in 2010, in which a methane explosion claimed 29 lives – the country's worst mining accident in more than a century. By the wishes of the families of the men killed in the accident, the site of the mine has been folded into Paparoa National Park and their memorial will be a new 'Great Walk', opening in 2018.

POPULATION: **4.83 MILLION**

AREA: **268,021 SQ KM**

GDP: **$268.1 BILLION**

INFLATION: **1.9% (2017)**

UNEMPLOYMENT: **4.8% (2017)**

if New Zealand were 100 people

65 would be European
15 would be Maori
12 would be Asian
7 would be Pacific Islanders
1 would be Other

where they live
(% of New Zealanders)

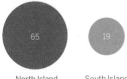

North Island South Island

Australia Rest of the World Travelling

population per sq km

NEW ZEALAND AUSTRALIA USA

👤 ≈ 3 people

History

Historians continue to unravel New Zealand's early history...with much of what they discover confirming traditional Māori narratives. In less than a thousand years NZ produced two new peoples: the Polynesian Māori and European New Zealanders (also known by their Māori name, 'Pākehā'). New Zealand shares some of its history with the rest of Polynesia, and with other European settler societies. This cultural intermingling has created unique features along the way.

Māori Settlement

The Ministry for Culture & Heritage's history website (www. nzhistory.net.nz) is an excellent source of info on NZ history.

The first settlers of NZ were the Polynesian forebears of today's Māori. Archaeologists and anthropologists continue to search for the details, but the most widely accepted evidence suggests they arrived in the 13th century. The DNA of Polynesian rat bones, dated to centuries earlier, has been written off as unreliable (and certainly not conclusive evidence of earlier settlement). Most historians now agree on 1280 as the Māori's likeliest arrival date. Scientists have sequenced the DNA of settlers buried at the Wairau Bar archaeological site on the South Island, and confirmed the settlers as originating from east Polynesia (though work is ongoing to pinpoint their origins more precisely). The genetic diversity of the buried settlers suggests a fairly large-scale settlement – a finding consistent with Māori narratives about numerous vessels reaching the islands.

Similarities in language between Māori and Tahitian indicate close contact in historical times. Māori is about as similar to Tahitian as Spanish is to French, despite the 4294km separating these island groups.

Prime sites for first settlement were warm coastal gardens for the food plants brought from Polynesia (kumara or sweet potato, gourd, yam and taro); sources of workable stone for knives and adzes; and areas with abundant big game. New Zealand has no native land mammals apart from a few species of bat, but 'big game' is no exaggeration: the islands were home to a dozen species of moa (a large flightless bird), the largest of which weighed up to 240kg, about twice the size of an ostrich...preyed upon by *Harpagornis moorei*, a whopping 15kg eagle that is now extinct. Other species of flightless birds and large sea mammals, such as fur seals, were easy game for hunters from small Pacific islands. The first settlers spread far and fast, from the top of the North Island to the bottom of the

TIMELINE	AD 1280	1500–1642	1642
	Based on evidence from archaeological digs, the most likely arrival date of east Polynesians in NZ, now known as Māori.	The 'classic period' of Māori culture, where weapon-making and artistic techniques were refined. Many remain cultural hallmarks to this day.	First European contact: Abel Tasman arrives on an expedition from the Dutch East Indies (Indonesia) but leaves in a hurry after a sea skirmish with Māori.

THE MYTHICAL MORIORI

One of NZ's most persistent legends is that Māori found mainland NZ already occupied by a more peaceful and racially distinct Melanesian people, known as the Moriori, whom they exterminated. This myth has been regularly debunked by scholars since the 1920s, but somehow hangs on.

To complicate matters, there were real 'Moriori', and Māori did treat them badly. The real Moriori were the people of the Chatham Islands, a windswept group about 900km east of the mainland. They were, however, fully Polynesian, and descended from Māori – 'Moriori' was their version of the same word. Mainland Māori arrived in the Chathams in 1835, as a spin-off of the Musket Wars, killing some Moriori and enslaving the rest, but they did not exterminate them.

South Island within the first 100 years. High-protein diets are likely to have boosted population growth.

By about 1400, however, with big-game supply dwindling, Māori economics turned from big game to small game – forest birds and rats – and from hunting to farming and fishing. A good living could still be made, but it required detailed local knowledge, steady effort and complex communal organisation, hence the rise of the Māori tribes. Competition for resources increased, conflict did likewise, and this led to the building of increasingly sophisticated *pā* (fortified villages), complete with wells and food storage pits. Vestiges of *pā* earthworks can still be seen around the country (on the hilltops of Auckland, for example).

Around 1500 is considered the dawn of the 'classic period', when Māori developed a social structure and aesthetic that was truly distinct, rather than an offshoot of the parent Polynesian culture. Māori had no metals and no written language (and no alcoholic drinks or drugs). Traditional Māori culture from these times endures, including performance art like *kapa haka* (cultural dance) and unmistakeable visual art, notably woodcarving, weaponry and *pounamu* (greenstone).

Spiritual life was similarly distinctive. Below Ranginui (sky father) and Papatūānuku (earth mother) were various gods of land, forest and sea, joined by deified ancestors over time. The mischievous demigod Māui was particularly important. In legend, he vanquished the sun and fished up the North Island before meeting his death between the thighs of the goddess Hine-nui-te-pō in an attempt to bring immortality to humankind.

Rumours of late survivals of the giant moa bird abound, but none has been authenticated. In recent years there has been enthusiasm around attempting to 'de-extinct' the moa using DNA samples, though scientists see conserving existing species as the bigger priority. Spoilsports.

1769	1772	1790s	1818–36
European contact recommences with visits by James Cook and Jean de Surville. Despite violence, both manage to communicate with Māori. This time NZ's link with the outside world proves permanent.	Marion du Fresne's French expedition arrives; it stays for some weeks at the Bay of Islands. Relations with Māori start well, but a breach of Māori *tapu* (sacred law) leads to violence.	Whaling ships and sealing gangs arrive in the country. Relations are established with Māori, with Europeans depending on the contact for essentials, such as food, water and protection.	Intertribal Māori 'Musket Wars' take place: tribes acquire muskets and win bloody victories against tribes without them. The wars taper off, probably due to the equal distribution of weapons.

Enter Europe

The first authenticated contact between Māori and European explorers took place in 1642. Seafarer Abel Tasman had just claimed Van Diemen's Land (Tasmania) for the Dutch when rough winds steered his ships east, where he sighted New Zealand. Tasman's two ships were searching for southern land and anything valuable it might contain. Tasman was instructed to pretend to any natives he might meet 'that you are by no means eager for precious metals, so as to leave them ignorant of the value of the same'.

When Tasman's ships anchored in the bay, local Māori came out in their canoes to make the traditional challenge: friends or foes? The Dutch blew their trumpets, unwittingly challenging back. When a boat was lowered to take a party between the two ships, it was attacked and four crewmen were killed. Having not even set foot on the land, Tasman sailed away and didn't return; nor did any other European for 127 years. But the Dutch did leave a name: initially 'Statenland', later changed to 'Nova Zeelandia' by cartographers.

Contact between Māori and Europeans was renewed in 1769, when English and French explorers arrived, under James Cook and Jean de Surville – Cook narrowly pipped the latter to the post, naming Doubtless Bay before the French party dropped anchor there. The first French exploration ended sourly, with mistrust between the ailing French seamen and Māori, one of whom they took prisoner (he died at sea). Bloody skirmishes took place during a second French expedition, led by Marc-Joseph Marion du Fresne, when cultural misunderstandings led to violent reprisals; later expeditions were more fruitful. Meanwhile Cook made two more visits between 1773 and 1777. Exploration continued, motivated by science, profit and political rivalry.

Unofficial visits, by whaling ships in the north and seal-hunting gangs in the south, began in the 1790s (though Māori living in New Zealand's interior remained largely unaffected). The first Christian missionaries established themselves in the Bay of Islands in 1814, followed by dozens of others – Anglican, Methodist and Catholic. Europe brought such things as pigs and potatoes, which benefited Māori and were even used as currency. Trade in flax and timber generated small European–Māori settlements by the 1820s. Surprisingly, the most numerous category of 'European' visitor was probably American. New England whaling ships favoured the Bay of Islands for rest and recreation, which meant sex and drink. Their favourite haunt, the little town of Kororāreka (now Russell), was known as 'Gomorrah, the scourge of the Pacific'. As a result, New England visitors today might well have distant relatives among the local Māori.

Abel Tasman named NZ 'Statenland', assuming it was connected to Staten Island near Argentina. It was subsequently named after the province of Zeeland in Tasman's native Holland.

One of the first European women to settle in New Zealand was Charlotte Badger, a convict mutineer who fled to the Bay of Islands in 1806 and refused to return to European society.

1837	1840	1844	1858
European settlers introduce possums from Australia to NZ, creating a possum population boom that comes to threaten native flora and bird life.	Starting at Waitangi in the Bay of Islands on 6 February, around 500 chiefs countrywide sign the Treaty of Waitangi to 'settle' sovereignty once and for all. NZ becomes a nominal British colony.	Young Ngāpuhi chief Hone Heke challenges British sovereignty, first by cutting down the British flag at Kororāreka (now Russell), then by sacking the town itself. The ensuing Northland war continues until 1846.	The Waikato chief Te Wherowhero is installed as the first Māori King.

One or two dozen bloody clashes dot the history of Māori–European contact before 1840 but, given the number of visits, interracial conflict was modest. Europeans needed Māori protection, food and labour, and Māori came to need European articles, especially muskets. Whaling stations and mission stations were linked to local Māori groups by intermarriage, which helped keep the peace. Most warfare was between

CAPTAIN JAMES COOK

Countless obelisks, faded plaques and graffiti-covered statues remember the renowned navigator James Cook (1728–79). It's impossible to travel the Pacific without encountering the captain's image and his controversial legacy in the lands he opened to the West.

Cook came from an extremely pinched and provincial background. The son of a day labourer in rural Yorkshire, he was born in a mud cottage, had little schooling and seemed destined for farm work. Instead, Cook went to sea as a teenager, worked his way up from coal-ship servant to naval officer, and attracted notice for his exceptional charts of Canada. But Cook remained a little-known second lieutenant until, in 1768, the Royal Navy chose him to command a daring voyage to the South Seas.

In a converted coal ship called Endeavour, Cook sailed to Tahiti and then became the first European to land in New Zealand and the east coast of Australia. While he was there Cook sailed and mapped NZ's coastline in full – with impressive accuracy. The ship almost sank after striking the Great Barrier Reef, and 40% of the crew died from disease and accidents, but somehow the Endeavour arrived home in 1771. On a return voyage (1772–75), Cook became the first navigator to pierce the Antarctic Circle and circled the globe near its southernmost latitude, demolishing the ancient myth that a vast, populous and fertile continent surrounded the South Pole.

Cook's travels made an enormous contribution to world thought. During his voyages, Cook and his crew took astronomical measurements. Botanists accompanied him on his voyages, diligently recording and studying the flora they encountered. Cook was also remarkable for completing a round-the-world voyage without any of his crew dying of scurvy – adding 'nutrition' to his impressive roster of specialist subjects.

But these achievements exist beneath a long shadow. Cook's travels spurred colonisation of the Pacific, and within a few decades of his death, missionaries, whalers, traders and settlers began transforming (and often devastating) island cultures. As a result, many indigenous people now revile Cook as an imperialist villain who introduced disease, dispossession and other ills to the region (hence the frequent vandalising of Cook monuments). However, as islanders revive traditional crafts and practices, from tattooing to tapa (traditional barkcloth), they have turned to the art and writing of Cook and his men as a resource for cultural renewal. Significant geographical features in NZ bear his name, including Aoraki/Mt Cook, Cook Strait and Cook River, along with countless streets and hotels.

For good and ill, a Yorkshire farm boy remains one of the single most significant figures in shaping the modern Pacific.

1860–69	1861	1863–64	1867
The Taranaki wars, starting with the controversial swindling of Māori land by the government at Waitara, and continuing with outrage over the confiscation of more land as a result.	Gold discovered in Otago by Gabriel Read, an Australian prospector. As a result, the population of Otago climbs from less than 13,000 to over 30,000 in six months.	Waikato Land War. Up to 5000 Māori resist an invasion mounted by 20,000 imperial, colonial and 'friendly' Māori troops. Despite surprising successes, Māori are defeated and much land is confiscated.	All Māori men (rather than individual landowners) are granted the right to vote.

Māori and Māori: the terrible intertribal 'Musket Wars' of 1818–36. Because Northland had the majority of early contact with Europe, its Ngāpuhi tribe acquired muskets first. Under their great general Hongi Hika, Ngāpuhi then raided south, winning bloody victories against tribes without muskets. Once they acquired muskets, these tribes then saw off Ngāpuhi, but also raided further south in their turn. The domino effect continued to the far south of the South Island in 1836. The missionaries claimed that the Musket Wars then tapered off through their influence, but the restoration of the balance of power through the equal distribution of muskets was probably more important.

The Māori population for 1769 has been estimated at between 85,000 and 110,000. The Musket Wars killed perhaps 20,000, and new diseases (including typhoid, tuberculosis and venereal disease) did considerable damage, too. Fortunately NZ had the natural quarantine of distance: infected Europeans often recovered or died during the long voyage, and smallpox, for example, which devastated indigenous North Americans, never arrived. By 1840 Māori had been reduced to about 70,000, a decline of at least 20%. Māori bent under the weight of European contact, but they certainly did not break.

Growing Pains

Māori tribes valued the profit and prestige brought by the Pākehā and wanted both, along with protection from foreign powers. Accepting nominal British authority was the way to get them. New Zealand was appointed its first British Resident, James Busby, in 1833, though his powers were largely symbolic. Busby selected the country's first official flag and established the Declaration of the Independence of New Zealand. But Busby was too ineffectual to curb rampant colonisation.

By 1840 the British government was overcoming its reluctance to undertake potentially expensive intervention in NZ. The British were eager to secure their commercial interests and they also believed, wrongly but sincerely, that Māori could not handle the increasing scale of unofficial European contact. In 1840 the two peoples struck a deal, symbolised by the treaty first signed at Waitangi on 6 February that year. The Treaty of Waitangi now has a standing not dissimilar to that of the Constitution in the US, but is even more contested. The original problem was a discrepancy between British and Māori understandings of it. The English version promised Māori full equality as British subjects in return for complete rights of government. The Māori version also promised that Māori would retain their chieftainship, which implied local rights of government. The problem was not great at first, because the Māori version applied outside the small European settlements. But as those settlements grew, conflict brewed.

'I believe we were all glad to leave New Zealand. It is not a pleasant place. Amongst the natives there is absent that charming simplicity...and the greater part of the English are the very refuse of society.' Charles Darwin, writing about his 1835 visit to Kororāreka (Russell).

The Waitangi Treaty Grounds, where the Treaty of Waitangi was first signed in 1840, is now a tourist attraction for Kiwis and non-Kiwis alike. Each year on 6 February, Waitangi hosts treaty commemorations and protests.

1868–72	1886–87	1893	1901
East Coast war. Te Kooti, having led an escape from his prison on the Chatham Islands, leads a holy guerrilla war in the Urewera region. He finally retreats to establish the Ringatū Church.	Tuwharetoa tribe gifts the mountains of Ruapehu, Ngauruhoe and Tongariro to the government to establish NZ's first national park.	NZ becomes the first country in the world to grant the vote to women, following a campaign led by Kate Sheppard, who petitioned the government for years.	NZ politely declines the invitation to join the new Commonwealth of Australia, but thanks for asking.

LAND WARS

Starting in Northland and moving throughout the North Island, the New Zealand Wars had many complex causes, but *whenua* (land) was the one common factor. In these conflicts, also referred to as the Land Wars or Māori Wars, Māori fought both for and against the NZ government, on whose side stood the Imperial British Army, Australians and NZ's own Armed Constabulary. Land confiscations imposed on the Māori as punishment for involvement in these wars are still the source of conflict today, with the government struggling to finance compensation for what are now acknowledged to have been illegal seizures.

In 1840 there were only about 2000 Europeans in NZ, with the shanty town of Kororāreka as the capital and biggest settlement. By 1850 six new settlements had been formed, with 22,000 settlers between them. About half of these had arrived under the auspices of the New Zealand Company and its associates. The company was the brainchild of Edward Gibbon Wakefield, who also influenced the settlement of South Australia. Wakefield hoped to short-circuit the barbarous frontier phase of settlement with 'instant civilisation', but his success was limited. From the 1850s his settlers, who included a high proportion of upper-middle-class gentlefolk, were swamped by succeeding waves of immigrants that continued to wash in until the 1880s. These people were part of the great British and Irish diaspora that also populated Australia and much of North America, but the NZ mix was distinctive. Lowland Scots settlers were more prominent in NZ than elsewhere, for example, with the possible exception of parts of Canada. New Zealand's Irish, even the Catholics, tended to come from the north of Ireland. New Zealand's English tended to come from the counties close to London. Small groups of Germans, Scandinavians and Chinese made their way in, though the last faced increasing racial prejudice from the 1880s, when the Pākehā population reached half a million.

Much of the mass immigration from the 1850s to the 1870s was assisted by the provincial and central governments, which also mounted large-scale public works schemes, especially in the 1870s under Julius Vogel. In 1876 Vogel abolished the provinces on the grounds that they were hampering his development efforts. The last imperial governor with substantial power was the talented but machiavellian George Grey, who ended his second governorship in 1868. Thereafter, the governors (governors-general from 1917) were largely just nominal heads of state; the head of government, the premier or prime minister, had more power. The central government, originally weaker than the provincial governments, the imperial governor and the Māori tribes, eventually exceeded the power of all three.

'Kaore e mau te rongo – ake, ake!' (Peace never shall be made – never, never!) War chief Rewi Maniapoto in response to government troops at the battle of Orakau, 1864

1908	1914–18	1931	1935–49
NZ physicist Ernest Rutherford is awarded the Nobel Prize in chemistry for 'splitting the atom', investigating the disintegration of elements and the chemistry of radioactive substances.	NZ's contribution to WWI is staggering: for a country of just over one million people, about 100,000 NZ men serve overseas. Some 60,000 become casualties, mostly on the Western Front in France.	A massive earthquake in Napier and Hastings kills at least 256 people.	First Labour government in power, under Michael Savage. This government creates NZ's pioneering version of the welfare state, and also takes some independent initiatives in foreign policy.

The Māori tribes did not go down without a fight. Indeed, their resistance was one of the most formidable ever mounted against European expansion. The first clash took place in 1843 in the Wairau Valley, now a wine-growing district. A posse of settlers set out to enforce the myth of British control, but encountered the reality of Māori control. Twenty-two settlers were killed, including Wakefield's brother, Arthur, along with about six Māori. In 1845 more serious fighting broke out in the Bay of Islands, when Hōne Heke sacked a British settlement. Heke and his ally Kawiti baffled three British punitive expeditions, using a modern variant of the traditional *pā* fortification. Vestiges of these innovative earthworks can still be seen at Ruapekapeka (south of Kawakawa). Governor Grey claimed victory in the north, but few were convinced at the time. Grey had more success in the south, where he arrested the formidable Ngāti Toa chief Te Rauparaha, who until then wielded great influence on both sides of Cook Strait. Pākehā were able to swamp the few Māori living in the South Island, but the fighting of the 1840s confirmed that the North Island at that time comprised a European fringe around an independent Māori heartland.

In the 1850s settler population and aspirations grew, and fighting broke out again in 1860. The wars burned on sporadically until 1872 over much of the North Island. In the early years the King Movement, seeking to establish a monarchy that would allow Māori to assume a more equal footing with the European settlers, was the backbone of resistance. In later years some remarkable prophet-generals, notably Titokowaru and Te Kooti, took over. Most wars were small-scale, but the Waikato war of 1863–64 was not. This conflict, fought at the same time as the American Civil War, involved armoured steamships, ultra-modern heavy artillery, and 10 proud British regular regiments. Despite the odds, Māori forces won several battles, such as that at Gate Pā, near Tauranga, in 1864. But in the end they were ground down by European numbers and resources. Māori political, though not cultural, independence ebbed away in the last decades of the 19th century. It finally expired when police invaded its last sanctuary, the Urewera Mountains, in 1916.

From Gold Rush to Welfare State

From the 1850s to the 1880s, despite conflict with Māori, the Pākehā economy boomed. A gold rush on the South Island made Dunedin NZ's biggest town, and a young, mostly male population chased their fortunes along the West Coast. Fretting over the imbalance in this frontier society, the British government tried to entice women to settle in NZ. Huge amounts of wool were exported and there were unwise levels of overseas borrowing for development of railways and roads. By 1886 the population

---

Maurice Shadbolt's *Season of the Jew* (1987) is a semi-fictionalised story of bloody campaigns led by warrior Te Kooti against the British in Poverty Bay in the 1860s. Te Kooti and his followers compared themselves to the Israelites cast out of Egypt. For more about the NZ Wars, visit www.newzealand wars.co.nz.

Former NZ Prime Minister Julius Vogel (1835–99) wrote a science fiction novel *Anno Domini 2000* (1889) in which he imagines a utopian society led by women. Very prescient, considering NZ was the first country to give women the vote...

1936	1939–45	1930s	1953
NZ aviatrix Jean Batten becomes the first aviator to fly solo directly from Britain to NZ.	NZ troops back Britain and the Allied war effort during WWII; from 1942 as many as 45,000 American soldiers camp in NZ to guard against Japanese attack.	Maurice Schlesinger begins producing the Buzzy Bee, NZ's most famous children's toy.	New Zealander Edmund Hillary, with Tenzing Norgay, 'knocks the bastard off': the pair become the first men to reach the summit of Mt Everest.

reached a tipping point: the population of non-Māori people were mostly born in NZ. Many still considered Britain their distant home, but a new identity was taking shape.

Depression followed in 1879, when wool prices slipped and gold production thinned out. Unemployment pushed some of the working population to Australia, and many of those who stayed suffered miserable working conditions. There was still cause for optimism: NZ successfully exported frozen meat in 1882, raising hopes of a new backbone for the economy. Forests were enthusiastically cleared to make way for farmland.

In 1890 the Liberals, NZ's first organised political party, came to power. They stayed there until 1912, helped by a recovering economy. For decades, social reform movements such as the Woman's Christian Temperance Union (WCTU) had lobbied for women's freedom, and NZ became the first country in the world to give women the vote in 1893. (Another major WCTU push, for countrywide prohibition, didn't take off.) Old-age pensions were introduced in 1898 but these social leaps forward didn't bring universal good news. Pensions only applied for those falling within a very particular definition of 'good character', and the pension reforms deliberately excluded the population of Chinese settlers who had arrived to labour in the goldfields. Meanwhile, the Liberals were obtaining more and more Māori land for settlement. By now, the non-Māori population outnumbered the Māori by 17 to one.

Revered NZ Prime Minister (1893–1906) Richard 'King Dick' Seddon popularised the country's self-proclaimed nickname 'Godzone' with his famous final telegraph: 'Just leaving for God's own country'.

Nation-Building

New Zealand had backed Britain in the Boer War (1899–1902) and WWI (1914–18), with dramatic losses in WWI. However, the bravery of AN-ZAC (Australian and New Zealander Army Corps) forces in the failed Gallipoli campaign endures as a nation-building moment for NZ. In the 1930s NZ's experience of the Great Depression was as grim as any. The derelict farmhouses still seen in rural areas often date from this era. In 1935 a second reforming government took office, campaigning on a platform of social justice: the First Labour government, led by Australian-born Michael Joseph Savage. In WWII NZ formally declared war on Germany: 140,000 or so New Zealanders fought in Europe and the Middle East, while at home, women took on increasing roles in the labour force.

By the 1930s giant ships were regularly carrying frozen meat, cheese and butter, as well as wool, on regular voyages from NZ to Britain. As the NZ economy adapted to the feeding of London, cultural links were also enhanced. New Zealand children studied British history and literature, not their own. New Zealand's leading scientists and writers, such as Ernest Rutherford and Katherine Mansfield, gravitated to Britain. Average

Wellington-born Nancy Wake (codenamed 'The White Mouse') led a guerrilla attack against the Nazis with a 7000-strong army. Her honours included being the Gestapo's most wanted person and a highly decorated Allied servicewoman, and she was memorialised as 'the socialite who killed a Nazi with her bare hands'.

1974	1981	1985	1992
Pacific Island migrants who have outstayed visas are subjected to Dawn Raids (crackdowns by immigration police) under Robert Muldoon and the National government. Raids continue until the early 1980s.	Springbok rugby tour divides the nation. Many New Zealanders show a strong anti-apartheid stance by protesting the games. Other Kiwis feel that sport and politics should not mix and support the tour.	*Rainbow Warrior* sunk in Auckland Harbour by French government agents, preventing the Greenpeace protest ship from sailing to Moruroa, where the French government is conducting nuclear testing.	Government begins reparations for land confiscated in the Land Wars, confirming Māori fishing rights in the 'Sealord deal'. Major reparations follow, including those for the Waikato land confiscations.

living standards in NZ were normally better than in Britain, as were the welfare and lower-level education systems. New Zealanders had access to British markets and culture, and they contributed their share to the latter as equals. The list of 'British' writers, academics, scientists, military leaders, publishers and the like who were actually New Zealanders is long.

New Zealand prided itself on its affluence, equality and social harmony. But it was also conformist, even puritanical. The 1953 Marlon Brando movie, *The Wild One,* was banned until 1977. Full Sunday trading was not allowed until 1989. Licensed restaurants hardly existed in 1960, nor did supermarkets or TV. Notoriously, from 1917 to 1967, pubs were obliged to shut at 6pm (which, ironically, paved the way for a culture of fast, heavy drinking before closing time). Yet puritanism was never the whole story. Opposition to Sunday trading stemmed not so much from belief in the sanctity of the sabbath, but from the belief that workers should have weekends, too. Six o'clock closing was a standing joke in rural areas. There was always something of a Kiwi counterculture, even before imported countercultures took root from the 1960s onward.

In 1973 'Mother England' ran off and joined the budding EU. New Zealand was beginning to develop alternative markets to Britain, and alternative exports to wool, meat and dairy products. Wide-bodied jet aircraft were allowing the world and NZ to visit each other on an increasing scale. Women were beginning to penetrate first the upper reaches of the workforce and then the political sphere. Gay people came out of the closet, despite vigorous efforts by moral conservatives to push them back in. University-educated youths were becoming more numerous and more assertive.

New Zealand's staunch anti-nuclear stance earned it the nickname 'The Mouse that Roared'.

Scottish influence can still be felt in NZ, particularly in the south of the South Island. New Zealand has more Scottish pipe bands per capita than Scotland itself.

The Modern Age

From the 1930s, Māori experienced both a population explosion and massive urbanisation. Life expectancy was lengthening, the birth rate was high, and Māori were moving to cities for occupations formerly filled by Pākehā servicemen. Almost 80% of Māori were urban dwellers by 1986, a staggering reversal of the status quo that brought cultural displacement but simultaneously triggered a movement to strengthen pride in Māori identity. Immigration was broadening, too, first allowing in Pacific Islanders for their labour, and then (East) Asians for their money.

1995	2004	2010	2011
Peter Blake and Russell Coutts win the America's Cup for NZ, sailing *Black Magic;* red socks become a matter of national pride.	Māori TV begins broadcasting – for the first time a channel committed to NZ content and the revitalisation of Māori language and culture hits the small screen.	A cave-in at Pike River coalmine on the South Island's West Coast kills 29 miners.	A severe earthquake strikes Christchurch, killing 185 people and badly damaging the central business district.

Then, in 1984, NZ's next great reforming government was elected – the Fourth Labour government, led nominally by David Lange, and in fact by Roger Douglas, the Minister of Finance. This government adopted a more-market economic policy (dubbed 'Rogernomics'), delighting the right, and an anti-nuclear foreign policy, delighting the left. New Zealand's numerous economic controls were dismantled with breakneck speed. Middle NZ was uneasy about the anti-nuclear policy, which threatened NZ's ANZUS alliance with Australia and the US. But in 1985 French spies sank the anti-nuclear protest ship *Rainbow Warrior* in Auckland Harbour, killing one crewman. The lukewarm American condemnation of the French act brought middle NZ in behind the anti-nuclear policy, which became associated with national independence. Other New Zealanders were uneasy about the more-market economic policy, but failed to come up with a convincing alternative. Revelling in their new freedom, NZ investors engaged in a frenzy of speculation, and suffered even more than the rest of the world from the economic crash of 1987.

From the 1990s, a change to points-based immigration was weaving an increasingly multicultural tapestry in NZ. Numbers of incoming Brits fell but new arrivals increased, particularly from Asia but also from North Africa, the Middle East and various European countries. By 2006 more than 9% of the population was Asian.

By 2017 NZ had a new face to the world. Helmed by Jacinda Ardern, a coalition government was formed by Labour and NZ First, with support from the Green Party. New Zealand's third woman prime minister is faced with a balancing act between her governing parties while tackling the housing crisis and effecting bigger investment in education and health. It's no wonder that Ardern's ascendancy has been touted as the dawn of a new period of major reform.

In 2015 there was a public referendum to decide between five proposed designs for a new national flag, and the winner was a black- and blue-backed silver fern. During a second referendum in 2016, Kiwis decided that on reflection, they preferred the original flag – if it ain't broke...

2011	2013	2013	2015
NZ hosts and wins the Rugby World Cup for just the second time; brave France succumbs 8–7 in the final.	New Zealand becomes one of just 15 countries in the world to legally recognise same-sex marriage.	Auckland teenager Ella Yelich-O'Connor, aka Lorde, hits No 1 on the US music charts with her mesmeric, chant-like tune 'Royals'.	New Zealand's beloved All Blacks win back-to-back Rugby World Cups in England, defeating arch-rivals Australia 34–17 in the final.

Environment

New Zealand's landforms have a diversity that you would expect to find across an entire continent: snow-dusted mountains, drowned glacial valleys, rainforests, dunelands and an otherworldly volcanic plateau. Straddling the boundary of two great colliding slabs of the earth's crust – the Pacific plate and the Indo-Australian plate – NZ is a plaything for nature's strongest forces.

The Land

New Zealand is a young country – its present shape is less than 10,000 years old. Having broken away from the supercontinent of Gondwanaland (which included Africa, Australia, Antarctica and South America) some 85 million years ago, it endured continual uplift and erosion, buckling and tearing, and the slow fall and rise of the sea as ice ages came and went.

Nature Guide to the New Zealand Forest by J Dawson and R Lucas is a beautifully photographed foray into NZ's forests, home to ancient species dating from the time of the dinosaurs.

Evidence of NZ's tumultuous past is everywhere. The South Island's mountainous spine – the 650km-long ranges of the Southern Alps – grew from the clash between plates at a rate of 20km over three million years; in geological terms, that's a sprint. Despite NZ's highest peak, Aoraki/Mt Cook, losing 10m from its summit overnight in a 1991 landslide (and a couple of dozen more metres to erosion), the Alps are overall believed to be some of the fastest-growing mountains in the world.

Volcanic New Zealand

The North Island's most impressive landscapes have been wrought by volcanoes. Auckland is built on an isthmus peppered by some 48 scoria cones (cinder cones, or volcanic vents). The city's biggest and most recently formed volcano, 600-year-old Rangitoto Island, is a short ferry ride from the downtown wharves. Some 300km further south, the classically shaped cone of snowcapped Mt Taranaki overlooks tranquil dairy pastures.

The Department of Conservation website (www. doc.govt.nz) has useful information on the country's national parks, tracks and walkways. It also lists backcountry huts and campsites.

But the real volcanic heartland runs through the centre of the North Island, from the restless bulk of Mt Ruapehu in Tongariro National Park, northeast through the Rotorua lake district out to NZ's most active volcano, White Island, in the Bay of Plenty. Called the Taupo Volcanic Zone, this great 350km-long rift valley – part of a volcano chain known as the 'Pacific Ring of Fire' – has been the seat of massive eruptions that have left their mark on the country physically and culturally. The volcano that created Lake Taupo last erupted 1800 years ago in a display that was the most violent anywhere on the planet within the past 5000 years.

You can experience the aftermath of volcanic destruction on a smaller scale at **Te Wairoa (the Buried Village)** (☑07-362 8287; www.buriedvillage. co.nz; 1180 Tarawera Rd; adult/child $35/10; ☺9am-5pm), near Rotorua on the shores of Lake Tarawera. Here, partly excavated and open to the public, lie the remains of a 19th-century Māori village overwhelmed when nearby Mt Tarawera erupted without warning. The famous Pink and White Terraces, spectacular naturally formed pools (and one of several claimants

NEW ZEALAND ENVIRONMENTAL CARE CODE

Toitu te whenua (leave the land undisturbed). To support this approach, the Department of Conservation (DOC) has developed an Environmental Care Code that includes the following directives:

Protect plants & wildlife Treat forests and animal life with care and respect; they are unique and often rare.

Remove rubbish Litter is unattractive, harmful to wildlife and can increase vermin and disease. Don't burn plastic waste as some types will create ozone-harming gases.

Don't pollute lakes When cleaning and washing, take the water and wash well away from the water source. This way the water drains into the soil, which acts as a filter.

Take care with fires Summer fire bans are common, so use a portable fuel stove instead. If you use a fire, keep it small, use only dead wood, put it out by dousing it with water and check the ashes to be sure nothing is smouldering.

Camp carefully When camping, leave no trace of your visit.

Keep to the track By keeping to the track (where one exists) you lessen the chance of damaging fragile plants.

Consider others Be considerate of others who also want to enjoy the environment, particularly in huts and campsites. Always be prepared to make room for others.

Respect the country's cultural heritage Many places in NZ have a spiritual and historical significance. Treat these places with respect.

to the title 'eighth wonder of the world'), were destroyed overnight by the same upheaval.

Born of geothermal violence, **Waimangu Volcanic Valley** (☏07-366 6137; www.waimangu.co.nz; 587 Waimangu Rd; adult/child walk $39/12, cruise $45/12; ⊗8.30am-5pm, last admission 3pm) is the place to go to experience hot earth up close and personal amid geysers, silica pans, bubbling mud pools and the world's biggest hot spring. Alternatively, wander around Rotorua's **Whakarewarewa village** (☏07-349 3463; www.whakarewarewa. com; 17 Tryon St; adult/child $40/18, incl hāngi $70/40; ⊗8.30am-5pm), where descendants of Māori displaced by the eruption live in the middle of steaming vents and prepare food for visitors in boiling pools.

The South Island can also see some evidence of volcanism – if the remains of the old volcanoes of Banks Peninsula weren't there to repel the sea, the vast Canterbury Plains, built from alpine sediment washed down the rivers from the Alps, would have eroded long ago.

Earthquakes

Not for nothing has New Zealand been called 'the Shaky Isles'. Earthquakes are common, but most only rattle the glassware. A few have wrecked major towns. In 1931 an earthquake measuring 7.9 on the Richter scale levelled the Hawke's Bay city of Napier, causing huge damage and loss of life. Napier was rebuilt almost entirely in then-fashionable art-deco architectural style.

On the South Island, in September 2010 Christchurch was rocked by a magnitude 7.1 earthquake. Less than six months later, in February 2011, a magnitude 6.3 quake destroyed much of the city's historic heart and claimed 185 lives, making it the country's second-deadliest natural disaster. Then in November 2016 an earthquake measuring 7.8 on the Richter scale struck Kaikoura – further up the coast – resulting in two deaths and widespread damage to local infrastructure.

Flora & Fauna

New Zealand's long isolation has allowed it to become a veritable warehouse of unique and varied plants. Separation of NZ's landmass occurred before mammals appeared on the scene, leaving birds and insects to evolve in spectacular ways. As one of the last places on earth to be colonised by humans, NZ was for millennia a safe laboratory for risky evolutionary strategies. But the arrival of Māori, and later Europeans, brought new threats and sometimes extinction.

The now-extinct flightless moa, the largest of which grew to 3.5m tall and weighed more than 200kg, browsed open grasslands much as cattle do today (skeletons can be seen at Auckland Museum), while the smaller kiwi still ekes out a nocturnal living rummaging among forest leaf litter for insects and worms. One of the country's most ferocious-looking insects, the mouse-sized giant weta, meanwhile, has taken on a scavenging role elsewhere filled by rodents.

Many endemic creatures, including moa and the huia, an exquisite songbird, were driven to extinction, and the vast forests were cleared for timber and to make way for agriculture. Destruction of habitat and the introduction of exotic animals and plants have taken a terrible environmental toll – and New Zealanders are now fighting a rearguard battle to save what remains.

Native Birds & Animals

Pause in any NZ forest and listen: this country is aflutter with melodious feathered creatures. The country's first Polynesian settlers found little in the way of land mammals – just two species of bat – and most of NZ's present mammals are introduced species. New Zealand's birds generally aren't flashy, but they have an understated beauty that reveals itself in more delicate details: the lacy plumage of rare white heron (kōtuku), the bespectacled appearance of a silvereye or the golden frowns of Fiordland penguins.

The most beautiful songbird is the tui, a nectar-eater with an inventive repertoire that includes clicks, grunts and chuckles. Notable for the white throat feathers that stand out against its dark plumage, the tui often feeds on flax flowers in suburban gardens but is most at home in densely tangled forest ('bush' to New Zealanders). The bellbird (korimako) is also musical; it's common in both native and exotic forests everywhere except Northland (though it is more likely to be heard than seen). Its call is a series of liquid bell notes, most often sounded at dawn or dusk. Fantails (pīwakawaka) are also common on forest trails, swooping and jinking to catch insects stirred up by passing hikers.

At ground level, the most famous native bird is of course the kiwi, NZ's national emblem, with a rounded body and a long, distinctive bill with nostrils at the tip for sniffing out food. Sightings in the wild require patience and luck but numerous sanctuaries (p316) allow a peep of this iconic bird. Look out for other land birds like pukeko, elegant swamp-hens with blue plumage and bright-red beaks. They're readily seen along wetland margins and even on the sides of roads nearby – be warned, they have little road sense. Far rarer (though not dissimilar in appearance) is the takahe, a flightless bird thought extinct until a small colony was discovered in 1948. It's worth seeking them out at Te Anau's **bird sanctuary** (Te Anau Bird Sanctuary; www.doc.govt.nz; Te Anau–Manapouri Rd; ⊙dawn-dusk) FREE.

If you spend any time in the South Island high country, you are likely to spot the kea (unless it finds you first). A dark-green parrot with red underwings and a sense of mischief, its bold antics are a source of frustration and delight to New Zealanders, who crowned the kea 'Bird of the

Year' in 2017. Kea are particularly common in car parks along the Milford Hwy, and in the West Coast's glacier country, where they hang out for food scraps or tear rubber from car windscreens (we've also seen them nibbling at ski bindings in winter sports resorts around Queenstown: consider yourself warned). Resist the urge to feed them, as it's hugely damaging to their health.

ENVIRONMENTAL ISSUES IN NEW ZEALAND

New Zealand's reputation as an Eden, replete with pristine wilderness and ecofriendly practices, has been repeatedly placed under the microscope. The industry most visible to visitors, tourism, appears studded in green accolades, with environmental best practices employed in areas as broad as heating insulation in hotels to minimum-impact wildlife-watching. But mining, offshore oil and gas exploration, pollution, biodiversity loss, conservation funding cuts and questionable urban planning have provided endless hooks for bad-news stories.

Water quality is arguably the most serious environmental issue faced by New Zealanders. More than a quarter of the country's lakes and rivers have been deemed unsafe for swimming, and research from diverse sources confirms that the health of waterways is in decline. The primary culprit is 'dirty dairying' – cow effluent leaching into freshwater ecosystems, carrying with it high levels of nitrates, as well as bacteria and parasites such as *E. coli* and giardia. A 2017 report by the Ministry for the Environment and Statistics showed that nitrate levels in water were worsening at 55% of monitored river sites, and that urban waterways were in an especially dire state – with levels of harmful bacteria more than 20 times higher than in forest areas. A government push to make 90% of rivers and lakes swimmable by 2040 was met with initial scepticism about the metrics involved, but it's hoped that it will provide an impetus to make NZ's waterways worthy of the country's eco-conscious reputation.

Another ambitious initiative is Predator Free 2050, which aims to rid NZ of introduced animals that prey on native flora and fauna. The worst offenders are possums, stoats and rats, which eat swaths of forest and kill wildlife, particularly birds. Controversy rages at the Department of Conservation's (DOC) use of 1080 poison (sodium fluoroacetate) to control these pests, despite it being sanctioned by prominent environmental groups, such as Forest & Bird, as well as the Parliamentary Commissioner for the Environment. Vehement opposition to 1080 is expressed by such diverse camps as hunters and animal-rights activists, who cite detriments such as by-kill and the potential for poison passing into waterways. Proponents of its use argue that it's biodegradable and that aerial distribution of 1080 is the only cost-effective way to target predators across vast, inaccessible parts of NZ. Still, 'Ban 1080' signs remain common in rural communities and the controversy is likely to continue.

As well as its damaging impact on waterways, the $12 billion dairy industry – the country's biggest export earner – generates 48% of NZ's greenhouse gas emissions. Some farmers are cleaning up their act, lowering emissions through improved management of fertilisers and higher-quality feed, and major players DairyNZ and Fonterra have pledged support. But when it comes to contributing to climate change, the dairy industry isn't NZ's only dirty habit. New Zealand might be a nation of avid recyclers and solar-panel enthusiasts, but it also has the world's fourth-highest ratio of motor vehicles to people.

There have been fears about safeguarding the principal legislation governing the NZ environment, the 1991 *Resource Management Act*, in the face of proposed amendments. NGOs and community groups – ever-vigilant and already making major contributions to the welfare of NZ's environment – will find plenty to keep them occupied in coming years. With eco-conscious Jacinda Ardern leading a coalition government from 2017, New Zealanders have reason to be hopeful of a greener future – Ardern has pledged an ambitious goal of reducing net greenhouse gas emissions to zero by 2050. More trains, 100% renewable energy sources and planting 100 million trees per year – goals worthy of NZ's clean, green reputation.

And what of the native bats? Populations of both short-tailed and long-tailed bats are declining at frightening speed, though Kahurangi National Park and Nelson are believed to be home to small populations. DOC (Department of Conservation) is hard at work protecting bats, including ambitious plans to resettle them on predator-free islands. If you spot a bat, count yourself lucky – and consider telling DOC.

Marine Mammal–Watching

Kaikoura, on the northeast coast of the South Island, is NZ's nexus of marine mammal–watching. The main attraction here is whale-watching. The sperm whale, a toothed whale that can grow up to 18m long, is pretty much a year-round resident here. Depending on the season you may also see migrating humpback whales, pilot whales, blue whales and southern right whales. Other mammals – including fur seals and dusky dolphins – are seen year-round.

Kaikoura is also a hotspot for swimming with dolphins, with pods of up to 500 dusky dolphins commonly seen. Dolphin swimming is common elsewhere in NZ, with the animals gathering off the North Island near Whakatane, Paihia, Tauranga and in the Hauraki Gulf, and off

KIWI SPOTTING

A threatened species, the kiwi is also nocturnal and difficult to see in the wild; the odds are best in Trounson Kauri Park in Northland and on Stewart Island. If you are patient and can step lightly on a multi-hour evening guided walk, you have a good chance of seeing them with **Okarito Kiwi Tours** (☑03-753 4330; www.okaritokiwitours.co.nz; 53 The Strand; 3-5hr tours $75) ✎ on the West Coast. They can also be observed in many artificially dark 'kiwi houses':

Auckland Zoo (☑09-360 3805; www.aucklandzoo.co.nz; Motions Rd; adult/child $28/12; ◷9.30am-5pm, last entry 4.15pm) ✎

Kiwi North, Whangarei (☑09-438 9630; www.kiwinorth.co.nz; 500 SH14, Maunu; adult/child $20/5; ◷10am-4pm) ✎

Rainbow Springs, Rotorua (☑07-350 0440; www.rainbowsprings.co.nz; 192 Fairy Springs Rd, Fairy Springs; 24hr passes adult/child/family $40/20/99; ◷8.30am-10pm) ✎

Otorohanga Kiwi House & Native Bird Park (☑07-873 7391; www.kiwihouse.org.nz; 20 Alex Telfer Dr; adult/child $24/8; ◷9am-5pm, kiwi feedings 10.30am,1.30pm & 3.30pm daily)

National Aquarium of New Zealand, Napier (☑06-834 1404; www.nationalaquarium. co.nz; 546 Marine Pde; adult/child/family $20/10.50/57; ◷9am-5pm, feedings 10am & 2pm, last entry 4.30pm)

West Coast Wildlife Centre, Franz Josef (p219)

Ngā Manu, Waikanae (☑04-293 4131; www.ngamanu.co.nz; 74 Ngā Manu Reserve Rd; adult/child/family $18/8/38; ◷10am-5pm; 👪) ✎

Pukaha Mt Bruce National Wildlife Centre, near Masterton (p135)

Wellington Zoo (☑04-381 6755; www.wellingtonzoo.com; 200 Daniell St, Newtown; adult/child $24/12; ◷9.30am-5pm; 👪) ✎

Orana Wildlife Park, Christchurch (☑03-359 7109; www.oranawildlifepark.co.nz; 793 McLeans Island Rd, McLeans Island; adult/child $34.50/9.50; ◷10am-5pm)

Willowbank Wildlife Reserve, Christchurch (☑03-359 6226; www.willowbank.co.nz; 60 Hussey Rd, Northwood; adult/child $29.50/12; ◷9.30am-7pm Oct-Apr, to 5pm May-Sep) ✎

Kiwi Birdlife Park, Queenstown (☑03-442 8059; www.kiwibird.co.nz; Brecon St; adult/child $49/24; ◷9am-5pm, shows 11am, 1.30pm & 4pm)

National Kiwi Centre, Hokitika (☑03-755 5251; www.thenationalkiwicentre.co.nz; 64 Tancred St; adult/child $24/12; ◷9am-5pm Dec-Feb, to 4.30pm Mar-Nov; 👪)

Akaroa on the South Island's Banks Peninsula. Seal swimming also happens in Kaikoura and in Abel Tasman National Park.

But these kinds of wildlife encounters are controversial. Whale populations around the world have declined rapidly over the past 200 years: the same predictable migration habits that once made the giants easy prey for whalers nowadays make them easy targets for whale-watchers. As NZ's whale-watching industry has grown, so has concern over its impact. At the centre of the debate is the practice of swimming with whales and dolphins. While it's undoubtedly one of the more unusual experiences you can have on the planet, many observers suggest that human interaction with these marine mammals has a disruptive effect on behaviours and breeding patterns. Taking a longer view, others say that given humanity's historic propensity for slaughtering whales by the tens of thousands, it's time we gave them a little peace and quiet.

The Department of Conservation's guidelines and protocols ensure that all operators are licensed and monitored, and forbids swimming with dolphin pods that have vulnerable young calves. If it's truly a bucket-list essential for you, give yourself a few days to do it so that there is no pressure on the operator to 'chase' marine mammals to keep you happy. And if you feel your whale-, dolphin- or seal-swim operator has 'hassled' the animals or breached the boundaries in any way (like loud noises, feeding them or circling them), report them to DOC immediately.

NZ's Ancient Lizard

The largest native reptile in NZ is the tuatara, a crested lizard that can grow up to 50cm long. Thought to be unchanged for more than 220 million years, these endearing creatures can live for up to a century. Meet them at Auckland Zoo (p316), Invercargill's **Southland Museum** (⌨03-219 9069; www.southlandmuseum.com; Queens Park, 108 Gala St; ⊘9am-5pm Mon-Fri, from 10am Sat & Sun) FREE, Hokitika's National Kiwi Centre (p316), and other zoos and sanctuaries around NZ.

Trees

No visitor to NZ (particularly Australians) can last long without hearing about the damage done to the bush by that bad-mannered Australian import, the brushtail possum. The long list of mammal pests introduced to NZ, whether accidentally or for a variety of misguided reasons, includes deer, rabbits, stoats, pigs and goats. But by far the most destructive is the possum. At their height, 70 million possums were chewing through millions of tonnes of foliage a year. Following efforts by the DOC to control their numbers, the possum population has almost halved but they remain an enormous threat to native flora (and to bird life...possums prey on chicks and eggs).

Among favoured possum food is the colourful kowhai, a small-leaved tree growing to 11m, which in spring has drooping clusters of bright-yellow flowers (informally considered NZ's national flower); the pohutukawa, a beautiful coastal tree of the northern North Island that bursts into vivid red flower in December, earning the nickname 'Christmas tree'; and a similar crimson-flowered tree, the rata. Rata species are found on both islands; the northern rata starts life as a climber on a host tree (that it eventually chokes).

The few remaining pockets of mature centuries-old kauri are stately emblems of former days. Their vast trunks and towering, epiphyte-festooned limbs reach well over 50m high, reminders of why they were sought after in colonial days for spars and building timber. The best place to see the remaining giants is Northland's Waipoua Forest, home to the largest swath of kauri in the country. These mighty trees are under threat from fungus-like kauri dieback disease, so be diligent about following signs that direct you to clean your boots to stem the disease's spread.

Other native timber trees include the distinctive rimu (red pine) and the long-lived totara (favoured for Māori war canoes). NZ's perfect pine-growing conditions encouraged one of the country's most successful imports, *Pinus radiata*, which grow to maturity in 35 years (and sometimes less). Plantation forests are now widespread through the central North Island – the southern hemisphere's biggest, Kaingaroa Forest, lies southeast of Rotorua.

You won't get far into the bush without coming across tree ferns. NZ has an impressive 200 species of ferns, and almost half grow nowhere else on the planet. Most easily recognised are the mamaku (black tree fern) – which grows to 20m and can be seen in damp gullies throughout the country – and the 10m-high ponga (silver tree fern) with its distinctive white underside. The silver fern is a national symbol and adorns sporting and corporate logos, as well as shop signs, clothing and jewellery.

National Parks

More than 85,000 sq km of NZ – almost one-third of the country – is protected and managed within parks and reserves. Almost every conceivable landscape is present: from mangrove-fringed inlets in the north to the snow-topped volcanoes of the Central Plateau, and from the forested fastness of the Urewera ranges in the east to the Southern Alps' majestic mountains, glaciers and fiords. The 13 national parks and more than 30 marine reserves and parks, along with numerous forest parks, offer huge scope for wilderness experiences, ranging from climbing, skiing and mountain biking to tramping, kayaking and trout fishing.

Three places are World Heritage Areas: NZ's Subantarctic Islands; Tongariro National Park (on the North Island); and Te Wāhipounamu (Southwest New Zealand), an amalgam of several national parks in southwest NZ that boast the world's finest surviving Gondwanaland plants and animals in their natural habitats.

Access to the country's wild places is relatively straightforward, though huts on walking tracks require passes and may need to be booked in advance. In practical terms, there is little difference for travellers between a national park and a forest park, though pets are generally not allowed in national parks without a permit. Disability-assist dogs can be taken into dog-controlled areas without a permit. Camping is possible in all parks, but may be restricted to dedicated camping grounds – check with DOC first.

B Heather and H Robertson's *Field Guide to the Birds of New Zealand* is a comprehensive guide for birdwatchers and a model of helpfulness for anyone even casually interested in the country's remarkable bird life. Another good guide is *Birds of New Zealand: Locality Guide* by Stuart Chambers.

New Zealand is one of the most spectacular places in the world to see geysers. On the North Island, Rotorua's short-lived Waimangu geyser, formed after the 1886 Mt Tarawera eruption, was once the world's largest, often gushing to a dizzying height of 400m.

Survival Guide

Directory A-Z

Accessible Travel

Kiwi accommodation generally caters fairly well for travellers with mobility issues, with most hostels, hotels and motels equipped with one or two wheelchair-accessible rooms. (B&Bs aren't required to have accessible rooms.) Many tourist attractions similarly provide wheelchair access, with wheelchairs often available. Most i-SITE visitor centres can advise on suitable attractions in the locality.

Tour operators with accessible vehicles operate from most major centres. Key cities are also serviced by 'kneeling' buses (buses that hydraulically stoop down to kerb level to allow easy access), and many taxi companies offer wheelchair-accessible vans. Large car-hire firms (Avis, Hertz etc) provide cars with hand controls at no extra charge (but advance notice is required). Air New Zealand is also very well equipped to accommodate travellers in wheelchairs.

Download Lonely Planet's free Accessible Travel guides from http://lptravel.to/AccessibleTravel.

Children

Thanks in part to its hut system, range of tracks and lack of critters that bite or sting, NZ is well suited for a tramping holiday with children. Along some tracks, such as the Heaphy, Routeburn and Lake Waikaremoana, it would be unusual not to have kids in the huts each night.

The huts mean that children (and parents) can carry less gear and start each day with dry clothes, ensuring a comfortable experience in the bush. DOC also encourages families to go tramping by not charging children under the age of 11 for huts or campsites, and offering a 50% discount to older kids (free at Great Walk huts).

The key to a successful tramp with kids is to carefully select the track to match their level of endurance. Children younger than 10 years do best on tracks that are well benched and bridged, and where the next hut is only four or five hours away at most. An excellent introduction to overnight hiking is the Sunrise Track (p124). An alternative for parents with very young children (ages four to six) not up for the rigours of tramping every day is to use a hut as a base camp, taking them on day walks. NZ also has a wide range of day walks near that towns that are well suited to children, be it a full day across the Tongariro Alpine Crossing (p95), a heady climb to Roys Peak (p262), or a simple cafe-fuelled wander through Karangahake Gorge (p82). DOC has created a set list of great day hikes (p66), most of which will hold the attention of young minds.

The other important thing about tramping with children is to make sure you pack enough food. After a day outdoors, parents are often shocked to see their children consume twice as much as they would at home.

For helpful general tips, see Lonely Planet's *Travel with Children*.

Climate

Lying between 34°S and 47°S, NZ is squarely in the 'Roaring Forties' latitude, meaning it has a prevailing and continual wind blowing over it from west to east, ranging from gentle freshening breezes to occasional raging winter gales. Coming across the Tasman Sea, this breeze is relatively warm and moisture-laden. When it hits NZ's mountains the wind is swept upwards, where it cools and dumps its moisture. When the wind comes from the south (from Antarctica) it's icy cold – a southerly wind always means cold weather.

Rainfall The South and North Islands, because of their different geological features, have two distinct patterns of rainfall. On the South Island the Southern Alps act as a barrier for the moisture-laden winds

Auckland

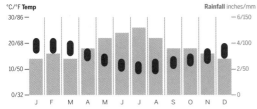

Christchurch

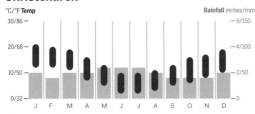

Queenstown

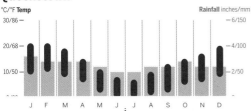

coming across the Tasman Sea. This creates a wet climate on the western side of the mountains and a dry climate on the eastern side – annual rainfall is more than 7500mm in parts of the west but only about 330mm across some of the east, even though they're not far apart. On the North Island, the western sides of the high volcanoes also get a lot more rain than the eastern sides, although since there's no complete barrier (as there is in the Southern Alps) the rain shadow is not as pronounced. Rainfall is more evenly distributed over the North Island, averaging around 1300mm per year. On the North Island rain falls throughout the year – typically, rainy days alternate with fine days, which is enough to keep the landscape perennially green.

Snow Snow is mostly seen in the mountains, and it can snow above the bushline any time of year. On the South Island there can also be snowfalls at sea level in winter, particularly in the far south.

Regional variations The South Island is a few degrees cooler than the North Island. It's quite warm and pleasant in Northland (the far north of the North Island) at any time of year; it's almost always a few degrees warmer than the rest of the country. Higher altitudes are always considerably cooler.

Unpredictability One of the most important things trampers need to know about NZ's climate is that it's a maritime climate, rather than the continental climate typical of larger land masses. This means the weather can change with amazing rapidity.

Customs Regulations

For the low-down on what you can and can't bring into NZ, see the New Zealand Customs Service website (www.customs.govt.nz). Per-person duty-free allowances:

➡ Three 1125mL (max) bottles of spirits or liqueur

➡ 4.5L of wine or beer

➡ 50 cigarettes, or 50g of tobacco or cigars

➡ Dutiable goods up to the value of $700

It's a good idea to declare any unusual medicines. Tramping gear (boots, tents etc) will be checked and may need to be cleaned before being allowed in. You must declare any plant or animal products (including anything made of wood), and food of any kind. Weapons and firearms are either prohibited or require a permit and safety testing. Don't take these rules lightly – noncompliance penalties will really hurt your hip pocket.

Electricity

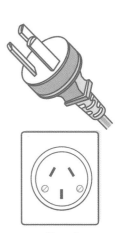

Type I
230V/50Hz

Emergency & Important Numbers

Regular NZ phone numbers have a two-digit area code followed by a seven-digit number. When dialling within a region, the area code is still required. Drop the initial 0 if dialling from abroad. If you're calling the police but don't speak English well, ask for Language Line, which may be able to hook you up with a translator.

NZ country code	☑64
International access code from NZ	☑00
Emergency (Ambulance, Fire, Police)	☑111
Directory Assistance (charges apply)	☑018

Entry & Exit Formalities

Disembarkation in New Zealand is generally a straightforward affair, with only the usual customs declarations and luggage-carousel scramble to endure. Under the Orwellian title of 'Advance Passenger Screening', documents that used to be checked after you touched down in NZ (passport, visa etc) are now checked before you board your flight – make sure all your documentation is in order so that your check-in is stress-free.

Customs Regulations

For the low-down on what you can and can't bring into NZ, see the New Zealand Customs Service website (www.customs.govt.nz). Per-person duty-free allowances:

➡ Three 1125mL (max) bottles of spirits or liqueur

➡ 4.5L of wine or beer

➡ 50 cigarettes, or 50g of tobacco or cigars

➡ Dutiable goods up to the value of $700

It's a good idea to declare any unusual medicines. Tramping gear (boots, tents etc) will be checked and may need to be cleaned before being allowed in. You must declare any plant or animal products (including anything made of wood), and food of any kind. Weapons and firearms are either prohibited or require a permit and safety testing. Don't take these rules lightly – noncompliance penalties will really hurt your hip pocket.

Visas

Citizens of 60 countries, including Australia, the UK, the US and most EU countries, don't need visas for NZ (length-of-stay allowances vary). See www.immigration. govt.nz.

Visa application forms are available from NZ diplomatic missions overseas, travel agents and **Immigration New Zealand** (☑09-914 4100, 0508 558 855; www. immigration.govt.nz). Immigration New Zealand has more than 25 offices overseas, including the US, UK and Australia; consult the website.

Food & Drink

New Zealand is a mighty fine place to wine and dine. From country pubs to chic restaurants, the emphasis is on home-grown ingredients like lamb, seafood and venison, with a thriving vegetarian and vegan food scene to cleanse the palate. Dining choices depend on destination: you'll be spoilt for choice in Auckland while little seaside towns might have just a bakery and pub to pick from.

Most eating options (p322) are casual walk-ups (pubs, cafes and takeaways) but book top-end restaurants well in advance.

Restaurants Open for dinner and lunch. 'Modern NZ' = locally sourced, top-quality fare with international influences.

Cafes Locally roasted beans, expert baristas, savvy breakfast-to-lunch food and family-friendly.

Takeaways Fish and chips, kebabs, burgers...the big internationals are here, but quality local outfits give them a run for their money.

Pubs & bars You can get a bite to eat at most Kiwi bars and pubs – from standard stodge to delicately wrought tapas and farmer-sized steaks.

Supermarkets In all sizeable towns – often open until 9pm.

On the liquid front, NZ wine is world class (especially sauvignon blanc and pinot noir), and you'll be hard-pressed to find a NZ town of any size without decent espresso. NZ's craft beer scene (www.soba.org.nz) is also riding the same wave of popularity as the rest of the world.

Most large urban centres have at least one dedicated vegetarian cafe or restaurant. See the NZ Vegetarian Society (www.vegetarian.org. nz) restaurant guide for listings. Beyond this, almost all restaurants and cafes offer vegetarian menu choices (although sometimes only one or two). Many eateries also provide gluten-free and vegan options.

EATING PRICE RANGES

The following price ranges refer to the average price of a main course.

$ less than $15

$$ $15–35

$$$ more than $35

Most small and medium-sized NZ towns will have at least one supermarket (eg New World, Pak'nSave or Countdown). When planning for a tramp, try to make sure you stock up where there is a decent supermarket rather than relying on a small corner shop or dairy.

There are numerous farmers markets held around NZ, usually at weekends. These are excellent places to meet local producers and source fresh regional produce. Check out www.farmersmarkets.org.nz for details.

Health

New Zealand poses minimal health risks to travellers. Diseases such as malaria and typhoid are unheard of, poisonous snakes and other dangerous animals are absent, and there are currently no dangerous insect-borne diseases. The biggest risks to travellers involve exploring the great outdoors: trampers must be clued in on rapid-changing weather and diligent about sharing any plans to visit remote areas, while drivers must exert extreme caution on NZ's notoriously winding roads.

For information about staying safe on the trail, see the Safety in the Outdoors chapter (p38).

Insurance

➡ A watertight travel-insurance policy covering theft, loss and medical problems is essential. Some policies specifically exclude designated 'dangerous activities', such as scuba diving, bungy jumping, white-water rafting, skiing and even tramping. Make sure your policy covers you fully.

➡ It's worth mentioning that under NZ law, you cannot sue for personal injury (other than

PRACTICALITIES

Electricity To plug yourself into the electricity supply (230V AC, 50Hz), use a three-pin adaptor (the same as in Australia; different from British three-pin adaptors).

Newspapers Check out Auckland's *New Zealand Herald* (www.nzherald.co.nz), Wellington's *Dominion Post* (www.stuff.co.nz/dominion-post) or Christchurch's *The Press* (www.stuff.co.nz/the-press).

TV Watch one of the national government-owned TV stations – including TVNZ 1, TVNZ 2, Māori TV or the 100% Māori-language Te Reo.

Radio Tune in to Radio New Zealand (www.radionz.co.nz) for news, current affairs, classical and jazz. Radio Hauraki (www.hauraki.co.nz) cranks out rock.

DVDs Kiwi DVDs are encoded for Region 4, which includes Australia, the Pacific, Mexico, Central America, the Caribbean and South America.

Smoking Like much of the Western world, smoking rates in NZ have been on the slide in recent decades. Smoking on public transport and in restaurants, cafes, bars and pubs is banned.

Goods & Services Tax (GST) A flat 15% tax applies to all domestic goods and services. NZ prices listed by Lonely Planet include GST. There's no GST refund available when you leave NZ.

Weights & measures New Zealand uses the metric system.

exemplary damages). Instead, the country's Accident Compensation Corporation (www.acc.co.nz) administers an accident compensation scheme that provides accident insurance for NZ residents and visitors to the country, regardless of fault. This scheme, however, does not negate the necessity for your own comprehensive travel-insurance policy, as it doesn't cover you for such things as income loss, treatment at home or ongoing illness.

➡ Consider a policy that pays doctors or hospitals directly, rather than you paying on the spot and claiming later. If you have to claim later, keep all documentation. Some policies ask you to call (reverse charges) to a centre in your home country where an immediate assessment

of your problem is made. Check that the policy covers ambulances and emergency medical evacuations by air.

➡ Worldwide travel insurance is available at www.lonelyplanet.com/travel-insurance. You can buy, extend and claim online anytime – even if you're already on the road.

Internet Access

Getting online in NZ is easy in all but remote locales. Expect abundant wi-fi in cafes and accommodation in big towns and cities, but thrifty download limits elsewhere.

Wireless Access

Wi-fi You'll be able to find wi-fi access around the country, from hotel rooms and pub beer gardens to hostel dorms. Usually you have to be a guest or customer to log in; you'll be issued with an access code. Sometimes it's free, sometimes there's a charge, and often there's a limit on time or data.

Hotspots The country's main telecommunications company is Spark New Zealand (www.spark. co.nz), which has more than 1000 wireless hotspots around the country. You can purchase prepaid access cards or a pre-paid number from the login page at any wireless hotspot using your credit card. See Spark's website for hotspot listings.

Equipment & ISPs If you've brought your tablet or laptop, consider buying a prepay USB modem (aka a 'dongle') with a local SIM card: both Spark and Vodafone (www.vodafone.co.nz) sell these from around $50.

Internet Cafes

There are fewer internet cafes around these days than there were five years ago, but you'll still find them in the bigger cities (frequented more by gamers than tourists). Access costs anywhere from $3 to $6 per hour.

Similarly, most hostels and holiday parks have done away with actual computers in favour of wi-fi. Most hotels, motels, B&Bs and holiday parks also offer wi-fi, sometimes free but usually for a small charge.

Legal Matters

If you are questioned or arrested by police, it's your right to ask why, to refrain from making a statement, and to consult a lawyer in private.

Plans are brewing for a referendum on whether personal use of cannabis should be decriminalised, but at the time of writing it was still illegal. Anyone caught carrying this or other illicit drugs will have the book thrown at them.

Drink-driving is a serious offence and remains a significant problem in NZ. The legal blood alcohol limit is 0.05% for drivers aged 20 years and over, and zero for those under 20.

LGBT+ Travellers

The gay tourism industry in NZ isn't as high profile as it is in some other developed nations, but LGBT communities are prominent in Auckland and Wellington, with myriad support organisations across both islands. New Zealand has progressive laws protecting human rights: same-sex marriage and adoption by same-sex couples were legalised in 2013, while the legal minimum age for sex between consenting persons is 16.

Generally speaking, Kiwis are fairly relaxed and accepting about gender fluidity, but that's not to say that homophobia doesn't exist. Rural communities tend to be more conservative; here public displays of affection should probably be avoided.

Maps

New Zealand's **Automobile Association** (AA; ☑0800 500 444; www.aa.co.nz/travel) produces excellent city, town, regional, island and highway maps, available from its local offices. The AA also produces a detailed *New Zealand Road Atlas*. Other reliable countrywide atlases, available from visitor information centres and bookshops, are published by Hema and KiwiMaps.

Land Information New Zealand (www.linz.govt.nz) publishes several exhaustive map series, including street, country and holiday maps, national park and forest park maps, and topographical trampers' maps. For information about topo maps for tramping, see the Safety in the Outdoor chapter (p39).

Online, log onto AA Maps (www.aamaps.co.nz) or search on Wises (www.wises. co.nz) to pinpoint exact NZ addresses.

Money

Credit cards are used for most purchases in NZ, and are accepted in most hotels and restaurants. ATMs are widely available in cities and larger towns.

ATMs & Eftpos

Branches of the country's major banks across both islands have ATMs, but you won't find them everywhere (eg not in small towns).

Many NZ businesses use Eftpos (electronic funds transfer at point of sale), allowing you to use your bank card (credit or debit) to make direct purchases and often withdraw cash as well. Eftpos is available practically everywhere: just like at an ATM, you'll need a PIN.

Credit Cards

Credit cards (Visa, Master-Card) are widely accepted for everything from a hostel bed to a bungy jump, and are pretty much essential for car hire. Credit cards can also be used for over-the-counter cash advances at banks and from ATMs, but be aware that such transactions incur charges. Diners Club and American Express cards are not as widely accepted.

Currency

New Zealand's currency is the NZ dollar, comprising 100 cents. There are 10c, 20c, 50c, $1 and $2 coins, and $5, $10, $20, $50 and $100 notes. Prices are often marked in single cents and then rounded to the nearest 10c when you hand over your money.

Debit Cards

Debit cards enable you to draw money directly from your home bank account using ATMs, banks or Eftpos facilities. Any card connected to the international banking network (Cirrus, Maestro, Visa Plus and Eurocard) should work with your PIN. Fees will vary depending on your home bank; check before you leave. Alternatively, companies such as Travelex offer debit cards with set withdrawal fees and a balance you can top up from your personal bank account while on the road.

Money Changers
Changing foreign currency (and to a lesser extent old-fashioned travellers cheques) is usually no problem at NZ banks or at licensed money changers (eg Travelex) in major tourist areas, cities and airports.

Tipping
Tipping is completely optional in NZ.

Guides Your kayaking guide or tour group leader will happily accept tips; up to $10 is fine.

Restaurants The total on your bill is all you need to pay (though sometimes a service charge is factored in). If you like, reward good service with 5% to 10%.

Taxis If you round up your fare, don't be surprised if the driver hands back your change.

Travellers Cheques
Amex, Travelex and other international brands of travellers cheques are a bit old hat these days, but they're still easily exchanged at banks and money changers. Present your passport for identification when cashing them; shop around for the best rates.

Opening Hours
Opening hours vary seasonally depending on where you are. Most places close on Christmas Day and Good Friday.

Banks 9am–4.30pm Monday to Friday, some also 9am–noon Saturday

Cafes 7am–4pm

Post offices 8.30am–5pm Monday to Friday; larger branches also 9.30am–noon Saturday

Pubs & bars noon–late ('late' varies by region, and by day)

Restaurants noon–2.30pm and 6.30pm–9pm

Shops & businesses 9am–5.30pm Monday to Friday and 9am to noon or 5pm Saturday

Supermarkets 8am–7pm, often 9pm or later in cities

Post
The services offered by **New Zealand Post** (☑0800 501 501; www.nzpost.co.nz) are reliable and reasonably inexpensive. See the website for info on national and international zones and rates, plus post office (or 'post shop') locations.

Public Holidays
New Zealand's main public holidays are as follows:

New Year 1 and 2 January
Waitangi Day 6 February
Easter Good Friday and Easter Monday; March/April
Anzac Day 25 April
Queen's Birthday First Monday in June
Labour Day Fourth Monday in October
Christmas Day 25 December
Boxing Day 26 December

In addition, each NZ province has its own anniversary-day holiday. The dates of these provincial holidays vary: when they fall on Friday to Sunday, they're usually observed the following Monday; if they fall on Tuesday to Thursday, they're held on the preceding Monday. To see an up-to-date list of provincial anniversaries during the year you travel, see www.govt.nz/browse/work/public-holidays-and-work/public-holidays-and-anniversary-dates.

Safe Travel
New Zealand is no more dangerous than other developed countries, but take normal safety precautions, especially after dark on city streets and in remote areas.

➡ Kiwi roads are often made hazardous by map-distracted tourists, wide-cornering campervans and traffic-ignorant sheep.

➡ Major fault lines run the length of NZ, causing occasional earthquakes.

➡ Avoid leaving valuables in vehicles: theft is a problem, even in remote areas.

➡ New Zealand's climate is unpredictable: hypothermia is a risk in high-altitude areas.

➡ At the beach, beware of rips and undertows, which can drag swimmers out to sea.

➡ New Zealand's sandflies are an itchy annoyance. Use repellent in coastal and lakeside areas.

Government Travel Advice
The following government websites offer travel advisories and information on current hotspots:

Australian Department of Foreign Affairs & Trade (www.smarttraveller.gov.au)

British Foreign & Commonwealth Office (www.gov.uk/fco)

Dutch Ministry of Foreign Affairs (www.government.nl/ministries/ministry-of-foreign-affairs)

Foreign Affairs, Trade & Development Canada (www.international.gc.ca)

German Federal Foreign Office (www.auswaertiges-amt.de)

Japanese Ministry of Foreign Affairs (www.mofa.go.jp)

US Department of State (www.travel.state.gov)

Telephone

New Zealand uses regional two-digit area codes for long-distance calls, which can be made from any payphone. If you're making a local call (ie to someone else in the same town), you don't need to dial the area code. But if you're dialling within a region (even if it's to a nearby town with the same area code), you do have to dial the area code.

To make international calls from NZ (which is possible on payphones), you need to dial the international access code 00, then the country code and the area code (without the initial '0'). So for a London number, for example, you'd dial 00-44-20, then the number. If dialling NZ from overseas, the country code is 64, followed by the appropriate area code minus the initial '0'.

Time

New Zealand is 12 hours ahead of GMT/UTC and two hours ahead of Australian Eastern Standard Time. The Chathams are 45 minutes ahead of NZ's main islands.

In summer, NZ observes daylight saving time: clocks are wound forward by one hour on the last Sunday in September; clocks are wound back on the first Sunday of April.

Toilets

Toilets in NZ are sit-down Western style. Public toilets are plentiful, and are usually reasonably clean with working locks and plenty of toilet paper.

See www.toiletmap.co.nz for public-toilet locations around the country.

Tourist Information

The website for the official national tourism body, Tourism New Zealand (www.newzealand.com), is an excellent place for pre-trip research. The site has information in several languages, including German, Spanish, French, Chinese and Japanese.

Princes Wharf i-SITE (☑09-365 9914; www.aucklandnz.com; Princes Wharf; ⊗9am-5pm) Auckland's main official information centre.

Auckland International Airport i-SITE (☑09-365 9925; www.aucklandnz.com; International Arrivals Hall; ⊗6.30am-10.30pm)

Christchurch i-SITE (☑03-379 9629; www.christchurchnz.com; Arts Centre, 28 Worcester Blvd; ⊗8.30am-5pm)

Christchurch Airport i-SITE (☑03-741 3980; www.christchurchnz.com; International Arrivals Hall; ⊗8am-6pm)

Queenstown i-SITE (☑03-442 4100; www.queenstownisite.co.nz; cnr Shotover & Camp Sts; ⊗8.30am-8pm)

Visitor Information Centres

Almost every NZ city or town seems to have a visitor information centre. The bigger centres stand united within the outstanding i-SITE network (www.newzealand.com/travel/i-sites), affiliated with Tourism New Zealand. i-SITEs have trained staff, information on local activities and attractions, and free brochures and maps. Staff can also book activities, transport and accommodation.

There's also an excellent network of DOC visitor centres to help you plan activities, make bookings and buy maps – and generally pick the brains of knowledgeable DOC staff for local track conditions and recommendations. Visitor centres also usually have displays on local lore, flora and fauna.

Volunteering

New Zealand presents an array of active, outdoorsy volunteer opportunities for travellers to get some dirt under their fingernails and participate in conservation programs. These programs can include anything from tree planting and weed removal to track construction, habitat conservation and fencing. Ask about local opportunities at any regional i-SITE visitor information centre, join one of the programs run by DOC (www.doc.govt.nz/getting-involved), or check out these online resources:

➡ www.conservation volunteers.org.nz

➡ www.helpx.net

➡ www.nature.org.nz

➡ www.volunteeringnz.org.nz

➡ www.wwf.org.nz

Women Travellers

New Zealand is generally a very safe place for female travellers, although the usual sensible precautions apply (for both sexes): avoid walking alone at night; never hitchhike alone; and if you're out on the town, have a plan for how to get back to your accommodation safely. Sexual harassment is not a widely reported problem in NZ, but of course that doesn't mean it doesn't happen. See www.women travel.co.nz for tours aimed at solo women.

Transport

GETTING THERE & AWAY

New Zealand is a long way from almost everywhere – most travellers jet in from afar. Flights, cars and tours can be booked online at lonelyplanet.com/bookings.

Entering the Country/Region

Disembarkation in New Zealand is generally a straightforward affair, with only the usual customs declarations and luggage-carousel scramble to endure. Under the Orwellian title of 'Advance Passenger Screening', documents that used to be checked after you touched down in NZ (passport, visa etc) are now checked before you board your flight – make sure all your documentation is in order so that your check-in is stress-free.

Passport

There are no restrictions when it comes to foreign citizens entering NZ. If you have a current passport and visa (or don't require one), you should be fine.

Air

New Zealand's abundance of year-round activities means that airports here are busy most of the time: if you want to fly at a particularly popular time of year (eg over the Christmas period), book well in advance.

The high season for flights into NZ is during summer (December to February), with slightly less of a premium on fares over the shoulder months (October/November and March/April). The low season generally tallies with the winter months (June to August), though this is still a busy time for airlines ferrying ski bunnies and powder hounds.

Airports & Airlines

A number of NZ airports handle international flights, with Auckland receiving the most traffic:

Auckland Airport (AKL; ☑09-275 0789; www.aucklandairport.co.nz; Ray Emery Dr, Mangere)

Christchurch Airport (CHC; ☑03-358 5029; www.christchurchairport.co.nz; 30 Durey Rd)

Dunedin Airport (DUD; ☑03-486 2879; www.dnairport.co.nz; 25 Miller Rd, Momona; ☎)

Queenstown Airport (ZQN; ☑03-450 9031; www.queenstownairport.co.nz; Sir Henry Wrigley Dr, Frankton)

Wellington Airport (WLG; ☑04-385 5100; www.wellingtonairport.co.nz; Stewart Duff Dr, Rongotai)

Note that Hamilton, Rotorua and Palmerston North airports are capable of handling direct international

arrivals and departures, but are not currently doing so.

AIRLINES FLYING TO & FROM NEW ZEALAND

New Zealand's international carrier is Air New Zealand (www.airnewzealand.co.nz), which flies to runways across Europe, North America, eastern Asia, Australia and the Pacific, and has an extensive network across NZ.

Winging in with direct flights from Australia, Virgin Australia (www.virginaustralia.com), Qantas (www.qantas.com.au), Jetstar (www.jetstar.com) and Air New Zealand are the key players.

Joining Air New Zealand from North America, other operators include Air Canada (www.aircanada.com) and American Airlines (www.aa.com) – the latter has direct flights from Los Angeles to Auckland.

From Europe, the options are a little broader, with British Airways (www.britishairways.com), Lufthansa (www.lufthansa.com) and Virgin Atlantic (www.virginatlantic.com) entering the fray. Flights go via major Middle Eastern or Asian airports. Several other airlines stop in NZ on broader round-the-world routes.

CLIMATE CHANGE & TRAVEL

Every form of transport that relies on carbon-based fuel generates CO2, the main cause of human-induced climate change. Modern travel is dependent on aeroplanes, which might use less fuel per kilometre per person than most cars but travel much greater distances. The altitude at which aircraft emit gases (including CO_2) and particles also contributes to their climate change impact. Many websites offer 'carbon calculators' that allow people to estimate the carbon emissions generated by their journey and, for those who wish to do so, to offset the impact of the greenhouse gases emitted with contributions to portfolios of climate-friendly initiatives throughout the world. Lonely Planet offsets the carbon footprint of all staff and author travel.

From Asia and the Pacific there are myriad options, with direct flights from China, Japan, Singapore, Malaysia, Thailand and Pacific Island nations.

Land

It is not possible to travel here by land.

Sea

Cruise Ship If you're travelling from Australia and content with a slow pace, try P&O (www.pocruises.com.au) and Princess (www.princess.com) for cruises to New Zealand.

Cargo Ship If you don't need luxury, a berth on a cargo ship or freighter to/from New Zealand is a quirky way to go. Freighter Expeditions (www.freighterexpeditions.com.au) offers cruises to New Zealand from Singapore (49 days return) and Antwerp in Belgium (32 days one way).

Yacht It is possible (though by no means straightforward) to make your way between NZ, Australia and the Pacific Islands by crewing on a yacht. Try asking around at harbours, marinas, and yacht and sailing clubs. Popular yachting harbours in NZ include the Bay of Islands and Whangarei (both in Northland), Auckland and Wellington. March and April are the best months to look for boats heading to Australia. From Fiji, October to November is a peak departure season to beat the cyclones that soon follow in that neck of the woods.

GETTING AROUND

New Zealand is long and skinny, and many roads are two-lane country byways: getting from A to B requires some thought.

Car Travel at your own tempo, explore remote areas and visit regions with no public transport. Hire cars in major towns. Drive on the left; the steering wheel is on the right (...in case you can't find it).

Bus Reliable, frequent services to most destinations around the country (usually cheaper than flying), though services thin out in rural areas.

Plane Fast-track your holiday with affordable, frequent, fast internal flights. You can carbon-offset your flights if you're feeling guilty.

Train Reliable, regular services (if not fast or cheap) along specific routes on both islands.

Air

Those who have limited time to get between NZ's attractions can make the most of a widespread (and very reliable and safe) network of intra- and inter-island flights.

Airlines in New Zealand

The country's major domestic carrier, Air New Zealand, has an aerial network covering most of the country, often operating under the Air New Zealand Link moniker on less-popular routes.

Australia-based Jetstar also flies between main urban areas. Between them, these two airlines carry the vast majority of domestic passengers in NZ.

Beyond this, several small-scale regional operators provide essential transport services to outlying islands, such as Great Barrier Island (in the Hauraki Gulf) to Stewart Island and the Chathams. There are also plenty of scenic- and charter-flight operators around NZ, not listed here. Operators include the following:

Air Chathams (0800 580 127; www.airchathams.co.nz) Services to the remote Chatham Islands from Wellington, Christchurch and Auckland. Auckland–Whakatane flights also available.

Air New Zealand (0800 737 000; www.airnewzealand.co.nz) Offers flights between 20-plus domestic destinations, plus myriad overseas hubs.

Air2there.com (0800 777 000; www.air2there.com) Connects destinations across Cook Strait, including Paraparaumu, Wellington, Nelson and Blenheim.

Barrier Air (0800 900 600; www.barrierair.kiwi) Flies the skies over Great Barrier Island, Auckland and Kaitaia (and seasonally, Tauranga and Whitianga).

FlyMySky (0800 222 123; www.flymysky.co.nz) At least three flights daily from Auckland to Great Barrier Island.

Golden Bay Air (0800 588 885; www.goldenbayair.co.nz) Flies regularly to Takaka in Golden Bay from Wellington and

Nelson. Also connects to Karamea for Heaphy Track trampers.

Jetstar (☎0800 800 995; www.jetstar.com) Joins the dots between key tourism centres: Auckland, Wellington, Christchurch, Dunedin, Queenstown, Nelson, Napier, New Plymouth and Palmerston North.

Sounds Air (☎0800 505 005; www.soundsair.co.nz) Numerous flights daily between Picton and Wellington, plus flights from Wellington to Blenheim, Nelson, Westport and Taupo. Also flies Blenheim to Christchurch, Kaikoura, Paraparaumu and Napier, and Nelson to Paraparaumu.

Stewart Island Flights (☎03-218 9129; www.stewartisland flights.co.nz) Flies between Invercargill and Stewart Island three times daily.

Sunair (☎0800 786 247; www.sunair.co.nz) Flies to Whitianga from Ardmore (near Auckland), Great Barrier Island and Tauranga, plus numerous other North Island connections between Hamilton, Rotorua, Gisborne and Whakatane.

Air Passes

Available exclusively to travellers from the USA or Canada who have bought an Air New Zealand fare to NZ from the USA, Canada, Australia or the Pacific Islands, Air New Zealand offers the good-value New Zealand Explorer Pass (www.airnewzealand.com/explorer-pass). The pass lets you fly between up to 37 destinations in New Zealand, Australia and the South Pacific islands (including Norfolk Island, Tonga, New Caledonia, Samoa, Vanuatu, Tahiti, Fiji, Niue and the Cook Islands). Fares are broken down into four discounted, distance-based zones: zone one flights start at US$99 (eg Auckland to Wellington); zone two from US$129 (eg Auckland to Queenstown); zone three from US$214 (eg Wellington to Sydney); and zone four from US$295 (eg Auckland to Tahiti). You can buy the pass before you travel, or after you arrive in NZ.

Arriving in New Zealand

Auckland Airport Airbus Express buses run into the city every 10 to 30 minutes, 24 hours. Door-to-door shuttle buses run 24 hours (from $35). A taxi into the city costs $80 to $90 (45 minutes).

Wellington Airport Airport Flyer buses ($9) run into the city every 10 to 20 minutes from around 7am to 9pm. Door-to-door shuttle buses run 24 hours (from $20). A taxi into the city costs around $30 (20 minutes).

Christchurch Airport
Christchurch Metro Purple Line runs into the city regularly from around 7am to 11pm. Door-to-door shuttles run 24 hours (from $23). A taxi into the city costs around $45 to $65 (20 minutes).

Bicycle

Touring cyclists proliferate in NZ, particularly over summer. The country is clean, green and relatively uncrowded, and has lots of cheap accommodation (including camping) and abundant freshwater. The roads are generally in good nick, and the climate is usually not too hot or cold. Road traffic is the biggest danger: trucks overtaking too close to cyclists are a particular threat. Bikes and cycling gear are readily available to hire or buy in the main centres, and bicycle-repair shops are common.

By law all cyclists must wear an approved safety helmet (or risk a fine); it's also vital to have good, reflective safety clothing. Cyclists who use public transport will find that major bus lines and trains only take bicycles on a 'space available' basis (in cities, usually outside rush hour) and may charge up to $10. Some of the smaller shuttle bus companies, on the other hand, make sure they have storage space for bikes, which they carry for a surcharge.

If importing your own bike or transporting it by plane

within NZ, check with the relevant airline for costs and the degree of dismantling and packing required.

See www.nzta.govt.nz/walking-cycling-and-public-transport for more bike safety and legal tips, and the New Zealand Cycle Trail (Nga Haerenga; www.nzcycletrail.com) – a network of 22 'Great Rides' across NZ.

Hire

Rates offered by most outfits for hiring road or mountain bikes are usually around $20 per hour to $60 per day. Longer-term hire may be available by negotiation. You can often hire bikes from your accommodation (hostels, holiday parks etc), or hire more reputable machines from bike shops in the larger towns.

Buying a Bike

Bicycles can be readily bought in NZ's larger cities, but prices for newer models are high. For a decent hybrid bike or rigid mountain bike you'll pay anywhere from $800 to $1800, though you can get a cheap one for around $500 (but you still then need to buy panniers, helmet, lock etc, and the cost quickly climbs). Other options include the post-Christmas sales and midyear stocktakes, when newish cycles can be heavily discounted.

Boat

New Zealand may be an island nation but there's virtually no long-distance water transport around the country. Obvious exceptions include the boat services between Auckland and various islands in the Hauraki Gulf, the inter-island ferries that cross the Cook Strait between Wellington and Picton, and the passenger ferry that negotiates Foveaux Strait between Bluff and the town of Oban on Stewart Island.

If you're cashed-up, consider the cruise liners that

chug around the NZ coastline as part of broader South Pacific itineraries: P&O Cruises (www.pocruises.com.au) is a major player.

Bus

Bus travel in NZ is easygoing and well organised, with services transporting you to the far reaches of both islands (including the start/end of various walking tracks)...but it can be expensive, tedious and time-consuming.

New Zealand's main bus company is **InterCity** (www.intercity.co.nz), which can drive you to just about anywhere on the North and South Islands. **Naked Bus** (📞09-979 1616; https://nakedbus.com) has similar routes and remains the main competition. Both bus lines offer fares as low as $1(!). InterCity also has a South Island sightseeing arm called **Newmans Coach Lines** (www.newmanscoach.co.nz), travelling between Queenstown, Christchurch and the West Coast glaciers.

Privately run shuttle buses can transport travellers to some trailheads or collect them from the end point of a tramp; advance booking essential.

Reservations

Over summer (December to February), school holidays and public holidays, book well in advance on popular routes (a week or two ahead if possible). At other times, a day or two ahead is usually fine. The best prices are generally available online, booked a few weeks in advance.

Seat Classes & Smoking

There are no allocated economy or luxury classes on NZ buses (very democratic), and smoking on the bus is a definite no-no.

Naked Bus has a sleeper class on overnight services between Auckland and Wellington (stopping at Hamilton and Palmerston North) where you can lie flat in a 1.8m-long bed (bring a sleeping bag, pillowcase and maybe earplugs). See http://nakedbus.com/nz/home/sleeper-bus for details.

Bus Passes

If you're covering a lot of ground, both InterCity and Naked Bus offer bus passes (respectively, priced by hours and number of trips). This can be cheaper than paying as you go, but do the maths before buying and note that you'll be locked into using one network. Passes are usually valid for 12 months.

On fares other than bus passes, InterCity offers a discount of around 10% for YHA, ISIC, HI, Nomads, BBH or VIP backpacker card holders. Senior discounts only apply for NZ citizens.

Shuttle Buses

As well as InterCity and Naked Bus, regional shuttle buses fill in the gaps between the smaller towns and often to the trailheads for tramps. Operators include the following (see www.tourism.net.nz/transport/bus-and-coach-services for a complete list), offering regular scheduled services and/or bus tours and charters:

Abel Tasman Travel (www.abeltasmantravel.co.nz) Traverses the roads between Nelson, Motueka, Golden Bay and Abel Tasman National Park.

Atomic Shuttles (www.atomictravel.co.nz) Has services throughout the South Island, including to Christchurch, Dunedin, Invercargill, Picton, Nelson, Greymouth, Hokitika, Queenstown and Wanaka.

Catch-a-Bus South (www.catchabussouth.co.nz) Invercargill and Bluff to Dunedin and Queenstown.

Cook Connection (www.cookconnect.co.nz) Triangulates between Mt Cook, Twizel and Lake Tekapo.

East West Coaches (www.eastwestcoaches.co.nz) Offers a service between Christchurch and Westport via Lewis Pass.

Go Kiwi Shuttles (www.go-kiwi.co.nz) Links Auckland with Whitianga on the Coromandel Peninsula daily.

Hanmer Connection (www.hanmerconnection.co.nz) Daily services between Hanmer Springs and Christchurch.

Headfirst Travel (www.travelheadfirst.com) Does a loop from Rotorua to Waitomo (with an option to finish in Auckland).

Tracknet (www.tracknet.net) Summer track transport (Milford, Hollyford, Routeburn, Kepler) with Queenstown, Te Anau and Invercargill connections.

Trek Express (www.trekexpress.co.nz) Shuttle services to all tramping tracks in the top half of the South Island (eg Heaphy, Abel Tasman, Old Ghost Road).

West Coast Shuttle (www.westcoastshuttle.co.nz) Daily bus from Greymouth to Christchurch and back.

Bus Tours

Clock up some kilometres with like-minded fellow travellers. The following operators run fixed-itinerary bus tours, nationwide or on the North or South Islands. Accommodation, meals and hop-on/hop-off flexibility are often included. Styles vary from activity-focused itineraries through to hangover-mandatory backpacker buses.

Adventure Tours New Zealand (www.adventuretours.com.au/new-zealand) Four 11- to 22-day NZ tours of North or South Island, or both.

Bottom Bus (www.travelheadfirst.com/local-legends/bottom-bus) South Island nether-region tours ex-Dunedin, Invercargill and Queenstown.

Flying Kiwi (www.flyingkiwi.com) Good-fun, activity-based trips around NZ with camping and cabin accommodation from a few days to a few weeks.

Haka Tours (www.hakatours.com) Three- to 24-day tours with adventure, snow or mountain-biking themes.

Kirra Tours (www.kirratours.co.nz) Upmarket coach tours (graded 'Classic' or 'Platinum' by price) from an operator with 50 years in the business.

Kiwi Experience (www.kiwiexperience.com) A major hop-on/hop-off player with eco-friendly credentials. Myriad tours cover the length and breadth of NZ.

Stray Travel (www.straytravel.com) A wide range of flexible hop-on/hop-off passes and tours.

Car & Motorcycle

The best way to explore NZ in depth is to have your own wheels. It's easy to hire cars and campervans, though it's worth noting that fuel costs can be eye-watering. Alternatively, if you're in NZ for a few months, you might consider buying your own vehicle.

Automobile Association (AA)

New Zealand's **Automobile Association** (AA; ☑0800 500 444; www.aa.co.nz/travel) provides emergency breakdown services, distance calculators and accommodation guides (from holiday parks to motels and B&Bs).

Members of overseas automobile associations should bring their membership cards – many of these bodies have reciprocal agreements with the AA.

Driving Licences

International visitors to NZ can use their home-country driving licence – if your licence isn't in English, it's a good idea to carry a certified translation with you. Alternatively, use an International Driving Permit (IDP), which will usually be issued on the spot (valid for 12 months) by your home country's automobile association.

Fuel

Fuel (petrol, aka gasoline) is available from service stations across NZ: unless you're cruising around in something from the 1970s, you'll be filling up with 'unleaded', or LPG (gas). LPG is not always stocked by rural suppliers; if you're on gas, it's safer to have dual-fuel capability. Aside from remote locations like Milford Sound and Mt Cook, petrol prices don't vary much from place to place: per-litre costs at the time of research were hovering above $2.

Hire

CAMPERVAN

Check your rear-view mirror on any far-flung NZ road and you'll probably see a shiny white campervan (aka mobile home, motor home, RV), packed with liberated travellers, mountain bikes and portable barbecues, cruising along behind you.

Most towns of any size have a campground or holiday park with powered sites (where you can plug your vehicle in) for around $35 per night. There are also 250-plus vehicle-accessible Department of Conservation (DOC; www.doc.govt.nz) campsites around NZ, priced at up to $21 per adult. Weekly campsite passes for hired campervans slice up to 50% off the price of stays in DOC campgrounds; check the website for info.

You can hire campervans from dozens of companies. Prices vary with season, vehicle size and length of hire, and it pays to book months in advance.

A small van for two people typically has a minikitchen and foldout dining table, the latter transforming into a double bed when dinner is done and dusted. Larger, 'superior' two-berth vans include shower and toilet. Four- to six-berth campervans are the size of trucks (and similarly sluggish) and,

besides the extra space, usually contain a toilet and shower.

Over summer, rates offered by the main firms for two-/four-/six-berth vans booked three months in advance start at around $120/150/230 per day (though they rise much higher, depending on model) for hire for two weeks or more. Rates drop to $60/75/100 per day during winter.

Major operators include the following:

Apollo (☑0800 113 131, 09-889 2976; www.apollocamper.co.nz)

Britz (☑09-255 3910, 0800 081 032; www.britz.co.nz) Also does 'Britz Bikes' (add a mountain or city bike from $12 per day).

Maui (☑09-255 3910, 0800 688 558; www.maui-rentals.com)

Wilderness Motorhomes (☑09-282 3606; www.wilderness.co.nz)

BACKPACKER VAN RENTALS

Budget players in the campervan industry offer slick deals and funky (often gregariously spray-painted), well-kitted-out vehicles for backpackers. Rates are competitive (from $30/60 per day for a two-/four-berth van from May to September; from $90/170 per day from December to February). Operators include the following:

Escape Campervans (☑0800 216 171; www.escaperentals.co.nz)

Hippie Camper (☑0800 113 131; www.hippiecamper.co.nz)

Jucy (☑09-374 4360, 0800 399 736; www.jucy.co.nz)

Mighty Cars & Campers (☑0800 422 505; www.mightycampers.co.nz)

Spaceships (☑09-526 2130, 0800 772 237; www.spaceshipsrentals.co.nz)

Tui Sleeper Vans (☑03-359 4731; www.sleepervans.co.nz)

CAR

Competition between car-hire companies in NZ is torrid, particularly in the big cities and Picton. Remember that if you want to travel far, you need unlimited kilometres. Some (but not all) companies require drivers to be at least 21 years old – ask around.

International car-hire firms don't generally allow you to take their vehicles between islands on the Cook Strait ferries. Instead, you leave your car at either Wellington or Picton terminal and pick up another car once you've crossed the strait. This saves you paying to transport a vehicle on the ferries, and is a pain-free exercise. However, some local car-hire firms (such as Apex) are fine with you taking your rental vehicle on the ferry and will even book your ferry ticket for you.

INTERNATIONAL RENTAL COMPANIES

The big multinational companies have offices in most major cities, towns and airports. Firms sometimes offer one-way rentals (eg collect a car in Auckland, leave it in Wellington), but there are usually restrictions and fees.

The major companies offer a choice of either unlimited kilometres, or 100km (or so) per day free, plus so many cents per subsequent kilometre. Daily rates in main cities typically start at around $40 per day for a compact, late-model, Japanese car, and from $70 for medium-sized cars (including GST, unlimited kilometres and insurance).

Avis (☑0800 655 111, 09-526 2847; www.avis.co.nz)

Budget (☑09-529 7788, 0800 283 438; www.budget.co.nz)

Europcar (☑0800 800 115; www.europcar.co.nz)

Hertz (☑0800 654 321; www.hertz.co.nz)

Thrifty (☑03-359 2721, 0800 737 070; www.thrifty.co.nz)

LOCAL RENTAL COMPANIES

Local hire firms proliferate. These are almost always cheaper than the big boys – sometimes half the price – but the cheap rates may come with serious restrictions: vehicles are often older, depots might be further away from airports/city centres, and with less formality sometimes comes a less-protective legal structure for renters.

Rentals from local firms start at around $30 or $40 per day for the smallest option. It's cheaper if you hire for a week or more, and there are often low-season and weekend discounts.

Affordable, independent operators with national networks include the following:

a2b Car Rentals (☑0800 545 000, 09-254 4397; www.a2b-car-rental.co.nz)

Ace Rental Cars (☑0800 502 277, 09-303 3112; www.acerentalcars.co.nz)

Apex Rentals (☑03-595 2315, 0800 500 660; www.apexrentals.co.nz)

Ezi Car Rental (☑0800 545 000, 09-254 4397; www.ezicar rental.co.nz)

Go Rentals (☑0800 467 368, 09-974 1598; www.gorentals.co.nz)

Omega Rental Cars (☑09-377 5573, 0800 525 210; www.omegarentalcars.com)

Pegasus Rental Cars (☑0800 803 580; www.rentalcars.co.nz)

Transfercar (☑09-630 7533; www.transfercar.co.nz) Relocation specialists with massive money-saving deals on one-way car hire.

MOTORCYCLE

Born to be wild? New Zealand has great terrain for motorcycle touring, despite the fickle weather in some regions. Most of the country's motorcycle-hire shops are in Auckland and Christchurch, where you can hire anything from a little 50cc moped (aka nifty-fifty) to a throbbing

750cc touring motorcycle and beyond. Recommended operators (who also run guided tours) offer rates around $100 per day:

New Zealand Motorcycle Rentals & Tours (☑09-486 2472; www.nzbike.com)

Te Waipounamu Motorcycle Tours (☑03-372 3537; www.motorcycle-hire.co.nz)

Insurance

Rather than risk paying out wads of cash if you have an accident, you can take out your own comprehensive insurance policy, or (the usual option) pay an additional fee per day to the hire company to reduce your excess. This brings the amount you must pay in the event of an accident down from around $1500 or $2000 to around $200 or $300. Smaller operators offering cheap rates often have a compulsory insurance excess, taken as a credit-card bond, of around $900.

Many insurance agreements won't cover the cost of damage to glass (including the windscreen) or tyres, and insurance coverage is often invalidated on beaches and certain rough (4WD) unsealed roads – read the fine print.

See www.acc.co.nz for info on NZ's Accident Compensation Corporation insurance scheme (fault-free personal injury insurance).

Purchase

Planning a long trip? Buying a car then selling it at the end of your travels can be one of the cheapest and best ways to see NZ. Auckland is the easiest place to buy a car, followed by Christchurch: scour the hostel noticeboards. Turners Auctions (www.turners.co.nz) is NZ's biggest car-auction operator, with 11 locations.

BUY-BACK DEALS

You can avoid the hassle of buying/selling a vehicle privately by entering into a buy-back arrangement with a dealer. Predictably, dealers often find sneaky ways of knocking down the return-sale price, which may be 50% less than what you paid, so hiring or buying and selling a vehicle yourself (if you have the time) is usually a better bet.

LEGALITIES

Make sure your prospective vehicle has a Warrant of Fitness (WoF) and registration valid for a reasonable period: see the New Zealand Transport Agency website (www.nzta.govt.nz) for details.

Buyers should also take out third-party insurance, covering the cost of repairs to another vehicle in an accident that is your fault: try the **Automobile Association** (AA; ☑0800 500 444; www.aa.co.nz/travel). New Zealand's no-fault Accident Compensation Corporation (www.acc.co.nz) scheme covers personal injury, but make sure you have travel insurance, too.

If you're considering buying a car and want someone to check it out for you, various companies inspect cars for around $150; find them at car auctions, or they will come to you. Try Vehicle Inspection New Zealand (☑09-573 3230, 0800 468 469; www.vinz.co.nz) or the AA.

Before you buy it's wise to confirm ownership of the vehicle, and find out if there's anything dodgy about it (eg stolen, or outstanding debts). The AA's LemonCheck (☑09-420 3090; www.lemoncheck.co.nz) offers this service.

Road Hazards

There's an unusually high percentage of international drivers involved in road accidents in NZ – something like 30% of accidents involve a nonlocal driver. Kiwi traffic is usually pretty light, but it's easy to get stuck behind a slow-moving truck or campervan – pack plenty of patience, and know your road rules before you get behind the wheel. There are also lots of slow wiggly roads, one-way bridges and plenty of gravel roads, all of which require a more cautious driving approach. And watch out for sheep!

To check road conditions, call ☑0800 444 449 or see www.nzta.govt.nz/traffic.

Road Rules

➧ Kiwis drive on the left-hand side of the road; cars are right-hand drive. Give way to the right at intersections.

➧ All vehicle occupants must wear a seatbelt or risk a fine. Small children must be belted into approved safety seats.

➧ Always carry your licence when driving.

➧ Drink-driving is a serious offence and remains a significant problem in NZ, despite widespread campaigns and severe penalties. The legal blood-alcohol limit is 0.05% for drivers aged over 20, and 0% (zero) for those under 20.

➧ At single-lane bridges (of which there are a surprisingly large number), a smaller red arrow pointing in your direction of travel means that you give way.

➧ Speed limits on the open road are generally 100km/h; in built-up areas the limit is usually 50km/h. Speed cameras and radars are used extensively.

➧ Be aware that not all rail crossings have barriers or alarms. Approach slowly and look both ways.

➧ Don't pass other cars when the centre line is yellow.

➧ It's illegal to drive while using a mobile phone.

Hitching & Ride-Sharing

Hitchhiking is never entirely safe, and we don't recommend it. Travellers who hitch should understand that they are taking a small but potentially serious risk. That said, it's not unusual to see hitchhikers along NZ country roads.

Alternatively, check hostel noticeboards for ride-share opportunities.

Local Transport

New Zealand's larger cities have extensive bus services but, with a few honourable exceptions, they are mainly daytime, weekday operations; weekend services can be infrequent or nonexistent. Negotiating inner-city Auckland is made easier by Link buses; Hamilton has a free city-centre loop bus; Christchurch has city buses and the historic tramway. Most main cities have late-night buses for boozy Friday and Saturday nights. Don't expect local bus services in more remote areas.

The only cities with decent local train services are Auckland and Wellington, with four and five suburban routes respectively.

The main cities have plenty of taxis and even small towns may have a local service. Taxis are metered, and are generally reliable and trustworthy.

Train

New Zealand train travel is all about the journey, not about getting anywhere in a hurry. **Great Journeys of New Zealand** (☑0800 872 467, 04-495 0775; www.greatjourneysofnz.co.nz) operates four routes, listed below. It's best to reserve online or by phone; reservations can be made directly through Great Journeys of New Zealand (operated by KiwiRail), or at most train stations, travel agents and visitor information centres. Cheaper fares appear if you book online within NZ. All services are for day travel (no sleeper services).

Capital Connection Weekday commuter service between Palmerston North and Wellington.

Coastal Pacific Track damage during the 2016 earthquakes put this scenic Christchurch–Picton route out of action, but when we went to press it was estimated to return in 2018.

Northern Explorer Between Auckland and Wellington: southbound on Mondays, Thursdays and Saturdays; northbound on Tuesdays, Fridays and Sundays.

TranzAlpine Over the Southern Alps between Christchurch and Greymouth – one of the world's most famous train rides.

Train Passes

A Scenic Journeys Rail Pass allows unlimited travel on all of Great Journeys of New Zealand's rail services, including passage on the Wellington–Picton *Interislander* ferry. There are two types of pass, both requiring you to book your seats a minimum of 24 hours before you want to travel. Both have discounts for kids.

Fixed Pass Limited-duration fares for one/two/three weeks, costing $629/729/829 per adult.

Freedom Pass Affords you travel on a certain number of days over a 12-month period; a three-/seven-/10-day pass costs $439/969/1299.

Accommodation

B&Bs

Bed and breakfast (B&B) accommodation in NZ pops up in the middle of cities, in rural hamlets and on stretches of isolated coastline, with rooms on offer in everything from suburban bungalows to stately manors.

Breakfast may be 'continental' (a standard offering of cereal, toast and tea or coffee, or a heartier version with yoghurt, fruit, home-baked bread or muffins), or a stomach-loading cooked meal (eggs, bacon, sausages – though, with notice, vegetarians are increasingly being well catered for). Some B&B hosts may also cook dinner for guests and advertise dinner, bed and breakfast (DB&B) packages.

B&B tariffs are typically in the $120 to $200 bracket (per double), though some places cost upwards of $300 per double. Some hosts charge cheeky prices for what is, in essence, a bedroom in their home. Off-street parking is often a bonus in the big cities.

Camping & Holiday Parks

Campers and campervan drivers converge on NZ's hugely popular 'holiday parks', slumbering in powered and unpowered sites, cheap bunk rooms (dorm rooms), cabins

(shared bathroom facilities) and self-contained units (often called motels or tourist flats). Well-equipped communal kitchens, dining areas, games and TV rooms, and playgrounds often feature. In cities, holiday parks are usually a fair way from the action, but in smaller towns they can be impressively central or near lakes, beaches, rivers and forests.

The nightly cost of holiday-park tent sites is usually $15 to $20 per adult, with children charged half price; powered campervan sites can be anything from a couple of dollars more to around the $40 mark. Cabin/unit accommodation normally ranges from $70 to $120 per double. Unless noted otherwise, Lonely Planet lists campsite, campervan site, hut and cabin prices for two people.

DOC & Freedom Camping

A fantastic option for those in campervans is the 250-plus vehicle-accessible 'Conservation Campsites' run by the Department of Conservation (DOC; www.

doc.govt.nz), with fees ranging from free (basic toilets and fresh water) to $21 per adult (flush toilets and showers). DOC publishes free brochures with detailed descriptions and instructions to find every campsite (even GPS coordinates). Pick up copies from DOC offices before you hit the road, or visit the website.

New Zealand is so photogenic, it's tempting to just pull off the road at a gorgeous viewpoint and camp the night. But never assume it's OK to camp somewhere: always ask a local or check with the local i-SITE, DOC office or commercial campground. If you are 'freedom camping', treat the area with respect. If your chosen campsite doesn't have toilet facilities and neither does your campervan, it's illegal for you to sleep there (your campervan must also have an on-board grey-water storage system). Legislation allows for $200 instant fines for camping in prohibited areas or improper disposal of waste (in cases where dumping waste could damage the environment, fees are up to $10,000). See www.camping.org.nz for more freedom-camping tips and consider downloading the free Campermate App (www.campermate.co.nz), which flags drinking-water sources, public toilets, freedom-camping spots and locals happy to rent their driveway to campervans.

Farmstays

Farmstays open the door to the agricultural side of NZ life, with visitors encouraged to get some dirt beneath their fingernails at orchards, and dairy, sheep and cattle farms. Costs can vary widely, with bed and breakfast generally costing $80 to $140. Some farms have separate cottages where you can fix your own food; others offer low-cost, shared, backpacker-style accommodation.

Farm Helpers in NZ (www.fhinz.co.nz) produces a booklet ($25) that lists around 350 NZ farms providing lodging in exchange for four to six hours' work per day.

WWOOFing

If you don't mind getting your hands dirty, an economical way of travelling around NZ involves doing some voluntary work as a member of the international **Willing Workers On Organic Farms** (WWOOF; ☑03-544 9890; www. wwoof.co.nz; ◷9am-3pm Mon-Fri) scheme. Down on the

farm, in exchange for a short, hard day's work, owners provide food, accommodation and some hands-on organic farming experience. Contact farm owners a week or two beforehand to arrange your stay, as you would for a hotel or hostel – don't turn up unannounced!

A one-year online membership costs $40 for an individual or a couple. A farm-listing book, which is mailed to you, costs an extra $10 to $30, depending on where in the world your mailbox is. You should have a Working Holiday Visa when you visit NZ, as the immigration department considers WWOOFers to be working.

Hostels

New Zealand is packed to the rafters with backpacker hostels, both independent and part of large chains, ranging from small, homestay-style affairs with a handful of beds to refurbished hotels and towering modern structures in the big cities. Hostel bed prices listed by Lonely Planet are nonmember rates, usually $25 to $35 per night.

Budget Backpacker Hostels
(www.bbh.co.nz) A network of more than 160 hostels. Membership costs $45 for 12 months and entitles you to stay at member hostels at rates listed in the annual (free) *BBH Backpacker Accommodation* booklet. Nonmembers pay an extra $4 per night. Pick up a

membership card from any member hostel or order one online ($50).

YHA New Zealand (www.yha. co.nz) Around 40 hostels in prime NZ locations. The YHA is part of the Hostelling International network (www.hihostels.com), so if you're already an HI member in your own country, membership entitles you to use NZ hostels. If you don't already have a home membership, you can join at major NZ YHA hostels or online for $25, valid for 12 months (it's free for under 18s). Nonmembers pay an extra $3 or more per night. Membership has other perks, such as discounts on some car-hire providers, travel insurers, DOC hut passes and more.

Base Backpackers (www. stayatbase.com) Chain with nine-plus hostels around NZ: Bay of Islands, Auckland, Rotorua, Taupo, Wellington, Wanaka, Queenstown, Dunedin and Christchurch. Expect clean dorms, women-only areas and party opportunities aplenty. Offers a flexible 10-night 'Base Jumping' accommodation package for $289, bookable online.

VIP Backpackers (www.vip backpackers.com) International organisation affiliated with around 20 NZ hostels (not BBH or YHA), mainly in the cities and tourist hot spots. For around $61 (including postage), you'll receive a 12-month membership entitling you to a $1 discount off nightly accommodation and discounts with affiliated activity and tour providers. Join online or at VIP hostels.

Haka Lodge (www.hakalodge. com) A local chain on the way up, with snazzy hostels in Auckland, Queenstown, Christchurch, Taupo and Paihia. Rates are comparable to other hostels around NZ, and quality is high. Tours are also available.

Pubs, Hotels & Motels

The least expensive form of NZ hotel accommodation is the humble pub. Some are full of character (and characters); others are grotty,

---

PRICE RANGES

The following price ranges refer to a double room with bathroom during high season. Price ranges generally increase by 20% to 25% in Auckland, Wellington and Christchurch. Here you can still find budget accommodation at up to $120 per double, but midrange stretches from $120 to $250, with top-end rooms more than $250.

$ less than $120

$$ $120–$200

$$$ more than $200

DOC HUTS & CAMPSITES

Huts

DOC maintains a network of more than 950 huts in its national parks, conservation areas and reserves. The majority of these operate on a first-come, first-served basis and fall into three categories, paid for with Backcountry Hut Passes or hut tickets:

Serviced Huts ($15) Equipped with mattresses, water supply, toilets, hand-washing facilities and heating with fuel available; may have gas cooking facilities and a warden.

Standard Huts ($5) Mattresses, water supply and toilets; wood heaters are provided at huts below the bushline.

Basic Huts or 'Bivvy' (free) Very basic enclosed shelter with limited facilities.

There are two other categories of huts. Great Walk Huts ($24 to $80) are the most comfortable, with mattresses, water supply, toilets, hand-washing facilities and heating with fuel available. They may have solar lighting, gas cooking facilities and a hut warden. Bookings are essential and can be made via **Great Walks Bookings** (☎0800 694 732; www.greatwalks.co.nz) or in person at any DOC visitor centre. Most of these huts revert to Serviced or Standard Huts out of the Great Walks season.

There are also private club huts that are open to the public, such as those owned by the New Zealand Alpine Club (NZAC). These have mattresses, a water supply, toilets and hand-washing facilities. They may have heating and cooking facilities. Backcountry Hut Passes and hut tickets are generally not valid at club huts and bookings may be required.

Campsites

There are also plenty of campsites throughout the DOC estate, which are either paid for in cash when you arrive at the campsite, or to a camp warden, or in some cases when you book via www.doc.govt.nz. They fall into the following categories:

Backcountry campsites (free) With toilets and a water supply, which may be from a stream. They may have picnic tables, cooking shelters or fireplaces.

Basic campsites (free) Very limited facilities, so you need to be fully self-sufficient. There are basic toilets and water from a tank, stream or lake. Access may be by road or boat.

Standard campsite ($6) With toilets (usually the composting or pit variety), water supply (tap, stream or lake) and vehicle or boat access. Wood barbecues and fireplaces, showers (cold), picnic tables, a cooking shelter and rubbish bins may be provided.

Scenic campsite ($10) Located in high-use locations, these have toilets, tap-water supply and vehicle or boat access. Wood barbecues and fireplaces, cold showers, picnic tables, a cooking shelter and rubbish bins may be provided.

Serviced campsite ($15) With flush toilets, tap water, kitchen/cooking bench, hot showers, rubbish collection and road access for all types of vehicles. Laundry facilities, barbecues, fireplaces, cookers and picnic tables may be available.

In addition, all Great Walks (except the Milford Track) have **Great Walk Campsites** ($6 to $20) near huts or in designated areas. There are nearly 60 Great Walk campsites offering basic facilities, including toilets, hand-washing sinks and a water supply. Some have picnic tables and cooking shelters. These are very popular and must be booked in advance.

Backcountry camping where there are no facilities is permitted on most tracks (excluding Great Walks). You can also camp near huts, and use their water and toilet facilities, although camping outside a Serviced Hut costs $5.

ramshackle places that are best avoided (especially by women travelling solo). Check whether there's a band playing the night you're staying – you could be in for a sleepless night. In the cheapest pubs, singles/doubles might cost as little as $45/70 (with a shared bathroom down the hall); $70/90 is more common.

At the top end of the hotel scale are five-star international chains, resort complexes and architecturally splendorous boutique hotels, all of which charge a hefty premium for their mod cons, snappy service and/or historic opulence. We quote

HUT ETIQUETTE

Located everywhere from forest deep to mountain high, DOC's backcountry huts are a very special part of the NZ tramping experience. Using them is a privilege and a pleasure – as long as everyone follows a few simple guidelines.

Share the bunks When huts are crowded, everybody needs to shift across on the platform bunks and share the mattresses; nobody wants to sleep on the bare floor. It's important to remember that purchasing a hut ticket does not guarantee you a bunk.

Be quiet in the evening and early morning Huts in the middle of the bush are not places for blaring music, excessive drinking or all-night partying. Be considerate of trampers who hit the sack early or sleep in late. Try to minimise your use of torches at night and early in the morning.

Take out your rubbish Carry out your rubbish and do not leave half-burnt garbage in the fireplace. As the hut signs urge, 'pack it in and pack it out'.

Replace firewood Wood stoves in huts are primarily for heat on cold nights. If you must light a fire, make sure to restock the wood box with both kindling and logs for the next trampers, who may arrive wet and cold.

Conserve water Most huts are equipped with rainwater tanks, which can run dry during hot summers. Use water sparingly.

Keep huts clean Leave muddy boots and gaiters outside. Before leaving in the morning, clean the counters and tables and sweep the floor.

Pack earplugs In larger huts along popular tracks, somebody will inevitably snore at night. If you're a light sleeper, pack earplugs.

Pay your hut fees Huts in NZ are extremely affordable. But to maintain the system, everybody needs to pay for the privilege, either with hut tickets or a pass.

'rack rates' (official advertised rates) for such places, but discounts and special deals often apply.

New Zealand's towns have a glut of nondescript low-rise motels and 'motor lodges', charging $90 to $200 for double rooms. These tend to be squat structures skulking by highways on the edges of towns. Most are modernish (though decor is often mired in the early 2000s or earlier) and have basic facilities, namely tea- and coffee-making equipment, fridge and TV. Prices vary with standard.

Rental Accommodation

The basic Kiwi holiday home is called a 'bach' (short for 'bachelor', as they were historically used by single men as hunting and fishing hideouts); in Otago and Southland they're known as 'cribs'. These are simple self-contained cottages that can be rented in rural and coastal areas, often in isolated locations, and sometimes include surf, fishing or other outdoor gear hire in the cost. Prices are typically $90 to $180 per night, which isn't bad for a whole house or self-contained bungalow. For more upmarket holiday houses, expect to pay anything from $180 to $400 per double.

Booking Services

Local visitor information centres around NZ provide reams of accommodation information, sometimes in the form of folders detailing facilities and up-to-date prices; many can also make bookings on your behalf.

Lonely Planet (www.lonely planet.com/new-zealand/hotels) Recommendations and bookings.

Automobile Association (www.aa.co.nz/travel) Online accommodation bookings (especially good for motels, B&Bs and holiday parks).

Jasons (www.jasons.co.nz) Long-running travel service with myriad online-booking options.

New Zealand Bed & Breakfast (www.bnb.co.nz) The name says it all.

Bed & Breakfast New Zealand (www.bed-and-breakfast.co.nz) B&B and self-contained accommodation directory.

Rural Holidays NZ (www.ruralholidays.co.nz) Farm and homestay listings across NZ.

Book a Bach (www.bookabach.co.nz) Apartment and holiday-house bookings (and maybe even a bach or two!).

Holiday Houses (www.holiday houses.co.nz) Holiday-house rentals NZ wide.

New Zealand Apartments (www.nzapartments.co.nz) Rental listings for upmarket apartments of all sizes.

Glossary

bach – holiday home

backcountry – anywhere away from roads or other major infrastructure

benched track – a trail cut and levelled to create even terrain

billy – small pot

bivouac, bivvy – rudimentary shelter under a rock ledge, or a small hut

bluff – steep or precipitous land feature, cliff

bouldering – hopping from one boulder to the next, often along a river where there is no trail

bridle – a track that also accommodates horses

burn – small river

bush – forest

bushline – boundary between the last patches of forest and the alpine area

cairn – stack of rocks marking a track, *route* or *fork*

cirque – rounded, high ridge or bowl formed by glacial action

contour – a line on a map connecting land points with the same elevation

dairy – small convenience store/newsagent

DOC – Department of Conservation (or Te Papa Atawhai); government department that administers conservation estate

flat – open, level area of grass or gravel

ford – to cross a stream or river where there is no bridge

fork – an alternative track leading off from a junction

gorge – narrow ravine, where a river or stream often flows

graded – levelled track for easier tramping

Great Walks – a set of nine of NZ's most popular outdoor adventures

head – uppermost part of a valley

iwi – tribe

longdrop – outdoor toilet or privy

moraine – an accumulation of debris deposited by a glacier

pa – fortified Maori village, usually on a hilltop

Pakeha – European settler

permolat – metal disks nailed to trees to aid navigation

pounamu – greenstone or jade

ridgeline – crest of a ridge, which is often used for travel above the *bushline*

route – unformed track requiring significant *backcountry* and navigational skills and experience

saddle – low point on a ridge or between two peaks providing passage from one catchment to another

scree – slope of loose stones found in alpine areas

scroggin – trail mix

slip – an area where large volumes of earth and rocks have 'slipped' from the hillside

snow pole – post used to mark a *route* above the *bushline*

spur – side trail; small ridge that leads up from a valley to the main ridge

swing bridge – bridge over a river or creek, held by heavy wire cables

switchback – zigzagging track that is designed to reduce the steepness of a climb or descent

tarn – small alpine lake

terrace – raised flat area often featuring a bluff-like edge

torch – flashlight

tramp – bushwalk, trek, hike

trig – triangular marker used by surveyors; also called trig point or trig station

true left/right – the left/right side of a waterway as seen when facing downstream

walkwire – cable set-up for crossing streams and rivers

white spirits – white gas that is used in camping stove

Behind the Scenes

SEND US YOUR FEEDBACK

We love to hear from travellers – your comments keep us on our toes and help make our books better. Our well-travelled team reads every word on what you loved or loathed about this book. Although we cannot reply individually to your submissions, we always guarantee that your feedback goes straight to the appropriate authors, in time for the next edition. Each person who sends us information is thanked in the next edition – the most useful submissions are rewarded with a selection of digital PDF chapters.

Visit **lonelyplanet.com/contact** to submit your updates and suggestions or to ask for help. Our award-winning website also features inspirational travel stories, news and discussions.

Note: We may edit, reproduce and incorporate your comments in Lonely Planet products such as guidebooks, websites and digital products, so let us know if you don't want your comments reproduced or your name acknowledged. For a copy of our privacy policy visit lonelyplanet.com/privacy.

WRITER THANKS

Andrew Bain

Big thanks to an army of DOC staff who provided invaluable help with this edition. To Lizzy Sutcliffe for being my go-between, Phil Brownie for my update, and to DOC staff across the country, including Des Williams, Lizzie Coates, Trish Grant, Amy Rutledge, James Barsdell, Fiona Oliphant, Sarah Ensor, Jennifer Ross, Ray Bellringer, Jayne Ramage, Jess Curtis, Sarah Keeble, Sorrel Hoskin, Neil Murray, Margot Ferrier, Graeme Kates, Helen Dodson and Jose Watson. Thanks also to Derek Brenchley at the Ngai Tūhoe, Phil Rossiter at the Old Ghost Road, Nathan Watson at the NZ Mountain Safety Council, Emily Thorn at Auckland Council, Cedric Wedderburn at the Hump Ridge Track and Heather Macfarlane at the Kaikoura Coast Track. To Jason and Megan Hopper for a whole bunch of stuff, including the excellent company on the trails, I owe you one.

ACKNOWLEDGEMENTS

Climate map data adapted from Peel MC, Finlayson BL & McMahon TA (2007) 'Updated World Map of the Köppen-Geiger Climate Classification', Hydrology and Earth System Sciences, 11, 163344.

Cover photograph: Routeburn Track, Mt Aspiring National Park, Top-Pics TBK/Alamy ©

THIS BOOK

This 8th edition of Lonely Planet's *Hiking & Tramping in New Zealand* guidebook was researched and written by Andrew Bain, with contributions from Brett Atkinson, Peter Dragicevic, Samantha Forge, Anita Isalska and Sofia Levin. The previous edition was written by Sarah Bennett and Lee Slater, and earlier editions were written by Jim DuFresne. This guidebook was produced by the following:

Destination Editor Tasmin Waby

Senior Product Editor Kate Chapman

Product Editor Jessica Ryan

Senior Cartographer Diana Von Holdt

Book Designer Gwen Cotter

Assisting Editors Michelle Bennett, Nigel Chin, Peter Cruttenden, Melanie Dankel, Andrea Dobbin, Jennifer Hattam, Jodie Martire, Lou McGregor, Kristin Odijk, Monique Perrin, Simon Williamson

Cartographer Michael Garrett

Cover Researcher Naomi Parker

Thanks to Izzy Bowles, Jakob Burger, Jennifer Carey, Daniel Corbett, Paul Cuchurean, Shona Gray, Jane Grisman, Liz Heynes, Andi Jones, Sandie Kestell, Emiel Konings, Claire Naylor, Karyn Noble, Kirsten Rawlings, Angela Tinson, Tracy Whitmey

Index

Map Pages **000**
Photo Pages **000**

LONELY PLANET IN THE WILD

Send your 'Lonely Planet in the Wild' photos to social@lonelyplanet.com
We share the best on our Facebook page every week!

Map Legend

Sights

- Beach
- Bird Sanctuary
- Buddhist
- Castle/Palace
- Christian
- Confucian
- Hindu
- Islamic
- Jain
- Jewish
- Monument
- Museum/Gallery/Historic Building
- Ruin
- Shinto
- Sikh
- Taoist
- Winery/Vineyard
- Zoo/Wildlife Sanctuary
- Other Sight

Activities, Courses & Tours

- Bodysurfing
- Diving
- Canoeing/Kayaking
- Course/Tour
- Sento Hot Baths/Onsen
- Skiing
- Snorkelling
- Surfing
- Swimming/Pool
- Walking
- Windsurfing
- Other Activity

Sleeping

- Sleeping
- Camping
- Hut/Shelter

Eating

- Eating

Drinking & Nightlife

- Drinking & Nightlife
- Cafe

Entertainment

- Entertainment

Shopping

- Shopping

Information

- Bank
- Embassy/Consulate
- Hospital/Medical
- Internet
- Police
- Post Office
- Telephone
- Toilet
- Tourist Information
- Other Information

Geographic

- Beach
- Gate
- Hut/Shelter
- Lighthouse
- Lookout
- Mountain/Volcano
- Oasis
- Park
- Pass
- Picnic Area
- Waterfall

Population

- Capital (National)
- Capital (State/Province)
- City/Large Town
- Town/Village

Transport

- Airport
- Border crossing
- Bus
- Cable car/Funicular
- Cycling
- Ferry
- Metro station
- Monorail
- Parking
- Petrol station
- Subway station
- Taxi
- Train station/Railway
- Tram
- Underground station
- Other Transport

Routes

- Tollway
- Freeway
- Primary
- Secondary
- Tertiary
- Lane
- Unsealed road
- Road under construction
- Plaza/Mall
- Steps
- Tunnel
- Pedestrian overpass
- Walking Tour
- Walking Tour detour
- Path/Walking Trail

Boundaries

- International
- State/Province
- Disputed
- Regional/Suburb
- Marine Park
- Cliff
- Wall

Hydrography

- River, Creek
- Intermittent River
- Canal
- Water
- Dry/Salt/Intermittent Lake
- Reef

Areas

- Airport/Runway
- Beach/Desert
- Cemetery (Christian)
- Cemetery (Other)
- Glacier
- Mudflat
- Park/Forest
- Sight (Building)
- Sportsground
- Swamp/Mangrove

Note: Not all symbols displayed above appear on the maps in this book

OUR STORY

A beat-up old car, a few dollars in the pocket and a sense of adventure. In 1972 that's all Tony and Maureen Wheeler needed for the trip of a lifetime – across Europe and Asia overland to Australia. It took several months, and at the end – broke but inspired – they sat at their kitchen table writing and stapling together their first travel guide, *Across Asia on the Cheap*. Within a week they'd sold 1500 copies. Lonely Planet was born.

Today, Lonely Planet has offices in Franklin, London, Melbourne, Oakland, Dublin, Beijing and Delhi, with more than 600 staff and writers. We share Tony's belief that 'a great guidebook should do three things: inform, educate and amuse'.

OUR WRITERS

Andrew Bain

Andrew prefers adventure to avarice and can usually be found walking when he should be working. His writing and photography feature in magazines and newspapers around the world, and his writing has won multiple awards, including Best Adventure Story and Best Australian Story (three times) from the Australian Society of Travel Writers. He was formerly commissioning editor of Lonely Planet's outdoor adventure series of titles, and is the author of *Headwinds*, the story of his 20,000-kilometre cycle journey around Australia, and Lonely Planet's *A Year of Adventures*.

Jim DuFresne

Jim first came to New Zealand more than 20 years ago in search of high peaks and wild places. He found both, along with some fine trout fishing, and has been returning ever since with his backpack and fly rod in hand. Jim began his writing career as the sports and outdoors editor of the *Juneau Empire* and was the first Alaskan sportswriter to win a national award from Associated Press. Today he lives in Michigan and feeds his appetite for the alpine world with frequent trips to Alaska and New Zealand, having authored Lonely Planet's *Alaska*, *Hiking in Alaska* and previous editions of this guidebook.

Contributing Writers

Brett Atkinson Brett is based in Auckland, New Zealand, but is frequently on the road for Lonely Planet. He's a full-time travel and food writer, specialising in adventure travel, unusual destinations and surprising angles on more well known destinations.

Peter Dragicevic Over the last decade Peter has written dozens of guidebooks for Lonely Planet on an oddly disparate collection of countries, all of which he's come to love. He calls Auckland, New Zealand his home.

Samantha Forge Samantha became hooked on travel at the age of 17, when she arrived in London with an overstuffed backpack and a copy of Lonely Planet's *Europe on a Shoestring*. After a stint in Paris, she moved back to Australia and now works as a freelance writer and editor.

Anita Isalska After several merry years as a staff writer and editor – a few of them in Lonely Planet's London office – Anita now works freelance between Australia, the UK and any Alpine chalet with good wi-fi.

Sofia Levin Sofia is a Melbourne-based journalist with an insatiable appetite for food and travel. A regular contributor to Lonely Planet, Sofia also runs Word Salad – a social media and copywriting business, plus has an Insta-famous toy poodle, @lifeofjinkee.

Published by Lonely Planet Global Limited
CRN 554153
8th edition – Dec 2018
ISBN 978 1 78657 269 1
© Lonely Planet 2018   Photographs © as indicated 2018
10 9 8 7 6 5 4 3 2 1
Printed in China